D1105249

Brown Brothers

BENJAMIN FRANKLIN

His autobiography was the first piece of American literature to be hailed with enthusiasm abroad. It reveals Franklin's genius not only as a writer but as a business man, scientist, philosopher, and statesman.

# BEACON LIGHTS OF LITERATURE

## *BOOK TWO*

*By*

RUDOLPH W. CHAMBERLAIN

Editor of the Citizen-Advertiser, Auburn, New York
Co-editor of Progressive Readings in Prose
Formerly instructor in English at Chauncy Hall School, Boston,
and at Syracuse University

IROQUOIS PUBLISHING COMPANY, INC.
*Home Office:* SYRACUSE, NEW YORK
NEW YORK CHICAGO ATLANTA DALLAS

*Printed in the United States of America*
6.34 C

# TO TEACHERS OF ENGLISH

The *Beacon Lights of Literature* series has resulted from the widespread belief that the study of literature in secondary schools should be so organized as to arouse and maintain student interest and, at the same time, present in a broad way the historical developments so necessary to an understanding and enjoyment of whatever may be read in school or afterward. The series is composed of four books, one for each of the high school years. Each book provides sufficient reading for one year's work, and, in addition, offers many helpful suggestions for continued reading. In order to meet the requirements of the alert teacher, a great variety of material is given in each book. This is more than sufficient to satisfy even the most comprehensive literature requirements for one year, and is designed to lure students into voluntary exploration of new reading fields.

## Selection and Organization of Material in Book Two

Book Two of the *Beacon Lights of Literature* series has six sections: Autobiography, the Novel, Diary and Letters, English Poetry from Charles II to George III, the Story-Essay, and Modern Short Stories. The selection of this material has been based on a survey of the recommendations of the foremost educational authorities throughout the country. In *Beacon Lights,* dull, useless and boring selections have been excluded in favor of those that combine interest with value as outstanding examples of type or of period. This material has been most carefully prepared and provides a background which enables the student to appreciate and enjoy what he reads.

Book Two may be used as a treasury of prose and poetry, to be read for pure interest without regard to order. The arrangement as printed, however, has been carefully devised, especially within each large section. In order to encourage students to reading that is not haphazard, the majority of teachers require a textbook that is organized on some clearly defined principles. *Beacon Lights* shows the natural developments of the various types by using a chronological order within each large section. Introductions that picture the historical background of the various periods demonstrate that literature is not a mass of unrelated fragments but a continuous stream. Presented in this fashion, as a living, growing thing, literature becomes an exciting study full of adventure and romance.

Today's trends in the teaching of literature definitely show that teachers are concerning themselves increasingly with the *relationships* that are evident in literature. It used to be that the selections read in a single year frequently had little relation to one another. Adaptation of the material to the maturity of the student seemed to be the only criterion in selecting it. Now it has been realized that a second, greater factor must be taken into consideration: organization of the material in type and period of historical development. If a student studies each unit separately with only vague intimations of its relationship to what has preceded and what will follow, he will have little comprehension of literature in its broader aspects.

The present trend is definitely away from the old-fashioned notion of specializing in English literature one year and American literature another year. *Beacon Lights,* therefore, presents the two concurrently. When, however, it is desirable to study a special development, a period of English literature or of American literature is treated as a unit.

The logical, well-planned arrangement and the thought-provoking presentation of the *Beacon Lights of Literature* series are possible only when the four years' work is co-ordinated and unified under a single editorial program. The knowledge that the student will read each book of the series in succession permits a logical organization of material impossible when separate classics, representing various editorial points of view, are used as the basis of study.

Today educational authorities unanimously agree that in the tenth year the student should be introduced to some things that are new, and renew acquaintance with some which he has met before. The Short Story, Poetry, and the Novel are widely recommended for study during this year. *Beacon Lights,* Book Two, contains a splendid section of Modern Short Stories, including an introduction to the better magazine fiction of today. A valuable contribution is the concluding group of short short stories representing the most recent development in the short story form.

The Poetry section of Book Two is unique. It gives a brief, interesting survey of English poetry from Charles II to the reign of George III, showing the gradual breakdown of the old standards of classicism represented by Pope, the rebirth of a more healthy spirit in the transitional work of Gray, Cowper, and Goldsmith, and finally the upflaming of pure romanticism in Blake. The student is prepared to understand and enjoy this period of English poetry by the preceding section, which provides colorful pictures of English life during the century between the Restoration and the American Revolution. The great age of Charles II is vividly re-created through the inimitable diary of Samuel Pepys; and the first half of the eighteenth century is brought to life in the gossipy letters of Horace Walpole, the famous letters on proper behavior written by Lord Chesterfield to his son, and characteristic passages from Boswell's *Life of Johnson.* Thus the student, besides getting a picture of the general trend of poetic form and spirit, sees one of the most interesting periods in English history unfold before his eyes.

It is unnecessary to say much concerning the novel included in Book Two. *Silas Marner* is a student favorite. Students like to read it, and teachers like to teach it. It tells the interesting story of interesting people in an interesting way—and it goes under the surface, into the minds of its characters. Students in the tenth year are prepared and eager for this.

### Presentation by the Teacher

Three procedures are open to the teacher. She may cover the entire course, with classroom work based in part on the Questions and Exercises supplied by the editor. She may concentrate on certain sections or parts of sections and assign the remainder in whole or in part as collateral reading. Or she may use the entire book as fresh ground to be explored by the pupils under her guidance. In the last case, her presentation will be conditioned by the personal preferences of the individual students. Because of the great variety of material offered in Book Two, it will be possible to reach the student at his own level of interest and encourage him to venture further into the pages of the volume.

The lists of suggested readings given at the end of each section are offered chiefly as an inducement to voluntary reading but may, if desired, be used for collateral assignments. These lists include titles of selections similar in subject, method, or atmosphere to the selections contained in the book. In these lists of interesting books, there is a splendid spur to outside reading for which every teacher will be extremely thankful.

## Conclusion

With Book Two, the principles upon which the *Beacon Lights of Literature* series is based, become evident. All the approved new trends in teaching have been recognized. The selections have been chosen with the mental maturity of the student, the appreciation by the student, and the interest to the student always in mind.

The material has been organized in such a way that continuity and historical values have been very largely preserved. The zest which pervades the introductions, questions, and exercises will, it is believed, capture the interest of the student and solve many of the problems which confront the teacher of English literature.

Special attention has been paid to mechanical matters of make-up and binding in the *Beacon Lights* series. An attractive book invites the youthful reader, and pride of ownership may result in the founding of a library of his own. The four books in the *Beacon Lights* series form a splendid beginning for a private library—a "six-inch library" that comprises the best works of the best authors. Within this small space there is confined a world in itself, a thrilling world, whose paths invite one to set out on journeys of fascinating adventure.

Iroquois Publishing Company, Inc.

# CONTENTS



## SECTION ONE

### AUTOBIOGRAPHY



## SECTION TWO

### THE NOVEL

# ILLUSTRATIONS

# *Autobiography*

Brown Brothers

**Franklin the Printer's 'Prentice**

As a boy Franklin served as apprentice in his brother's printing shop. Here he not only learned the printing trade but also contributed articles to his brother's newspaper.

# AUTOBIOGRAPHY

With the reading of an autobiography the student of English prose literature passes from the familiar Narration of Fiction to Narration of Fact. Quite properly, his study began with short stories, novels, and plays which deal with imagined characters and events woven into a fictitious plot. In this play of imagination there is a universal appeal, an invitation to experience through the magic of the printed page the adventures of the hero and heroine the author has invented. Fiction owes a great deal of its charm to the fact that while it did not happen exactly as related, it might have happened—and why not to us?

Thoughtful readers find a different but none the less stimulating pleasure in Narration of Fact. Here the author must deal with actual events and persons. He cannot ignore the facts as he finds them or invent others. He cannot change destiny to suit his own fancy. The story has already been lived; it is for him to recreate it in words.

This does not mean that imagination is unessential. It is as important as the accurate report of what happened. Names and dates and events are only a small part of the task. To write a worth while Narrative of Fact, an author must have the gift of conjuring up the period in which his characters lived—what people were doing, what they were thinking about, what songs they were singing, what their pastimes were, what political ideas were popular, who was cheered and who was hissed, and why men laughed or cried. Against this background he must make his characters stand out as individuals, with all their nobility and meanness, their hopes and their disappointments, human beings like ourselves caught in the old struggle for existence and triumphing or going down to defeat as circumstances or their own natures dictate.

There are three fields for Narration of Fact: history, biography, autobiography. History has developed from simple chronicles stating baldly the chief incidents of wars or reigns into complex forms, uniting research for facts long buried or forgotten with an analysis of those facts and the causes back of the historical events. Biography, too, has changed in recent years. Originally, it was a straight-forward recital of the facts of another person's life. Today many authors also borrow from fiction the use of dialogue, the inclusion of trivial incidents that show the great man off his guard, and the chatty style of the novelist. Although eagerness to arouse interest has sometimes led to an over-emphasis of the man's faults and vices, this very sensationalism and vividness of treatment has won an increasingly large number of biography readers.

Autobiography differs from both history and biography in the peculiarly intimate relation between the author and his subject. The author is his own subject. He is telling his own story, trying to explain himself to his generation and to posterity—why he did this, why he did not do that. He tells how he felt in such and such a crisis and reveals personal motives often hidden from the biographer.

Autobiography gives the writer great freedom both in form and content. He can gossip pleasantly about the people he has known or discuss seriously the problems of his time. He does not have to worry much about digressions if he can tell his story with an eye to its human values, for we are interested more in personalities than in institutions or theories. We want to know about *him*. The more he discovers himself to us, the better we like it and the more valuable is his contribution to letters.

Although not every one has a life story worth relating to a large reading public, many of us, if we had the vision to grasp it and the art to paint it, might leave behind us a valuable picture of our epoch, fragmentary perhaps, yet dealing with certain phases of life in our generation that deserve recording. It is possible that a growing realization of this truth is partly responsible for the increase in autobiographical writings in recent years.

Autobiography, however, has one great obstacle to overcome. It is extremely difficult for a man properly to appreciate his own importance. He is inclined to exaggerate or underestimate. Few have a well-developed sense of self-criticism, and all autobiography is necessarily biased. Benjamin Franklin, a man whom destiny placed in positions of great responsibility during our colonial development, had not only a story to tell but the honesty and the art to tell it truthfully and entertainingly. He was neither a braggart nor an apologist. He set down his great accomplishments with decent pride, and humbly revealed his sins and shortcomings. As a record of the times, but even more as a portrait of one of our national idols, Franklin's *Autobiography* is a document of inestimable value.

# THE AUTOBIOGRAPHY OF BENJAMIN FRANKLIN

## THE AUTHOR

## 1706–1790

It would be folly to anticipate the *Autobiography* itself by giving an account of Benjamin Franklin's life or presenting a lengthy interpretation of his character. It is all there, so far as the account goes, for the thoughtful reader. At the point where Franklin discontinued his work, a biographical sketch has been added to give the essential facts of his later career.

It is important to realize at the outset, however, how crucial was the period in which Franklin lived and how great a part he played in bringing thirteen colonies, often at odds with each other, into a compact union. He was born less than a century after the Pilgrims landed at Plymouth. William Penn had established the Colony of Pennsylvania only twenty-five years before. The total population of the colonies was less than 300,000, only enough to form a moderately large city in our day. Except for a few towns, the country was still a wilderness. Communication was difficult, and transportation was confined to dangerous voyages by boat along the coast or down the streams, and to travel on horseback through the forest. The first regular stagecoach line between Philadelphia and New York was not established until half a century later, and even then the trip took three days, with six more required to reach Boston.

Franklin's life extended from shortly after the beginning of the eighteenth century to shortly before its close. In that time, the colonies grew from struggling little states to a nation. In spite of great differences of temperament between the residents of the South and of the North, there was the common bond of race and a feeling that their destinies were linked. At first loyal to their King, the colonists bore oppression with fortitude, pleading through their representatives for privileges they believed should be theirs. When it was evident that their petitions would not be granted, it was with indignation tinged with regret that they severed all governmental ties with the homeland and declared for independence.

During these troublous times Benjamin Franklin was the great spokesman for the colonies. His benevolent face and quaint, rather stout figure were familiar in the courts of both England and France; and his homely wisdom found a ready hearing in an age when democratic sentiments were the vogue. A statesman and philosopher had risen from an obscure family to take rank with Washington and Jefferson among our patriots and to win a name as well among our pioneer authors and scientists.

Versatility was one of the fascinating characteristics of Franklin. By trade he was a printer and binder. He operated a paper mill and owned a bookshop. For a time he dealt in indentured servants and slaves, though in his later years he became one of the pioneer advocates of the abolition of slavery. He is recognized today as the greatest of Colonial writers. It was probably a natural transition for a printer of his temperament to proceed to creative writing. Consider the curious assortment of subjects with which he was familiar! He published a newspaper and an almanac. He devised maxims that found their way into a nation's copy-books. He wrote essays on politics, science, and philosophy. In the composition of the *Autobiography* alone he covered many fields of thought. To enlarge his horizon he taught himself to read French, Spanish, Italian, and Latin. He learned to play the harp, the guitar, and the violin. He even invented a new musical instrument, the harmonica, which he mistakenly believed might replace the piano. It was a device consisting of half spheres of glass of different sizes that could be played as one plays on water tumblers partly filled with water.

As an author Franklin holds a high place, for he was the first American to write a book of international importance—the *Autobiography*. Admirable as this work and his other serious efforts are, there is even greater charm in some of his lighter essays and gay letters. He began at an early age with the composition of rimes, but, as he says himself, "escaped being a poet, most probably a very bad one," by his father's ridicule. His prose was modeled after that of the *Spectator Papers,* written by Addison and Steele. It was clear, direct, and often satirical. The wit that characterizes such youthful pieces as the newspaper articles he wrote under the signature of "Silence Dogood" and that came to best utterance in the sayings of Poor Richard justifies the statement that American humor began with Franklin. For all his sense of humor, he had a strong urge to teach a lesson and rarely failed to drag in a moral by the hair of its head. Typical of the light yet sincere touch with which he treated serious subjects is the epitaph he wrote for himself in 1728 while in his early twenties:

The Body of
B. Franklin, Printer
(Like the Cover of an old Book
Its Contents torn out
And stript of its Lettering and Gilding)
Lies here, Food for Worms.
But the Work shall not be lost;
For it will (as he believed) appear once more,
In a new and more elegant Edition
Revised and corrected
By the Author

When one remembers that Franklin was largely self-taught, his achievements in science seem almost miraculous. His experiments led to the first understanding of the nature of electricity. Most scientists had hitherto thought electricity a kind of fluid. Franklin studied wind movements, the Gulf Stream, shooting stars, sun spots, and a host of other phenomena, rarely failing to contribute something worth while to our knowledge.

Besides these investigations, he was continually inventing or perfecting devices for the comfort and well-being of mankind. A certain type of small, open-fire stove, a favorite with our grandfathers, bears his name, though he called it the Pennsylvania Fire-place. In spite of its immediate popularity, Franklin refused to patent it, believing that everyone should benefit by inventions. It was he who designed bifocal spectacles, which have two kinds of lenses to adjust vision to both long and short distances. The lightning rod was the product of his brain. He built a machine, called a mangle, for pressing clothes, and constructed a simplified clock with only three wheels and two pinions which told the hours, minutes, and seconds. Franklin delved into nature's secrets with the same patience and curiosity with which he probed men's minds. His own mind was always open to truth, eager for more knowledge.

This intellectual energy resulted in a variety of projects, ranging from the founding of an academy that later developed into the University of Pennsylvania to the establishment of the first circulating library; from a scheme to operate a swimming school in England to the organization of a philosophical society. Franklin was a citizen in the best sense of the word: one who feels a responsibility toward the community in which he lives. However far from home his missions took him, he never became too great for the humble role of townsman. To his civic pride and initiative Philadelphia owes the introduction of proper paving and cleaning of its streets, and the establishment of a city police force and a volunteer fire brigade—all sound, practical, home-town improvements.

One test of a man's character is the attitude of other people toward him. Every one liked Franklin, apparently, though a few of Philadelphia's grand ladies, remembering his humble origin and slow rise, affected a certain scorn. This superior feeling was no doubt increased by his own indelicacies of speech and conduct and his wife's lack of education and culture. Nevertheless, he was at home in a humble cottage or in a Paris salon. As a struggling youth in a strange city he attracted the attention of no less a person than the governor of the colony. In his maturity even his political adversaries admired him. In the brilliant society of the French capital he impressed the men and captivated the ladies. Whether or not he would have had the same social success in Paris had his wife "Debby" been there, we leave it to the ladies to decide. Mrs. Franklin had an unfortunate habit of addressing her husband in public as "Pappy," a nickname that his enemies were quick to take advantage of.

As it was, he numbered among his intimates most of the great and near-great in Paris and London. He had humor, wisdom, tolerance, and sympathy, yet was a man's man, enjoying life. Though striving for temperance in all things, he was sometimes led into indiscretions. In short, a very human, lovable, honest, shrewd, and witty Ben Franklin.

## THE STORY

In an autobiography the author and the story are so closely knit that it is difficult to draw a line between them. If the author does a good job, he and the story are one. Few persons, however, are willing to tell the whole truth about themselves. They trim up the account for their readers. Fortunately, there are some notable exceptions.

Jean Jacques Rousseau is one of them. All his curious thoughts, reveries, noble and ignoble deeds, mistakes, and achievements Rousseau set down for us in an autobiography he called his *Confessions.* He seemed to take delight in revealing everything. Another exception is Samuel Pepys, a petty official in the British admiralty under Charles II. His autobiography, in the form of a diary, he wrote in cipher, little thinking that years later men would find the key to his shorthand and elevate him from obscurity to a figure of great literary importance.

Though Benjamin Franklin is deservedly one of the great American patriots and heroes, he had his faults. Even in his own time he was subjected to personal attacks because of his failure to keep to the path of rectitude he had laid out for himself. In Philadelphia some of his enemies called him "the old rogue." In the most exclusive society he was tolerated largely because of his personal magnetism and the high rank which he had attained. His wife, who lacked the social graces, was rarely received by the aristocratic families.

No one realized his shortcomings better than Franklin himself. Though he might have excused himself on the ground that his faults were the faults of his time, he strove honestly to record them in his autobiography; not because he loved to make a show of himself and his occasional waywardness or because he intended the confessions for no other eyes but his own, but because he felt he was teaching a lesson to his descendants and to his countrymen. That is the big difference between Franklin, and Rousseau and Pepys. The American author was moved by a high moral purpose. Beneath the humor there was a serious-minded thinker with a strong conviction of right and wrong. Never content to skim the surface, he went to the bottom of things. He wanted a reason for everything. Believing that experience is the greatest teacher, he wrote down what he had learned as a guide for future conduct. One of the delightful things about his *Autobiography* is the balance between the great and good things and the small and not-so-good things. It is a portrait of a real man, not a saint or rogue. Because his greatness so far outreaches his littleness, Franklin will always be a popular hero in Europe as well as in America.

How the *Autobiography* came to be written and what happened to the manuscript makes an interesting story in itself. Publication of his memoirs did not at first occur to Franklin. When the first installment was written, he intended the document solely for his own family and friends. Later, advised by others, he realized the historical importance of his recollections and decided to publish them. From that point on he wrote with a larger audience in mind.

In 1771 during the second of those long sojourns in England whither business for the colonies had taken him, Franklin found himself enjoying a holiday at the country house of his close friend, Bishop Jonathan Shipley of St. Asaph's. Though grateful for the rest which this interlude in affairs of state brought him, he was not one to remain idle. It was here that he conceived the idea of putting into writing some recollections of his family and of his own varied career. He set to work without the slightest suspicion that this was the beginning of a great American classic. When he had brought the *Autobiography* through the year 1730 he sent the manuscript to his son William, then governor of New Jersey. Apparently he had no intention of continuing the account and even if he had, the press of work and the responsibility which fell upon him in the short period before the outbreak of the Revolution must have made it well-nigh impossible.

William Franklin, however, was not having an easy time. Because he was a Tory, supporting the King in the colonial disputes, he was unpopular with his neighbors. In time he found it more comfortable to leave the colonies and take residence in England. Either through neglect or accident he permitted the manuscript to get out of his hands. Fortunately, it came into good keeping, for about a dozen years later Franklin, now in Paris, received a letter from Mr. Abel James, a Quaker friend in Pennsylvania, enclosing the pages he had written at Bishop Shipley's. James and other friends urged Franklin to complete the *Autobiography* as a duty to himself and to posterity.

Inspired by such advice, Franklin set to work anew but succeeded at this time (1784) in finishing only a few pages. Not until four years later when he was at home did he again take up the task, bringing the account down to the year 1757. Thereafter he wrote no more until the last year of his life when, suffering from a combination of maladies, he painfully added a few more pages relating the conclusion of his first mission to London ending in 1762.

When Franklin died in April of 1790, the *Autobiography* together with miscellaneous books and papers was bequeathed to his grandson, William Temple Franklin. Franklin had taken so vital a part in negotiations with France and England and was besides so brilliant a figure in social and literary circles that both in America and in England the publication of his memoirs was awaited with keen interest. Yet it was not until 1817, nearly three decades after the death of the great man, that a mutilated version of the *Autobiography* appeared in English.

(In 1791 a French translation of the first part of the manuscript had been published in Paris, a strange fate for a document so American in spirit.)

What happened to the manuscript in the meantime is rather mysterious. Most students have blamed the grandson, Temple Franklin, for the unnecessary delay. Some even charge him with entering into a deal with the British government to suppress or modify portions of the memoirs that might reflect on that nation. Though there is not a great deal of evidence to prove this latter accusation, it is true that Temple Franklin allowed other interests to intervene, apparently little realizing how precious a trust had been given into his hands.

Moreover, he was careless and neglectful, for when the *Autobiography* was at last published, it was not from the original but from an incomplete copy. The last few pages were lacking. In a well-meaning but misguided spirit he took it upon himself to alter some twelve hundred of Franklin's own words. In nearly every case he substituted the niceties of speech demanded by his own generation for the homely phraseology of Franklin. Times had changed, and good taste, in Temple Franklin's opinion, required more delicate expressions than his famous grandsire sometimes employed. Under his editing, "footed it to London" was changed to the conventional "walked to London"; "like a pig poisoned" became "with astonishment"; and "sotting with brandy" turned circumspectly to "drinking of brandy." Other changes of a similar nature sacrificed vividness to elegance, frankness to propriety.

More than seventy-five years after Franklin passed away, John Bigelow, then American ambassador to the French court, found the original manuscript in the possession of a French family, purchased it, and brought out the first complete, authentic edition in 1868. The following reprint follows Mr. Bigelow's text.

Regret that Franklin did not complete his *Autobiography* and that it was left for others to finish the account of his later life is tempered by the satisfaction that so large a portion of his personal recollections has been preserved. Without question the work ranks with the great biographies of literature. Had Franklin been able to bring it through the Revolutionary period, we may be sure that his intimate records would have captured the spirit of those stirring times with greater vividness than is possible for the historian.

Notwithstanding this incompleteness, we see the development of a rich personality against a background of movement and color; the struggles, customs, prejudices and beliefs of a pioneer people, hemmed in by the sea on the one hand and a virgin forest filled with hostile savages on the other; and finally the growth of a national consciousness that is to lead to a war for independence waged between people of the same race and speech. Through it all, however, the most interesting subject is Benjamin Franklin himself.

# THE AUTOBIOGRAPHY OF BENJAMIN FRANKLIN

## CHAPTER I[1]

### THE BOY FRANKLIN

Reasons for writing *Autobiography*—Ancestry—Early Days in Boston—The Printer Apprentice—His Reading—First Essay in Journalism

*Twyford, at the Bishop of St. Asaph's,*[2] *1771.*

DEAR SON:[3] I have ever had pleasure in obtaining any little anecdotes of my ancestors. You may remember the inquiries I made among the remains of my relations when you were with me in England,[4] and the journey I undertook for that purpose. Imagining it may be equally agreeable to you to know the circumstances of my life, many of which you are yet unacquainted with, and expecting the enjoyment of a week's uninterrupted leisure in my present country retirement, I sit down to write them for you. To which I have besides some other inducements. Having emerged from the poverty and obscurity in which I was born and bred, to a state of affluence and some degree of reputation in the world, and having gone so far through life with a considerable share of felicity, the conducing means[5] I made use of, which with the blessing of God so well succeeded, my posterity may like to know, as they may find some of them suitable to their own situations, and therefore fit to be imitated.

That felicity, when I reflected on it, has induced me sometimes to say, that were it offered to my choice, I should have no objection

---

[1] CHAPTER I—Franklin made no chapter divisions in his manuscript. The scheme followed here has been arranged by the editor.

[2] BISHOP OF ST. ASAPH'S—Franklin began the writing of his *Autobiography* at the country home of his friend, Jonathan Shipley, Bishop of St. Asaph, who was a friend of the colonies. Franklin's letters to the Bishop's daughter Georgiana show the delightful intimacy that sprang up between the aging man and this attractive and intelligent girl.

[3] DEAR SON—William Franklin, the only surviving son, then royal governor of New Jersey.

[4] WHEN YOU WERE WITH ME IN ENGLAND—In 1757 William accompanied his father on the latter's first mission to England, spending several years studying law in London.

[5] CONDUCING MEANS—The means employed (to gain his affluence, etc.). *Means* is object of *to know,* following.

to a repetition of the same life from its beginning, only asking the advantages authors have in a second edition to correct some faults of the first. So I might, besides correcting the faults, change some sinister accidents and events of it for others more favorable. But though this were denied, I should still accept the offer. Since such a repetition is not to be expected, the next thing most like living one's life over again seems to be a recollection of that life, and to make that recollection as durable as possible by putting it down in writing.

Hereby, too, I shall indulge the inclination so natural in old men, to be talking of themselves and their own past actions; and I shall indulge it without being tiresome to others, who, through respect to age, might conceive themselves obliged to give me a hearing, since this may be read or not as any one pleases. And, lastly (I may as well confess it, since my denial of it will be believed by nobody), perhaps I shall a good deal gratify my own vanity. Indeed, I scarce ever heard or saw the introductory words, "Without vanity I may say," etc., but some vain thing immediately followed. Most people dislike vanity in others, whatever share they have of it themselves; but I give it fair quarter[6] wherever I meet with it, being persuaded that it is often productive of good to the possessor, and to others that are within his sphere of action; and therefore, in many cases, it would not be altogether absurd if a man were to thank God for his vanity among the other comforts of life.

And now I speak of thanking God, I desire with all humility to acknowledge that I owe the mentioned happiness of my past life to His kind providence, which led me to the means I used and gave them success. My belief of this induces me to *hope,* though I must not *presume,* that the same goodness will still be exercised toward me, in continuing that happiness, or enabling me to bear a fatal reverse, which I may experience as others have done; the complexion of my future fortune being known to Him only in whose power it is to bless to us even our afflictions.

The notes one of my uncles (who had the same kind of curiosity in collecting family anecdotes) once put into my hands furnished me with several particulars relating to our ancestors. From these notes I learned that the family had lived in the same village, Ecton,

[6] GIVE IT FAIR QUARTER—Give it proper respect.

in Northamptonshire, for three hundred years, and how much longer he knew not (perhaps from the time when the name of Franklin,[7] that before was the name of an order of people, was assumed by them as a surname when others took surnames all over the kingdom), on a freehold of about thirty acres, aided by the smith's business, which had continued in the family till his time, the eldest son being always bred to that business; a custom which he and my father followed as to their eldest sons. When I searched the registers at Ecton, I found an account of their births, marriages, and burials from the year 1555 only, there being no registers kept in that parish at any time preceding. By that register I perceived that I was the youngest son of the youngest son for five generations back. My grandfather, Thomas, who was born in 1598, lived at Ecton till he grew too old to follow business longer, when he went to live with his son John, a dyer at Banbury, in Oxfordshire, with whom my father served an apprenticeship.[8] There my grandfather died and lies buried. We saw his gravestone in 1758. His eldest son Thomas lived in the house at Ecton, and left it with the land to his only child, a daughter, who, with her husband, one Fisher, of Wellingborough, sold it to Mr. Isted, now lord of the manor there. My grandfather had four sons that grew up, viz.: Thomas, John, Benjamin, and Josiah. I will give you what account I can of them, at this distance from my papers, and if these are not lost in my absence, you will among them find many more particulars.

Thomas was bred a smith under his father; but, being ingenious, and encouraged in learning (as all my brothers were) by an Esquire Palmer, then the principal gentleman in that parish, he qualified himself for the business of scrivener;[9] became a considerable man in the county; was a chief mover of all public spirited undertakings for the county or town of Northampton, and his own village, of which many instances were related of him; and much

---

[7] FRANKLIN—Name formerly applied in England to persons who were freeholders; that is, middle class landowners. Later, occupations or class orders were taken over as surnames, or family names: John, the smith, became John Smith; Henry, the carpenter, Henry Carpenter; and William, the franklin, William Franklin. It is interesting to note that while the Franklins were humble folk, the Washingtons, who also came originally from Northamptonshire, belonged to the aristocracy.

[8] SERVED AN APPRENTICESHIP—Bound himself to work for a certain time without pay to learn a trade; in this case, dyeing.

[9] SCRIVENER—Professional writer who drew up contracts and other legal documents.

taken notice of and patronized by the then Lord Halifax.[10] He died in 1702, January 6, old style,[11] just four years to a day before I was born. The account we received of his life and character from some old people at Ecton, I remember, struck you as something extraordinary, from its similarity to what you knew of mine. "Had he died on the same day," you said, "one might have supposed a transmigration."[12]

John was bred a dyer, I believe, of woolens. Benjamin was bred a silk dyer, serving an apprenticeship at London. He was an ingenious man. I remember him well, for when I was a boy he came over to my father in Boston, and lived in the house with us some years. He lived to a great age. His grandson, Samuel Franklin, now lives in Boston. He left behind him two quarto volumes, in manuscript,[13] of his own poetry, consisting of little occasional pieces addressed to his friends and relations, of which the following, sent to me, is a specimen.[14] He had formed a short-hand of his own which he taught me, but, never practicing it, I have now forgot it. I was named after this uncle, there being a particular affection between him and my father. He was very pious, a great attender of sermons of the best preachers which he took down in his short-hand, and had with him many volumes of them. He was also much of a politician; too much, perhaps, for his station. There fell lately into my hands, in London, a collection he had made of all the principal pamphlets relating to public affairs, from 1641 to 1717; many of the volumes are wanting as appears by the numbering, but there still remain eight volumes in folio,[15] and twenty-four in quarto and in octavo. A dealer in old books met with them, and knowing me by my sometimes buying of him,

---

[10] LORD HALIFAX—Charles Montagu, also from Northamptonshire, who was a friend of many famous writers of the day, among them Addison, Swift, and Pope.

[11] OLD STYLE—According to the Julian calendar, established by Julius Cæsar in 46 B.C. Astronomers having discovered that ten days had been lost by this system, Pope Gregory reformed the calendar in 1582. England, however, did not adopt "new style," or the Gregorian calendar, until 1752. By that time eleven days had been lost, and Franklin's birthday shifted automatically from Jan. 6 to Jan. 17.

[12] TRANSMIGRATION—The doctrine that at death the soul passes into the body of an animal or a new-born baby.

[13] QUARTO VOLUMES, IN MANUSCRIPT—Books bound with sheets folded twice to make four leaves, in his own handwriting.

[14] THE FOLLOWING . . . IS A SPECIMEN—Franklin noted in the margin of his manuscript: "Here insert it," but the specimen of Uncle Benjamin's verse was never included.

[15] FOLIO—Bound with sheets folded once to make two leaves. For quarto, see note 13. In an octavo volume the sheets are folded three times to make eight leaves.

he brought them to me. It seems my uncle must have left them here when he went to America, which was above fifty years since. There are many of his notes in the margins.

This obscure family of ours was early in the Reformation,[16] and continued Protestants through the reign of Queen Mary,[17] when they were sometimes in danger of trouble on account of their zeal against popery. They had got an English Bible, and to conceal and secure it, it was fastened open with tapes under and within the cover of a joint-stool. When my great-great-grandfather read it to his family, he turned up the joint-stool upon his knees, turning over the leaves then under the tapes. One of the children stood at the door to give notice if he saw the apparitor coming, who was an officer of the spiritual court. In that case the stool was turned down again upon its feet, when the Bible remained concealed under it as before. This anecdote I had from my uncle Benjamin. The family continued all of the Church of England[18] till about the end of Charles the Second's reign, when some of the ministers that had been outed for non-conformity[19] holding conventicles in Northamptonshire, Benjamin and Josiah adhered to them, and so continued all their lives: the rest of the family remained with the Episcopal Church.

Josiah, my father, married young, and carried his wife with three children into New England, about 1682. The conventicles having been forbidden by law, and frequently disturbed, induced some considerable men of his acquaintance to remove to that country, and he was prevailed with to accompany them thither, where they expected to enjoy their mode of religion with freedom. By the same wife he had four children more born there, and by

---

[16] Reformation—A great religious revolution that started early in the sixteenth century with Martin Luther in Germany and spread gradually to other countries. It resulted in the establishment of the Protestant Church.

[17] Queen Mary—Daughter of Henry VIII of England whose persecution of Protestants in an effort to re-establish the Roman Catholic Church won her the name of Bloody Mary. She reigned 1553–1558, and was followed by Queen Elizabeth, another daughter of Henry VIII, who in turn persecuted the Catholics.

[18] Church of England—The Protestant Church in England established under Henry VIII.

[19] Outed for non-conformity—Expelled for not adhering to the regulations of the Church of England and for holding their own religious assemblies (conventicles), often in secret. By the time of Charles II (1660–1685) the Protestant Church in England had split just as the Catholic Church had split during the Reformation. Those who broke away from the established Church of England and formed sects of their own were called Dissenters.

a second wife ten more, in all seventeen,[20] of which I remember thirteen sitting at one time at his table, who all grew up to be men and women, and married. I was the youngest son, and the youngest child but two, and was born in Boston,[21] New England. My mother, the second wife, was Abiah Folger, daughter of Peter Folger, one of the first settlers of New England, of whom honorable mention is made by Cotton Mather, in his church history of that country, entitled "Magnalia Christi Americana,"[22] as *"a godly, learned Englishman,"* if I remember the words rightly. I have heard that he wrote sundry small occasional pieces, but only one of them was printed, which I saw now many years since. It was written in 1675, in the homespun verse of that time and people, and addressed to those then concerned in the government there. It was in favor of liberty of conscience, and in behalf of the Baptists, Quakers, and other sectaries[23] that had been under persecution, ascribing the Indian wars, and other distresses that had befallen the country, to that persecution, as so many judgments of God to punish so heinous an offense, and exhorting a repeal of those uncharitable laws. The whole appeared to me as written with a good deal of decent plainness and manly freedom. The six concluding lines I remember, though I have forgotten the two first of the stanza; but the purport of them was, that his censures proceeded from good-will, and therefore he would be known to be the author.

Because to be a libeller
  I hate it with my heart;
From Sherburne town, where now I dwell
  My name I do put here;
Without offense your real friend,
  It is Peter Folgier.

---

[20] IN ALL SEVENTEEN—Though Josiah was one of five brothers, and the father of ten sons, when the eighteenth century ended, William Franklin was the only descendant entitled to the surname. Benjamin Franklin's line was carried on through his daughter, Sarah, who became Mrs. Richard Bache (bāch).

[21] BORN IN BOSTON—1706, in a small house in Milk Street opposite the famous Old South Church, now in the center of Boston's business district. This house was burned in 1810.

[22] "MAGNALIA CHRISTI AMERICANA"—Cotton Mather's *Ecclesiastical History of New England.*

[23] BAPTISTS, QUAKERS, AND OTHER SECTARIES—Though the Puritans had migrated to New England that they might worship God in their own way, they were intolerant of other creeds, among them the Baptists and Quakers. Peter Folger evidently sympathized with Roger Williams, Anne Hutchinson, and others who were banished for their teachings. When Anne Hutchinson was murdered by the Indians, the Puritan preachers believed it was divine vengeance.

My elder brothers were all put apprentices to different trades. I was put to the grammar-school at eight years of age, my father intending to devote me, as the tithe of his sons,[24] to the service of the Church. My early readiness in learning to read (which must have been very early, as I do not remember when I could not read), and the opinion of all his friends that I should certainly make a good scholar, encouraged him in this purpose of his. My uncle Benjamin, too, approved of it, and proposed to give me all his short-hand volumes of sermons, I suppose as a stock to set up with, if I would learn his character.[25] I continued, however, at the grammar-school not quite one year, though in that time I had risen gradually from the middle of the class of that year to be the head of it, and further, was removed into the next class above it, in order to go with that into the third at the end of the year. But my father, in the mean time, from a view of the expense of a college education, which having so large a family he could not well afford, and the mean living many so educated were afterwards able to obtain,—reasons that he gave to his friends in my hearing,—altered his first intention, took me from the grammar-school, and sent me to a school for writing and arithmetic, kept by a then famous man, Mr. George Brownell, very successful in his profession generally, and that by mild, encouraging methods. Under him I acquired fair writing pretty soon, but I failed in the arithmetic, and made no progress in it. At ten years old I was taken home to assist my father in his business, which was that of a tallow-chandler and soap-boiler;[26] a business he was not bred to, but had assumed on his arrival in New England, and on finding his dyeing trade would not maintain his family, being in little request. Accordingly, I was employed in cutting wick for the candles, filling the dipping mould and the moulds for cast candles, attending the shop, going of errands, etc.

I disliked the trade, and had a strong inclination for the sea, but my father declared against it; however, living near the water, I was much in and about it, learnt early to swim well, and to manage boats; and when in a boat or canoe with other boys, I was

---

[24] Tithe of his sons—As Franklin was one of ten sons, giving him to the church would have been like giving a tithe, or tenth part, to religious uses.

[25] Character—Shorthand system.

[26] Tallow-chandler and soap-boiler—A maker and merchant of candles and soap.

commonly allowed to govern,[27] especially in any case of difficulty; and upon other occasions I was generally a leader among the boys, and sometimes led them into scrapes, of which I will mention one instance, as it shows an early projecting public spirit, though not then justly conducted.

There was a salt marsh that bounded part of the mill pond, on the edge of which, at high water, we used to stand to fish for minnows. By much trampling, we had made it a mere quagmire. My proposal was to build a wharf there fit for us to stand upon, and I showed my comrades a large heap of stones, which were intended for a new house near the marsh, and which would very well suit our purpose. Accordingly, in the evening, when the workmen were gone, I assembled a number of my playfellows, and working with them diligently, like so many emmets, sometimes two or three to a stone, we brought them all away and built our little wharf. The next morning the workmen were surprised at missing the stones, which were found in our wharf. Inquiry was made after the removers; we were discovered and complained of; several of us were corrected by our fathers; and, though I pleaded the usefulness of the work, mine convinced me that nothing was useful which was not honest.

I think you may like to know something of his person and character. He had an excellent constitution of body, was of middle stature, but well set, and very strong. He was ingenious, could draw prettily, was skilled a little in music, and had a clear, pleasing voice, so that when he played psalm tunes on his violin and sung withal, as he sometimes did in an evening after the business of the day was over, it was extremely agreeable to hear. He had a mechanical genius, too, and, on occasion, was very handy in the use of other tradesmen's tools; but his great excellence lay in a sound understanding and solid judgment in prudential matters,[28] both in private and public affairs. In the latter, indeed, he was never employed, the numerous family he had to educate and the straitness of his circumstances keeping him close to his trade; but I remember well his being frequently visited by leading people, who consulted him for his opinion in affairs of the town or of the church he belonged to, and showed a good deal of respect for his

[27] GOVERN—Steer.

[28] PRUDENTIAL MATTERS—Matters requiring good judgment.

judgment and advice. He was also much consulted by private persons about their affairs when any difficulty occurred, and frequently chosen an arbitrator between contending parties. At his table he liked to have, as often as he could, some sensible friend or neighbor to converse with, and always took care to start some ingenious or useful topic for discourse, which might tend to improve the minds of his children. By this means he turned our attention to what was good, just, and prudent in the conduct of life; and little or no notice was ever taken of what related to the victuals on the table, whether it was well or ill dressed, in or out of season, of good or bad flavor, preferable or inferior to this or that other thing of the kind, so that I was brought up in such a perfect inattention to those matters as to be quite indifferent what kind of food was set before me, and so unobservant of it, that to this day if I am asked I can scarce tell a few hours after dinner what I dined upon. This has been a convenience to me in traveling, where my companions have been sometimes very unhappy for want of a suitable gratification of their more delicate, because better instructed, tastes and appetites.

My mother had likewise an excellent constitution; she suckled all her ten children. I never knew either my father or mother to have any sickness but that of which they died, he at eighty-nine, and she at eighty-five years of age. They lie buried together at Boston,[29] where I some years since placed a marble over their grave, with this inscription:—

JOSIAH FRANKLIN,
and
ABIAH his wife,
lie here interred.
They lived lovingly together in wedlock
fifty-five years.
Without an estate, or any gainful employment,
By constant labor and industry,
with God's blessing,
They maintained a large family
comfortably,
and brought up thirteen children
and seven grandchildren
reputably.

---

[29] **BURIED TOGETHER AT BOSTON—In the old burial ground on Tremont Street just north of Park Street, only a few steps from the Common.**

From this instance, reader,
Be encouraged to diligence in thy calling,
And distrust not Providence.
He was a pious and prudent man;
She, a discreet and virtuous woman.
Their youngest son,
In filial regard to their memory,
Places this stone.
J. F. born 1655, died 1744, Ætat[30] 89.
A. F. born 1667, died 1752, —85.

By my rambling digressions I perceive myself to be grown old. I used to write more methodically. But one does not dress for private company as for a public ball.[31] 'Tis perhaps only negligence.

To return: I continued thus employed in my father's business for two years, that is, till I was twelve years old; and my brother John, who was bred to that business, having left my father, married, and set up for himself at Rhode Island, there was all appearance that I was destined to supply his place, and become a tallow-chandler. But my dislike to the trade continuing, my father was under apprehensions that if he did not find one for me more agreeable, I should break away and get to sea, as his son Josiah had done, to his great vexation. He therefore sometimes took me to walk with him, and see joiners, bricklayers, turners, braziers, etc., at their work, that he might observe my inclination, and endeavor to fix it on some trade or other on land. It has ever since been a pleasure to me to see good workmen handle their tools, and it has been useful to me, having learned so much by it as to be able to do little jobs myself in my house when a workman could not readily be got, and to construct little machines for my experiments, while the intention of making the experiment was fresh and warm in my mind. My father at last fixed upon the cutler's trade, and my uncle Benjamin's son Samuel, who was bred to that business in London, being about that time established in Boston, I was sent to be with him some time on liking. But his expectations of a fee[32] with me displeasing my father, I was taken home again.

[30] ÆTAT—At the age of, Latin.

[31] BUT ONE . . . PUBLIC BALL—Here is evidence that at this time Franklin had no thought of publishing his memoirs.

[32] EXPECTATIONS OF A FEE—Samuel Franklin evidently demanded pay for teaching his cousin the trade.

From a child I was fond of reading, and all the little money that came into my hands was ever laid out in books. Pleased with the "Pilgrim's Progress,"[33] my first collection was of John Bunyan's works in separate little volumes. I afterward sold them to enable me to buy R. Burton's "Historical Collections"; they were small chapmen's books,[34] and cheap, forty or fifty in all. My father's little library consisted chiefly of books in polemic divinity,[35] most of which I read, and have since often regretted that, at a time when I had such a thirst for knowledge, more proper books had not fallen in my way, since it was now resolved I should not be a clergyman. Plutarch's "Lives" there was in which I read abundantly, and I still think that time spent to great advantage. There was also a book of De Foe's, called an "Essay on Projects," and another of Dr. Mather's, called "Essays to do Good," which perhaps gave me a turn of thinking that had an influence on some of the principal future events of my life.

This bookish inclination at length determined my father to make me a printer, though he had already one son (James) of that profession. In 1717 my brother James returned from England with a press and letters to set up his business in Boston. I liked it much better than that of my father, but still had a hankering for the sea. To prevent the apprehended effect of such an inclination, my father was impatient to have me bound to my brother. I stood out some time, but at last was persuaded, and signed the indentures[36] when I was yet but twelve years old. I was to serve as an apprentice till I was twenty-one years of age, only I was to be allowed journeyman's[37] wages during the last year. In a little time I made great proficiency in the business, and became a useful hand to my brother. I now had access to better books. An acquaintance with the apprentices of booksellers enabled me sometimes to borrow a small one, which I was careful to return soon and clean. Often

---

[33] *Pilgrim's Progress,* ETC.—Allegory of the Christian life; Burton's *Historical Collections,* a series of books giving historical sketches in popular style; Plutarch's *Lives,* biographical accounts of famous Greeks and Romans, written in the first century A. D.; De Foe's *Essay on Projects,* a discussion of business and social practices in the early eighteenth century: Mather's *Essays to Do Good,* sermons urging a Christian life, with the prophecy that the world would come to an end in 1716.

[34] CHAPMEN'S BOOKS—Cheap volumes sold by peddlers.

[35] POLEMIC DIVINITY—Questions of religious dispute.

[36] INDENTURES—Contracts binding an apprentice to a master of a trade.

[37] JOURNEYMAN'S—When an apprentice has served his term, he becomes a journeyman and receives wages.

I sat up in my room reading the greatest part of the night, when the book was borrowed in the evening and to be returned early in the morning, lest it should be missed or wanted.

And after some time an ingenious tradesman, Mr. Matthew Adams, who had a pretty collection of books, and who frequented our printing-house, took notice of me, invited me to his library, and very kindly lent me such books as I chose to read. I now took a fancy to poetry, and made some little pieces; my brother, thinking it might turn to account, encouraged me, and put me on composing occasional ballads.[38] One was called *The Lighthouse Tragedy* and contained an account of the drowning of Captain Worthilake, with his two daughters; the other was a sailor's song, on the taking of *Teach* (or Blackbeard), the pirate. They were wretched stuff, in the Grub Street[39] ballad style; and when they were printed he sent me about the town to sell them. The first sold wonderfully, the event being recent, having made a great noise. This flattered my vanity; but my father discouraged me by ridiculing my performances, and telling me verse-makers were generally beggars. So I escaped being a poet, most probably a very bad one; but as prose writing has been of great use to me in the course of my life, and was a principal means of my advancement, I shall tell you how, in such a situation, I acquired what little ability I have in that way.

There was another bookish lad in the town, John Collins by name, with whom I was intimately acquainted. We sometimes disputed, and very fond we were of argument, and very desirous of confuting one another, which disputatious turn, by the way, is apt to become a very bad habit, making people often extremely disagreeable in company by the contradiction that is necessary to bring it into practice; and thence, besides souring and spoiling the conversation, is productive of disgusts and perhaps enmities where you may have occasion for friendship. I had caught it by reading my father's books of dispute about religion. Persons of good sense, I have since observed, seldom fall into it, except lawyers, university men, and men of all sorts that have been bred at Edinburgh.[40]

---

[38] OCCASIONAL BALLADS—Verse written to celebrate a contemporary event, and being hastily done and usually without inspiration, rarely of literary merit.

[39] GRUB STREET—A street in London where lived many writers, most of whom were poor and not greatly talented; hence applied to any literary work of mediocre merit.

[40] BRED AT EDINBURGH—Rather a curious taunt, if seriously meant, at the Scots for their love of dispute.

A question was once, somehow or other, started between Collins and me, of the propriety of educating the female sex[41] in learning, and their abilities for study. He was of opinion that it was improper, and that they were naturally unequal to it. I took the contrary side, perhaps a little for dispute's sake. He was naturally more eloquent, had a ready plenty of words; and sometimes, as I thought, bore me down more by his fluency than by the strength of his reasons. As we parted without settling the point, and were not to see one another again for some time, I sat down to put my arguments in writing, which I copied fair and sent to him. He answered, and I replied. Three or four letters of a side had passed, when my father happened to find my papers and read them. Without entering into the discussion, he took occasion to talk to me about the manner of my writing; observed that, though I had the advantage of my antagonist in correct spelling and pointing (which I owed to the printing-house) I fell far short in elegance of expression, in method, and in perspicuity, of which he convinced me by several instances. I saw the justice of his remarks, and thence grew more attentive to the manner in writing, and determined to endeavor at improvement.

About this time I met with an odd volume of the *Spectator*.[42] It was the third. I had never before seen any of them. I bought it, read it over and over, and was much delighted with it. I thought the writing excellent, and wished, if possible, to imitate it. With this view I took some of the papers, and making short hints of the sentiment in each sentence, laid them by a few days, and then, without looking at the book, tried to complete the papers again, by expressing each hinted sentiment at length, and as fully as it had been expressed before, in any suitable words that should come to hand. Then I compared my *Spectator* with the original, discovered some of my faults and corrected them. But I found I wanted a stock of words, or a readiness in recollecting and using them, which I thought I should have acquired before that time if I had gone

[41] EDUCATING THE FEMALE SEX—One of the subjects dealt with in De Foe's *Essay on Projects.*

[42] *Spectator*—A periodical of the early eighteenth century containing informal essays written chiefly by Addison and Steele. Sir Roger de Coverley is the most famous of the characters appearing in these papers. Franklin was a great admirer of Addison, following Dr. Johnson's advice that whoever wishes to attain a familiar, elegant English style must give his days and nights to the volumes of Addison.

on making verses; since the continual occasion for words of the same import, but of different length, to suit the measure, or of different sound for the rhyme, would have laid me under a constant necessity of searching for variety, and also have tended to fix that variety in my mind, and make me master of it. Therefore I took some of the tales and turned them into verse; and, after a time, when I had pretty well forgotten the prose, turned them back again. I also sometimes jumbled my collections of hints into confusion, and after some weeks endeavored to reduce them into the best order, before I began to form the full sentences and complete the paper. This was to teach me method in the arrangement of thoughts. By comparing my work afterwards with the original, I discovered many faults and amended them; but I sometimes had the pleasure of fancying that, in certain particulars of small import, I had been lucky enough to improve the method or the language, and this encouraged me to think I might possibly in time come to be a tolerable English writer, of which I was extremely ambitious. My time for these exercises and for reading was at night, after work, or before it began in the morning, or on Sundays, when I contrived to be in the printing-house alone, evading as much as I could the common attendance on public worship which my father used to exact of me when I was under his care, and which indeed I still thought a duty, though I could not, as it seemed to me, afford time to practice it.

When about sixteen years of age I happened to meet with a book, written by one Tryon, recommending a vegetable diet. I determined to go into it. My brother, being yet unmarried, did not keep house, but boarded himself and his apprentices in another family. My refusing to eat flesh occasioned an inconveniency, and I was frequently chid for my singularity. I made myself acquainted with Tryon's manner of preparing some of his dishes, such as boiling potatoes or rice, making hasty pudding, and a few others, and then proposed to my brother that if he would give me, weekly, half the money he paid for my board, I would board myself. He instantly agreed to it and I presently found that I could save half what he paid me. This was an additional fund for buying books. But I had another advantage in it. My brother and the rest going from the printing-house to their meals, I remained there alone, and dispatching presently my light repast, which often was no more than a biscuit or a slice of bread, a handful of raisins or a tart from the pastry-cook's, and a glass of water, had the rest of the time till their return for study, in which I made the greater progress, from that greater clearness of head and quicker apprehension which usually attend temperance in eating and drinking.

And now it was that, being on some occasion made ashamed of my ignorance in figures, which I had twice failed in learning when at school, I took Cocker's book of arithmetic, and went through the whole by myself with great ease. I also read Seller's and Shermy's books of navigation, and became acquainted with the little geometry they contain, but never proceeded far in that science. And I read about this time Locke[43] *On Human Understanding,* and the *Art of Thinking,* by Messrs. du Port Royal.[44]

While I was intent on improving my language, I met with an English grammar (I think it was Greenwood's), at the end of which there were two little sketches of the arts of rhetoric and logic, the latter finishing with a specimen of a dispute in the Socratic method;[45] and soon after I procured Xenophon's[46] "Memorable Things of Socrates," wherein there are many instances of the same method. I was charmed with it, adopted it, dropped my abrupt contradiction and positive argumentation, and put on the humble inquirer and doubter. And being then, from reading Shaftesbury and Collins,[47] become a real doubter in many points of our religious doctrine, I found this method safest for myself and very embarrassing to those against whom I used it. Therefore I took a delight in it, practiced it continually, and grew very artful and expert in drawing people, even of superior knowledge, into concessions, the consequences of which they did not foresee, entangling them in difficulties out of which they could not extricate themselves, and so obtaining victories that neither myself nor my cause always deserved. I continued this method some few years, but gradually

---

[43] LOCKE—John Locke, noted English philosopher.

[44] MESSRS. DU PORT ROYAL—Society of scholars who lived at the Abbey of Port Royal, near Paris.

[45] SOCRATIC METHOD—A method of argumentation based on the use of questions adroitly designed to lead an opponent into contradictions. The name comes from Socrates, Greek philosopher, who employed the method with great success.

[46] XENOPHON'S—Xenophon, famous Greek author of the *Anabasis,* kept a record of some of Socrates' debates.

[47] SHAFTESBURY AND COLLINS—Authors of religious and philosophic tracts in Franklin's time.

left it, retaining only the habit of expressing myself in terms of modest diffidence; never using, when I advanced anything that may possibly be disputed, the words *certainly, undoubtedly,* or any others that give the air of positiveness to an opinion; but rather say, I conceive or apprehend a thing to be so and so; it appears to me, or *I should think it so or so,* for such and such reasons; or *I imagine it to be so;* or *it is so if I am not mistaken.* This habit, I believe, has been of great advantage to me when I have had occasion to inculcate my opinions, and persuade men into measures that I have been from time to time engaged in promoting; and as the chief ends of conversation are to *inform,* or to be *informed,* to *please* or to *persuade,* I wish well-meaning, sensible men would not lessen their power of doing good by a positive, assuming manner, that seldom fails to disgust, tends to create opposition, and to defeat every one of those purposes for which speech was given to us, to wit, giving or receiving information or pleasure. For if you would inform, a positive and dogmatical manner in advancing your sentiments may provoke contradiction and prevent a candid attention. If you wish information and improvement from the knowledge of others, and yet at the same time express yourself as firmly fixed in your present opinions, modest, sensible men who do not love disputation will probably leave you undisturbed in the possession of your error. And by such a manner you can seldom hope to recommend yourself in *pleasing* your hearers, or to persuade those whose concurrence you desire. Pope[48] says judiciously:—

> Men should be taught as if you taught them not,
> And things unknown propos'd as things forgot;

farther recommending to us

> To speak, tho' sure, with seeming diffidence.

And he might have coupled with this line that which he has coupled with another, I think less properly,

> For want of modesty is want of sense.

---

[48] **Pope—Alexander Pope, greatest English poet of the time. His poetry, written in polished heroic couplets, was witty, often satiric, and immensely popular. The quotation is from his *Essay on Criticism*.**

If you ask, Why less properly? I must repeat the lines,—

> Immodest words admit of no defense,
> For want of modesty is want of sense.

Now, is not want of sense (where a man is so unfortunate as to want it) some apology for his want of modesty? And would not the lines stand more justly thus?

> Immodest words admit but this defense,
> That want of modesty is want of sense.

This, however, I should submit to better judgments.

My brother had, in 1720 or 1721, begun to print a newspaper. It was the second[49] that appeared in America, and was called the *New England Courant.* The only one before it was the *Boston News-Letter.* I remember his being dissuaded by some of his friends from the undertaking, as not likely to succeed, one newspaper being, in their judgment, enough for America. At this time (1771) there are not less than five-and-twenty. He went on, however, with the undertaking, and after having worked in composing the types and printing off the sheets, I was employed to carry the papers through the streets to the customers.

He had some ingenious men among his friends, who amused themselves by writing little pieces for this paper, which gained it credit and made it more in demand, and these gentlemen often visited us. Hearing their conversations, and their accounts of the approbation their papers were received with, I was excited to try my hand among them; but being still a boy, and suspecting that my brother would object to printing anything of mine in his paper if he knew it to be mine, I contrived to disguise my hand, and writing an anonymous paper, I put it in at night under the door of the printing-house. It was found in the morning, and communicated to his writing friends when they called in as usual. They read it, commented on it in my hearing, and I had the exquisite pleasure of finding it met with their approbation, and that in their different guesses at the author, none were named but men of some character among us for learning and ingenuity. I suppose now

---

[49] THE SECOND—Franklin erred. It was the fourth. The *New England Courant* has been called "the ancestor of yellow journalism," because it attacked the government, Harvard College, religion, etc., with irreverence and often malice.

that I was rather lucky in my judges, and that perhaps they were not really so very good ones as I then esteemed them.

Encouraged, however, by this, I wrote and conveyed in the same way to the press several more papers[50] which were equally approved; and I kept my secret till my small fund of sense for such performances was pretty well exhausted, and then I discovered it, when I began to be considered a little more by my brother's acquaintance, and in a manner that did not quite please him, as he thought, probably with reason, that it tended to make me too vain. And, perhaps, this might be one occasion of the differences that we began to have about this time. Though a brother, he considered himself as my master, and me as his apprentice, and, accordingly, expected the same services from me as he would from another, while I thought he demeaned me too much in some he required of me, who from a brother expected more indulgence. Our disputes were often brought before our father, and I fancy I was either generally in the right, or else a better pleader, because the judgment was generally in my favor. But my brother was passionate, and had often beaten me, which I took extremely amiss; and, thinking my apprenticeship very tedious, I was continually wishing for some opportunity of shortening it, which at length offered in a manner unexpected.*

One of the pieces in our newspaper on some political point,[51] which I have now forgotten, gave offence to the Assembly.[52] He was taken up, censured, and imprisoned for a month, by the speaker's warrant,[53] I suppose, because he would not discover his author. I too was taken up and examined before the council; but, though I did not give them any satisfaction, they contented themselves with admonishing me, and dismissed me, considering me,

* I fancy his harsh and tyrannical treatment of me might be a means of impressing me with that aversion to arbitrary power that has stuck to me through my whole life.—B. F.

---

[50] Several more papers—Among these were the letters Franklin wrote over the signature of Mrs. Silence Dogood (see Introduction, "The Author").

[51] Some political point—The *Courant* ridiculed Cotton Mather and other Puritan ministers who were trying to introduce inoculation as a preventive for smallpox, and attacked the government itself. This may well have been the chief reason for the imprisonment of James Franklin, though there were other offenses. It is interesting to note that Benjamin Franklin later advocated inoculation, his own son having died of the disease.

[52] Assembly—The legislative body that governed Massachusetts. Its members were elected by the people.

[53] Speaker's warrant—Warrant issued by the chairman of the Assembly.

perhaps, as an apprentice who was bound to keep his master's secrets.

During my brother's confinement, which I resented a good deal, notwithstanding our private differences, I had the management of the paper; and I made bold to give our rulers some rubs in it, which my brother took very kindly, while others began to consider me in an unfavorable light, as a young genius that had a turn for libelling and satire. My brother's discharge was accompanied with an order of the House (a very odd one), that *"James Franklin should no longer print the paper called the* NEW ENGLAND COURANT."

There was a consultation held in our printing-house among his friends, what he should do in this case. Some proposed to evade the order by changing the name of the paper; but my brother seeing inconveniences in that, it was finally concluded on as a better way, to let it be printed for the future under the name of BENJAMIN FRANKLIN; and to avoid the censure of the Assembly, that might fall on him as still printing it by his apprentice, the contrivance was that my old indenture should be returned to me, with a full discharge on the back of it, to be shown on occasion, but to secure to him the benefit of my service, I was to sign new indentures for the remainder of the term, which were to be kept private. A very flimsy scheme it was; however, it was immediately executed, and the paper went on accordingly, under my name for several months.

## CHAPTER II

### SEEKING HIS FORTUNE

The Runaway 'Prentice—Arrival in Philadelphia—Meeting with Miss Read—Keimer the Printer—A Governor's Patronage—Boston Revisited—Franklin's Friends

At length, a fresh difference arising between my brother and me, I took upon me to assert my freedom, presuming that he would not venture to produce the new indentures. It was not fair in me to take this advantage, and this I therefore reckon one of the first errata[1] of my life; but the unfairness of it weighed little with me, when under the impressions of resentment for the blows his passion

[1] ERRATA—Wilful missteps.

too often urged him to bestow upon me, though he was otherwise not an ill-natured man. Perhaps I was too saucy and provoking.

When he found I would leave him, he took care to prevent my getting employment in any other printing-house of the town, by going round and speaking to every master, who accordingly refused to give me work. I then thought of going to New York, as the nearest place where there was a printer; and I was rather inclined to leave Boston when I reflected that I had already made myself a little obnoxious to the governing party, and from the arbitrary proceedings of the Assembly in my brother's case, it was likely I might, if I stayed, soon bring myself into scrapes; and further, that my indiscreet disputations about religion began to make me pointed at with horror by good people as an infidel or atheist. I determined on the point, but my father now siding with my brother, I was sensible that if I attempted to go openly, means would be used to prevent me. My friend Collins, therefore, undertook to manage a little for me. He agreed with the captain of a New York sloop for my passage under the notion of my being a young acquaintance of his that had got into trouble. So I sold some of my books to raise a little money, was taken on board privately, and as we had a fair wind, in three days I found myself in New York, near three hundred miles from home, a boy of but seventeen,[2] without the least recommendation to, or knowledge of, any person in the place, and with very little money in my pocket.

My inclinations for the sea were by this time worn out, or I might now have gratified them. But, having a trade, and supposing myself a pretty good workman, I offered my service to the printer in the place, old Mr. William Bradford,[3] who had been the first printer in Pennsylvania, but removed from thence upon the quarrel of George Keith. He could give me no employment, having little to do, and help enough already; but says he, "My son at Philadelphia has lately lost his principal hand, Aquila Rose, by death; if you go thither, I believe he may employ you." Philadelphia was a hundred miles further; I set out, however, in a boat for Amboy, leaving my chest and things to follow me round by sea.

---

[2] A BOY OF BUT SEVENTEEN—As Franklin was born in 1706, this places the year as 1723.

[3] WILLIAM BRADFORD—Bradford had come over to William Penn's Quaker colony in 1685 and moved from Philadelphia to New York in 1693.

In crossing the bay, we met with a squall that tore our rotten sails to pieces, prevented our getting into the Kill,[4] and drove us upon Long Island. In our way, a drunken Dutchman, who was a passenger too, fell overboard; when he was sinking, I reached through the water to his shock pate,[5] and drew him up, so that we got him in again. His ducking sobered him a little, and he went to sleep, taking first out of his pocket a book, which he desired I would dry for him. It proved to be my old favorite author, Bunyan's *Pilgrim's Progress,* in Dutch, finely printed on good paper, with copper cuts, a dress better than I had ever seen it wear in its own language. I have since found that it has been translated into most of the languages of Europe, and suppose it has been more generally read than any other book, except perhaps the Bible. Honest John was the first that I know of who mixed narration and dialogue; a method of writing very engaging to the reader, who in the most interesting parts finds himself, as it were, brought into the company and present at the discourse. De Foe in his *Crusoe,* his *Moll Flanders, Religious Courtship, Family Instructor,* and other pieces, has imitated it with success, and Richardson[6] has done the same in his *Pamela,* etc.

When we drew near the island, we found it was at a place where there could be no landing, there being a great surf on the stony beach. So we dropped anchor, and swung round towards the shore. Some people came down to the water edge and hallooed to us, as we did to them; but the wind was so high, and the surf so loud, that we could not hear so as to understand each other. There were canoes on the shore, and we made signs, and hallooed that they should fetch us; but they either did not understand us, or thought it impracticable, so they went away, and night coming on, we had no remedy but to wait till the wind should abate; and, in the mean time, the boatman and I concluded to sleep, if we could; and so crowded into the scuttle,[7] with the Dutchman, who was still wet; and the spray beating over the head of our boat, leaked through to us, so that we were soon almost as wet as he. In this manner we lay all night, with very little rest; but the wind abating the

[4] KILL—Channel between Staten Island and New Jersey.

[5] SHOCK PATE—Hair of his head.

[6] DE FOE . . . RICHARDSON—The English novel begins with the work of these two writers.

[7] SCUTTLE—Hatchway, or opening in the deck.

next day, we made a shift to reach Amboy before night, having been thirty hours on the water, without victuals, or any drink but a bottle of filthy rum, the water we sailed on being salt.

In the evening I found myself very feverish, and went into bed; but having read somewhere that cold water drank plentifully was good for a fever, I followed the prescription, sweat plentifully most of the night, my fever left me, and in the morning, crossing the ferry, I proceeded on my journey on foot, having fifty miles to Burlington,[8] where I was told I should find boats that would carry me the rest of the way to Philadelphia.

It rained very hard all the day; I was thoroughly soaked, and by noon a good deal tired; so I stopped at a poor inn, where I stayed all night, beginning now to wish that I had never left home. I cut so miserable a figure, too, that I found by the questions asked me, I was suspected to be some runaway servant, and in danger of being taken up on that suspicion. However, I proceeded the next day, and got in the evening to an inn, within eight or ten miles of Burlington, kept by one Dr. Brown. He entered into conversation with me while I took some refreshment, and, finding I had read a little, became very sociable and friendly. Our acquaintance continued as long as he lived. He had been, I imagine, an itinerant doctor, for there was no town in England, or country in Europe, of which he could not give a very particular account. He had some letters,[9] and was ingenious, but much of an unbeliever, and wickedly undertook, some years after, to travesty the Bible in doggerel verse, as Cotton[10] had done Virgil. By this means he set many of the facts in a very ridiculous light, and might have hurt weak minds if his work had been published; but it never was.

At his house I lay that night, and the next morning reached Burlington, but had the mortification to find that the regular boats were gone a little before my coming, and no other expected to go before Tuesday, this being Saturday; wherefore I returned to an old woman in the town, of whom I had bought gingerbread to eat on the water, and asked her advice. She invited me to lodge at her house till a passage by water should offer; and being tired with my foot travelling, I accepted the invitation. She, understanding

[8] Burlington—Town on Delaware River, less than 20 miles from Philadelphia.

[9] Letters—Learning.

[10] Cotton—The English minor poet, Charles Cotton, who burlesqued the *Æneid*.

I was a printer, would have had me stay at that town and follow my business, being ignorant of the stock necessary to begin with. She was very hospitable, gave me a dinner of ox-cheek with great good-will, accepting only of a pot of ale in return; and I thought myself fixed till Tuesday should come. However, walking in the evening by the side of the river, a boat came by, which I found was going towards Philadelphia, with several people in her. They took me in, and, as there was no wind, we rowed all the way; and about midnight, not having yet seen the city, some of the company were confident we must have passed it, and would row no farther; the others knew not where we were; so we put toward the shore, got into a creek, landed near an old fence, with the rails of which we made a fire, the night being cold, in October, and there we remained till daylight. Then one of the company knew the place to be Cooper's Creek, a little above Philadelphia, which we saw as soon as we got out of the creek, and arrived there about eight or nine o'clock on the Sunday morning, and landed at the Market Street wharf.

I have been the more particular in this description of my journey, and shall be so of my first entry into that city, that you may in your mind compare such unlikely beginnings with the figure I have since made there. I was in my working-dress, my best clothes being to come round by sea. I was dirty from my journey; my pockets were stuffed out with shirts and stockings, and I knew no soul nor where to look for lodging. I was fatigued with traveling, rowing, and want of rest; I was very hungry; and my whole stock of cash consisted of a Dutch dollar, and about a shilling in copper. The latter I gave the people of the boat for my passage, who at first refused it on account of my rowing; but I insisted on their taking it, a man being sometimes more generous when he has but a little money than when he has plenty, perhaps through fear of being thought to have but little.

Then I walked up the street, gazing about till near the market-house I met a boy with bread. I had made many a meal on bread, and inquiring where he got it, I went immediately to the baker's he directed me to, in Second Street, and asked for biscuit, intending such as we had in Boston; but they, it seems were not made in Philadelphia. Then I asked for a three-penny loaf, and was told they had none such. So not considering or knowing the difference of money, and the greater cheapness nor the names of his bread, I bade him give me three-penny worth of any sort. He gave me, accordingly, three great puffy rolls. I was surprised at the quantity, but took it, and having no room in my pockets, walked off with a roll under each arm, and eating the other. Thus I went up Market Street as far as Fourth Street, passing by the door of Mr. Read, my future wife's father; when she, standing at the door, saw me, and thought I made, as I certainly did, a most awkward, ridiculous appearance. Then I turned and went down Chestnut Street and part of Walnut Street, eating my roll all the way, and coming round, found myself again at Market Street wharf, near the boat I came in, to which I went for a draught of the river water; and being filled with one of my rolls, gave the other two to a woman and her child that came down the river in the boat with us, and were waiting to go farther.

Thus refreshed, I walked again up the street, which by this time had many clean-dressed people in it, who were all walking the same way. I joined them, and thereby was led into the great meeting-house of the Quakers near the market. I sat down among them, and after looking round a while and hearing nothing said,[11] being very drowsy through labor and want of rest the preceding night, I fell fast asleep, and continued so till the meeting broke up, when one was kind enough to rouse me. This was, therefore, the first house I was in or slept in, in Philadelphia.

Walking down again toward the river, and looking in the faces of people, I met a young Quaker man, whose countenance I liked, and, accosting him, requested he would tell me where a stranger could get lodging. We were then near the sign of the Three Mariners. "Here," says he, "is one place that entertains strangers, but it is not a reputable house; if thee wilt walk with me, I'll show thee a better." He brought me to the Crooked Billet in Water Street. Here I got a dinner; and while I was eating it, several sly questions were asked me, as it seemed to be suspected from my youth and appearance that I might be some runaway.

After dinner, my sleepiness returned, and being shown to a bed, I lay down without undressing, and slept till six in the evening, was called to supper, went to bed again very early, and slept

[11] Hearing nothing said—In Quaker meetings no one speaks until "the spirit moves" him.

soundly till next morning. Then I made myself as tidy as I could, and went to Andrew Bradford the printer's. I found in the shop the old man his father, whom I had seen at New York, and who, traveling on horseback, had got to Philadelphia before me. He introduced me to his son, who received me civilly, gave me a breakfast, but told me he did not at present want a hand, being lately supplied with one; but there was another printer in town, lately set up, one Keimer, who, perhaps, might employ me; if not, I should be welcome to lodge at his house, and he would give me a little work to do now and then till fuller business should offer.

The old gentleman said he would go with me to the new printer; and when we found him, "Neighbor," says Bradford, "I have brought to see you a young man of your business; perhaps you may want such a one." He asked me a few questions, put a composing stick[12] in my hand to see how I worked, and then said he would employ me soon, though he had just then nothing for me to do; and taking old Bradford, whom he had never seen before, to be one of the town's people that had a good will for him, entered into a conversation on his present undertaking and prospects; while Bradford, not discovering that he was the other printer's father, on Keimer's saying he expected soon to get the greatest part of the business into his own hands, drew him on by artful questions, and starting little doubts, to explain all his views, what interests he relied on, and in what manner he intended to proceed. I, who stood by and heard all, saw immediately that one of them was a crafty old sophister,[13] and the other a mere novice. Bradford left me with Keimer, who was greatly surprised when I told him who the old man was.

Keimer's printing-house, I found, consisted of an old shattered press, and one small, worn-out font of English,[14] which he was then using himself, composing an Elegy on Aquila Rose, before mentioned, an ingenious young man, of excellent character, much respected in the town, clerk of the Assembly, and a pretty poet. Keimer made verses, too, but very indifferently. He could not be said to write them, for his manner was to compose them in the types directly out of his head. So there being no copy, but one

[12] Composing stick—A narrow tray on which the compositor sets up the type.

[13] Sophister—A shrewd fellow adept in tricky reasoning.

[14] Font of English—A whole set (font) of type known to printers as "English." Other types are Caslon, Gothic, Ionic, etc.

pair of cases,[15] and the Elegy likely to require all the letters, no one could help him. I endeavored to put his press (which he had not yet used, and of which he understood nothing) into order fit to be worked with; and promising to come and print off his Elegy as soon as he should have got it ready, I returned to Bradford's, who gave me a little job to do for the present, and there I lodged and dieted. A few days after, Keimer sent for me to print off the Elegy. And now he had got another pair of cases, and a pamphlet to reprint, on which he set me to work.

These two printers I found poorly qualified for their business. Bradford had not been bred to it, and was very illiterate; and Keimer, though something of a scholar, was a mere compositor, knowing nothing of presswork. He had been one of the French prophets, and could act their enthusiastic agitations.[16] At this time he did not profess any particular religion, but something of all on occasion; was very ignorant of the world, and had, as I afterward found, a good deal of the knave in his composition. He did not like my lodging at Bradford's while I worked with him. He had a house indeed, but without furniture, so he could not lodge me; but he got me a lodging at Mr. Read's before mentioned, who was the owner of his house; and my chest and clothes being come by this time, I made rather a more respectable appearance in the eyes of Miss Read than I had done when she first happened to see me eating my roll in the street.

I began now to have some acquaintance among the young people of the town that were lovers of reading, with whom I spent my evenings very pleasantly; and gaining money by my industry and frugality, I lived very agreeably, forgetting Boston as much as I could, and not desiring that any there should know where I resided except my friend Collins, who was in my secret, and kept it when I wrote to him. At length, an incident happened that sent me back again much sooner than I had intended. I had a brother-in-law, Robert Holmes,[17] master of a sloop that traded between Boston and Delaware. He being at Newcastle, forty miles below Philadelphia, heard there of me, and wrote me a letter mentioning the concern of

---

[15] CASES—Trays for holding sets of type.

[16] FRENCH PROPHETS . . . ENTHUSIASTIC AGITATIONS—Keimer evidently belonged to one of the Protestant sects of France whose religious emotion put them in a frenzy.

[17] ROBERT HOLMES—He had married Franklin's elder sister, Mary.

my friends in Boston at my abrupt departure, assuring me of their good-will to me, and that everything would be accommodated to my mind if I would return, to which he exhorted me very earnestly. I wrote an answer to his letter, thanked him for his advice, but stated my reasons for quitting Boston fully and in such a light as to convince him I was not so wrong as he had apprehended.

Sir William Keith,[18] governor of the province, was then at Newcastle, and Captain Holmes, happening to be in company with him when my letter came to hand, spoke to him of me, and showed him the letter. The governor read it, and seemed surprised when he was told my age. He said I appeared a young man of promising parts, and therefore should be encouraged; the printers at Philadelphia were wretched ones; and, if I would set up there, he made no doubt I should succeed; for his part, he would procure me the public business, and do me every other service in his power. This my brother-in-law afterwards told me in Boston, but I knew as yet nothing of it; when, one day, Keimer and I being at work together near the window, we saw the governor and another gentleman (which proved to be Colonel French of Newcastle), finely dressed, come directly across the street to our house, and heard them at the door.

Keimer ran down immediately, thinking it a visit to him; but the governor inquired for me, came up, and with a condescension and politeness I had been quite unused to made me many compliments, desired to be acquainted with me, blamed me kindly for not having made myself known to him when I first came to the place, and would have me away with him to the tavern, where he was going with Colonel French to taste, as he said, some excellent Madeira.[19] I was not a little surprised, and Keimer stared like a pig poisoned. I went, however, with the governor and Colonel French to a tavern, at the corner of Third Street, and over the Madeira he proposed my setting up my business, laid before me the probabilities of success, and both he and Colonel French assured me I should have their interest and influence in procuring the public business of both governments.[20] On my doubting whether my father

---

[18] SIR WILLIAM KEITH—Governor of Pennsylvania 1717–1726. He put through some good measures, but in 1728 was forced to flee from America to escape creditors. He died in 1749 while in prison for debt in the famous Old Bailey, London prison.

[19] MADEIRA—A wine made on the island of Madeira, off the northwest coast of Africa.

[20] BOTH GOVERNMENTS—Those of Pennsylvania and Delaware.

would assist me in it, Sir William said he would give me a letter to him, in which he would state the advantages, and he did not doubt of prevailing with him. So it was concluded I should return to Boston in the first vessel, with the governor's letter recommending me to my father. In the mean time the intention was to be kept a secret, and I went on working with Keimer as usual, the governor sending for me now and then to dine with him,[21] a very great honor I thought it, and conversing with me in the most affable, familiar, and friendly manner imaginable.

About the end of April, 1724, a little vessel offered for Boston. I took leave of Keimer as[22] going to see my friends. The governor gave me an ample letter, saying many flattering things of me to my father, and strongly recommending the project of my setting up at Philadelphia as a thing that must make my fortune. We struck on a shoal in going down the bay, and sprung a leak; we had a blustering time at sea, and were obliged to pump almost continually, at which I took my turn. We arrived safe, however, at Boston in about a fortnight. I had been absent seven months, and my friends had heard nothing of me; for my brother Holmes was not yet returned, and had not written about me. My unexpected appearance surprised the family; all were, however, very glad to see me, and made me welcome, except my brother. I went to see him at his printing-house. I was better dressed than ever while in his service, having a genteel new suit from head to foot, a watch, and my pockets lined with near five pounds sterling[23] in silver. He received me not very frankly, looked me all over, and turned to his work again.

The journeymen were inquisitive where I had been, what sort of a country it was, and how I liked it. I praised it much, and the happy life I led in it, expressing strongly my intention of returning to it; and one of them asking what kind of money we had there, I produced a handful of silver, and spread it before them, which was a kind of raree-show[24] they had not been used to, paper being

---

[21] TO DINE WITH HIM—An extraordinary favor for a mere journeyman printer. Even as a boy Franklin attracted the attention of men of importance.

[22] AS—As if.

[23] FIVE POUNDS STERLING—English money worth about $25, but in purchasing power in Franklin's time equivalent to several times that amount as compared to present-day values. The English pound was worth approximately $5.

[24] RAREE-SHOW—Show carried about in a box and exhibited in the streets.

the money of Boston.[25] Then I took an opportunity of letting them see my watch; and, lastly (my brother still grum and sullen), I gave them a piece of eight to drink,[26] and took my leave. This visit of mine offended him extremely; for, when my mother some time after spoke to him of a reconciliation, and of her wishes to see us on good terms together, and that we might live for the future as brothers, he said I had insulted him in such a manner before his people that he could never forget or forgive it. In this, however, he was mistaken.

My father received the governor's letter with some apparent surprise, but said little of it to me for some days, when Captain Holmes returning he showed it to him, asked him if he knew Keith, and what kind of man he was; adding his opinion that he must be of small discretion to think of setting a boy up in business who wanted yet three years of being at man's estate. Holmes said what he could in favor of the project, but my father was clear in the impropriety of it, and at last gave a flat denial to it. Then he wrote a civil letter to Sir William, thanking him for the patronage he had so kindly offered me, but declining to assist me as yet in setting up, I being, in his opinion, too young to be trusted with the management of a business so important, and for which the preparation must be so expensive.

My friend and companion Collins, who was a clerk in the post-office, pleased with the account I gave him of my new country, determined to go thither also; and, while I waited for my father's determination, he set out before me by land to Rhode Island, leaving his books, which were a pretty collection of mathematics and natural philosophy,[27] to come with mine and me to New York, where he proposed to wait for me.

My father, though he did not approve Sir William's proposition, was yet pleased that I had been able to obtain so advantageous a character from a person of such note where I had resided, and that I had been so industrious and careful as to equip myself so handsomely in so short a time; therefore, seeing no prospect of an accommodation between my brother and me, he gave his consent

---

[25] Paper being the money of Boston—It was not until 1795 that the first metal money was coined in the United States. Before that, the money authorized by the colonies was all paper, but foreign coins were often accepted as currency.

[26] A piece of eight to drink—A Spanish dollar with which to buy drink.

[27] Natural philosophy—The old term for the science of physics.

to my returning again to Philadelphia, advised me to behave respectfully to the people there, endeavor to obtain the general esteem, and avoid lampooning and libelling, to which he thought I had too much inclination; telling me, that by steady industry and a prudent parsimony I might save enough by the time I was one-and-twenty to set me up; and that, if I came near the matter, he would help me out with the rest. This was all I could obtain, except some small gifts as tokens of his and my mother's love, when I embarked again for New York, now with their approbation and their blessing.

The sloop putting in at Newport, Rhode Island, I visited my brother John,[28] who had been married and settled there some years. He received me very affectionately, for he always loved me. A friend of his, one Vernon, having some money due to him in Pennsylvania, about thirty-five pounds currency,[29] desired I would receive it for him, and keep it till I had his directions what to remit it in. Accordingly, he gave me an order. This afterward occasioned me a good deal of uneasiness.

At New York I found my friend Collins, who had arrived there some time before me. We had been intimate from children, and had read the same books together; but he had the advantage of more time for reading and studying, and a wonderful genius for mathematical learning, in which he far outstripped me. While I lived in Boston, most of my hours of leisure for conversation were spent with him, and he continued a sober as well as an industrious lad; was much respected for his learning by several of the clergy and other gentlemen, and seemed to promise making a good figure in life. But during my absence, he had acquired a habit of sotting with brandy; and I found by his own account, and what I heard from others, that he had been drunk every day since his arrival at New York, and behaved very oddly. He had gamed, too, and lost his money, so that I was obliged to discharge his lodgings, and defray his expenses to and at Philadelphia, which proved extremely inconvenient to me.

---

[28] MY BROTHER JOHN—One of his favorite brothers. Later Benjamin started him and another brother, Peter, in their father's trade of soap and candle making. When Franklin became deputy postmaster general, he appointed John postmaster of Boston and Peter postmaster of Philadelphia. Franklin's habit of appointing his relations to important offices (see "Franklin's Later Life") earned him unfavorable criticism.

[29] POUNDS CURRENCY—The colonial paper pound, worth about one-third less than the English pound sterling.

The then governor of New York, Burnet[30] (son of Bishop Burnet), hearing from the captain that a young man, one of his passengers, had a great many books, desired he would bring me to see him. I waited upon him accordingly, and should have taken Collins with me but that he was not sober. The governor treated me with great civility, showed me his library, which was a very large one, and we had a good deal of conversation about books and authors. This was the second governor who had done me the honor to take notice of me; which, to a poor boy like me, was very pleasing.

We proceeded to Philadelphia. I received on the way Vernon's money, without which we could hardly have finished our journey. Collins wished to be employed in some counting-house; but, whether they discovered his dramming by his breath, or by his behavior, though he had some recommendations, he met with no success in any application, and continued lodging and boarding at the same house with me, and at my expense. Knowing I had that money of Vernon's, he was continually borrowing of me, still promising repayment as soon as he should be in business. At length he had got so much of it that I was distressed to think what I should do in case of being called on to remit it.

His drinking continued, about which we sometimes quarrelled; for, when a little intoxicated, he was very fractious. Once, in a boat on the Delaware with some other young men, he refused to row in his turn. "I will be rowed home," says he. "We will not row you," says I. "You must, or stay all night on the water," says he, "just as you please." The others said, "Let us row; what signifies it?" But, my mind being soured with his other conduct, I continued to refuse. So he swore he would make me row, or throw me overboard; and coming along, stepping on the thwarts, toward me, when he came up and struck at me, I clapped my hand under his leg, and, rising, pitched him head-foremost into the river. I knew he was a good swimmer, and so was under little concern about him; but before he could get round to lay hold of the boat, we had with a few strokes pulled her out of his reach; and ever when he drew near the boat, we asked if he would row,

---

30 BURNET—William Burnet, then governor of New York and New Jersey, and later of Massachusetts and New Hampshire. His father, Bishop of Salisbury, was author of several histories.

striking a few strokes to slide her away from him. He was ready to die with vexation, and obstinately would not promise to row. However, seeing him at last beginning to tire we lifted him in and brought him home dripping wet in the evening. We hardly exchanged a civil word afterwards, and a West India captain, who had a commission to procure a tutor for the sons of a gentleman at Barbadoes, happening to meet with him, agreed to carry him thither. He left me then, promising to remit me the first money he should receive in order to discharge the debt; but I never heard of him after.

The breaking into this money of Vernon's was one of the first great errata of my life; and this affair showed that my father was not much out in his judgment when he supposed me too young to manage business of importance. But Sir William, on reading his letter, said he was too prudent. There was a great difference in persons; and discretion did not always accompany years, nor was youth always without it. "And since he will not set you up," says he, "I will do it myself. Give me an inventory of the things necessary to be had from England, and I will send for them. You shall repay me when you are able; I am resolved to have a good printer here, and I am sure you must succeed." This was spoken with such an appearance of cordiality that I had not the least doubt of his meaning what he said. I had hitherto kept the proposition of my setting up a secret in Philadelphia, and I still kept it. Had it been known that I depended on the governor, probably some friend, that knew him better, would have advised me not to rely on him, as I afterwards heard it as his known character to be liberal of promises which he never meant to keep.[31] Yet, unsolicited as he was by me, how could I think his generous offers insincere? I believed him one of the best men in the world.

I presented him an inventory of a little printing-house, amounting by my computation to about one hundred pounds sterling. He liked it, but asked me if my being on the spot in England to choose the types, and see that everything was good of the kind, might not be of some advantage. "Then," says he, "when there, you may make acquaintances, and establish correspondences in the book-

---

[31] PROMISES WHICH HE NEVER MEANT TO KEEP—In spite of seeking to win popularity by promises he could not always fulfill, Keith was more friendly to the people than most of the governors.

selling and stationery way." I agreed that this might be advantageous. "Then," says he, "get yourself ready to go with Annis,"[32] which was the annual ship, and the only one at that time usually passing between London and Philadelphia. But it would be some months before Annis sailed, so I continued working with Keimer, fretting about the money Collins had got from me, and in daily apprehensions of being called upon by Vernon, which, however, did not happen for some years after.

I believe I have omitted mentioning that, in my first voyage from Boston, being becalmed off Block Island, our people set about catching cod, and hauled up a great many. Hitherto I had stuck to my resolution of not eating animal food, and on this occasion I considered, with my master Tryon, the taking every fish as a kind of unprovoked murder, since none of them had, or ever could do us any injury that might justify the slaughter. All this seemed very reasonable. But I had formerly been a great lover of fish, and, when this came hot out of the frying-pan, it smelt admirably well. I balanced some time between principle and inclination, till I recollected that, when the fish were opened, I saw smaller fish taken out of their stomachs; then thought I, "If you eat one another, I don't see why we mayn't eat you." So I dined upon cod very heartily, and continued to eat with other people, returning only now and then occasionally to a vegetable diet. So convenient a thing it is to be a reasonable creature, since it enables one to find or make a reason for everything one has a mind to do.

Keimer and I lived on a pretty good familiar footing, and agreed tolerably well, for he suspected nothing of my setting up. He retained a great deal of his old enthusiasm and loved argumentation. We therefore had many disputations. I used to work him so with my Socratic method, and trepanned[33] him so often by questions apparently so distant from any point we had in hand, and yet by degrees led to the point, and brought him into difficulties and contradictions, that at last he grew ridiculously cautious, and would hardly answer me the most common question, without asking first, *"What do you intend to infer from that?"* However, it gave him so high an opinion of my abilities in the confuting way, that he seriously proposed my being his colleague in a project he had of

---

[32] Annis—Captain Annis of the "annual ship."

[33] Trepanned—Perforated. We might say, "peppered him."

setting up a new sect. He was to preach the doctrines, and I was to confound all opponents. When he came to explain with me upon the doctrines, I found several conundrums which I objected to, unless I might have my way a little, too, and introduce some of mine.

Keimer wore his beard at full length, because somewhere in the Mosaic law[34] it is said, *"Thou shalt not mar the corners of thy beard."* He likewise kept the Seventh day, Sabbath;[35] and these two points were essentials with him. I disliked both; but agreed to admit them upon condition of his adopting the doctrine of using no animal food. "I doubt," said he, "my constitution will not bear that." I assured him it would, and that he would be the better for it. He was usually a great glutton, and I promised myself some diversion in half starving him. He agreed to try the practice, if I would keep him company. I did so, and we held it for three months. We had our victuals dressed, and brought to us regularly by a woman in the neighborhood, who had from me a list of forty dishes, to be prepared for us at different times, in all of which there was neither fish, flesh, nor fowl, and the whim suited me the better at this time from the cheapness of it, not costing us above eighteen pence sterling[36] each per week. I have since kept several Lents most strictly, leaving the common diet for that and that for the common, abruptly without the least inconvenience, so that I think that there is little in the advice of making those changes by easy gradations. I went on pleasantly, but poor Keimer suffered grievously, tired of the project, longed for the flesh-pots of Egypt,[37] and ordered a roast pig. He invited me and two women friends to dine with him; but, it being too soon upon the table, he could not resist the temptation, and ate the whole before we came.

I had made some courtship during this time to Miss Read. I had a great respect and affection for her, and had some reason to believe she had the same for me; but as I was about to take a long voyage, and we were both very young, only a little above eighteen, it was thought most prudent by her mother to prevent our going too

[34] Mosaic law—Laws the Lord gave Moses. The quotation is based on Leviticus 19:27.

[35] The Seventh day, Sabbath—Saturday, observed by the Jews and some Christians as a day of rest and worship.

[36] Eighteen pence sterling—Thirty-six cents. Remember that would buy much more then than now.

[37] Flesh-pots of Egypt—Meat, feasting. See Exodus 16:3.

far at present, as a marriage, if it was to take place, would be more convenient after my return, when I should be, as I expected, set up in my business. Perhaps, too, she thought my expectations not so well founded as I imagined them to be.

My chief acquaintances at this time were Charles Osborne, Joseph Watson, and James Ralph, all lovers of reading. The two first were clerks to an eminent scrivener or conveyancer in the town, Charles Brockden; the other was clerk to a merchant. Watson was a pious, sensible young man, of great integrity; the others rather more lax in their principles of religion, particularly Ralph, who as well as Collins, had been unsettled by me, for which they both made me suffer. Osborne was sensible, candid, frank, sincere and affectionate to his friends, but in literary matters, too fond of criticizing. Ralph was ingenious, genteel in his manners, and extremely eloquent; I think I never knew a prettier talker. Both of them were great admirers of poetry, and began to try their hands in little pieces. Many pleasant walks we four had together on Sundays into the woods, near Schuylkill, where we read to one another, and conferred on what we read.

Ralph was inclined to pursue the study of poetry, not doubting but he might become eminent in it and make his fortune by it, alleging that the best poets must, when they first began to write, make as many faults as he did. Osborne dissuaded him, assured him he had no genius for poetry, and advised him to think of nothing beyond the business he was bred to; that in the mercantile way, though he had no stock, he might by his diligence and punctuality recommend himself to employment as a factor,[38] and in time acquire wherewith to trade on his own account. I approved the amusing one's self with poetry now and then, so far as to improve one's language, but no farther.

On this it was proposed that we should each of us, at our next meeting, produce a piece of our own composing, in order to improve by our mutual observations, criticisms, and corrections. As language and expression were what we had in view, we excluded all considerations of invention by agreeing that the task should be a version of the eighteenth Psalm, which describes the descent of a Deity. When the time of our meeting drew nigh, Ralph called on me first, and let me know his piece was ready. I told him I

[38] FACTOR—Agent operating on a commission basis.

had been busy, and having little inclination, had done nothing. He then showed me his piece for my opinion, and I much approved it, as it appeared to me to have great merit. "Now," says he, "Osborne never will allow the least merit in anything of mine, but makes a thousand criticisms out of mere envy. He is not so jealous of you; I wish, therefore, you would take this piece, and produce it as yours; I will pretend not to have had time, and so produce nothing. We shall then see what he will say to it." It was agreed, and I immediately transcribed it, that it might appear in my own hand.

We met; Watson's performance was read; there were some beauties in it, but many defects. Osborne's was read; it was much better; Ralph did it justice; remarked some faults, but applauded the beauties. He himself had nothing to produce. I was backward; seemed desirous of being excused; had not had sufficient time to correct, etc.; but no excuse could be admitted; produce I must. It was read and repeated; Watson and Osborne gave up the contest, and joined in applauding it. Ralph only made some criticisms, and proposed some amendments; but I defended my text. Osborne was against Ralph, and told him he was no better a critic than poet; so he dropped the argument. As they two went home together, Osborne expressed himself still more strongly in favor of what he thought my production; having restrained himself before, as he said, lest I should think it flattery. "But who would have imagined," said he, "that Franklin had been capable of such a performance; such painting, such force, such fire! He has even improved the original. In his common conversation he seems to have no choice of words;[39] he hesitates and blunders; and yet, good God! how he writes!" When we next met, Ralph discovered the trick we had played him, and Osborne was a little laughed at.

This transaction fixed Ralph in his resolution of becoming a poet. I did all I could to dissuade him from it, but he continued scribbling verses till Pope cured him.[40] He became, however, a pretty good prose writer. More of him hereafter. But, as I may not have occasion again to mention the other two, I shall just

---

[39] No choice of words—Franklin never did become a fluent orator. When in the Assembly and Continental Congress he spoke seldom, always briefly, even haltingly, but to the point, making his impression by modesty and sound sense.

[40] Till Pope cured him—Shortly after this, Ralph accompanied Franklin to England, where his mediocre verses were ridiculed by Pope in his *Dunciad*. Ralph made his best mark in political and historical writings. See page 141.

remark here, that Watson died in my arms a few years after, much lamented, being the best of our set. Osborne went to the West Indies, where he became an eminent lawyer and made money, but died young. He and I had made a serious agreement, that the one who happened first to die should, if possible, make a friendly visit to the other, and acquaint him how he found things in that separate state. But he never fulfilled his promise.

## CHAPTER III

### London Adventures

A Governor's Promises—Meeting Famous Men—James Ralph's Troubles—The Water-American—Watt's Printing-house—Swimming—The Merchant's Clerk

The governor, seeming to like my company, had me frequently to his house, and his setting me up was always mentioned as a fixed thing. I was to take with me letters recommendatory to a number of his friends, besides the letter of credit to furnish me with the necessary money for purchasing the press and types, paper, etc. For these letters I was appointed to call at different times, when they were to be ready; but a future time was still named. Thus he went on till the ship, whose departure too had been several times postponed, was on the point of sailing. Then, when I called to take my leave and receive the letters, his secretary, Dr. Baird, came out to me and said the governor was extremely busy in writing, but would be down at Newcastle before the ship, and there the letters would be delivered to me.

Ralph, though married, and having one child, had determined to accompany me in this voyage. It was thought he intended to establish a correspondence, and obtain goods to sell on commission; but I found afterwards, that, through some discontent with his wife's relations, he purposed to leave her on their hands, and never return again. Having taken leave of my friends, and interchanged some promises with Miss Read, I left Philadelphia in the ship, which anchored at Newcastle. The governor was there; but when I went to his lodging, the secretary came to me from him with the civilest message in the world, that he could not then see me, being engaged in business of the utmost importance, but should send the letters to me on board, wished me heartily a good voyage and a speedy return, etc. I returned on board a little puzzled, but still not doubting.

Mr. Andrew Hamilton,[1] a famous lawyer of Philadelphia, had taken passage in the same ship for himself and son, and with Mr. Denham, a Quaker merchant, and Messrs. Onion and Russel, masters of an iron work in Maryland, had engaged the great cabin; so that Ralph and I were forced to take up with a berth in the steerage, and none on board knowing us, were considered as ordinary persons. But Mr. Hamilton and his son (it was James, since governor) returned from Newcastle to Philadelphia, the father being recalled by a great fee to plead for a seized ship; and, just before we sailed, Colonel French coming on board, and showing me great respect, I was more taken notice of, and, with my friend Ralph, invited by the other gentlemen to come into the cabin, there being now room. Accordingly, we removed thither.

Understanding that Colonel French had brought on board the governor's dispatches, I asked the captain for those letters that were to be under my care. He said all were put into the bag together and he could not then come at them; but, before we landed in England, I should have an opportunity of picking them out, so I was satisfied for the present, and we proceeded on our voyage. We had a sociable company in the cabin, and lived uncommonly well, having the addition of all Mr. Hamilton's stores, who had laid in plentifully. In this passage Mr. Denham contracted a friendship for me that continued during his life. The voyage was otherwise not a pleasant one, as we had a great deal of bad weather.

When we came into the Channel, the captain kept his word with me, and gave me an opportunity of examining the bag for the governor's letters. I found none upon which my name was put as under my care. I picked out six or seven, that, by the handwriting, I thought might be the promised letters, especially as one of them was directed to Basket, the king's printer, and another to some stationer. We arrived in London the 24th of December, 1724. I waited upon the stationer, who came first in my way, delivering the letter as from Governor Keith. "I don't know such a person," says

[1] ANDREW HAMILTON—Philadelphia lawyer of Scottish birth who became attorney general of Pennsylvania and leader of the colonial bar. "Smart as a Philadelphia lawyer" became a by-word. He and his son-in-law built as a private enterprise the State House, later known as Independence Hall.

he; but, opening the letter, "Oh! this is from Riddlesden. I have lately found him to be a complete rascal, and I will have nothing to do with him, nor receive any letters from him." So, putting the letter into my hand, he turned on his heel and left me to serve some customer. I was surprised to find these were not the governor's letters; and, after recollecting and comparing circumstances, I began to doubt his sincerity. I found my friend Denham, and opened the whole affair to him. He let me into Keith's character; told me there was not the least probability that he had written any letters for me; that no one, who knew him, had the smallest dependence on him; and he laughed at the notion of the governor's giving me a letter of credit, having, as he said, no credit to give. On my expressing some concern about what I should do, he advised me to endeavor getting some employment in the way of my business. "Among the printers here," said he, "you will improve yourself, and when you return to America, you will set up to greater advantage."

We both of us happened to know, as well as the stationer, that Riddlesden, the attorney, was a very knave. He had half ruined Miss Read's father by persuading him to be bound for him.[2] By this letter it appeared there was a secret scheme on foot to the prejudice of Hamilton (supposed to be then coming over with us); and that Keith was concerned in it with Riddlesden. Denham, who was a friend of Hamilton's, thought he ought to be acquainted with it; so, when he arrived in England, which was soon after, partly from resentment and ill-will to Keith and Riddlesden, and partly from good-will to him, I waited on him, and gave him the letter. He thanked me cordially, the information being of importance to him; and from that time he became my friend, greatly to my advantage afterwards on many occasions.

But what shall we think of a governor's playing such pitiful tricks, and imposing so grossly on a poor ignorant boy! It was a habit he had acquired. He wished to please everybody; and, having little to give, he gave expectations. He was otherwise an ingenious, sensible man, a pretty good writer, and a good governor for the people, though not for his constituents, the proprietaries,[3] whose

---

[2] To be bound for him—To guarantee payment of a debt.

[3] Proprietaries—Descendants and heirs of the persons to whom the land was originally granted by the King.

instructions he sometimes disregarded. Several of our best laws were of his planning and passed during his administration.

Ralph and I were inseparable companions. We took lodgings together in Little Britain[4] at three shillings and sixpence a week—as much as we could then afford. He found some relations, but they were poor, and unable to assist him. He now let me know his intentions of remaining in London, and that he never meant to return to Philadelphia. He had brought no money with him, the whole he could muster having been expended in paying his passage. I had fifteen pistoles;[5] so he borrowed occasionally of me to subsist while he was looking out for business. He first endeavored to get into the playhouse, believing himself qualified for an actor; but Wilkes,[6] to whom he applied, advised him candidly not to think of that employment, as it was impossible he should succeed in it. Then he proposed to Roberts, a publisher in Paternoster Row,[7] to write for him a weekly paper like the *Spectator,* on certain conditions, which Roberts did not approve. Then he endeavored to get employment as a hackney writer, to copy for the stationers and lawyers about the Temple,[8] but could find no vacancy.

I immediately got into work at Palmer's, then a famous printing-house in Bartholomew Close, and here I continued near a year. I was pretty diligent, but spent with Ralph a good deal of my earnings in going to plays and other places of amusement. We had together consumed all my pistoles, and now just rubbed on from hand to mouth. He seemed quite to forget his wife and child, and I, by degrees, my engagements with Miss Read, to whom I never wrote more than one letter, and that was to let her know I was not likely soon to return. This was another of the great errata of my life, which I should wish to correct if I were to live it over again. In fact, by our expenses, I was constantly kept unable to pay my passage.

At Palmer's I was employed in composing for the second edition of Wollaston's "Religion of Nature." Some of his reasonings not appearing to me well founded, I wrote a little metaphysical piece

---

[4] LITTLE BRITAIN—Small neighborhood in the heart of London, a famous quarter for booksellers. See essay on Little Britain in Irving's *Sketch Book,* page 546.

[5] FIFTEEN PISTOLES—A pistole was a Spanish coin worth about $4.

[6] WILKES—Comedy actor and manager of Drury Lane Theater, London.

[7] PATERNOSTER ROW—London street which was the center of the publishing business.

[8] THE TEMPLE—A group of buildings, on the site of the old Knights Templars headquarters, where many lawyers have their offices.

in which I made remarks on them. It was entitled "A Dissertation[9] on Liberty and Necessity, Pleasure and Pain." I inscribed it to my friend Ralph; I printed a small number. It occasioned my being more considered by Mr. Palmer as a young man of some ingenuity, though he seriously expostulated with me upon the principles of my pamphlet, which to him appeared abominable. My printing this pamphlet was another erratum. While I lodged in Little Britain, I made an acquaintance with one Wilcox, a bookseller, whose shop was at the next door. He had an immense collection of second-hand books. Circulating libraries were not then in use; but we agreed that, on certain reasonable terms, which I have now forgotten, I might take, read, and return any of his books. This I esteemed a great advantage, and I made as much use of it as I could.

My pamphlet by some means falling into the hands of one Lyons, a surgeon, author of a book entitled "The Infallibility of Human Judgment," it occasioned an acquaintance between us. He took great notice of me, called on me often to converse on those subjects, carried me to the Horns, a pale-ale house in —— Lane, Cheapside,[10] and introduced me to Dr. Mandeville,[11] author of the "Fable of the Bees," who had a club there, of which he was the soul, being a most facetious, entertaining companion. Lyons, too, introduced me to Dr. Pemberton, at Batson's Coffee-house,[12] who promised to give me an opportunity, some time or other, of seeing Sir Isaac Newton,[13] of which I was extremely desirous; but this never happened.

I had brought over a few curiosities, among which the principal was a purse made of the asbestos, which purifies by fire. Sir Hans Sloane[14] heard of it, came to see me, and invited me to his house in Bloomsbury Square, where he showed me all his curiosities, and

---

[9] A DISSERTATION—Franklin, passing through a period of doubt, argued in this paper against the probability of the immortality of the soul.

[10] CHEAPSIDE—Another famous street in the heart of London.

[11] DR. MANDEVILLE—Bernard Mandeville, a Dutch physician living in London, who shocked the conservatives with his witty writings on religious and moral subjects.

[12] COFFEE-HOUSE—A restaurant which usually became a rendezvous for a group of intimates gathered about one or more of the important figures of the day. It became practically a club where the patrons discussed literary, political, or scientific subjects.

[13] SIR ISAAC NEWTON—English scientist and mathematician, one of whose great achievements was the discovery of the law of gravitation.

[14] SIR HANS SLOANE—British physician and naturalist who succeeded Sir Isaac Newton as president of the Royal Society, an association of scientists. His great library, which he bequeathed to the nation, became the nucleus of the British Museum.

persuaded me to let him add that to the number, for which he paid me handsomely. . . .

Ralph . . . being still out of business . . . now took a resolution of going from London, to try for a country school, which he thought himself well qualified to undertake, as he wrote an excellent hand, and was a master of arithmetic and accounts. This, however, he deemed a business below him, and confident of future better fortune, when he should be unwilling to have it known that he once was so meanly employed, he changed his name, and did me the honor to assume mine; for I soon after had a letter from him, acquainting me that he was settled in a small village (in Berkshire, I think it was, where he taught reading and writing to ten or a dozen boys, at sixpence each per week) . . . and desiring me to write to him, directing for Mr. Franklin, schoolmaster at such a place.

He continued to write frequently, sending me large specimens of an epic poem which he was then composing, and desiring my remarks and corrections. These I gave him from time to time, but endeavored rather to discourage his proceeding. One of Young's "Satires" was then just published. I copied and sent him a great part of it, which set in a strong light the folly of pursuing the Muses with any hope of advancement by them. All was in vain; sheets of the poem continued to come by every post. In the mean time . . . another affair made a breach between us; and, when he returned again to London, he let me know he thought I had cancelled all the obligations he had been under to me. So I found I was never to expect his repaying me what I lent to him, or advanced for him. This, however, was not then of much consequence, as he was totally unable; and in the loss of his friendship I found myself relieved from a burden. I now began to think of getting a little money beforehand, and, expecting better work, I left Palmer's to work at Watts's, near Lincoln's Inn Fields,[15] a still greater printing-house. Here I continued all the rest of my stay in London.

At my first admission into this printing-house I took to working at press, imagining I felt a want of the bodily exercise I had been used to in America, where presswork is mixed with composing. I

[15] LINCOLN'S INN FIELDS—Largest square in London and site of an eighteenth century theater of that name.

drank only water; the other workmen, near fifty in number, were great guzzlers of beer. On occasion, I carried up and down stairs a large form of types in each hand, when others carried but one in both hands. They wondered to see, from this and several instances, that the *Water-American,* as they called me, was *stronger* than themselves, who drank *strong* beer! We had an alehouse boy who attended always in the house to supply the workmen. My companion at the press drank every day a pint before breakfast, a pint at breakfast with his bread and cheese, a pint between breakfast and dinner, a pint at dinner, a pint in the afternoon about six o'clock, and another when he had done his day's work. I thought it a detestable custom; but it was necessary, he supposed, to drink *strong* beer, that he might be *strong* to labor. I endeavored to convince him that the bodily strength afforded by beer could only be in proportion to the grain or flour of the barley dissolved in the water of which it was made; that there was more flour in a pennyworth of bread; and therefore, if he would eat that with a pint of water, it would give him more strength than a quart of beer. He drank on, however, and had four or five shillings to pay out of his wages every Saturday night for that muddling liquor; an expense I was free from. And thus these poor devils kept themselves always under.

Watts, after some weeks, desiring to have me in the composing-room, I left the pressmen; a new bien venu, or sum for drink, being five shillings, was demanded of me by the compositors. I thought it an imposition, as I had paid below;[16] the master thought so too, and forbade my paying it. I stood out two or three weeks, was accordingly considered as an excommunicate, and had so many little pieces of private mischief done me, by mixing my sorts,[17] transposing my pages, breaking my matter, etc., etc., if I were ever so little out of the room, and all ascribed to the chapel ghost,[18] which they said ever haunted those not regularly admitted, that, notwithstanding the master's protection, I found myself obliged to comply and pay the money, convinced of the folly of being on ill terms with those one is to live with continually.

---

[16] BELOW—In the press room. Franklin was working on the floor above in the composing room, where the type was set up.

[17] SORTS—Sets of type.

[18] CHAPEL GHOST—Ghost of the printing office. After hazing Franklin by mixing his type, etc., the men pretended the ghost had done the mischief.

I was now on a fair footing with them, and soon acquired considerable influence. I proposed some reasonable alterations in their chapel laws, and carried them against all opposition. From my example, a great part of them left their muddling breakfast of beer, and bread, and cheese, finding they could, with me, be supplied from a neighboring house with a large porringer of hot water-gruel, sprinkled with pepper, crumbed with bread, and a bit of butter in it, for the price of a pint of beer, viz., three half-pence. This was a more comfortable as well as cheaper breakfast, and kept their heads clearer. Those who continued sotting with beer all day were often, by not paying, out of credit at the alehouse, and used to make interest with me to get beer; their *light,* as they phrased it, *being out.*[19] I watched the pay-table on Saturday night, and collected what I stood engaged for them, having to pay sometimes near thirty shillings a week on their accounts. This, and my being esteemed a pretty good riggite, that is, a jocular, verbal satirist, supported my consequence in the society. My constant attendance (I never making a St. Monday[20]) recommended me to the master; and my uncommon quickness at composing occasioned my being put upon all work of dispatch, which was generally better paid. So I went on now very agreeably.

My lodging in Little Britain being too remote, I found another in Duke Street, opposite to the Romish chapel. It was two pair of stairs backwards, at an Italian warehouse. A widow lady kept the house. She had a daughter, and a maid servant, and a journeyman who attended the warehouse, but lodged abroad. After sending to inquire my character at the house where I last lodged, she agreed to take me in at the same rate, 3*s.* 6*d.* per week; cheaper, as she said, from the protection she expected in having a man lodge in the house. She was a widow, an elderly woman; had been bred a Protestant, being a clergyman's daughter, but was converted to the Catholic religion by her husband, whose memory she much revered; had lived much among people of distinction, and knew a thousand anecdotes of them as far back as the times of Charles the Second. She was lame in her knees with the gout, and, therefore, seldom stirred out of her room, so sometimes wanted company;

---

[19] THEIR LIGHT . . . BEING OUT—Slang. They were "broke" and could get no more credit.

[20] ST. MONDAY—A Monday taken off by workmen after a week-end of dissipation.

and hers was so highly amusing to me, that I was sure to spend an evening with her whenever she desired it. Our supper was only half an anchovy each, on a very little strip of bread and butter, and half a pint of ale between us; but the entertainment was in her conversation. My always keeping good hours, and giving little trouble in the family, made her unwilling to part with me; so that, when I talked of a lodging I had heard of, nearer my business, for two shillings a week, which, intent as I now was on saving money, made some difference, she bid me not think of it, for she would abate me two shillings a week for the future; so I remained with her at one shilling and sixpence as long as I stayed in London.

In a garret of her house there lived a maiden lady of seventy, in the most retired manner, of whom my landlady gave me this account: that she was a Roman Catholic, had been sent abroad when young, and lodged in a nunnery with an intent of becoming a nun; but, the country not agreeing with her, she returned to England, where, there being no nunnery, she had vowed to lead the life of a nun, as near as might be done in those circumstances. Accordingly she had given all her estate to charitable uses, reserving only twelve pounds a year to live on, and out of this sum she still gave a great deal in charity, living herself on water-gruel only, and using no fire but to boil it. She had lived many years in that garret, being permitted to remain there gratis by successive Catholic tenants of the house below, as they deemed it a blessing to have her there. A priest visited her to confess her every day. "I have asked her," says my landlady, "how she, as she lived, could possibly find so much employment for a confessor?" "Oh," said she, "it is impossible to avoid *vain thoughts*." I was permitted once to visit her. She was cheerful and polite, and conversed pleasantly. The room was clean, but had no other furniture than a mattress, a table with a crucifix and book, a stool which she gave me to sit on, and a picture over the chimney of Saint Veronica displaying her handkerchief,[21] with the miraculous figure of Christ's bleeding face on it, which she explained to me with great seriousness. She looked

[21] SAINT VERONICA DISPLAYING HER HANDKERCHIEF—According to tradition, Veronica was a woman of Jerusalem who in pity gave Christ her handkerchief with which to wipe His brow as He carried the cross on the way to Calvary. The image of His face is supposed to have been marked upon the handkerchief, which ever since has had miraculous healing powers.

pale, but was never sick; and I give it as another instance on how small an income life and health may be supported.

At Watts's printing-house I contracted an acquaintance with an ingenious young man, one Wygate, who, having wealthy relations, had been better educated than most printers; was a tolerable Latinist, spoke French, and loved reading. I taught him and a friend of his to swim at twice going into the river, and they soon became good swimmers. They introduced me to some gentlemen from the country, who went to Chelsea[22] by water to see the College and Don Saltero's curiosities.[23] In our return, at the request of the company, whose curiosity Wygate had excited, I stripped and leaped into the river, and swam from near Chelsea to Blackfriar's,[24] performing on the way many feats of activity, both upon and under water, that surprised and pleased those to whom they were novelties.

I had from a child been ever delighted with this exercise, had studied and practised all Thevenot's motions[25] and positions, added some of my own, aiming at the graceful and easy as well as the useful. All these I took this occasion of exhibiting to the company, and was much flattered by their admiration; and Wygate, who was desirous of becoming a master, grew more and more attached to me on that account, as well as from the similarity of our studies. He at length proposed to me travelling all over Europe together, supporting ourselves everywhere by working at our business. I was once inclined to it; but, mentioning it to my good friend Mr. Denham, with whom I often spent an hour when I had leisure, he dissuaded me from it, advising me to think only of returning to Pennsylvania, which he was now about to do.

I must record one trait of this good man's character. He had formerly been in business at Bristol, but failed in debt to a number of people, compounded[26] and went to America. There, by a close

---

[22] CHELSEA—Then a London suburb, now part of the city.

[23] DON SALTERO'S CURIOSITIES—A collection of curios exhibited by one James Salter, formerly valet to Sir Hans Sloane from whom he had received most of the display. Salter ran a barber shop and coffee-house which became a popular resort.

[24] FROM NEAR CHELSEA TO BLACKFRIAR'S—A distance of about three miles. Blackfriar's was a locality in old London, site of the famous Elizabethan theater of that name.

[25] THEVENOT'S MOTIONS—The art of swimming as explained by the French writer, Thevenot.

[26] COMPOUNDED—Effected a compromise with his creditors; that is, paid what he could on the dollar.

application to business as a merchant, he acquired a plentiful fortune in a few years. Returning to England in the ship with me, he invited his old creditors to an entertainment, at which he thanked them for the easy composition they had favored him with, and, when they expected nothing but the treat, every man at the first remove found under his plate an order on a banker for the full amount of the unpaid remainder with interest.

He now told me he was about to return to Philadelphia, and should carry over a great quantity of goods in order to open a store there. He proposed to take me over as his clerk, to keep his books, in which he would instruct me, copy his letters, and attend the store. He added that, as soon as I should be acquainted with mercantile business, he would promote me by sending me with a cargo of flour and bread, etc., to the West Indies, and procure me commissions from others which would be profitable; and if I managed well, would establish me handsomely. The thing pleased me; for I was grown tired of London, remembered with pleasure the happy months I had spent in Pennsylvania, and wished again to see it; therefore I immediately agreed on the terms of fifty pounds a year, Pennsylvania money,[27] less, indeed, than my present gettings as a compositor, but affording a better prospect.

I now took leave of printing, as I thought, forever, and was daily employed in my new business, going about with Mr. Denham among the tradesmen to purchase various articles, and seeing them packed up, doing errands, calling upon workmen to dispatch, etc.; and when all was on board, I had a few days' leisure. On one of these days, I was, to my surprise, sent for by a great man I knew only by name, a Sir William Wyndham,[28] and I waited upon him. He had heard by some means or other of my swimming from Chelsea to Blackfriar's, and of my teaching Wygate and another young man to swim in a few hours. He had two sons, about to set out on their travels; he wished to have them first taught swimming, and proposed to gratify me handsomely if I would teach them. They were not yet come to town, and my stay was uncertain, so I could not undertake it; but from this incident, I thought it likely

---

[27] Fifty pounds . . . Pennsylvania money—About $165. The Pennsylvania pound was worth only about $3.30, while the British pound was worth about $5.

[28] Sir William Wyndham—English politician who had been dismissed from a ministry post on suspicion of having been involved in a political plot following the death of Queen Anne.

that if I were to remain in England and open a swimming-school I might get a good deal of money; and it struck me so strongly that, had the overture been sooner made me, probably I should not so soon have returned to America. After many years, you and I had something of more importance to do with one of these sons of Sir William Wyndham, become Earl of Egremont, which I shall mention in its place.[29]

Thus I spent about eighteen months in London; most part of the time I worked hard at my business, and spent but little upon myself except in seeing plays and in books. My friend Ralph had kept me poor; he owed me about twenty-seven pounds, which I was now never likely to receive; a great sum out of my small earnings! I loved him, notwithstanding, for he had many amiable qualities. I had by no means improved my fortune; but I had picked up some very ingenious acquaintances, whose conversation was of great advantage to me; and I had read considerably.

We sailed from Gravesend on the 23d of July, 1726. For the incidents of the voyage, I refer you to my Journal,[30] where you will find them all minutely related. Perhaps the most important part of that journal is the *plan* to be found in it which I formed at sea, for regulating my future conduct in life. It is the more remarkable, as being formed when I was so young, and yet being pretty faithfully adhered to quite through to old age.

## CHAPTER IV

### The Master Printer

Return to Printing—Quarrel with Keimer—Firm of Franklin & Meredith—The Junto—Venture in Journalism—Friends in the Assembly—Independence at Last—Marriage—The Circulating Library

We landed in Philadelphia on the 11th of October, where I found sundry alterations. Keith was no longer governor, being superseded by Major Gordon. I met him walking the streets as a common citizen. He seemed a little ashamed at seeing me, but passed without saying anything. I should have been as much

[29] Which . . . in its place—The *Autobiography* stops just short of the period in which these dealings would have been related.

[33] My Journal—A copy of the Journal was found among Franklin's papers, but the plan mentioned was lacking.

ashamed at seeing Miss Read, had not her friends, despairing with reason of my return after the receipt of my letter,[1] persuaded her to marry another, one Rogers, a potter, which was done in my absence. With him, however, she was never happy, and soon parted from him, refusing to bear his name, it now being said that he had another wife. He was a worthless fellow, though an excellent workman, which was the temptation to her friends. He got into debt, ran away in 1727 or 1728, went to the West Indies, and died there. Keimer had got a better house, a shop well supplied with stationery, plenty of new types, a number of hands, though none good, and seemed to have a great deal of business.

Mr. Denham took a store in Water Street, where we opened our goods; I attended the business diligently, studied accounts, and grew in a little time expert at selling. We lodged and boarded together; he counselled me as a father, having a sincere regard for me. I respected and loved him, and we might have gone on together very happy; but in the beginning of February, 1727, when I had just passed my twenty-first year, we both were taken ill. My distemper was a pleurisy, which very nearly carried me off. I suffered a good deal, gave up the point in my own mind, and was rather disappointed when I found myself recovering, regretting, in some degree, that I must now, some time or other, have all that disagreeable work to do over again. I forget what his distemper was; it held him a long time, and at length carried him off. He left me a small legacy in a nuncupative will[2] as a token of his kindness for me, and he left me once more to the wide world; for the store was taken into the care of his executors, and my employment under him ended.

My brother-in-law, Holmes, being now at Philadelphia, advised my return to my business; and Keimer tempted me, with an offer of large wages by the year, to come and take the management of his printing-house, that he might better attend his stationer's shop. I had heard a bad character of him in London from his wife and her friends, and was not fond of having any more to do with him. I tried for further employment as a merchant's clerk; but not readily meeting with any, I closed again with Keimer. I found in

---

[1] My letter—See page 50.

[2] Nuncupative will—A will drafted in an emergency without full legal procedure of signature, witnesses, etc.

his house these hands: Hugh Meredith, a Welsh Pennsylvanian, thirty years of age, bred to country work; honest, sensible, had a great deal of solid observation, was something of a reader, but given to drink. Stephen Potts, a young countryman of full age,[3] bred to the same, of uncommon natural parts, and great wit and humor, but a little idle. These he had agreed with at extremely low wages per week, to be raised a shilling every three months, as they would deserve by improving in their business; and the expectation of these high wages, to come on hereafter, was what he had drawn them in with. Meredith was to work at press, Potts at bookbinding, which he, by agreement, was to teach them, though he knew neither one nor the other. John ——, a wild Irishman, brought up to no business, whose service, for four years, Keimer had purchased from the captain of a ship;[4] he, too, was to be made a pressman. George Webb, an Oxford scholar, whose time for four years he had likewise bought, intending him for a compositor, of whom more presently; and David Harry, a country boy, whom he had taken apprentice.

I soon perceived that the intention of engaging me at wages so much higher than he had been used to give was to have these raw, cheap hands formed through me; and as soon as I had instructed them, then they being all articled to him, he should be able to do without me. I went on, however, very cheerfully, put his printing-house in order, which had been in great confusion, and brought his hands by degrees to mind their business and to do it better.

It was an odd thing to find an Oxford scholar in the situation of a bought servant. He was not more than eighteen years of age, and gave me this account of himself; that he was born in Gloucester, educated at a grammar-school there, had been distinguished among the scholars for some apparent superiority in performing his part, when they exhibited plays; belonged to the Witty Club there, and had written some pieces in prose and verse, which were printed in the Gloucester newspapers; thence he was

---

[3] Of full age—Having reached one's majority, commonly 21 years.

[4] Whose service . . . captain of a ship—Emigrants to America sometimes contracted with the ship's captain to work for a specified time in payment for their passage. On arrival, the captain sold his rights in these "indentured or bought servants" to some one in the colonies. That Franklin himself dealt for a time in indentures, buying and selling bonded servants for a profit, is proved by advertisements in his newspaper, the *Pennsylvania Gazette*.

sent to Oxford where he continued about a year, but not well satisfied, wishing of all things to see London, and become a player. At length, receiving his quarterly allowance of fifteen guineas,[5] instead of discharging his debts he walked out of town, hid his gown[6] in a furze bush, and footed it to London, where, having no friend to advise him, he fell into bad company, soon spent his guineas, found no means of being introduced among the players, grew necessitous, pawned his clothes, and wanted bread. Walking the street very hungry, and not knowing what to do with himself, a crimp's bill[7] was put into his hand, offering immediate entertainment and encouragement to such as would bind themselves to serve in America. He went directly, signed the indentures, was put into the ship, and came over, never writing a line to acquaint his friends what was become of him. He was lively, witty, good-natured, and a pleasant companion, but idle, thoughtless, and imprudent to the last degree.

John the Irishman soon ran away; with the rest I began to live very agreeably, for they all respected me the more, as they found Keimer incapable of instructing them, and that from me they learned something daily. We never worked on Saturday, that being Keimer's Sabbath, so I had two days for reading. My acquaintance with ingenious people in the town increased. Keimer himself treated me with great civility and apparent regard, and nothing now made me uneasy but my debt to Vernon, which I was yet unable to pay, being hitherto but a poor economist. He, however, kindly made no demand of it.

Our printing-house often wanted sorts, and there was no letter-founder[8] in America. I had seen types cast at James's, in London, but without much attention to the manner; however, I now contrived a mould, made use of the letters we had as puncheons, struck the matrices[9] in lead, and thus supplied in a pretty tolerable

---

[5] FIFTEEN GUINEAS—About $77. A guinea was worth 21 shillings, one more shilling than a pound sterling. Though the coin has passed out of currency, English prices are still quoted in terms of guineas.

[6] GOWN—The academic gown worn by Oxford students.

[7] CRIMP'S BILL—An advertisement circulated by crimps, agents who for a commission lured men into the marine service or induced them to sign indentures for labor in the colonies.

[8] LETTER-FOUNDER—One who casts type. Franklin became the first letter-founder in America.

[9] PUNCHEONS . . . MATRICES—Dies . . . molds.

way all deficiencies. I also engraved several things on occasion; I made the ink; I was warehouseman, and everything, and, in short, quite a factotum.[10]

But, however serviceable I might be, I found that my services became every day of less importance, as the other hands improved in the business; and when Keimer paid my second quarter's wages, he let me know that he felt them too heavy, and thought I should make an abatement. He grew by degrees less civil, put on more of the master, frequently found fault, was captious, and seemed ready for an outbreaking. I went on, nevertheless, with a good deal of patience, thinking that his incumbered circumstances were partly the cause. At length a trifle snapped our connections; for, a great noise happening near the court-house, I put my head out of the window to see what was the matter. Keimer, being in the street, looked up and saw me, called out to me in a loud voice and angry tone to mind my business, adding some reproachful words, that nettled me the more for their publicity, all the neighbors who were looking out on the same occasion being witnesses how I was treated. He came up immediately into the printing-house, continued the quarrel, high words passed on both sides, he gave me the quarter's warning we had stipulated, expressing a wish that he had not been obliged to so long a warning. I told him his wish was unnecessary, for I would leave him that instant; and so, taking my hat, walked out of doors, desiring Meredith, whom I saw below, to take care of some things I left, and bring them to my lodgings.

Meredith came accordingly in the evening, when we talked my affair over. He had conceived a great regard for me, and was very unwilling that I should leave the house while he remained in it. He dissuaded me from returning to my native country, which I began to think of; he reminded me that Keimer was in debt for all he possessed; that his creditors began to be uneasy; that he kept his shop miserably, sold often without profit for ready money, and often trusted without keeping accounts; that he must therefore fail, which would make a vacancy I might profit of. I objected my want of money. He then let me know that his father had a high opinion of me, and from some discourse that had passed between them, he was sure would advance money to set us up, if I would enter into

[10] Factotum—Jack-of-all-trades.

partnership with him. "My time," says he, "will be out with Keimer in the spring; by that time we may have our press and types in from London. I am sensible I am no workman; if you like it, your skill in the business shall be set against the stock I furnish, and we will share the profits equally."

The proposal was agreeable, and I consented. His father was in town and approved of it, the more as he saw I had great influence with his son, had prevailed on him to abstain long from dram-drinking, and he hoped might break him of that wretched habit entirely, when we came to be so closely connected. I gave an inventory to the father, who carried it to a merchant; the things were sent for, the secret was to be kept till they should arrive, and in the mean time I was to get work, if I could, at the other printing-house. But I found no vacancy there, and so remained idle a few days, when Keimer, on a prospect of being employed to print some paper money in New Jersey, which would require cuts and various types that I only could supply, and apprehending Bradford might engage me and get the job from him, sent me a very civil message, that old friends should not part for a few words, the effect of sudden passion, and wishing me to return. Meredith persuaded me to comply, as it would give more opportunity for his improvement under my daily instructions; so I returned, and we went on more smoothly than for some time before. The New Jersey job was obtained, I contrived a copper-plate press[11] for it, the first that had been seen in the country; I cut several ornaments and checks[12] for the bills. We went together to Burlington,[13] where I executed the whole to satisfaction; and he received so large a sum for the work as to be enabled thereby to keep his head much longer above water.

At Burlington I made an acquaintance with many principal people of the province. Several of them had been appointed by the Assembly a committee to attend the press, and take care that no more bills were printed than the law directed. They were, therefore, by turns, constantly with us, and generally he who attended brought with him a friend or two for company. My mind

---

[11] COPPER-PLATE PRESS—Press for striking off impressions from copper plates. Used for such fine work as printing paper money.

[12] ORNAMENTS AND CHECKS—Intricate designs engraved on the copper plate so that the printed money could not be counterfeited. Compare with the modern process.

[13] BURLINGTON—See page 32, note 8.

having been much more improved by reading than Keimer's, I suppose it was for that reason my conversation seemed to be more valued. They had me to their houses, introduced me to their friends, and showed me much civility; while he, though the master, was a little neglected. In truth, he was an odd fish; ignorant of common life, fond of rudely opposing received opinions, slovenly to extreme dirtiness, enthusiastic in some points of religion, and a little knavish withal.

We continued there near three months, and by that time I could reckon among my acquired friends, Judge Allen,[14] Samuel Bustill, the secretary of the province, Isaac Pearson, Joseph Cooper, and several of the Smiths, members of Assembly, and Isaac Decow, the surveyor-general. The latter was a shrewd, sagacious old man, who told me that he began for himself, when young, by wheeling clay for the brickmakers, learned to write after he was of age, carried the chain for surveyors, who taught him surveying, and he had now by his industry acquired a good estate; and says he, "I forsee that you will soon work this man out of his business, and make a fortune in it at Philadelphia." He had not then the least intimation of my intention to set up there or anywhere. These friends were afterwards of great use to me, as I occasionally was to some of them. They all continued their regard for me as long as they lived.

We had not been long returned to Philadelphia before the new types arrived from London. We settled with Keimer, and left him by his consent before he heard of it. We found a house to hire near the market, and took it. To lessen the rent, which was then but twenty-four pounds a year, though I have since known it to let for seventy, we took in Thomas Godfrey, a glazier, and his family, who were to pay a considerable part of it to us, and we to board with them. We had scarce opened our letters and put our press in order, before George House, an acquaintance of mine, brought a countryman to us, whom he had met in the street inquiring for a printer.

All our cash was now expended in the variety of particulars we had been obliged to procure, and this countryman's five shillings, being our first-fruits, and coming so seasonably gave

[14] JUDGE ALLEN, ETC.—Note again Franklin's ability to attract men of high learning and importance.

me more pleasure than any crown[15] I have since earned; and the gratitude I felt toward House has made me often more ready than perhaps I should otherwise have been to assist young beginners.

There are croakers in every country, always boding its ruin. Such a one then lived in Philadelphia; a person of note, an elderly man, with a wise look and a very grave manner of speaking. His name was Samuel Mickle. This gentleman, a stranger to me, stopped one day at my door, and asked me if I was the young man who had lately opened a new printing-house. Being answered in the affirmative, he said he was sorry for me, because it was an expensive undertaking, and the expense would be lost; for Philadelphia was a sinking place, the people already half bankrupts, or near being so; all appearances to the contrary, such as new buildings and the rise of rents, being to his certain knowledge fallacious; for they were, in fact, among the things that would soon ruin us. And he gave me such a detail of misfortunes now existing, or that were soon to exist, that he left me half melancholy. Had I known him before I engaged in this business, probably I never should have done it. This man continued to live in this decaying place, and to declaim in the same strain, refusing for many years to buy a house there, because all was going to destruction; and at last I had the pleasure of seeing him give five times as much for one as he might have bought it for when he first began his croaking.

I should have mentioned before that, in the autumn of the preceding year, I had formed most of my ingenious acquaintance into a club of mutual improvement, which we called the JUNTO;[16] we met on Friday evenings. The rules that I drew up required that every member, in his turn, should produce one or more queries on any point of Morals, Politics, or Natural Philosophy, to be discussed by the company; and once in three months produce and read an essay of his own writing, on any subject he pleased. Our debates were to be under the direction of a president, and to be conducted in the sincere spirit of inquiry after truth, without fondness for dispute, or desire of victory; and to prevent warmth, all expressions of positiveness in opinions, or direct contradiction,

---

[15] CROWN—English coin worth five shillings, or about $1.25.

[16] THE JUNTO—The debating club which later developed into the American Philosophical Society.

were after some time made contraband, and prohibited under small pecuniary penalties.

The first members were Joseph Breintnal, a copier of deeds for the scriveners, a good-natured, friendly, middle-aged man, a great lover of poetry, reading all he could meet with, and writing some that was tolerable; very ingenious in many little nicknackeries, and of sensible conversation.

Thomas Godfrey, a self-taught mathematician, great in his way, and afterward inventor of what is now called Hadley's Quadrant.[17] But he knew little out of his way, and was not a pleasing companion; as, like most great mathematicians I have met with, he expected universal precision in everything said, or was forever denying or distinguishing upon trifles, to the disturbance of all conversation. He soon left us.

Nicholas Scull, a surveyor, afterward surveyor-general, who loved books, and sometimes made a few verses.

William Parsons, bred a shoemaker, but, loving reading, had acquired a considerable share of mathematics, which he first studied with a view to astrology,[18] and afterwards laughed at it. He also became surveyor-general.

William Maugridge, a joiner, a most exquisite mechanic, and a solid, sensible man.

Hugh Meredith, Stephen Potts, and George Webb I have characterized before.

Robert Grace, a young gentleman of some fortune, generous, lively, and witty; a lover of punning and of his friends.

And William Coleman, then a merchant's clerk, about my age, who had the coolest, clearest head, the best heart, and the exactest morals of almost any man I ever met with. He became afterwards a merchant of great note, and one of our provincial judges. Our friendship continued without interruption to his death, upward of forty years; and the club continued almost as long, and was the best school of philosophy, morality, and politics that then existed in the province; for our queries, which were read the week preceding their discussion, put us upon reading with attention upon the several subjects, that we might speak more to the purpose; and

[17] QUADRANT—An instrument for measuring altitudes. It is used in astronomy, navigation, and surveying.

[18] ASTROLOGY—The so-called science, still believed in by many, that treats of the influence of the stars on human affairs and professes to foretell events.

here, too, we acquired better habits of conversation, everything being studied in our rules which might prevent our disgusting each other. From hence the long continuance of the club, which I shall have frequent occasion to speak further of hereafter.

But my giving this account of it here is to show something of the interest I had, every one of these exerting themselves in recommending business to us. Breintnal particularly procured us from the Quakers the printing of forty sheets of their history, the rest being done by Keimer; and upon this we worked exceedingly hard, for the price was low. It was a folio, in pica, with long primer[19] notes. I composed of it a sheet a day, and Meredith worked it off at press; it was often eleven at night, and sometimes later, before I had finished my distribution[20] for the next day's work, for the little jobs sent in by our other friends now and then put us back. But so determined I was to continue doing a sheet a day of the folio, that one night, when, having imposed my forms,[21] I thought my day's work over, one of them by accident was broken, and two pages reduced to pi, I immediately distributed and composed it over again before I went to bed; and this industry, visible to our neighbors, began to give us character and credit; particularly, I was told, that mention being made of the new printing-office at the merchants' Every-night club, the general opinion was that it must fail, there being already two printers in the place, Keimer and Bradford; but Dr. Baird (whom you and I saw many years after at his native place, St. Andrew's in Scotland) gave a contrary opinion; "For the industry of that Franklin," says he, "is superior to anything I ever saw of the kind; I see him still at work when I go home from club, and he is at work again before his neighbors are out of bed." This struck the rest, and we soon after had offers from one of them to supply us with stationery; but as yet we did not choose to engage in shop business.

I mention this industry the more particularly and the more freely, though it seems to be talking in my own praise, that those of my posterity who shall read it may know the use of that virtue, when they see its effects in my favor throughout this relation.

---

[19] Pica . . . long primer—Pica type is one-sixth of an inch high, and long primer is slightly smaller.

[20] Distribution—Putting the used type back into its proper letter compartments.

[21] Imposed my forms—Locked up the page of composed type in a frame for printing. When set material is accidentally disarranged, it is called "pi" or pied type.

George Webb, who had found a female friend that lent him wherewith to purchase his time of Keimer, now came to offer himself as a journeyman to us. We could not then employ him; but I foolishly let him know as a secret that I soon intended to begin a newspaper, and might then have work for him. My hopes of success, as I told him, were founded on this, that the then only newspaper, printed by Bradford, was a paltry thing, wretchedly managed, no way entertaining, and yet was profitable to him; I therefore thought a good paper would scarcely fail of good encouragement. I requested Webb not to mention it; but he told it to Keimer, who immediately, to be beforehand with me, published proposals for printing one himself, on which Webb was to be employed. I resented this; and to counteract them, as I could not yet begin our paper, I wrote several pieces of entertainment for Bradford's paper, under the title of the BUSY BODY,[22] which Breintnal continued some months. By this means the attention of the public was fixed on that paper, and Keimer's proposals, which we burlesqued and ridiculed, were disregarded. He began his paper, however, and, after carrying it on three quarters of a year, with at most only ninety subscribers, he offered it to me for a trifle; and I, having been ready some time to go on with it, took it in hand[23] directly; and it proved in a few years extremely profitable to me.

I perceive that I am apt to speak in the singular number, though our partnership still continued. The reason may be that, in fact, the whole management of the business lay upon me. Meredith was no compositor, a poor pressman, and seldom sober. My friends lamented my connection with him, but I was to make the best of it.

Our first papers made a quite different appearance from any before in the province; a better type, and better printed; but some spirited remarks of my writing, on the dispute[24] then going on between Governor Burnet and the Massachusetts Assembly, struck the principal people, occasioned the paper and the manager of it

[22] BUSY BODY—These letters were similar in style to those Franklin had written over the signature, Mrs. Dogood, but were not so bitter and sarcastic.

[23] TOOK IT IN HAND—Franklin and Meredith purchased the paper and continued it as the *Pennsylvania Gazette,* a wise abbreviation of Keimer's cumbersome *Universal Instructor in all Arts and Sciences and Pennsylvania Gazette.*

[24] DISPUTE—Massachusetts had been accustomed to reward its royal governors with a grant or gift according to their several abilities. When Burnet arrived with an order to demand a flat salary of about $5,000 a year, the Assembly refused, and a controversy arose. Franklin's "spirited remarks" showed a great deal of journalistic shrewdness, for he managed to praise both factions and seriously offend neither.

to be much talked of, and in a few weeks brought them all to be our subscribers.

Their example was followed by many, and our number went on growing continually. This was one of the first good effects of my having learned a little to scribble; another was, that the leading men, seeing a newspaper now in the hands of one who could also handle a pen, thought it convenient to oblige and encourage me. Bradford still printed the votes, and laws, and other public business. He had printed an address of the House to the governor in a coarse, blundering manner; we reprinted it elegantly and correctly, and sent one to every member. They were sensible of the difference: it strengthened the hands of our friends in the House, and they voted us their printers for the year ensuing.

Among my friends in the House I must not forget Mr. Hamilton, before mentioned, who was then returned from England, and had a seat in it. He interested himself for me strongly in that instance, as he did in many others afterward, continuing his patronage till his death.

Mr. Vernon, about this time, put me in mind of the debt I owed him, but did not press me. I wrote him an ingenuous letter of acknowledgment, craved his forbearance a little longer, which he allowed me, and as soon as I was able, I paid the principal with interest, and many thanks; so that erratum was in some degree corrected.

But now another difficulty came upon me which I had never the least reason to expect. Mr. Meredith's father, who was to have paid for our printing-house, according to the expectations given me, was able to advance only one hundred pounds currency, which had been paid, and a hundred more was due to the merchant, who grew impatient, and sued us all. We gave bail, but saw that, if the money could not be raised in time, the suit must soon come to a judgment and execution, and our hopeful prospects must, with us, be ruined, as the press and letters must be sold for payment, perhaps at half price.

In this distress two true friends, whose kindness I have never forgotten, nor ever shall forget while I can remember anything, came to me separately, unknown to each other, and, without any application from me, offering each of them to advance me all the money that should be necessary to enable me to take the whole business upon myself, if that should be practicable; but they did not like my continuing the partnership with Meredith, who, as they said, was often seen drunk in the streets, and playing at low games in ale-houses, much to our discredit. These two friends were William Coleman and Robert Grace. I told them I could not propose a separation while any prospect remained of the Merediths' fulfilling their part of our agreement, because I thought myself under great obligations to them for what they had done, and would do if they could; but, if they finally failed in their performance, and our partnership must be dissolved, I should then think myself at liberty to accept the assistance of my friends.

Thus the matter rested for some time, when I said to my partner, "Perhaps your father is dissatisfied at the part you have undertaken in this affair of ours, and is unwilling to advance for you and me what he would for you alone. If that is the case, tell me, and I will resign the whole to you, and go about my business." "No," said he, "my father has really been disappointed, and is really unable; and I am unwilling to distress him further. I see this is a business I am not fit for. I was bred a farmer, and it was a folly in me to come to town, and put myself, at thirty years of age, an apprentice to learn a new trade. Many of our Welsh people are going to settle in North Carolina, where land is cheap. I am inclined to go with them, and follow my old employment. You may find friends to assist you. If you will take the debts of the company upon you, return to my father the hundred pounds he has advanced, pay my little personal debts, and give me thirty pounds and a new saddle, I will relinquish the partnership, and leave the whole in your hands."

I agreed to this proposal; it was drawn up in writing, signed, and sealed immediately. I gave him what he demanded, and he went soon after to Carolina, from whence he sent me next year two long letters, containing the best account that had been given of that country, the climate, the soil, husbandry, etc., for in those matters he was very judicious. I printed them in the papers, and they gave great satisfaction to the public.

As soon as he was gone, I recurred to my two friends; and because I would not give an unkind preference to either, I took half of what each had offered, and I wanted, of one, and half of the other; paid off the company's debts, and went on with the business in my own name, advertising that the partnership was dissolved. I think this was in or about the year 1729.[25]

About this time there was a cry among the people for more paper money, only fifteen thousand pounds being extant in the province, and that soon to be sunk.[26] The wealthy inhabitants opposed any addition, being against all paper currency, from an apprehension that it would depreciate, as it had done in New England, to the prejudice of all creditors. We had discussed this point in our Junto, where I was on the side of an addition, being persuaded that the first small sum struck in 1723 had done much good by increasing the trade, employment, and number of inhabitants in the province, since I now saw all the old houses inhabited, and many new ones building; whereas I remembered well that when I first walked about the streets of Philadelphia, eating my roll, I saw most of the houses in Walnut Street, between Second and Front streets, with bills on their doors "To be let"; and many likewise in Chestnut Street and other streets, which made me think the inhabitants of the city were deserting it one after another.

Our debates possessed me so fully of the subject that I wrote and printed an anonymous pamphlet on it, entitled "The Nature and Necessity of a Paper Currency." It was well received by the common people in general; but the rich men disliked it, for it increased and strengthened the clamor for more money, and they happening to have no writers among them that were able to answer it, their opposition slackened, and the point was carried by a majority in the House. My friends there, who conceived I had been of some service, thought fit to reward me by employing me in printing the money;[27] a very profitable job and a great help to me. This was another advantage gained by my being able to write.

The utility of this currency became by time and experience so evident as never afterwards to be much disputed; so that it grew soon to fifty-five thousand pounds, and in 1739 to eighty thousand pounds, since which it arose during war to upwards of three hundred and fifty thousand pounds, trade, building, and inhabitants all

[25] ABOUT THE YEAR 1729—Remember that Franklin was writing this account from memory and sometimes was inaccurate. It was July 14, 1730, that the partnership was dissolved.

[26] SOON TO BE SUNK—Probably meaning soon to be reduced or perhaps called in.

[27] THOUGHT FIT . . . PRINTING THE MONEY—One is inclined to suspect that shrewd business sense contributed to Franklin's enthusiasm for more paper currency now that he was an established printer of such money.

the while increasing, though I now think there are limits beyond which the quantity may be hurtful.

I soon after obtained, through my friend Hamilton, the printing of the Newcastle paper money, another profitable job as I then thought it; small things appearing great to those in small circumstances; and these, to me, were really great advantages, as they were great encouragements. He procured for me, also, the printing of the laws and votes of that government,[28] which continued in my hands as long as I followed the business.

I now opened a little stationer's shop. I had in it blanks of all sorts, the correctest that ever appeared among us, being assisted in that by my friend Breintnal. I had also paper, parchment, chapmen's books, etc. One Whitemash, a compositor I had known in London, an excellent workman, now came to me, and worked with me constantly and diligently; and I took an apprentice, the son of Aquila Rose.

I began now gradually to pay off the debt I was under for the printing-house. In order to secure my credit and character as a tradesman, I took care not only to be in *reality* industrious and frugal, but to avoid all appearances to the contrary. I dressed plainly; I was seen at no places of idle diversion. I never went out a fishing or shooting; a book, indeed, sometimes debauched me from my work, but that was seldom, snug, and gave no scandal; and, to show that I was not above my business, I sometimes brought home the paper I purchased at the stores through the streets on a wheelbarrow. Thus being esteemed an industrious, thriving young man, and paying duly for what I bought, the merchants who imported stationery solicited my custom; others proposed supplying me with books, and I went on swimmingly. In the mean time, Keimer's credit and business declining daily, he was at last forced to sell his printing-house to satisfy his creditors. He went to Barbadoes, and there lived some years in very poor circumstances.

His apprentice, David Harry, whom I had instructed while I worked with him, set up in his place at Philadelphia, having bought his materials. I was at first apprehensive of a powerful rival in Harry, as his friends were very able, and had a good deal of interest. I therefore proposed a partnership to him, which he, fortunately for me, rejected with scorn. He was very proud, dressed like a

[28] THAT GOVERNMENT—Newcastle was in Delaware colony.

gentleman, lived expensively, took much diversion and pleasure abroad, ran in debt, and neglected his business; upon which, all business left him; and finding nothing to do, he followed Keimer to Barbadoes, taking the printing-house with him. There this apprentice employed his former master as a journeyman; they quarreled often; Harry went continually behindhand, and at length was forced to sell his types and return to his country work in Pennsylvania. The person that bought them employed Keimer to use them, but in a few years he died.

There remained now no competitor with me at Philadelphia but the old one, Bradford, who was rich and easy, did a little printing now and then by straggling hands, but was not very anxious about the business. However, as he kept the post-office, it was imagined he had better opportunities of obtaining news; his paper was thought a better distributor of advertisements than mine, and therefore had many more, which was a profitable thing to him, and a disadvantage to me; for, though I did indeed receive and send papers by the post, yet the public opinion was otherwise, for what I did send was by bribing the riders,[29] who took them privately, Bradford being unkind enough to forbid it, which occasioned some resentment on my part; and I thought so meanly of him for it that, when I afterward came into his situation, I took care never to imitate it.

I had hitherto continued to board with Godfrey, who lived in part of my house with his wife and children, and had one side of the shop for his glazier's business, though he worked little, being always absorbed in his mathematics. Mrs. Godfrey projected a match for me with a relation's daughter, took opportunities of bringing us often together, till a serious courtship on my part ensued, the girl being in herself very deserving. The old folks encouraged me by continual invitations to supper, and by leaving us together, till at length it was time to explain. Mrs. Godfrey managed our little treaty. I let her know that I expected as much money with their daughter as would pay off my remaining debt for the printing-house, which I believe was not then above a hundred pounds. She brought me word they had no such sum to spare; I said they might mortgage their house in the loan-office. The

[29] Riders—Post-riders who carried the mail, that being then the swiftest means of transportation.

answer to this, after some days, was, that they did not approve the match; that, on inquiry of Bradford, they had been informed the printing business was not a profitable one; the types would soon be worn out, and more wanted; that S. Keimer and D. Harry had failed one after the other, and I should probably soon follow them; and, therefore, I was forbidden the house, and the daughter shut up.

Whether this was a real change of sentiment or only artifice, on a supposition of our being too far engaged in affection to retract, and therefore that we should steal a marriage, which would leave them at liberty to give or withhold what they pleased, I know not; but I suspected the latter, resented it, and went no more. Mrs. Godfrey brought me afterward some more favorable accounts of their disposition, and would have drawn me on again; but I declared absolutely my resolution to have nothing more to do with that family. This was resented by the Godfreys; we differed, and they removed, leaving me the whole house, and I resolved to take no more inmates.

But this affair having turned my thoughts to marriage, I looked round me and made overtures of acquaintance in other places; but soon found that the business of a printer being generally thought a poor one, I was not to expect money with a wife, unless with such a one as I should not otherwise think agreeable. A friendly correspondence as neighbors and old acquaintances had continued between me and Mrs. Read's family, who all had a regard for me from the time of my first lodging in their house. I was often invited there and consulted in their affairs, wherein I sometimes was of service. I pitied poor Miss Read's unfortunate situation, who was generally dejected, seldom cheerful, and avoided company. I considered my giddiness and inconstancy when in London as in a great degree the cause of her unhappiness, though the mother was good enough to think the fault more her own than mine, as she had prevented our marrying before I went thither, and persuaded the other match[30] in my absence. Our mutual affection was revived, but there were now great objections to our union. The match was indeed looked upon as invalid, a preceding wife being said to be living in England; but this could not easily be proved, because of the distance; and though there was a report of his death, it was not certain. Then, though it should be true, he had left many debts,

---

[30] THE OTHER MATCH—See page 59.

which his successor might be called upon to pay. We ventured, however, over all these difficulties, and I took her to wife, September 1, 1730. None of the inconveniences happened that we had apprehended; she proved a good and faithful helpmate, assisted me much by attending the shop; we throve together, and have ever mutually endeavored to make each other happy.[31] Thus I corrected that great erratum as well as I could.

About this time, our club meeting, not at a tavern, but in a little room of Mr. Grace's, set apart for that purpose, a proposition was made by me that, since our books were often referred to in our disquisitions upon the queries, it might be convenient to us to have them all together where we met, that upon occasion they might be consulted; and by thus clubbing our books to a common library, we should, while we liked to keep them together, have each of us the advantage of using the books of all the other members, which would be nearly as beneficial as if each owned the whole. It was liked and agreed to, and we filled one end of the room with such books as we could best spare. The number was not so great as we expected; and though they had been of great use, yet some inconveniences occurring for want of due care of them, the collection, after about a year, was separated, and each took his books home again.

And now I set on foot my first project of a public nature, that for a subscription library. I drew up the proposals, got them put into form by our great scrivener, Brockden, and by the help of my friends in the Junto, procured fifty subscribers of forty shillings each to begin with, and ten shillings a year for fifty years, the term our company was to continue. We afterwards obtained a charter, the company being increased to one hundred; this was the mother of all the North American subscription libraries, now so numerous. It is become a great thing itself, and continually increasing.[32] These libraries have improved the general conversation of the Americans, made the common tradesmen and farmers as intelligent as most gentlemen from other countries, and perhaps

---

[31] WE THROVE . . . EACH OTHER HAPPY—In spite of great differences in temperament, talents, and training, the marriage was a happy one. In his correspondence Franklin addressed his wife as "My dear child," or "My dear Debby," and Mrs. Franklin in her illiterate way signed herself "Your afeckshonet wife."

[32] CONTINUALLY INCREASING—From this small beginning the "Library Company of Philadelphia" has grown to the great Philadelphia Library housing over a quarter of a million books.

have contributed in some degree to the stand so generally made throughout the colonies in defence of their privileges.[33]

Mem°. Thus far was written with the intention expressed in the beginning and therefore contains several little family anecdotes of no importance to others. What follows was written many years after in compliance with the advice contained in these letters, and accordingly intended for the public. The affairs of the Revolution occasioned the interruption.—*Franklin.*

*Continuation of the account of my life, begun at Passy, near Paris, 1784.—Franklin.*

The books were imported;[34] the library was opened one day in the week for lending to the subscribers, on their promissory notes to pay double the value if not duly returned. The institution soon manifested its utility, was imitated by other towns, and in other provinces. The libraries were augmented by donations; reading became fashionable; and our people, having no public amusements to divert their attention from study, became better acquainted with books, and in a few years were observed by strangers to be better instructed and more intelligent than people of the same rank generally are in other countries.

When we were about to sign the above-mentioned articles, which were to be binding on us, our heirs, etc., for fifty years, Mr. Brockden, the scrivener, said to us, "You are young men, but it is scarcely probable that any of you will live to see the expiration of the term fixed in the instrument." A number of us, however, are yet living; but the instrument was after a few years rendered null by a charter that incorporated and gave perpetuity to the company.

The objections and reluctances I met with in soliciting the subscriptions made me soon feel the impropriety of presenting one's self as the proposer of any useful project, that might be supposed to raise one's reputation in the smallest degree above that of one's neighbors, when one has need of their assistance to accomplish that project. I therefore put myself as much as I could out of sight, and stated it as a scheme of a *number of friends,* who

[33] PRIVILEGES—This marks the conclusion of the first part of the *Autobiography* begun and finished in 1771 during his visit to the Twyford country home of Dr. Shipley, Bishop of St. Asaph's. It is in the form of a letter to his son William, then governor of New Jersey.

[34] THE BOOKS WERE IMPORTED—When Franklin took up the account 13 years later, he had with him no copy of what he had previously written, and he repeated the story of the library's establishment. The first few paragraphs have therefore been omitted.

had requested me to go about and propose it to such as they thought lovers of reading. In this way my affair went on more smoothly, and I ever after practised it on such occasions; and from my frequent successes can heartily recommend it. The present little sacrifice of your vanity will afterwards be amply repaid. If it remains a while uncertain to whom the merit belongs, some one more vain than yourself will be encouraged to claim it, and then even envy will be disposed to do you justice by plucking those assumed feathers, and restoring them to their right owner.

This library afforded me the means of improvement by constant study, for which I set apart an hour or two each day, and thus repaired in some degree the loss of the learned education my father once intended for me. Reading was the only amusement I allowed myself. I spent no time in taverns, games, or frolics of any kind; and my industry in my business continued as indefatigable as it was necessary. I was indebted for my printing-house; I had a young family coming on to be educated, and I had to contend for business with two printers, who were established in the place before me. My circumstances, however, grew daily easier. My original habits of frugality continuing, and my father having, among his instructions to me when a boy, frequently repeated a proverb of Solomon, "Seest thou[35] a man diligent in his calling, he shall stand before kings, he shall not stand before mean men," I from thence considered industry as a means of obtaining wealth and distinction, which encouraged me, though I did not think that I should ever literally *stand before kings,* which, however, has since happened; for I have stood before five, and even had the honor of sitting down with one, the King of Denmark, to dinner.

## CHAPTER V

### Morality and Religion

Fundamental Beliefs—Ideas on Church Attendance—Scheme for Improving His Character—Difficulty with Order—Comment on Humility

We have an English proverb that says, *"He that would thrive, must ask his wife."* It was lucky for me that I had one as much disposed to industry and frugality as myself. She assisted me cheerfully in my business, folding and stitching pamphlets, tending

[35] "Seest thou . . ." etc.—Proverbs 22:29.

shop, purchasing old linen rags for the paper makers, etc., etc. We kept no idle servants, our table was plain and simple, our furniture of the cheapest. For instance, my breakfast was a long time bread and milk (no tea), and I ate it out of a twopenny earthen porringer, with a pewter spoon. But mark how luxury will enter families, and make a progress, in spite of principle: being called one morning to breakfast, I found it in a china bowl, with a spoon of silver! They had been bought for me without my knowledge by my wife, and had cost her the enormous sum of three-and-twenty shillings, for which she had no other excuse or apology to make, but that she thought *her* husband deserved a silver spoon and china bowl as well as any of his neighbors. This was the first appearance of plate and china in our house, which afterward, in a course of years, as our wealth increased, augmented gradually to several hundred pounds in value.

I had been religiously educated as a Presbyterian; and though some of the dogmas of that persuasion, such as *the eternal decrees of God, election, reprobation, etc.,* appeared to me unintelligible, others doubtful, and I early absented myself from the public assemblies of the sect, Sunday being my studying day, I never was without some religious principles. I never doubted, for instance, the existence of the Deity; that He made the world, and governed it by His providence; that the most acceptable service of God was the doing good to man; that our souls are immortal; and that all crime will be punished, and virtue rewarded, either here or hereafter. These I esteemed the essentials of every religion; and being to be found in all the religions we had in our country, I respected them all, though with different degrees of respect, as I found them more or less mixed with other articles, which, without any tendency to inspire, promote, or confirm morality, served principally to divide us, and make us unfriendly to one another. This respect to all, with an opinion that the worst had some good effects, induced me to avoid all discourse that might tend to lessen the good opinion another might have of his own religion; and as our province increased in people, and new places of worship were continually wanted, and generally erected by voluntary contribution, my mite for such purpose, whatever might be the sect, was never refused.

It was about this time I conceived the bold and arduous project of arriving at moral perfection. I wished to live without committing any fault at any time; I would conquer all that either natural inclination, custom, or company might lead me into. As I knew, or thought I knew, what was right and wrong, I did not see why I might not always do the one and avoid the other. But I soon found I had undertaken a task of more difficulty than I had imagined. While my care was employed in guarding against one fault, I was often surprised by another; habit took the advantage of inattention; inclination was sometimes too strong for reason. I concluded, at length, that the mere speculative conviction that it was our interest to be completely virtuous was not sufficient to prevent our slipping; and that the contrary habits must be broken, and good ones acquired and established, before we can have any dependence on a steady, uniform rectitude of conduct. For this purpose I therefore contrived the following method.

In the various enumerations of the moral virtues I had met with in my reading, I found the catalogue more or less numerous, as different writers included more or fewer ideas under the same name. Temperance, for example, was by some confined to eating and drinking, while by others it was extended to mean the moderating every other pleasure, appetite, inclination, or passion, bodily or mental, even to our avarice and ambition. I proposed to myself, for the sake of clearness, to use rather more names, with fewer ideas annexed to each, than a few names with more ideas; and I included under thirteen names of virtues all that at that time occurred to me as necessary or desirable, and annexed to each a short precept, which fully expressed the extent I gave to its meaning.

These names of virtues, with their precepts were:—

1. TEMPERANCE

Eat not to dulness; drink not to elevation.

2. SILENCE

Speak not but what may benefit others or yourself; avoid trifling conversation.

3. ORDER

Let all your things have their places; let each part of your business have its time.

4. RESOLUTION

Resolve to perform what you ought; perform without fail what you resolve.

5. Frugality

Make no expense but to do good to others or yourself; *i. e.*, waste nothing.

6. Industry

Lose no time; be always employed in something useful; cut off all unnecessary actions.

7. Sincerity

Use no hurtful deceit; think innocently and justly; and, if you speak, speak accordingly.

8. Justice

Wrong none by doing injuries, or omitting the benefits that are your duty.

9. Moderation

Avoid extremes; forbear resenting injuries so much as you think they deserve.

10. Cleanliness

Tolerate no uncleanliness in body, clothes, or habitation.

11. Tranquillity

Be not disturbed at trifles, or at accidents common or unavoidable.

12. Chastity

13. Humility

Imitate Jesus and Socrates.

My intention being to acquire the *habitude* of all these virtues, I judged it would be well not to distract my attention by attempting the whole at once, but to fix it on one of them at a time; and, when I should be master of that, then to proceed to another, and so on, till I should have gone through the thirteen; and as the previous acquisition of some might facilitate the acquisition of certain others, I arranged them with that view, as they stand above. *Temperance* first, as it tends to procure that coolness and clearness of head, which is so necessary where constant vigilance was to be kept up, and guard maintained against the unremitting attraction of ancient habits, and the force of perpetual temptations. This being acquired and established, silence would be more easy; and my desire being to gain knowledge at the same time that I improved in virtue, and considering that in conversation it was obtained rather by the use of the ears than of the tongue, and therefore wishing to break a habit I was getting into of prattling, punning, and joking, which only made me acceptable to trifling company, I gave *Silence* the second place. This and the next, *Order,* I expected would allow me more time for attending to my project and my studies. *Resolution,* once become habitual, would keep me firm in my endeavors to obtain all the subsequent virtues; *Frugality* and *Industry* freeing me from my remaining debt, and producing affluence and independence, would make more easy the practice of *Sincerity* and *Justice,* etc., etc. Conceiving then, that, agreeably to the advice of Pythagoras[1] in his "Golden Verses," daily examination would be necessary, I contrived the following method for conducting that examination.

I made a little book, in which I allotted a page for each of the virtues. I ruled each page with red ink, so as to have seven columns, one for each day of the week, marking each column with a letter for the day. I crossed these columns with thirteen red lines, marking the beginning of each line with the first letter of one of the virtues, on which line, and in its proper column, I might mark, by a little black spot, every fault I found upon examination to have been committed respecting that virtue upon that day.

I determined to give a week's strict attention to each of the virtues successively. Thus, in the first week, my great guard was to avoid every the least offence against *Temperance,* leaving the other virtues to their ordinary chance, only marking every evening the faults of the day. Thus, if in the first week I could keep my first line, marked T, clear of spots, I supposed the habit of that virtue so much strengthened, and its opposite weakened, that I might venture extending my attention to include the next, and for the following week keep both lines clear of spots. Proceeding thus to the last, I could go through a course complete in thirteen weeks, and four courses in a year. And like him who, having a garden to weed, does not attempt to eradicate all the bad herbs at once, which would exceed his reach and his strength, but works on one of the beds at a time, and, having accomplished the first, proceeds to a second, so I should have, I hoped, the encouraging pleasure of seeing on my pages the progress I made in virtue, by clearing successively my lines of their spots, till in the end, by a number

[1] PYTHAGORAS—Famous Greek philosopher.

of courses, I should be happy in viewing a clean book, after a thirteen weeks' daily examination.

And conceiving God to be the fountain of wisdom, I thought it right and necessary to solicit his assistance for obtaining it; to this end I formed the following little prayer, which was prefixed to my tables of examination, for daily use.

*O powerful Goodness! bountiful Father! merciful Guide! Increase in me that wisdom which discovers my truest interest. Strengthen my resolutions to perform what that wisdom dictates. Accept my kind offices to thy other children as the only return in my power for thy continual favors to me.*

I entered upon the execution of this plan for self-examination, and continued it with occasional intermissions for some time. I was surprised to find myself so much fuller of faults than I had imagined; but I had the satisfaction of seeing them diminish. To avoid the trouble of renewing now and then my little book, which, by scraping out the marks on the paper of old faults to make room for new ones in a new course, became full of holes, I transferred my tables and precepts to the ivory leaves of a memorandum book, on which the lines were drawn with red ink, that made a durable stain, and on those lines I marked my faults with a black lead pencil, which marks I could easily wipe out with a wet sponge. After a while I went through one course only in a year, and afterward only one in several years, till at length I omitted them entirely, being employed in voyages and business abroad, with a multiplicity of affairs that interfered; but I always carried my little book with me.

My scheme of *Order* gave me the most trouble; and I found that, though it might be practicable where a man's business was such as to leave him the disposition of his time, that of a journeyman printer, for instance, it was not possible to be exactly observed by a master, who must mix with the world, and often receive people of business at their own hours. *Order,* too, with regard to places for things, papers, etc., I found extremely difficult to acquire. I had not been early accustomed to it, and having an exceeding good memory, I was not so sensible of the inconvenience attending want of method. This article, therefore, cost me so much painful attention, and my faults in it vexed me so much, and I made so little progress in amendment, and had such frequent relapses,[2] that I was almost ready to give up the attempt, and content myself with a faulty character in that respect, like the man who, in buying an axe of a smith, my neighbor, desired to have the whole of its surface as bright as the edge. The smith consented to grind it bright for him if he would turn the wheel; he turned, while the smith pressed the broad face of the axe hard and heavily on the stone, which made the turning of it very fatiguing. The man came every now and then from the wheel to see how the work went on, and at length would take his axe as it was, without farther grinding. "No," said the smith, "turn on, turn on; we shall have it bright by and by; as yet, it is only speckled." "Yes," says the man, *"but I think I like a speckled axe best."* And I believe this may have been the case with many, who, having, for want of some such means as I employed, found the difficulty of obtaining good and breaking bad habits in other points of vice and virtue, have given up the struggle, and concluded that *"a speckled axe was best"*; for something, that pretended to be reason, was every now and then suggesting to me that such extreme nicety as I exacted of myself might be a kind of foppery in morals, which, if it were known, would make me ridiculous; that a perfect character might be attended with the inconvenience of being envied and hated; and that a benevolent man should allow a few faults in himself, to keep his friends in countenance.

In truth, I found myself incorrigible with respect to order; and now I am grown old, and my memory bad, I feel very sensibly the want of it. But, on the whole, though I never arrived at the perfection I had been so ambitious of obtaining, but fell far short of it, yet I was, by the endeavor, a better and a happier man than I otherwise should have been if I had not attempted it; as those who aim at perfect writing by imitating the engraved copies, though they never reach the wished-for excellence of those copies, their hand is mended by the endeavor, and is tolerable while it continues fair and legible.

It may be well my posterity should be informed that to this little artifice, with the blessing of God, their ancestor owed the constant felicity of his life, down to his seventy-ninth year, in which this is written. What reverses may attend the remainder is

[2] FREQUENT RELAPSES—Refer to John Adams' report of Franklin's administration of affairs in Paris, "Franklin's Later Life," page 157.

in the hand of Providence; but, if they arrive, the reflection on past happiness enjoyed ought to help his bearing them with more resignation. To temperance he ascribes his long-continued health, and what is still left to him of a good constitution; to industry and frugality, the early easiness of his circumstances and acquisition of his fortune, with all that knowledge that enabled him to be a useful citizen, and obtained for him some degree of reputation among the learned; to sincerity and justice, the confidence of his country and the honorable employs it conferred upon him; and to the joint influence of the whole mass of the virtues, even in the imperfect state he was able to acquire them, all that evenness of temper, and that cheerfulness in conversation, which makes his company still sought for, and agreeable even to his younger acquaintance. I hope, therefore, that some of my descendants may follow the example and reap the benefit.

It will be remarked that, though my scheme was not wholly without religion, there was in it no mark of any of the distinguishing tenets of any particular sect. I had purposely avoided them; for, being fully persuaded of the utility and excellency of my method, and that it might be serviceable to people in all religions, and intending some time or other to publish it, I would not have anything in it that should prejudice any one, of any sect, against it.

My list of virtues contained at first but twelve; but a Quaker friend having kindly informed me that I was generally thought proud; that my pride showed itself frequently in conversation; that I was not content with being in the right when discussing any point, but was overbearing, and rather insolent, of which he convinced me by mentioning several instances; I determined endeavoring to cure myself, if I could, of this vice or folly among the rest, and I added *Humility* to my list, giving an extensive meaning to the word.

I cannot boast of much success in acquiring the *reality* of this virtue, but I had a good deal with regard to the *appearance* of it. I made it a rule to forbear all direct contradiction to the sentiments of others, and all positive assertion of my own. I even forbade myself, agreeably to the old laws of our Junto, the use of every word or expression in the language that imported a fixed opinion, such as *certainly, undoubtedly,* etc., and I adopted, instead of them, *I conceive, I apprehend,* or *I imagine* a thing to be so or so;

or it *so appears to me at present.* When another asserted something that I thought an error, I denied myself the pleasure of contradicting him abruptly, and of showing immediately some absurdity in his proposition; and in answering I began by observing that in certain cases or circumstances his opinion would be right, but in the present case there *appeared* or *seemed* to me some difference, etc. I soon found the advantage of this change in my manner; the conversations I engaged in went on more pleasantly. The modest way in which I proposed my opinions procured them a readier reception and less contradiction; I had less mortification when I was found to be in the wrong, and I more easily prevailed with others to give up their mistakes and join with me when I happened to be in the right.

And this mode, which I at first put on with some violence to natural inclination, became at length so easy, and so habitual to me, that perhaps for these fifty years past no one has ever heard a dogmatical expression escape me.[3] And to this habit (after my character of integrity) I think it principally owing that I had early so much weight with my fellow-citizens when I proposed new institutions, or alterations in the old, and so much influence in public councils when I became a member; for I was but a bad speaker, never eloquent, subject to much hesitation in my choice of words, hardly correct in language, and yet I generally carried my points.

In reality, there is, perhaps, no one of our natural passions so hard to subdue as pride. Disguise it, struggle with it, beat it down, stifle it, mortify it as much as one pleases, it is still alive, and will every now and then peep out and show itself; you will see it, perhaps, often in this history; for, even if I could conceive that I had completely overcome it, I should probably be proud of my humility.

[Thus far written at Passy, 1784.]

---

[3] FOR THESE FIFTY YEARS . . . ESCAPE ME—It was Franklin's modest behavior that so often won him his point. It is interesting to note his confession that this humility was more *appearance* than *reality.*

# CHAPTER VI

## THE PUBLIC-SPIRITED CITIZEN

*Poor Richard's Almanack*—Study of Languages—Offices in the Colony—Public Improvements in Philadelphia—Whitefield's Eloquence—Public Defence—Franklin and the Quakers

In 1732 I first published my Almanack,[1] under the name of *Richard Saunders.* It was continued by me about twenty-five years, commonly called *Poor Richard's Almanack.* I endeavored to make it both entertaining and useful; and it accordingly came to be in such demand that I reaped considerable profit from it, vending annually near ten thousand. And observing that it was generally read, scarce any neighborhood in the province being without it, I considered it as a proper vehicle for conveying instruction among the common people, who bought scarcely any other books. I therefore filled all the little spaces that occurred between the remarkable days in the calendar with proverbial sentences, chiefly such as inculcated industry and frugality as the means of procuring wealth, and thereby securing virtue; it being more difficult for a man in want to act always honestly, as, to use here one of those proverbs, *"it is hard for an empty sack to stand upright."*

These proverbs, which contained the wisdom of many ages and nations, I assembled and formed into a connected discourse prefixed to the Almanack of 1757,[2] as the harangue of a wise old man to the people attending an auction. The bringing all these scattered counsels thus into a focus enabled them to make greater impression. The piece, being universally approved, was copied in all the newspapers of the continent; reprinted in Britain on a broadside, to be stuck up in houses; two translations were made of it in French, and great numbers bought by the clergy and gentry, to distribute gratis among their poor parishioners and tenants. In Pennsylvania,

[1] ALMANACK—In those days almanacs, even more than newspapers, were the "literature of the masses" in both England and America. Published annually, they provided not only information concerning eclipses, tides, motions of the sun and moon, but bits of humor, wise sayings, and long-distance weather predictions. The popularity of an almanac depended on the ingenuity of the writer, or philomath as he was called. Franklin first arranged with his tenant, the mathematician Thomas Godfrey, to write the copy, but after the quarrel (see pages 73–74) Godfrey took his MS. to a rival printer. Thereupon Franklin determined to be his own philomath, chose the name of a seventeenth century almanac writer, Richard Saunders, and began his famous publication. The name, Poor Richard, is fashioned after that of another almanac, Poor Robin.

[2] ALMANACK OF 1757—Written in 1757 for the calendar year 1758. This was the 25th and last issue.

as it discouraged useless expense in foreign superfluities, some thought it had its share of influence in producing that growing plenty of money which was observable for several years after its publication.

I considered my newspaper, also, as another means of communicating instruction, and in that view frequently reprinted in it extracts from the *Spectator,* and other moral writers; and sometimes published little pieces of my own, which had been first composed for reading in our Junto.

In the conduct of my newspaper, I carefully excluded all libelling and personal abuse, which is of late years become so disgraceful to our country.[3] Whenever I was solicited to insert anything of that kind, and the writers pleaded, as they generally did, the liberty of the press, and that a newspaper was like a stage-coach, in which any one who would pay had a right to a place, my answer was, that I would print the piece separately if desired, and the author might have as many copies as he pleased to distribute himself, but that I would not take upon me to spread his detraction; and that, having contracted with my subscribers to furnish them with what might be either useful or entertaining, I could not fill their papers with private altercation, in which they had no concern, without doing them manifest injustice. Now, many of our printers make no scruple of gratifying the malice of individuals by false accusations of the fairest characters among ourselves, augmenting animosity even to the producing of duels; and are, moreover, so indiscreet as to print scurrilous reflections on the government of neighboring states, and even on the conduct of our best national allies, which may be attended with the most pernicious consequences. These things I mention as a caution to young printers, and that they may be encouraged not to pollute their presses and disgrace their profession by such infamous practices, but refuse steadily, as they may see by my example that such a course of conduct will not, on the whole, be injurious to their interests.

In 1733 I sent one of my journeymen to Charleston, South Carolina, where a printer was wanting. I furnished him with a

---

[3] IN THE CONDUCT . . TO OUR COUNTRY—Note the change which has come over Franklin since he wrote those first articles in Boston. He is now condemning the very fault of which he was guilty as a youth.

press and letters, on an agreement of partnership, by which I was to receive one third of the profits of the business, paying one third of the expense. He was a man of learning, and honest but ignorant in matters of account; and, though he sometimes made me remittances, I could get no account from him, nor any satisfactory statement of our partnership while he lived. On his decease, the business was continued by his widow, who, being born and bred in Holland, where, as I have been informed, the knowledge of accounts makes a part of female education, she not only sent me as clear a statement as she could find of the transactions past, but continued to account with the greatest regularity and exactness every quarter afterwards, and managed the business with such success, that she not only brought up reputably a family of children, but, at the expiration of the term, was able to purchase of me the printing-house, and establish her son in it.

I mention this affair chiefly for the sake of recommending that branch of education for our young females,[4] as likely to be of more use to them and their children, in case of widowhood, than either music or dancing, by preserving them from losses by imposition of crafty men, and enabling them to continue, perhaps, a profitable mercantile house, with established correspondence, till a son is grown up fit to undertake and go on with it, to the lasting advantage and enriching of the family.

About the year 1734 there arrived among us from Ireland a young Presbyterian preacher, named Hemphill, who delivered with a good voice, and apparently extempore, most excellent discourses, which drew together considerable numbers of different persuasions, who joined in admiring them. Among the rest, I became one of his constant hearers, his sermons pleasing me, as they had little of the dogmatical kind, but inculcated strongly the practice of virtue, or what in the religious style are called good works. Those, however, of our congregation, who considered themselves as orthodox Presbyterians, disapproved his doctrine, and were joined by most of the old clergy, who arraigned him of heterodoxy[5] before the synod, in order to have him silenced. I became his zealous partisan, and contributed all I could to raise a party in his favor, and we combated

---

[4] EDUCATION FOR OUR YOUNG FEMALES—A subject in which Franklin was deeply interested.

[5] HETERODOXY—Lack of orthodox, or accepted, belief.

for him a while with some hopes of success. There was much scribbling pro and con upon the occasion; and finding that, though an elegant preacher, he was but a poor writer, I lent him my pen and wrote for him two or three pamphlets, and one piece in the *Gazette* of April, 1735. Those pamphlets, as is generally the case with controversial writings, though eagerly read at the time, were soon out of vogue, and I question whether a single copy of them now exists.

During the contest an unlucky occurrence hurt his cause exceedingly. One of our adversaries having heard him preach a sermon that was much admired, thought he had somewhere read the sermon before, or at least a part of it. On search, he found that part quoted at length, in one of the *British Reviews,* from a discourse of Dr. Foster's.[6] This detection gave many of our party disgust, who accordingly abandoned his cause, and occasioned our more speedy discomfiture in the synod. I stuck by him, however, as I rather approved his giving us good sermons composed by others, than bad ones of his own manufacture, though the latter was the practice of our common teachers. He afterward acknowledged to me that none of those he preached were his own; adding, that his memory was such as enabled him to retain and repeat any sermon after one reading only. On our defeat, he left us in search elsewhere of better fortune, and I quitted the congregation, never joining it after, though I continued many years my subscription for the support of its ministers.

I had begun in 1733 to study languages. I soon made myself so much a master of the French as to be able to read the books with ease. I then undertook the Italian. An acquaintance, who was also learning it, used often to tempt me to play chess with him. Finding this took up too much of the time I had to spare for study, I at length refused to play any more, unless on this condition, that the victor in every game should have a right to impose a task, either in parts of the grammar to be got by heart, or in translations, etc., which tasks the vanquished was to perform upon honor, before our next meeting. As we played pretty equally, we thus beat one another into that language. I afterwards, with a little painstaking, acquired as much of the Spanish as to read their books also.

---

[6] Dr. Foster's—The Rev. James Foster was one of the greatest London preachers of the time.

I have already mentioned that I had only one year's instruction in a Latin school, and that when very young, after which I neglected that language entirely. But when I had attained an acquaintance with the French, Italian, and Spanish, I was surprised to find, on looking over a Latin Testament, that I understood so much more of that language than I had imagined, which encouraged me to apply myself again to the study of it, and I met with more success, as those preceding languages had greatly smoothed my way.

From these circumstances, I have thought that there is some inconsistency in our common mode of teaching languages. We are told that it is proper to begin first with the Latin, and, having acquired that, it will be more easy to attain those modern languages which are derived from it; and yet we do not begin with the Greek, in order more easily to acquire the Latin. It is true that, if you can clamber and get to the top of a staircase without using the steps, you will more easily gain them in descending; but certainly, if you begin with the lowest you will with more ease ascend to the top; and I would therefore offer it to the consideration of those who superintend the education of our youth, whether, since many of those who begin with the Latin quit the same after spending some years without having made any great proficiency, and what they have learned becomes almost useless, so that their time has been lost, it would not have been better to have begun with the French, proceeding to the Italian, etc.; for, though, after spending the same time, they should quit the study of languages and never arrive at the Latin, they would, however, have acquired another tongue or two, that, being in modern use, might be serviceable to them in common life.

After ten years' absence from Boston, and having become easy in my circumstances, I made a journey thither to visit my relations, which I could not sooner well afford. In returning, I called at Newport to see my brother, then settled there with his printing-house. Our former differences were forgotten, and our meeting was very cordial and affectionate. He was fast declining in his health, and requested of me that, in case of his death, which he apprehended not far distant, I would take home his son, then but ten years of age, and bring him up to the printing business. This I accordingly performed, sending him a few years to school before I took him into the office. His mother carried on the business till he was grown up, when I assisted him with an assortment of new types, those of his father being in a manner worn out. Thus it was that I made my brother ample amends for the service I had deprived him of by leaving him so early.

In 1736 I lost one of my sons, a fine boy of four years old, by the small-pox, taken in the common way. I long regretted bitterly, and still regret that I had not given it to him by inoculation.[7] This I mention for the sake of parents who omit that operation, on the supposition that they should never forgive themselves if a child died under it; my example showing that the regret may be the same either way, and that therefore, the safer should be chosen.

Our club, the Junto, was found so useful, and afforded such satisfaction to the members, that several were desirous of introducing their friends, which could not well be done without exceeding what we had settled as a convenient number, viz., twelve. We had from the beginning made it a rule to keep our institution a secret, which was pretty well observed. The intention was to avoid applications of improper persons for admittance, some of whom, perhaps, we might find it difficult to refuse. I was one of those who were against any addition to our number, but, instead of it, made in writing a proposal that every member separately should endeavor to form a subordinate club, with the same rules respecting queries, etc., and without informing them of the connection with the Junto. The advantages proposed were, the improvement of so many more young citizens by the use of our institutions; our better acquaintance with the general sentiments of the inhabitants on any occasion, as the Junto member might propose what queries we should desire, and was to report to the Junto what passed in his separate club; the promotion of our particular interests in business by more extensive recommendation, and the increase of our influence in public affairs, and our power of doing good by spreading through the several clubs the sentiments of the Junto.

The project was approved, and every member undertook to form his club, but they did not all succeed. Five or six only were completed, which were called by different names, as the Vine, the Union, the Band, etc. They were useful to themselves, and afforded us

---

[7] Inoculation—A method for producing immunity from smallpox by giving the patient a light case of the disease. Vaccination was not introduced until several years after Franklin's death. See page 28. note 51.

a good deal of amusement, information, and instruction, besides answering, in some considerable degree, our views of influencing the public opinion on particular occasions, of which I shall give some instances in course of time as they happened.

My first promotion was my being chosen, in 1736, clerk of the General Assembly.[8] The choice was made that year without opposition; but the year following, when I was again proposed (the choice, like that of the members, being annual), a new member made a long speech against me, in order to favor some other candidate. I was, however, chosen, which was the more agreeable to me, as, besides the pay for the immediate service as clerk, the place gave me a better opportunity of keeping up an interest among the members, which secured to me the business of printing the votes, laws, paper money, and other occasional jobs for the public, that, on the whole, were very profitable.

I therefore did not like the opposition of this new member, who was a gentleman of fortune and education, with talents that were likely to give him, in time, great influence in the House, which indeed afterwards happened. I did not, however, aim at gaining his favor by paying any servile respect to him, but, after some time, took this other method. Having heard that he had in his library a certain very scarce and curious book, I wrote a note to him, expressing my desire of perusing that book, and requesting he would do me the favor of lending it to me for a few days. He sent it immediately, and I returned it in about a week with another note, expressing strongly my sense of the favor. When we next met in the House, he spoke to me (which he had never done before), and with great civility; and he ever after manifested a readiness to serve me on all occasions, so that we became great friends, and our friendship continued to his death. This is another instance of the truth of an old maxim I had learned, which says, *"He that has once done you a kindness will be more ready to do you another, than he whom you yourself have obliged."* And it shows how much more profitable it is prudently to remove, than to resent, return, and continue inimical proceedings.

In 1737, Colonel Spotswood, late governor of Virginia, and then postmaster-general, being dissatisfied with the conduct of his

---

[8] General Assembly—The Pennsylvania Legislature elected by the people. Note how openly Franklin confesses to using his office for promoting his private business.

deputy[9] at Philadelphia, respecting some negligence in rendering, and inexactitude of his accounts, took from him the commission and offered it to me. I accepted it readily, and found it of great advantage; for though the salary was small it facilitated the correspondence that improved my newspaper, increased the number demanded, as well as the advertisements to be inserted, so that it came to afford me a considerable income. My old competitor's newspaper declined proportionably, and I was satisfied without retaliating his refusal, while postmaster, to permit my papers being carried by the riders. Thus he suffered greatly from his neglect in due accounting; and I mention it as a lesson to those young men who may be employed in managing affairs for others, that they should always render accounts, and make remittances, with great clearness and punctuality. The character of observing such a conduct is the most powerful of all recommendations to new employments and increase of business.

I began now to turn my thoughts a little to public affairs, beginning, however, with small matters. The city watch[10] was one of the first things that I conceived to want regulation. It was managed by the constables of the respective wards in turn; the constable warned a number of housekeepers to attend him for the night. Those who chose never to attend paid him six shillings a year to be excused, which was supposed to be for hiring substitutes, but was, in reality, much more than was necessary for that purpose, and made the constableship a place of profit; and the constable, for a little drink, often got such ragamuffins about him as a watch that respectable housekeepers did not choose to mix with. Walking the rounds, too, was often neglected, and most of the nights spent in tippling. I thereupon wrote a paper to be read in Junto, representing these irregularities, but insisting more particularly on the inequality of this six-shilling tax of the constables, respecting the circumstances of those who paid it, since a poor widow housekeeper, all whose property to be guarded by the watch did not perhaps exceed the value of fifty pounds, paid as much as the wealthiest merchant, who had thousands of pounds' worth of goods in his stores.

[9] His deputy—Andrew Bradford, publisher of the *Mercury*, rival newspaper.

[10] City watch—Constables and deputies chosen from the citizens, who patrolled the streets at night. Franklin began the first real city police service paid for with a property tax.

On the whole, I proposed as a more effectual watch, the hiring of proper men to serve constantly in that business; and as a more equitable way of supporting the charge, the levying a tax that should be proportioned to the property. This idea, being approved by the Junto, was communicated to the other clubs, but as arising in each of them; and though the plan was not immediately carried into execution, yet, by preparing the minds of people for the change, it paved the way for the law obtained a few years after, when the members of our clubs were grown into more influence.

About this time I wrote a paper (first to be read in Junto, but it was afterward published) on the different accidents and carelessness by which houses were set on fire, with cautions against them, and means proposed of avoiding them. This was much spoken of as a useful piece, and gave rise to a project, which soon followed it, of forming a company for the more ready extinguishing of fires, and mutual assistance in removing and securing of goods when in danger. Associates in this scheme were presently found, amounting to thirty. Our articles of agreement obliged every member to keep always in good order, and fit for use, a certain number of leather buckets, with strong bags and baskets (for packing and transporting of goods), which were to be brought to every fire; and we agreed to meet once a month and spend a social evening together, in discoursing and communicating such ideas as occurred to us upon the subject of fires, as might be useful in our conduct on such occasions.

The utility of this institution soon appeared, and many more desiring to be admitted than we thought convenient for one company, they were advised to form another, which was accordingly done; and this went on, one new company being formed after another, till they became so numerous as to include most of the inhabitants who were men of property; and now, at the time of my writing this, though upward of fifty years[11] since its establishment, that which I first formed, called the Union Fire Company, still subsists and flourishes, though the first members are all deceased but myself and one, who is older by a year than I am. The small fines that have been paid by members for absence at the monthly meetings have been applied to the purchase of fire-engines,

---

[11] FIFTY YEARS—Only comparatively recently have paid city fire departments taken the place of volunteer companies serving without regular salaries.

ladders, fire-hooks, and other useful implements for each company, so that I question whether there is a city in the world better provided with the means of putting a stop to beginning conflagrations; and, in fact, since these institutions, the city has never lost by fire more than one or two houses at a time, and the flames have often been extinguished before the house in which they began had been half consumed.

In 1739 arrived among us from Ireland the Reverend Mr. Whitefield,[12] who had made himself remarkable there as an itinerant preacher. He was at first permitted to preach in some of our churches; but the clergy, taking a dislike to him, soon refused him their pulpits, and he was obliged to preach in the fields. The multitudes of all sects and denominations that attended his sermons were enormous, and it was matter of speculation to me, who was one of the number, to observe the extraordinary influence of his oratory on his hearers, and how much they admired and respected him, notwithstanding his common abuse of them, by assuring them they were naturally *half beasts and half devils.* It was wonderful to see the change soon made in the manners of our inhabitants. From being thoughtless or indifferent about religion, it seemed as if all the world were growing religious, so that one could not walk through the town in an evening without hearing psalms sung in different families of every street.

And it being found inconvenient to assemble in the open air, subject to its inclemencies, the building of a house to meet in was no sooner proposed, and persons appointed to receive contributions, but sufficient sums were soon received to procure the ground and erect the building, which was one hundred feet long and seventy broad, about the size of Westminster Hall;[13] and the work was carried on with such spirit as to be finished in a much shorter time than could have been expected. Both house and ground were vested in trustees, expressly for the use of any preacher of any religious persuasion who might desire to say something to the people at Philadelphia; the design in building not being to accommodate any

---

[12] Reverend Mr. Whitefield (hwĭt′fēld)—One of the greatest English religious reformers. At first associated with the Wesley Methodists, he disagreed on points of doctrine, and being barred from the English Church, preached in the open air to vast audiences. At the time of this visit to America (he made seven in all) he was only twenty-five years old.

[13] Westminster Hall—The great hall in Westminster Palace, London.

particular sect, but the inhabitants in general; so that even if the Mufti of Constantinople[14] were to send a missionary to preach Mohammedanism to us, he would find a pulpit at his service.

Mr. Whitefield, in leaving us, went preaching all the way through the Colonies to Georgia. The settlement of that province had lately been begun, but, instead of being made with hardy, industrious husbandmen accustomed to labor, the only people fit for such an enterprise, it was with families of broken shopkeepers and other insolvent debtors, many of indolent and idle habits, taken out of the jails,[15] who, being set down in the woods, unqualified for clearing land, and unable to endure the hardships of a new settlement, perished in numbers, leaving many helpless children unprovided for. The sight of their miserable situation inspired the benevolent heart of Mr. Whitefield with the idea of building an Orphan House there, in which they might be supported and educated. Returning northward, he preached up this charity, and made large collections, for his eloquence had a wonderful power over the hearts and purses of his hearers, of which I myself was an instance.

I did not disapprove of the design, but, as Georgia was then destitute of materials and workmen, and it was proposed to send them from Philadelphia at a great expense, I thought it would have been better to have built the house here, and brought the children to it. This I advised; but he was resolute in his first project, rejected my counsel, and I therefore refused to contribute. I happened soon after to attend one of his sermons, in the course of which I perceived he intended to finish with a collection, and I silently resolved he should get nothing from me. I had in my pocket a handful of copper money, three or four silver dollars, and five pistoles in gold. As he proceeded I began to soften, and concluded to give the coppers. Another stroke of his oratory made me ashamed of that, and determined me to give the silver; and he finished so admirably, that I emptied my pocket wholly into the collector's dish, gold and all. At this sermon there was also one of our club, who, being of my sentiments respecting the building in Georgia, and suspecting a collection might be intended, had, by precaution, emptied his

---

[14] Mufti of Constantinople—Official expounders or interpreters of Mohammedan law.

[15] With families of . . . out of the jails—Georgia, the last of the thirteen colonies to be settled, was founded by Gen. James Oglethorpe in 1733 with a company composed chiefly of persons recruited from the English debtors' prisons. As it was a poor group with which to start a colony, there was much trouble and suffering.

pockets before he came from home. Towards the conclusion of the discourse, however, he felt a strong desire to give, and applied to a neighbor, who stood near him, to borrow some money for the purpose. The application was unfortunately made to perhaps the only man in the company who had the firmness not to be affected by the preacher. His answer was, *"At any other time, Friend Hopkinson, I would lend to thee freely; but not now, for thee seems to be out of thy right senses."*

Some of Mr. Whitefield's enemies affected to suppose that he would apply these collections to his own private emolument; but I, who was intimately acquainted with him (being employed in printing his sermons and journals, etc.), never had the least suspicion of his integrity, but am to this day decidedly of opinion that he was in all his conduct a perfectly honest man; and methinks my testimony in his favor ought to have the more weight, as we had no religious connection. He used, indeed, sometimes to pray for my conversion, but never had the satisfaction of believing that his prayers were heard. Ours was a mere civil friendship, sincere on both sides, and lasted to his death.

My business was now continually augmenting, and my circumstances growing daily easier, my newspaper having become very profitable, as being for a time almost the only one in this and the neighboring provinces. I experienced, too, the truth of the observation, *"that after getting the first hundred pounds, it is more easy to get the second,"* money itself being of a prolific nature.

The partnership at Carolina having succeeded, I was encouraged to engage in others, and to promote several of my workmen, who had behaved well, by establishing them with printing-houses in different colonies, on the same terms with that in Carolina. Most of them did well, being enabled at the end of our term, six years, to purchase the types of me and go on working for themselves, by which means several families were raised. Partnerships often finish in quarrels; but I was happy in this, that mine were all carried on and ended amicably, owing, I think, a good deal to the precaution of having very explicitly settled, in our articles, everything to be done by or expected from each partner, so that there was nothing to dispute, which precaution I would therefore recommend to all who enter into partnerships; for, whatever esteem partners may have for, and confidence in each other at the time of the contract, little jealousies and disgusts may arise, with ideas of inequality in the care and burden of the business, etc., which are attended often with breach of friendship and of the connection, perhaps with lawsuits and other disagreeable consequences.

I had, on the whole, abundant reason to be satisfied with my being established in Pennsylvania. There were, however, two things that I regretted, there being no provision for defence, nor for a complete education of youth: no militia, nor any college. I therefore, in 1743, drew up a proposal for establishing an academy; and at that time, thinking the Reverend Mr. Peters, who was out of employ, a fit person to superintend such an institution, I communicated the project to him; but he, having more profitable views in the service of the proprietaries,[16] which succeeded, declined the undertaking; and, not knowing another at that time suitable for such a trust, I let the scheme lie a while dormant. I succeeded better the next year, 1744, in proposing and establishing a Philosophical Society.[17] The paper I wrote for that purpose will be found among my writings, when collected.

With respect to defence, Spain having been several years at war[18] against Great Britain, and being at length joined by France, which brought us into great danger, and the labored and long-continued endeavor of our governor, Thomas, to prevail with our Quaker Assembly[19] to pass a militia law, and make other provisions for the security of the province, having proved abortive, I determined to try what might be done by a voluntary association of the people. To promote this, I first wrote and published a pamphlet, entitled Plain Truth, in which I stated our defenceless situation in strong lights, with the necessity of union and discipline for our defence, and promised to propose in a few days an associ-

---

[16] Proprietaries—The proprietaries of Pennsylvania still had vast tracts of their own which they contended should be exempt from taxation. They employed many agents to look out for their interests.

[17] A Philosophical Society—Still in existence under the name, American Philosophical Society. It was an outgrowth of the Junto, six of the nine founders being members of Franklin's debating society.

[18] War—War of the Austrian Succession (1741–1748) to defend Maria Theresa's rights in her Austrian dominions. It was almost a world war, for Austria, Britain, Russia, Hungary, and Poland were arrayed against France, Prussia, Spain, Sardinia, and Bavaria. The conflict spread to America, where it was known as King George's War.

[19] Quaker Assembly—The Pennsylvania Legislature was at this time controlled by the Quakers, or Friends, a religious sect opposed to bearing arms. Franklin's campaign for defence followed raids by French and Spanish privateers up the Delaware River, threatening Philadelphia itself.

ation, to be generally signed for that purpose. The pamphlet had a sudden and surprising effect. I was called upon for the instrument of association, and having settled the draft of it with a few friends, I appointed a meeting of the citizens in the large building[20] before mentioned. The house was pretty full; I had prepared a number of printed copies, and provided pens and ink dispersed all over the room. I harangued them a little on the subject, read the paper, and explained it, and then distributed the copies, which were eagerly signed, not the least objection being made.

When the company separated, and the papers were collected, we found above twelve hundred hands; and other copies being dispersed in the country, the subscribers amounted at length to upward of ten thousand. These all furnished themselves as soon as they could with arms, formed themselves into companies and regiments, chose their own officers, and met every week to be instructed in the manual exercise,[21] and other parts of military discipline. The women, by subscriptions among themselves, provided silk colors, which they presented to the companies, painted with different devices and mottoes, which I supplied.

The officers of the companies composing the Philadelphia regiment, being met, chose me for their colonel; but, conceiving myself unfit, I declined that station, and recommended Mr. Lawrence, a fine person and man of influence, who was accordingly appointed. I then proposed a lottery[22] to defray the expense of building a battery below the town, and furnishing it with cannon. It filled expeditiously, and the battery was soon erected, the merlons[23] being framed of logs and filled with earth. We bought some old cannon from Boston, but these not being sufficient, we wrote to England for more, soliciting, at the same time, our proprietaries for some assistance, though without much expectation of obtaining it.

Meanwhile Colonel Lawrence, William Allen, Abram Taylor, Esquire, and myself were sent to New York by the associators, commissioned to borrow some cannon of Governor Clinton. He at

---

[20] Large building—The one built for Whitefield.

[21] Manual exercise—Drill in handling weapons.

[22] Lottery—A gambling system often employed in the early days to raise money for states, colleges, and other institutions. Legislation finally put a stop to it, though a state lottery continued in Louisiana until the 1890's. Lotteries are still conducted on the sly for private profit.

[23] Merlons—Walls or ramparts of a fort.

first refused us peremptorily; but at dinner with his council, where there was great drinking of Madeira wine, as the custom of that place then was, he softened by degrees, and said he would lend us six. After a few more bumpers he advanced to ten; and at length he very good-naturedly conceded eighteen. They were fine cannon, eighteen-pounders, with their carriages, which we soon transported and mounted on our battery, where the associators kept a nightly guard while the war lasted, and among the rest I regularly took my turn of duty there as a common soldier.

My activity in these operations was agreeable to the governor and council; they took me into confidence, and I was consulted by them in every measure wherein their concurrence was thought useful to the association. Calling in the aid of religion, I proposed to them the proclaiming a fast, to promote reformation, and implore the blessing of Heaven on our undertaking. They embraced the motion; but, as it was the first fast ever thought of in the province, the secretary had no precedent from which to draw the proclamation. My education in New England, where a fast is proclaimed every year, was here of some advantage: I drew it in the accustomed style; it was translated into German,[24] printed in both languages, and divulged through the province. This gave the clergy of the different sects an opportunity of influencing their congregations to join in the association, and it would probably have been general among all but Quakers if the peace had not soon intervened.

It was thought by some of my friends that, by my activity in these affairs, I should offend that sect, and thereby lose my interest in the Assembly of the province, where they formed a great majority. A young gentleman, who had likewise some friends in the House, and wished to succeed me as their clerk, acquainted me that it was decided to displace me at the next election; and he, therefore, in good will, advised me to resign, as more consistent with my honor than being turned out. My answer to him was that I had read or heard of some public man who made it a rule never to ask for an office, and never to refuse one when offered to him. "I approve," says I, "of his rule, and will practise it with a small addition: I shall never *ask,* never *refuse,* nor ever *resign* an office.

---

[24] TRANSLATED INTO GERMAN—Many Germans had emigrated to Pennsylvania. Their descendants, still called mistakenly "Pennsylvania Dutch," have a peculiar dialect of their own.

If they will have my office of clerk to dispose of to another, they shall take it from me. I will not, by giving it up, lose my right of some time or other making reprisals on my adversaries." I heard, however, no more of this; I was chosen again unanimously as usual at the next election. Possibly, as they disliked my late intimacy with the members of council, who had joined the governors in all the disputes about military preparations, with which the House had long been harassed, they might have been pleased if I would voluntarily have left them; but they did not care to displace me on account merely of my zeal for the association, and they could not well give another reason.

Indeed, I had some cause to believe that the defence of the country was not disagreeable to any of them, provided they were not required to assist in it. And I found that a much greater number of them than I could have imagined, though against offensive war were clearly for the defensive. Many pamphlets *pro* and *con* were published on the subject, and some by good Quakers, in favor of defence, which I believe convinced most of their younger people.

My being many years in the Assembly, the majority of which were constantly Quakers, gave me frequent opportunities of seeing the embarrassment given them by their principle against war, whenever application was made to them, by order of the crown, to grant aids for military purposes. They were unwilling to offend government, on the one hand, by a direct refusal; and their friends, the body of the Quakers, on the other, by a compliance contrary to their principles; hence a variety of evasions to avoid complying, and modes of disguising the compliance when it became unavoidable. The common mode at last was to grant money under the phrase of its being "for the king's use," and never to inquire how it was applied.

To avoid this kind of embarrassment, the Quakers have of late years been gradually declining the public service in the Assembly and in the magistracy, choosing rather to quit their power than their principle.

## CHAPTER VII

### Achievements and Honors

The Pennsylvania Fireplace—Founding an Academy—Political Promotion—Raising Money for a Hospital—Interest in City Streets—Appointment as Postmaster General—Honorary Degrees

In order of time, I should have mentioned before, that having, in 1742, invented an open stove[1] for the better warming of rooms, and at the same time saving fuel, as the fresh air admitted was warmed in entering, I made a present of the model to Mr. Robert Grace,[2] one of my early friends, who, having an iron-furnace, found the casting of the plates for these stoves a profitable thing, as they were growing in demand. To promote that demand, I wrote and published a pamphlet, entitled *An Account of the new-invented Pennsylvania Fireplaces; wherein their Construction and Manner of Operation is particularly explained; their Advantages above every other Method of warming Rooms demonstrated; and all Objections that have been raised against the Use of them answered and obviated,* etc. This pamphlet had a good effect. Governor Thomas was so pleased with the construction of this stove, as described in it, that he offered to give me a patent for the sole vending of them for a term of years; but I declined it from a principle which has ever weighed with me on such occasions, viz., *That, as we enjoy great advantages from the inventions of others, we should be glad of an opportunity to serve others by any invention of ours; and this we should do freely and generously.*

An ironmonger in London, however, assuming a good deal of my pamphlet, and working it up into his own, and making some small changes in the machine, which rather hurt its operation, got a patent for it there, and made, as I was told, a little fortune by it. And this is not the only instance of patents taken out for my inventions by others, though not always with the same success, which I never contested, as having no desire of profiting by patents myself, and hating disputes. The use of these fireplaces in very

---

[1] An open stove—Until Franklin invented his stove, the usual method of heating was the open fireplace which let much of the heat escape up the chimney. The Franklin stove was an iron box which was set in the fireplace and extended out into the room. The fire was built in the iron box, which soon became very hot. The hot iron radiated much more heat into the room than the old fireplace had done.

[2] Robert Grace—See page 70.

many houses, both of this and the neighboring colonies, has been, and is, a great saving of wood to the inhabitants.

Peace being concluded, and the association[3] business therefore at an end, I turned my thoughts again to the affair of establishing an academy. The first step I took was to associate in the design a number of active friends, of whom the Junto furnished a good part; the next was to write and publish a pamphlet, entitled *Proposals relating to the Education of Youth in Pennsylvania.* This I distributed among the principal inhabitants gratis; and as soon as I could suppose their minds a little prepared by the perusal of it, I set on foot a subscription for opening and supporting an academy; it was to be paid in quotas yearly for five years; by so dividing it, I judged the subscription might be larger, and I believe it was so, amounting to no less, if I remember right, than five thousand pounds.

In the introduction to these proposals, I stated their publication, not as an act of mine, but of some *public-spirited gentlemen,* avoiding as much as I could, according to my usual rule, the presenting myself to the public as the author of any scheme for their benefit.

The subscribers, to carry the project into immediate execution, chose out of their number twenty-four trustees, and appointed Mr. Francis, then attorney-general, and myself to draw up constitutions for the government of the academy; which being done and signed, a house was hired, masters engaged, and the schools opened, I think, in the same year, 1749.

The scholars increasing fast, the house was soon found too small, and we were looking out for a piece of ground, properly situated, with intention to build, when Providence threw into our way a large house ready built, which, with a few alterations, might well serve our purpose. This was the building before mentioned, erected by the hearers of Mr. Whitefield, and was obtained for us in the following manner.

It is to be noted that the contributions to this building being made by people of different sects, care was taken in the nomination of trustees, in whom the building and ground was to be vested, that a predominancy should not be given to any sect, lest in time that predominancy might be a means of appropriating the whole to the

---

[3] PEACE . . . ASSOCIATION—After the signing of the treaty terminating King George's War, Franklin's association for defence had nothing more to do.

use of such sect, contrary to the original intention. It was therefore that one of each sect was appointed, viz., one Church-of-England man, one Presbyterian, one Baptist, one Moravian,[4] etc., those, in case of vacancy by death, were to fill it by election from among the contributors. The Moravian happened not to please his colleagues, and on his death they resolved to have no other of that sect. The difficulty then was, how to avoid having two of some other sect, by means of the new choice.

Several persons were named, and for that reason not agreed to. At length one mentioned me, with the observation that I was merely an honest man, and of no sect at all, which prevailed with them to choose me. The enthusiasm which existed when the house was built had long since abated, and its trustees had not been able to procure fresh contributions for paying the ground-rent, and discharging some other debts the building had occasioned, which embarrassed them greatly. Being now a member of both sets of trustees, that for the building and that for the academy, I had a good opportunity of negotiating with both, and brought them finally to an agreement, by which the trustees for the building were to cede it to those of the academy, the latter undertaking to discharge the debt, to keep forever open in the building a large hall for occasional preachers, according to the original intention, and maintain a free school for the instruction of poor children. Writings were accordingly drawn, and on paying the debts the trustees of the academy were put in possession of the premises; and by dividing the great and lofty hall into stories, and different rooms above and below for the several schools, and purchasing some additional ground, the whole was soon made fit for our purpose, and the scholars removed into the building. The care and trouble of agreeing with the workmen, purchasing materials, and superintending the work, fell upon me; and I went through it the more cheerfully, as it did not then interfere with my private business, having the year before taken a very able, industrious, and honest partner, Mr. David Hall, with whose character I was well acquainted, as he had worked for me four years. He took off my hands all care of the printing office, paying me punctually my share of the profits. This partnership continued eighteen years, successfully for us both.

[4] MORAVIAN—One of the religious sects formed in Bohemia among the followers of John Huss, Protestant reformer.

The trustees of the academy, after a while, were incorporated by a charter from the governor; their funds were increased by contributions in Britain and grants of land from the proprietaries, to which the Assembly has since made considerable addition; and thus was established the present University of Philadelphia.[5] I have been continued one of its trustees from the beginning, now near forty years, and have had the very great pleasure of seeing a number of the youth who have received their education in it, distinguished by their improved abilities, serviceable in public stations, and ornaments to their country.

When I disengaged myself, as above mentioned, from private business, I flattered myself that by the sufficient though moderate fortune I had acquired, I had secured leisure during the rest of my life for philosophical studies[6] and amusements. I purchased all Dr. Spence's apparatus, who had come from England to lecture here, and I proceeded in my electrical experiments with great alacrity; but the public, now considering me as a man of leisure, laid hold of me for their purposes, every part of our civil government, and almost at the same time, imposing some duty upon me. The governor put me into the commission of the peace; the corporation of the city chose me of the common council, and soon after an alderman; and the citizens at large chose me a burgess to represent them in Assembly. This latter station was the more agreeable to me, as I was at length tired with sitting there to hear debates, in which, as clerk, I could take no part, and which were often so unentertaining that I was induced to amuse myself with making magic squares or circles,[7] or anything to avoid weariness; and I conceived my becoming a member would enlarge my power of doing good. I would not, however, insinuate that my ambition was not flattered by all these promotions; it certainly was; for, considering my low beginning, they were great things to me; and they were still more pleasing, as being so many spontaneous testimonies of the public good opinion, and by me entirely unsolicited.

---

[5] UNIVERSITY OF PHILADELPHIA—Later changed to University of Pennsylvania.

[6] PHILOSOPHICAL STUDIES—Scientific studies, especially physics.

[7] MAGIC SQUARES OR CIRCLES—Franklin's interest in mathematics led him to the construction of squares cut into small rectangles by horizontal and vertical lines, each rectangle containing a figure, and the sum of each column reading up and down or across or sometimes diagonally totaling the same amount. He also worked out a similar puzzle with circles.

The office of justice of the peace I tried a little, by attending a few courts, and sitting on the bench to hear causes; but finding that more knowledge of the common law than I possessed was necessary to act in that station with credit, I gradually withdrew from it, excusing myself by my being obliged to attend the higher duties of a legislator in the Assembly. My election to this trust was repeated every year for ten years, without my ever asking any elector for his vote, or signifying, either directly or indirectly, any desire of being chosen. On taking my seat in the House, my son was appointed their clerk.[8]

The year following, a treaty being to be held with the Indians at Carlisle,[9] the governor sent a message to the House, proposing that they should nominate some of their members, to be joined with some members of council, as commissioners for that purpose. The House named the speaker (Mr. Norris) and myself; and, being commissioned, we went to Carlisle, and met the Indians accordingly.

As those people are extremely apt to get drunk, and, when so, are very quarrelsome and disorderly, we strictly forbade the selling any liquor to them; and when they complained of this restriction, we told them that if they would continue sober during the treaty, we would give them plenty of rum when business was over. They promised this, and they kept their promise because they could get no liquor, and the treaty was conducted very orderly, and concluded to mutual satisfaction. They then claimed and received the rum; this was in the afternoon: they were near one hundred men, women, and children, and were lodged in temporary cabins, built in the form of a square, just without the town. In the evening, hearing a great noise among them, the commissioners walked out to see what was the matter. We found they had made a great bonfire in the middle of the square; they were all drunk, men and women, quarrelling and fighting. Their dark-colored bodies, half naked, seen only by the gloomy light of the bonfire, running after and beating one another with firebrands, accompanied by their horrid yellings, formed a scene the most resembling our ideas of hell that could well be imagined; there was no appeasing the tumult, and we retired to our lodging. At midnight a number of them came thundering at our door, demanding more rum, of which we took no notice.

[8] SON . . . APPOINTED . . . CLERK—Franklin never hesitated to use political influence for the advancement of his own relatives.

[9] CARLISLE—Town in Pennsylvania a little southwest of Harrisburg. From 1879 to 1918 it was the seat of the U. S. Indian Training and Industrial School.

The next day, sensible they had misbehaved in giving us that disturbance, they sent three of their old counsellors to make their apology. The orator acknowledged the fault, but laid it upon the rum; and then endeavored to excuse the rum by saying, "*The Great Spirit, who made all things, made everything for some use, and whatever use he designed anything for, that use it should always be put to. Now, when he made rum, he said, 'Let this be for the Indians to get drunk with,' and it must be so.*" And, indeed, if it be the design of Providence to extirpate these savages in order to make room for cultivators of the earth, it seems not improbable that rum may be the appointed means. It has already annihilated all the tribes who formerly inhabited the sea-coast.

In 1751, Dr. Thomas Bond, a particular friend of mine, conceived the idea of establishing a hospital in Philadelphia (a very beneficent design, which has been ascribed to me, but was originally his) for the reception and cure of poor sick persons, whether inhabitants of the province or strangers. He was zealous and active in endeavoring to procure subscriptions for it, but the proposal being a novelty in America, and at first not well understood, he met but with small success.

At length he came to me with the compliment that he found there was no such thing as carrying a public-spirited project through without my being concerned in it. "For," says he, "I am often asked by those to whom I propose subscribing, Have you consulted Franklin upon this business? And what does he think of it? And when I tell them that I have not (supposing it rather out of your line), they do not subscribe, but say they will consider of it." I inquired into the nature and probable utility of his scheme, and receiving from him a very satisfactory explanation, I not only subscribed to it myself, but engaged heartily in the design of procuring subscriptions from others. Previously, however, to the solicitation I endeavored to prepare the minds of the people by writing on the subject in the newspapers, which was my usual custom in such cases, but which he had omitted.

The subscriptions afterwards were more free and generous; but, beginning to flag, I saw they would be insufficient without some assistance from the Assembly, and therefore proposed to petition for it, which was done. The country members did not at first relish the project; they objected that it could only be serviceable to the city, and therefore the citizens alone should be at the expense of it; and they doubted whether the citizens themselves generally approved of it. My allegation on the contrary, that it met with such approbation as to leave no doubt of our being able to raise two thousand pounds by voluntary donations, they considered as a most extravagant supposition, and utterly impossible.

On this I formed my plan; and, asking leave to bring in a bill for incorporating the contributors according to the prayer of their petition, and granting them a blank sum of money, which leave was obtained chiefly on the consideration that the House could throw the bill out if they did not like it, I drew it so as to make the important clause a conditional one, viz., "And be it enacted, by the authority aforesaid, that when the said contributors shall have met and chosen their managers and treasurer, *and shall have raised by their contributions a capital stock of —— value* (the yearly interest of which is to be applied to the accommodating of the sick poor in the said hospital, free of charge for diet, attendance, advice, and medicines), *and shall make the same appear to the satisfaction of the speaker of the Assembly for the time being,* that *then* it shall and may be lawful for the said speaker, and he is hereby required, to sign an order on the provincial treasurer for the payment of two thousand pounds, in two yearly payments, to the treasurer of the said hospital, to be applied to the founding, building, and finishing of the same."

This condition carried the bill through; for the members who had opposed the grant, and now conceived they might have the credit of being charitable without the expense, agreed to its passage; and then, in soliciting subscriptions among the people, we urged the conditional promise of the law as an additional motive to give, since every man's donation would be doubled; thus the clause worked both ways. The subscriptions accordingly soon exceeded the requisite sum, and we claimed and received the public gift, which enabled us to carry the design into execution. A convenient and handsome building was soon erected; the institution has by constant experience been found useful, and flourishes to this day; and I do not remember any of my political manœuvres, the success of which gave me at the time more pleasure, or wherein, after thinking of it, I more easily excused myself for having made some use of cunning.

Our city, though laid out with a beautiful regularity, the streets large, straight, and crossing each other at right angles, had the disgrace of suffering those streets to remain long unpaved, and in wet weather the wheels of heavy carriages ploughed them into a quagmire, so that it was difficult to cross them; and in dry weather the dust was offensive. I had lived near what was called the Jersey Market, and saw with pain the inhabitants wading in mud while purchasing their provisions. A strip of ground down the middle of that market was at length paved with brick, so that, being once in the market, they had firm footing, but were often over shoes in dirt to get there. By talking and writing on the subject, I was at length instrumental in getting the street paved with stone between the market and the bricked foot pavement, that was on each side next the houses. This, for some time, gave an easy access to the market dry-shod; but the rest of the street not being paved, whenever a carriage came out of the mud upon this pavement, it shook off and left its dirt upon it, and it was soon covered with mire, which was not removed, the city as yet having no scavengers.[10]

After some inquiry, I found a poor, industrious man who was willing to undertake keeping the pavement clean by sweeping it twice a week, carrying off the dirt from before all the neighbors' doors, for the sum of sixpence per month, to be paid by each house. I then wrote and printed a paper setting forth the advantages to the neighborhood that might be obtained by this small expense; the greater ease in keeping our houses clean, so much dirt not being brought in by people's feet; the benefit to the shops by more custom, etc., etc., as buyers could more easily get at them; and by not having, in windy weather, the dust blown in upon their goods, etc., etc. I sent one of these papers to each house, and in a day or two went round to see who would subscribe an agreement to pay these sixpences; it was unanimously signed, and for a time well executed. All the inhabitants of the city were delighted with the cleanliness of the pavement that surrounded the market, it being a convenience to all, and this raised a general desire to have all the streets paved, and made the people more willing to submit to a tax for that purpose.

After some time I drew a bill for paving the city, and brought it into the Assembly. It was just before I went to England, in

[10] SCAVENGERS—Men employed to clean the streets.

1757, and did not pass till I was gone, and then with an alteration in the mode of assessment, which I thought not for the better, but with an additional provision for lighting as well as paving the streets, which was a great improvement. It was by a private person, the late Mr. John Clifton, his giving a sample of the utility of lamps, by placing one at his door, that the people were first impressed with the idea of enlighting all the city. The honor of this public benefit has also been ascribed to me, but it belongs truly to that gentleman. I did but follow his example, and have only some merit to claim respecting the form of our lamps, as differing from the globe lamps we were at first supplied with from London. Those we found inconvenient in these respects: they admitted no air below; the smoke, therefore, did not readily go out above, but circulated in the globe, lodged on its inside, and soon obstructed the light they were intended to afford; giving, besides, the daily trouble of wiping them clean; and an accidental stroke on one of them would demolish it and render it totally useless. I therefore suggested the composing them of four flat panes, with a long funnel above to draw up the smoke, and crevices admitting air below, to facilitate the ascent of the smoke; by this means they were kept clean, and did not grow dark in a few hours, as the London lamps do, but continued bright till morning, and an accidental stroke would generally break out a single pane, easily repaired.

I have sometimes wondered that the Londoners did not, from the effect holes in the bottom of the globe lamps used at Vauxhall[11] have in keeping them clean, learn to have such holes in their street lamps. But, these holes being made for another purpose, viz., to communicate flame more suddenly to the wick by a little flax hanging down through them, the other use, of letting in air, seems not to have been thought of; and therefore, after the lamps have been lit a few hours, the streets of London are very poorly illuminated.

The mention of these improvements puts me in mind of one I proposed, when in London, to Dr. Fothergill, who was among the best men I have known, and a great promoter of useful projects. I had observed that the streets, when dry, were never swept, and the light dust carried away; but it was suffered to accumulate till wet weather reduced it to mud, and then, after lying some days

---

[11] VAUXHALL—Famous public garden in London established after the Restoration in 1660. Its amusements have been described by many British novelists and dramatists.

so deep on the pavement that there was no crossing but in paths kept clean by poor people with brooms, it was with great labor raked together and thrown up into carts open above, the sides of which suffered some of the slush at every jolt on the pavement to shake out and fall, sometimes to the annoyance of foot-passengers. The reason given for not sweeping the dusty streets was, that the dust would fly into the windows of shops and houses.

An accidental occurrence had instructed me how much sweeping might be done in a little time. I found at my door in Craven Street,[12] one morning, a poor woman sweeping my pavement with a birch broom; she appeared very pale and feeble, as just come out of a fit of sickness. I asked who employed her to sweep there; she said, "Nobody; but I am very poor and in distress, and I sweeps before gentlefolkses doors, and hopes they will give me something." I bid her sweep the whole street clean, and I would give her a shilling; this was at nine o'clock; at twelve she came for the shilling. From the slowness I saw at first in her working I could scarce believe that the work was done so soon, and sent my servant to examine it, who reported that the whole street was swept perfectly clean, and all the dust placed in the gutter, which was in the middle; and the next rain washed it quite away, so that the pavement and even the kennel[13] were perfectly clean.

I then judged that, if that feeble woman could sweep such a street in three hours, a strong, active man might have done it in half the time. And here let me remark the convenience of having but one gutter in such a narrow street, running down its middle, instead of two, one on each side, near the footway; for where all the rain that falls on a street runs from the sides and meets in the middle, it forms there a current strong enough to wash away all the mud it meets with; but when divided into two channels, it is often too weak to cleanse either, and only makes the mud it finds more fluid, so that the wheels of carriages and feet of horses throw and dash it upon the foot-pavement, which is thereby rendered foul and slippery, and sometimes splash it upon those who are walking.

Some may think these trifling matters not worth minding or relating; but when they consider that though dust blown into the

[12] Craven Street—During both of Franklin's sojourns in London he resided in Craven Street with a Mrs. Stevenson, more as a member of the family than as a lodger. His correspondence with the daughter Mary is as delightful as that with Georgiana Shipley.

[13] Kennel—Gutter.

eyes of a single person, or into a single shop on a windy day, is but of small importance, yet the great number of the instances in a populous city, and its frequent repetitions give it weight and consequence, perhaps they will not censure very severely those who bestow some attention to affairs of this seemingly low nature. Human felicity is produced not so much by great pieces of good fortune that seldom happen, as by little advantages that occur every day. Thus, if you teach a poor young man to shave himself, and keep his razor in order, you may contribute more to the happiness of his life than in giving him a thousand guineas. The money may be soon spent, the regret only remaining of having foolishly consumed it; but in the other case, he escapes the frequent vexation of waiting for barbers, and of their sometimes dirty fingers, offensive breaths, and dull razors; he shaves when most convenient to him, and enjoys daily the pleasure of its being done with a good instrument. With these sentiments I have hazarded the few preceding pages, hoping they may afford hints which some time or other may be useful to a city I love, having lived many years in it very happily, and perhaps to some of our towns in America.

Having been for some time employed by the postmaster-general of America as his comptroller in regulating several offices, and bringing the officers to account, I was, upon his death in 1753, appointed, jointly with Mr. William Hunter, to succeed him, by a commission from the postmaster-general in England. The American office never had hitherto paid anything to that of Britain. We were to have six hundred pounds a year between us, if we could make that sum out of the profits of the office. To do this a variety of improvements[14] were necessary; some of these were inevitably at first expensive, so that in the first four years the office became above nine hundred pounds in debt to us. But it soon after began to repay us; and before I was displaced by a freak of the ministers,[15] of which I shall speak hereafter, we had brought it to yield *three times* as much clear revenue to the crown as the post-office of

[14] Improvements—To put the postoffice system on a paying basis, Franklin rode through the colonies studying conditions, then put swifter post-riders into the service, increased the number of mails, permitted newspapers to be carried for a charge, and reduced postal rates. The added use made of the mail service soon brought a profit.

[15] A freak of the ministers—The *Autobiography* was not brought down far enough to include this incident. In 1774 the British cabinet removed Franklin because of the Hutchinson letters. See "Franklin's Later Life" (pages 155–156).

Ireland. Since that imprudent transaction, they have received from it—not one farthing!

The business of the post-office occasioned my taking a journey this year to New England, where the College of Cambridge,[16] of their own motion, presented me with the degree of Master of Arts. Yale College, in Connecticut, had before made me a similar compliment. Thus, without studying in any college, I came to partake of their honors. They were conferred in consideration of my improvements and discoveries in the electric branch of natural philosophy.

## CHAPTER VIII

### The Pennsylvania Statesman

Franklin's Plan of Union—Quarrel with the Proprietaries—Furnishing Supplies for Braddock—Franklin's Warning and Braddock's Defeat—Financial Responsibilities

In 1754, war with France being again apprehended, a congress of commissioners from the different colonies was, by an order of the Lords of Trade,[1] to be assembled at Albany, there to confer with the chiefs of the Six Nations[2] concerning the means of defending both their country and ours. Governor Hamilton, having received this order, acquainted the House with it, requesting they would furnish proper presents for the Indians, to be given on this occasion; and naming the speaker (Mr. Norris) and myself to join Mr. Thomas Penn[3] and Mr. Secretary Peters as commissioners to act for Pennsylvania. The House approved the nomination, and provided the goods for the present, though they did not much like treating out of the provinces; and we met the other commissioners at Albany about the middle of June.

In our way thither, I projected and drew a plan for the union of all the colonies under one government, so far as might be necessary for defence and other important general purposes. As we passed through New York, I had there shown my project to

---

[16] College of Cambridge—Harvard.

[1] Lords of Trade—British body supervising colonial affairs.

[2] Six Nations—The powerful Iroquois Confederacy of Central New York, comprising the Mohawks, Oneidas, Onondagas, Cayugas, Senecas, and Tuscaroras.

[3] Thomas Penn—One of the proprietaries and son of William Penn, founder of the Colony.

Mr. James Alexander and Mr. Kennedy, two gentlemen of great knowledge in public affairs, and, being fortified by their approbation, I ventured to lay it before the Congress. It then appeared that several of the commissioners had formed plans of the same kind. A previous question was first taken, whether a union should be established, which passed in the affirmative unanimously. A committee was then appointed, one member from each colony, to consider the several plans, and report. Mine happened to be preferred, and, with a few amendments, was accordingly reported.

By this plan the general government was to be administered by a president-general, appointed and supported by the crown, and a grand council was to be chosen by the representatives of the people of the several colonies, met in their respective assemblies. The debates upon it in Congress went on daily, hand in hand with the Indian business. Many objections and difficulties were started, but at length they were all overcome, and the plan was unanimously agreed to, and copies ordered to be transmitted to the Board of Trade[4] and to the assemblies of the several provinces. Its fate was singular: the assemblies did not adopt it, as they all thought there was too much *prerogative*[5] in it, and in England it was judged to have too much of the *democratic*. The Board of Trade therefore did not approve of it, nor recommend it for the approbation of his majesty; but another scheme was formed, supposed to answer the same purpose better, whereby the governors of the provinces, with some members of their respective councils, were to meet and order the raising of troops, building of forts, etc., and to draw on the treasury of Great Britain for the expense, which was afterwards to be refunded by an act of Parliament laying a tax on America.

Being the winter following in Boston, I had much conversation with Governor Shirley[6] upon both the plans. The different and contrary reasons of dislike to my plan make me suspect that it was really the true medium; and I am still of opinion it would have been happy for both sides the water if it had been adopted. The colonies, so united, would have been sufficiently strong to have

---

[4] BOARD OF TRADE—Same as Lords of Trade.

[5] PREROGATIVE—Too much power granted the king. Since both sides turned down the plan, thinking it gave the other too much authority, Franklin's scheme must have been a fair compromise.

[6] GOVERNOR SHIRLEY—William Shirley of Massachusetts Bay Colony, who succeeded General Braddock as Commander-in-chief of the British forces in America.

defended themselves; there would then have been no need of troops from England; of course, the subsequent pretence for taxing America, and the bloody contest it occasioned, would have been avoided. But such mistakes are not new: history is full of the errors of states and princes.

> Look round the habitable world, how few
> Know their own good, or, knowing it, pursue![7]

Those who govern, having much business on their hands, do not generally like to take the trouble of considering and carrying into execution new projects. The best public measures are therefore seldom *adopted from previous wisdom, but forced by the occasion.*

The Governor of Pennsylvania, in sending it down to the Assembly, expressed his approbation of the plan, "as appearing to him to be drawn up with great clearness and strength of judgment, and therefore recommended it as well worthy of their closest and most serious attention." The House, however, by the management of a certain member, took it up when I happened to be absent, which I thought not very fair, and reprobated it without paying any attention to it at all, to my no small mortification.

In my journey to Boston this year, I met at New York with our new governor, Mr. Morris, just arrived there from England, with whom I had been before intimately acquainted. He brought a commission to supersede Mr. Hamilton, who, tired with the disputes his proprietary instructions subjected him to, had resigned. Mr. Morris asked me if I thought he must expect as uncomfortable an administration. I said, "No; you may, on the contrary, have a very comfortable one, if you will only take care not to enter into any dispute with the Assembly." "My dear friend," says he, pleasantly, "how can you advise my avoiding disputes? You know I love disputing; it is one of my greatest pleasures; however, to show the regard I have for your counsel, I promise you I will, if possible, avoid them." He had some reason for loving to dispute, being eloquent, an acute sophister, and therefore generally successful in argumentative conversation. He had been brought up to it from a boy, his father, as I have heard, accustoming his children to dispute with one another for his diversion, while sitting at table

[7] LOOK . . . PURSUE—From Dryden's translations of the Latin poet, Juvenal.

after dinner; but I think the practice was not wise; for, in the course of my observation, these disputing, contradicting, and confuting people are generally unfortunate in their affairs. They get victory sometimes, but they never get good will, which would be of more use to them. We parted, he going to Philadelphia, and I to Boston.

In returning, I met at New York with the votes of the Assembly, by which it appeared that, notwithstanding his promise to me, he and the House were already in high contention; and it was a continual battle between them as long as he retained the government. I had my share of it; for, as soon as I got back to my seat in the Assembly, I was put on every committee for answering his speeches and messages, and by the committees always desired to make the drafts. Our answers, as well as his messages, were often tart, and sometimes indecently abusive; and as he knew I wrote for the Assembly, one might have imagined that, when we met, we could hardly avoid cutting throats; but he was so good-natured a man that no personal difference between him and me was occasioned by the contest, and we often dined together.

These public quarrels were all at bottom owing to the proprietaries, our hereditary governors, who, when any expense was to be incurred for the defence of their province, with incredible meanness instructed their deputies[8] to pass no act for levying the necessary taxes, unless their vast estates were in the same act expressly excused; and they had even taken bonds of these deputies to observe such instructions. The Assemblies for three years held out against this injustice, though constrained to bend at last. At length Captain Denny, who was Governor Morris's successor, ventured to disobey those instructions: how that was brought about I shall show hereafter.

But I am got forward too fast with my story: there are still some transactions to be mentioned that happened during the administration of Governor Morris.

War[9] being in a manner commenced with France, the government of Massachusetts Bay projected an attack upon Crown Point,[10] and sent Mr. Quincy[11] to Pennsylvania, and Mr. Pownall,

---

[8] THEIR DEPUTIES—The acting governors sent over by the proprietaries.

[9] WAR—The French and Indian War (1754–1763).

[10] CROWN POINT—Fortified trading post in northeastern New York on Lake Champlain.

[11] MR. QUINCY—Josiah Quincy of Boston, who was to play a large part in bringing about the Revolution. His family has been famous in American history.

afterward Governor Pownall, to New York, to solicit assistance. As I was in the Assembly, knew its temper, and was Mr. Quincy's countryman, he applied to me for my influence and assistance. I dictated his address to them, which was well received. They voted an aid of ten thousand pounds, to be laid out in provisions. But the governor refusing his assent to their bill (which included this with other sums granted for the use of the crown), unless a clause were inserted exempting the proprietary estate from bearing any part of the tax that would be necessary, the Assembly, though very desirous of making their grant to New England effectual, were at a loss how to accomplish it. Mr. Quincy labored hard with the governor to obtain his assent, but he was obstinate.

I then suggested a method of doing the business without a governor, by orders on the trustees of the Loan Office,[12] which, by law, the Assembly had the right of drawing. There was, indeed, little or no money at that time in the office, and therefore I proposed that the orders should be payable in a year, and to bear an interest of five per cent. With these orders I supposed the provisions might easily be purchased. The Assembly, with very little hesitation, adopted the proposal. The orders were immediately printed, and I was one of the committee directed to sign and dispose of them. The fund for paying them was the interest of all the paper currency then extant in the province upon loan, together with the revenue arising from the excise, which being known to be more than sufficient, they obtained instant credit, and were not only received in payment for the provisions, but many moneyed people, who had cash lying by them, vested it in those orders, which they found advantageous, as they bore interest while upon hand, and might on any occasion be used as money, so that they were eagerly all bought up, and in a few weeks none of them were to be seen. Thus this important affair was by my means completed. Mr. Quincy returned thanks to the Assembly in a handsome memorial,[13] went home highly pleased with the success of his embassy, and ever after bore for me the most cordial and affectionate friendship.[14]

---

[12] Loan office—A department that handled funds invested by private individuals in the government of the colony.

[13] Memorial—Written expression of thanks.

[14] Friendship—Josiah Quincy went to England in 1774 and was in close touch with Franklin during the months preceding the Revolution. He died on the voyage home the following spring.

The British government, not choosing to permit the union of the colonies as proposed at Albany, and to trust that union with their defence, lest they should thereby grow too military and feel their own strength, suspicions and jealousies at this time being entertained of them, sent over General Braddock with two regiments of regular English troops for that purpose. He landed at Alexandria, in Virginia, and thence marched to Fredericktown, in Maryland, where he halted for carriages. Our Assembly apprehending, from some information, that he had conceived violent prejudices against them, as averse to the service, wished me to wait upon him, not as from them, but as postmaster-general, under the guise of proposing to settle with him the mode of conducting with most celerity and certainty the dispatches between him and the governors of the several provinces, with whom he must necessarily have continual correspondence, and of which they proposed to pay the expense. My son accompanied me on this journey.

We found the general at Fredericktown, waiting impatiently for the return of those he had sent through the back parts of Maryland and Virginia to collect wagons. I stayed with him several days, dined with him daily, and had full opportunity of removing all his prejudices, by the information of what the Assembly had before his arrival actually done, and were still willing to do, to facilitate his operations. When I was about to depart, the returns of wagons to be obtained were brought in, by which it appeared that they amounted only to twenty-five, and not all of those were in serviceable condition. The general and all the officers were surprised, declared the expedition was then at an end, being impossible, and exclaimed against the ministers for ignorantly landing them in a country destitute of the means of conveying their stores, baggage, etc., not less than one hundred and fifty wagons being necessary.

I happened to say I thought it was a pity they had not been landed rather in Pennsylvania, as in that country almost every farmer had his wagon. The general eagerly laid hold of my words, and said, "Then you, sir, who are a man of interest there, can probably procure them for us; and I beg you will undertake it." I asked what terms were to be offered the owners of the wagons; and I was desired to put on paper the terms that appeared to me necessary. This I did, and they were agreed to, and a commission and instructions accordingly prepared immediately. What those terms were will appear in the advertisement I published as soon as I arrived at Lancaster, which being, from the great and sudden effect it produced, a piece of some curiosity, I shall insert it at length, as follows:

ADVERTISEMENT

Lancaster, *April* 26, 1755

Whereas, one hundred and fifty wagons, with four horses to each wagon, and fifteen hundred saddle or pack horses, are wanted for the service of his majesty's forces now about to rendezvous at Will's Creek, and his excellency General Braddock having been pleased to empower me to contract for the hire of the same, I hereby give notice that I shall attend for that purpose at Lancaster from this day to next Wednesday evening, and at York from next Thursday morning till Friday evening, where I shall be ready to agree for wagons and teams, or single horses, on the following terms, viz.: 1. That there shall be paid for each wagon, with four good horses and a driver, fifteen shillings per diem; and for each able horse with a pack-saddle or other saddle and furniture, two shillings per diem; and for each able horse without a saddle, eighteen pence per diem. 2. That the pay commence from the time of their joining the forces at Will's Creek, which must be on or before the 20th of May ensuing, and that a reasonable allowance be paid over and above for the time necessary for their travelling to Will's Creek and home again after their discharge. 3. Each wagon and team, and every saddle or pack horse, is to be valued by indifferent[15] persons chosen between me and the owner; and in case of the loss of any wagon, team, or other horse in the service, the price according to such valuation is to be allowed and paid. 4. Seven days' pay is to be advanced and paid in hand by me to the owner of each wagon and team or horse, at the time of contracting, if required, and the remainder to be paid by General Braddock, or by the paymaster of the army, at the time of their discharge, or from time to time, as it shall be demanded. 5. No drivers of wagons, or persons taking care of the hired horses, are on any account to be called upon to do the duty of soldiers, or be otherwise employed than in conducting or taking care of their carriages or horses. 6. All oats, Indian corn,

[15] INDIFFERENT—Disinterested.

or other forage that wagons or horses bring to the camp, more than is necessary for the subsistence of the horses, is to be taken for the use of the army, and a reasonable price paid for the same.

Note. — My son, William Franklin, is empowered to enter into like contracts with any person in Cumberland county.

B. Franklin

*To the Inhabitants of the Counties of Lancaster, York, and Cumberland*

Friends and Countrymen:

Being occasionally at the camp at Frederick a few days since, I found the general and officers extremely exasperated on account of their not being supplied with horses and carriages, which had been expected from this province, as most able to furnish them; but, through the dissensions between our governor and Assembly, money had not been provided, nor any steps taken for that purpose.

It was proposed to send an armed force immediately into these counties to seize as many of the best carriages and horses as should be wanted, and compel as many persons into the service as would be necessary to drive and take care of them.

I apprehended that the progress of British soldiers through these counties on such an occasion, especially considering the temper they are in, and their resentment against us, would be attended with many and great inconveniences to the inhabitants, and therefore more willingly took the trouble of trying first what might be done by fair and equitable means. The people of these back counties have lately complained to the Assembly that a sufficient currency was wanting; you have an opportunity of receiving and dividing among you a very considerable sum; for, if the service of this expedition should continue, as it is more than probable it will, for one hundred and twenty days, the hire of these wagons and horses will amount to upward of thirty thousand pounds, which will be paid you in silver and gold of the king's money.

The service will be light and easy, for the army will scarce march above twelve miles per day, and the wagons and baggage-horses, as they carry those things that are absolutely necessary to the welfare of the army, must march with the army, and no faster; and are, for the army's sake, always placed where they can be most secure, whether in a march or in a camp.

If you are really, as I believe you are, good and loyal subjects to his majesty, you may now do a most acceptable service, and make it easy to yourselves; for three or four of such as can not separately spare from the business of their plantations a wagon and four horses and a driver, may do it together, one furnishing the wagon, another one or two horses, and another the driver, and divide the pay proportionately between you; but if you do not this service to your king and country voluntarily, when such good pay and reasonable terms are offered to you, your loyalty will be strongly suspected. The king's business must be done; so many brave troops, come so far for your defence, must not stand idle through your backwardness to do what may be reasonably expected from you; wagons and horses must be had; violent measures will probably be used, and you will be left to seek for a recompense where you can find it, and your case, perhaps, be little pitied or regarded.

I have no particular interest in this affair, as, except the satisfaction of endeavoring to do good, I shall have only my labor for my pains. If this method of obtaining the wagons and horses is not likely to succeed, I am obliged to send word to the general in fourteen days; and I suppose Sir John St. Clair, the hussar, with a body of soldiers, will immediately enter the province for the purpose, which I shall be sorry to hear, because I am very sincerely and truly your friend and well-wisher,[16]

B. FRANKLIN

I received of the general about eight hundred pounds, to be disbursed in advance-money to the wagon owners, etc.; but that sum being insufficient, I advanced upward of two hundred pounds more, and in two weeks the one hundred and fifty wagons, with two hundred and fifty-nine carrying horses, were on their march for the camp. The advertisement promised payment according to the valuation, in case any wagon or horse should be lost. The owners, however, alleging they did not know General Braddock, or what dependence might be had on his promise, insisted on my bond for the performance, which I accordingly gave them.

While I was at the camp, supping one evening with the officers of Colonel Dunbar's regiment, he represented to me his concern for

[16] WELL-WISHER—Note the combination of threat, flattery, and mercenary lure in this document.

the subalterns, who, he said, were generally not in affluence, and could ill afford, in this dear country, to lay in the stores that might be necessary in so long a march, through a wilderness, where nothing was to be purchased. I commiserated their case, and resolved to endeavor procuring them some relief. I said nothing, however, to him of my intention, but wrote the next morning to the committee of the Assembly, who had the disposition of some public money, warmly recommending the case of these officers to their consideration, and proposing that a present should be sent them of necessaries and refreshments. My son, who had some experience of a camp life, and of its wants, drew up a list for me, which I enclosed in my letter. The committee approved, and used such diligence that, conducted by my son, the stores arrived at the camp as soon as the wagons. They consisted of twenty parcels, each containing:

6 lbs. loaf sugar.
6 lbs. good Muscovado do.[17]
1 lb. good green tea.
1 lb. good bohea do.
6 lbs. good ground coffee.
6 lbs. chocolate.
½ cwt. best white biscuit.
½ lb. pepper.
1 quart best white wine vinegar.
1 Gloucester cheese.
1 keg containing 20 lbs. good butter.
2 doz. old Madeira wine.
2 gallons Jamaica spirits.
1 bottle flour of mustard.
2 well-cured hams.
½ dozen dried tongues.
6 lbs. rice.
6 lbs. raisins.

These twenty parcels, well packed, were placed on as many horses, each parcel, with the horse, being intended as a present for one officer. They were very thankfully received, and the kindness acknowledged by letters to me from the colonels of both regiments, in the most grateful terms. The general, too, was highly satisfied with my conduct in procuring him the wagons, etc., and readily paid my account of disbursements, thanking me repeatedly, and requesting my farther assistance in sending provisions after him. I undertook this also, and was busily employed in it till we heard of his defeat, advancing for the service of my own money upwards of one thousand pounds sterling, of which I sent him an account. It came to his hands, luckily for me, a few days before the battle, and he returned me immediately an order on the paymaster for the round

[17] Do.—Ditto; hence, Muscovado (brown) sugar; and below, bohea (black) tea.

sum of one thousand pounds, leaving the remainder to the next account. I consider this payment as good luck, having never been able to obtain that remainder, of which more hereafter.

This general was, I think, a brave man, and might probably have made a figure as a good officer in some European war. But he had too much self-confidence, too high an opinion of the validity of regular troops, and too mean a one of both Americans and Indians. George Croghan, our Indian interpreter, joined him on his march with one hundred of those people, who might have been of great use to his army as guides, scouts, etc., if he had treated them kindly; but he slighted and neglected them, and they gradually left him.

In conversation with him one day, he was giving me some account of his intended progress. "After taking Fort Duquesne,"[18] says he, "I am to proceed to Niagara; and, having taken that, to Frontenac,[19] if the season will allow time; and I suppose it will, for Duquesne can hardly detain me above three or four days; and then I see nothing that can obstruct my march to Niagara." Having before revolved in my mind the long line his army must make in their march by a very narrow road, to be cut for them through the woods and bushes, and also what I had read of a former defeat of fifteen hundred French, who invaded the Iroquois country, I had conceived some doubts and some fears for the event of the campaign. But I ventured only to say, "To be sure, sir, if you arrive well before Duquesne, with these fine troops, so well provided with artillery, that place not yet completely fortified, and as we hear with no very strong garrison, can probably make but a short resistance. The only danger I apprehend of obstruction to your march is from ambuscades of Indians, who, by constant practice, are dexterous in laying and executing them; and the slender line, near four miles long, which your army must make, may expose it to be attacked by surprise in its flanks, and to be cut like a thread into several pieces, which, from their distance, can not come up in time to support each other."

[18] FORT DUQUESNE—Built by the French on the present site of Pittsburgh at the junction of the Allegheny and Monongahela Rivers. After the French burned it in 1758 to prevent its falling into the hands of the English, it was rebuilt and called Fort Pitt after the prime minister of England. The settlement which later sprang up around the fort developed rapidly because of the natural advantages of its location.

[19] FRONTENAC—A French fort in Canada on Lake Ontario, the present site of Kingston, an important port on the Great Lakes.

He smiled at my ignorance, and replied, "These savages may, indeed, be a formidable enemy to your raw American militia,[20] but upon the king's regular and disciplined troops, sir, it is impossible they should make any impression." I was conscious of an impropriety in my disputing with a military man in matters of his profession, and said no more. The enemy, however, did not take the advantage of his army which I apprehended its long line of march exposed it to, but let it advance without interruption till within nine miles of the place; and then, when more in a body (for it had just passed a river, where the front had halted till all were come over), and in a more open part of the woods than any it had passed, attacked its advanced guard by a heavy fire from behind trees and bushes, which was the first intelligence the general had of an enemy's being near him. This guard being disordered, the general hurried the troops up to their assistance, which was done in great confusion, through wagons, baggage, and cattle; and presently the fire came upon their flank: the officers, being on horseback, were more easily distinguished, picked out as marks, and fell very fast; and the soldiers were crowded together in a huddle, having or hearing no orders, and standing to be shot at till two-thirds of them were killed; and then, being seized with a panic, the whole fled with precipitation.

The wagoners took each a horse out of his team and scampered; their example was immediately followed by others; so that all the wagons, provisions, artillery, and stores were left to the enemy. The general, being wounded, was brought off with difficulty; his secretary, Mr. Shirley, was killed by his side; and out of eighty-six officers, sixty-three were killed or wounded, and seven hundred and fourteen men killed out of eleven hundred. These eleven hundred had been picked men from the whole army; the rest had been left behind with Colonel Dunbar, who was to follow with the heavier part of the stores, provisions, and baggage. The flyers, not being pursued, arrived at Dunbar's camp, and the panic they brought with them instantly seized him and all his people; and, though he had now above one thousand men, and the enemy who had beaten Braddock did not at most exceed four hundred Indians and French together, instead of proceeding, and endeavoring to recover some

---

[20] Raw American militia—Including a young Virginian officer named George Washington, who also warned Braddock of his danger.

of the lost honor, he ordered all the stores, ammunition, etc., to be destroyed, that he might have more horses to assist his flight towards the settlements, and less lumber to remove. He was there met with requests from the governors of Virginia, Maryland, and Pennsylvania, that he would post his troops on the frontiers, so as to afford some protection to the inhabitants; but he continued his hasty march through all the country, not thinking himself safe till he arrived at Philadelphia, where the inhabitants could protect him. This whole transaction gave us Americans the first suspicion that our exalted ideas of the prowess of British regulars had not been well founded.

In their first march, too, from their landing till they got beyond the settlements, they had plundered and stripped the inhabitants, totally ruining some poor families, besides insulting, abusing, and confining the people if they remonstrated. This was enough to put us out of conceit of[21] such defenders, if we had really wanted any. How different was the conduct of our French friends in 1781, who, during a march through the most inhabited part of our country from Rhode Island to Virginia, near seven hundred miles, occasioned not the smallest complaint for the loss of a pig, a chicken, or even an apple.

Captain Orme, who was one of the general's aides-de-camp, and, being grievously wounded, was brought off with him, and continued with him to his death, which happened in a few days, told me that he was totally silent all day, and at night only said, *"Who would have thought it?"* That he was silent again the following day, saying only at last, *"We shall better know how to deal with them another time,"* and died in a few minutes after.

The secretary's papers, with all the general's orders, instructions, and correspondence, falling into the enemy's hands, they selected and translated into French a number of the articles, which they printed, to prove the hostile intentions of the British court before the declaration of war. Among these I saw some letters of the general to the ministry, speaking highly of the great service I had rendered the army, and recommending me to their notice. David Hume,[22] too, who was some years after secretary to Lord Hertford, when minister in France, and afterward to General Conway, when

[21] PUT US OUT OF CONCEIT OF—Take away our desire for.
[22] DAVID HUME—Noted British philosopher and author.

secretary of state, told me he had seen among the papers in that office, letters from Braddock highly recommending me. But the expedition having been unfortunate, my service, it seems, was not thought of much value, for those recommendations were never of any use to me.

As to rewards from himself, I asked only one, which was that he would give orders to his officers not to enlist any more of our bought servants,[23] and that he would discharge such as had been already enlisted. This he readily granted, and several were accordingly returned to their masters, on my application. Dunbar, when the command devolved on him, was not so generous. He being at Philadelphia, on his retreat or rather flight, I applied to him for the discharge of the servants of three poor farmers of Lancaster county that he had enlisted, reminding him of the late general's orders on that head. He promised me that if the masters would come to him at Trenton, where he should be in a few days on his march to New York, he would there deliver their men to them. They accordingly were at the expense and trouble of going to Trenton, and there he refused to perform his promise, to their great loss and disappointment.

As soon as the loss of the wagons and horses was generally known, all the owners came upon me for the valuation which I had given bond to pay. Their demands gave me a great deal of trouble, my acquainting them that the money was ready in the paymaster's hands, but that orders for paying it must first be obtained from General Shirley, and my assuring them that I had applied to that general by letter, but he being at a distance, an answer could not soon be received, and they must have patience; all this was not sufficient to satisfy, and some began to sue me. General Shirley at length relieved me from this terrible situation by appointing commissioners to examine the claims, and ordering payment. They amounted to near twenty thousand pound, which to pay would have ruined me.

Before we had the news of this defeat, the two Doctors Bond [24] came to me with a subscription paper for raising money to defray the expense of a grand firework which it was intended to exhibit

---

[23] Bought servants—See page 60, note 4.

[24] Two Doctors Bond—One of these, Thomas, is the man who promoted the hospital in Philadelphia.

at a rejoicing on receipt of the news of our taking Fort Duquesne. I looked grave, and said it would, I thought, be time enough to prepare for the rejoicing when we knew we should have occasion to rejoice. They seemed surprised that I did not immediately comply with their proposal. "Why!" says one of them, "you surely don't suppose that the fort will not be taken?" "I don't know that it will not be taken, but I know that the events of war are subject to great uncertainty." I gave them the reasons of my doubting; the subscription was dropped, and the projectors thereby missed the mortification they would have undergone if the firework had been prepared. Dr. Bond, on some other occasion afterward, said that he did not like Franklin's forebodings.

## CHAPTER IX

### Service in the Field

More Trouble with the Proprietaries—In Charge of Frontier Defence—Building the Forts—The Moravians—Promotion to Colonel—Franklin and Governor Morris

Governor Morris, who had continually worried the Assembly with message after message before the defeat of Braddock, to beat them into the making of acts to raise money for the defence of the province without taxing, among others, the proprietary estates, and had rejected all their bills for not having such an exempting clause, now redoubled his attacks with more hope of success, the danger and necessity being greater. The Assembly, however, continued firm, believing they had justice on their side, and that it would be giving up an essential right if they suffered the governor to amend their money-bills. In one of the last, indeed, which was for granting fifty thousand pounds, his proposed amendment was only of a single word. The bill expressed "that all estates, real and personal, were to be taxed, those of the proprietaries *not* excepted." His amendment was, for *"not"* read *"only"*: a small but very material alteration. However, when the news of this disaster reached England, our friends there, whom we had taken care to furnish with all the Assembly's answers to the governor's messages, raised a clamor against the proprietaries for their meanness and injustice in giving their governor such instructions; some going so far as to say that by obstructing the defence of their province they forfeited their right to it. They were intimidated by this, and sent orders to their receiver-general to add five thousand pounds of their money to whatever sum might be given by the Assembly for such purpose.

This, being notified to the House, was accepted in lieu of their share of a general tax, and a new bill was formed, with an exempting clause, which passed accordingly. By this act I was appointed one of the commissioners for disposing of the money, sixty thousand pounds. I had been active in modelling the bill and procuring its passage, and had, at the same time, drawn a bill for establishing and disciplining a voluntary militia, which I carried through the House without much difficulty, as care was taken in it to leave the Quakers at their liberty. To promote the association necessary to form the militia, I wrote a dialogue, stating and answering all the objections I could think of to such a militia, which was printed, and had, as I thought, great effect.

While the several companies in the city and country were forming, and learning their exercise, the governor prevailed with me to take charge of our Northwestern frontier, which was infested by the enemy, and provide for the defence of the inhabitants by raising troops and building a line of forts. I undertook this military business, though I did not conceive myself well qualified for it. He gave me a commission with full powers, and a parcel of blank commissions for officers, to be given to whom I thought fit. I had but little difficulty in raising men, having soon five hundred and sixty under my command. My son, who had in the preceding war been an officer in the army raised against Canada, was my aide-de-camp, and of great use to me. The Indians had burned Gnadenhut,[1] a village settled by the Moravians, and massacred the inhabitants; but the place was thought a good situation for one of the forts.

In order to march thither, I assembled the companies at Bethlehem,[2] the chief establishment of those people. I was surprised to find it in so good a posture of defence; the destruction of Gnadenhut had made them apprehend danger. The principal

[1] GNADENHUT—Or Gnadenhütten, a Moravian village in the Lehigh Valley, near Bethlehem, Pa., which is fifty miles from Philadelphia.

[2] BETHLEHEM—Bethlehem is now a center of the steel industry.

buildings were defended by a stockade. They had purchased a quantity of arms and ammunition from New York, and had even placed quantities of small paving stones between the windows of their high stone houses for their women to throw down upon the heads of any Indians that should attempt to force into them. The armed brethren, too, kept watch, and relieved as methodically as any garrison town. In conversation with the bishop, Spangenberg, I mentioned this my surprise; for, knowing they had obtained an act of Parliament exempting them from military duties in the colonies, I had supposed they were conscientiously scrupulous of bearing arms. He answered me that it was not one of their established principles, but that, at the time of their obtaining that act, it was thought to be a principle with many of their people. On this occasion, however, they, to their surprise, found it adopted by but a few. It seems they were either deceived in themselves or deceived the Parliament; but common sense, aided by present danger, will sometimes be too strong for whimsical opinions.

It was the beginning of January when we set out upon this business of building forts. I sent one detachment toward the Minisink,[3] with instructions to erect one for the security of that upper part of the country, and another to the lower part, with similar instructions; and I concluded to go myself with the rest of my force to Gnadenhut, where a fort was thought more immediately necessary. The Moravians procured me five wagons for our tools, stores, baggage, etc.

Just before we left Bethlehem, eleven farmers, who had been driven from their plantations by the Indians, came to me requesting a supply of firearms, that they might go back and fetch off their cattle. I gave them each a gun with suitable ammunition. We had not marched many miles before it began to rain, and it continued raining all day; there were no habitations on the road to shelter us till we arrived near night at the house of a German, where, and in his barn, we were all huddled together, as wet as water could make us. It was well we were not attacked in our march, for our arms were of the most ordinary sort, and our men could not keep their gunlocks dry. The Indians are dexterous in contrivances for that purpose, which we had not. They met that day the eleven poor farmers above mentioned, and killed ten of

[3] MINISINK—Indian name for part of the Delaware River valley.

them. The one who escaped informed us that his and his companions' guns would not go off, the priming being wet with the rain.

The next day being fair, we continued our march and arrived at the desolated Gnadenhut. There was a saw-mill near, round which were left several piles of boards, with which we soon hutted ourselves; an operation the more necessary at that inclement season as we had no tents. Our first work was to bury more effectually the dead we found there, who had been half interred by the country people.

The next morning our fort was planned and marked out, the circumference measuring four hundred and fifty-five feet, which would require as many palisades to be made of trees, one with another, of a foot diameter each. Our axes, of which we had seventy, were immediately set to work to cut down trees, and, our men being dexterous in the use of them, great dispatch was made. Seeing the trees fall so fast, I had the curiosity to look at my watch when two men began to cut at a pine; in six minutes they had it upon the ground, and I found it of fourteen inches diameter. Each pine made three palisades of eighteen feet long, pointed at one end. While these were preparing, our other men dug a trench all round, of three feet deep, in which the palisades were to be planted; and our wagons, the bodies being taken off, and the fore and hind wheels separated by taking out the pin which united the two parts of the perch, we had ten carriages, with two horses each, to bring the palisades from the woods to the spot. When they were set up, our carpenters built a stage of boards all round within, about six feet high, for the men to stand on when to fire through the loopholes. We had one swivel gun, which we mounted on one of the angles, and fired it as soon as fixed, to let the Indians know, if any were within hearing, that we had such pieces; and thus our fort, if such a magnificent name may be given to so miserable a stockade, was finished in a week, though it rained so hard every other day that the men could not work.

This gave me occasion to observe that when men are employed they are best contented; for on the days they worked they were good-natured and cheerful, and, with the consciousness of having done a good day's work, they spent the evening jollily; but on our idle days they were mutinous and quarrelsome, finding fault with their pork, the bread, etc., and in continual ill-humor, which put me in mind of a sea-captain, whose rule it was to keep his men constantly at work; and when his mate once told him that they had done everything, and there was nothing further to employ them about, *"Oh," says he, "make them scour the anchor."*

This kind of fort, however contemptible, is a sufficient defence against Indians, who have no cannon. Finding ourselves now posted securely, and having a place to retreat to on occasion, we ventured out in parties to scour the adjacent country. We met with no Indians, but we found the places on the neighboring hills where they had lain to watch our proceedings. There was an art in their contrivance of those places that seems worth mention. It being winter, a fire was necessary for them; but a common fire on the surface of the ground would by its light have discovered their position at a distance. They had therefore dug holes in the ground about three feet in diameter and somewhat deeper. We saw where they had with their hatchets cut off the charcoal from the sides of burnt logs lying in the woods. With these coals they had made small fires in the bottom of the holes, and we observed among the weeds and grass the prints of their bodies, made by their lying all round, with their legs hanging down in the holes to keep their feet warm, which with them is an essential point. This kind of fire, so managed, could not discover them, either by its light, flame, sparks, or even smoke: it appeared that their number was not great, and it seems they saw we were too many to be attacked by them with prospect of advantage.

We had for our chaplain a zealous Presbyterian minister, Mr. Beatty,[4] who complained to me that the men did not generally attend his prayers and exhortations. When they enlisted, they were promised, besides pay and provisions, a gill of rum a day, which was punctually served out to them, half in the morning and the other half in the evening; and I observed they were as punctual in attending to receive it; upon which I said to Mr. Beatty, "It is, perhaps, below the dignity of your profession to act as steward of the rum, but if you were to deal it out and only just after prayers, you would have them all about you." He liked the thought, undertook

[4] MR. BEATTY—Rev. Charles Beatty had come over from Ireland when very young and started as a peddler in Philadelphia and vicinity. Coming under the influence of the Rev. William Tennent, he studied for the ministry and later did missionary work among the Indians. He died of yellow fever in the Barbadoes.

the office, and, with the help of a few hands to measure out the liquor, executed it to satisfaction, and never were prayers more generally and more punctually attended; so that I thought this method preferable to the punishment inflicted by some military laws for non-attendance on divine service.

I had hardly finished this business, and got my fort well stored with provisions, when I received a letter from the governor, acquainting me that he had called the Assembly, and wished my attendance there, if the posture of affairs on the frontiers was such that my remaining there was no longer necessary. My friends, too, of the Assembly, pressing me by their letters to be, if possible, at the meeting, and my three intended forts being now completed, and the inhabitants contented to remain on their farms under that protection, I resolved to return; the more willingly, as a New England officer, Colonel Clapham, experienced in Indian war, being on a visit to our establishment, consented to accept the command. I gave him a commission, and, parading the garrison, had it read before them, and introduced him to them as an officer who, from his skill in military affairs, was much more fit to command them than myself; and, giving them a little exhortation, took my leave. I was escorted as far as Bethlehem, where I rested a few days to recover from the fatigue I had undergone. The first night, being in a good bed, I could hardly sleep, it was so different from my hard lodging on the floor of our hut at Gnaden, wrapped only in a blanket or two.

While at Bethlehem, I inquired a little into the practice of the Moravians: some of them had accompanied me, and all were very kind to me. I found they worked for a common stock,[5] ate at common tables, and slept in common dormitories, great numbers together. In the dormitories I observed loopholes, at certain distances all along just under the ceiling, which I thought judiciously placed for change of air. I was at their church, where I was entertained with good music, the organ being accompanied with violins, hautboys, flutes, clarinets, etc. I understood that their sermons were not usually preached to mixed congregations of men, women, and children, as is our common practice, but that they assembled sometimes the married men, at other times their wives, then the

[5] Worked for a common stock—Pooled all their earnings in a common fund for the use of the community.

young men, the young women, and the little children, each division by itself. The sermon I heard was to the latter, who came in and were placed in rows on benches; the boys under the conduct of a young man, their tutor, and the girls conducted by a young woman. The discourse seemed well adapted to their capacities, and was delivered in a pleasing, familiar manner, coaxing them, as it were, to be good. They behaved very orderly, but looked pale and unhealthy, which made me suspect they were kept too much within doors, or not allowed sufficient exercise.

I inquired concerning the Moravian marriages, whether the report was true that they were by lot. I was told that lots were used only in particular cases; that generally, when a young man found himself disposed to marry, he informed the elders of his class, who consulted the elder ladies that governed the young women. As these elders of the different sexes were well acquainted with the tempers and dispositions of their respective pupils, they could best judge what matches were suitable, and their judgments were generally acquiesced in; but if, for example, it should happen that two or three young women were found to be equally proper for the young man, the lot was then recurred to. I objected, if the matches are not made by the mutual choice of parties, some of them may chance to be very unhappy. "And so they may," answered my informer, "if you let the parties choose for themselves"; which, indeed, I could not deny.

Being returned[6] to Philadelphia, I found the association went on swimmingly, the inhabitants that were not Quakers having pretty generally come into it, formed themselves into companies, and chose their captains, lieutenants, and ensigns, according to the new law. Dr. B.[7] visited me, and gave me an account of the pains he had taken to spread a general good liking to the law, and ascribed much to those endeavors. I had had the vanity to ascribe all to my *Dialogue;*[8] however, not knowing but that he might be in the right, I let him enjoy his opinion, which I take to be generally the best way in such cases. The officers, meeting, chose me to be colonel of the regiment, which I this time accepted. I forget how many companies we had, but we paraded about twelve hundred well-looking

[6] Being returned—Franklin has spent scarcely more than a month on the frontier.
[7] Dr. B.—Probably Dr. Bond, before-mentioned.
[8] *Dialogue*—See page 128.

men, with a company of artillery, who had been furnished with six brass field-pieces, which they had become so expert in the use of as to fire twelve times in a minute. The first time I reviewed my regiment they accompanied me to my house, and would salute me with some rounds fired before my door, which shook down and broke several glasses of my electrical apparatus. And my new honor proved not much less brittle; for all our commissions were soon after broken by a repeal of the law in England.

During this short time of my colonelship, being about to set out on a journey to Virginia, the officers of my regiment took it into their heads that it would be proper for them to escort me out of town, as far as the Lower Ferry. Just as I was getting on horseback they came to my door, between thirty and forty, mounted, and all in their uniforms. I had not been previously acquainted with the project, or I should have prevented it, being naturally averse to the assuming of state on any occasion; and I was a good deal chagrined at their appearance, as I could not avoid their accompanying me. What made it worse was, that, as soon as we began to move, they drew their swords and rode with them naked all the way. Somebody wrote an account of this to the proprietor, and it gave him great offence. No such honor had been paid him when in the province, nor to any of his governors; and he said it was only proper to princes[9] of the blood royal, which may be true for aught I know, who was, and still am, ignorant of the etiquette in such cases.

This silly affair, however, greatly increased his rancor against me, which was before not a little, on account of my conduct in the Assembly respecting the exemption of his estate from taxation, which I had always opposed very warmly, and not without severe reflections on his meanness and injustice of contending for it. He accused me to the ministry as being the great obstacle to the king's service, preventing, by my influence in the House, the proper form of the bills for raising money, and he instanced this parade with my officers as a proof of my having an intention to take the government of the province out of his hands by force. He also applied to Sir Everard Fawkener, the postmaster-general, to deprive me of my office; but it had no other effect than to procure from Sir Everard a gentle admonition.

---

[9] PRINCES—The reader cannot fail to observe that Franklin, in recalling the incident, derived a certain satisfaction from the display in his honor.

Notwithstanding the continual wrangle between the governor and the House, in which I, as a member, had so large a share, there still subsisted a civil intercourse between that gentleman and myself, and we never had any personal difference. I have sometimes since thought that his little or no resentment against me, for the answers it was known I drew up to his messages, might be the effect of professional habit, and that, being bred a lawyer, he might consider us both as merely advocates for contending clients in a suit, he for the proprietaries and I for the Assembly. He would, therefore, sometimes call in a friendly way to advise with me on difficult points, and sometimes, though not often, take my advice.

We acted in concert to supply Braddock's army with provisions; and when the shocking news arrived of his defeat, the governor sent in haste for me to consult with him on measures for preventing the desertion of the back counties. I forget now the advice I gave; but I think it was that Dunbar should be written to, and prevailed with, if possible, to post his troops on the frontiers for their protection, till, by re-enforcements from the colonies, he might be able to proceed on the expedition. And, after my return from the frontier, he would have had me undertake the conduct of such an expedition with provincial troops, for the reduction of Fort Duquesne, Dunbar and his men being otherwise employed; and he proposed to commission me as general. I had not so good an opinion of my military abilities as he professed to have, and I believe his professions must have exceeded his real sentiments; but probably he might think that my popularity would facilitate the raising of the men, and my influence in Assembly, the grant of money to pay them, and that, perhaps, without taxing the proprietary estate. Finding me not so forward to engage as he expected, the project was dropped, and he soon after left the government, being superseded by Captain Denny.

## CHAPTER X

### Franklin the Scientist

First Studies in Electricity—The Philadelphia Experiments—His Reputation Abroad—Election to Royal Society

Before I proceed in relating the part I had in public affairs under this new governor's administration, it may not be amiss here to give some account of the rise and progress of my philosophical reputation.[1]

In 1746, being at Boston, I met there with a Dr. Spence,[2] who was lately arrived from Scotland, and showed me some electric experiments. They were imperfectly performed, as he was not very expert; but, being on a subject quite new to me, they equally surprised and pleased me. Soon after my return to Philadelphia, our library company received from Mr. Collinson,[3] Fellow of the Royal Society[4] of London, a present of a glass tube, with some account of the use of it in making such experiments. I eagerly seized the opportunity of repeating what I had seen at Boston; and, by much practice, acquired great readiness in performing those, also, which we had an account of from England, adding a number of new ones. I say much practice, for my house was continually full, for some time, with people who came to see these new wonders.

To divide a little this incumbrance among my friends, I caused a number of similar tubes to be blown at our glass-house, with which they furnished themselves, so that we had at length several performers. Among these, the principal was Mr. Kinnersley, an ingenious neighbor, who, being out of business, I encouraged to undertake showing the experiments for money, and drew up for him two lectures, in which the experiments were ranged in such order, and accompanied with such explanations in such method, as that the foregoing should assist in comprehending the following. He procured an elegant apparatus for the purpose, in which all the little machines that I had roughly made for myself were nicely formed by instrument-makers. His lectures were well attended, and gave great satisfaction; and after some time he went through the colonies, exhibiting them in every capital town, and picked up some money. In the West India islands, indeed, it was with difficulty the experiments could be made, from the general moisture of the air.[5]

---

[1] PHILOSOPHICAL REPUTATION—Reputation as a scientist.

[2] DR. SPENCE—See page 105.

[3] MR. COLLINSON—Peter Collinson, English scientist. Franklin made many friendships with such men.

[4] ROYAL SOCIETY—Formed in London, 1660, for "the improvement of natural knowledge." Still in existence, it has numbered among its members most of the world's famous scientists.

[5] MOISTURE OF THE AIR—Since in these early experiments electricity was generated by rubbing a long glass tube with a piece of silk, a damp climate seriously interfered with the demonstrations.

Obliged as we were to Mr. Collinson for his present of the tube, etc., I thought it right he should be informed of our success in using it, and wrote him several letters containing accounts of our experiments. He got them read in the Royal Society, where they were not at first thought worth so much notice as to be printed in their Transactions. One paper, which I wrote for Mr. Kinnersley, on the sameness of lightning with electricity,[6] I sent to Dr. Mitchel, an acquaintance of mine, and one of the members also of that society, who wrote me word that it had been read but was laughed at by the connoisseurs. The papers, however, being shown to Dr. Fothergill, he thought them of too much value to be stifled, and advised the printing of them. Mr. Collinson then gave them to *Cave* for publication in his Gentleman's Magazine; but he chose to print them separately in a pamphlet, and Dr. Fothergill wrote the preface. Cave, it seems, judged rightly for his profit, for by the additions that arrived afterward they swelled to a quarto volume, which has had five editions, and cost him nothing for copy-money.[7]

It was, however, some time before those papers were much taken notice of in England. A copy of them happening to fall into the hands of the Count de Buffon, a philosopher deservedly of great reputation in France, and, indeed, all over Europe, he prevailed with M.[8] Dalibard to translate them into French, and they were printed at Paris. The publication offended the Abbé Nollet,[9] preceptor in natural philosophy to the royal family, and an able experimenter, who had formed and published a theory of electricity, which then had the general vogue. He could not at first believe that such a work came from America, and said it must have been fabricated by his enemies at Paris, to decry his system. Afterwards, having been assured that there really existed such a person as Franklin at Philadelphia, which he had doubted, he wrote and published a volume of letters, chiefly addressed to me, defending his theory,

---

[6] LIGHTNING . . . ELECTRICITY—In June, 1752, Franklin proved the sameness of lightning and electricity by his famous kite experiment. In the meantime, Buffon, Dalibard, and De Lor (see following pages), following one of Franklin's own suggestions, had demonstrated the same thing with very long iron rods.

[7] COPY-MONEY—Payment to the authors of the articles.

[8] M.—Monsieur, French equivalent of our Mr. The plural is Messrs. or MM.

[9] ABBÉ NOLLET—Jean Antoine Nollet (1700–1770). French physicist of peasant origin, who entered holy orders and attained rank of abbé. Noted for his experimental research in electricity. In 1734 he was made a member of the Royal Society.

and denying the verity of my experiments, and of the positions deduced from them.

I once purposed answering the abbé, and actually began the answer; but, on consideration that my writings contained a description of experiments which any one might repeat and verify, and if not to be verified, could not be defended; or of observations offered as conjectures, and not delivered dogmatically, therefore not laying me under any obligation to defend them; and reflecting that a dispute between two persons, writing in different languages, might be lengthened greatly by mistranslations, and thence misconceptions of one another's meaning, much of one of the abbé's letters being founded on an error in the translation, I concluded to let my papers shift for themselves, believing it was better to spend what time I could spare from public business in making new experiments, than in disputing about those already made. I therefore never answered M. Nollet, and the event gave me no cause to repent my silence; for my friend M. le Roy, of the Royal Academy of Sciences, took up my cause and refuted him; my book was translated into the Italian, German, and Latin languages; and the doctrine it contained was by degrees universally adopted by the philosophers of Europe, in preference to that of the abbé; so that he lived to see himself the last of his sect, except Monsieur B——, of Paris, his *élève*[10] and immediate disciple.

What gave my book the more sudden and general celebrity was the success of one of its proposed experiments, made by Messrs. Dalibard and De Lor at Marly, for drawing lightning from the clouds. This engaged the public attention everywhere. M. de Lor, who had an apparatus for experimental philosophy, and lectured in that branch of science, undertook to repeat what he called the *Philadelphia Experiments;* and, after they were performed before the king and court, all the curious of Paris flocked to see them. I will not swell this narrative with an account of that capital experiment, nor of the infinite pleasure I received in the success of a similar one I made soon after with a kite at Philadelphia, as both are to be found in the histories of electricity.

Dr. Wright, an English physician, when at Paris, wrote to a friend, who was of the Royal Society, an account of the high esteem my experiments were in among the learned abroad, and of

[10] *Élève*—Pupil.

their wonder that my writings had been so little noticed in England. The society, on this, resumed the consideration of the letters that had been read to them; and the celebrated Dr. Watson[11] drew up a summary account of them, and of all I had afterwards sent to England on the subject, which he accompanied with some praise of the writer. This summary was then printed in their Transactions; and some members of the society in London, particularly the very ingenious Mr. Canton, having verified the experiment of procuring lightning from the clouds by a pointed rod, and acquainting them with the success, they soon made me more than amends for the slight with which they had before treated me. Without my having made any application for that honor, they chose me a member, and voted that I should be excused the customary payments,[12] which would have amounted to twenty-five guineas; and ever since have given me their Transactions gratis. They also presented me with the gold medal of Sir Godfrey Copley[13] for the year 1753, the delivery of which was accompanied by a very handsome speech of the president, Lord Macclesfield, wherein I was highly honored.

## CHAPTER XI

### First Mission to England

Relations with Governor Denny—Agent for Pennsylvania—Lord Loudoun's Character—Voyage to London—Champion of the Colonies—Diplomatic Victory

Our new governor, Captain Denny, brought over for me the before-mentioned medal from the Royal Society, which he presented to me at an entertainment given him by the city. He accompanied it with very polite expressions of his esteem for me, having, as he said, been long acquainted with my character. After dinner, when the company, as was customary at that time, were engaged in drinking, he took me aside into another room, and acquainted me that he had been advised by his friends in England to cultivate a friend-

---

[11] Dr. Watson—Sir William Watson, famous for his studies in electricity.

[12] Excused the customary payments—In a letter to his son, written in 1767, Franklin explains that this exemption was voted because he had not, as was customary, applied for admission to the Royal Society, but had been voluntarily honored by the society.

[13] Gold medal of Sir Godfrey Copley—Awarded annually for achievements in science from a fund established in 1709 by Sir Godfrey Copley.

ship with me, as one who was capable of giving him the best advice, and of contributing most effectually to the making his administration easy; that he therefore desired of all things to have a good understanding with me, and he begged me to be assured of his readiness on all occasions to render me every service that might be in his power. He said much to me, also, of the proprietor's good disposition towards the province, and of the advantage it might be to us all, and to me in particular, if the opposition that had been so long continued to his measures was dropped, and harmony restored between him and the people; in effecting which, it was thought no one could be more serviceable than myself; and I might depend on adequate acknowledgments and recompenses, etc., etc. The drinkers, finding we did not return immediately to the table, sent us a decanter of Madeira, which the governor made liberal use of, and in proportion became more profuse of his solicitations and promises.

My answers were to this purpose: that my circumstances, thanks to God, were such as to make proprietary favors unnecessary to me; and that, being a member of the Assembly, I could not possibly accept of any; that, however, I had no personal enmity to the proprietary, and that, whenever the public measures he proposed should appear to be for the good of the people, no one should espouse and forward them more zealously than myself; my past opposition having been founded on this, that the measures which had been urged were evidently intended to serve the proprietary interest, with great prejudice to that of the people; that I was much obliged to him (the governor) for his professions of regard to me, and that he might rely on everything in my power to make his administration as easy as possible, hoping at the same time that he had not brought with him the same unfortunate instructions his predecessor had been hampered with.

On this he did not then explain himself; but when he afterwards came to do business with the Assembly, they appeared again, the disputes were renewed, and I was as active as ever in the opposition, being the penman, first, of the request to have a communication of the instructions, and then of the remarks upon them, which may be found in the votes of the time, and in the Historical Review[1]

[1] Historical Review—*Historical Review of Pennsylvania,* written by Franklin's son William and widely circulated. It was a survey of the quarrels between the Assembly and the proprietaries and governors.

I afterward published. But between us personally no enmity arose; we were often together; he was a man of letters, had seen much of the world, and was very entertaining and pleasing in conversation. He gave me the first information that my old friend Jas. Ralph was still alive; that he was esteemed one of the best political writers in England; had been employed in the dispute between Prince Frederic[2] and the king, and had obtained a pension of three hundred a year; that his reputation was indeed small as a poet, Pope having damned his poetry in the *Dunciad*,[3] but his prose was thought as good as any man's.

The Assembly finally finding the proprietary obstinately persisted in manacling their deputies with instructions inconsistent not only with the privileges of the people, but with the service of the crown, resolved to petition the king[4] against them, and appointed me their agent[5] to go over to England, to present and support the petition. The House had sent up a bill to the governor, granting a sum of sixty thousand pounds for the king's use (ten thousand pounds of which was subjected to the orders of the then general, Lord Loudoun[6]), which the governor absolutely refused to pass in compliance with his instructions.

I had agreed with Captain Morris, of the packet at New York, for my passage, and my stores were put on board, when Lord Loudoun arrived at Philadelphia, expressly, as he told me, to endeavor an accommodation between the governor and Assembly, that his majesty's service might not be obstructed by their dissensions. Accordingly, he desired the governor and myself to meet him, that he might hear what was to be said on both sides. We met and discussed the business. In behalf of the Assembly, I urged all the various arguments that may be found in the public papers of that time, which were of my writing, and are printed with the minutes of the Assembly; and the governor pleaded his instruc-

---

[2] PRINCE FREDERIC—Son of George II and father of George III. As Crown Prince, Frederick defied his father and aided in bringing England into the War of the Austrian Succession.

[3] *Dunciad*—See page 46, note 40.

[4] PETITION THE KING—First, to give the Assembly the right to tax the proprietary estates; and second, to suggest that the king take over the province from the proprietors. Luckily, the second suggestion was never adopted, for under George III the colony could have expected nothing but oppression.

[5] THEIR AGENT—Isaac Norris, speaker of the Assembly, was also appointed, but because of ill health could not accompany Franklin to England.

[6] LORD LOUDOUN—Then Commander-in-chief of the British forces in America.

tions; the bond he had given to observe them, and his ruin if he disobeyed, yet seemed not unwilling to hazard himself[7] if Lord Loudoun would advise it. This his lordship did not choose to do, though I once thought I had nearly prevailed with him to do it; but finally he rather chose to urge the compliance of the Assembly; and he entreated me to use my endeavors with them for that purpose, declaring that he would spare none of the king's troops for the defence of our frontiers, and that, if we did not continue to provide for that defence ourselves they must remain exposed to the enemy.

I acquainted the House with what had passed, and, presenting them with a set of resolutions I had drawn up, declaring our rights, and that we did not relinquish our claim to those rights, but only suspended the exercise of them on this occasion through *force,* against which we protested, they at length agreed to drop that bill, and frame another conformable to the proprietary instructions. This of course the governor passed, and I was then at liberty to proceed on my voyage. But, in the mean time, the packet had sailed with my sea-stores, which was some loss to me, and my only recompense was his lordship's thanks for my service, all the credit of obtaining the accommodation falling to his share.

He set out for New York before me; and, as the time for dispatching the packet-boats was at his disposition, and there were two then remaining there, one of which he said, was to sail very soon, I requested to know the precise time, that I might not miss her by any delay of mine. His answer was, "I have given out that she is to sail on Saturday next; but I may let you know, *entre nous,*[8] that if you are there by Monday morning, you will be in time, but do not delay longer." By some accidental hindrance at a ferry, it was Monday noon before I arrived, and I was much afraid she might have sailed, as the wind was fair; but I was soon made easy by the information that she was still in the harbor and would not move till the next day. One would imagine that I was now on the very point of departing for Europe. I thought so; but I was not then so well acquainted with his lordship's character, of which *indecision* was one of the strongest features. I shall give

[7] Not unwilling to hazard himself—Governor Denny was apparently a reasonable man but was under oath to the proprietaries. It was he who finally took the step that made possible Franklin's triumph in England. (See page 152, note 32.)

[8] *Entre nous*—French for "just between ourselves."

some instances. It was about the beginning of April that I came to New York, and I think it was near the end of June before we sailed. There were then two of the packet-boats which had been long in port, but were detained for the general's letters, which were always to be ready to-morrow. Another packet arrived; she too was detained; and before we sailed, a fourth was expected. Ours was the first to be dispatched, as having been there longest. Passengers were engaged in all, and some extremely impatient to be gone, and the merchants uneasy about their letters and the orders they had given for insurance (it being war time[9]) for fall goods; but their anxiety availed nothing; his lordship's letters were not ready; and yet whoever waited on him found him always at his desk, pen in hand, and concluded he must needs write abundantly.

Going myself one morning to pay my respects, I found in his antechamber one Innis, a messenger of Philadelphia, who had come from thence express with a packet from Governor Denny for the General. He delivered to me some letters from my friends there, which occasioned my inquiring when he was to return, and where he lodged, that I might send some letters by him. He told me he was ordered to call to-morrow at nine for the general's answer to the governor, and should set off immediately. I put my letters into his hands the same day. A fortnight after I met him again in the same place. "So, you are soon returned, Innis?" *"Returned!* no, I am not *gone* yet." "How so?" "I have called here by order every morning these two weeks past for his lordship's letter, and it is not yet ready." "Is it possible, when he is so great a writer? For I see him constantly at his escritoire." "Yes," says Innis, "but he is like St. George on the signs,[10] *always on horseback, and never rides on."* This observation of the messenger was, it seems, well founded; for, when in England, I understood that Mr. Pitt[11] gave it as one reason for removing this general, and sending Generals Amherst and Wolfe,[12] *that the minister never heard from him, and could not know what he was doing.*

---

[9] War time—The Seven Years' War, so-called in Europe, corresponding to the French and Indian War in America.

[10] St. George on the signs—St. George is a favorite name for British inns and taverns. On the signboard St. George is usually pictured astride a horse.

[11] Mr. Pitt—William Pitt (the elder), then prime minister. Before the Revolution he fought vainly for a change of policy toward the colonies.

[12] Generals Amherst and Wolfe—Lord Jeffrey Amherst, after whom Amherst College is named, and James Wolfe, hero of the taking of Quebec.

This daily expectation of sailing, and all the three packets going down to Sandy Hook, to join the fleet there, the passengers thought it best to be on board, lest by a sudden order the ships should sail, and they be left behind. There, if I remember right, we were about six weeks, consuming our sea-stores, and obliged to procure more. At length the fleet sailed, the General and all his army on board, bound to Louisburg, with intent to besiege and take that fortress;[13] all the packet-boats in company ordered to attend the General's ship, ready to receive his dispatches when they should be ready. We were out five days before we got a letter with leave to part, and then our ship quitted the fleet and steered for England. The other two packets he still detained, carried them with him to Halifax, where he stayed some time to exercise the men in sham attacks upon sham forts, then altered his mind as to besieging Louisburg, and returned to New York, with all his troops, together with the two packets above mentioned, and all their passengers. During his absence the French and savages had taken Fort George, on the frontier of that province, and the savages had massacred many of the garrison after capitulation.

I saw afterwards in London Captain Bonnell, who commanded one of those packets. He told me that when he had been detained a month, he acquainted his lordship that his ship had grown foul,[14] to a degree that must necessarily hinder her fast sailing, a point of consequence for a packet-boat, and requested an allowance of time to heave her down and clean her bottom. He was asked how long time that would require. He answered, three days. The general replied, "If you can do it in one day, I give you leave: otherwise not; for you must certainly sail the day after to-morrow." So he never obtained leave, though detained afterwards from day to day during full three months.

I saw also in London one of Bonnell's passengers, who was so enraged against his lordship for deceiving and detaining him so long at New York, and then carrying him to Halifax and back again, that he swore he would sue him for damages. Whether he did or not, I never heard; but, as he represented the injury to his affairs, it was very considerable.

---

[13] TAKE THAT FORTRESS—It was not until the next year (1758) that Wolfe and Amherst captured Louisburg.

[14] GROWN FOUL—Her bottom covered with barnacles that make slow sailing.

On the whole, I wondered much how such a man came to be intrusted with so important a business as the conduct of a great army; but, having since seen more of the great world, and the means of obtaining, and motives for giving places, my wonder is diminished. General Shirley, on whom the command of the army devolved upon the death of Braddock, would, in my opinion, if continued in place, have made a much better campaign than that of Loudoun in 1757, which was frivolous, expensive, and disgraceful to our nation beyond conception; for, though Shirley was not a bred soldier, he was sensible and sagacious in himself, and attentive to good advice from others, capable of forming judicious plans, and quick and active in carrying them into execution. Loudoun, instead of defending the colonies with his great army, left them totally exposed, while he paraded idly at Halifax, by which means Fort George was lost; besides, he deranged all our mercantile operations, and distressed our trade, by a long embargo on the exportation of provisions, on pretence of keeping supplies from being obtained by the enemy, but in reality for beating down their price in favor of the contractors, in whose profits, it was said, perhaps from suspicion only, he had a share. And, when at length the embargo was taken off, by neglecting to send notice of it to Charleston, the Carolina fleet was detained near three months longer, whereby their bottoms were so much damaged by the worm[15] that a great part of them foundered in their passage home.

Shirley was, I believe, sincerely glad of being relieved from so burdensome a charge as the conduct of an army must be to a man unacquainted with military business. I was at the entertainment given by the city of New York to Lord Loudoun, on his taking upon him the command. Shirley, though thereby superseded, was present also. There was a great company of officers, citizens, and strangers, and, some chairs having been borrowed in the neighborhood, there was one among them very low, which fell to the lot of Mr. Shirley. Perceiving it as I sat by him, I said, "They have given you, sir, too low a seat." "No matter," says he, "Mr. Franklin, I find *a low seat* the easiest."

While I was, as afore mentioned, detained at New York, I received all the accounts of the provisions, etc., that I had furnished to Braddock, some of which accounts could not sooner be

[15] THE WORM—A sea borer that eats into the hulls of vessels.

obtained from the different persons I had employed to assist in the business. I presented them to Lord Loudoun, desiring to be paid the balance. He caused them to be regularly examined by the proper officer, who, after comparing every article with its voucher, certified them to be right; and the balance due for which his lordship promised to give me an order on the paymaster. This was, however, put off from time to time; and, though I called often for it by appointment, I did not get it. At length, just before my departure, he told me he had, on better consideration, concluded not to mix his accounts with those of his predecessors. "And you," says he, "when in England, have only to exhibit your accounts at the treasury, and you will be paid immediately."

I mentioned, but without effect, the great and unexpected expense I had been put to by being detained so long at New York, as a reason for my desiring to be presently paid; and on my observing that it was not right I should be put to any further trouble or delay in obtaining the money I had advanced, as I charged no commission for my service, "O, sir," says he, "you must not think of persuading us that you are no gainer; we understand better those affairs, and know that every one concerned in supplying the army finds means, in the doing it, to fill his own pockets." I assured him that was not my case, and that I had not pocketed a farthing;[16] but he appeared clearly not to believe me; and, indeed, I have since learnt that immense fortunes are often made in such employments. As to my balance, I am not paid it to this day, of which more hereafter.

Our captain of the packet had boasted much, before we sailed, of the swiftness of his ship; unfortunately, when we came to sea, she proved the dullest of ninety-six sail, to his no small mortification. After many conjectures respecting the cause, when we were near another ship almost as dull as ours, which, however, gained upon us, the captain ordered all hands to come aft, and stand as near the ensign staff as possible. We were, passengers included, about forty persons. While we stood there, the ship mended her pace, and soon left her neighbor far behind, which proved clearly what our captain suspected, that she was loaded too much by the head.[17]

[16] NOT POCKETED A FARTHING—Though Franklin was sometimes suspected of fraud because his accounts were muddled, it is agreed that he himself never profited illegally from his public transactions. Rather, as in this case, he lost money which he had personally advanced.

[17] BY THE HEAD—Forward, near the bow, as opposed to aft, near the stern.

The casks of water, it seems, had been all placed forward; these he therefore ordered to be moved further aft, on which the ship recovered her character, and proved the best sailer in the fleet.

The captain said she had once gone at the rate of thirteen knots, which is accounted thirteen miles per hour. We had on board, as a passenger, Captain Kennedy, of the Navy, who contended that it was impossible, and that no ship ever sailed so fast, and that there must have been some error in the division of the log-line,[18] or some mistake in heaving the log. A wager ensued between the two captains, to be decided when there should be sufficient wind. Kennedy thereupon examined rigorously the log-line, and, being satisfied with that, he determined to throw the log himself. Accordingly some days after, when the wind blew very fair and fresh, and the captain of the packet, Lutwidge, said he believed she then went at the rate of thirteen knots, Kennedy made the experiment, and owned his wager lost.

The above fact I give for the sake of the following observation. It has been remarked, as an imperfection in the art of ship-building, that it can never be known, till she is tried, whether a new ship will or will not be a good sailer; for that the model of a good-sailing ship has been exactly followed in a new one, which has proved, on the contrary, remarkably dull. I apprehend that this may partly be occasioned by the different opinions of seamen respecting the modes of lading, rigging, and sailing of a ship; each has his system; and the same vessel, laden by the judgment and orders of one captain, shall sail better or worse than when by the orders of another. Besides, it scarce ever happens that a ship is formed, fitted for the sea, and sailed by the same person. One man builds the hull, another rigs her, a third lades and sails her. No one of these has the advantage of knowing all the ideas and experience of the others, and, therefore, cannot draw just conclusions from a combination of the whole.

Even in the simple operation of sailing when at sea, I have often observed different judgments in the officers who commanded the successive watches, the wind being the same. One would have the sails trimmed sharper or flatter than another, so that they seemed to have no certain rule to govern by. Yet I think a set of experi-

[18] LOG-LINE—The log is an instrument for measuring the rate of a ship's speed. Originally a triangular block fastened to a line and heaved from the stern.

ments might be instituted, first, to determine the most proper form of the hull for swift sailing; next, the best dimensions and properest place for the masts; then the form and quantity of sails, and their position, as the wind may be; and, lastly, the disposition of the lading. This is an age of experiments, and I think a set accurately made and combined would be of great use. I am persuaded, therefore, that ere long some ingenious philosopher will undertake it, to whom I wish success.

We were several times chased[19] in our passage, but outsailed everything, and in thirty days had soundings. We had a good observation, and the captain judged himself so near our port, Falmouth,[20] that, if we made a good run in the night, we might be off the mouth of that harbor in the morning, and by running in the night might escape the notice of the enemy's privateers, who often cruised near the entrance of the channel. Accordingly, all the sail was set that we could possibly make, and the wind being very fresh and fair, we went right before it, and made great way. The captain, after his observation, shaped his course, as he thought, so as to pass wide of the Scilly Isles;[21] but it seems there is sometimes a strong indraught setting up St. George's Channel,[22] which deceives seamen and caused the loss of Sir Cloudesley Shovel's squadron. This indraught was probably the cause of what happened to us.

We had a watchman placed in the bow, to whom they often called, "*Look well out before there,*" and he as often answered, "*Ay, ay*"; but perhaps had his eyes shut, and was half asleep at the time, they sometimes answering, as is said, mechanically; for he did not see a light just before us, which had been hid by the studding-sails from the man at the helm, and from the rest of the watch, but by an accidental yaw of the ship was discovered, and occasioned a great alarm, we being very near it, the light appearing to me as big as a cart-wheel. It was midnight, and our captain fast asleep; but Captain Kennedy, jumping upon deck, and seeing the danger, ordered the ship to wear round,[23] all sails standing; an

[19] CHASED—By hostile French craft.

[20] FALMOUTH—Port in Cornwall close to the southwestern tip of England.

[21] SCILLY ISLES—Group of islands off southwest England, first land to be sighted by boats sailing from the United States to England.

[22] ST. GEORGE'S CHANNEL—Between Ireland and Wales.

[23] WEAR ROUND—A dangerous maneuver in a stiff breeze, consisting of coming about by turning the bow away from the wind instead of into it, the usual tactics. Modern sailors call it jibing.

operation dangerous to the masts, but it carried us clear, and we escaped shipwreck, for we were running right upon the rocks on which the lighthouse was erected. This deliverance impressed me strongly with the utility of lighthouses, and made me resolve to encourage the building more of them in America, if I should live to return there.

In the morning it was found by the soundings, etc., that we were near our port, but a thick fog hid the land from our sight. About nine o'clock the fog began to rise, and seemed to be lifted up from the water like the curtain at a play-house, discovering underneath, the town of Falmouth, the vessels in its harbor, and the fields that surrounded it. This was a most pleasing spectacle to those who had been so long without any other prospects than the uniform view of a vacant ocean, and it gave us the more pleasure as we were now free from the anxieties which the state of war occasioned.

I set out immediately, with my son, for London, and we only stopped a little by the way to view Stonehenge[24] on Salisbury Plain, and Lord Pembroke's house and gardens,[25] with his very curious antiquities at Wilton. We arrived in London the 27th of July, 1757.[26]

As soon as I was settled in a lodging Mr. Charles[27] had provided for me, I went to visit Dr. Fothergill,[28] to whom I was strongly recommended, and whose counsel respecting my proceedings I was advised to obtain. He was against an immediate complaint to the government, and thought the proprietaries should first be personally applied to, who might possibly be induced by the interposition and

---

[24] Stonehenge—A circle of great stones, located near Salisbury through which Franklin would pass on the way to London from Falmouth. These stones are believed to have been placed there for some religious purpose by the Druids (the officials of an ancient pagan religion).

[25] Lord Pembroke's house and gardens—Still one of the show-places of England, and associated with such names as Sir Philip Sidney, William Shakespeare, Edmund Spenser, and Ben Jonson.

[26] July, 1757—The *Autobiography* as originally published ends at this point. The few remaining pages, written in 1790, the last year of Franklin's life, were not discovered until 1867 when they came into the hands of John Bigelow, American Ambassador to France. Bigelow bought the manuscript of the *Autobiography* from the French family who owned it, and brought out the first complete edition in English in 1868. See Introduction, "The Story."

[27] Mr. Charles—London agent for Pennsylvania, who established Franklin with Mrs. Stevenson at No. 7 Craven Street.

[28] Dr. Fothergill—Fashionable physician of London who had helped popularize Franklin's scientific articles in England.

persuasion of some private friends, to accommodate matters amicably. I then waited on my old friend and correspondent, Mr. Peter Collinson, who told me that John Hanbury, the great Virginia merchant, had requested to be informed when I should arrive, that he might carry me to Lord Granville's, who was then President of the Council, and wished to see me as soon as possible. I agreed to go with him the next morning. Accordingly Mr. Hanbury called for me and took me in his carriage to that nobleman's, who received me with great civility; and after some questions respecting the present state of affairs in America and discourse thereupon, he said to me: "You Americans have wrong ideas of the nature of your constitution; you contend that the king's instructions to his governors are not laws, and think yourselves at liberty to regard or disregard them at your own discretion. But those instructions are not like the pocket instructions given to a minister going abroad, for regulating his conduct in some trifling point of ceremony. They are first drawn up by judges learned in the laws; they are then considered, debated, and perhaps amended in Council after which they are signed by the king. They are then, so far as they relate to you, the law of the land, for the king is the legislator of the colonies." I told his lordship this was new doctrine to me. I had always understood from our charters that our laws were to be made by our Assemblies, to be presented indeed to the king for his royal assent, but that being once given the king could not repeal or alter them. And as the Assemblies could not make permanent laws without his assent, so neither could he make a law for them without theirs. He assured me I was totally mistaken. I did not think so, however, and his lordship's conversation having a little alarmed me as to what might be the sentiments of the court concerning us, I wrote it down as soon as I returned to my lodgings. I recollected that about twenty years before, a clause in a bill brought into Parliament by the ministry had proposed to make the king's instructions laws in the colonies, but the clause was thrown out by the Commons, for which we adored them as our friends and friends of liberty, till by their conduct towards us in 1765 it seemed that they had refused that point of sovereignty to the king only that they might reserve it for themselves.

After some days, Dr. Fothergill having spoken to the proprietaries, they agreed to a meeting with me at Mr. T. Penn's house in Spring Garden.[29] The conversation at first consisted of mutual declarations of disposition to reasonable accommodations, but I suppose each party had its own ideas of what should be meant by *reasonable*. We then went into consideration of our several points of complaint, which I enumerated. The proprietaries justified their conduct as well as they could, and I the Assembly's. We now appeared very wide, and so far from each other in our opinions as to discourage all hope of agreement. However, it was concluded that I should give them the heads of our complaints in writing, and they promised then to consider them. I did so soon after, but they put the paper into the hands of their solicitor, Ferdinand John Paris, who managed for them all their law business in their great suit[30] with the neighboring proprietary of Maryland, Lord Baltimore, which had subsisted seventy years, and wrote for them all their papers and messages in their dispute with the Assembly. He was a proud, angry man, and as I had occasionally in the answers of the Assembly treated his papers with some severity, they being really weak in point of argument and haughty in expression, he had conceived a mortal enmity to me, which discovering itself whenever we met, I declined the proprietary's proposal that he and I should discuss the heads of complaint between our two selves and refused treating with any one but them. They then by his advice put the paper into the hands of the Attorney and Solicitor-General for their opinion and counsel upon it, where it lay unanswered a year wanting eight days, during which time I made frequent demands of an answer from the proprietaries, but without obtaining any other than that they had not yet received the opinion of the Attorney and Solicitor-General. What it was when they did receive it I never learnt, for they did not communicate it to me, but sent a long message to the Assembly drawn and signed by Paris, reciting my paper, complaining of its want of formality, as a rudeness on my part, and giving a flimsy justification of their conduct, adding that they should be willing to accommodate matters if the

[29] T. Penn's house in Spring Garden—The son of William Penn, founder of Pennsylvania, lived in the fashionable part of London. In the quarrels between the Assembly and the proprietors he showed himself grasping and short-sighted, his demands for exemption of the proprietary estates from taxation being one of the disputes that led to the Declaration of Independence.

[30] Suit—Over the boundary line between Maryland and Pennsylvania, finally settled in 1767 by two English surveyors, Charles Mason and Jeremiah Dixon; hence, the Mason and Dixon Line, still referred to as a boundary between the North and the South.

Assembly would send out *some person of candor* to treat with them for that purpose, intimating thereby that I was not such.

The want of formality or rudeness was, probably, my not having addressed the paper to them with their assumed titles of True and Absolute Proprietaries of the Province of Pennsylvania, which I omitted as not thinking it necessary in a paper, the intention of which was only to reduce to a certainty by writing, what in conversation I had delivered *viva voce.*[31]

But during this delay, the Assembly having prevailed with Governor Denny to pass an act[32] taxing the proprietary estate in common with the estates of the people, which was the grand point in dispute, they omitted answering the message.

When this act however came over, the proprietaries, counselled by Paris, determined to oppose its receiving the royal assent. Accordingly they petitioned the king in Council, and a hearing was appointed in which two lawyers were employed by them against the act, and two by me in support of it. They alleged that the act was intended to load the proprietary estate in order to spare those of the people, and that if it were suffered to continue in force, and the proprietaries, who were in odium with the people, left to their mercy in proportioning the taxes, they would inevitably be ruined. We replied that the act had no such intention, and would have no such effect. That the assessors were honest and discreet men under an oath to assess fairly and equitably, and that any advantage each of them might expect in lessening his own tax by augmenting that of the proprietaries was too trifling to induce them to perjure themselves. This is the purport of what I remember as urged by both sides, except that we insisted strongly on the mischievous consequences that must attend a repeal, for that the money, £100,000, being printed and given to the king's use, expended in his service, and now spread among the people, the repeal would strike it dead in their hands to the ruin of many, and the total discouragement of future grants, and the selfishness of the proprietors in soliciting such a general catastrophe, merely from a groundless fear of their estate being taxed too highly, was insisted on in the strongest terms. On this, Lord Mansfield, one of the counsel, rose, and beckoning me

---

[31] *Viva voce*—By word of mouth, orally. Latin.

[32] Pass an act—Governor Denny's agreement to this act, which authorized an issue of paper money, was a fortunate thing for Franklin. Without it, he might never have won his point with the proprietaries.

took me into the clerk's chamber, while the lawyers were pleading, and asked me if I was really of opinion that no injury would be done the proprietary estate in the execution of the act. I said, certainly. "Then," says he, "you can have little objection to enter into an engagement to assure that point." I answered, "None at all." He then called in Paris, and after some discourse his lordship's proposition was accepted on both sides; a paper to the purpose was drawn up by the Clerk of the Council, which I signed with Mr. Charles, who was also an Agent of the Province for their ordinary affairs, when Lord Mansfield returned to the Council Chamber, where finally the law was allowed to pass. Some changes were however recommended, and we also engaged they should be made by a subsequent law, but the Assembly did not think them necessary; for one year's tax having been levied by the act before the order of Council arrived, they appointed a committee to examine the proceedings of the assessors, and on this committee they put several particular friends of the proprietaries. After a full enquiry, they unanimously signed a report that they found the tax had been assessed with perfect equity.

The Assembly looked into my entering into the first part of the engagement as an essential service to the Province, since it secured the credit of the paper money then spread over all the country. They gave me their thanks in form when I returned. But the proprietaries were enraged at Governor Denny for having passed the act, and turned him out with threats of suing him for breach of instructions which he had given bond to observe. He, however, having done it at the instance of the General,[33] and for His Majesty's service, and having some powerful interest at court, despised the threats and they were never put in execution.[34] . . .

(UNFINISHED)

[33] THE GENERAL—The Solicitor General of Great Britain.

[34] EXECUTION—The last word Franklin wrote in his *Autobiography*. He still had nearly 30 years to cover, filled with far more exciting and historically important events than any he had related.

## FRANKLIN'S LATER LIFE

The eighteenth century was a period of revolutionary sentiments. Everywhere the old ideas were losing their hold. Traditions were being swept aside. Even the "divine right of kings" was being questioned. First the common people began to wonder whether the ruling class had a right to oppress them, and second they took steps to put an end to it. Then came the Declaration of Independence with its bold assertion of the right of every man to life, liberty, and the pursuit of happiness; and with it, the American Revolution.

Even more violent forces were at work in France. A few years after the American colonies had won independence, the Parisian populace turned on their masters and in an orgy of blood overthrew the French empire. For several years tumult and terror reigned. Even in England the spirit of revolt, in thought more than in action, spread rapidly. Such men as Wordsworth, Coleridge, and others eagerly accepted the ideas underlying the French Revolution, though they were soon disillusioned by the excesses and brutalities to which those ideas led.

Of the moderate views of this exciting century Franklin was a distinguished representative. He was a democrat through and through, in dress, in conduct, in philosophy. He represented the common people and their aspirations. Through his *Poor Richard's Almanack,* published between 1732 and 1757, he spread his doctrine of common sense living, until "as Poor Richard says" became a stock phrase. Because he translated much of the world's wisdom into proverbs intelligible to humble people, he has been called "the Sir Roger de Coverley of the masses."

Franklin was never a militant revolutionist. Violence he abhorred. Even when his own country was engaged in a struggle for liberty he wrote: "I have been apt to think, that there never has been, nor ever will be, any such thing as a *good* war, or a *bad* peace." Another time he anticipated the Hague Tribunal and the World Court by observing sadly: "All wars are follies, very expensive, and very mischievous ones . . . When will mankind be convinced of this and agree to settle their differences by arbitration?" Until shortly before the outbreak of the Revolution he sought to conciliate, not inflame, but when he saw that conflict was inevitable he threw all his energies and resources into the cause of freedom.

Franklin liked the English. On his first mission to London he found them so agreeable that parting brought a sadness. On the eve of his sailing he wrote: "I am now waiting here only for a wind to waft me to America, but cannot leave this happy island and my friends in it without extreme regret, though I am going to a country and a people that I love." Some of his admiration wore off on subsequent visits to "this happy island." He found himself thwarted in his efforts to bring about a more sympathetic treatment of the colonies by His Majesty's officers. Furthermore, he suffered the fate of all who seek the middle of the road, for he complained that he was suspected "in England of being too much of an American, and in America of being too much of an Englishman."

The *Autobiography* brings the story down to the conclusion of his first mission to England in 1762, though the final incidents are but briefly sketched in the few pages written in the last year of his life. In 1757 Franklin had been sent by the Pennsylvania Assembly to protest against the system of proprietors, descendants of William Penn, whose property in the colony had been exempt from taxation. After several years of negotiation Franklin finally obtained a compromise which admitted the right of Pennsylvania to tax the proprietors' estates.

Only two years after his return to Philadelphia, Franklin was again chosen by the colony to seek from the king a recall of the charter which gave the proprietors the right to appoint and instruct the governors of Pennsylvania. Though he failed in this, he was immediately plunged into a controversy of far greater significance. The British government had determined to tax the colonies notwithstanding the fact that they were not represented in Parliament. In spite of all that Franklin could do, in 1765 Parliament passed the Stamp Act, a measure for raising revenue by requiring government stamps on all legal documents used by the British Colonies in America.

Even Franklin failed to anticipate the storm this caused in America. He seems to have believed the law would be accepted docilely, for he sent over some stamped papers for his business partner to sell. In Philadelphia this created against Franklin an outcry that was not stilled until he was called before the House of Commons and questioned concerning the act and its effect on the colonists. So shrewdly did he answer and refute his examiners that the British government made haste to repeal the law. Again Franklin had won the day.

At this point he wanted to return to America, having had enough of disputes and negotiations, but the Pennsylvania Assembly reappointed him its agent in London. During the next few years Georgia, New Jersey, and Massachusetts likewise chose him to represent them in England. Instead of a brief sojourn of a few months as he had originally contemplated, he remained ten years. In the meantime he worked for reconciliation, yet curiously he was himself responsible for one phase of the widening breach.

One day Franklin complained to an English acquaintance about the sending of troops to Boston and other measures taken by the British government against the colonists. To his surprise, this friend undertook to prove that England was acting upon the advice of certain colonial leaders residing in America. Franklin was shown a number of letters from various colonials, among them several written by Governor Hutchinson of Massachusetts to William Whately, member of Parliament. One of them stated that "there must be an abridgment of what are called English liberties." This obviously referred to the increasing legislative power which the colonial Assemblies had won from the king.

Seeing an opportunity to abate the bitterness of the colonies against the British government, Franklin obtained permission to send the letters to some prominent persons in Massachusetts with the promise that they should not be copied or published. To his embarrassment, this pledge was broken. The letters were printed and distributed in Boston without his consent or knowledge. On both sides of the water there was intense excitement. Massachusetts started a movement to oust Governor Hutchinson. In London two men fought a duel over the matter, and finally to save further bloodshed Franklin took sole responsibility for obtaining the letters and transmitting them to the colonies. As a reward for this honorable act, he was publicly denounced as a thief, subjected to violent personal attack, and removed from his office of deputy postmaster general.

These were dark days for Franklin. His effort to reconcile the colonies and the mother country had resulted in even greater bitterness. His wife Deborah had died during his long stay in London. War was daily growing more imminent. He himself was close on seventy, weary of all the uproar and disputing. Still he stuck to his post until 1775 when strained relations made further negotiations impossible.

On his return to Philadelphia he found that the attacks upon him in England had greatly increased his popularity at home. Honors and responsibilities were heaped upon him. He was elected to the Continental Congress, the Pennsylvania Assembly, and the Pennsylvania Convention. To compensate him for the loss of his post under the Crown, Congress appointed him postmaster general. Realizing that conciliation was now impossible, Franklin drafted a Plan of Union for the colonies, the first practical step toward the formation of a confederation. About the same time he served on a number of commissions, one of which purposed to persuade Canada to join with the colonies in the revolt against the mother country. This ended in utter failure. As one of a committee of five he aided in drafting the Declaration of Independence, though the author of that document was Thomas Jefferson.

A still greater task soon confronted him. In September, 1776, he was appointed with Silas Deane and Arthur Lee on a commission to obtain money, supplies, and, if possible, military assistance from France. Though the commissioners had equal powers, most of the responsibility fell on Franklin's shoulders. He was greeted in Paris with an enthusiasm that has rarely been equaled. People struggled to get a glimpse of him. At first cautious, the French government gave aid secretly through Beaumarchais, a striking figure in the political and literary life of the period. It was his play, *The Barber of Seville,* that forecast the French Revolution. Because the American Congress never fully repaid him, Beaumarchais lost most of his fortune for his services to us.

It was not until Burgoyne's surrender that the French government decided to support openly the cause of the colonies. Early in 1778 a treaty was signed making France an ally in the struggle against England. This event had much to do with the final success of the Revolution. In this triumph of American diplomacy Franklin's personality was the major factor; but though the man wielded a powerful influence on French public opinion, he was slack in administration of detail. When John Adams, who was to become second president of the United States, came to Paris to succeed Silas Deane, he found affairs in almost hopeless confusion. There were few records of transactions. Expenses had been incurred without proper authorization. Large sums were still due the colonies, but account books were lacking. A nephew whom Franklin had appointed to an important post was responsible for a number of the irregularities.

While it was inevitable that much of the blame for this state of affairs should fall on Franklin, the bitter attacks of Arthur Lee, his fellow commissioner, were unjustified. Franklin never profited from these operations. Whatever his shortcomings as an executive, he was probably the only man who could have won the undivided support of the French people. In Paris he was more popular than any French hero of the time, not excepting Voltaire.

All during the war Franklin was busy. He had to deal with England for the exchange of prisoners, a difficult task in view of the British contention that all the colonists were traitors. He had to work out the great financial problems of the conflict, find money to pay the soldiers, and strengthen credit abroad. Finally in 1781, after the surrender of Lord Cornwallis at Yorktown, he was named one of the commission to negotiate peace. At first conducting the negotiations alone, he was later joined by John Adams and John Jay. Three of the important points Franklin insisted upon were incorporated in the final draft of the treaty: independence, extension of the western boundaries to the Mississippi River, and fishing rights on the banks of Newfoundland. A fourth point, cession of Canada to the United States, was ruled out by Adams and Jay.

When Franklin returned to America in 1785 he was nearly eighty years old, worn out by his heavy burdens, afflicted by a serious malady, and longing for rest. But there was no leisure for him yet. For three full years he acted as president of the Commonwealth of Pennsylvania. In addition he attended for four months of 1787 the Constitutional Convention of which he had been chosen a member. Though none of his pet ideas was adopted (he favored a single chamber in Congress and unsalaried executives), his serene spirit and common sense aided greatly in bringing about those compromises essential to the adoption of the Constitution. This has been called his most brilliant feat of statesmanship.

And now his work was done. With resignation he awaited the end. It came to him on April 17, 1790, but not before he had affixed his signature to a petition urging Congress to abolish slavery in the United

States and so remove "this inconsistency from the character of the American people." It was his last public act. Franklin lies with his wife in Christ Church Burial Ground, Philadelphia, under a stone bearing the inscription, unassuming as the man himself:

BENJAMIN AND DEBORAH FRANKLIN

---

## FRANKLIN'S WILL

The will Benjamin Franklin drew up at the age of eighty-two is an extraordinary document, showing clearly how sincere was his affection for the land of his birth and how deep his interest in human progress. At Franklin's death, his estate was estimated to be worth $150,000, most of it in properties. After providing for his relatives and friends, he devised plans for putting the remainder to the best possible public use, as follows:

One hundred pounds sterling to the directors of the free schools at Boston, where he had received his early education, the money to be continued at interest forever and the income applied to the purchase of silver medals given annually as honorary rewards for high scholarship. The award of these medals is still part of the graduation exercises in Boston high schools.

One thousand pounds sterling to the City of Boston and a like amount to the City of Philadelphia, the income to be loaned at interest to young married workmen who have faithfully served their apprenticeship. Franklin directed that at the end of one hundred years a certain amount of this increasing fund should be devoted to public works and the rest continued at interest for another hundred years. The stipulations of the will applied alike to Boston, his native city, and Philadelphia, his city by adoption, except that to the Philadelphians Franklin recommended devoting the hundred-year interest increase to piping fresh water from a nearby creek and to making the Schuylkill River completely navigable.

It is interesting to note that the money for these latter bequests was to be derived from the accumulated salary due Franklin as President of Pennsylvania. He had refused to accept any pay, believing there should be no offices of profit in a democratic state. Though few workmen made use of the loan privilege, the funds grew steadily. In 1891, after the first hundred years at interest, the Boston fund was over $391,000. All but $72,000 was spent in the erection of the Franklin Union, a splendid modern building devoted to vocational education. By 1991 that $72,000 will have grown to more than $2,000,000. Again a large part of it will be available for public improvements, and, though Franklin was wise enough not to insist further, the city and state will probably continue the system forever.

## QUESTIONS

### Chapter I

1. What were the circumstances leading to the writing of the *Autobiography?*
2. What was Franklin's estimate of his own life? Was he fully content with it, or would he have chosen to live it over, differently?
3. Did Franklin have any pride in ancestry? Was there anything in his ancestry to account for his unusual talents? Did his brothers and sisters show any great genius?
4. What advantages or disadvantages did he have as a boy? Compare or contrast his early life with that of some other great American.
5. How did he undertake to educate himself? What was the chief factor in his early development?
6. What books did the boy read? What can you say of Franklin's opportunity for finding reading material as compared with your own?
7. Did Franklin show any qualities of leadership as a boy? Any spirit of adventure? Any initiative? Explain.
8. What were Franklin's first experiences in finding a trade? What was his special talent?
9. In the quarrels between Benjamin and James was the fault all on one side?
10. What was Franklin's attitude toward religion while he was a printer's apprentice? What had been the faith of his ancestors?
11. Do you think the Assembly was justified in forbidding James Franklin to publish the *New England Courant?* Was it ethical to print the newspaper under Benjamin's name?
12. What were Franklin's first efforts in creative writing? Did they have merit? Did they give promise of future achievements?

### Chapter II

1. Who assisted Franklin on his trip from Boston to Philadelphia, including his first day in the latter city? What was there about the boy to win such attention? Is hospitality and kindliness to strangers as common today as it was then?
2. What incidents of the trip are most vivid? Could Franklin tell a story well? What can you say of his observation of detail?
3. Why did Franklin feel that Philadelphia was a good city in which to enter the printing trade? What was the importance of the city? How did the two master printers rank?
4. Is there anything to show that Franklin was homesick? Was he glad to be free from parental and brotherly discipline? Did he like his home? Could he have made as great a success had he remained in Boston?
5. What is the first definite evidence that Franklin is an extraordinary young man? What sort of friends did he make? How did he value friendship: for friendship's sake or for the help his friends could give him?
6. What impression did he make on his first visit to Boston? Did he pose a little? Do you think his father's refusal to approve Governor Keith's plan was wise? What do you think would have been the result had Franklin been set up in business for himself at this time?
7. What was Franklin's attitude toward women? Was he attractive to

them? Did they attract him? Was his affair with Miss Read love at first sight? Did the two have much in common?

8. What is your opinion of the friends of Franklin's youth? Were they satisfied with the existing government, orthodox religious doctrines, etc., or were they rebels? What does this indicate concerning Franklin's views?
9. What did Franklin have to say of spiritualism? What do you infer from it?

## Chapter III

1. How did Franklin chance to make friends with the great lawyer, Andrew Hamilton?
2. What comment can you make on the system of delivering letters sent from America to England? Was Franklin justified in showing Riddlesden's letter to Hamilton?
3. Why did Franklin call the writing of his pamphlet on *Liberty and Necessity, Pleasure and Pain* "another erratum"?
4. What famous men did Franklin meet in London? Was it accident or merit that brought him such attention? Is it as easy today to make the acquaintance of great men?
5. Did Franklin have any difficulty in finding employment in London? What was the secret of the "Water-American's" success?
6. Why did Franklin remain so long in London? What were his sentiments toward Miss Read at this time?
7. Do you think Mr. Denham was wise in dissuading Franklin from touring Europe with Wygate?
8. Of what value to Franklin was this London adventure?

## Chapter IV

1. If Mr. Denham had lived, would Franklin the merchant have achieved as great a success as did Franklin the printer? For which occupation was he better fitted? Why?
2. How did Franklin's quarrel with Keimer prove a stepping-stone to prosperity?
3. How did Franklin show his ingenuity in improving the crude printing equipment of the time?
4. What was Franklin's opinion of "croakers"? Was Franklin himself apt to be too optimistic, or was he conservative, cautious about new enterprises, and calculating?
5. For what purpose did Franklin write the *Busy Body* papers? What indiscretion was indirectly the cause of them?
6. How did Franklin attract attention to his newspaper, the *Pennsylvania Gazette,* and increase its circulation? What friend was particularly instrumental in getting government jobs for Franklin & Meredith?
7. What incident occurred which shows the great confidence Franklin's friends had in him? How was their confidence rewarded?
8. Do you think that Franklin at the age of twenty-four was qualified to write a paper on such a difficult subject as the necessity of a paper currency? Was there any factor that might, consciously or unconsciously, have prejudiced him in favor of an additional issue of paper money? Explain.

9. What was Franklin's attitude toward his competitors in the printing business? Was rivalry keen? Did he rejoice in the losses of his competitors? How did he learn from their failures? What unfair methods did Bradford employ against Franklin?
10. What did Franklin look for in a wife? Was he romantic, or did practical considerations enter in? Why did he back out of the affair with Mrs. Godfrey's relation? Why did he marry Mrs. Rogers (the former Miss Read)? What was his feeling for her? Was it a fortunate union for both? Was it a happy union?
11. What was Franklin's first public project, and of what importance was it?

## Chapter V

1. Do you think Franklin's plan for arriving at "moral perfection" is practical?
2. Does Franklin's list include all the essential virtues? Would you add any others? Do you agree with the order of the list?
3. What was his scheme for attaining the virtues he listed? What caused him the greatest difficulty?
4. For what two things did Franklin petition God in his prayer? What does he believe is the only way in which a man can repay his Creator?
5. What were Franklin's views on *Humility?* Note the distinction he draws between *reality* and *appearance.* Would you call Franklin a humble man? Support your answers by references to the text of the *Autobiography.*

## Chapter VI

1. Why was *Poor Richard's Almanack* so great a success? What was the feature of the last issue (for the year 1758)? For how many years did he publish his *Almanack?* What two virtues did he particularly stress in his sayings?
2. What was Franklin's plan for expanding his printing business?
3. What were Franklin's views on education for women? On the preaching of borrowed sermons?
4. Did Franklin hold any grudge against his brother James? Did he really feel indebted to his brother? What great service did he render James later?
5. What personal advantage did Franklin gain through the Junto? What was the educational value of the Junto?
6. How do you suppose Franklin came to be chosen clerk of the General Assembly? Was he a shrewd politician? How did he conciliate opponents?
7. Why did Franklin jump at the chance to be deputy postmaster general?
8. What qualities in Whitefield did Franklin admire? Did Whitefield appeal more to the heart or to the head? What was his influence on Franklin? Mention one incident which showed Franklin's scientific spirit.
9. How did Franklin chance to be drawn into military affairs? What was his own estimate of himself as a soldier? Was he fitted physically and mentally for such a calling? What do you think of his system of defence?
10. Why was Franklin an ideal man to deal with the Quakers? How did the colony obtain the financial support of the Quakers for military expenditures?

## Chapter VII

1. Of what importance was Franklin's invention of an open stove?
2. Was Franklin's attitude toward patenting inventions reasonable? Was it good ethics? Was it good business? What is usually the result of neglecting to apply for a patent? What happened in this case?
3. How was Franklin's broad-mindedness demonstrated in his project for founding an academy? What later development proved the wisdom of his course?
4. Do you think that the many public trusts given to Franklin at this time were due to political influence or appreciation of his ability?
5. Why did he dislike the office of clerk of the Assembly? In what way was his nervous energy shown?
6. How logical was the argument of the Indian orator in defense of the night rioting?
7. What was the secret of Franklin's success in raising funds? What sort of projects did he elect to support?
8. What, in Franklin's opinion, is the relation of "trifling matters" to "human felicity"? Is his homely illustration appropriate? How many proverbs can you recall that have to do with the importance of trifles?
9. Why did Harvard and Yale confer the honorary degree of Master of Arts upon Franklin? What does this indicate concerning his position in the American colonies at this time?

## Chapter VIII

1. Is there anything curious or significant in the fact that as early as 1754 Franklin drew up a plan of union for the colonies? What was his purpose? Was any thought of colonial independence in his mind? Why did the plan fail of adoption both in England and in the colonies?
2. What did Franklin think of argumentative conversation? Did he himself like to dispute? How did he get along personally with the governors whom he often attacked in the Assembly?
3. Though Franklin failed in his efforts at colonial union, he did succeed in inducing Pennsylvania to give assistance to Massachusetts against France. How did he manage it, and how was the necessary money raised?
4. What were the risks Franklin took in engaging to supply Braddock with horses and wagons? What do you think of the effectiveness of his published advertisements? What was their tone? To what emotions did he appeal?
5. What was Franklin's estimate of Braddock? Was Braddock a brave soldier? What was his chief fault? What was Franklin's warning? What young Virginian officer vainly urged Braddock to abandon the British type of fighting for Indian methods? How was Franklin personally concerned in Braddock's defeat?
6. Why did Franklin seek to prevent the enlistment of "bought servants"?

## Chapter IX

1. How did the defeat of Braddock assist the Assembly in its conflict with the Governor? How did the proprietaries compromise without yielding in principle? Was it wise for the Assembly to accept this compromise?
2. Do you think Franklin was qualified to superintend the construction of forts on the frontier? Base your answer on the results he achieved.

3. Were Franklin and his company in any danger at Gnadenhut? Were there any signs of Indians? Did Franklin handle his men well? Give examples. What do you imagine was their opinion of him?
4. What human failing did Dr. B. have? How did Franklin deal with it? Did Franklin show any signs of the same failing?
5. Why did such a simple thing as a military escort cause Franklin so much trouble? What does this incident show as to the temper of the British and colonists at this time?
6. What were Franklin's personal relations with Governor Morris? What expression of confidence in Franklin's ability did the Governor make?

### Chapter X

1. What was Franklin's chief contribution to our knowledge of electricity? By whom was the incandescent lamp invented? Does Franklin share any of that honor? What, aside from astonishment, would be Franklin's impression of Broadway if he could visit it today?
2. What was the attitude of contemporary scientists toward Franklin's theories and experiments? Why was the Abbé Nollet so bitter? What attitude did Franklin take toward his opponents in science?
3. How was Franklin honored, and what unusual circumstance proved his high standing in the scientific world?
4. Is there anything unusual in the fact that Franklin possessed both a literary and a scientific talent? What other men have been famous in letters and in one or more of the branches of science?
5. What was Franklin's training in science? Of what importance is school preparation for the boy of scientific leanings? What do you think of the value of the Edison scholarships for developing scientific geniuses?

### Chapter XI

1. Why did the governors of Pennsylvania in turn seek to win Franklin's support? What method did Captain Denny employ? What made his approach to Franklin easy? What news did he bring of an old friend?
2. For what purpose did the Assembly send Franklin to England? What was the immediate cause? What was the fundamental dispute? What qualities made Franklin a good agent for the colonies?
3. Was Lord Loudoun negligent by nature, or did he have some secret purpose in delaying the packet-boat on which Franklin was to sail? What other incidents show the indecision in his character? With what other character in the *Autobiography* would you compare Lord Loudoun?
4. What remark shows that as he grew older Franklin had been disillusioned concerning the capacity of men in responsible positions? To what did he attribute the advancement of incompetent men? Is the same true today? If so, do you think the abuse greater or less than in Franklin's time?
5. What side-light on Loudoun's character is provided by his answer to Franklin's plea for payment of the money advanced for provisions for Braddock? What was Franklin's reward for his part in obtaining supplies?
6. What were Franklin's observations on sailing and boat-building?
7. Why and by whom was Franklin's ship chased? What improvements for the protection of ships did Franklin resolve to urge when he should return to America?

8. Why was Franklin disturbed by Lord Granville's views on the American situation? Do you think he felt a good case might be made for Granville's interpretation?
9. Why did the proprietaries demand that the Assembly send over "some person of candor" to treat with them? What incident in the Assembly finally gave Franklin the upper hand in the negotiations? What was the great point that Franklin won in the agreement?
10. What is your opinion of Governor Denny in comparison with the previous governors? Was there any justice in the arguments of the proprietaries? What properties today are exempt from taxation? Is real estate owned by individuals or money-making concerns ever exempted?

## GENERAL QUESTIONS

1. What is the chief difference between biography and autobiography?
2. What were Franklin's motives in writing the *Autobiography?*
3. What was the history of the manuscript?
4. What part in the *Autobiography* does Franklin's son William play?
5. In how many important fields of endeavor was Franklin active? Would you say that because he was a jack-of-all-trades he was master of none?
6. Why is Franklin ranked as one of the greatest of our patriots? Why has he been called "the first American"?
7. If Franklin had been born in our times, do you think he would have been so successful in business? In politics? Why?
8. Why was Franklin able to influence so many people both in America and Europe? What were the qualities of his leadership?
9. What mistakes did Franklin admit having made? Can you point to any other "errata" not confessed as mistakes?
10. Was Franklin a man's man? Was he fond of sports? Hunting and fishing? Games? Swimming? Did he have the competitive spirit?
11. In the *Autobiography* is Franklin fair both to himself and others whom he portrays? Does he give praise where praise is due? Is his own estimate of himself exaggerated, too humble, or accurate?
12. Would Franklin have made an entertaining dinner guest? Why? What other American statesmen have been noted for their wit?
13. What in your opinion was Franklin's greatest achievement during the period covered by the *Autobiography* (1706–1760)? What was the greatest in his later period (1760–1790)?
14. Name at least five outstanding figures in American history. Which ones can be compared to Franklin in origin, training, capacity, or temperament? Which ones differ greatly from Franklin?
15. How would you rank the *Autobiography* in interest value with other works of non-fiction you have read? What is the historical value of the *Autobiography?*

## EXERCISES

**Exercises preceded by a star are designed for assignment at the discretion of the teacher, or for any student who volunteers.**

### Chapter I

1. Give a brief character sketch of Franklin's father, mother, and Uncle Benjamin.
2. Write an essay on the subject: Self Education versus School Training.

*3. Contrast Franklin and Washington with regard to ancestry, advantages, and character.

4. Explain Franklin's views on vanity.
5. Comment on Benjamin's relations with his brother James, the printer.

*6. Give your views on "the freedom of the press" with particular reference to the *New England Courant.*

7. Explain the terms: apprentice, journeyman, master.
8. Trace the incidents leading to Franklin's departure for New York.
9. Write an essay on the subject: Franklin, a Boy's Boy.

### Chapter II

1. In the rôle of Benjamin, write a letter to Franklin Senior explaining why you ran away from home.

*2. Report on the means of transportation in Franklin's time.

3. As Miss Read, write a letter to a girl friend describing Franklin as she first saw him.
4. Contrast the two Philadelphia printers, Bradford and Keimer.
5. Comment on the incident of Vernon's money: the trusting of so large a sum to a mere lad; Franklin's use of the borrowed money; the effect of this experience upon Franklin.
6. Discuss Franklin's views on a vegetable diet.

*7. Write an essay on the thought expressed in the statement on page 43: "so convenient a thing it is to be a reasonable creature, since it enables one to find or make a reason for everything one has a mind to do."

*8. Explain Franklin's "Socratic method" of argumentation.

9. Write brief character studies of Collins, Governor Keith, James Ralph.

### Chapter III

1. Imagine yourself a newspaper reporter assigned to interview Franklin at his lodgings in Little Britain. Write an interview giving his impressions of his first trip across the ocean, his disappointment at finding no letter of credit, and his opinion of London life.
2. Give your own opinion of James Ralph's actions and Franklin's treatment of this friend.
3. Give examples showing Franklin's pride in his mental capacity and physical prowess.

*4. Write a description, partly imaginary but based on the details Franklin has given, of the garret room in which the Roman Catholic lady lived. Be sure your details are in keeping with the character of the occupant.

5. In the role of Franklin, write a letter to Miss Read explaining your continued residence in London.
6. Comment on Mr. Denham's wisdom and honesty.

7. Explain how Franklin finally saved enough money to buy his passage back to America.
8. Although few of us meet so many famous men as the young Franklin did in London, all of us have made the acquaintance of several interesting personalities. Write an essay on the topic: *Interesting People I Have Met.*

### Chapter IV

1. List the shortcomings that prevented Meredith and Webb from achieving the same measure of success as Franklin.
2. Show how Keimer's meanness in money matters proved his own undoing.
3. Give a brief account of the firm of Franklin & Meredith, its origin, its first efforts to get business, the role played by each of the two partners, and the break-up of the firm.

*4. Write a leading article for the first number of Franklin's *Pennsylvania Gazette,* explaining to the public what the policies of the newspaper will be.

5. Show the significance of the final settlement of the debt to Vernon, with special relation to the character of both Vernon and Franklin.

*6. Comment on Franklin's policy of *appearing* as well as *being* industrious and frugal. Give your own opinion as to the value and fitness of the wheelbarrow delivery. Contrast with the present business practice of always appearing prosperous, with comment on the value of credit.

7. Write an account of Mrs. Godfrey's attempt at match-making, Franklin's reasons for withdrawing from the affair, and the results.
8. In the United States the masses are better educated than in any other country in the world. Explain Franklin's contribution to this extensive education.

### Chapter V

1. Give Franklin's views on church attendance.
2. Mention any incident thus far related that illustrates Franklin's difficulty with *Order,* No. 3 in his list of virtues. Consult "Franklin's Later Life" for further examples.
3. Explain the use of Franklin's little notebook.
4. Write an essay entitled: *Speckled Axes.*

### Chapter VI

1. Explain the meaning of the proverb: "It is hard for an empty sack to stand upright."
2. Summarize Franklin's views on the proper conduct of a newspaper. Did his first newspaper writings in Boston conform to these principles? Explain.
3. Show how Franklin became a "capitalist"; that is, how he made his money earn more money by investment.

*4. Give your own opinion of Franklin's plan for teaching languages. Indicate whether or not his views are being adopted today.

5. Contrast Franklin's attitude toward inoculation at this time with the views expressed in the *New England Courant* during his boyhood in Boston.
6. List the public improvements in which Franklin had a hand at this time, commenting on those which have been of lasting value.

*7. Report on the founding of Georgia and early conditions in that colony.

8. Write an essay on the topic: *Franklin and the Quakers.* Do not simply repeat the incidents mentioned in the *Autobiography.* Interpret the Quaker character and describe Franklin's methods of winning support for his defence measures.
9. Franklin was now in the prime of life. From among the following adjectives select those that most accurately describe him: frugal, thrifty, miserly; proud, humble, self-respecting; moral, religious; practical, idealistic; dissembling, sincere; cunning, shrewd, subtle; placid, excitable, self-controlled; ambitious, grasping, smug.

## Chapter VII

1. Debate the proposition: Resolved, That inventions should not be patented, but should be used, without restriction, for the benefit of humanity.
2. Point out the various means by which Franklin obtained financial independence while still in his early forties.
3. Write in your own words a description of the Indian riot at Carlisle.

*4. From the account given here and from pictures or data to be found in the library, describe a typical city street of Franklin's time, telling something of the types of buildings as well as giving a picture of the roadway itself. Compare with a modern street.

5. Franklin admitted that he had difficulty in achieving *Order.* Sometimes his administration of business affairs resulted in confusion, yet he must have had considerable executive ability. Cite one instance of his success in reorganizing a system, and show how he obtained his results.

## Chapter VIII

*1. To illustrate his point in arguing for union of the colonies against France, Franklin devised an emblem depicting a snake cut into various parts, each representing a colony. Beneath was the motto: *Join, or Die.* Write an interpretation of his symbolic picture.

*2. Apply the following proposition of Franklin's to some event of present-day politics: "The best public measures are . . . seldom adopted from previous wisdom, but forced by the occasion."

3. Explain why England sent British soldiers to defend the colonies.
4. Write a narrative sketch of Braddock's defeat, bringing into the account several names of historical importance.
5. Compare the conduct of the British regulars during Dunbar's retreat with that of the French soldiers some 25 years later. Show what effect the former incident had on colonial sentiment.

## Chapter IX

1. Suggest reasons to explain why Governor Morris appointed Franklin, one of his most active opponents in the Assembly, to take charge of defense preparations on the Northwestern Frontier.
2. Review Franklin's account of the Moravians, their customs, doctrines, mode of living, etc. Cite instances that show Franklin as an unbiased observer, eager to find and report the truth.
3. Discuss Franklin's contention that men are happiest when employed, with comment, favorable or unfavorable, on recent agitation for a five-day working week.

*4. In the character of Franklin, write a letter to Mr. T. Penn, son of William Penn and owner of vast tracts in Pennsylvania, explaining the incident of the military escort which gave offense to the proprietaries.
5. One of the greatest controversies of the time was the quarrel between the Assembly and the proprietaries. It is suggested that the class be divided into two groups, one group writing arguments supporting the Assembly, the other taking the side of the proprietaries. The writers of the three or four best papers in each group may be permitted to engage in a classroom debate on the subject.

### Chapter X

1. Report on the scientific studies and achievements of Franklin.
2. Explain how Franklin's scientific theories were made popular in England.
3. Point out passages preceding this chapter in which Franklin's scientific spirit is revealed.
4. Write an essay on the importance of any one of Franklin's inventions.

### Chapter XI

1. Comment on Franklin's reply to Captain Denny, with special attention to (1) its noble spirit, and (2) its shrewdness.
2. Explain the significance of Innis's remark concerning Lord Loudoun: "He is like St. George on the signs, always on horseback, and never rides on."
*3. Narrate an incident in Franklin's own experience as office holder that might account for his attitude regarding appointments to important posts.
4. Explain the double meaning of the following bit of repartee:
   Franklin: They have given you, sir, too low a seat.
   Shirley: No matter, Mr. Franklin, I find a low seat the easiest.
5. As Franklin, write a letter to "Dear Debby," giving a vivid account of the escape from shipwreck. From your own imagination elaborate the details Franklin has given.
*6. As Franklin, write a letter to the Pennsylvania Assembly reporting the progress of the negotiations, with side lights on the characters of several men opposed to him. Also suggest a motive for the proprietors' demand that some other agent be sent to England in place of Franklin.

## GENERAL EXERCISES

1. Cite passages from the *Autobiography* showing Franklin's (1) industry, (2) honesty, (3) generosity, (4) familiarity with printing and publishing, (5) belief in his own worth, (6) humor, (7) ability to handle men, (8) shrewdness in business, (9) public spirit, and (10) tact and diplomacy.
2. Explain the force of the following words, phrases, and sentences: hope, presume, page 12, lines 29–30; he never fulfilled his promise, 47, 7; you, 58, 4; I like a speckled axe best, 83, 12; proud of my humility, 85, 30–31; He that has once done you a kindness will be more ready to do you another, than he whom you yourself have obliged, 92, 31–33; I have no particular interest in this affair, 121, 16; ignorance, 124, 1; scour the anchor, 131, 5; some person of candor, 152, 1.

*3. Divide the *Autobiography* into the several sections that were written at different times. Noting the date when each section was composed, study each installment to find differences in (1) style, and (2) point of view.
4. Make a synopsis of the important events in Franklin's career, placing the date of each (year only) at the left-hand side of the page.
5. Show how circumstance or accident several times changed Franklin's career.
6. Franklin had little liking for military affairs, yet contributed important services in each of the three wars that occurred in America during his lifetime. Explain in detail.
*7. Write a book review of the *Autobiography* with special mention of style, vividness of narration, background, character analysis, author's purpose, and general value as a literary and historical work.
8. Trace Franklin's change of views on (1) religion, (2) loyalty to the king, (3) slavery, and (4) one phase of medical science.
*9. Imagine a meeting between Franklin and Edison. Write a dialogue in which Edison comments on some modern developments in electricity, and Franklin gives his reactions.
10. Write an essay comparing Franklin with the man you consider the greatest living American.
*11. Write a brief outline for a five-act play based on Franklin's life, noting briefly what incidents you would include in each act. Remember to use only such incidents as advance the plot, reveal character, or give essential information as to background.
12. Report on some other autobiography or biography which you have read.

## SELECTED READINGS FROM FRANKLIN

### LETTERS

The collected letters of a man constitute an informal autobiography. They are often more valuable for an understanding of him than is his own written account. An autobiography proper is usually composed in retrospect and marked with a certain effort to appear to advantage before the readers. Letters, on the contrary, are written when the events related are fresh in mind. With few exceptions, they are intended for the eyes of the recipient only. As a consequence, we see the great man in his intimate moments, giving free rein to his thoughts, chatting of great or little affairs, assuming no attitude to impress the crowd.

Of late, the art of letter-writing has fallen off measurably. Apparently we have not the time for prolonged correspondence, and our letters are curt and business-like, or politely formal. In Franklin's time, notwithstanding the fact that education had not yet reached the masses, many people took great pride in their correspondence. Perhaps they posed a little, put on a show of literary style and high emotion; yet even these little tricks are revealing.

The letters of Franklin are among the best written during his time. Though having a literary flavor, they show a simplicity and sincerity that must have endeared him to his correspondents. We find him lamenting in a droll way the death of Georgiana Shipley's pet squirrel; scolding his wife gently for not having written him and adding the postscript, "I have scratched out the loving words, being writ in haste, by mistake, when I forgot I was angry;" advising Polly Stevenson on her reading; and complimenting the Marquis de Lafayette on his improvement in handwriting. Echoes of the Revolution sound through his correspondence with Robert Livingston, John Jay, John Adams, and other patriots. Philosophy and science are favorite themes. Though he rarely misses an opportunity to preach his reader a lesson, his shrewd wit and sprightly humor are disarming.

The following letters are typical of hundreds which Franklin wrote and from which is derived much of our knowledge of his friendships, his experiments in science, and his diplomatic career. Even in these few selections, chosen to represent the several stages of his life from the point where the *Autobiography* leaves off till his death in 1790, the real man, the Benjamin Franklin known and loved by his friends, stands out more clearly than in the many volumes written by his biographers.

#### Memories of England

In 1762, after a five-year residence in London, Franklin returned to America. Though he was delighted to see once more his friends and family in Philadelphia, he looked back with a feeling close to longing upon those happy days in Craven Street. Even in his busy life he had time to remember the little circle of which he had become the center—Mrs. Stevenson, her daughter Mary, and their friends. When, about six months after his arrival in America, he wrote Mary (Polly) this letter, he had not the slightest suspicion that in another year and a half he would be with them all again and would spend ten years in the little house in Craven Street.

*Phila., 25 March, 1763.*

MY DEAR POLLEY,

Your pleasing favour of Nov. 11 is now before me. It found me as you suppos'd it would, happy with my American friends and family about me; and it made me more happy in showing me that I am not yet forgotten by the dear friends I left in England. And indeed, why should I fear they will ever forget me, when I feel so strongly that I shall ever remember them! . . .

Of all the enviable things England has, I envy it most its people. Why should that petty island, which compar'd to America, is but like a stepping-stone in a brook, scarce enough of it above water to keep one's shoes dry; why, I say, should that little island enjoy in almost every neighborhood, more sensible, virtuous, and elegant minds, than we can collect in ranging 100 leagues of our vast forests? But 'tis said the arts delight to travel westward. You have effectually defended us in this glorious war,[1] and in time you will improve us. After the first cares for the necessaries of life are over, we shall come to think of the embellishments. Already some of our young geniuses begin to lisp attempts at printing, poetry, and musick. . .

I do not wonder at the behaviour you mention of Dr. Smith towards me, for I have long since known him thoroughly. I made that man my enemy by doing him too much kindness. 'Tis the honestest way of acquiring an enemy. And, since 'tis convenient to have at least one enemy, who by his readiness to revile one on all occasions, may make one careful of one's conduct, I shall keep him an enemy for that purpose; and shall observe your good mother's advice, never again to receive him as a friend. . .

Adieu, my dear Polly, and believe me as ever, with the sincerest esteem and regard, your truly affectionate friend and humble servant,

B. FRANKLIN.

[1] THIS GLORIOUS WAR—The French and Indian War, 1754–63, by which France lost to England all her possessions east of the Mississippi.

## Sarah Franklin Falls in Love

As young girls will, Franklin's daughter Sarah, called Sally by her friends, grew up and fell in love. The suitor for her hand was Richard Bache, a young Philadelphia business man, later Deputy Postmaster General of Pennsylvania. As mothers will, Mrs. Franklin worried and wondered whether or not it would be a good match. In those days parents had a great deal to say concerning a daughter's choice of a husband. Debby could not talk it over with Franklin. For a second time the colony had sent him to England as its agent, and he had been away nearly three years. In her perplexity she sent him a letter by a Captain Falconer, asking his advice. The following is Franklin's reply. It is interesting to remember that Sarah and Richard Bache were married and that the Franklin line has come down to our time through that union.

*London, 22 June, 1767.*

My dear Child,

Captain Falconer is arrived, and came yesterday to see me and bring my letters. I was extremely glad of yours, because I had none by the packet. It seems now as if I should stay here another winter, and therefore I must leave it to your judgment to act in the affair of our daughter's match as shall seem best. If you think it a suitable one, I suppose the sooner it is completed the better. In that case, I would advise that you do not make an expensive feasting wedding, but conduct everything with frugality and economy, which our circumstances now require to be observed in all our expenses. For, since my partnership with Mr. Hall[2] has expired, a great source of our income is cut off; and, if I should lose the post-office,[3] which, among the many changes here, is far from being unlikely, we should be reduced to our rents and interest of money for a subsistence, which will by no means afford the chargeable housekeeping and entertainments we have been used to.

For my own part, I live here as frugally as possible, not to be destitute of the comforts of life, making no dinners for anybody, and contenting myself with a single dish when I dine at home; and yet such is the dearness of living here in every article, that my

---

[2] Mr. Hall—David Hall, for eighteen years Franklin's partner in the highly profitable printing business in Philadelphia. In 1766 he bought out Franklin.

[3] Lose the post-office—Franklin's fear that the King would remove him from the office of joint deputy postmaster general of the colonies was realized in 1774 after the unfortunate episode of the Hutchinson letters. This partly explains his gentle remonstrance at the size of Debby's expense account.

expenses amaze me. I see, too, by the sums you have received in my absence, that yours are very great; and I am very sensible that your situation naturally brings you a great many visitors, which occasions an expense not easily to be avoided, especially when one has been long in the practice and habit of it. But, when people's incomes are lessened, if they cannot proportionably lessen their outgoings, they must come to poverty. If we were young enough to begin business again, it might be another matter; but I doubt we are past it, and business not well managed ruins one faster than no business. In short, with frugality and prudent care we may subsist decently on what we have, and leave it entire to our children; but without such care we shall not be able to keep it together; it will melt away like butter in the sunshine, and we may live long enough to feel the miserable consequences of our indiscretion.

I know very little of the gentleman or his character, nor can I at this distance. I hope his expectations are not great of any fortune to be had with our daughter before our death. I can only say that, if he proves a good husband to her and a good son to me, he shall find me as good a father as I can be: but at present I suppose you would agree with me, that we cannot do more than fit her out handsomely in clothes and furniture, not exceeding in the whole five hundred pounds in value. For the rest, they must depend, as you and I did, on their own industry and care, as what remains in our hands will be barely sufficient for our support, and not enough for them when it comes to be divided at our decease.

I suppose the blue room is too blue, the wood being of the same color with the paper, and so looks too dark. I would have you finish it as soon as you can, thus: paint the wainscot a dead white, paper the walls blue, and tack the gilt border round just above the surbase and under the cornice. If the paper is not equally colored when pasted on, let it be brushed over again with the same color, and let the papier maché musical figures be tacked to the middle of the ceiling. When this is done, I think it will look very well.

I am glad to hear that Sally keeps up and increases the number of her friends. The best wishes of a fond father for her happiness always attend her. I am, my dear Debby, your affectionate husband,

B. FRANKLIN.

## Epitaph for a Pet Squirrel

In 1771, seven years after Franklin had returned to England on his second mission, he visited the Shipleys at Twyford. Bishop Jonathan Shipley was a man of some importance both in the church and in politics, having a seat in the House of Lords. A lovely wife and five charming daughters made up his family.

Franklin's visit had three results. First, Bishop Shipley, for all his aristocratic tendencies, became through Franklin's influence a firm friend of America. In the years that followed, his courageous utterances in favor of the Colonies won him the ill will of the King, George III, and probably lost him the prized appointment as Archbishop of Canterbury. Secondly, Franklin formed a friendship that lasted till death. And finally, as we know, the *Autobiography* was begun here, probably at the urging of the Shipleys.

Of the five daughters, Georgiana was Franklin's favorite. On the occasion of his first visit to Twyford, she was but fifteen, high-spirited, talented. Talent always attracted Franklin. The correspondence between the elderly statesman and this young girl is a tribute to the splendid qualities of each.

One day Franklin presented Georgiana with a gray squirrel which his wife had sent him from America. Unfortunately for both the squirrel and its owner, a dog decided that a scampering animal which had escaped from its cage was proper prey, and promptly dispatched it. Tearfully Georgiana buried him in the garden and erected a little monument. Shortly afterward, she received this letter from Franklin.

*London, 26 September, 1772.*

Dear Miss,

I lament with you most sincerely the unfortunate end of poor Mungo. Few squirrels were better accomplished; for he had a good education, had travelled far, and seen much of the world. As he had the honor of being, for his virtues, your favorite, he should not go, like common skuggs,[4] without an elegy or an epitaph. Let us give him one in the monumental style and measure, which, being neither prose nor verse, is perhaps the properest for grief; since to use common language would look as if we were not affected, and to make rhymes would seem trifling in sorrow.

EPITAPH

Alas! poor Mungo!
Happy wert thou, hadst thou known
Thy own felicity.

[4] Skuggs—Common name by which squirrels were known in England, as cats are called puss.

Remote from the fierce bald eagle,
Tyrant of thy native woods,
Thou hadst nought to fear from his piercing talons,
Nor from the murdering gun
Of the thoughtless sportsman.

Safe in thy wired castle,
Grimalkin[5] never could annoy thee.
Daily wert thou fed with the choicest viands,
By the fair hand of an indulgent mistress;
But, discontented,
Thou wouldst have more freedom.
Too soon, alas! didst thou obtain it;
And wandering,
Thou art fallen by the fangs of wanton, cruel Ranger!

Learn hence,
Ye who blindly seek more liberty,
Whether subjects, sons, squirrels, or daughters,
That apparent restraint may be real protection,
Yielding peace and plenty
With security.

You see, my dear Miss, how much more decent and proper this broken style is, than if we were to say, by way of epitaph,—

Here Skugg
Lies snug
As a bug
In a rug.

And yet, perhaps, there are people in the world of so little feeling as to think that this would be a good enough epitaph for poor Mungo.

If you wish it, I shall procure another to succeed him, but perhaps you will now choose some other amusement.

Remember me affectionately to all the good family, and believe me ever your affectionate friend,

B. FRANKLIN.

## LONGINGS FOR HOME

Franklin returned from his second mission to England in May, 1775, barely two weeks after the battles of Lexington and Concord. Immediately he was plunged into the preparations for the War of

[5] GRIMALKIN—Cat.

Independence. Besides serving on many commissions he drafted a plan of union and aided in formulating the Declaration of Independence. Nevertheless, his residence in America was even shorter than last time. In October, 1776, in the seventieth year of his age, he sailed for France as head of a commission to win the sympathy and support of the French government.

For nearly eight years and a half he carried on, sick, tired, old, yet sticking to his job until the final ratification of the peace treaty. The following excerpts from his letters of this period give us a glimpse of his mind, now brightened by the homage of the gay people he had learned to love, now depressed by cares, attacks of jealous enemies, and a longing for home.

The first excerpt is part of a letter addressed to his daughter Sarah and her husband, Richard Bache; the second is addressed to Mr. Bache, whom he calls son.

*Passy, 14 May, 1781.*[6]

Dear Son and Daughter,

. . . It is not my purpose to return immediately home, unless ordered; chusing rather to remain here till the Peace, among a People that love me & whom I love, than to hazard an English Prison. My proper situation indeed would be in my own house, with my Daughter to take care of me & nurse me in case of Illness, and with her Child to amuse me; but as this cannot well be at present, we must manage as we can. My Friend and Neighbor M. Veillard[7] has sent his Son to live some time in Philadelphia; he is a very deserving young Man. Do you, My Daughter, be a Mother to him, and his Mother and Sister will be Daughter to me. It is a most amiable Family. . . .

*Passy, 26 December, 1782.*[8]

Dear Son,

You will hear of the progress made too, and a Peace from various quarters. It is not yet concluded, and perhaps it may be some time first. But as soon as it is, I hope to be permitted to return home, there being nothing there I more desire than to spend my last days with my Family & lay my bones next in America. . . .

---

[6] Passy, etc.—From an original letter in the possession of Dennis Percy McCarthy of Syracuse, N. Y., a direct descendant of Franklin.

[7] M. Veillard (vĕ'ā-yár)—He urged Franklin to continue his memoirs begun at the Shipleys.

[8] Passy, etc.—This letter is likewise part of the McCarthy collection.

## Peace and War

Though Franklin took an active part in three wars, he was a man of peace. In this letter to Sir Joseph Banks, famous naturalist who for nearly quarter of a century was president of the Royal Society, he gives expression to a thought that disturbed many after the World War of 1914–1918.

*Passy, 27 July, 1783.*

Dear Sir,

I join with you most cordially in rejoicing at the return of peace. I hope it will be lasting, and that mankind will at length, as they call themselves reasonable creatures, have reason and sense enough to settle their differences without cutting throats; for, in my opinion, there never was a good war, or a bad peace. What vast additions to the conveniences and comforts of living might mankind have acquired, if the money spent in wars had been employed in works of public utility! What an extension of agriculture, even to the tops of our mountains; what rivers rendered navigable, or joined by canals; what bridges, aqueducts, new roads, and other public works, edifices and improvements, rendering England a complete paradise, might have been obtained by spending those millions in doing good, which in the last war have been spent in doing mischief,—in bringing misery into thousands of families, and destroying the lives of so many thousands of working people, who might have performed useful labor!

## A Reconciliation

During the war years Franklin not only suffered physical pain because of his malady but was tormented in mind by the desertion of William Franklin. What hours of anguish he must have spent thinking of his only son, a sworn enemy to the cause for which he was giving the best years of his life! When the war was over, Franklin was glad to effect a reconciliation, yet he could not conceal his mortification that the family name should be coupled with the Tory cause. In this very human letter, showing traces of affection but with an undertone of sad reproof, he expresses his willingness to forget—as well as he can.

Father and son met the following year in England and then parted never to meet again. Franklin returned to Philadelphia. William remained in London, where he lived to the ripe old age of eighty-two. If they ever wrote to each other after this parting, the letters are lost. Franklin never quite reconciled himself to his son's disloyalty. In the first article of his will, which bequeaths to William certain lands in Nova Scotia, he adds with a touch of bitterness: "The part he acted against me in the late war, which is of public notoriety, will account for my leaving him no more of an estate he endeavoured to deprive me of."

*Passy, 16 August, 1784.*

DEAR SON,

I received your letter of the 22d ultimo, and am glad to find that you desire to revive the affectionate intercourse that formerly existed between us. It will be very agreeable to me; indeed, nothing has ever hurt me so much, and affected me with such keen sensations, as to find myself deserted in my old age by my only son; and not only deserted, but to find him taking up arms against me in a cause wherein my good fame, fortune, and life were all at stake. You conceived, you say, that your duty to your king and regard for your country required this. I ought not to blame you for differing in sentiment with me in public affairs. We are men, all subject to errors. Our opinions are not in our own power; they are formed and governed much by circumstances that are often as inexplicable as they are irresistible. Your situation was such that few would have censured your remaining neuter, though there are natural duties which precede political ones, and cannot be extinguished by them.

This is a disagreeable subject. I drop it; and we will endeavor, as you propose, mutually to forget what has happened relating to it, as well as we can. . . .

## POST-WAR PROBLEMS

Even after the signing of the Peace Treaty in its final form at Paris, 1783, Franklin was not permitted to return home. A multitude of official duties remained to be done, difficult tasks in view of the inexperience of the United States in diplomatic affairs and the poor condition of the treasury. In this letter to a colleague, William Carmichael, he reveals not only problems with which he is wrestling but also his own nobility of spirit and self sacrifice for his country.

*Passy, 26 August, 1784.*[9]

DEAR FRIEND,

. . . Mr. Jefferson is arrived. He has brought Commissions joining him with Mr. Adams and myself for treating with the several European Powers. Mr. Adams too is arrived here and has taken a house near me. . . . I have long complained as well as you

[9] PASSY, ETC.—From the McCarthy collection.

of the Silence of Congress. Mr. Jefferson tells me that is merely owing to the Want of a Secretary for Foreign Affairs; it being almost impossible for the Congress as a Body to write and answer Letters. They have sometimes attempted it by appointing Committees; but when the Committees brought in Drafts of the intended Letters, there were so many proposed Changes, so much Disputing and Voting, that much Time was Devour'd and nothing well done at last. This Evil will now be remedy'd if Mr. Jay[10] accepts that Office, which they have voted him.

I accepted your Bill: Your Appointments ought always to be regularly paid, but it would not be amiss for you to consider whether it is not possible for you to retrench your Expenses: For the Congress are become parsimonious, and have curtail'd the Salaries of all their Servants. . . . As Money is not my Object, being near my Journey's End, and having enough to pay the remaining Turnpikes and Post Chaises, I shall stick to the Service so long as the Congress requires it of me, tho' they were to give me nothing. . . .

Yours most Affectionately,

BENJAMIN FRANKLIN.

## HOME AGAIN!

When Franklin returned to Philadelphia, he found waiting for him a packet of three letters from Mrs. Mary Hewson, the former Polly Stevenson. They had been written ten years before and had arrived shortly after he sailed for France. These old letters, he wrote Polly, "broke out upon me, *like words,* that had been, as somebody says, *congealed in northern air.*" Franklin's reply, though not mentioning his election as President of Pennsylvania a few months before, gives a pleasing picture of the old patriot in the family circle. At the age of eighty he sits down for a few hours of peace and contentment.

*Philadelphia, 6 May, 1786.*

MY DEAR FRIEND,

A long winter has passed, and I have not had the pleasure of a line from you, acquainting me with your and your children's welfare, since I left England. I suppose you have been in Yorkshire, out of the way and knowledge of opportunities; for I will not think you have forgotten me. . . .

---

[10] MR. JAY—John Jay, who with Franklin and John Adams negotiated the peace treaty.

I have found my family here in health, good circumstances, and well respected by their fellow citizens. The companions of my youth are indeed almost all departed, but I find an agreeable society among their children and grandchildren. I have public business enough to preserve me from *ennui*,[11] and private amusement besides in conversation, books, my garden, and *cribbage*. Considering our well-furnished, plentiful market as the best of gardens, I am turning mine, in the midst of which my house stands, into grass-plats, and gravel-walks, with trees and flowering shrubs. Cards we sometimes play here in long winter evenings, but it is as they play at chess,—not for money, but for honor, or the pleasure of beating one another. This will not be quite a novelty to you, as you may remember we played together in that manner during the winter you helped me to pass so agreeably at Passy. I have, indeed, now and then a little compunction in reflecting that I spend time so idly; but another reflection comes to relieve me, "You know the soul is immortal; why, then, should you be such a niggard of a little time, when you have a whole eternity before you?" So, being easily convinced, and, like other reasonable creatures, satisfied with a small reason when it is in favor of doing what I have a mind to do, I shuffle the cards again, and begin another game.

As to public amusements, we have neither plays nor operas, but we had yesterday a kind of oratorio, as you will see by the enclosed papers; and we have assemblies, balls, and concerts, besides little parties at one another's houses, in which there is sometimes dancing, and frequently good music; so that we jog on in life as pleasantly as you do in England, anywhere but in London; for there you have plays performed by good actors. That, however, is, I think, the only advantage London has over Philadelphia. . . .

With sincere and very great esteem, I am ever, my dear friend, yours most affectionately,

B. Franklin.

## Farewell to Washington

The end is approaching. Looking back over the years, Franklin may well take pride in what he has accomplished. Even during these last few years he has served as President of Pennsylvania and as delegate to the Constitutional Convention. Now he is trying to add a

[11] *Ennui*—Tedium, boredom.

few more pages to his *Autobiography*. He seems to realize that but a few more months are left to him. What more fitting conclusion for this section than an exchange of letters between the two greatest figures of the Revolution: Franklin and Washington! When these letters were penned, Washington was just beginning his first administration as President of the United States. Each writer knew that it was a last farewell.

*Philadelphia, 16 Sept., 1789.*

My malady renders my sitting up to write rather painful to me; but I cannot let my son-in-law, Mr. Bache, part for New York, without congratulating you by him on the recovery of your health, so precious to us all, and on the growing strength of our new government under your administration. For my personal ease, I should have died two years ago; but, though those years have been spent in excruciating pain, I am pleased that I have lived them, since they have brought me to see our present situation. I am now finishing my eighty-fourth year, and probably with it my career in this life; but whatever state of existence I am placed in hereafter, if I retain any memory of what has passed here, I shall with it retain the esteem, respect, and affection, with which I have long been, my dear friend, yours most sincerely,

B. FRANKLIN.

*New York, 23 September, 1789.*

DEAR SIR:

The affectionate congratulations on the recovery of my health, and the warm expressions of personal friendship, which were contained in your letter of the 16th instant, claim my gratitude. And the consideration, that it was written when you were afflicted with a painful malady, greatly increases my obligation for it.

Would to God, my dear Sir, that I could congratulate you upon the removal of that excruciating pain, under which you labor, and that your existence might close with as much ease to yourself, as its continuance has been beneficial to our country and useful to mankind; or, if the united wishes of a free people, joined with the earnest prayers of every friend to science and humanity, could relieve the body from pains or infirmities, that you could claim an exemption on this score. But this cannot be, and you have within yourself the only resource to which we can confidently apply for relief, a philosophic mind.

If to be venerated for benevolence, if to be admired for talents, if to be esteemed for patriotism, if to be beloved for philanthropy, can gratify the human mind, you must have the pleasing consolation to know that you have not lived in vain. And I flatter myself that it will not be ranked among the least grateful occurrences of your life to be assured, that, so long as I retain my memory, you will be recollected with respect, veneration, and affection by your sincere friend,

GEORGE WASHINGTON.

Even from the grave Franklin spoke to Washington through a bequest whose actual worth was little but whose sentimental value the President must have fully appreciated:

"My fine crabtree walking stick, with a gold head curiously wrought in the form of the cap of liberty, I give to my friend, and the friend of mankind, General Washington. If it were a sceptre he has merited it; and would become it. It was a present to me from that excellent woman Madame de Forbach, the Dowager Duchess of Deux-Ponts, connected with some verses which should go with it."

## QUESTIONS

1. What does the letter to Polly Stevenson (March 25, 1763) indicate concerning Franklin's attitude toward England? How did that attitude change in later years? What does this letter show concerning the state of American arts at this time?
2. What emotion underlies the epitaph on "Poor Mungo"? What does Franklin mean by "monumental style"?
3. What do you think were Franklin's real feelings toward his son William? How might William have defended himself on the charge of being disloyal?
4. What was the standing of the United States among the nations for the first few years after the signing of the peace treaty in 1783? What were some of Franklin's problems?
5. Who was Mrs. Mary Hewson? What traits in Franklin's character may account for the devotion of many women much younger than he?
6. Why should two men of such different birth and training as Franklin and Washington be attracted to each other? Do you believe their feeling for each other was sincere? Why?
7. Have these selected readings revealed to you any phase of Franklin's personality not evident in the *Autobiography?* If so, what?

## EXERCISES

Exercises preceded by a star are designed for assignment at the discretion of the teacher, or for any student who volunteers.

1. Discuss the general application of Franklin's statement (to Polly, March 25, 1763): "I made that man my enemy by doing him too much kindness."
2. In Franklin's letter to his wife concerning the expected marriage of their daughter Sarah, point out passages that are particularly revealing of the author's character.
3. Choosing either the affirmative or negative side, write the synopsis of an argument based on Franklin's proposition: "There never was a good war, or a bad peace." (The writers of the three or four best arguments on each side may, if time permits, debate the issue in class.)

*4. In the character of William Franklin, write the letter which you imagine may have brought Benjamin Franklin's reply of Aug. 16, 1784.

5. Describe Franklin's home life after his return to Philadelphia in the autumn of 1785.

## SUGGESTED READING LIST

Other Autobiographies:

Roosevelt's *Autobiography*
*The Making of an American,* Jacob Riis
*The Story of My Boyhood and Youth,* John Muir
*Up from Slavery,* Booker T. Washington
*The Americanization of Edward Bok*
*The Promised Land,* Mary Antin
*The Story of My Life,* Helen Keller
*Twenty Years at Hull-house,* Jane Addams
*My Autobiography,* Benito Mussolini
*The Autobiography of Lincoln Steffens*

Biographies:

*The God-like Daniel,* Samuel Hopkins Adams
*Abraham Lincoln,* Carl Schurz
*Abraham Lincoln, the Prairie Years,* Carl Sandburg
*The Magnificent Idler* (Walt Whitman), T. Cameron Rogers
*Roosevelt: The Story of a Friendship,* Owen Wister

Reference Books:

*Benjamin Franklin,* John T. Morse, Jr. (American Statesmen Series)
*The True Benjamin Franklin,* Sidney George Fisher
*The Many-sided Franklin,* Paul Leicester Ford
*Benjamin Franklin,* E. L. Dudley
*Franklin, the Apostle of Modern Times,* Bernard Faÿ
*Benjamin Franklin,* Phillips Russell
*Four Great Americans,* James Baldwin
*Makers of America,* Emma Lilian Dana
*Washington, Jefferson, and Franklin on War,* Edwin D. Mead
*American Statesmen,* Edward Howard Griggs
*Franklin in France,* Edward E. Hale
*Sayings of Poor Richard,* Comp. by Paul Leicester Ford
*My Dear Girl;* the Correspondence of Benjamin Franklin with Polly Stevenson, Georgiana, and Catherine Shipley, Edit. by James Madison Stifler

# The Novel

Publishers' Photo Service, N. Y.

GEORGE ELIOT

George Eliot was the pen name of Marian Evans, one of the first of the great women novelists. As a writer, she was interested in the thoughts rather than the deeds of men, and her characters reflect her own deep and sympathetic understanding of human nature.

# THE NOVEL

## 1. History of the Novel

It was at the beginning of the eighteenth century that the English novel first took form. Its immediate ancestor was that popular classic, Defoe's *Robinson Crusoe,* published in 1719. Long before that, however, there had been *tales,* simple narratives of events in chronological order with little attempt at organization or climax or psychology; and *fables,* which taught a moral through personified virtues and vices or through animals acting like human beings. Tales were either very long with many episodes loosely strung together, or else so short as to be mere anecdotes.

Though Defoe shows some progress in arranging his material in orderly fashion, the true novel does not begin until more than twenty years later. In 1740 appeared Samuel Richardson's *Pamela;* the second year following, Henry Fielding published *Joseph Andrews.* With the composition of these books, the two great types of English novel are established; for Richardson's *Pamela* is almost wholly romantic, while Fielding's *Joseph Andrews* is largely realistic. The former deals with the none too honorable attentions of a man of high social standing to a pretty country lass in his mother's service. As the sub-title, *Virtue Rewarded,* indicates, it shows the triumph of virtue over evil in true romantic style, with sentiment and passion lending high color to the narrative. Fielding, on the other hand, started with intent to ridicule the extravagant emotions of *Pamela* but ended more than half seriously by giving us an accurate picture of contemporary life and manners. It was, in fact, the beginning of the realistic novel.

Let us understand at the outset that though we may call a certain period romantic or realistic, there are always some representatives of both schools; and that though a certain book is classified as romantic or realistic, it may possibly contain features of both. Periods we designate by their general trend; books, by their general character. For example, *Silas Marner* is distinctly in the realistic tradition of *Joseph Andrews,* yet, as will be shown later on, a few of the romantic devices remain. These two streams, romance and realism, come down through the years, sometimes one prevailing, sometimes the other; but neither disappears.

Following the course of the romantic novel from Richardson, one encounters such famous names as Sir Walter Scott; James Fenimore Cooper, the American novelist; and Victor Hugo, the French master of fiction. Rather curiously, the two English novelists who carried on the realistic tradition of Fielding were both women—Jane Austen and George Eliot. For the development of a stern realism, however, one must look to France. There, a number of writers took their realism so seriously that they compiled endless notebooks of conversations heard and incidents observed, from which they concocted their novels. They were microscopic in their observation and rejected nothing simply because it seemed unimportant. To them everything in life was worth while material for literature.

When George Eliot was born, in 1819, the world had seen the French Revolution that shattered old ideas of government and social distinctions, and the rise and fall of Napoleon. These stirring times found an echo in England in an outburst of romantic literature. Byron, Shelley, and Keats were doing in poetry what other writers were doing in prose. By 1830, however, the tide of romance was beginning to ebb. A new age of reason was being ushered in. Intellectualism gained ground against sentimentality. Discoveries of science gave new impetus to the movement, so that by the accession of Queen Victoria in 1837 the ground had been prepared for a new kind of literature. Victorian literature, it was called in England, and though realism never attained the vogue there that it did in France, most of the English writers of this period show the trend of the times.

George Eliot was not interested in the actual facts of life for their own sake, as are many of the realists, but as a means to the discovery of an underlying purpose that will explain life. She was first of all a moralist. Actions reflect what is going on in the mind, and the mind was her battle-ground, the real setting for her stories. As the historical novel tends to be romantic, so the psychological novel that deals with states of mind tends to be realistic. The actions of the persons involved are limited by their own characters. The author dare not go beyond that even for the sake of being interesting. Romantic writers often have a wicked character reform in a moment and reap the rewards of his conversion; but the realist knows that is not reasonable. The habits and thoughts of a life-time cannot be discarded without a long struggle. To be convincing, the psychological novel must be true to the facts of mental life as well as accurate in the presentation of action and in the description of persons and places.

## 2. Analysis of the Novel

A novel, like a short story, may be analyzed on the basis of plot, character, and setting. Usually one of these factors predominates. Sometimes a fourth factor enters in: thesis, or the moral the author wishes to convey. Most of the great writers, like Shakespeare, strive for no definite lesson; the very truthfulness of their picture of life is sufficient, for life is the greatest of teachers. Among those who write fiction with the frank purpose of driving home a moral, George Eliot comes closer to artistic success than the average. Not only do her fidelity of characterization and vividness of setting win our interest, but even her moral comment, so searching and honest, has a certain appeal absent from most thesis fiction.

Because of the broad scope of a novel, an author can, if he chooses, carry his chief characters through experiences that leave him a far different man at the end from what he was at the beginning. This is called character development. *Silas Marner* covers a period of more than thirty years. During that time Silas has grown from a young man to a man of fifty-five. And he looks even older. His experiences have aged and changed him. He has a different outlook on life. The progress of this transformation is the most interesting feature of the novel, as it is in all novels whose emphasis is on character rather than plot or setting. Plot in *Silas Marner* holds a very minor position. The real movement of the story is in the realm of the mental, not the physical. Setting, because it has a very definite influence on character, is second in importance to character.

Point of view is another factor to be considered. The story may be told in the first person from the point of view of one or more of the characters; or it may be told in the third person from the point of view of an author who assumes knowledge not only of what is happening in various places but of what is passing through the minds of all the characters. Now, it is obvious that a psychological novel of the *Silas Marner* type cannot be related by one of the participants in the story. It must be told by the author if the mental processes of the characters are to be revealed. If Silas Marner or Godfrey Cass had told the story of the weaver of Raveloe, think what we should have lost, for neither could have known what the other was thinking. Stories of adventure and vigorous action, on the contrary, often gain in vividness by the use of the first person, for the "I" puts the reader on familiar terms with the narrator.

For emphasis a novelist sometimes starts his story with a passage of exciting action; still more often he brings it to an end with a dramatic flourish. George Eliot scorns both these devices. She begins *Silas Marner* in a leisurely fashion and concludes it in a quiet key. Throughout she makes no attempt to surprise the reader. If she does not tell outright what is to happen, one can usually conjecture. Rightly, she relies on suspense, not mystery, for the effectiveness of a psychological novel.

Of one expedient, however, she makes abundant use, almost to the point of abuse. That is contrast (or antithesis) not only between characters but between sets of circumstances. Note a few of them: the "staring white-faced creatur" that is Silas and the laughing golden-haired child; the naturally good, though weak, Godfrey and his wholly vicious brother, Dunstan; the sweet, beautiful Nancy Lammeter and her homely, good-natured sister, Priscilla; the splendid hospitality at Squire Cass's mansion on New Year's Eve and the tragic atmosphere at the Stone-pits, hard by Silas's rude cottage.

Technique, or the author's method of construction, and literary style are to be considered in any study of a novel, but since these are so closely related to the work itself, they will be treated later in the section devoted to The Story. There remains a final estimate of the lasting value of a literary production. Some novels, stories, and plays have a contemporary interest only; that is, they deal with certain subjects in such a way that only the people of that era find them absorbing. "Dated" is the term critics are accustomed to apply to such narratives, for in form and content they belong to an earlier age than ours. Though George Eliot drew characters that belonged to a small circle (the English midland counties) and though she treated the problems of her time with the spirit and point of view of her time, her novels, while not widely popular now, have a permanent interest.

Her characters may be extremely individual, yet have an undeniable trace of the universal in them. They typify, to a certain degree, the physical and mental traits of a class that is always with us: the humble workers of the world, sometimes ignorant yet with a faculty of driving straight to the heart of a matter as if instinct had taken the place of reasoning. Though customs and manners have changed, even the petty aristocracy of Raveloe, represented by Squire Cass, has its counterpart today. As for the problems presented—our own age has not outgrown the moral issues dealt with in *Silas Marner;* for George Eliot was one of the first "moderns."

# SILAS MARNER

## GEORGE ELIOT

## 1819–1880

### THE AUTHOR

The assistant editor of *The Westminster Review,* a periodical devoted to the expression of liberal thought, sat in her lodgings in the Strand, London, and looked disconsolately at the thick German volume at her side. Mary Ann Evans, or Marian Evans as she preferred to be called, was dispirited. The very notion of reading and abridging that ponderous book sickened her. A review of an article on taxation was awaiting her editorial pencil. Her sense of duty, always strong, reminded her that her own translation of Feuerbach's *Essence of Christianity* was still in an incomplete state. Tomorrow there would be meetings of associations, interviews with authors, great and near-great, and perhaps an hour stolen from her tasks for a chat with that brilliant young man, George Henry Lewes, whom Mr. Herbert Spencer, the eminent philosopher, had recently introduced to her.

She was enjoying her associations with the famous literary men of the period, among them Carlyle; J. S. Mill, the political economist; Francis Newman (whom she called "our blessed St. Francis"); and Froude, the historian. Yet in spite of herself the interminable procession of dull pages waiting for her revision had begun to weary her. Even her own interest in science and philosophy could not brighten the gloom of some of those articles. She wondered why. Could it be true that the ripening friendship with Mr. Lewes was distracting her attention from daily tasks?

It was an autumn day in 1853. Already the shadows were beginning to fall across the manuscript pages on the desk before her. But it was more than the dusk that blurred the characters. In imagination she sped back through the years to her childhood in Warwickshire, when with her brother she had rambled through the meadows bordering the canal and searched for gypsy camps in the little groves of that midland county. The district had not the charm of southern England or the eerie fascination of the moorlands to the north where for miles the silence was unbroken save for the bleat of shaggy-haired sheep. For pictures of that region we must read the novels of the Brontë sisters. Where Marian Evans lived, midway between Nuneaton and Coventry, there were no mountains or lakes or rivers; simply a landscape of fields and hedgerows whose monotony was interrupted by an occasional thicket, canal, coal pit, and a few industrial towns where hand-looms hummed from morning till night.

A plain, unpretentious country, yet Marian Evans found a quiet joy in its recollection. Her father had been agent for one of the rural estates, and she had often accompanied him on his trips through the country. From these jaunts she had stored up memories of solid, conservative Britishers, stubborn, unchanging, yet most human; of country squires carrying on the tradition of English hospitality in their park-surrounded mansions; of red-cheeked buxom lasses courted by awkward swains, and of motherly matrons not quite effaced by their domestic slavery. She remembered them now with affection, these rural friends of her youth, though she no longer held their unquestioning faith or believed life so simple as she once had done.

The years had brought a great change to Marian Evans. After an adequate schooling in a village near her home and later at Nuneaton, a rather drab town at the outskirts of England's great industrial district, she had continued her education at Coventry. Some years after the death of her mother she and her father went there to live. Though Coventry was not far from her birthplace, she met a different kind of society—men and women who were interested in philosophical and moral problems, many of them liberal in their thought, indeed radical compared with the people among whom she had grown up. Her own temperament was reflective, and she was soon pondering many of the religious questions of the day. The time came when her religious doubts threatened a serious break with her father, but the two were soon reconciled and lived together until his death in 1849.

Having had a thorough grounding in French and German, she read much foreign literature, and when only twenty-five began the translation of Strauss's *Life of Christ*. Her ripening talents soon caught the attention of discerning critics. Following the publication of one of her articles in *The Westminster Review* for January, 1851, she was offered the post of assistant editor and promptly accepted. Though for the past three years she had lived in a literary atmosphere, her own creative genius was scarcely realized. Perhaps this present dissatisfaction with the dull manuscripts before her was due in part to a suppressed desire for a fuller expression than editorial labors permitted.

These memories came thronging upon her that autumn afternoon; yet woven into them was a name, a face, that she could not banish. George Henry Lewes, unhappily married and deserted, had first admired, then loved Marian Evans. She could not deny to herself that she returned his affection; yet what was she to do? Flaunt convention, exile herself from the properly shocked society of London, and cleave to the man she loved; or sink into herself, forego his needful companionship, and try to forget? Soon she must decide.

Whatever judgment one may pass on Marian Evans, she was a woman of high moral purpose and an almost burdening sense of duty. When she violated age-old ordinances and joined in partnership with Lewes, she felt justified by a higher law than her critics ever dreamed of. From that July day in 1854 when she left England with Lewes for a stay in Germany, until his death in 1878, they lived an almost ideal romance. The dedication of George Eliot's novel *Romola* reveals the true nature of their attachment: "To the Husband, whose perfect love has been the best source of her insight and strength, this manuscript is given by his devoted wife, the writer."

This is not extravagant praise. It was Lewes who discovered Marian Evans' talent and inspired her to attempt the writing of fiction. Near the end of 1856 Lewes sent his wife's first story, *The Sad Fortunes of the Rev. Amos Barton,* to John Blackwood, editor of *Blackwood's Magazine,* telling him it was the work of a talented friend, George Eliot by name. This was the first use of the pseudonym, or pen name, under which all her later novels were to be published. When the story appeared the following January, all the great writers of the time hailed a new genius. Only Dickens, however, had the insight to discern that the writer was a woman. *The Sad Fortunes of the Rev. Amos Barton* was the first of a series of narratives later collected as *Scenes from Clerical Life.* Most of the scenes and portraits were authentic, being remembered from childhood days in Warwickshire.

From this beginning George Eliot went on to greater things. Before five years had passed, *Adam Bede, The Mill on the Floss,* and *Silas Marner* had been published. After two visits to Florence, Italy, she wrote the historical novel *Romola,* for which a publisher offered the astounding sum of $50,000. *Felix Holt, The Spanish Gypsy* (a dramatic poem), *Middlemarch,* and *Daniel Deronda* followed. These, with essays, sketches, and poems, comprise her productions. Though not a large output, compared to the works of Scott, Thackeray, and Dickens, it elevated her to the front rank of nineteenth century novelists. That George Eliot is not so widely read today as are her contemporaries is not surprising, for her insistence on the relation of art and morals (that is, the principle that a novel should present some noble teaching) does not appeal to modern taste. Indeed, it is obvious that her works suffer from an artistic point of view because of her increasing intentness on ethical problems.

When Lewes died, George Eliot was prostrated. His encouragement had meant much to her. He had been a kindly critic and a beloved husband. Now she felt much alone. In her bereavement a friend, Mrs. Cross, gave her sympathy and understanding. In May, 1880, George Eliot married Mrs. Cross's son, John Walter Cross. Before the year was out, she died. Though their union had been short-lived, Cross immediately devoted himself to the writing of a three-volume life of George Eliot as told chiefly in her own letters and diaries. Most of our knowledge of the novelist has come from this source.

A lofty but mediocre poet, a conscientious but uninspired essayist, George Eliot found her happiest literary expression in the medium of the novel. Here her deep and sympathetic understanding of human nature was reflected in the words and deeds of intensely human characters.

Before leaving George Eliot, let us have a word portrait of her from the pen of Leslie Stephen.

"Her personal appearance was intellectually attractive, and had a peculiar pathetic charm. She looked fragile, overweighted perhaps by thought, and with traces of the depression of which she so often complains in her letters. Her abundant hair, auburn-brown, in later years streaked with grey, was covered by a kind of lace mantilla. She could not be called beautiful, [but her gaze] was one 'in which simple human fellowship expressed itself as a strongly-felt bond.' . . . Her features were strongly marked, with a rather large mouth and jaw; her eyes a grey-blue, with very variable expression; her hands were finely formed; her voice low and very musical—a 'contralto,' it is said in singing; and the whole appearance expressive of a singular combination of power with intense sensibility."

## IMPORTANT DATES IN GEORGE ELIOT'S LIFE

| | |
|---|---|
| 1819 | Born at Arbury Farm, Warwickshire, England |
| 1820 | Moved to Griff, nearby |
| 1825 | Sent to school at Attleboro, a neighboring village |
| 1827 | Sent to school at Nuneaton |
| 1832 | Sent to school at Coventry |
| 1836 | Death of George Eliot's mother, Mrs. Evans |
| 1840 | Publication of first verses in *Christian Observer* |
| 1841 | Moved to Coventry with her father |
| 1844–1846 | Translating Strauss's *Life of Christ* |
| 1849 | Death of George Eliot's father |
| 1849–1850 | Sojourn in Geneva, Switzerland |
| 1851–1854 | Assistant editor of *Westminster Review* |
| 1854 | Translation of Feuerbach's *Essence of Christianity* |
| 1854 | Union with George Henry Lewes |
| 1858 | *Scenes from Clerical Life* |
| 1858 | *Adam Bede* |
| 1860 | *The Mill on the Floss* |
| 1861 | *Silas Marner* |
| 1863 | *Romola* |
| 1866 | *Felix Holt* |
| 1868 | *The Spanish Gypsy* |
| 1872 | *Middlemarch* |
| 1876 | *Daniel Deronda* |
| 1878 | Death of George Henry Lewes |
| 1880, May | Marriage to J. W. Cross |
| 1880, Dec. | Died in Chelsea, London |

## THE STORY

### 1. The Type

In the Introduction George Eliot has been classified as a realistic writer. In comparison with such thoroughly romantic authors as Sir Walter Scott she undoubtedly belongs to the school which seeks to paint people as they are and events as they happen; but one cannot place all English writers into definite groups. The boundary lines overlap. Something of the romantic tradition remains in *Silas Marner,* yet the impression the author leaves is one of genuine realism.

Among the first things the reader will notice in this novel is the author's preoccupation with states of mind. The events that occur are not half so important as the effect of those events upon the characters. We are really more interested in what Silas Marner and Godfrey Cass think about the things that happen to them than in the things themselves. It is only natural, therefore, that the physical plot should be slender. You can tell the outward story of *Silas Marner* in a few sentences, but such a recital would miss the chief significance.

In this type of writing, the psychological novel, few have equalled George Eliot. The type itself necessitates a certain kind of realism. The characters must look and act like real persons. Their reasoning and their actions must be logical and convincing, or the reader will reject the whole book. In *Silas Marner* the actions of the characters flow from their own natures. The author has conceived the characters and invented the situations, but she is not free to tell them how they shall meet these situations. They must go their own way, for better or worse. In a sense, they have become independent of the author.

Silas acts as he does because his mind works that way. The same is true of the other persons, even down to the simple villagers. Their actions ring true. You could not expect them to behave differently. Heredity and environment and their own natures hold them inexorably to the course they follow, as Fate drove the heroes in Greek drama. Life in Raveloe follows the old grooves. Custom and prejudice and faith have been handed down through generations. The surroundings of the village prescribe a certain mode of living. Cause and effect. That is George Eliot's creed.

The very scene chosen by the novelist shows the trend toward realism. Here is a bit of genuine English landscape inhabited by recognizable English people. No knights on snorting chargers. No fair ladies imprisoned in castles. No heroes out of ancient times possessing all the virtues. Just simple country folk, rude in speech and dress, hard-headed, with the good and bad mixed in them, yet with few exceptions appealing to our sympathy and liking. We smile at them it is true, for the author presents their short-comings with delicious irony. But we don't grow bitter. George Eliot never patronizes her characters. She meets them on their own ground, and no note of superiority or contempt creeps into her portrayal.

If the setting is not remote, neither is the time, from George Eliot's point of view. Except for the "cut-back" to Silas's early life, the period covered by the novel is that of the author's own youth. She is reporting from her own memory and observation. She well recalls the era of economic depression that followed the Napoleonic Wars. Faces from her childhood float into her mind and thence into the pages of the book. Though imaginatively presented, people and places and time are real—authentic pictures far removed from the elaborately touched-up canvases of *Ivanhoe*.

There is another mark of realism in *Silas Marner*. In spite of a passion for inserting her own reflections on situations and their moral significance, George Eliot leaves her characters severely alone. They live, move, and have their being in their own world. The author does not weep over their sorrows or laugh at their follies. They are presented objectively, without the intrusion of the novelist's own personality. Because of this strict detachment, George Eliot never becomes sentimental. Here are these people, she is saying to the reader; let them win your tears or your smiles if they can. I will not interfere. So faithfully does George Eliot keep to this principle that we have an illusion of their actual existence, as if the roofs of their little cottages were transparent and from above we watched their comings and goings.

It is interesting to note that practically all the characters are in the grip of strong religious convictions. Though the author herself had long since abandoned orthodox beliefs, pinning her faith to a principle of creative goodness in human nature, she realized that to these people their conceptions of God and the hereafter were indisputable realities, necessary for their contentment in life. She does not scoff, even though she disbelieves; even though she knows the reader will disbelieve, for there is much of the purely superstitious in the Raveloe creed. This, too, is a detachment rarely found among romantic writers.

So much for the realistic elements in *Silas Marner*. There are also traces of romance. Some realists complain that George Eliot too much ignores the more brutal aspect of life in Raveloe. They would have her tell all, even emphasize the drab and the vicious. The true realist, however, does not need to be a photographer. He also may choose his detail so long as that detail is faithful to character and period and general conditions. It is enough for George Eliot's purpose to *suggest* the other side of the picture in the brief history of Molly. The novelist's restraint in avoiding too idealized pictures on the one hand and too degraded pictures on the other is in keeping with true realism. We must look elsewhere for romantic tendencies.

George Eliot worked on the old romantic principle that good is always rewarded and evil always punished. Though she would doubtlessly call it cause and effect, it is nothing more than a modern adaptation of retribution. Note how all the important characters in *Silas Marner* get their just deserts in direct proportion to their sins and good deeds. Silas Marner atones with fifteen years of solitude for his lapse from faith. Only when he devotes himself to a little waif do happiness and his stolen gold return. Godfrey Cass, too weak-willed to confess the one great sin of his youth, may marry the lady of his choice but is denied the blessing of children and must hear his daughter by a first marriage call another Father. Molly, the drug addict, whom Godfrey married in an evil moment, takes an overdose of laudanum and dies in the snow. But Dunstan Cass is the worst sinner. He blackmails his brother after maneuvering him into the disgraceful marriage. He steals Silas's gold. The fate that overtakes him is in keeping with the enormity of his crimes.

In the character of Dunstan there is another suspicion of romanticism. Though George Eliot has no idealized heroes such as appear in *Ivanhoe* and *The Tale of Two Cities,* she has come perilously near the type of melodramatic villain. Dunstan is all black. No slight gleam of goodness or decency shines through his wickedness. He serves his evil purpose in the plot and disappears, unlamented.

Distinguish carefully between the acts of the persons and the events which the author has invented and over which the persons have no control. In *Silas Marner* the actions performed by the persons themselves grow out of their characters. It is the external happenings devised by the author in the name of retribution (a realist would call it Chance) that force the moral George Eliot wishes to teach. In her role of narrator she introduces events that will prove her theory of the consequences of right and wrong. Long ago the author of the Book of Job raised such doubts concerning the justice man receives in this life that it is debatable whether or not a realist should carry the principle of retribution to the extreme attempted by George Eliot.

## 2. The Background

"In the early years of this century . . ." wrote George Eliot, "a linen weaver, named Silas Marner, worked at his vocation . . . near the village of Raveloe." Thus the chief character, the period, and the setting of the story are at once established. Though the novelist was not born until near the end of the second decade of the eighteenth century, she must have heard a great deal about the years that had preceded.

At the very turn of the century Napoleon had suddenly made himself all-powerful in France. He had dreams of conquering the world, like Alexander. The wars that he waged in his great project brought to England a prosperity she had rarely known. She grew exceedingly rich by selling food and supplies to the continental armies. Agriculture and industry flourished. It was easy to make a living, and there was employment for everybody. People were content not only with themselves but with their government, for England had made herself supreme on the seas and her armies had been victorious in Spain.

By the time Silas Marner lost his gold, however, conditions had changed. The end of the Napoleonic Wars, following the final defeat of Bonaparte at Waterloo in 1815, instead of ushering in an age of plenty brought suffering and poverty and unrest. The rise of the factory with its machines that could do the work of many men made unemployment a serious problem now that the boom of the war period had passed. Prices fell. The government was controlled by the land-owning class, and there were few laws to protect the working men. The death penalty was imposed for hundreds of offenses. Riots occurred. At length, the ministry was forced to introduce laws giving more power to the common people. This democratic movement was greatly aided by the Reform Bill of 1832 which decreased the representation of the landed gentry in the House of Commons and transferred power to the middle class. From that time on, the growth of democracy in England was rapid. When Victoria, a girl of eighteen, came to the throne in 1837, she regained through her charm and dignity much of the popularity of the Crown lost under Georges III and IV.

There were some sections of England, however, in which only the echo of these events was heard. Off the main routes of travel, these communities kept to their old customs. Men lived, worked, and died as their fathers and grandfathers had done before them. The new factory system meant little to them. The village was self-sustaining. Food was obtained from the fields and dairies. Hand-work, done by artisans in their own homes or little shops, provided the necessities of life. The women not only helped with the farming but spun thread and sometimes wove cloth, though there were professional weavers, like Silas Marner, who were patronized by those who could afford it. The roads were none too good. Travel was mainly by horseback or wagon, and few cared to undertake the discomforts of a long journey. Nearly three-quarters of a century was to pass before the introduction of the telephone. The only means of communication was the mail, carried by post-riders or stage; but who was there to write to such remote villagers?

In these communities there was usually one man who owned most of the land. Like others of his class he had little faith in democratic government. The land owners should rule. In prosperous times, the squire, as he was called, had an easy time of it. He hired men to work his fields or rented his property to tenants. His hospitality was lavish, as the New Year's Eve party given by Squire Cass at Red House bears witness. When prosperity waned, however, a great many country gentlemen found their estates badly encumbered. They had farmed poorly and lived extravagantly. With the drop in rents and prices, it was often impossible to keep the estate together, and it diminished acre by acre leaving the owner proud but poor.

Raveloe was such a village. It was "nestled in a snug well-wooded hollow, quite an hour's journey on horseback from any turnpike, where it was never reached by the vibrations of the coach-horn or of public opinion." Physically isolated, it was also intellectually remote from the trend of current thought. Its people held to the orthodox views of the Church of England without bothering their heads about the "movement," that is, the separation of a group, commonly called Dissenters, who disapproved of some of the forms and beliefs of the established church. The Dissenters, themselves divided into several sects such as the Methodists, Presbyterians, and Baptists, were at first forbidden to congregate and had to worship in secret. Later they were granted religious freedom but were still subjected to some persecution. Their houses of worship were called "chapels," to distinguish them from the "churches" of the regular faith. Although the new movement was apparently well under way in Lantern Yard during Silas Marner's youth, the people of Raveloe had scarcely heard of it. Even Dolly Winthrop thought Silas no better than a heathen when she learned some of his earlier beliefs.

On the surface, life in Raveloe seems serene, but when George Eliot lifts the veil, one sees that in spite of different manners and customs, the residents have much the same problems that we have today. Intimately connected with the setting as the story is, the moral issues rise above Raveloe and leap the bounds of the nineteenth century. They have a significance for all times and for all peoples.

## 3. The Technique

Some critics have called *Silas Marner* George Eliot's masterpiece. The novel was finished in February, 1861, when the author was thirty-nine and nearing the height of her powers. Though it is much shorter than most of her works, her art seems to have been improved by space limitation. There is in it a nobility of conception brightened by a vein of rich humor. The character analysis, in which she always excelled, is well-nigh perfect. Dialogue is brisk, most of it in the dialect of the region. Notwithstanding the moral tags and even distribution of penalties and rewards, one feels that the progress of the action is both logical and inevitable. To produce such results, a mind capable of great intellectual power and deep sympathy must have been brought to bear on the problem.

George Eliot's technique, or method of construction, appears to better advantage in *Silas Marner* than in almost anything else she ever wrote. The plot is compact, beautifully wrought, and admirably adapted to her purpose: the unfolding of character and the emphasizing of a moral. If the reader looks beneath the surface of the story, he will find two series of events, at first unrelated to each other, then linked by a single character, and finally tied together by a major knot. Instead of telling the story as a whole in strict time order, with all the characters grouped together, George Eliot has separated the story into two strands which meet at various points and finally unite permanently. This is not uncommon in a novel; sometimes there are three or more stories thus woven together, but one of them usually predominates in interest and importance.

In *Silas Marner* the incidents in the life of the weaver form the first and most important strand of the plot. The events surrounding life at the Cass mansion form the second. The two are brought into contact by Dunstan and later by Eppie, child of Godfrey Cass's secret marriage. The strands separate for a time but always return. The chief purpose behind the movement of both strands is the redemption of Silas from his hopeless, ingrowing self.

The literary style of the novel is suitable to the subject and method, yet is not particularly distinguished. Crisp and life-like in the dialogue passages, it tends to become involved whenever the author takes up the narration or interposes analytical comment. It is rarely brilliant, though at times the reader is stimulated by the accuracy with which a thought is expressed. George Eliot is never a stylist. She uses few striking turns of phrase or novel devices of vocabulary and diction. There is none of the tricky punctuation, such as dots, stars, and spacing, popular with many writers today. It is simply a serviceable style in the conventional Victorian manner. Beyond that we need not look.

For the thoughtful reader George Eliot has an elusive charm quite different from that of her more widely-read contemporaries. Moralist she may be, but her knowledge of the hearts and minds of a certain class of society and her sure handling of psychology strike a responsive chord in our own feelings and intellects. Though we are told she was subject to fits of depression, there is a strain of optimism in all her novels, a conviction that at the last good will emerge triumphant. William Blake was of the opinion that because Milton wrote better of Satan and his demons than of God and His angels, the poet was on the side of the devil without knowing it. By the same token one may also venture the guess that because George Eliot wrote more easily of good than she did of evil, she was, for all her religious heresy, on the side of heaven. And this, let us hasten to add, is independent of the lectures on ethics and morals with which she so frequently adorns her narratives.*

* Because *Silas Marner* presents problems of a more difficult nature than the student has hitherto met in his study of literature, it is suggested that this introductory material be assigned for reading only, prior to a study of the novel itself, and that it be carefully studied at the conclusion of the work on this section.

# SILAS MARNER:
## THE WEAVER OF RAVELOE

## PART I

### CHAPTER I

In the days when the spinning-wheels hummed busily in the farmhouses—and even great ladies, clothed in silk and thread-lace, had their toy spinning-wheels of polished oak—there might be seen, in districts far away among the lanes, or deep in the bosom of the hills, certain pallid undersized men, who, by the side of the brawny country-folk, looked like the remnants of a disinherited race. The shepherd's dog barked fiercely when one of these alien-looking men appeared on the upland, dark against the early winter sunset; for what dog likes a figure bent under a heavy bag?—and these pale men rarely stirred abroad without that mysterious burden. The shepherd himself, though he had good reason to believe that the bag held nothing but flaxen thread, or else the long rolls of strong linen spun from that thread, was not quite sure that this trade of weaving, indispensable though it was, could be carried on entirely without the help of the Evil One. In that far-off time superstition clung easily round every person or thing that was at all unwonted, or even intermittent and occasional merely, like the visits of the pedlar or the knife-grinder. No one knew where wandering men had their homes or their origin; and how was a man to be explained unless you at least knew somebody who knew his father and mother? To the peasants of old times, the world outside their own direct experience was a region of vagueness and mystery: to their untravelled thought a state of wandering was a conception as dim as the winter life of the swallows that came back with the spring; and even a settler, if he came from distant parts, hardly ever ceased to be viewed with a remnant of distrust, which would have prevented any surprise if a long course of inoffensive conduct on his part had ended in the commission of a crime; especially if he had any reputation for knowledge, or showed any skill in handicraft. All cleverness, whether in the rapid use of that difficult instrument the tongue, or in some other art unfamiliar to villagers, was in itself suspicious: honest folk, born and bred in a visible manner, were mostly not overwise or clever—at least, not beyond such a matter as knowing the signs of the weather; and the process by which rapidity and dexterity of any kind were acquired was so wholly hidden that they partook of the nature of conjuring. In this way it came to pass that those scattered linen-weavers—emigrants from the town into the country—were to the last regarded as aliens by their rustic neighbors, and usually contracted the eccentric habits which belong to a state of loneliness.

In the early years of this century, such a linen-weaver, named Silas Marner, worked at his vocation in a stone cottage that stood among the nutty hedgerows near the village of Raveloe, and not far from the edge of a deserted stone-pit.[1] The questionable sound of Silas's loom, so unlike the natural cheerful trotting of the winnowing-machine, or the simpler rhythm of the flail, had a half-fearful fascination for the Raveloe boys, who would often leave off their nutting or birds'-nesting to peep in at the window of the stone cottage, counterbalancing a certain awe at the mysterious action of the loom by a pleasant sense of scornful superiority, drawn from the mockery of its alternating noises, along with the bent, tread-mill attitude of the weaver. But sometimes it happened that Marner, pausing to adjust an irregularity in his thread, became aware of the small scoundrels, and, though chary of his time, he liked their intrusion so ill that he would descend from his loom, and, opening the door, would fix on them a gaze that was always enough to make them take to their legs in terror. For how was it possible to believe that those large brown protuberant eyes in Silas Marner's pale face really saw nothing very distinctly that was not close to them, and not rather that their dreadful stare could dart cramp,[2] or rickets, or a wry mouth at any boy who happened to be in the rear? They had, perhaps, heard their fathers and mothers hint that Silas Marner could cure folks' rheumatism if he had a mind, and add, still more darkly, that if you could only speak the devil fair[3] enough, he might save you the cost of the doctor. Such strange lingering echoes of the old demon-worship might perhaps even now be caught by the diligent listener among

[1] Deserted stone-pit—Abandoned stone quarry. Remember this feature of the surroundings, for it plays an important part in the story.

[2] Dart cramp, etc.—Cast a spell, in the form of these bodily ailments.

[3] Speak the devil fair—Speak well of Silas lest he bewitch you.

the gray-haired peasantry; for the rude mind with difficulty associates the ideas of power and benignity. A shadowy conception of power that by much persuasion can be induced to refrain from inflicting harm, is the shape most easily taken by the sense of the Invisible in the minds of men who have always been pressed close by primitive wants,[4] and to whom a life of hard toil has never been illuminated by any enthusiastic religious faith.[5] To them pain and mishap present a far wider range of possibilities than gladness and enjoyment: their imagination is almost barren of the images that feed desire and hope, but is all overgrown by recollections that are a perpetual pasture to fear. "Is there anything you can fancy that you would like to eat?" I once said to an old laboring man, who was in his last illness, and who had refused all the food his wife had offered him. "No," he answered, "I've never been used to nothing but common victual, and I can't eat that." Experience had bred no fancies in him that could raise the phantasm of appetite.

And Raveloe was a village where many of the old echoes lingered, undrowned by new voices. Not that it was one of those barren parishes lying on the outskirts of civilization—inhabited by meagre sheep and thinly scattered shepherds: on the contrary, it lay in the rich central plain of what we are pleased to call Merry England, and held farms which, speaking from a spiritual point of view, paid highly desirable tithes.[6] But it was nestled in a snug well-wooded hollow, quite an hour's journey on horseback from any turnpike, where it was never reached by the vibrations of the coach-horn or of public opinion. It was an important-looking village, with a fine old church and large churchyard in the heart of it, and two or three large brick-and-stone homesteads, with well-walled orchards and ornamental weathercocks, standing close upon the road, and lifting more imposing fronts than the rectory, which peeped from among the trees on the other side of the churchyard,—a village which showed at once the summits of its social life, and told the practised eye that there was no great park and manor-

[4] PRIMITIVE WANTS—Bare necessities of life.

[5] ENTHUSIASTIC RELIGIOUS FAITH—A reference to the religious awakening brought about by the Wesleys, Whitefield, and others. Although George Eliot had lost the simple faith of her youth, she realized that even the superstitions of these narrow-minded people should be looked upon with compassion, for they were part of an inherited tradition. In this passage, the author momentarily forsakes the role of narrator for that of moralist.

[6] TITHES—A tenth part of the yearly harvest was commonly given to the church.

house[7] in the vicinity, but that there were several chiefs in Raveloe who could farm badly quite at their ease,[8] drawing enough money from their bad farming, in those war times, to live in a rollicking fashion, and keep a jolly Christmas, Whitsun,[9] and Easter tide.

It was fifteen years since Silas Marner had first come to Raveloe; he was then simply a pallid young man, with prominent, short-sighted brown eyes, whose appearance would have had nothing strange for people of average culture and experience, but for the villagers near whom he had come to settle it had mysterious peculiarities which corresponded with the exceptional nature of his occupation and his advent from an unknown region called "North'ard." So had his way of life:—he invited no comer to step across his door-sill, and he never strolled into the village to drink a pint at the Rainbow,[10] or to gossip at the wheelwright's; he sought no man or woman, save for the purposes of his calling, or in order to supply himself with necessaries; and it was soon clear to the Raveloe lasses that he would never urge one of them to accept him against her will—quite as if he had heard them declare that they would never marry a dead man come to life again. This view of Marner's personality was not without another ground than his pale face and unexampled eyes; for Jem Rodney, the mole-catcher, averred that, one evening as he was returning homeward, he saw Silas Marner leaning against a stile with a heavy bag on his back, instead of resting the bag on the stile as a man in his senses would have done; and that, on coming up to him, he saw that Marner's eyes were set like a dead man's, and he spoke to him, and shook him, and his limbs were stiff, and his hands clutched the bag as if they'd been made of iron; but just as he had made up his mind that the weaver was dead, he came all right again, like, as you might say, in the winking of an eye, and said "Good-night," and walked off. All this Jem swore he

---

[7] No great park and manor-house—This indicates that the society of Raveloe did not rank very high, for if any of the great nobles had possessed estates in this neighborhood, there would have been the customary manor-house surrounded by a park. There are only two social classes represented in Raveloe: the moderately well-off land owners, such as Squire Cass, and the peasants. This condition was typical of rural English life in such remote places as Raveloe.

[8] Who could farm badly quite at their ease—At the time of the Napoleonic wars the prices of grain and raw materials exported by England to the Continent were so high that English farmers could still make a profit with slipshod methods and small crops.

[9] Whitsun—The seventh Sunday after Easter.

[10] The Rainbow—Name of the village tavern.

had seen, more by token that it was the very day he had been mole-catching on Squire Cass's land, down by the old saw-pit. Some said Marner must have been in a "fit," a word which seemed to explain things otherwise incredible; but the argumentative Mr. Macey, clerk of the parish, shook his head, and asked if anybody was ever known to go off in a fit and not fall down. A fit was a stroke, wasn't it? and it was in the nature of a stroke to partly take away the use of a man's limbs and throw him on the parish, if he'd got no children to look to. No, no; it was no stroke that would let a man stand on his legs, like a horse between the shafts, and then walk off as soon as you can say "Gee!" But there might be such a thing as a man's soul being loose from his body,[11] and going out and in, like a bird out of its nest and back; and that was how folks got overwise, for they went to school in this shell-less state to those who could teach them more than their neighbors could learn with their five senses and the parson.[12] And where did Master Marner get his knowledge of herbs from—and charms, too, if he liked to give them away? Jem Rodney's story was no more than what might have been expected by anybody who had seen how Marner had cured Sally Oates, and made her sleep like a baby, when her heart had been beating enough to burst her body for two months and more, while she had been under the doctor's care. He might cure more folks if he would; but he was worth speaking fair, if it was only to keep him from doing you a mischief.

It was partly to this vague fear that Marner was indebted for protecting him from the persecution that his singularities might have drawn upon him, but still more to the fact that, the old linen-weaver in the neighboring parish of Tarley being dead, his handicraft made him a highly welcome settler to the richer housewives of the district, and even to the more provident cottagers, who had their little stock of yarn at the year's end. Their sense of his usefulness would have counteracted any repugnance or suspicion which was not confirmed by a deficiency in the quality or the tale[13] of the cloth he wove for them. And the years had rolled on

[11] SOUL . . . LOOSE FROM HIS BODY—Mr. Macey's unwillingness to accept a rational explanation of the fit that overtakes Silas must have been typical of most, if not all, the inhabitants of this superstitious community. In what follows note other incidents that seem to support the villagers' belief in the weaver's supernatural powers.

[12] WENT TO SCHOOL . . . THE PARSON—In a disembodied (shell-less) state people were taught supernatural things, probably by Satan himself.

[13] THE TALE—The count; hence, the amount.

without producing any change in the impressions of the neighbors concerning Marner, except the change from novelty to habit. At the end of fifteen years the Raveloe men said just the same things about Silas Marner as at the beginning; they did not say them quite so often, but they believed them much more strongly when they did say them. There was only one important addition which the years had brought: it was, that Master Marner had laid by a fine sight of money somewhere, and that he could buy up "bigger men" than himself.

But while opinion concerning him had remained nearly stationary, and his daily habits had presented scarcely any visible change, Marner's inward life had been a history and a metamorphosis,[14] as that of every fervid nature must be when it has fled, or been condemned, to solitude. His life, before he came to Raveloe,[15] had been filled with the movement, the mental activity, and the close fellowship, which, in that day as in this, marked the life of an artisan early incorporated in a narrow religious sect, where the poorest layman has the chance of distinguishing himself by gifts of speech, and has, at the very least, the weight of a silent voter in the government of his community. Marner was highly thought of in that little hidden world, known to itself as the church assembling in Lantern Yard;[16] he was believed to be a young man of exemplary life and ardent faith; and a peculiar interest had been centred in him ever since he had fallen, at a prayer-meeting, into a mysterious rigidity and suspension of consciousness, which, lasting for an hour or more, had been mistaken for death. To have sought a medical explanation for this phenomenon would have been held by Silas himself, as well as by his minister and fellow-members, a willful self-exclusion from the spiritual significance[17] that might lie therein. Silas was evidently

---

[14] METAMORPHOSIS—Change.

[15] BEFORE HE CAME TO RAVELOE—Note George Eliot's method of introducing Silas. Having presented him in the surroundings in which the main action will occur, she drops back fifteen years to reveal, as in a "cut-back" in a motion picture, the events of his early life.

[16] LANTERN YARD—A small neighborhood, hidden at the end of a dark, narrow alley, in the industrial town where Silas had lived.

[17] SPIRITUAL SIGNIFICANCE—This is a different explanation from that offered by Mr. Macey of Raveloe. Mr. Macey is superstitious through simple ignorance, and fears evil powers. The friends of Silas at Lantern Yard are pious—too pious to deny the possible spiritual significance of his seizure. To Raveloe it is the Devil; to Lantern Yard it is God. Neither accepts fully such a simple explanation as sickness.

a brother selected for a peculiar discipline; and though the effort to interpret this discipline was discouraged by the absence, on his part, of any spiritual vision during his outward trance, yet it was believed by himself and others that its effect was seen in an accession of light and fervor. A less truthful man than he might have been tempted into the subsequent creation of a vision in the form of resurgent memory; a less sane man might have believed in such a creation; but Silas was both sane and honest, though, as with many honest and fervent men, culture had not defined any channels for his sense of mystery, and so it spread itself over the proper pathway of inquiry and knowledge. He had inherited from his mother some acquaintance with medicinal herbs and their preparation,—a little store of wisdom which she had imparted to him as a solemn bequest,—but of late years he had had doubts about the lawfulness of applying this knowledge, believing that herbs could have no efficacy without prayer, and that prayer might suffice without herbs; so that his inherited delight to wander through the fields in search of foxglove and dandelion and coltsfoot began to wear to him the character of a temptation.

Among the members of his church there was one young man, a little older than himself, with whom he had long lived in such close friendship that it was the custom of their Lantern Yard brethren to call them David and Jonathan.[18] The real name of the friend was William Dane, and he, too, was regarded as a shining instance of youthful piety, though somewhat given to over-severity towards weaker brethren, and to be so dazzled by his own light as to hold himself wiser than his teachers. But whatever blemishes others might discern in William, to his friend's mind he was faultless; for Marner had one of those impressible self-doubting natures which, at an inexperienced age, admire imperativeness and lean on contradiction. The expression of trusting simplicity in Marner's face, heightened by that absence of special observation, that defenceless, deer-like gaze which belongs to large prominent eyes, was strongly contrasted by the self-complacent suppression of inward triumph that lurked in the narrow slanting eyes and compressed lips of William Dane. One of the most frequent topics of conversation between the two friends was Assurance of salvation: Silas confessed that he could never arrive at anything higher than hope

[18] DAVID AND JONATHAN—Devoted friends (I Samuel, XVIII).

mingled with fear, and listened with longing wonder when William declared that he had possessed unshaken assurance ever since, in the period of his conversion, he had dreamed that he saw the words "calling and election sure" standing by themselves on a white page in the open Bible. Such colloquies have occupied many a pair of pale-faced weavers, whose unnurtured souls have been like young winged things, fluttering forsaken in the twilight.

It had seemed to the unsuspecting Silas[19] that the friendship had suffered no chill even from his formation of another attachment of a closer kind. For some months he had been engaged to a young servant woman, waiting only for a little increase to their mutual savings in order to their marriage; and it was a great delight to him that Sarah did not object to William's occasional presence in their Sunday interviews. It was at this point in their history that Silas's cataleptic fit occurred during the prayer-meeting; and amidst the various queries and expressions of interest addressed to him by his fellow-members, William's suggestion alone jarred with the general sympathy towards a brother thus singled out for special dealings. He observed that, to him, this trance looked more like a visitation of Satan than a proof of divine favor, and exhorted his friend to see that he hid no accursed thing within his soul. Silas, feeling bound to accept rebuke and admonition as a brotherly office, felt no resentment, but only pain, at his friend's doubts concerning him; and to this was soon added some anxiety at the perception that Sarah's manner towards him began to exhibit a strange fluctuation between an effort at an increased manifestation of regard and involuntary signs of shrinking and dislike. He asked her if she wished to break off their engagement; but she denied this: their engagement was known to the church, and had been recognized in the prayer-meetings; it could not be broken off without strict investigation, and Sarah could render no reason that would be sanctioned by the feeling of the community. At this time the senior deacon was taken dangerously ill, and, being a childless widower, he was tended night and day by some of the younger brethren or sisters. Silas frequently took his turn in the

[19] Unsuspecting Silas—By such phrases the author takes the reader into her confidence. When the reader learns later of William Dane's treachery, he is not at all surprised. George Eliot is not interested in creating an atmosphere of mystery. She wishes to portray the relations and reactions of a group of characters, one to another, and does not hesitate to foreshadow events that are to come.

night-watching with William, the one relieving the other at two in the morning. The old man, contrary to expectation, seemed to be on the way to recovery, when one night Silas, sitting up by his bedside, observed that his usual audible breathing had ceased. The candle was burning low, and he had to lift it to see the patient's face distinctly. Examination convinced him that the deacon was dead—had been dead some time, for the limbs were rigid. Silas asked himself if he had been asleep, and looked at the clock: it was already four in the morning. How was it that William had not come? In much anxiety he went to seek for help, and soon there were several friends assembled in the house, the minister among them, while Silas went away to his work, wishing he could have met William to know the reason of his non-appearance. But at six o'clock, as he was thinking of going to seek his friend, William came, and with him the minister. They came to summon him to Lantern Yard, to meet the church members there; and to his inquiry concerning the cause of the summons the only reply was, "You will hear." Nothing further was said until Silas was seated in the vestry, in front of the minister, with the eyes of those who to him represented God's people fixed solemnly upon him. Then the minister, taking out a pocket-knife, showed it to Silas, and asked him if he knew where he had left that knife? Silas said he did not know that he had left it anywhere out of his own pocket—but he was trembling at this strange interrogation. He was then exhorted not to hide his sin, but to confess and repent. The knife had been found in the bureau by the departed deacon's bedside—found in the place where the little bag of church money had lain, which the minister himself had seen the day before. Some hand had removed that bag; and whose hand could it be, if not that of the man to whom the knife belonged? For some time Silas was mute with astonishment; then he said, "God will clear me: I know nothing about the knife being there, or the money being gone. Search me and my dwelling: you will find nothing but three pound five of my own savings, which William Dane knows I have had these six months." At this William groaned, but the minister said, "The proof is heavy against you, brother Marner. The money was taken in the night last past, and no man was with our departed brother but you, for William Dane declares to us that he was hindered by sudden sickness from going to take his place as usual, and you yourself said that he had not come; and, moreover, you neglected the dead body."

"I must have slept," said Silas. Then, after a pause, he added, "Or I must have had another visitation like that which you have all seen me under, so that the thief must have come and gone while I was not in the body, but out of the body. But, I say again, search me and my dwelling, for I have been nowhere else."

The search was made, and it ended—in William Dane's finding the well-known bag, empty, tucked behind the chest of drawers in Silas's chamber! On this William exhorted his friend to confess, and not to hide his sin any longer. Silas turned a look of keen reproach on him, and said, "William, for nine years that we have gone in and out together, have you ever known me tell a lie? But God will clear me."

"Brother," said William, "how do I know what you may have done in the secret chambers of your heart, to give Satan an advantage over you?"

Silas was still looking at his friend. Suddenly a deep flush came over his face, and he was about to speak impetuously, when he seemed checked again by some inward shock that sent the flush back and made him tremble. But at last he spoke feebly, looking at William.

"I remember now—the knife wasn't in my pocket."

William said, "I know nothing of what you mean." The other persons present, however, began to inquire where Silas meant to say that the knife was, but he would give no further explanation; he only said, "I am sore stricken; I can say nothing. God will clear me."

On their return to the vestry there was further deliberation. Any resort to legal measures for ascertaining the culprit was contrary to the principles of the church in Lantern Yard, according to which prosecution was forbidden to Christians, even had the case held less scandal to the community. But the members were bound to take other measures for finding out the truth, and they resolved on praying and drawing lots.[20] This resolution can be a ground of surprise only to those who are unacquainted with that obscure

[20] Drawing lots—The drawing of lots to discover an unknown sinner was used by the children of Israel during their wanderings. This probably explains why the people of Lantern Yard took the method seriously.

religious life which has gone on in the alleys of our towns. Silas knelt with his brethren, relying on his own innocence being certified by immediate divine interference, but feeling that there was sorrow and mourning behind for him even then—that his trust in man had been cruelly bruised. *The lots declared that Silas Marner was guilty.* He was solemnly suspended from church membership, and called upon to render up the stolen money: only on confession, as the sign of repentance, could he be received once more within the folds of the church. Marner listened in silence. At last, when every one rose to depart, he went towards William Dane, and said, in a voice shaken by agitation,—

"The last time I remember using my knife was when I took it out to cut a strap for you. I don't remember putting it in my pocket again. *You* stole the money, and you have woven the plot to lay the sin at my door. But you may prosper, for all that; there is no just God that governs the earth righteously, but a God of lies, that bears witness against the innocent."

There was a general shudder at this blasphemy.

William said meekly, "I leave our brethren to judge whether this is the voice of Satan or not. I can do nothing but pray for you, Silas."

Poor Marner went out with that despair in his soul, that shaken trust in God and man, which is little short of madness to a loving nature. In the bitterness of his wounded spirit, he said to himself, "*She* will cast me off too." And he reflected that, if she did not believe the testimony against him, her whole faith must be upset, as his was. To people accustomed to reason about the forms in which their religious feeling has incorporated itself, it is difficult to enter into that simple, untaught state of mind in which the form and the feeling have never been severed by an act of reflection. We are apt to think it inevitable that a man in Marner's position should have begun to question the validity of an appeal to the divine judgment by drawing lots; but to him this would have been an effort of independent thought such as he had never known; and he must have made the effort at a moment when all his energies were turned into the anguish of disappointed faith. If there is an angel who records the sorrows of men as well as their sins, he knows how many and deep are the sorrows that spring from false ideas for which no man is culpable.

Marner went home, and for a whole day sat alone, stunned by despair, without any impulse to go to Sarah and attempt to win her belief in his innocence. The second day he took refuge from benumbing unbelief by getting into his loom and working away as usual; and before many hours were past, the minister and one of the deacons came to him with the message from Sarah, that she held her engagement to him at an end. Silas received the message mutely, and then turned away from the messengers to work at his loom again. In little more than a month from that time, Sarah was married to William Dane; and not long afterwards it was known to the brethren in Lantern Yard that Silas Marner had departed from the town.

## CHAPTER II

Even people whose lives have been made various[1] by learning sometimes find it hard to keep a fast hold on their habitual views of life, on their faith in the Invisible—nay, on the sense that their past joys and sorrows are a real experience, when they are suddenly transported to a new land, where the beings around them know nothing of their history, and share none of their ideas—where their mother earth shows another lap, and human life has other forms than those on which their souls have been nourished. Minds that have been unhinged from their old faith and love have perhaps sought this Lethean[2] influence of exile, in which the past becomes dreamy because its symbols have all vanished, and the present, too, is dreamy because it is linked with no memories. But even *their* experience may hardly enable them thoroughly to imagine what was the effect on a simple weaver like Silas Marner, when he left his own country and people and came to settle in Raveloe. Nothing could be more unlike his native town, set within sight of the wide-spread hillsides, than this low, wooded region, where he felt hidden even from the heavens by the screening trees and hedgerows. There was nothing here, when he rose in the deep morning quiet and looked out on the dewy brambles and rank tufted grass, that seemed to have any relation with that life centring in Lantern Yard, which had once been to him the altar-place of high dispensations.

---

[1] VARIOUS—In this sense, many-sided.

[2] LETHEAN—Referring to the River Lethe in Hades, a drink from whose stream was supposed to bring forgetfulness.

The whitewashed walls; the little pews where well-known figures entered with a subdued rustling, and where first one well-known voice and then another, pitched in a peculiar key of petition, uttered phrases at once occult and familiar, like the amulet[3] worn on the heart; the pulpit where the minister delivered unquestioned doctrine, and swayed to and fro, and handled the book in a long-accustomed manner; the very pauses between the couplets of the hymn, as it was given out, and the recurrent swell of voices in song: these things had been the channel of divine influences to Marner—they were the fostering home of his religious emotions—they were Christianity and God's kingdom upon earth. A weaver who finds hard words in his hymn-book knows nothing of abstraction; as the little child knows nothing of parental love, but only knows one face and one lap towards which it stretches its arms for refuge and nurture.

And what could be more unlike that Lantern Yard world than the world in Raveloe?—orchards looking lazy with neglected plenty; the large church in the wide churchyard, which men gazed at lounging at their own doors in service-time; the purple-faced farmers jogging along the lanes or turning in at the Rainbow; homesteads, where men supped heavily and slept in the light of the evening hearth, and where women seemed to be laying up a stock of linen for the life to come. There were no lips in Raveloe from which a word could fall that would stir Silas Marner's benumbed faith to a sense of pain.[4] In the early ages of the world, we know, it was believed that each territory was inhabited and ruled by its own divinities, so that a man could cross the bordering heights and be out of the reach of his native gods, whose presence was confined to the streams and the groves and the hills among which he had lived from his birth. And poor Silas was vaguely conscious of something not unlike the feeling of primitive men, when they fled thus, in fear or in sullenness, from the face of an unpropitious deity. It seemed to him that the Power he had vainly trusted in among the streets and at the prayer-meetings was very far away from this land in which he had taken refuge, where men lived in careless abundance, knowing and needing nothing of that trust which, for him, had been turned to bitterness. The little light he possessed

[3] AMULET—Charm, often worn over the heart, as protection against evil; hence, both occult (supernatural) and familiar.

[4] THERE WERE NO LIPS . . . PAIN—No one in Raveloe could appeal to Marner's small remnant of faith, even to the point of bringing him regrets.

spread its beams so narrowly, that frustrated belief was a curtain broad enough to create for him the blackness of night.

His first movement after the shock had been to work in his loom; and he went on with this unremittingly, never asking himself why, now he was come to Raveloe, he worked far on into the night to finish the tale of Mrs. Osgood's table-linen sooner than she expected—without contemplating beforehand the money she would put into his hand for the work. He seemed to weave, like the spider, from pure impulse, without reflection. Every man's work, pursued steadily, tends in this way to become an end in itself, and so to bridge over the loveless chasms of his life. Silas's hand satisfied itself with throwing the shuttle, and his eye with seeing the little squares in the cloth complete themselves under his effort. Then there were the calls of hunger; and Silas, in his solitude, had to provide his own breakfast, dinner, and supper, to fetch his own water from the well, and put his own kettle on the fire; and all these immediate promptings helped, along with the weaving, to reduce his life to the unquestioning activity of a spinning insect. He hated the thought of the past; there was nothing that called out his love and fellowship toward the strangers he had come amongst; and the future was all dark, for there was no Unseen Love that cared for him. Thought was arrested by utter bewilderment now its old narrow pathway was closed, and affection seemed to have died under the bruise that had fallen on its keenest nerves.

But at last Mrs. Osgood's table-linen was finished, and Silas was paid in gold. His earnings in his native town, where he worked for a wholesale dealer, had been after a lower rate; he had been paid weekly, and of his weekly earnings a large proportion had gone to objects of piety and charity. Now, for the first time in his life, he had five bright guineas put into his hand; no man expected a share of them, and he loved no man that he should offer him a share. But what were the guineas to him who saw no vista beyond countless days of weaving? It was needless for him to ask that, for it was pleasant to him to feel them in his palm, and look at their bright faces, which were all his own: it was another element of life, like the weaving and the satisfaction of hunger, subsisting quite aloof from the life of belief and love from which he had been cut off. The weaver's hand had known the touch of hard-won money even before the palm had grown to its full breadth; for twenty years, mysterious money had stood to him as the symbol of earthly good, and the immediate object of toil. He had seemed to love it little in the years when every penny had its purpose for him; for he loved the *purpose* then. But now, when all purpose was gone, that habit of looking towards the money and grasping it with a sense of fulfilled effort made a loam that was deep enough for the seeds of desire; and as Silas walked homeward across the fields in the twilight, he drew out the money, and thought it was brighter in the gathering gloom.

About this time an incident happened which seemed to open a possibility of some fellowship with his neighbors. One day, taking a pair of shoes to be mended, he saw the cobbler's wife seated by the fire, suffering from the terrible symptoms of heart-disease and dropsy, which he had witnessed as the precursors of his mother's death. He felt a rush of pity at the mingled sight and remembrance, and, recalling the relief his mother had found from a simple preparation of foxglove, he promised Sally Oates to bring her something that would ease her, since the doctor did her no good. In this office of charity, Silas felt, for the first time since he had come to Raveloe, a sense of unity between his past and present life, which might have been the beginning of his rescue from the insect-like existence into which his nature had shrunk. But Sally Oates's disease had raised her into a personage of much interest and importance among the neighbors, and the fact of her having found relief from drinking Silas Marner's "stuff" became a matter of general discourse. When Doctor Kimble gave physic, it was natural that it should have an effect; but when a weaver, who came from nobody knew where, worked wonders with a bottle of brown waters, the occult character of the process was evident. Such a sort of thing had not been known since the Wise Woman[5] at Tarley died; and she had charms as well as "stuff": everybody went to her when their children had fits. Silas Marner must be a person of the same sort, for how did he know what would bring back Sally Oates's breath, if he didn't know a fine sight more than that? The Wise Woman had words that she muttered to herself, so that you couldn't hear what they were, and if she tied a bit of red thread round the child's

[5] Wise Woman—A woman who used herbs and charms for healing. These poor creatures were often thought to be witches.

toe the while, it would keep off the water in the head. There were women in Raveloe, at that present time, who had worn one of the Wise Woman's little bags round their necks, and, in consequence, had never had an idiot child, as Ann Coulter had. Silas Marner could very likely do as much, and more; and now it was all clear how he should have come from unknown parts, and be so "comical-looking." But Sally Oates must mind and not tell the doctor, for he would be sure to set his face against Marner: he was always angry about the Wise Woman, and used to threaten those who went to her that they should have none of his help any more.

Silas now found himself and his cottage suddenly beset by mothers who wanted him to charm away the whooping-cough, or bring back the milk, and by men who wanted stuff against the rheumatics or the knots in the hands; and, to secure themselves against a refusal, the applicants brought silver in their palms. Silas might have driven a profitable trade in charms as well as in his small list of drugs; but money on this condition was no temptation to him: he had never known an impulse towards falsity, and he drove one after another away with growing irritation, for the news of him as a wise man had spread even to Tarley, and it was long before people ceased to take long walks for the sake of asking his aid. But the hope in his wisdom was at length changed into dread, for no one believed him when he said he knew no charms and could work no cures, and every man and woman who had an accident or a new attack after applying to him, set the misfortune down to Master Marner's ill-will and irritated glances. Thus it came to pass that his movement of pity towards Sally Oates, which had given him a transient sense of brotherhood, heightened the repulsion between him and his neighbors, and made his isolation more complete.

Gradually the guineas, the crowns, and the half-crowns grew to a heap, and Marner drew less and less for his own wants, trying to solve the problem of keeping himself strong enough to work sixteen hours a day on as small an outlay as possible. Have not men, shut up in solitary imprisonment, found an interest in marking the moments by straight strokes of a certain length on the wall, until the growth of the sum of straight strokes, arranged in triangles, has become a mastering purpose? Do we not wile away moments of inanity or fatigued waiting by repeating some trivial movement or sound, until the repetition has bred a want, which is incipient habit? That will help us to understand how the love of accumulating money grows an absorbing passion in men whose imaginations, even in the very beginning of their hoard, showed them no purpose beyond it. Marner wanted the heaps of ten to grow into a square, and then into a larger square; and every added guinea, while it was itself a satisfaction, bred a new desire. In this strange world, made a hopeless riddle to him, he might, if he had had a less intense nature, have sat weaving, weaving—looking towards the end of his pattern, or towards the end of his web, till he forgot the riddle, and everything else but his immediate sensations; but the money had come to mark off his weaving into periods, and the money not only grew, but it remained with him. He began to think it was conscious of him, as his loom was, and he would on no account have exchanged those coins, which had become his familiars,[6] for other coins with unknown faces. He handled them, he counted them, till their form and color were like the satisfaction of a thirst to him; but it was only in the night, when his work was done, that he drew them out to enjoy their companionship. He had taken up some bricks in his floor underneath his loom, and here he had made a hole in which he set the iron pot that contained his guineas and silver coins, covering the bricks with sand whenever he replaced them. Not that the idea of being robbed presented itself often or strongly to his mind: hoarding was common in country districts in those days; there were old laborers in the parish of Raveloe who were known to have their savings by them, probably inside their flock-beds;[7] but their rustic neighbors, though not all of them as honest as their ancestors in the days of King Alfred, had not imaginations bold enough to lay a plan of burglary. How could they have spent the money in their own village without betraying themselves? They would be obliged to "run away"—a course as dark and dubious as a balloon journey.

So, year after year, Silas Marner had lived in this solitude, his guineas rising in the iron pot, and his life narrowing and hardening itself more and more into a mere pulsation of desire and satisfaction that had no relation to any other being. His life had reduced itself to the functions of weaving and hoarding, without any contempla-

---

[6] His familiars—His intimate companions.

[7] Flock-beds—Beds with mattresses stuffed with wool or cotton.

tion of an end towards which the functions tended. The same sort of process has perhaps been undergone by wiser men, when they have been cut off from faith and love—only, instead of a loom and a heap of guineas, they have had some erudite research, some ingenious project, or some well-knit theory. Strangely Marner's face and figure shrank and bent themselves into a constant mechanical relation to the objects of his life, so that he produced the same sort of impression as a handle or a crooked tube, which has no meaning standing apart. The prominent eyes that used to look trusting and dreamy now looked as if they had been made to see only one kind of thing that was very small, like tiny grain, for which they hunted everywhere: and he was so withered and yellow that, though he was not yet forty, the children always called him "Old Master Marner."

Yet even in this stage of withering a little incident happened which showed that the sap of affection was not all gone. It was one of his daily tasks to fetch his water from a well a couple of fields off, and for this purpose, ever since he came to Raveloe, he had had a brown earthenware pot, which he held as his most precious utensil, among the very few conveniences he had granted himself. It had been his companion for twelve years, always standing on the same spot, always lending its handle to him in the early morning, so that its form had an expression for him of willing helpfulness, and the impress of its handle on his palm gave a satisfaction mingled with that of having the fresh clear water. One day as he was returning from the well he stumbled against the step of the stile, and his brown pot, falling with force against the stones that overarched the ditch below him, was broken in three pieces. Silas picked up the pieces and carried them home with grief in his heart. The brown pot could never be of use to him any more, but he stuck the bits together and propped the ruin in its old place for a memorial.

This is the history of Silas Marner until the fifteenth year after he came to Raveloe. The livelong day he sat in his loom, his ear filled with its monotony, his eyes bent close down on the slow growth of sameness in the brownish web, his muscles moving with such even repetition that their pause seemed almost as much a constraint as the holding of his breath. But at night came his revelry: at night he closed his shutters, and made fast his doors, and drew forth his gold. Long ago the heap of coins had become too large for the iron pot to hold them, and he had made for them two thick leather bags, which wasted no room in their resting-place, but lent themselves flexibly to every corner. How the guineas shone as they came pouring out of the dark leather mouths! The silver bore no large proportion in amount to the gold, because the long pieces of linen which formed his chief work were always partly paid for in gold, and out of the silver he supplied his own bodily wants, choosing always the shillings and sixpences to spend in this way. He loved the guineas best, but he would not change the silver—the crowns and half-crowns that were his own earnings, begotten by his labor; he loved them all. He spread them out in heaps and bathed his hands in them; then he counted them and set them up in regular piles, and felt their rounded outline between his thumb and fingers, and thought fondly of the guineas that were only half earned by the work in his loom, as if they had been unborn children—thought of the guineas that were coming slowly through the coming years, through all his life, which spread far away before him, the end quite hidden by countless days of weaving. No wonder his thoughts were still with his loom and his money when he made his journeys through the fields and the lanes to fetch and carry home his work, so that his steps never wandered to the hedge-banks and the lane-side in search of the once familiar herbs: these, too, belonged to the past, from which his life had shrunk away, like a rivulet that has sunk far down from the grassy fringe of its old breadth into a little shivering thread, that cuts a groove for itself in the barren sand.

But about the Christmas of that fifteenth year a second great change came over Marner's life, and his history became blent in a singular manner with the life of his neighbors.

## CHAPTER III

The greatest man in Raveloe was Squire Cass, who lived in the large red house, with the handsome flight of stone steps in front and the high stables behind it, nearly opposite the church. He was only one among several landed parishioners, but he alone was honored with the title of Squire; for though Mr. Osgood's family was also understood to be of timeless origin—the Raveloe imagination having never ventured back to that fearful blank when there were no Osgoods—still he merely owned the farm he occupied; whereas Squire Cass had a tenant or two, who complained of the game to him quite as if he had been a lord.[1]

It was still that glorious war-time[2] which was felt to be a peculiar favor of Providence towards the landed interests, and the fall of prices had not yet come to carry the race of small squires and yeomen down that road to ruin for which extravagant habits and bad husbandry were plentifully anointing their wheels. I am speaking now in relation to Raveloe and the parishes that resembled it; for our old-fashioned country life had many different aspects, as all life must have when it is spread over a various surface, and breathed on variously by multitudinous currents, from the winds of heaven to the thoughts of men, which are forever moving and crossing each other, with incalculable results. Raveloe lay low among the bushy trees and the rutted lanes, aloof from the currents of industrial energy and Puritan earnestness: the rich ate and drank freely, accepting gout and apoplexy[3] as things that ran mysteriously in respectable families, and the poor thought that the rich were entirely in the right of it to lead a jolly life; besides, their feasting caused a multiplication of orts,[4] which were the heirlooms of the poor. Betty Jay scented the boiling of Squire Cass's hams, but her longing was arrested by the unctuous liquor in which they were boiled; and when the seasons brought round the great merrymakings, they were regarded on all hands as a fine thing for the poor. For the Raveloe feasts were like the rounds of beef and the barrels of ale—they were on a large scale, and lasted a good while, especially in the winter-time. After ladies had packed up their best gowns and top-knots in bandboxes, and had incurred the risk of fording streams on pillions[5] with the precious burden in rainy or snowy weather, when there was no knowing how high the water would rise, it was not to be supposed that they looked forward to a brief pleasure. On this ground it was always contrived in the dark seasons, when there was little work to be done, and the hours were

---

[1] Who complained . . . lord—All the game was protected. The peasants had not the right to kill the very animals which destroyed their crops, for these animals provided hunting sport for the landed gentry. Moreover, the hunters often did more damage to crops than the game.

[2] That glorious war-time—Period of the Napoleonic Wars.

[3] Gout and apoplexy—Illnesses which came as a penalty of high living.

[4] Orts—Odd bits and leavings.

[5] Pillions—Cushions placed behind a man's saddle for a woman rider.

long, that several neighbors should keep open house in succession. So soon as Squire Cass's standing dishes diminished in plenty and freshness, his guests had nothing to do but to walk a little higher up the village to Mr. Osgood's, at the Orchards, and they found hams and chines[6] uncut, pork-pies with the scent of the fire in them, spun butter in all its freshness—everything, in fact, that appetites at leisure could desire, in perhaps greater perfection, though not in greater abundance, than at Squire Cass's.

For the Squire's wife had died long ago, and the Red House was without that presence of the wife and mother which is the fountain of wholesome love and fear in parlor and kitchen; and this helped to account not only for there being more profusion than finished excellence in the holiday provisions, but also for the frequency with which the proud Squire condescended to preside in the parlor of the Rainbow rather than under the shadow of his own dark wainscot; perhaps, also, for the fact that his sons had turned out rather ill. Raveloe was not a place where moral censure was severe, but it was thought a weakness in the Squire that he had kept all his sons at home in idleness; and though some license was to be allowed to young men whose fathers could afford it, people shook their heads at the courses of the second son, Dunstan, commonly called Dunsey Cass, whose taste for swopping and betting might turn out to be a sowing of something worse than wild oats. To be sure, the neighbors said, it was no matter what became of Dunsey,—a spiteful, jeering fellow, who seemed to enjoy his drink the more when other people went dry,—always provided that his doings did not bring trouble on a family like Squire Cass's, with a monument in the church,[7] and tankards older than King George. But it would be a thousand pities if Mr. Godfrey, the eldest, a fine, open-faced, good-natured young man, who was to come into the land some day,[8] should take to going along the same road with his brother, as he had seemed to do of late. If he went on in that way, he would lose Miss Nancy Lammeter; for it was well known that she had looked very shyly on him ever since last Whitsuntide

[6] CHINES—Portions of meat, especially the backs of beeves.

[7] WITH A MONUMENT IN THE CHURCH—A tablet in memory of deceased members of the family. This indicates the importance of the Squire's family.

[8] COME INTO THE LAND SOME DAY—The first-born son of English as well as of Continental families was, unless disinherited, the sole heir to the property of a family. The exception to this was in the case of personal effects which could be distributed at will.

twelvemonth, when there was so much talk about his being away from home days and days together. There was something wrong, more than common—that was quite clear; for Mr. Godfrey didn't look half so fresh-colored and open as he used to do. At one time everybody was saying, What a handsome couple he and Miss Nancy Lammeter would make! and if she could come to be mistress at the Red House there would be a fine change, for the Lammeters had been brought up in that way, that they never suffered a pinch of salt to be wasted, and yet everybody in their household had of the best, according to his place. Such a daughter-in-law would be a saving to the old Squire, if she never brought a penny to her fortune; for it was to be feared that, notwithstanding his incomings, there were more holes in his pocket than the one where he put his own hand in. But if Mr. Godfrey didn't turn over a new leaf, he might say "Good-by" to Miss Nancy Lammeter.

It was the once hopeful Godfrey who was standing, with his hands in his side-pockets and his back to the fire, in the dark wainscoted parlor, one late November afternoon, in that fifteenth year of Silas Marner's life at Raveloe. The fading gray light fell dimly on the walls decorated with guns, whips, and foxes' brushes,[9] on coats and hats flung on the chairs, on tankards sending forth a scent of flat ale, and on a half-choked fire, with pipes propped up in the chimney-corners: signs of a domestic life destitute of any hallowing charm, with which the look of gloomy vexation on Godfrey's blond face was in sad accordance. He seemed to be waiting and listening for some one's approach, and presently the sound of a heavy step, with an accompanying whistle, was heard across the large empty entrance-hall.

The door opened, and a thick-set, heavy-looking young man entered, with the flushed face and the gratuitously[10] elated bearing which mark the first stage of intoxication. It was Dunsey, and at the sight of him Godfrey's face parted with some of its gloom to take on the more active expression of hatred. The handsome brown spaniel that lay on the hearth retreated under the chair in the chimney-corner.[11]

---

[9] Foxes' brushes—Fox-tails.

[10] Gratuitously—In this sense, without reason.

[11] The . . . spaniel . . . chimney-corner—Note the choice of detail used by George Eliot to turn the reader against Dunstan Cass.

"Well, Master Godfrey, what do you want with me?" said Dunsey, in a mocking tone. "You're my elders and betters, you know; I was obliged to come when you sent for me."

"Why, this is what I want—and just shake yourself sober and listen, will you?" said Godfrey savagely. He had himself been drinking more than was good for him, trying to turn his gloom into uncalculating anger. "I want to tell you, I must hand over that rent of Fowler's to the Squire, or else tell him I gave it you; for he's threatening to distrain[12] for it, and it'll all be out soon, whether I tell him or not. He said, just now, before he went out, he should send word to Cox to distrain, if Fowler didn't come and pay up his arrears this week. The Squire's short o' cash, and in no humor to stand any nonsense; and you know what he threatened, if ever he found you making away with his money again. So, see and get the money, and pretty quickly, will you?"

"Oh!" said Dunsey sneeringly, coming nearer to his brother and looking in his face. "Suppose, now, you get the money yourself, and save me the trouble, eh? Since you was so kind as to hand it over to me, you'll not refuse me the kindness to pay it back for me: it was your brotherly love made you do it, you know."

Godfrey bit his lips and clenched his fist. "Don't come near me with that look, else I'll knock you down."

"Oh no, you won't," said Dunsey, turning away on his heel, however. "Because I'm such a good-natured brother, you know. I might get you turned out of house and home, and cut off with a shilling any day. I might tell the Squire how his handsome son was married to that nice young woman, Molly Farren, and was very unhappy because he couldn't live with his drunken wife, and I should slip into your place as comfortable as could be. But, you see, I don't do it—I'm so easy and good-natured. You'll take any trouble for me. You'll get the hundred pounds[13] for me—I know you will."

"How can I get the money?" said Godfrey, quivering. "I haven't a shilling to bless myself with. And it's a lie that you'd slip into my place: you'd get yourself turned out too, that's all. For if you begin telling tales, I'll follow. Bob's my father's favorite—you know that very well. He'd only think himself well rid of you."

---

[12] Distrain—Seize some property as security for the debt.
[13] Hundred pounds—About $500.

"Never mind," said Dunsey, nodding his head sideways as he looked out of the window. "It'ud be very pleasant to me to go in your company—you're such a handsome brother, and we've always been so fond of quarrelling with one another I shouldn't know what to do without you. But you'd like better for us both to stay at home together; I know you would. So you'll manage to get that little sum o' money, and I'll bid you good-by, though I'm sorry to part."

Dunstan was moving off, but Godfrey rushed after him and seized him by the arm, saying, with an oath,—

"I tell you, I have no money: I can get no money."

"Borrow of old Kimble."

"I tell you, he won't lend me any more, and I shan't ask him."

"Well then, sell Wildfire."

"Yes, that's easy talking. I must have the money directly."

"Well, you've only got to ride him to the hunt to-morrow. There'll be Bryce and Keating there, for sure. You'll get more bids than one."

"I dare say, and get back home at eight o'clock, splashed up to the chin. I'm going to Mrs. Osgood's birthday dance."

"Oho!" said Dunsey, turning his head on one side, and trying to speak in a small mincing treble. "And there's sweet Miss Nancy coming; and we shall dance with her, and promise never to be naughty again, and be taken into favor, and"—

"Hold your tongue about Miss Nancy, you fool," said Godfrey, turning red, "else I'll throttle you."

"What for?" said Dunsey, still in an artificial tone, but taking a whip from the table and beating the butt-end of it on his palm. "You've a very good chance. I'd advise you to creep up her sleeve again: it'ud be saving time if Molly should happen to take a drop too much laudanum some day, and make a widower of you. Miss Nancy wouldn't mind being a second, if she didn't know it. And you've got a good-natured brother, who'll keep your secret well, because you'll be so very obliging to him."

"I'll tell you what it is," said Godfrey, quivering, and pale again, "my patience is pretty near at an end. If you'd a little more sharpness in you, you might know that you may urge a man a bit too far, and make one leap as easy as another. I don't know but what it is so now: I may as well tell the Squire everything myself—

I should get you off my back, if I got nothing else. And, after all, he'll know some time. She's been threatening to come herself and tell him. So, don't flatter yourself that your secrecy's worth any price you choose to ask. You drain me of money till I have got nothing to pacify *her* with, and she'll do as she threatens some day. It's all one. I'll tell my father everything myself, and you may go to the devil."

Dunsey perceived that he had overshot his mark, and that there was a point at which even the hesitating Godfrey might be driven into decision. But he said, with an air of unconcern,—

"As you please; but I'll have a draught of ale first." And ringing the bell, he threw himself across two chairs, and began to rap the window-seat with the handle of his whip.

Godfrey stood, still with his back to the fire, uneasily moving his fingers among the contents of his side-pockets, and looking at the floor. That big muscular frame of his held plenty of animal courage, but helped him to no decision when the dangers to be braved were such as could neither be knocked down nor throttled. His natural irresolution and moral cowardice were exaggerated by a position in which dreaded consequences seemed to press equally on all sides, and his irritation had no sooner provoked him to defy Dunstan and anticipate all possible betrayals, than the miseries he must bring on himself by such a step seemed more unendurable to him than the present evil. The results of confession were not contingent,[14] they were certain; whereas betrayal was not certain. From the near vision of that certainty he fell back on suspense and vacillation with a sense of repose. The disinherited son of a small squire, equally disinclined to dig and to beg,[15] was almost as helpless as an uprooted tree, which, by the favor of earth and sky, has grown to a handsome bulk on the spot where it first shot upward. Perhaps it would have been possible to think of digging with some cheerfulness if Nancy Lammeter were to be won on those terms, but since he must irrevocably lose *her* as well as the inheritance, and must break every tie but the one that degraded him and left him without motive for trying to recover his better self, he could

---

[14] NOT CONTINGENT—Not dependent on circumstances.

[15] DISINCLINED TO DIG AND TO BEG—As a member of a family which belonged to the ranks of the landed gentry, Godfrey would have considered himself degraded if he had been obliged to earn his living—except, possibly, in the ministry or the army. This sentiment, though waning, still has its echo in English and Continental aristocratic circles.

imagine no future for himself on the other side of confession but that of "'listing for a soldier,"—the most desperate step, short of suicide, in the eyes of respectable families. No! he would rather trust to casualties than to his own resolve—rather go on sitting at the feast and sipping the wine he loved, though with the sword hanging over him[16] and terror in his heart, than rush away into the cold darkness where there was no pleasure left. The utmost concession to Dunstan about the horse began to seem easy, compared with the fulfilment of his own threat. But his pride would not let him recommence the conversation otherwise than by continuing the quarrel. Dunstan was waiting for this, and took his ale in shorter draughts than usual.

"It's just like you," Godfrey burst out, in a bitter tone, "to talk about my selling Wildfire in that cool way—the last thing I've got to call my own, and the best bit of horse-flesh I ever had in my life. And if you'd got a spark of pride in you, you'd be ashamed to see the stables emptied, and everybody sneering about it. But it's my belief you'd sell yourself, if it was only for the pleasure of making somebody feel he'd got a bad bargain."

"Ay, ay," said Dunstan, very placably, "you do me justice, I see. You know I'm a jewel for 'ticing people into bargains. For which reason I advise you to let *me* sell Wildfire. I'd ride him to the hunt to-morrow for you, with pleasure. I shouldn't look so handsome as you in the saddle, but it's the horse they'll bid for, and not the rider."

"Yes, I dare say—trust my horse to you!"

"As you please," said Dunstan, rapping the window-seat again with an air of great unconcern. "It's *you* have got to pay Fowler's money; it's none of my business. You received the money from him when you went to Bramcote, and *you* told the Squire it wasn't paid. I'd nothing to do with that; you chose to be so obliging as to give it me, that was all. If you don't want to pay the money, let it alone; it's all one to me. But I was willing to accommodate you by undertaking to sell the horse, seeing it's not convenient to you to go so far to-morrow."

Godfrey was silent for some moments. He would have liked to spring on Dunstan, wrench the whip from his hand, and flog

[16] Sword hanging over him—Allusion to the sword which was suspended by a single hair over the head of Damocles.

him to within an inch of his life; and no bodily fear could have deterred him; but he was mastered by another sort of fear, which was fed by feelings stronger even than his resentment. When he spoke again, it was in a half-conciliatory tone.

"Well, you mean no nonsense about the horse, eh? You'll sell him all fair, and hand over the money? If you don't, you know, everything 'ull go to smash, for I've got nothing else to trust to. And you'll have less pleasure in pulling the house over my head, when your own skull's to be broken too."

"Ay, ay," said Dunstan, rising; "all right. I thought you'd come round. I'm the fellow to bring old Bryce up to the scratch. I'll get you a hundred and twenty for him, if I get you a penny."

"But it'll perhaps rain cats and dogs to-morrow, as it did yesterday, and then you can't go," said Godfrey, hardly knowing whether he wished for that obstacle or not.

"Not *it,*" said Dunstan. "I'm always lucky in my weather. It might rain if you wanted to go yourself. You never hold trumps, you know—I always do. You've got the beauty, you see, and I've got the luck, so you must keep me by you for your crooked six-pence;[17] you'll *ne*-ver get along without me."

"Confound you, hold your tongue!" said Godfrey impetuously. "And take care to keep sober to-morrow, else you'll get pitched on your head coming home, and Wildfire might be the worse for it."

"Make your tender heart easy," said Dunstan, opening the door. "You never knew me see double when I'd got a bargain to make; it 'ud spoil the fun. Besides whenever I fall, I'm warranted to fall on my legs."

With that, Dunstan slammed the door behind him, and left Godfrey to that bitter rumination on his personal circumstances which was now unbroken from day to day save by the excitement of sporting, drinking, card-playing, or the rarer and less oblivious pleasure of seeing Miss Nancy Lammeter. The subtle and varied pains springing from the higher sensibility that accompanies higher culture, are perhaps less pitiable than that dreary absence of impersonal enjoyment and consolation which leaves ruder minds to the perpetual urgent companionship of their own griefs and discontents. The lives of those rural forefathers whom we are apt to think very prosaic figures—men whose only work was to ride round their land,

[17] CROOKED SIX-PENCE—Considered a lucky pocket-piece.

getting heavier and heavier in their saddles, and who passed the rest of their days in the half-listless gratification of senses dulled by monotony—had a certain pathos in them nevertheless. Calamities came to *them* too, and their early errors carried hard consequences; perhaps the love of some sweet maiden, the image of purity, order, and calm, had opened their eyes to the vision of a life in which the days would not seem too long, even without rioting; but the maiden was lost, and the vision passed away, and then what was left to them, especially when they had become too heavy for the hunt, or for carrying a gun over the furrows, but to drink and get merry, or to drink and get angry, so that they might be independent of variety, and say over again with eager emphasis the things they had said already any time that twelvemonth? Assuredly, among these flushed and dull-eyed men there were some whom—thanks to their native human kindness—even riot could never drive into brutality; men who, when their cheeks were fresh, had felt the keen point of sorrow or remorse, had been pierced by the reeds they leaned on, or had lightly put their limbs in fetters from which no struggle could loose them; and under these sad circumstances, common to us all, their thoughts could find no resting-place outside the ever-trodden round of their own petty history.

That, at least, was the condition of Godfrey Cass in this six and twentieth year of his life. A movement of compunction, helped by those small indefinable influences which every personal relation exerts on a pliant nature, had urged him into a secret marriage, which was a blight on his life. It was an ugly story of low passion, delusion, and waking from delusion, which needs not to be dragged from the privacy of Godfrey's bitter memory. He had long known that the delusion was partly due to a trap laid for him by Dunstan, who saw in his brother's degrading marriage the means of gratifying at once his jealous hate and his cupidity. And if Godfrey could have felt himself simply a victim, the iron bit that destiny had put into his mouth would have chafed him less intolerably. If the curses he muttered half aloud when he was alone had had no other object than Dunstan's diabolical cunning, he might have shrunk less from the consequences of avowal. But he had something else to curse—his own vicious folly, which now seemed as mad and unaccountable to him as almost all our follies and vices do when their promptings have long passed away. For four years he had thought of Nancy Lammeter, and wooed her with tacit patient worship, as the woman who made him think of the future with joy: she would be his wife, and would make home lovely to him, as his father's home had never been; and it would be easy, when she was always near, to shake off those foolish habits that were no pleasures, but only a feverish way of annulling vacancy. Godfrey's was an essentially domestic nature, bred up in a home where the hearth had no smiles, and where the daily habits were not chastised by the presence of household order. His easy disposition made him fall in unresistingly with the family courses, but the need of some tender permanent affection, the longing for some influence that would make the good he preferred easy to pursue, caused the neatness, purity, and liberal orderliness of the Lammeter household, sunned by the smile of Nancy, to seem like those fresh bright hours of the morning, when temptations go to sleep, and leave the ear open to the voice of the good angel, inviting to industry, sobriety, and peace. And yet the hope of this paradise had not been enough to save him from a course which shut him out of it forever. Instead of keeping fast hold of the strong silken rope by which Nancy would have drawn him safe to the green banks, where it was easy to step firmly, he had let himself be dragged back into mud and slime, in which it was useless to struggle. He had made ties for himself which robbed him of all wholesome motive, and were a constant exasperation.

Still, there was one position worse than the present: it was the position he would be in when the ugly secret was disclosed; and the desire that continually triumphed over every other was that of warding off the evil day, when he would have to bear the consequences of his father's violent resentment for the wound inflicted on his family pride—would have, perhaps, to turn his back on that hereditary ease and dignity which, after all, was a sort of reason for living, and would carry with him the certainty that he was banished forever from the sight and esteem of Nancy Lammeter. The longer the interval, the more chance there was of deliverance from some, at least, of the hateful consequences to which he had sold himself; the more opportunities remained for him to snatch the strange gratification of seeing Nancy, and gathering some faint indications of her lingering regard. Towards this gratification he was impelled, fitfully, every now and then, after having passed weeks in which he had avoided her as the far-off, bright-winged prize, that only made him spring forward, and find his chain all the more galling. One of those fits of yearning was on him now, and it would have been strong enough to have persuaded him to trust Wildfire to Dunstan rather than disappoint the yearning, even if he had not had another reason for his disinclination towards the morrow's hunt. That other reason was the fact that the morning's meet was near Batherley, the market-town where the unhappy woman lived, whose image became more odious to him every day; and to his thought the whole vicinage was haunted by her. The yoke a man creates for himself by wrong-doing will breed hate in the kindliest nature; and the good-humored, affectionate-hearted Godfrey Cass was fast becoming a bitter man, visited by cruel wishes, that seemed to enter, and depart, and enter again, like demons who had found in him a ready-garnished home.

What was he to do this evening to pass the time? He might as well go to the Rainbow, and hear the talk about the cock-fighting: everybody was there, and what else was there to be done? Though, for his own part, he did not care a button for cock-fighting. Snuff, the brown spaniel, who had placed herself in front of him, and had been watching him for some time, now jumped up in impatience for the expected caress. But Godfrey thrust her away without looking at her, and left the room, followed humbly by the unresenting Snuff—perhaps because she saw no other career open to her.

## CHAPTER IV

Dunstan Cass, setting off in the raw morning, at the judiciously quiet pace of a man who is obliged to ride to cover on his hunter, had to take his way along the lane which, at its farther extremity, passed by the piece of uninclosed ground called the Stone-pit, where stood the cottage, once a stone-cutter's shed, now for fifteen years inhabited by Silas Marner. The spot looked very dreary at this season, with the moist trodden clay about it, and the red, muddy water high up in the deserted quarry. That was Dunstan's first thought as he approached it; the second was, that the old fool of a weaver, whose loom he heard rattling already, had a great deal of money hidden somewhere. How was it that he, Dunstan Cass, who had often heard talk of Marner's miserliness, had never thought of suggesting to Godfrey that he should frighten or persuade the old fellow into lending the money on the excellent security of the young Squire's prospects? The resource occurred to him now as so easy and agreeable, especially as Marner's hoard was likely to be large enough to leave Godfrey a handsome surplus beyond his immediate needs, and enable him to accommodate his faithful brother, that he had almost turned the horse's head towards home again. Godfrey would be ready enough to accept the suggestion: he would snatch eagerly at a plan that might save him from parting with Wildfire. But when Dunstan's meditation reached this point, the inclination to go on grew strong and prevailed. He didn't want to give Godfrey that pleasure: he preferred that Master Godfrey should be vexed. Moreover, Dunstan enjoyed the self-important consciousness of having a horse to sell, and the opportunity of driving a bargain, swaggering, and, possibly, taking somebody in. He might have all the satisfaction attendant on selling his brother's horse, and not the less have the further satisfaction of setting Godfrey to borrow Marner's money. So he rode on to cover.

Bryce and Keating were there, as Dunstan was quite sure they would be—he was such a lucky fellow.

"Heyday," said Bryce, who had long had his eye on Wildfire, "you're on your brother's horse to-day: how's that?"

"Oh, I've swopped with him," said Dunstan, whose delight in lying, grandly independent of utility,[1] was not to be diminished by the likelihood that his hearer would not believe him. "Wildfire's mine now."

"What! has he swopped with you for that big-boned hack of yours?" said Bryce, quite aware that he should get another lie in answer.

"Oh, there was a little account between us," said Dunsey carelessly, "and Wildfire made it even. I accommodated him by taking the horse, though it was against my will, for I'd got an itch for a mare o' Jortin's—as rare a bit o' blood as ever you threw your leg across. But I shall keep Wildfire, now I've got him, though I'd a bid of a hundred and fifty for him the other day, from a man over at Flitton—he's buying for Lord Cromleck—a fellow with a

---

[1] GRANDLY INDEPENDENT OF UTILITY—Dunstan lied for the joy of it, not caring much whether the lie was useful to him or not.

cast in his eye, and a green waistcoat. But I mean to stick to Wildfire: I shan't get a better at a fence in a hurry. The mare's got more blood, but she's a bit too weak in the hind-quarters."

Bryce of course divined that Dunstan wanted to sell the horse, and Dunstan knew that he divined it (horse-dealing is only one of many human transactions carried on in this ingenious manner); and they both considered that the bargain was in its first stage, when Bryce replied ironically,—

"I wonder at that now; I wonder you mean to keep him; for I never heard of a man who didn't want to sell his horse getting a bid of half as much again as the horse was worth. You'll be lucky if you get a hundred."

Keating rode up now, and the transaction became more complicated. It ended in the purchase of the horse by Bryce for a hundred and twenty, to be paid on the delivery of Wildfire, safe and sound, at the Batherley stables. It did occur to Dunsey that it might be wise for him to give up the day's hunting, proceed at once to Batherley, and, having waited for Bryce's return, hire a horse to carry him home with the money in his pocket. But the inclination for a run, encouraged by confidence in his luck, and by a draught of brandy from his pocket-pistol[2] at the conclusion of the bargain, was not easy to overcome, especially with a horse under him that would take the fences to the admiration of the field.[3] Dunstan, however, took one fence too many, and got his horse pierced with a hedge-stake. His own ill-favored person, which was quite unmarketable, escaped without injury; but poor Wildfire, unconscious of his price, turned on his flank, and painfully panted his last. It happened that Dunstan, a short time before, having had to get down to arrange his stirrup, had muttered a good many curses at this interruption, which had thrown him in the rear of the hunt near the moment of glory, and under this exasperation had taken the fences more blindly. He would soon have been up with the hounds again, when the fatal accident happened; and hence he was between eager riders in advance, not troubling themselves about what happened behind them, and far-off stragglers, who were as likely as not to pass quite aloof from the line of road in which Wildfire had fallen. Dunstan, whose nature it was to care more for immediate

[2] Pocket-pistol—Pocket flask.

[3] The field—All the riders.

annoyances than for remote consequences, no sooner recovered his legs, and saw that it was all over with Wildfire, than he felt a satisfaction at the absence of witnesses to a position which no swaggering could make enviable. Reinforcing himself, after his shake, with a little brandy and much swearing, he walked as fast as he could to a coppice on his right hand, through which it occurred to him that he could make his way to Batherley without danger of encountering any member of the hunt. His first intention was to hire a horse there and ride home forthwith, for to walk many miles without a gun in his hand, and along an ordinary road, was as much out of the question to him as to other spirited young men of his kind. He did not much mind about taking the bad news to Godfrey, for he had to offer him at the same time the resource of Marner's money; and if Godfrey kicked, as he always did, at the notion of making a fresh debt, from which he himself got the smallest share of advantage, why, he wouldn't kick long: Dunstan felt sure he could worry Godfrey into anything. The idea of Marner's money kept growing in vividness, now the want of it had become immediate; the prospect of having to make his appearance with the muddy boots of a pedestrian at Batherley, and to encounter the grinning queries of stablemen, stood unpleasantly in the way of his impatience to be back at Raveloe and carry out his felicitous plan; and a casual visitation of his waistcoat-pocket, as he was ruminating, awakened his memory to the fact that the two or three small coins his fore-finger encountered there were of too pale a color[4] to cover that small debt, without payment of which the stable-keeper had declared he would never do any more business with Dunsey Cass. After all, according to the direction in which the run had brought him, he was not so very much farther from home than he was from Batherley; but Dunsey, not being remarkable for clearness of head, was only led to this conclusion by the gradual perception that there were other reasons for choosing the unprecedented course of walking home. It was now nearly four o'clock, and a mist was gathering: the sooner he got into the road the better. He remembered having crossed the road and seen the finger-post only a little while before Wildfire broke down; so, buttoning his coat, twisting the lash of his hunting-whip compactly round the handle, and rapping the tops of his boots with a self-

[4] Too PALE A COLOR—Therefore not gold, but silver.

possessed air, as if to assure himself that he was not at all taken by surprise, he set off with the sense that he was undertaking a remarkable feat of bodily exertion, which somehow, and at some time, he should be able to dress up and magnify to the admiration of a select circle at the Rainbow. When a young gentleman like Dunsey is reduced to so exceptional a mode of locomotion as walking, a whip in his hand is a desirable corrective to a too bewildering dreamy sense of unwontedness in his position; and Dunstan, as he went along through the gathering mist, was always rapping his whip somewhere. It was Godfrey's whip, which he had chosen to take without leave because it had a gold handle; of course no one could see, when Dunstan held it, that the name *Godfrey Cass* was cut in deep letters on that gold handle—they could only see that it was a very handsome whip. Dunsey was not without fear that he might meet some acquaintance in whose eyes he would cut a pitiable figure, for mist is no screen when people get close to each other; but when he at last found himself in the well-known Raveloe lanes without having met a soul, he silently remarked that that was part of his usual good luck. But now the mist, helped by the evening darkness, was more of a screen than he desired, for it hid the ruts into which his feet were liable to slip—hid everything, so that he had to guide his steps by dragging his whip along the low bushes in advance of the hedgerow. He must soon, he thought, be getting near the opening at the Stone-pits, he should find it out by the break in the hedgerow. He found it out, however, by another circumstance which he had not expected—namely, by certain gleams of light, which he presently guessed to proceed from Silas Marner's cottage. That cottage and the money hidden within it had been in his mind continually during his walk, and he had been imagining ways of cajoling and tempting the weaver to part with the immediate possession of his money for the sake of receiving interest. Dunstan felt as if there must be a little frightening added to the cajolery, for his own arithmetical convictions were not clear enough to afford him any forcible demonstration as to the advantages of interest; and as for security, he regarded it vaguely as a means of cheating a man by making him believe that he would be paid. Altogether, the operation on the miser's mind was a task that Godfrey would be sure to hand over to his more daring and cunning brother: Dunstan had made up his mind to that; and by the time he saw the light gleaming through the chinks of Marner's shutters, the idea of a dialogue with the weaver had become so familiar to him, that it occurred to him as quite a natural thing to make the acquaintance forthwith. There might be several conveniences attending this course: the weaver had possibly got a lantern, and Dunstan was tired of feeling his way. He was still nearly three quarters of a mile from home, and the lane was becoming unpleasantly slippery, for the mist was passing into rain. He turned up the bank, not without some fear lest he might miss the right way, since he was not certain whether the light were in front or on the side of the cottage. But he felt the ground before him cautiously with his whip-handle, and at last arrived safely at the door. He knocked loudly, rather enjoying the idea that the old fellow would be frightened at the sudden noise. He heard no movement in reply: all was silence in the cottage. Was the weaver gone to bed, then? If so, why had he left a light? That was a strange forgetfulness in a miser. Dunstan knocked still more loudly, and, without pausing for a reply, pushed his fingers through the latch-hole, intending to shake the door and pull the latch-string[5] up and down, not doubting that the door was fastened. But, to his surprise, at this double motion the door opened, and he found himself in front of a bright fire, which lit up every corner of the cottage—the bed, the loom, the three chairs, and the table—and showed him that Marner was not there.

Nothing at that moment could be much more inviting to Dunsey than the bright fire on the brick hearth: he walked in and seated himself by it at once. There was something in front of the fire, too, that would have been inviting to a hungry man, if it had been in a different stage of cooking. It was a small bit of pork suspended from the kettle-hanger by a string passed through a large door-key, in a way known to primitive housekeepers unpossessed of jacks.[6] But the pork had been hung at the farthest extremity of the hanger, apparently to prevent the roasting from proceeding too rapidly during the owner's absence. The old staring simpleton had hot meat for his supper, then? thought Dunstan. People had always said he lived on mouldy bread, on purpose to

[5] THE LATCH-STRING—A leathern thong or stout string passed through the latch hole of a door so that the door could be opened from without provided it were not bolted.

[6] JACKS—Devices for turning the spit on which meat was placed for roasting. Some of these jacks were operated by a clock mechanism.

check his appetite. But where could he be at this time, and on such an evening, leaving his supper in this stage of preparation, and his door unfastened? Dunstan's own recent difficulty in making his way suggested to him that the weaver had perhaps gone outside his cottage to fetch in fuel, or for some such brief purpose, and had slipped into the Stone-pit. That was an interesting idea to Dunstan, carrying consequences of entire novelty. If the weaver was dead, who had a right to his money? Who would know where his money was hidden? *Who would know that anybody had come to take it away?* He went no farther into the subtleties of evidence: the pressing question, "Where *is* the money?" now took such entire possession of him as to make him quite forget that the weaver's death was not a certainty. A dull mind, once arriving at an inference that flatters a desire, is rarely able to retain the impression that the notion from which the inference started was purely problematic.[7] And Dunstan's mind was as dull as the mind of a possible felon usually is. There were only three hiding-places where he had ever heard of cottagers' hoards being found: the thatch,[8] the bed, and a hole in the floor. Marner's cottage had no thatch; and Dunstan's first act, after a train of thought made rapid by the stimulus of cupidity, was to go up to the bed; but while he did so, his eyes travelled eagerly over the floor, where the bricks, distinct in the firelight, were discernible under the sprinkling of sand. But not everywhere; for there was one spot, and one only, which was quite covered with sand, and sand showing the marks of fingers which had apparently been careful to spread it over a given space. It was near the treadles of the loom. In an instant Dunstan darted to that spot, swept away the sand with his whip, and, inserting the thin end of the hook between the bricks, found that they were loose. In haste he lifted up two bricks, and saw what he had no doubt was the object of his search; for what could there be but money in those two leathern bags? And, from their weight, they must be filled with guineas. Dunstan felt round the hole, to be certain that it held no more; then hastily replaced the bricks, and spread the sand over them. Hardly more than five minutes had passed since he entered the cottage, but it seemed to

[7] A DULL MIND . . . PROBLEMATIC—A stupid person may form a plan based on some imagined circumstance and forget later that circumstance itself is not a fact.

[8] THATCH—The straw of which the roofs of many country cottages in England are made.

Dunstan like a long while; and though he was without any distinct recognition of the possibility that Marner might be alive, and might reënter the cottage at any moment, he felt an undefinable dread laying hold on him as he rose to his feet with the bags in his hand. He would hasten out into the darkness, and then consider what he should do with the bags. He closed the door behind him immediately, that he might shut in the stream of light: a few steps would be enough to carry him beyond betrayal by the gleams from the shutter-chinks and the latch-hole. The rain and darkness had got thicker, and he was glad of it; though it was awkward walking with both hands filled, so that it was as much as he could do to grasp his whip along with one of the bags. But when he had gone a yard or two, he might take his time. So he stepped forward into the darkness.

## CHAPTER V

When Dunstan Cass turned his back on the cottage, Silas Marner was not more than a hundred yards away from it, plodding along from the village with a sack thrown round his shoulders as an overcoat, and with a horn lantern[1] in his hand. His legs were weary, but his mind was at ease, free from the presentiment of change. The sense of security more frequently springs from habit than from conviction, and for this reason it often subsists after such a change in the conditions as might have been expected to suggest alarm. The lapse of time during which a given event has not happened is, in this logic of habit, constantly alleged as a reason why the event should never happen, even when the lapse of time is precisely the added condition which makes the event imminent. A man will tell you that he has worked in a mine for forty years unhurt by an accident, as a reason why he should apprehend no danger, though the roof is beginning to sink; and it is often observable, that the older a man gets, the more difficult it is to him to retain a believing conception of his own death. This influence of habit was necessarily strong in a man whose life was so monotonous as Marner's—who saw no new people and heard of no new events to keep alive in him the idea of the unexpected and the

[1] HORN LANTERN—Before glass came into common use, the candle in the lantern was protected from the wind by horn scraped thin to allow the light to shine through.

changeful; and it explains, simply enough, why his mind could be at ease, though he had left his house and his treasure more defenceless than usual. Silas was thinking with double complacency of his supper: first, because it would be hot and savory; and, secondly, because it would cost him nothing. For the little bit of pork was a present from that excellent housewife, Miss Priscilla Lammeter, to whom he had this day carried home a handsome piece of linen; and it was only on occasion of a present like this that Silas indulged himself with roast meat. Supper was his favorite meal, because it came at his time of revelry, when his heart warmed over his gold; whenever he had roast meat, he always chose to have it for supper. But this evening, he had no sooner ingeniously knotted his string fast round his bit of pork, twisted the string according to rule over his door-key, passed it through the handle, and made it fast on the hanger, then he remembered that a piece of very fine twine was indispensable to his "setting up" a new piece of work in his loom early in the morning. It had slipped his memory, because, in coming from Mr. Lammeter's, he had not had to pass through the village; but to lose time by going on errands in the morning was out of the question. It was a nasty fog to turn out into, but there were things Silas loved better than his own comfort; so, drawing his pork to the extremity of the hanger, and arming himself with his lantern and his old sack, he set out on what, in ordinary weather, would have been a twenty minutes' errand. He could not have locked his door without undoing his well-knotted string and retarding his supper; it was not worth his while to make that sacrifice. What thief would find his way to the Stone-pits on such a night as this? and why should he come on this particular night, when he had never come through all the fifteen years before? These questions were not distinctly present in Silas's mind; they merely serve to represent the vaguely felt foundation of his freedom from anxiety.

He reached his door in much satisfaction that his errand was done: he opened it, and to his short-sighted eyes everything remained as he had left it, except that the fire sent out a welcome increase of heat. He trod about the floor while putting by his lantern and throwing aside his hat and sack, so as to merge the marks of Dunstan's feet on the sand in the marks of his own nailed boots. Then he moved his pork nearer to the fire, and sat down to the agreeable business of tending the meat and warming himself at the same time.

Any one who had looked at him as the red light shone upon his pale face, strange straining eyes, and meagre form, would perhaps have understood the mixture of contemptuous pity, dread, and suspicion with which he was regarded by his neighbors in Raveloe. Yet few men could be more harmless than poor Marner. In his truthful simple soul, not even the growing greed and worship of gold could beget any vice directly injurious to others. The light of his faith quite put out, and his affections made desolate, he had clung with all the force of his nature to his work and his money; and like all objects to which a man devotes himself, they had fashioned him into correspondence with themselves. His loom, as he wrought in it without ceasing, had in its turn wrought on him, and confirmed more and more the monotonous craving for its monotonous response. His gold, as he hung over it and saw it grow, gathered his power of loving together into a hard isolation like its own.

As soon as he was warm he began to think it would be a long while to wait till after supper before he drew out his guineas, and it would be pleasant to see them on the table before him as he ate his unwonted feast. For joy is the best of wine, and Silas's guineas were a golden wine of that sort.

He rose and placed his candle unsuspectingly on the floor near his loom, swept away the sand without noticing any change, and removed the bricks. The sight of the empty hole made his heart leap violently, but the belief that his gold was gone could not come at once—only terror, and the eager effort to put an end to the terror. He passed his trembling hand all about the hole trying to think it possible that his eyes had deceived him: then he held the candle in the hole and examined it curiously, trembling more and more. At last he shook so violently that he let fall the candle, and lifted his hands to his head, trying to steady himself, that he might think. Had he put his gold somewhere else, by a sudden resolution last night, and then forgotten it? A man falling into dark water seeks a momentary footing even on sliding stones; and Silas, by acting as if he believed in false hopes, warded off the moment of despair. He searched in every corner, he turned his bed over, and shook it, and kneaded it; he looked in his brick oven where he laid his sticks. When there was no other place to be searched, he kneeled down again, and felt once more all round the hole. There was no untried refuge left for a moment's shelter from the terrible truth.

Yes, there was a sort of refuge which always comes with the prostration of thought under an overpowering passion: it was that expectation of impossibilities, that belief in contradictory images, which is still distinct from madness, because it is capable of being dissipated by the external fact. Silas got up from his knees trembling, and looked round at the table: didn't the gold lie there after all? The table was bare. Then he turned and looked behind him—looked all round his dwelling, seeming to strain his brown eyes after some possible appearance of the bags, where he had already sought them in vain. He could see every object in his cottage—and his gold was not there.

Again he put his trembling hands to his head, and gave a wild ringing scream, the cry of desolation. For a few moments after, he stood motionless; but the cry had relieved him from the first maddening pressure of the truth. He turned, and tottered towards his loom, and got into the seat where he worked, instinctively seeking this as the strongest assurance of reality.

And now that all the false hopes had vanished, and the first shock of certainty was past, the idea of a thief began to present itself, and he entertained it eagerly, because a thief might be caught and made to restore the gold. The thought brought some new strength with it, and he started from his loom to the door. As he opened it, the rain beat in upon him, for it was falling more and more heavily. There were no footsteps to be tracked on such a night—footsteps? When had the thief come? During Silas's absence in the daytime the door had been locked, and there had been no marks of any inroad on his return by daylight. And in the evening, too, he said to himself, everything was the same as when he had left it. The sand and bricks looked as if they had not been moved. *Was* it a thief who had taken the bags? or was it a cruel power that no hands could reach,[2] which had delighted in making him a second time desolate? He shrank from this vaguer dread, and fixed his mind with struggling effort on the

[2] Cruel power that no hands could reach—Though Silas's religious faith has gone, his belief in the supernatural remains.

robber with hands, who could be reached by hands. His thoughts glanced at all the neighbors who had made any remarks, or asked any questions which he might now regard as a ground of suspicion. There was Jem Rodney, a known poacher, and otherwise disreputable; he had often met Marner in his journeys across the fields, and had said something jestingly about the weaver's money; nay, he had once irritated Marner, by lingering at the fire when he called to light his pipe, instead of going about his business. Jem Rodney was the man—there was ease in the thought. Jem could be found and made to restore the money: Marner did not want to punish him, but only to get back his gold which had gone from him, and left his soul like a forlorn traveller on an unknown desert. The robber must be laid hold of. Marner's ideas of legal authority were confused, but he felt that he must go and proclaim his loss; and the great people in the village—the clergyman, the constable, and Squire Cass—would make Jem Rodney, or somebody else, deliver up the stolen money. He rushed out in the rain, under the stimulus of this hope, forgetting to cover his head, not caring to fasten his door; for he felt as if he had nothing left to lose. He ran swiftly till want of breath compelled him to slacken his pace as he was entering the village at the turning close to the Rainbow.

The Rainbow, in Marner's view, was a place of luxurious resort for rich and stout husbands, whose wives had superfluous stores of linen; it was the place where he was likely to find the powers and dignities of Raveloe, and where he could most speedily make his loss public. He lifted the latch, and turned into the bright bar or kitchen on the right hand, where the less lofty customers of the house were in the habit of assembling, the parlor on the left being reserved for the more select society in which Squire Cass frequently enjoyed the double pleasure of conviviality and condescension. But the parlor was dark to-night, the chief personages who ornamented its circle being all at Mrs. Osgood's birthday dance, as Godfrey Cass was. And in consequence of this, the party on the high-screened[3] seats in the kitchen was more numerous than usual; several personages, who would otherwise have been admitted into the parlor and enlarged the opportunity of hectoring and condescension for their betters, being content this

[3] HIGH-SCREENED—High-backed.

evening to vary their enjoyment by taking their spirits-and-water where they could themselves hector and condescend in company that called for beer.

## CHAPTER VI

The conversation, which was at a high pitch of animation when Silas approached the door of the Rainbow, had, as usual, been slow and intermittent when the company first assembled. The pipes began to be puffed in a silence which had an air of severity; the more important customers, who drank spirits and sat nearest the fire, staring at each other as if a bet were depending on the first man who winked; while the beer-drinkers, chiefly men in fustian[1] jackets and smock-frocks, kept their eyelids down and rubbed their hands across their mouths, as if their draughts of beer were a funereal duty attended with embarrassing sadness. At last, Mr. Snell, the landlord, a man of a neutral disposition, accustomed to stand aloof from human differences as those of beings who were all alike in need of liquor, broke silence by saying in a doubtful tone to his cousin the butcher,—

"Some folks 'ud say that was a fine beast you druv in yesterday, Bob?"

The butcher, a jolly, smiling, red-haired man, was not disposed to answer rashly. He gave a few puffs before he spat and replied, "And they wouldn't be fur wrong, John."

After this feeble delusive thaw, the silence set in as severely as before.

"Was it a red Durham?" said the farrier,[2] taking up the thread of discourse after the lapse of a few minutes.

The farrier looked at the landlord, and the landlord looked at the butcher, as the person who must take the responsibility of answering.

"Red it was," said the butcher, in his good-humored husky treble, "and a Durham it was."

"Then you needn't tell *me* who you bought it of," said the farrier, looking round with some triumph; "I know who it is has got the red Durhams o' this country-side. And she'd a white star

[1] FUSTIAN—A kind of coarse cotton cloth.

[2] FARRIER—Veterinary. Today, farrier means blacksmith.

on her brow, I'll bet a penny?" The farrier leaned forward with his hands on his knees as he put this question, and his eyes twinkled knowingly.

"Well; yes—she might," said the butcher slowly, considering that he was giving a decided affirmative. "I don't say contrairy."

"I knew that very well," said the farrier, throwing himself backward again, and speaking defiantly; "if *I* don't know Mr. Lammeter's cows, I should like to know who does—that's all. And as for the cow you've bought, bargain or no bargain, I've been at the drenching[3] of her—contradick me who will."

The farrier looked fierce, and the mild butcher's conversational spirit was roused a little.

"I 'm not for contradicking no man," he said; "I 'm for peace and quietness. Some are for cutting long ribs—I'm for cutting 'em short, myself; but *I* don't quarrel with 'em. All I say is, it's a lovely carkiss—and anybody as was reasonable, it 'ud bring tears into their eyes to look at it."

"Well, it's the cow as I drenched, whatever it is," pursued the farrier angrily; "and it was Mr. Lammeter's cow, else you told a lie when you said it was a red Durham."

"I tell no lies," said the butcher, with the same mild huskiness as before, "and I contradick none—not if a man was to swear himself black: he's no meat o' mine, nor none o' my bargains. All I say is, it's a lovely carkiss. And what I say, I'll stick to; but I'll quarrel wi' no man."

"No," said the farrier, with bitter sarcasm, looking at the company generally; "and p'rhaps you aren't pig-headed; and p'rhaps you didn't say the cow was a red Durham; and p'rhaps you didn't say she'd got a star on her brow—stick to that, now you're at it."

"Come, come," said the landlord; "let the cow alone. The truth lies atween you: you're both right and both wrong, as I allays say. And as for the cow's being Mr. Lammeter's, I say nothing to that; but this I say, as the Rainbow's the Rainbow. And for the matter o' that, if the talk is to be o' the Lammeters, *you* know the most upo' that head, eh, Mr. Macey? You remember when first Mr. Lammeter's father come into these parts, and took the Warrens?"[4]

[3] DRENCHING—Forcing down a dose of medicine.

[4] THE WARRENS—Name of the Lammeter estate.

Mr. Macey, tailor and parish-clerk, the latter of which functions rheumatism had of late obliged him to share with a small-featured young man who sat opposite him, held his white head on one side, and twirled his thumbs with an air of complacency, slightly seasoned with criticism. He smiled pityingly, in answer to the landlord's appeal, and said,—

"Ay, ay; I know, I know; but I let other folks talk. I've laid by now, and gev up to the young uns. Ask them as have been to school at Tarley: they've learnt pernouncing; that's come up[5] since my day."

"If you're pointing at me, Mr. Macey," said the deputy-clerk, with an air of anxious propriety, "I'm nowise a man to speak out of my place. As the psalm says,—

'I know what's right, nor only so,
But also practise what I know.' "

"Well, then, I wish you'd keep hold o' the tune when it's set for you; if you're for prac*tis*ing, I wish you'd prac*tise* that," said a large, jocose-looking man, an excellent wheelwright in his week-day capacity, but on Sundays leader of the choir. He winked, as he spoke, at two of the company, who were known officially as the "bassoon" and the "key-bugle," in the confidence that he was expressing the sense of the musical profession in Raveloe.

Mr. Tookey, the deputy-clerk, who shared the unpopularity common to deputies, turned very red, but replied, with careful moderation: "Mr. Winthrop, if you'll bring me any proof as I'm in the wrong, I'm not the man to say I won't alter. But there's people set up their own ears for a standard, and expect the whole choir to follow 'em. There may be two opinions, I hope."

"Ay, ay," said Mr. Macey, who felt very well satisfied with this attack on youthful presumption; "you're right there, Tookey. There's allays two 'pinions: there's the 'pinion a man has of himsen, and there's the 'pinion other folks have on him. There'd be two 'pinions about a cracked bell, if the bell could hear itself."

"Well, Mr. Macey," said poor Tookey, serious amidst the general laughter, "I undertook to partially fill up the office of parish-clerk by Mr. Crackenthorp's desire, whenever your infirmities

[5] Come up—Started.

should make you unfitting; and it's one of the rights thereof to sing in the choir—else why have you done the same yourself?"

"Ah! but the old gentleman and you are two folks," said Ben Winthrop. "The old gentleman's got a gift. Why, the Squire used to invite him to take a glass, only to hear him sing the 'Red Rovier;' didn't he, Mr. Macey? It's a nat'ral gift. There's my little lad Aaron, he's got a gift—he can sing a tune off straight, like a throstle.[6] But as for you, Master Tookey, you'd better stick to your 'Amens:' your voice is well enough when you keep it up in your nose. It's your inside as isn't right made for music: it's no better nor a hollow stalk."

This kind of unflinching frankness was the most piquant form of joke to the company at the Rainbow, and Ben Winthrop's insult was felt by everybody to have capped Mr. Macey's epigram.

"I see what it is plain enough," said Mr. Tookey, unable to keep cool any longer. "There's a consperacy to turn me out o' the choir, as I shouldn't share the Christmas money—that's where it is. But I shall speak to Mr. Crackenthorp; I'll not be put upon by no man."

"Nay, nay, Tookey," said Ben Winthrop. "We'll pay you your share to keep out of it—that's what we'll do. There's things folks 'ud pay to be rid on, besides varmin."

"Come, come," said the landlord, who felt that paying people for their absence was a principle dangerous to society; "a joke's a joke. We're all good friends here, I hope. We must give and take. You're both right and you're both wrong, as I say. I agree wi' Mr. Macey here, as there's two opinions; and if mine was asked, I should say they're both right. Tookey's right and Winthrop's right, and they've only got to split the difference and make themselves even."

The farrier was puffing his pipe rather fiercely, in some contempt at this trivial discussion. He had no ear for music himself, and never went to church, as being of the medical profession, and likely to be in requisition for delicate cows. But the butcher, having music in his soul, had listened with a divided desire for Tookey's defeat, and for the preservation of the peace.

"To be sure," he said, following up the landlord's conciliatory view, "we're fond of our old clerk; it's nat'ral, and him used to

[6] THROSTLE—Thrush.

be such a singer, and got a brother as is known for the first fiddler in this country-side. Eh, it's a pity but what Solomon lived in our village, and could give us a tune when we liked; eh, Mr. Macey? I'd keep him in liver and lights for nothing—that I would."

"Ay, ay," said Mr. Macey, in the height of complacency; "our family 's been known for musicianers as far back as anybody can tell. But them things are dying out, as I tell Solomon every time he comes round; there's no voices like what there used to be, and there's nobody remembers what we remember, if it isn't the old crows."

"Ay, you remember when first Mr. Lammeter's father come into these parts, don't you, Mr. Macey?" said the landlord.

"I should think I did," said the old man, who had now gone through that complimentary process necessary to bring him up to the point of narration; "and a fine old gentleman he was—as fine, and finer nor the Mr. Lammeter as now is. He came from a bit north'ard, so far as I could ever make out. But there 's nobody rightly knows about those parts: only it couldn't be far north'ard, nor much different from this country, for he brought a fine breed o' sheep with him, so there must be pastures there, and everything reasonable. We heared tell as he'd sold his own land to come and take the Warrens, and that seemed odd for a man as had land of his own, to come and rent a farm in a strange place. But they said it was along of his wife's dying; though there's reasons in things as nobody knows on—that's pretty much what I've made out; yet some folks are so wise, they'll find you fifty reasons straight off, and all the while the real reason's winking at 'em in the corner, and they niver see 't. Howsomever, it was soon seen as we'd got a new parish'ner as know'd the rights and customs o' things, and kep' a good house, and was well looked on by everybody. And the young man—that's the Mr. Lammeter as now is, for he'd niver a sister—soon begun to court Miss Osgood, that's the sister o' the Mr. Osgood as now is, and a fine handsome lass she was—eh, you can't think—they pretend this young lass is like her, but that's the way wi' people as don't know what come before 'em. *I* should know, for I helped the old rector, Mr. Drumlow as was,—I helped him marry 'em."

Here Mr. Macey paused; he always gave his narrative in instalments, expecting to be questioned according to precedent.

"Ay, and a partic'lar thing happened, didn't it, Mr. Macey, so as you were likely to remember that marriage?" said the landlord, in a congratulatory tone.

"I should think there did—a *very* partic'lar thing," said Mr. Macey, nodding sideways. "For Mr. Drumlow—poor old gentleman, I was fond on him, though he'd got a bit confused in his head, what wi' age and wi' taking a drop o' summat warm when the service come of a cold morning. And young Mr. Lammeter, he'd have no way but he must be married in Janiwary, which, to be sure, 's a unreasonable time to be married in, for it isn't like a christening or a burying, as you can't help; and so Mr. Drumlow—poor old gentleman, I was fond on him—but when he come to put the questions, he put 'em by the rule o' contrairy, like, and he says, 'Wilt thou have this man to thy wedded wife?' says he, and then he says, 'Wilt thou have this woman to thy wedded husband?' says he. But the partic'larest thing of all is, as nobody took any notice on it but me, and they answered straight off 'Yes,' like as if it had been me saying 'Amen' i' the right place, without listening to what went before."

"But *you* knew what was going on well enough, didn't you, Mr. Macey? You were live enough, eh?" said the butcher.

"Lor' bless you!" said Mr. Macey, pausing, and smiling in pity at the impotence of his hearer's imagination; "why, I was all of a tremble; it was as if I'd been a coat pulled by the two tails, like; for I couldn't stop the parson, I couldn't take upon me to do that; and yet I said to myself, I says, 'Suppose they should n't be fast married, 'cause the words are contrairy?' and my head went working like a mill, for I was allays uncommon for turning things over and seeing all round 'em; and I says to myself, 'Is 't the meanin' or the words[7] as makes folks fast i' wedlock?' For the parson meant right, and the bride and bridegroom meant right. But then, when I come to think on it, meanin' goes but a little way i' most things, for you may mean to stick things together and your glue may be bad, and then where are you? And so I says to mysen, 'It isn't the meanin', it's the glue.' And I was worreted as if I'd got three bells to pull at once, when we went into the vestry, and

[7] Meanin' or the words—Mr. Macey's solution indicates how much faith the people of Raveloe put in creed. To them form was much more important than good intentions. That is, the correct wording of the marriage ceremony was necessary in Mr. Macey's opinion to "glue" the couple together in the sight of the Lord.

they begun to sign their names. But where 's the use o' talking?—you can't think what goes on in a 'cute man's inside."

"But you held in for all that, didn't you, Mr. Macey?" said the landlord.

"Ay, I held in tight till I was by mysen wi' Mr. Drumlow, and then I out wi' everything, but respectful, as I allays did. And he made light on it, and he says, 'Pooh, pooh, Macey, make yourself easy,' he says; 'it's neither the meaning nor the words—it's the re*ges*ter does it—that's the glue.' So you see he settled it easy; for parsons and doctors know everything by heart, like, so as they aren't worreted wi' thinking what's the rights and wrongs o' things, as I'n been many and many's the time. And sure enough the wedding turned out all right, on'y poor Mrs. Lammeter—that's Miss Osgood as was—died afore the lasses was growed up; but for prosperity and everything respectable, there's no family more looked on."

Every one of Mr. Macey's audience had heard this story many times, but it was listened to as if it had been a favorite tune, and at certain points the puffing of the pipes was momentarily suspended, that the listeners might give their whole minds to the expected words. But there was more to come; and Mr. Snell, the landlord, duly put the leading question.

"Why, old Mr. Lammeter had a pretty fortin, didn't they say, when he come into these parts?"

"Well, yes," said Mr. Macey; "but I dare say it's as much as this Mr. Lammeter 's done to keep it whole. For there was allays a talk as nobody could get rich on the Warrens: though he holds it cheap, for it 's what they call Charity Land."

"Ay, and there's few folks know so well as you how it come to be Charity Land, eh, Mr. Macey?" said the butcher.

"How should they?" said the old clerk, with some contempt. "Why, my grandfather made the grooms' livery for that Mr. Cliff as came and built the big stables at the Warrens. Why, they 're stables four times as big as Squire Cass's, for he thought o' nothing but hosses and hunting, Cliff didn't—a Lunnon[8] tailor, some folks said, as had gone mad wi' cheating. For he could n't ride; lor' bless you! they said he'd got no more grip o' the hoss than if his legs had been cross-sticks: my grandfather heared old

[8] LUNNON—London.

Squire Cass say so many and many a time. But ride he would, as if Old Harry[9] had been a-driving him; and he'd a son, a lad o' sixteen; and nothing would his father have him do, but he must ride and ride—though the lad was frighted, they said. And it was a common saying as the father wanted to ride the tailor out o' the lad, and make a gentleman on him—not but what I 'm a tailor myself, but in respect as God made me such, I 'm proud on it, for 'Macey, Tailor,' 's been wrote up over our door since afore the Queen's heads went out on the shillings.[10] But Cliff, he was ashamed o' being called a tailor, and he was sore vexed as his riding was laughed at, and nobody o' the gentlefolks hereabout could abide him. Howsomever, the poor lad got sickly and died, and the father did n't live long after him, for he got queerer nor ever, and they said he used to go out i' the dead o' the night, wi' a lantern in his hand, to the stables, and set a lot o' lights burning, for he got as he couldn't sleep; and there he'd stand, cracking his whip and looking at his hosses; and they said it was a mercy as the stables didn't get burnt down wi' the poor dumb creaturs in 'em. But at last he died raving, and they found as he 'd left all his property, Warrens and all, to a Lunnon Charity, and that 's how the Warrens come to be Charity Land; though, as for the stables, Mr. Lammeter never uses 'em—they're out o' all charicter—lor' bless you! if you was to set the doors a-banging in 'em, it 'ud sound like thunder half o'er the parish."

"Ay, but there's more going on in the stables than what folks see by daylight, eh, Mr. Macey?" said the landlord.

"Ay, ay; go that way of a dark night, that's all," said Mr. Macey, winking mysteriously, "and then make believe, if you like, as you didn't see lights i' the stables, nor hear the stamping o' the hosses, nor the cracking o' the whips, and howling, too, if it's tow'rt daybreak. 'Cliff's Holiday' has been the name of it ever sin' I were a boy; that 's to say, some said as it was the holiday Old Harry gev him from roasting, like. That 's what my father told me, and he was a reasonable man, though there's folks nowadays know what happened afore they were born better nor they know their own business."

---

[9] Old Harry—The devil.

[10] Afore the Queen's heads went out on the shillings—Each sovereign had coins minted bearing his or her image. Hence, in this case, since the time of Queen Anne.

"What do you say to that, eh, Dowlas?" said the landlord, turning to the farrier, who was swelling with impatience for his cue. "There's a nut for *you* to crack."

Mr. Dowlas was the negative spirit in the company, and was proud of his position.

"Say? I say what a man *should* say as doesn't shut his eyes to look at a finger-post. I say, as I'm ready to wager any man ten pound, if he 'll stand out wi' me any dry night in the pasture before the Warren stables, as we shall neither see lights nor hear noises, if it is n't the blowing of our own noses. That 's what I say, and I've said it many a time; but there's nobody 'ull ventur a ten-pun' note on their ghos'es as they make so sure of."

"Why, Dowlas, that's easy betting, that is," said Ben Winthrop. "You might as well bet a man as he wouldn't catch the rheumatise if he stood up to 's neck in the pool of a frosty night. It 'ud be fine fun for a man to win his bet as he'd catch the rheumatise. Folks as believe in Cliff's Holiday aren't a-goin to ventur near it for a matter o' ten pound."

"If Master Dowlas wants to know the truth on it," said Mr. Macey, with a sarcastic smile, tapping his thumbs together, "he's no call to lay any bet—let him go and stan' by himself—there's nobody 'ull hinder him; and then he can let the parish'ners know if they're wrong."

"Thank you! I 'm obliged to you," said the farrier, with a snort of scorn. "If folks are fools, it's no business o' mine. *I* don't want to make out the truth about ghos'es: I know it a'ready. But I'm not against a bet—everything fair and open. Let any man bet me ten pound as I shall see Cliff's Holiday, and I'll go and stand by myself. I want no company. I'd as lief do it as I'd fill this pipe."

"Ah, but who's to watch you, Dowlas, and see you do it? That's no fair bet," said the butcher.

"No fair bet?" replied Mr. Dowlas angrily. "I should like to hear any man stand up and say I want to bet unfair. Come now, Master Lundy, I should like to hear you say it."

"Very like you would," said the butcher. "But it's no business o' mine. You're none o' my bargains, and I aren't a-going to try and 'bate your price. If anybody 'll bid for you at your own vallying, let him. I'm for peace and quietness, I am."

"Yes, that's what every yapping cur is, when you hold a stick up at him," said the farrier. "But I'm afraid o' neither man nor ghost, and I'm ready to lay a fair bet. *I* aren't a turn-tail cur."

"Ay, but there's this in it, Dowlas," said the landlord, speaking in a tone of much candor and tolerance. "There's folks, i' my opinion, they can't see ghos'es, not if they stood as plain as a pike-staff before 'em. And there's reason i' that. For there's my wife, now, can't smell, not if she 'd the strongest o' cheese under her nose. I never see'd a ghost myself, but then I says to myself, 'Very like I haven't got the smell for 'em.' I mean, putting a ghost for a smell, or else contrairiways. And so, I'm for holding with both sides; for, as I say, the truth lies between 'em. And if Dowlas was to go and stand, and say he 'd never seen a wink o' Cliff's Holiday all the night through, I 'd back him; and if anybody said as Cliff's Holiday was certain sure, for all that, I'd back *him* too. For the smell's what I go by."

The landlord's analogical argument[11] was not well received by the farrier—a man intensely opposed to compromise.

"Tut, tut," he said, setting down his glass with refreshed irritation; "what's the smell got to do with it? Did ever a ghost give a man a black eye? That's what I should like to know. If ghos'es want me to believe in 'em, let 'em leave off skulking i' the dark and i' lone places—let 'em come where there 's company and candles."

"As if ghos'es 'ud want to be believed in by anybody so ignirant!" said Mr. Macey, in deep disgust at the farrier's crass incompetence to apprehend the conditions of ghostly phenomena.

## CHAPTER VII

Yet the next moment there seemed to be some evidence that ghosts had a more condescending disposition than Mr. Macey attributed to them, for the pale thin figure of Silas Marner was suddenly seen standing in the warm light, uttering no word, but looking round at the company with his strange unearthly eyes. The long pipes gave a simultaneous movement, like the antennæ of startled insects, and every man present, not excepting even the

[11] Analogical argument—Argument based on analogy or comparison; here, the landlord argues from his wife's inability to smell cheese the inability of some persons to see ghosts.

skeptical farrier, had an impression that he saw, not Silas Marner in the flesh, but an apparition; for the door by which Silas had entered was hidden by the high-screened seats, and no one had noticed his approach. Mr. Macey, sitting a long way off the ghost, might be supposed to have felt an argumentative triumph, which would tend to neutralize his share of the general alarm. Had he not always said that when Silas Marner was in that strange trance of his, his soul went loose from his body? Here was the demonstration; nevertheless, on the whole, he would have been as well contented without it. For a few moments there was a dead silence, Marner's want of breath and agitation not allowing him to speak. The landlord, under the habitual sense that he was bound to keep his house open to all company, and confident in the protection of his unbroken neutrality, at last took on himself the task of adjuring the ghost.

"Master Marner," he said, in a conciliatory tone, "what's lacking to you? What's your business here?"

"Robbed!" said Silas gaspingly. "I've been robbed! I want the constable—and the Justice—and Squire Cass—and Mr. Crackenthorp."

"Lay hold on him, Jem Rodney," said the landlord, the idea of a ghost subsiding; "he's off his head, I doubt. He's wet through."

Jem Rodney was the outermost man, and sat conveniently near Marner's standing-place; but he declined to give his services.

"Come and lay hold on him yourself, Mr. Snell, if you've a mind," said Jem rather sullenly. "He's been robbed, and murdered too,[1] for what I know," he added, in a muttering tone.

"Jem Rodney!" said Silas, turning and fixing his strange eyes on the suspected man.

"Ay, Master Marner, what do ye want wi' me?" said Jem, trembling a little, and seizing his drinking-can as a defensive weapon.

"If it was you stole my money," said Silas, clasping his hands entreatingly, and raising his voice to a cry, "give it me back,—and I won't meddle with you. I won't set the constable on you. Give it me back, and I'll let you—I'll let you have a guinea."

"Me stole your money!" said Jem angrily. "I'll pitch this can at your eye if you talk o' *my* stealing your money."

[1] Murdered too—Jem half suspects Silas is a ghost.

"Come, come, Master Marner," said the landlord, now rising resolutely, and seizing Marner by the shoulder, "if you've got any information to lay, speak it out sensible, and show as you're in your right mind, if you expect anybody to listen to you. You're as wet as a drownded rat. Sit down and dry yourself, and speak straightforrard."

"Ah, to be sure, man," said the farrier, who began to feel that he had not been quite on a par with himself and the occasion. "Let's have no more staring and screaming, else we'll have you strapped for a madman.[2] That was why I didn't speak at the first —thinks I, the man's run mad."

"Ay, ay, make him sit down," said several voices at once, well pleased that the reality of ghosts remained still an open question.

The landlord forced Marner to take off his coat, and then to sit down on a chair aloof from every one else, in the centre of the circle, and in the direct rays of the fire. The weaver, too feeble to have any distinct purpose beyond that of getting help to recover his money, submitted unresistingly. The transient fears of the company were now forgotten in their strong curiosity, and all faces were turned towards Silas, when the landlord, having seated himself again, said,—

"Now, then, Master Marner, what 's this you 've got to say— as you've been robbed? Speak out."

"He'd better not say again as it was me robbed him," cried Jem Rodney hastily. "What could I ha' done with his money? I could as easy steal the parson's surplice, and wear it."

"Hold your tongue, Jem, and let's hear what he's got to say," said the landlord. "Now, then, Master Marner."

Silas now told his story under frequent questioning, as the mysterious character of the robbery became evident.

This strangely novel situation of opening his trouble to his Raveloe neighbors, of sitting in the warmth of a hearth not his own, and feeling the presence of faces and voices which were his nearest promise of help, had doubtless its influence on Marner, in spite of his passionate preoccupation with his loss. Our consciousness rarely registers the beginning of a growth within us any more

---

[2] Strapped for a madman—The old method of dealing with the violently insane was to strap them to boards and then either starve or beat them in order to drive out the evil spirits which were supposed to cause madness.

than without us: there have been many circulations of the sap before we detect the smallest sign of the bud.

The slight suspicion with which his hearers at first listened to him gradually melted away before the convincing simplicity of his distress: it was impossible for the neighbors to doubt that Marner was telling the truth, not because they were capable of arguing at once from the nature of his statements to the absence of any motive for making them falsely, but because, as Mr. Macey observed, "Folks as had the devil to back 'em were not likely to be so mushed" as poor Silas was. Rather, from the strange fact that the robber had left no traces, and had happened to know the nick of time, utterly incalculable by mortal agents, when Silas would go away from home without locking his door, the more probable conclusion seemed to be, that his disreputable intimacy in that quarter, if it ever existed, had been broken up, and that, in consequence, this ill turn had been done to Marner by somebody it was quite in vain to set the constable after. Why this preternatural felon should be obliged to wait till the door was left unlocked was a question which did not present itself.

"It isn't Jem Rodney as has done this work, Master Marner," said the landlord. "You mustn't be a-casting your eye at poor Jem. There may be a bit of a reckoning against Jem for the matter of a hare or so, if anybody was bound to keep their eyes staring open, and niver to wink; but Jem's been a-sitting here drinking his can, like the decentest man i' the parish, since before you left your house, Master Marner, by your own account."

"Ay, ay," said Mr. Macey, "let's have no accusing o' the innicent. That isn't the law. There must be folks to swear again' a man before he can be ta'en up. Let's have no accusing o' the innicent, Master Marner."

Memory was not so utterly torpid in Silas that it could not be wakened by these words. With a movement of compunction, as new and strange to him as everything else within the last hour, he started from his chair and went close up to Jem, looking at him as if he wanted to assure himself of the expression in his face.

"I was wrong," he said; "yes, yes—I ought to have thought. There's nothing to witness against you, Jem. Only you'd been into my house oftener than anybody else, and so you came into my head. I don't accuse you— I won't accuse anybody—only," he added, lifting up his hands to his head, and turning away with bewildered misery, "I try—I try to think where my guineas can be."

"Ay, ay, they're gone where it's hot enough to melt 'em, I doubt," said Mr. Macey.

"Tchuh!" said the farrier. And then he asked, with a cross-examining air, "How much money might there be in the bags, Master Marner?"

"Two hundred and seventy-two pounds,[3] twelve and sixpence, last night when I counted it," said Silas, seating himself again, with a groan.

"Pooh! why, they'd be none so heavy to carry. Some tramp's been in, that's all; and as for the no footmarks, and the bricks and the sand being all right—why, your eyes are pretty much like a insect's, Master Marner; they're obliged to look so close, you can't see much at a time. It's my opinion as, if I'd been you, or you'd been me—for it comes to the same thing—you wouldn't have thought you'd found everything as you left it. But what I vote is, as two of the sensiblest o' the company should go with you to Master Kench, the constable's—he's ill i' bed, I know that much—and get him to appoint one of us his deppity; for that's the law, and I don't think anybody 'ull take upon him to contradick me there. It isn't much of a walk to Kench's; and then, if it's me as is deppity, I'll go back with you, Master Marner, and examine your premises; and if anybody's got any fault to find with that, I'll thank him to stand up and say it out like a man."

By this pregnant speech the farrier had reëstablished his self-complacency, and waited with confidence to hear himself named as one of the superlatively sensible men.

"Let us see how the night is, though," said the landlord, who also considered himself personally concerned in this proposition. "Why, it rains heavy still," he said, returning from the door.

"Well, I'm not the man to be afraid o' the rain," said the farrier. "For it'll look bad when Justice Malam hears as respectable men like us had a information laid before 'em and took no steps."

The landlord agreed with this view, and after taking the sense of the company, and duly rehearsing a small ceremony known in

[3] Two HUNDRED AND SEVENTY-TWO POUNDS—Silas's savings, therefore, amounted to about $1,350, a small fortune in those days for one of his profession.

high ecclesiastical life as the *nolo episcopari,*[4] he consented to take on himself the chill dignity of going to Kench's. But to the farrier's strong disgust, Mr. Macey now started an objection to his proposing himself as a deputy-constable; for that oracular old gentleman, claiming to know the law, stated, as a fact delivered to him by his father, that no doctor could be a constable.

"And you're a doctor, I reckon, though you're only a cow-doctor—for a fly's a fly, though it may be a hoss-fly," concluded Mr. Macey, wondering a little at his own " 'cuteness."

There was a hot debate upon this, the farrier being of course indisposed to renounce the quality of doctor, but contending that a doctor could be a constable if he liked—the law meant, he needn't be one if he didn't like. Mr. Macey thought this was nonsense, since the law was not likely to be fonder of doctors than of other folks. Moreover, if it was in the nature of doctors more than of other men not to like being constables, how came Mr. Dowlas to be so eager to act in that capacity?

"*I* don't want to act the constable," said the farrier, driven into a corner by this merciless reasoning; "and there's no man can say it of me, if he'd tell the truth. But if there's to be any jealousy and en*v*ying about going to Kench's in the rain, let them go as like it—you won't get me to go, I can tell you."

By the landlord's intervention, however, the dispute was accommodated. Mr. Dowlas consented to go as a second person disinclined to act officially; and so poor Silas, furnished with some old coverings, turned out with his two companions into the rain again, thinking of the long night hours before him, not as those do who long to rest, but as those who expect to "watch for the morning."

## CHAPTER VIII

When Godfrey Cass returned from Mrs. Osgood's party at midnight, he was not much surprised to learn that Dunsey had not come home. Perhaps he had not sold Wildfire, and was waiting for another chance—perhaps, on that foggy afternoon, he had preferred

---

[4] *Nolo episcopari*—I do not desire to be made a bishop. Part of the ritual in the ceremony of installing a bishop. Notwithstanding this statement, the candidate knows his installation will be completed. This phrase has come to typify any perfunctory refusal made for the sake of appearances. The landlord does not wish to appear over-anxious to go on this errand, but in reality the idea appeals to him.

housing himself at the Red Lion at Batherley for the night, if the run had kept him in that neighborhood; for he was not likely to feel much concern about leaving his brother in suspense. Godfrey's mind was too full of Nancy Lammeter's looks and behavior, too full of the exasperation against himself and his lot, which the sight of her always produced in him, for him to give much thought to Wildfire or to the probabilities of Dunstan's conduct.

The next morning the whole village was excited by the story of the robbery, and Godfrey, like every one else, was occupied in gathering and discussing news about it, and in visiting the Stone-pits. The rain had washed away all possibility of distinguishing footmarks, but a close investigation of the spot had disclosed, in the direction opposite to the village, a tinder-box, with a flint and steel, half sunk in the mud. It was not Silas's tinder-box, for the only one he had ever had was still standing on his shelf; and the inference generally accepted was, that the tinder-box in the ditch was somehow connected with the robbery. A small minority shook their heads, and intimated their opinion that it was not a robbery to have much light thrown on it by tinder-boxes, that Master Marner's tale had a queer look with it, and that such things had been known as a man's doing himself a mischief, and then setting the justice to look for the doer. But when questioned closely as to their grounds for this opinion, and what Master Marner had to gain by such false pretences, they only shook their heads as before, and observed that there was no knowing what some folks counted gain; moreover, that everybody had a right to their own opinions, grounds or no grounds, and that the weaver, as everybody knew, was partly crazy. Mr. Macey, though he joined in the defence of Marner against all suspicions of deceit, also pooh-poohed the tinder-box; indeed, repudiated it as a rather impious suggestion, tending to imply that everything must be done by human hands, and that there was no power which could make away with the guineas without moving the bricks. Nevertheless, he turned round rather sharply on Mr. Tookey, when the zealous deputy, feeling that this was a view of the case peculiarly suited to a parish-clerk, carried it still further, and doubted whether it was right to inquire into a robbery at all when the circumstances were so mysterious.

"As if," concluded Mr. Tookey—"as if there was nothing but what could be made out by justices and constables."

"Now, don't you be for overshooting the mark, Tookey," said Mr. Macey, nodding his head aside admonishingly. "That's what you're allays at; if I throw a stone and hit, you think there's summat better than hitting, and you try to throw a stone beyond. What I said was against the tinder-box; I said nothing against justices and constables, for they're o' King George's making, and it 'ud be ill-becoming a man in a parish office to fly out again' King George."

While these discussions were going on amongst the group outside the Rainbow a higher consultation was being carried on within, under the presidency of Mr. Crackenthorp, the rector, assisted by Squire Cass and other substantial parishioners. It had just occurred to Mr. Snell, the landlord,—he being, as he observed, a man accustomed to put two and two together,—to connect with the tinder-box which, as deputy-constable, he himself had had the honorable distinction of finding, certain recollections of a pedlar who had called to drink at the house about a month before, and had actually stated that he carried a tinder-box about with him to light his pipe. Here, surely, was a clue to be followed out. And as memory, when duly impregnated with ascertained facts, is sometimes surprisingly fertile, Mr. Snell gradually recovered a vivid impression of the effect produced on him by the pedlar's countenance and conversation. He had a "look with his eye" which fell unpleasantly on Mr. Snell's sensitive organism. To be sure, he didn't say anything particular,—no, except that about the tinder-box,—but it isn't what a man says, it's the way he says it. Moreover, he had a swarthy foreignness of complexion which boded little honesty.[1]

"Did he wear ear-rings?" Mr. Crackenthorp wished to know, having some acquaintance with foreign customs.

"Well—stay—let me see," said Mr. Snell, like a docile clairvoyant, who would really not make a mistake if she could help it. After stretching the corners of his mouth and contracting his eyes, as if he were trying to see the ear-rings, he appeared to give up the effort, and said, "Well, he'd got ear-rings in his box to sell, so it's nat'ral to suppose he might wear 'em. But he called at every house, a'most, in the village; there's somebody else, mayhap, saw 'em in his ears, though I can't take upon me rightly to say."

---

[1] SWARTHY FOREIGNNESS . . . LITTLE HONESTY—Again George Eliot impresses the reader with the fact that the villagers associate the unknown with evil.

Mr. Snell was correct in his surmise, that somebody else would remember the pedlar's ear-rings. For, on the spread of inquiry among the villagers, it was stated with gathering emphasis, that the parson had wanted to know whether the pedlar wore ear-rings in his ears, and an impression was created that a great deal depended on the eliciting of this fact. Of course every one who heard the question, not having any distinct image of the pedlar as *without* ear-rings, immediately had an image of him *with* ear-rings, larger or smaller, as the case might be; and the image was presently taken for a vivid recollection, so that the glazier's wife, a well-intentioned woman, not given to lying,[2] and whose house was among the cleanest in the village, was ready to declare, as sure as ever she meant to take the sacrament the very next Christmas that was ever coming, that she had seen big ear-rings, in the shape of the young moon, in the pedlar's two ears; while Jinny Oates, the cobbler's daughter, being a more imaginative person, stated not only that she had seen them too, but that they had made her blood creep, as it did at that very moment while there she stood.

Also, by way of throwing further light on this clue of the tinder-box, a collection was made of all the articles purchased from the pedlar at various houses, and carried to the Rainbow to be exhibited there. In fact, there was a general feeling in the village, that for the clearing-up of this robbery there must be a great deal done at the Rainbow, and that no man need offer his wife an excuse for going there while it was the scene of severe public duties.

Some disappointment was felt, and perhaps a little indignation also, when it became known that Silas Marner, on being questioned by the Squire and the parson, had retained no other recollection of the pedlar than that he had called at his door, but had not entered his house, having turned away at once when Silas, holding the door ajar, had said that he wanted nothing. This had been Silas's testimony, though he clutched strongly at the idea of the pedlar's being the culprit, if only because it gave him a definite image of a whereabout for his gold, after it had been taken away from its hiding-place: he could see it now in the pedlar's box. But it was observed with some irritation in the village, that anybody

---

[2] NOT GIVEN TO LYING—Note that the villagers are not malicious by nature. The little evil they do springs from the ignorance and the superstition which have been bred in them for generations.

but a "blind creatur" like Marner would have seen the man prowling about, for how came he to leave his tinder-box in the ditch close by, if he hadn't been lingering there? Doubtless, he had made his observations when he saw Marner at the door. Anybody might know—and only look at him—that the weaver was a half-crazy miser. It was a wonder the pedlar hadn't murdered him; men of that sort, with rings in their ears, had been known for murderers often and often; there had been one tried at the 'sizes,[3] not so long ago but what there were people living who remembered it.

Godfrey Cass, indeed, entering the Rainbow during one of Mr. Snell's frequently repeated recitals of his testimony, had treated it lightly, stating that he himself had bought a pen-knife of the pedlar, and thought him a merry grinning fellow enough; it was all nonsense, he said, about the man's evil looks.[4] But this was spoken of in the village as the random talk of youth, "as if it was only Mr. Snell who had seen something odd about the pedlar!" On the contrary, there were at least half a dozen who were ready to go before Justice Malam, and give in much more striking testimony than any the landlord could furnish. It was to be hoped Mr. Godfrey would not go to Tarley and throw cold water on what Mr. Snell said there, and so prevent the justice from drawing up a warrant. He was suspected of intending this, when, after mid-day, he was seen setting off on horseback in the direction of Tarley.

But by this time Godfrey's interest in the robbery had faded before his growing anxiety about Dunstan and Wildfire, and he was going, not to Tarley, but to Batherley, unable to rest in uncertainty about them any longer. The possibility that Dunstan had played him the ugly trick of riding away with Wildfire, to return at the end of a month, when he had gambled away or otherwise squandered the price of the horse, was a fear that urged itself upon him more, even, than the thought of an accidental injury; and now that the dance at Mrs. Osgood's was past, he was irritated with himself that he had trusted his horse to Dunstan. Instead of trying to still his fears he encouraged them, with that superstitious impression which clings to us all, that if we expect evil very strongly it is

[3] 'Sizes—The assizes, or county courts.

[4] Nonsense . . . evil looks—Note the two persons whom the author represents as having an unbiased opinion of the pedlar. One is Silas, whose honesty is too real even to be tempted by the promptings of imagination; the other is Godfrey Cass, whom the author reveals as calmly reasonable about things which do not closely concern himself.

the less likely to come;[5] and when he heard a horse approaching at a trot, and saw a hat rising above a hedge beyond an angle of the lane, he felt as if his conjuration had succeeded. But no sooner did the horse come within sight than his heart sank again. It was not Wildfire; and in a few moments more he discerned that the rider was not Dunstan, but Bryce, who pulled up to speak, with a face that implied something disagreeable.

"Well, Mr. Godfrey, that's a lucky brother of yours, that Master Dunsey, isn't he?"

"What do you mean?" said Godfrey hastily.

"Why, hasn't he been home yet?" said Bryce.

"Home?—no. What has happened? Be quick! What has he done with my horse?"

"Ah, I thought it was yours, though he pretended you had parted with it to him."

"Has he thrown him down and broken his knees?" said Godfrey, flushed with exasperation.

"Worse than that," said Bryce. "You see, I'd made a bargain with him to buy the horse for a hundred and twenty—a swinging price, but I always liked the horse. And what does he do but go and stake him,—fly at a hedge with stakes in it, atop of a bank with a ditch before it. The horse had been dead a pretty good while when he was found. So he hasn't been home since, has he?"

"Home?—no," said Godfrey, "and he'd better keep away. Confound me for a fool! I might have known this would be the end of it."

"Well, to tell you the truth," said Bryce, "after I'd bargained for the horse, it did come into my head that he might be riding and selling the horse without your knowledge, for I didn't believe it was his own. I knew Master Dunsey was up to his tricks sometimes. But where can he be gone? He's never been seen at Batherley. He couldn't have been hurt, for he must have walked off."

"Hurt?" said Godfrey bitterly. "He'll never be hurt—he's made to hurt other people."

"And so you *did* give him leave to sell the horse, eh?" said Bryce.

"Yes; I wanted to part with the horse—he was always a little

---

[5] EVIL . . . LESS LIKELY TO COME—If Godfrey is reasonable in his judgments of others' difficulties, he is not so when his own welfare is at stake.

too hard in the mouth for me," said Godfrey; his pride making him wince under the idea that Bryce guessed the sale to be a matter of necessity. "I was going to see after him—I thought some mischief had happened. I'll go back now," he added, turning the horse's head, and wishing he could get rid of Bryce; for he felt that the long-dreaded crisis in his life was close upon him. "You're coming on to Raveloe, aren't you?"

"Well, no, not now," said Bryce. "I *was* coming round there, for I had to go to Flitton, and I thought I might as well take you in my way, and just let you know all I knew myself about the horse. I suppose Master Dunsey didn't like to show himself till the ill news had blown over a bit. He's perhaps gone to pay a visit at the Three Crowns, by Whitbridge—I know he's fond of the house."

"Perhaps he is," said Godfrey, rather absently. Then rousing himself, he said, with an effort at carelessness, "We shall hear of him soon enough, I'll be bound."

"Well, here's my turning," said Bryce, not surprised to perceive that Godfrey was rather "down"; "so I'll bid you good-day, and wish I may bring you better news another time."

Godfrey rode along slowly, representing to himself the scene of confession to his father from which he felt that there was now no longer any escape. The revelation about the money must be made the very next morning; and if he withheld the rest, Dunstan would be sure to come back shortly, and, finding that he must bear the brunt of his father's anger, would tell the whole story out of spite, even though he had nothing to gain by it. There was one step, perhaps, by which he might still win Dunstan's silence and put off the evil day: he might tell his father that he had himself spent the money paid to him by Fowler; and as he had never been guilty of such an offence before, the affair would blow over after a little storming. But Godfrey could not bend himself to this. He felt that in letting Dunstan have the money he had already been guilty of a breach of trust hardly less culpable than that of spending the money directly for his own behoof; and yet there was a distinction between the two acts which made him feel that the one was so much more blackening than the other as to be intolerable to him.

"I don't pretend to be a good fellow," he said to himself; "but I'm not a scoundrel—at least, I'll stop short somewhere. I'll bear the consequences of what I *have* done sooner than make believe

I've done what I never would have done. I'd never have spent the money for my own pleasure—I was tortured into it."

Through the remainder of this day Godfrey, with only occasional fluctuations, kept his will bent in the direction of a complete avowal to his father, and he withheld the story of Wildfire's loss till the next morning, that it might serve him as an introduction to heavier matter. The old Squire was accustomed to his son's frequent absence from home, and thought neither Dunstan's nor Wildfire's non-appearance a matter calling for remark. Godfrey said to himself again and again, that if he let slip this one opportunity of confession, he might never have another; the revelation might be made even in a more odious way than by Dunstan's malignity,—*she* might come, as she had threatened to do. And then he tried to make the scene easier to himself by rehearsal: he made up his mind how he would pass from the admission of his weakness in letting Dunstan have the money to the fact that Dunstan had a hold on him which he had been unable to shake off, and how he would work up his father to expect something very bad before he told him the fact. The old Squire was an implacable man: he made resolutions in violent anger, and he was not to be moved from them after his anger had subsided—as fiery volcanic matters cool and harden into rock. Like many violent and implacable men, he allowed evils to grow under favor of his own heedlessness, till they pressed upon him with exasperating force, and then he turned round with fierce severity and became unrelentingly hard. This was his system with his tenants: he allowed them to get into arrears, neglect their fences, reduce their stock, sell their straw, and otherwise go the wrong way,—and then, when he became short of money in consequence of this indulgence, he took the hardest measures and would listen to no appeal. Godfrey knew all this, and felt it with the greater force because he had constantly suffered annoyance from witnessing his father's sudden fits of unrelentingness, for which his own habitual irresolution deprived him of all sympathy. (He was not critical on the faulty indulgence which preceded these fits; *that* seemed to him natural enough.) Still there was just the chance, Godfrey thought, that his father's pride might see this marriage in a light that would induce him to hush it up, rather than turn his son out and make the family the talk of the country for ten miles round.

This was the view of the case that Godfrey managed to keep before him pretty closely till midnight, and he went to sleep thinking that he had done with inward debating. But when he awoke in the still morning darkness he found it impossible to reawaken his evening thoughts; it was as if they had been tired out and were not to be roused to further work. Instead of arguments for confession, he could now feel the presence of nothing but its evil consequences: the old dread of disgrace came back—the old shrinking from the thought of raising a hopeless barrier between himself and Nancy—the old disposition to rely on chances which might be favorable to him, and save him from betrayal. Why, after all, should he cut off the hope of them by his own act? He had seen the matter in a wrong light yesterday. He had been in a rage with Dunstan, and had thought of nothing but a thorough break-up of their mutual understanding; but what it would be really wisest for him to do was to try and soften his father's anger against Dunsey, and keep things as nearly as possible in their old condition. If Dunsey did not come back for a few days (and Godfrey did not know but that the rascal had enough money in his pocket to enable him to keep away still longer), everything might blow over.

## CHAPTER IX

Godfrey rose and took his own breakfast earlier than usual, but lingered in the wainscoted parlor till his younger brothers had finished their meal and gone out, awaiting his father, who always took a walk with his managing-man before breakfast. Every one breakfasted at a different hour in the Red House, and the Squire was always the latest, giving a long chance to a rather feeble morning appetite before he tried it. The table had been spread with substantial eatables nearly two hours before he presented himself—a tall, stout man of sixty, with a face in which the knit brow and rather hard glance seemed contradicted by the slack and feeble mouth. His person showed marks of habitual neglect, his dress was slovenly; and yet there was something in the presence of the old Squire distinguishable from that of the ordinary farmers in the parish, who were perhaps every whit as refined as he, but, having slouched their way through life with a consciousness of being in the vicinity of their "betters," wanted that self-possession and authoritativeness of voice and carriage which belonged to a man who thought of superiors as remote existences, with whom he had personally little more to do than with America[1] or the stars. The Squire had been used to parish homage all his life, used to the presupposition that his family, his tankards, and everything that was his, were the oldest and best; and as he never associated with any gentry higher than himself, his opinion was not disturbed by comparison.

He glanced at his son as he entered the room, and said, "What, sir! haven't *you* had your breakfast yet?" but there was no pleasant morning greeting between them; not because of any unfriendliness, but because the sweet flower of courtesy is not a growth of such homes as the Red House.

"Yes, sir," said Godfrey, "I've had my breakfast, but I was waiting to speak to you."

"Ah! well," said the Squire, throwing himself indifferently into his chair, and speaking in a ponderous coughing fashion, which was felt in Raveloe to be a sort of privilege of his rank, while he cut a piece of beef, and held it up before the deerhound that had come in with him. "Ring the bell for my ale, will you? You youngsters' business is your own pleasure, mostly. There's no hurry about it for anybody but yourselves."

The Squire's life was quite as idle as his sons', but it was a fiction kept up by himself and his contemporaries in Raveloe that youth was exclusively the period of folly, and that their aged wisdom was constantly in a state of endurance mitigated by sarcasm. Godfrey waited, before he spoke again, until the ale had been brought and the door closed—an interval during which Fleet, the deerhound, had consumed enough bits of beef to make a poor man's holiday dinner.

"There's been a cursed piece of ill-luck with Wildfire," he began; "happened the day before yesterday."

"What! broke his knees?" said the Squire, after taking a draught of ale. "I thought you knew how to ride better than that, sir. I never threw a horse down in my life. If I had, I might ha' whistled for another, for *my* father wasn't quite so ready to unstring[2] as some other fathers I know of. But they must turn over a new

[1] America—Note how remote America seemed to the people of England at that time.

[2] Unstring—Open the purse-strings.

leaf—*they* must. What with mortgages and arrears I'm as short o' cash as a roadside pauper. And that fool Kimble says the newspaper's talking about peace. Why, the country wouldn't have a leg to stand on. Prices 'ud run down like a jack,[3] and I should never get my arrears, not if I sold all the fellows up. And there's that damned Fowler, I won't put up with him any longer; I've told Winthrop to go to Cox this very day. The lying scoundrel told me he'd be sure to pay me a hundred last month. He takes advantage because he's on that outlying farm and thinks I shall forget him."

The Squire had delivered this speech in a coughing and interrupted manner, but with no pause long enough for Godfrey to make it a pretext for taking up the word again. He felt that his father meant to ward off any request for money on the ground of the misfortune with Wildfire, and that the emphasis he had thus been led to lay on his shortness of cash and his arrears was likely to produce an attitude of mind the utmost unfavorable for his own disclosure. But he must go on now he had begun.

"It's worse than breaking the horse's knees—he's been staked and killed," he said, as soon as his father was silent, and had begun to cut his meat. "But I wasn't thinking of asking you to buy me another horse; I was only thinking I'd lost the means of paying you with the price of Wildfire as I'd meant to do. Dunsey took him to the hunt to sell him for me the other day, and after he'd made a bargain for a hundred and twenty with Bryce he went after the hounds, and took some fool's leap or other that did for the horse at once. If it hadn't been for that, I should have paid you a hundred pounds this morning."

The Squire had laid down his knife and fork and was staring at his son in amazement, not being sufficiently quick of brain to form a probable guess as to what could have caused so strange an inversion of the paternal and filial relations as this proposition of his son to pay him a hundred pounds.

"The truth is, sir—I'm very sorry—I was quite to blame," said Godfrey. "Fowler did pay that hundred pounds. He paid it to me when I was over there one day last month. And Dunsey bothered me for the money, and I let him have it, because I hoped I should be able to pay it you before this."

[3] Run down like a jack—Many jacks, or spits for roasting meat, were operated by a clock mechanism so crude that they would often run down rapidly.

The Squire was purple with anger before his son had done speaking, and found utterance difficult. "You let Dunsey have it, sir? And how long have you been so thick with Dunsey that you must *collogue*[4] with him to embezzle my money? Are you turning out a scamp? I tell you I won't have it. I'll turn the whole pack of you out of the house together, and marry again. I'd have you to remember, sir, my property's got no entail on it;[5] since my grandfather's time the Casses can do as they like with their land. Remember that, sir. Let Dunsey have the money! Why should you let Dunsey have the money? There's some lie at the bottom of it."

"There's no lie, sir," said Godfrey. "I wouldn't have spent the money myself, but Dunsey bothered me, and I was a fool and let him have it. But I meant to pay it whether he did or not. That's the whole story. I never meant to embezzle money, and I'm not the man to do it. You never knew me do a dishonest trick, sir."

"Where's Dunsey, then? What do you stand talking there for? Go and fetch Dunsey, as I tell you, and let him give account of what he wanted the money for, and what he's done with it. He shall repent it. I'll turn him out. I said I would, and I'll do it. He shan't brave me. Go and fetch him."

"Dunsey isn't come back, sir."

"What! did he break his own neck, then?" said the Squire with some disgust at the idea that, in that case, he could not fulfil his threat.

"No, he wasn't hurt, I believe, for the horse was found dead, and Dunsey must have walked off. I dare say we shall see him again by and by. I don't know where he is."

"And what must you be letting him have my money for? Answer me that," said the Squire, attacking Godfrey again, since Dunsey was not within reach.

"Well, sir, I don't know," said Godfrey hesitatingly. That was a feeble evasion, but Godfrey was not fond of lying, and, not being sufficiently aware that no sort of duplicity can long flourish without the help of vocal falsehoods, he was quite unprepared with invented motives.

"You don't know? I tell you what it is, sir. You've been up to some trick, and you've been bribing him not to tell," said the

---

[4] *Collogue*—Conspire.

[5] No entail on it—No requirement as to the Squire's disposal of the property.

Squire with a sudden acuteness which startled Godfrey, who felt his heart beat violently at the nearness of his father's guess. The sudden alarm pushed him on to take the next step—a very slight impulse suffices for that on a downward road.

"Why, sir," he said, trying to speak with careless ease, "it was a little affair between me and Dunsey; it's no matter to anybody else. It's hardly worth while to pry into young men's fooleries: it wouldn't have made any difference to you, sir, if I'd not had the bad luck to lose Wildfire. I should have paid you the money."

"Fooleries! Pshaw! it's time you'd done with fooleries. And I'd have you know, sir, you *must* ha' done with 'em," said the Squire, frowning and casting an angry glance at his son. "Your goings-on are not what I shall find money for any longer. There's my grandfather had his stables full o' horses, and kept a good house, too, and in worse times, by what I can make out; and so might I, if I hadn't four good for nothing fellows to hang on me like horse-leeches. I've been too good a father to you all—that's what it is. But I shall pull up, sir."

Godfrey was silent. He was not likely to be very penetrating in his judgments, but he had always had a sense that his father's indulgence had not been kindness, and had had a vague longing for some discipline that would have checked his own errant weakness and helped his better will. The Squire ate his bread and meat hastily, took a deep draught of ale, then turned his chair from the table, and began to speak again.

"It'll be all the worse for you, you know—you'd need try and help me keep things together."

"Well, sir, I've often offered to take the management of things, but you know you've taken it ill always, and seemed to think I wanted to push you out of your place."

"I know nothing o' your offering or o' my taking it ill," said the Squire, whose memory consisted in certain strong impressions unmodified by detail; "but I know one while you seemed to be thinking o' marrying, and I didn't offer to put any obstacles in your way, as some fathers would. I'd as lieve you married Lammeter's daughter as anybody. I suppose if I'd said you nay, you'd ha' kept on with it; but for want o' contradiction you've changed your mind. You're a shilly-shally fellow: you take after your poor mother. She never had a will of her own; a woman has no call for one, if she's got a proper man for her husband. But *your* wife had need have one, for you hardly know your own mind enough to make both your legs walk one way. The lass hasn't said downright she won't have you, has she?"

"No," said Godfrey, feeling very hot and uncomfortable; "but I don't think she will."

"Think! why haven't you the courage to ask her? Do you stick to it, you want to have *her*—that's the thing?"

"There's no other woman I want to marry," said Godfrey evasively.

"Well, then, let me make the offer for you, that's all, if you haven't the pluck to do it yourself. Lammeter isn't likely to be loath for his daughter to marry into *my* family, I should think. And as for the pretty lass, she wouldn't have her cousin—and there's nobody else, as I see, could ha' stood in your way."

"I'd rather let it be, please, sir, at present," said Godfrey, in alarm. "I think she's a little offended with me just now, and I should like to speak for myself. A man must manage these things for himself."

"Well, speak then and manage it, and see if you can't turn over a new leaf. That's what a man must do when he thinks o' marrying."

"I don't see how I can think of it at present, sir. You wouldn't like to settle me on one of the farms, I suppose, and I don't think she'd come to live in this house with all my brothers. It's a different sort of life to what she's been used to."

"Not come to live in this house? Don't tell me. You ask her, that's all," said the Squire, with a short, scornful laugh.

"I'd rather let the thing be at present, sir," said Godfrey. "I hope you won't try to hurry it on by saying anything."

"I shall do what I choose," said the Squire, "and I shall let you know I'm master; else you may turn out and find an estate to drop into somewhere else. Go out and tell Winthrop not to go to Cox's, but wait for me. And tell 'em to get my horse saddled. And, stop: look out and get that hack o' Dunsey's sold, and hand me the money, will you? He'll keep no more hacks at my expense. And if you know where he's sneaking—I dare say you do—you may tell him to spare himself the journey o' coming back home. Let him turn ostler and keep himself. He shan't hang on me any more."

"I don't know where he is; and if I did, it isn't my place to tell him to keep away," said Godfrey, moving towards the door.

"Confound it, sir, don't stay arguing, but go and order my horse," said the Squire, taking up a pipe.

Godfrey left the room, hardly knowing whether he were more relieved by the sense that the interview was ended without having made any change in his position, or more uneasy that he had entangled himself still further in prevarication and deceit. What had passed about his proposing to Nancy had raised a new alarm, lest by some after-dinner words of his father's to Mr. Lammeter he should be thrown into the embarrassment of being obliged absolutely to decline her when she seemed to be within his reach. He fled to his usual refuge, that of hoping for some unforeseen turn of fortune, some favorable chance which would save him from unpleasant consequences—perhaps even justify his insincerity by manifesting its prudence.

In this point of trusting to some throw of fortune's dice Godfrey can hardly be called old-fashioned. Favorable Chance is the god of all men who follow their own devices instead of obeying a law they believe in. Let even a polished man of these days get into a position he is ashamed to avow, and his mind will be bent on all the possible issues that may deliver him from the calculable results of that position. Let him live outside his income, or shirk the resolute honest work that brings wages, and he will presently find himself dreaming of a possible benefactor, a possible simpleton who may be cajoled into using his interest, a possible state of mind in some possible person not yet forthcoming. Let him neglect the responsibilities of his office, and he will inevitably anchor himself on the chance, that the thing left undone may turn out not to be of the supposed importance. Let him betray his friend's confidence, and he will adore that same cunning complexity called Chance, which gives him the hope that his friend will never know. Let him forsake a decent craft that he may pursue the gentilities of a profession to which nature never called him, and his religion will infallibly be the worship of blessed Chance, which he will believe in as the mighty creator of success. The evil principle deprecated in that religion is the orderly sequence by which the seed brings forth a crop after its kind.[6]

[6] KIND—George Eliot has dropped the story to comment on human frailty.

## CHAPTER X

Justice Malam was naturally regarded in Tarley and Raveloe as a man of capacious mind, seeing that he could draw much wider conclusions without evidence[1] than could be expected of his neighbors who were not on the Commission of the Peace. Such a man was not likely to neglect the clue of the tinder-box, and an inquiry was set on foot concerning a pedlar, name unknown, with curly black hair and a foreign complexion, carrying a box of cutlery and jewelry, and wearing large rings in his ears. But either because inquiry was too slow-footed to overtake him, or because the description applied to so many pedlars that inquiry did not know how to choose among them, weeks passed away, and there was no other result concerning the robbery than a gradual cessation of the excitement it had caused in Raveloe. Dunstan Cass's absence was hardly a subject of remark: he had once before had a quarrel with his father, and had gone off, nobody knew whither, to return at the end of six weeks, take up his old quarters unforbidden, and swagger as usual. His own family, who equally expected this issue, with the sole difference that the Squire was determined this time to forbid him the old quarters, never mentioned his absence, and when his Uncle Kimble or Mr. Osgood noticed it, the story of his having killed Wildfire, and committed some offence against his father, was enough to prevent surprise. To connect the fact of Dunsey's disappearance with that of the robbery occurring on the same day, lay quite away from the track of every one's thought—even Godfrey's, who had better reason than any one else to know what his brother was capable of. He remembered no mention of the weaver between them since the time, twelve years ago, when it was their boyish sport to deride him; and, besides, his imagination constantly created an *alibi* for Dunstan: he saw him continually in some congenial haunt, to which he had walked off on leaving Wildfire—saw him sponging on chance acquaintances, and meditating a return home to the old amusement of tormenting his elder brother. Even if any brain in Raveloe had put the said two facts together, I doubt whether a combination so injurious to the prescriptive respectability of a family with a mural monument[2] and venerable tankards would not have been suppressed as of unsound tendency. But Christmas

[1] CONCLUSIONS WITHOUT EVIDENCE—Typical of George Eliot's gentle irony.

[2] A MURAL MONUMENT—A monument set in a wall. See page 221, note 7.

puddings, brawn, and abundance of spirituous liquors, throwing the mental originality into the channel of nightmare, are great preservatives against a dangerous spontaneity of waking thought.

When the robbery was talked of at the Rainbow and elsewhere, in good company, the balance continued to waver between the rational explanation founded on the tinder-box and the theory of an impenetrable mystery that mocked investigation. The advocates of the tinder-box-and-pedlar view considered the other side a muddle-headed and credulous set, who, because they themselves were wall-eyed, supposed everybody else to have the same blank outlook; and the adherents of the inexplicable more than hinted that their antagonists were animals inclined to crow before they had found any corn,—mere skimming-dishes in point of depth,—whose clear-sightedness consisted in supposing there was nothing behind a barn-door because they couldn't see through it; so that, though their controversy did not serve to elicit the fact concerning the robbery, it elicited some true opinions of collateral importance.

But while poor Silas's loss served thus to brush the slow current of Raveloe conversation, Silas himself was feeling the withering desolation of that bereavement about which his neighbors were arguing at their ease. To any one who had observed him before he lost his gold it might have seemed that so withered and shrunken a life as his could hardly be susceptible of a bruise, could hardly endure any subtraction but such as would put an end to it altogether. But in reality it had been an eager life, filled with immediate purpose, which fenced him in from the wide, cheerless unknown. It had been a clinging life; and though the object round which its fibres had clung was a dead disrupted thing, it satisfied the need for clinging. But now the fence was broken down—the support was snatched away. Marner's thoughts could no longer move in their old round, and were baffled by a blank like that which meets a plodding ant when the earth has broken away on its homeward path. The loom was there, and the weaving, and the growing pattern in the cloth; but the bright treasure in the hole under his feet was gone; the prospect of handling and counting it was gone; the evening had no phantasm of delight to still the poor soul's craving. The thought of the money he would get by his actual work could bring no joy, for its meagre image was only a fresh reminder of his loss; and hope was too heavily crushed by the sudden blow for his imagination to dwell on the growth of a new hoard from that small beginning.

He filled up the blank with grief. As he sat weaving, he every now and then moaned low, like one in pain: it was the sign that his thoughts had come round again to the sudden chasm—to the empty evening time. And all the evening, as he sat in his loneliness by his dull fire, he leaned his elbows on his knees, and clasped his head with his hands, and moaned very low—not as one who seeks to be heard.

And yet he was not utterly forsaken in his trouble. The repulsion Marner had always created in his neighbors was partly dissipated by the new light in which this misfortune had shown him. Instead of a man who had more cunning than honest folks could come by, and, what was worse, had not the inclination to use that cunning in a neighborly way, it was now apparent that Silas had not cunning enough to keep his own. He was generally spoken of as a "poor mushed creatur"; and that avoidance of his neighbors, which had before been referred to his ill-will, and to a probable addiction to worse company, was now considered mere craziness.

This change to a kindlier feeling was shown in various ways. The odor of Christmas cooking being on the wind, it was the season when superfluous pork and black puddings[3] are suggestive of charity in well to do families; and Silas's misfortune had brought him uppermost in the memory of housekeepers like Mrs. Osgood. Mr. Crackenthorp, too, while he admonished Silas that his money had probably been taken from him because he thought too much of it and never came to church, enforced the doctrine by a present of pigs' pettitoes,[4] well calculated to dissipate unfounded prejudices against the clerical character. Neighbors, who had nothing but verbal consolation to give, showed a disposition not only to greet Silas, and discuss his misfortune at some length when they encountered him in the village, but also to take the trouble of calling at his cottage, and getting him to repeat all the details on the very spot; and then they would try to cheer him by saying, "Well, Master Marner, you're no worse off nor other poor folks, after all; and if you was to be crippled, the parish 'ud give you a 'lowance."

---

[3] Black puddings—Blood puddings resembling sausages.

[4] Pigs' pettitoes—Pigs' feet.

I suppose one reason why we are seldom able to comfort our neighbors with our words is that our good-will gets adulterated, in spite of ourselves, before it can pass our lips. We can send black puddings and pettitoes without giving them a flavor of our own egoism; but language is a stream that is almost sure to smack of a mingled soil. There was a fair proportion of kindness in Raveloe; but it was often of a beery and bungling sort, and took the shape least allied to the complimentary and hypocritical.

Mr. Macey, for example, coming one evening expressly to let Silas know that recent events had given him the advantage of standing more favorably in the opinion of a man whose judgment was not formed lightly, opened the conversation by saying, as soon as he had seated himself and adjusted his thumbs,—

"Come, Master Marner, why, you've no call to sit a-moaning. You're a deal better off to ha' lost your money, nor to ha' kep' it by foul means. I used to think, when you first come into these parts, as you were no better nor you should be; you were younger a deal than what you are now; but you were allays a staring, white-faced creatur, partly like a bald-faced calf, as I may say. But there's no knowing: it isn't every queer-looksed thing as Old Harry's had the making of—I mean, speaking o' toads and such; for they're often harmless, and useful against varmin. And it's pretty much the same wi' you, as fur as I can see. Though as to the yarbs[5] and stuff to cure the breathing, if you brought that sort o' knowledge from distant parts, you might ha' been a bit freer of it. And if the knowledge wasn't well come by, why, you might ha' made up for it by coming to church reg'lar; for, as for the children as the Wise Woman charmed, I've been at the christening of 'em again and again, and they took the water just as well. And that's reasonable; for if Old Harry's a mind to do a bit o' kindness for a holiday, like, who's got anything against it? That's my thinking; and I've been clerk o' this parish forty year, and I know, when the parson and me does the cussing of a Ash Wednesday,[6] there's no cussing o' folks as have a mind to be cured without a doctor, let Kimble say what he will. And so, Master Marner, as I was saying—for there's windings i' things as they may carry you to the fur end o' the

[5] Yarbs—Herbs.

[6] Does the cussing of a Ash Wednesday—Reference to a service read in the Church of England on Ash Wednesday, in which various types of sinners are cursed, or denounced.

prayer-book afore you get back to 'em—my advice is, as you keep up your sperrits; for as for thinking you're a deep un, and ha' got more inside you nor 'ull bear daylight, I'm not o' that opinion at all, and so I tell the neighbors. For, says I, you talk o' Master Marner making out a tale—why, it's nonsense, that is: it 'ud take a 'cute man to make a tale like that; and, says I, he looked as scared as a rabbit."

During this discursive address Silas had continued motionless in his previous attitude, leaning his elbows on his knees, and pressing his hands against his head. Mr. Macey, not doubting that he had been listened to, paused, in the expectation of some appreciatory reply, but Marner remained silent.[7] He had a sense that the old man meant to be good-natured and neighborly; but the kindness fell on him as sunshine falls on the wretched—he had no heart to taste it, and felt that it was very far off him.

"Come, Master Marner, have you got nothing to say to that?" said Mr. Macey at last, with a slight accent of impatience.

"Oh," said Marner, slowly, shaking his head between his hands, "I thank you—thank you—kindly."

"Ay, ay, to be sure; I thought you would," said Mr. Macey; "and my advice is—have you got a Sunday suit?"

"No," said Marner.

"I doubted it was so," said Mr. Macey. "Now, let me advise you to get a Sunday suit; there's Tookey, he's a poor creatur, but he's got my tailoring business, and some o' my money in it, and he shall make a suit at a low price, and give you trust, and then you can come to church, and be a bit neighborly. Why, you've never heared me say 'Amen' since you come into these parts, and I recommend you to lose no time, for it'll be poor work when Tookey has it all to himself, for I mayn't be equil to stand i' the desk at all come another winter." Here Mr. Macey paused, perhaps expecting some sign of emotion in his hearer, but not observing any, he went on. "And as for the money for the suit o' clothes, why, you get a matter of a pound a week at your weaving, Master Marner, and you're a young man, eh, for all you look so mushed. Why, you couldn't ha' been five and twenty when you come into these parts, eh?"

---

[7] SILENT—Note the contrast between Mr. Macey, typifying the garrulous neighbors, and Silas, so stunned by misfortune that he has lost most of his social sense.

Silas started a little at the change to a questioning tone, and answered mildly, "I don't know; I can't rightly say—it's a long while since."

After receiving such an answer as this it is not surprising that Mr. Macey observed, later on in the evening at the Rainbow, that Marner's head was "all of a muddle," and that it was to be doubted if he ever knew when Sunday came round, which showed him a worse heathen than many a dog.

Another of Silas's comforters, besides Mr. Macey, came to him with a mind highly charged on the same topic. This was Mrs. Winthrop, the wheelwright's wife. The inhabitants of Raveloe were not severely regular in their church-going, and perhaps there was hardly a person in the parish who would not have held that to go to church every Sunday in the calendar would have shown a greedy desire to stand well with Heaven, and get an undue advantage over their neighbors—a wish to be better than the "common run," that would have implied a reflection on those who had had godfathers and godmothers as well as themselves, and had an equal right to the burying-service.[8] At the same time it was understood to be requisite for all who were not household servants, or young men, to take the sacrament at one of the great festivals; Squire Cass himself took it on Christmas Day; while those who were held to be "good livers" went to church with greater, though still with moderate, frequency.

Mrs. Winthrop was one of these: she was in all respects a woman of scrupulous conscience, so eager for duties that life seemed to offer them too scantily unless she rose at half-past four, though this threw a scarcity of work over the more advanced hours of the morning, which it was a constant problem with her to remove. Yet she had not the vixenish temper which is sometimes supposed to be a necessary condition of such habits: she was a very mild, patient woman, whose nature it was to seek out all the sadder and more serious elements of life, and pasture her mind upon them. She was the person always first thought of in Raveloe when there was illness or death in a family, when leeches were to be applied,[9] or there was a sudden disappointment in a monthly nurse. She

[8] An equal right to the burying-service—Because they had been properly baptized. Unbaptized adults were denied the regular service.

[9] When leeches were to be applied—Bleeding was a favorite remedy for many ailments. For this purpose leeches, or blood-suckers, were often used.

was a "comfortable woman"—good-looking, fresh-complexioned, having her lips always slightly screwed, as if she felt herself in a sick-room with the doctor or the clergyman present. But she was never whimpering; no one had seen her shed tears; she was simply grave and inclined to shake her head and sigh, almost imperceptibly, like a funereal mourner who is not a relation. It seemed surprising that Ben Winthrop, who loved his quart-pot and his joke, got along so well with Dolly; but she took her husband's jokes and joviality as patiently as everything else, considering that "men *would* be so," and viewing the stronger sex in the light of animals whom it had pleased Heaven to make naturally troublesome, like bulls and turkey-cocks.

This good wholesome woman could hardly fail to have her mind drawn strongly towards Silas Marner now that he appeared in the light of a sufferer, and one Sunday afternoon she took her little boy Aaron with her, and went to call on Silas, carrying in her hand some small lard-cakes, flat paste-like articles, much esteemed in Raveloe. Aaron, an apple-cheeked youngster of seven, with a clean starched frill, which looked like a plate for the apples, needed all his adventurous curiosity to embolden him against the possibility that the big-eyed weaver might do him some bodily injury; and his dubiety was much increased when, on arriving at the Stone-pits, they heard the mysterious sound of the loom.

"Ah, it is as I thought," said Mrs. Winthrop sadly.

They had to knock loudly before Silas heard them, but when he did come to the door he showed no impatience, as he would once have done, at a visit that had been unasked for and unexpected. Formerly, his heart had been as a locked casket with its treasure inside; but now the casket was empty, and the lock was broken. Left groping in darkness, with his prop utterly gone, Silas had inevitably a sense, though a dull and half-despairing one, that if any help came to him it must come from without; and there was a slight stirring of expectation at the sight of his fellow-men, a faint consciousness of dependence on their good-will. He opened the door wide to admit Dolly, but without otherwise returning her greeting than by moving the armchair a few inches as a sign that she was to sit down in it. Dolly, as soon as she was seated, removed the white cloth that covered her lard-cakes, and said in her gravest way,—

"I'd a baking yisterday, Master Marner, and the lard-cakes turned out better nor common, and I'd ha' asked you to accept some if you'd thought well. I don't eat such things myself, for a bit o' bread's what I like from one year's end to the other, but men's stomichs are made so comical they want a change—they do, I know, God help 'em."

Dolly sighed gently as she held out the cakes to Silas, who thanked her kindly, and looked very close at them, absently, being accustomed to look so at everything he took into his hand—eyed all the while by the wondering bright orbs of the small Aaron, who had made an outwork[10] of his mother's chair, and was peeping round from behind it.

"There's letters pricked on 'em," said Dolly. "I can't read 'em myself, and there's nobody, not Mr. Macey himself, rightly knows what they mean; but they've a good meaning, for they're the same as is on the pulpit-cloth at church. What are they, Aaron, my dear?"

Aaron retreated completely behind his outwork.

"Oh, go, that's naughty," said his mother mildly. "Well, whativer the letters are, they've a good meaning; and it's a stamp as has been in our house, Ben says, ever since he was a little un, and his mother used to put it on the cakes, and I've allays put it on too; for if there's any good, we've need of it i' this world."

"It's I. H. S.,"[11] said Silas, at which proof of learning Aaron peeped round the chair again.

"Well, to be sure, you can read 'em off," said Dolly. "Ben's read 'em to me many and many a time, but they slip out o' my mind again; the more's the pity, for they're good letters, else they wouldn't be in the church; and so I prick 'em on all the loaves and all the cakes, though sometimes they won't hold because o' the rising—for, as I said, if there's any good to be got we've need of it i' this world—that we have; and I hope they'll bring good to you, Master Marner, for it's wi' that will[12] I brought you the cakes, and you see the letters have held better nor common."

Silas was as unable to interpret the letters as Dolly, but there

---

[10] An outwork—A fortification.

[11] I. H. S.—These letters stand for Jesus in Greek. They have often been thought of as the initials of various phrases, the most common being: *In Hoc Signo,* in this sign (conquer).

[12] Wi' that will—With that wish.

was no possibility of misunderstanding the desire to give comfort that made itself heard in her quiet tones. He said, with more feeling than before, "Thank you—thank you kindly." But he laid down the cakes and seated himself absently—drearily unconscious of any distinct benefit towards which the cakes and the letters, or even Dolly's kindness, could tend for him.

"Ah, if there's good anywhere, we've need of it," repeated Dolly, who did not lightly forsake a serviceable phrase. She looked at Silas pityingly as she went on. "But you didn't hear the church-bells this morning, Master Marner? I doubt you didn't know it was Sunday. Living so lone here, you lose your count, I daresay; and then, when your loom makes a noise, you can't hear the bells, more partic'lar now the frost kills the sound."

"Yes, I did; I heard 'em," said Silas, to whom Sunday bells were a mere accident of the day, and not part of its sacredness. There had been no bells in Lantern Yard.

"Dear heart!" said Dolly, pausing before she spoke again. "But what a pity it is you should work of a Sunday, and not clean yourself,—if you *didn't* go to church; for if you'd a roasting bit, it might be as you couldn't leave it, being a lone man. But there's the bakehus,[13] if you could make up your mind to spend a twopence on the oven now and then,—not every week, in course—I shouldn't like to do that myself,—you might carry your bit o' dinner there, for it's nothing but right to have a bit o' summat hot of a Sunday, and not to make it as you can't know your dinner from Saturday. But now, upo' Christmas Day, this blessed Christmas as is ever coming, if you was to take your dinner to the bakehus, and go to church, and see the holly and the yew, and hear the anthim, and then take the sacramen', you'd be a deal the better, and you'd know which end you stood on, and you could put your trust i' Them as knows better nor we do, seein' you'd ha' done what it lies on us all to do."

Dolly's exhortation, which was an unusually long effort of speech for her, was uttered in the soothing persuasive tone with which she would have tried to prevail on a sick man to take his medicine or a basin of gruel for which he had no appetite. Silas had never before been closely urged on the point of his absence from church, which

[13] Bakehus—A public oven where for a small sum the village housewives could have their baking done.

had only been thought of as a part of his general queerness; and he was too direct and simple to evade Dolly's appeal.

"Nay, nay," he said, "I know nothing o' church. I've never been to church."

"No!" said Dolly, in a low tone of wonderment. Then bethinking herself of Silas's advent from an unknown country, she said, "Could it ha' been as they'd no church where you was born?"

"Oh, yes," said Silas meditatively, sitting in his usual posture of leaning on his knees and supporting his head. "There was churches—a many—it was a big town. But I knew nothing of 'em—I went to chapel."[14]

Dolly was much puzzled at this new word, but she was rather afraid of inquiring further, lest "chapel" might mean some haunt of wickedness. After a little thought she said,—

"Well, Master Marner, it's niver too late to turn over a new leaf, and if you've niver had no church, there's no telling the good it'll do you. For I feel so set up and comfortable as niver was when I've been and heard the prayers, and the singing to the praise and glory o' God, as Mr. Macey gives out—and Mr. Crackenthorp saying good words, and more partic'lar on Sacramen' Day; and if a bit o' trouble comes, I feel as I can put up wi' it, for I've looked for help i' the right quarter, and gev myself up to Them as we must all give ourselves up to at the last; and if we'n done our part, it isn't to be believed as Them as are above us 'ull be worse nor we are, and come short o' Their'n."

Poor Dolly's exposition of her simple Raveloe theology fell rather unmeaningly on Silas's ears, for there was no word in it that could rouse a memory of what he had known as religion, and his comprehension was quite baffled by the plural pronoun, which was no heresy of Dolly's, but only her way of avoiding a presumptuous familiarity. He remained silent, not feeling inclined to assent to the part of Dolly's speech which he fully understood—her recommendation that he should go to church. Indeed, Silas was so unaccustomed to talk beyond the brief questions and answers necessary for the transaction of his simple business that words did not easily come to him without the urgency of a distinct purpose.

---

[14] CHAPEL—Silas, being a Dissenter, had gone to "chapel" not to "church." See "The Story" in the Introduction, page 199, for an explanation of the difference between the two.

But now, little Aaron, having become used to the weaver's awful presence, had advanced to his mother's side, and Silas, seeming to notice him for the first time, tried to return Dolly's signs of goodwill by offering the lad a bit of lard-cake. Aaron shrank back a little, and rubbed his head against his mother's shoulder, but still thought the piece of cake worth the risk of putting his hand out for it.

"Oh, for shame, Aaron," said his mother, taking him on her lap, however; "why, you don't want cake again yet awhile. He's wonderful hearty," she went on, with a little sigh; "that he is, God knows. He's my youngest, and we spoil him sadly, for either me or the father must allays hev him in our sight—that we must."

She stroked Aaron's brown head, and thought it must do Master Marner good to see such a "pictur of a child." But Marner, on the other side of the hearth, saw the neat-featured rosy face as a mere dim round, with two dark spots in it.

"And he's got a voice like a bird—you wouldn't think," Dolly went on; "he can sing a Christmas carril as his father's taught him; and I take it for a token as he'll come to good, as he can learn the good tunes so quick. Come, Aaron, stan' up and sing the carril to Master Marner, come."

Aaron replied by rubbing his forehead against his mother's shoulder.

"Oh, that's naughty," said Dolly gently. "Stan' up, when mother tells you, and let me hold the cake till you've done."

Aaron was not indisposed to display his talents, even to an ogre, under protecting circumstances, and after a few more signs of coyness, consisting chiefly in rubbing the backs of his hands over his eyes, and then peeping between them at Master Marner to see if he looked anxious for the "carril," he at length allowed his head to be duly adjusted, and standing behind the table which let him appear above it only as far as his broad frill, so that he looked like a cherubic head untroubled with a body, he began with a clear chirp and in a melody that had the rhythm of an industrious hammer,—

"God rest you merry, gentlemen,
Let nothing you dismay,
For Jesus Christ our Saviour
Was born on Christmas Day."

Dolly listened with a devout look, glancing at Marner in some confidence that this strain would help to allure him to church.

"That's Christmas music," she said, when Aaron had ended and had secured his piece of cake again. "There's no other music equil to the Christmas music—'Hark the erol angils sing.' And you may judge what it is at church, Master Marner, with the bassoon and the voices, as you can't help thinking you've got to a better place a'ready—for I wouldn't speak ill o' this world, seeing as Them put us in it as knows best; but what wi' the drink, and the quarrelling, and the bad illnesses, and the hard dying, as I've seen times and times, one's thankful to hear of a better. The boy sings pretty, don't he, Master Marner?"

"Yes," said Silas absently, "very pretty."

The Christmas carol, with its hammer-like rhythm, had fallen on his ears as strange music, quite unlike a hymn, and could have none of the effect Dolly contemplated. But he wanted to show her that he was grateful, and the only mode that occurred to him was to offer Aaron a bit more cake.

"Oh, no, thank you, Master Marner," said Dolly, holding down Aaron's willing hands. "We must be going home now. And so I wish you good-by, Master Marner; and if you ever feel anyways bad in your inside, as you can't fend for yourself,[15] I'll come and clean up for you, and get you a bit o' victual, and willing. But I beg and pray of you to leave off weaving of a Sunday, for it's bad for soul and body—and the money as comes i' that way 'ull be a bad bed to lie down on at the last, if it doesn't fly away, nobody knows where, like the white frost. And you'll excuse me being that free with you, Master Marner, for I wish you well—I do. Make your bow, Aaron."

Silas said "Good-by, and thank you kindly," as he opened the door for Dolly, but he couldn't help feeling relieved when she was gone—relieved that he might weave again and moan at his ease. Her simple view of life and its comforts, by which she had tried to cheer him, was only like a report of unknown objects, which his imagination could not fashion. The fountains of human love and of faith in a divine love had not yet been unlocked, and his soul was still the shrunken rivulet, with only this difference, that its

---

[15] FEND FOR YOURSELF—Provide for yourself. In this instance the meaning is: do your own housework.

little groove of sand was blocked up, and it wandered confusedly against dark obstruction.

And so, notwithstanding the honest persuasions of Mr. Macey and Dolly Winthrop, Silas spent his Christmas Day in loneliness, eating his meat in sadness of heart, though the meat had come to him as a neighborly present. In the morning he looked out on the black frost that seemed to press cruelly on every blade of grass, while the half-icy red pool[16] shivered under the bitter wind; but towards evening the snow began to fall, and curtained from him even that dreary outlook, shutting him close up with his narrow grief. And he sat in his robbed home through the livelong evening, not caring to close his shutters or lock his door, pressing his head between his hands and moaning, till the cold grasped him and told him that his fire was gray.

Nobody in this world but himself knew that he was the same Silas Marner who had once loved his fellow with tender love, and trusted in an unseen goodness. Even to himself that past experience had become dim.

But in Raveloe village the bells rang merrily, and the church was fuller than all through the rest of the year, with red faces among the abundant dark green boughs—faces prepared for a longer service than usual by an odorous breakfast of toast and ale. Those green boughs, the hymn and anthem never heard but at Christmas—even the Athanasian Creed,[17] which was discriminated from the others only as being longer and of exceptional virtue, since it was only read on rare occasions—brought a vague exulting sense, for which the grown men could as little have found words as the children, that something great and mysterious had been done for them in heaven above, and in earth below, which they were appropriating by their presence. And then the red faces made their way through the black biting frost to their own homes, feeling themselves free for the rest of the day to eat, drink, and be merry, and using that Christian freedom without diffidence.

At Squire Cass's family party that day nobody mentioned Dunstan—nobody was sorry for his absence, or feared it would be

[16] RED POOL—The water standing in the pit. Evidently the color of the reddish sandy soil was reflected in the water. There is an ominous suggestion in the description of this particular pool as "red."

[17] THE ATHANASIAN CREED—Long thought to have been composed by Athanasius, patriarch of Alexandria.

too long. The doctor and his wife, Uncle and Aunt Kimble, were there, and the annual Christmas talk was carried through without any omissions, rising to the climax of Mr. Kimble's experience when he walked the London hospitals thirty years back, together with striking professional anecdotes then gathered. Whereupon cards followed,[18] with Aunt Kimble's annual failure to follow suit, and Uncle Kimble's irascibility concerning the odd trick which was rarely explicable to him, when it was not on his side, without a general visitation of tricks to see that they were formed on sound principles; the whole being accompanied by a strong steaming odor of spirits-and-water.

But the party on Christmas Day, being a strictly family party, was not the preëminently brilliant celebration of the season at the Red House. It was the great dance on New Year's Eve that made the glory of Squire Cass's hospitality, as of his forefathers', time out of mind. This was the occasion when all the society of Raveloe and Tarley, whether old acquaintances separated by long rutty distances, or cooled acquaintances separated by misunderstandings concerning runaway calves, or acquaintances founded on intermittent condescension, counted on meeting and on comporting themselves with mutual appropriateness. This was the occasion on which fair dames who came on pillions sent their bandboxes before them, supplied with more than their evening costume; for the feast was not to end with a single evening, like a paltry town entertainment, where the whole supply of eatables is put on the table at once and bedding is scanty. The Red House was provisioned as if for a siege; and as for the spare feather-beds ready to be laid on floors, they were as plentiful as might naturally be expected in a family that had killed its own geese for many generations.

Godfrey Cass was looking forward to this New Year's Eve with a foolish reckless longing that made him half deaf to his importunate companion, Anxiety.

"Dunsey will be coming home soon: there will be a great blow-up, and how will you bribe his spite to silence?" said Anxiety.

"Oh, he won't come home before New Year's Eve, perhaps," said Godfrey; "and I shall sit by Nancy then and dance with her, and get a kind look from her in spite of herself."

---

[18] Cards followed—In their squabbles Uncle and Aunt Kimble are not very different from modern husbands and wives who play bridge of an evening.

"But money is wanted in another quarter," said Anxiety, in a louder voice, "and how will you get it without selling your mother's diamond pin? And if you don't get it . . .?"

"Well, but something may happen to make things easier. At any rate, there's one pleasure for me close at hand—Nancy is coming."

"Yes, and suppose your father should bring matters to a pass that will oblige you to decline marrying her—and to give your reasons?"

"Hold your tongue, and don't worry me. I can see Nancy's eyes, just as they will look at me, and feel her hand in mine already."

But Anxiety went on, though in noisy Christmas company, refusing to be utterly quieted even by much drinking.

## CHAPTER XI

Some women, I grant, would not appear to advantage seated on a pillion, and attired in a drab joseph[1] and a drab beaver bonnet, with a crown resembling a small stew-pan; for a garment suggesting a coachman's greatcoat, cut out under an exiguity[2] of cloth that would only allow of miniature capes, is not well adapted to conceal deficiences of contour, nor is drab a color that will throw sallow cheeks into lively contrast. It was all the greater triumph to Miss Nancy Lammeter's beauty that she looked thoroughly bewitching in that costume, as, seated on the pillion behind her tall, erect father, she held one arm round him, and looked down, with open-eyed anxiety, at the treacherous snow-covered pools and puddles, which sent up formidable splashings of mud under the stamp of Dobbin's foot. A painter would, perhaps, have preferred her in those moments when she was free from self-consciousness; but certainly the bloom on her cheeks was at its highest point of contrast with the surrounding drab when she arrived at the door of the Red House, and saw Mr. Godfrey Cass ready to lift her from the pillion. She wished her sister Priscilla had come up at the same time behind the servant, for then she would have contrived that Mr. Godfrey should have lifted off Priscilla first, and, in the mean

[1] JOSEPH—A woman's riding habit consisting of a long coat which buttoned down the front.

[2] EXIGUITY—Scantiness.

time, she would have persuaded her father to go round to the horse-block instead of alighting at the doorsteps. It was very painful when you had made it quite clear to a young man that you were determined not to marry him, however much he might wish it, that he would still continue to pay you marked attentions; besides, why didn't he always show the same attentions if he meant them sincerely, instead of being so strange as Mr. Godfrey Cass was, sometimes behaving as if he didn't want to speak to her, and taking no notice of her for weeks and weeks, and then, all on a sudden, almost making love again? Moreover, it was quite plain he had no real love for her, else he would not let people have *that* to say of him which they did say. Did he suppose that Miss Nancy Lammeter was to be won by any man, squire or no squire, who led a bad life? That was not what she had been used to see in her own father, who was the soberest and best man in that country-side, only a little hot and hasty now and then if things were not done to the minute.

All these thoughts rushed through Miss Nancy's mind, in their habitual succession, in the moments between her first sight of Mr. Godfrey Cass standing at the door and her own arrival there. Happily, the Squire came out too, and gave a loud greeting to her father, so that, somehow, under cover of this noise, she seemed to find concealment for her confusion and neglect of any suitably formal behavior while she was being lifted from the pillion by strong arms which seemed to find her ridiculously small and light. And there was the best reason for hastening into the house at once, since the snow was beginning to fall again, threatening an unpleasant journey for such guests as were still on the road. These were a small minority; for already the afternoon was beginning to decline, and there would not be too much time for the ladies who came from a distance to attire themselves in readiness for the early tea which was to inspirit them for the dance.

There was a buzz of voices through the house as Miss Nancy entered, mingled with the scrape of a fiddle preluding in the kitchen; but the Lammeters were guests whose arrival had evidently been thought of so much that it had been watched for from the windows, for Mrs. Kimble, who did the honors at the Red House on these great occasions, came forward to meet Miss Nancy in the hall, and conduct her upstairs. Mrs. Kimble was the Squire's sister, as well as the doctor's wife—a double dignity, with which her diameter was in direct proportion; so that a journey upstairs being rather fatiguing to her, she did not oppose Miss Nancy's request to be allowed to find her way alone to the Blue Room, where the Miss Lammeters' bandboxes had been deposited on their arrival in the morning.

There was hardly a bedroom in the house where feminine compliments were not passing and feminine toilettes going forward, in various stages, in space made scanty by extra beds spread upon the floor; and Miss Nancy, as she entered the Blue Room, had to make her little formal curtsy to a group of six. On the one hand, there were ladies no less important than the two Miss Gunns, the wine merchant's daughters from Lytherly, dressed in the height of fashion, with the tightest skirts and the shortest waists, and gazed at by Miss Ladbrook (of the Old Pastures) with a shyness not unsustained by inward criticism. Partly, Miss Ladbrook felt that her own skirt must be regarded as unduly lax by the Miss Gunns, and partly, that it was a pity the Miss Gunns did not show that judgment which she herself would show if she were in their place, by stopping a little on this side of the fashion. On the other hand, Mrs. Ladbrook was standing in skull-cap and front, with her turban in her hand, curtsying and smiling blandly and saying, "After you, ma'am" to another lady in similar circumstances, who had politely offered the precedence at the looking-glass.

But Miss Nancy had no sooner made her curtsy than an elderly lady came forward, whose full white muslin kerchief and mob-cap round her curls of smooth gray hair were in daring contrast with the puffed yellow satins and top-knotted caps of her neighbors. She approached Miss Nancy with much primness, and said, with a slow, treble suavity,—

"Niece, I hope I see you well in health." Miss Nancy kissed her aunt's cheek dutifully, and answered, with the same sort of amiable primness, "Quite well, I thank you, aunt, and I hope I see you the same."

"Thank you, niece, I keep my health for the present. And how is my brother-in-law?"

These dutiful questions and answers were continued until it was ascertained in detail that the Lammeters were all as well as usual, and the Osgoods likewise, also that niece Priscilla must certainly arrive shortly, and that travelling on pillions in snowy weather was unpleasant, though a joseph was a great protection. Then Nancy was formally introduced to her aunt's visitors, the Miss Gunns, as being the daughters of a mother known to *their* mother, though now for the first time induced to make a journey into these parts; and these ladies were so taken by surprise at finding such a lovely face and figure in an out-of-the-way country place, that they began to feel some curiosity about the dress she would put on when she took off her joseph. Miss Nancy, whose thoughts were always conducted with the propriety and moderation conspicuous in her manners, remarked to herself that the Miss Gunns were rather hard-featured than otherwise, and that such very low dresses as they wore might have been attributed to vanity if their shoulders had been pretty, but that, being as they were, it was not reasonable to suppose that they showed their necks from a love of display, but rather from some obligation not inconsistent with sense and modesty. She felt convinced, as she opened her box, that this must be her aunt Osgood's opinion, for Miss Nancy's mind resembled her aunt's to a degree that everybody said was surprising, considering the kinship was on Mr. Osgood's side; and though you might not have supposed it from the formality of their greeting, there was a devoted attachment and mutual admiration between aunt and niece. Even Miss Nancy's refusal of her cousin Gilbert Osgood (on the ground solely that he was her cousin), though it had grieved her aunt greatly, had not in the least cooled the preference which had determined her to leave Nancy several of her hereditary ornaments, let Gilbert's future wife be whom[3] she might.

Three of the ladies quickly retired, but the Miss Gunns were quite content that Mrs. Osgood's inclination to remain with her niece gave them also a reason for staying to see the rustic beauty's toilette. And it was really a pleasure—from the first opening of the bandbox, where everything smelt of lavender and rose leaves, to the clasping of the small coral necklace that fitted closely round her little white neck. Everything belonging to Miss Nancy was of delicate purity and nattiness: not a crease was where it had no

---

[3] WHOM—Some critics imply that George Eliot made a grammatical error in this use of the objective case. *Whom* is the correct form because the auxiliary verb *to be* takes the same case after it as before it.

business to be, not a bit of her linen professed whiteness without fulfilling its profession; the very pins on her pin-cushion were stuck in after a pattern from which she was careful to allow no aberration; and as for her own person, it gave the same idea of perfect unvarying neatness as the body of a little bird. It is true that her light brown hair was cropped behind like a boy's, and was dressed in front in a number of flat rings, that lay quite away from her face; but there was no sort of coiffure that could make Miss Nancy's cheek and neck look otherwise than pretty; and when at last she stood complete in her silvery twilled silk, her lace tucker, her coral necklace, and coral ear-drops, the Miss Gunns could see nothing to criticise except her hands, which bore the traces of butter-making, cheese-crushing, and even still coarser work. But Miss Nancy was not ashamed of that, for while she was dressing she narrated to her aunt how she and Priscilla had packed their boxes yesterday, because this morning was baking morning, and since they were leaving home, it was desirable to make a good supply of meat-pies for the kitchen; and as she concluded this judicious remark, she turned to the Miss Gunns that she might not commit the rudeness of not including them in the conversation. The Miss Gunns smiled stiffly, and thought what a pity it was that these rich country people, who could afford to buy such good clothes (really Miss Nancy's lace and silk were very costly), should be brought up in utter ignorance and vulgarity. She actually said "mate" for "meat," "'appen" for "perhaps," and "'oss" for "horse," which, to young ladies living in good Lytherly society, who habitually said 'orse, even in domestic privacy, and only said 'appen on the right occasions, was necessarily shocking. Miss Nancy, indeed, had never been to any school higher than Dame Tedman's: her acquaintance with profane literature[4] hardly went beyond the rhymes she had worked in her large sampler under the lamb and the shepherdess; and in order to balance an account, she was obliged to effect her subtraction by removing visible metallic shillings and sixpences from a visible metallic total. There is hardly a servant-maid in these days who is not better informed than Miss Nancy; yet she had the essential attributes of a lady,—high veracity, delicate honor in her dealings, deference to others, and refined personal habits,—and lest these should not suffice to convince

[4] PROFANE LITERATURE—Literature other than sacred or religious writings.

grammatical fair ones that her feelings can at all resemble theirs, I will add that she was slightly proud and exacting, and as constant in her affection towards a baseless opinion as towards an erring lover.

The anxiety about sister Priscilla, which had grown rather active by the time the coral necklace was clasped, was happily ended by the entrance of that cheerful-looking lady herself, with a face made blowsy[5] by cold and damp. After the first questions and greetings, she turned to Nancy and surveyed her from head to foot —then wheeled her round, to ascertain that the back view was equally faultless.

"What do you think o' *these* gowns, Aunt Osgood?" said Priscilla, while Nancy helped her to unrobe.

"Very handsome indeed, niece," said Mrs. Osgood, with a slight increase of formality. She always thought niece Priscilla too rough.

"I'm obliged to have the same as Nancy, you know, for all I'm five years older, and it makes me look yallow; for she never *will* have anything without I have mine just like it, because she wants us to look like sisters. And I tell her folks 'ull think it's my weakness makes me fancy as I shall look pretty in what she looks pretty in. For I *am* ugly—there's no denying that: I feature my father's family. But, law! I don't mind, do you?" Priscilla here turned to the Miss Gunns, rattling on in too much preoccupation with the delight of talking to notice that her candor was not appreciated. "The pretty uns do for fly-catchers—they keep the men off us. I've no opinion o' the men, Miss Gunn—I don't know what *you* have. And as for fretting and stewing about what *they*'ll think of you from morning till night, and making your life uneasy about what they're doing when they're out o' your sight—as I tell Nancy, it's a folly no woman need be guilty of, if she's got a good father and a good home: let her leave it to them as have got no fortin, and can't help themselves. As I say, Mr. Have-your-own-way is the best husband, and the only one I'd ever promise to obey. I know it isn't pleasant, when you've been used to living in a big way, and managing hogsheads and all that, to go and put your nose in by somebody else's fireside, or to sit down by yourself to a scrag[6] or a knuckle; but, thank God! my father's a sober man

[5] Blowsy—Ruddy.

[6] Scrag—A neck-piece of meat.

and likely to live; and if you've got a man by the chimney-corner, it doesn't matter if he's childish—the business needn't be broke up."

The delicate process of getting her narrow gown over her head without injury to her smooth curls obliged Miss Priscilla to pause in this rapid survey of life, and Mrs. Osgood seized the opportunity of rising and saying,—

"Well, niece, you'll follow us. The Miss Gunns will like to go down."

"Sister," said Nancy, when they were alone, "you've offended the Miss Gunns, I'm sure."

"What have I done, child?" said Priscilla, in some alarm.

"Why, you asked them if they minded about being ugly—you're so very blunt."

"Law, did I? Well, it popped out; it's a mercy I said no more, for I'm a bad un to live with folks when they don't like the truth. But as for being ugly, look at me, child, in this silver-colored silk—I told you how it 'ud be—I look as yallow as a daffadil. Anybody 'ud say you wanted to make a mawkin[7] of me."

"No, Priscy, don't say so. I begged and prayed of you not to let us have this silk if you'd like another better. I was willing to have *your* choice, you know I was," said Nancy, in anxious self-vindication.

"Nonsense, child! you know you'd set your heart on this; and reason good, for you're the color o' cream. It 'ud be fine doings for you to dress yourself to suit *my* skin. What I find fault with is that notion o' yours as I must dress myself just like you. But you do as you like with me—you always did from when first you begun to walk. If you wanted to go the field's length, the field's length you'd go; and there was no whipping you, for you looked as prim and innicent as a daisy all the while."

"Priscy," said Nancy gently, as she fastened a coral necklace, exactly like her own, round Priscilla's neck, which was very far from being like her own, "I'm sure I'm willing to give way as far as is right, but who shouldn't dress alike if it isn't sisters? Would you have us go about looking as if we were no kin to one another—us that have got no mother and not another sister in the world? I'd do what was right, if I dressed in a gown dyed with cheese-coloring; I'd rather you'd choose, and let me wear what pleases you."

[7] A MAWKIN—A scarecrow.

"There you go again! You'd come round to the same thing if one talked to you from Saturday night till Saturday morning. It'll be fine fun to see how you'll master your husband and never raise your voice above the singing o' the kettle all the while. I like to see the men mastered!"

"Don't talk *so,* Priscy," said Nancy, blushing. "You know I don't mean ever to be married."

"Oh, you never mean a fiddelstick's end!" said Priscilla, as she arranged her discarded dress, and closed her bandbox. "Who shall I have to work for when father's gone, if you are to go and take notions in your head and be an old maid, because some folks are no better than they should be? I have n't a bit o' patience with you—sitting on an addled egg forever, as if there was never a fresh un in the world. One old maid's enough out o' two sisters; and I shall do credit to a single life, for God A'mighty meant me for it. Come, we can go down now. I'm as ready as a mawkin *can* be—there's nothing a-wanting to frighten the crows, now I've got my ear-droppers in."

As the two Miss Lammeters walked into the large parlor together, any one who did not know the character of both might certainly have supposed that the reason why the square-shouldered, clumsy, high-featured Priscilla wore a dress the facsimile of her pretty sister's was either the mistaken vanity of the one, or the malicious contrivance of the other in order to set off her own rare beauty. But the good-natured self-forgetful cheeriness and common sense of Priscilla would soon have dissipated the one suspicion; and the modest calm of Nancy's speech and manners told clearly of a mind free from all disavowed devices.

Places of honor had been kept for the Miss Lammeters near the head of the principal tea-table in the wainscoted parlor, now looking fresh and pleasant with handsome branches of holly, yew, and laurel, from the abundant growths of the old garden; and Nancy felt an inward flutter, that no firmness of purpose could prevent, when she saw Mr. Godfrey Cass advancing to lead her to a seat between himself and Mr. Crackenthorp, while Priscilla was called to the opposite side between her father and the Squire. It certainly did make some difference to Nancy that the lover she had given up was the young man of quite the highest consequence in the parish—at home in a venerable and unique parlor, which was the extremity of grandeur in her experience, a parlor where *she* might one day have been mistress, with the consciousness that she was spoken of as "Madam Cass," the Squire's wife. These circumstances exalted her inward drama in her own eyes, and deepened the emphasis with which she declared to herself that not the most dazzling rank should induce her to marry a man whose conduct showed him careless of his character, but that, "love once, love always," was the motto of a true and pure woman, and no man should ever have any right over her which would be a call on her to destroy the dried flowers that she treasured, and always would treasure, for Godfrey Cass's sake. And Nancy was capable of keeping her word to herself under very trying conditions. Nothing but a becoming blush betrayed the moving thoughts that urged themselves upon her as she accepted the seat next to Mr. Crackenthorp; for she was so instinctively neat and adroit in all her actions, and her pretty lips met each other with such quiet firmness, that it would have been difficult for her to appear agitated.

It was not the rector's practice to let a charming blush pass without an appropriate compliment. He was not in the least lofty or aristocratic, but simply a merry-eyed, small-featured, gray-haired man, with his chin propped by an ample, many-creased white neckcloth, which seemed to predominate over every other point in his person, and somehow to impress its peculiar character on his remarks; so that to have considered his amenities apart from his cravat would have been a severe, and perhaps a dangerous, effort of abstraction.[8]

"Ha, Miss Nancy," he said, turning his head within his cravat, and smiling down pleasantly upon her, "when anybody pretends this has been a severe winter, I shall tell them I saw the roses blooming on New Year's Eve—eh, Godfrey, what do *you* say?"

Godfrey made no reply, and avoided looking at Nancy very markedly; for though these complimentary personalities were held to be in excellent taste in old-fashioned Raveloe society, reverent love has a politeness of its own which it teaches to men otherwise of small schooling. But the Squire was rather impatient at Godfrey's showing himself a dull spark in this way. By this advanced

---

[8] To have considered . . . abstraction—The author has found this humorous way of saying that the rector's compliments have about the same significance as his cravat, being purely decorative.

hour of the day, the Squire was always in higher spirits than we have seen him in at the breakfast-table, and felt it quite pleasant to fulfil the hereditary duty of being noisily jovial and patronizing: the large silver snuff-box was in active service, and was offered without fail to all neighbors from time to time, however often they might have declined the favor. At present, the Squire had only given an express welcome to the heads of families as they appeared; but always as the evening deepened, his hospitality rayed out more widely, till he had tapped the youngest guests on the back and shown a peculiar fondness for their presence, in the full belief that they must feel their lives made happy by their belonging to a parish where there was such a hearty man as Squire Cass to invite them and wish them well. Even in this early stage of the jovial mood, it was natural that he should wish to supply his son's deficiencies by looking and speaking for him.

"Ay, ay," he began, offering his snuff-box to Mr. Lammeter, who for the second time bowed his head and waved his hand in stiff rejection of the offer, "us old fellows may wish ourselves young to-night, when we see the mistletoe-bough in the White Parlor. It's true, most things are gone back'ard in these last thirty years—the country's going down since the old king fell ill.[9] But when I look at Miss Nancy here, I begin to think the lasses keep up their quality;—ding me if I remember a sample to match her, not when I was a fine young fellow, and thought a deal about my pigtail.[10] No offence to you, madam," he added, bending to Mrs. Crackenthorp, who sat by him, "I didn't know *you* when you were as young as Miss Nancy here."

Mrs. Crackenthorp—a small, blinking woman, who fidgeted incessantly with her lace, ribbons, and gold chain, turning her head about and making subdued noises, very much like a guinea-pig, that twitches its nose and soliloquizes in all company indiscriminately—now blinked and fidgeted towards the Squire, and said, "Oh, no—no offence."

This emphatic compliment of the Squire's to Nancy was felt by others besides Godfrey to have a diplomatic significance; and

---

[9] Since the old king fell ill—George III was completely insane during the latter years of his life. This passage dates the action as before 1820, the year when George III died.

[10] Pigtail—At this period (early 19th century) the custom of wearing the hair in a long queue had completely passed out.

her father gave a slight additional erectness to his back as he looked across the table at her with complacent gravity. That grave and orderly senior was not going to bate a jot of his dignity by seeming elated at the notion of a match between his family and the Squire's: he was gratified by any honor paid to his daughter; but he must see an alteration in several ways before his consent would be vouchsafed. His spare but healthy person, and high-featured firm face, that looked as if it had never been flushed by excess, was in strong contrast, not only with the Squire's, but with the appearance of the Raveloe farmers generally—in accordance with a favorite saying of his own, that "breed was stronger than pasture."

"Miss Nancy's wonderful like what her mother was, though; isn't she, Kimble?" said the stout lady of that name, looking round for her husband.

But Doctor Kimble (country apothecaries in old days enjoyed that title without authority of diploma), being a thin and agile man, was flitting about the room with his hands in his pockets, making himself agreeable to his feminine patients, with medical impartiality, and being welcomed everywhere as a doctor by hereditary right—not one of those miserable apothecaries who canvass for practice in strange neighborhoods, and spend all their income in starving their one horse, but a man of substance, able to keep an extravagant table like the best of his patients. Time out of mind the Raveloe doctor had been a Kimble; Kimble was inherently a doctor's name; and it was difficult to contemplate firmly the melancholy fact that the actual Kimble had no son, so that his practice might one day be handed over to a successor, with the incongruous name of Taylor or Johnson. But in that case the wiser people in Raveloe would employ Dr. Blick, of Flitton—as less unnatural.

"Did you speak to me, my dear?" said the authentic doctor, coming quickly to his wife's side; but, as if foreseeing that she would be too much out of breath to repeat her remark, he went on immediately—"Ha, Miss Priscilla, the sight of you revives the taste of that super-excellent pork-pie. I hope the batch isn't near an end."

"Yes, indeed, it is, doctor," said Priscilla; "but I'll answer for it the next shall be as good. My pork-pies don't turn out well by chance."

"Not as your doctoring does, eh, Kimble?—because folks forget to take your physic, eh?" said the Squire, who regarded physic and doctors as many loyal churchmen regard the church and the clergy—tasting a joke against them when he was in health, but impatiently eager for their aid when anything was the matter with him. He tapped his box, and looked round with a triumphant laugh.

"Ah, she has a quick wit, my friend Priscilla has," said the doctor, choosing to attribute the epigram to a lady rather than allow a brother-in-law that advantage over him. "She saves a little pepper to sprinkle over her talk—that's the reason why she never puts too much into her pies. There's my wife now, she never has an answer at her tongue's end; but if I offend her, she's sure to scarify my throat with black pepper the next day, or else give me the colic with watery greens. That's an awful tit-for-tat." Here the vivacious doctor made a pathetic grimace.

"Did you ever hear the like?" said Mrs. Kimble, laughing above her double chin with much good-humor, aside to Mrs. Crackenthorp, who blinked and nodded, and amiably intended to smile, but the intention lost itself in small twitchings and noises.

"I suppose that's the sort of tit-for-tat adopted in your profession, Kimble, if you've a grudge against a patient," said the rector.

"Never do have a grudge against our patients," said Mr. Kimble, "except when they leave us; and then, you see, we haven't the chance of prescribing for 'em. Ha, Miss Nancy," he continued, suddenly skipping to Nancy's side, "you won't forget your promise? You're to save a dance for me, you know."

"Come, come, Kimble, don't you be too for'ard," said the Squire. "Give the young uns fair play. There's my son Godfrey'll be wanting to have a round with you if you run off with Miss Nancy. He's bespoke her for the first dance, I'll be bound. Eh, sir! what do you say?" he continued, throwing himself backward, and looking at Godfrey. "Haven't you asked Miss Nancy to open the dance with you?"

Godfrey, sorely uncomfortable under this significant insistence about Nancy, and afraid to think where it would end by the time his father had set his usual hospitable example of drinking before and after supper, saw no course open but to turn to Nancy and say, with as little awkwardness as possible,—

"No, I've not asked her yet, but I hope she'll consent—if somebody else hasn't been before me."

"No, I've not engaged myself," said Nancy quietly, though blushingly. (If Mr. Godfrey founded any hopes on her consenting to dance with him he would soon be undeceived, but there was no need for her to be uncivil.)

"Then I hope you've no objections to dancing with me," said Godfrey, beginning to lose the sense that there was anything uncomfortable in this arrangement.

"No, no objections," said Nancy, in a cold tone.

"Ah, well, you're a lucky fellow, Godfrey," said Uncle Kimble; "but you're my godson, so I won't stand in your way. Else I'm not so very old, eh, my dear?" he went on, skipping to his wife's side again. "You wouldn't mind my having a second after you were gone,—not if I cried a good deal first?"

"Come, come, take a cup o' tea and stop your tongue, do," said good-humored Mrs. Kimble, feeling some pride in a husband who must be regarded as so clever and amusing by the company generally. If he had only not been irritable at cards!

While safe, well-tested personalities were enlivening the tea in this way, the sound of the fiddle approaching within a distance at which it could be heard distinctly made the young people look at each other with sympathetic impatience for the end of the meal.

"Why, there's Solomon in the hall," said the Squire, "and playing my fav'rite tune, *I* believe—'The flaxen-headed ploughboy' —he's for giving us a hint as we aren't enough in a hurry to hear him play. Bob," he called out to his third long-legged son, who was at the other end of the room, "open the door, and tell Solomon to come in. He shall give us a tune here."

Bob obeyed, and Solomon walked in, fiddling as he walked, for he would on no account break off in the middle of a tune.

"Here, Solomon," said the Squire, with loud patronage. "Round here, my man. Ah, I knew it was 'The flaxen-headed ploughboy:' there's no finer tune."

Solomon Macey, a small, hale old man with an abundant crop of long white hair reaching nearly to his shoulders, advanced to the indicated spot, bowing reverently while he fiddled, as much as to say that he respected the company, though he respected the key-note more. As soon as he had repeated the tune and lowered his fiddle, he bowed again to the Squire and the rector, and said, "I hope I see your honor and your reverence well, and wishing you health and long life and a happy New Year. And wishing the same to you, Mr. Lammeter, sir; and to the other gentlemen, and the madams, and the young lasses."

As Solomon uttered the last words, he bowed in all directions solicitously, lest he should be wanting in due respect. But thereupon he immediately began to prelude, and fell into the tune which he knew would be taken as a special compliment by Mr. Lammeter.

"Thank ye, Solomon, thank ye," said Mr. Lammeter, when the fiddle paused again. "That's 'Over the hills and far away,' that is. My father used to say to me whenever we heard that tune, 'Ah, lad, *I* come from over the hills and far away.' There's a many tunes I don't make head or tail of; but that speaks to me like the blackbird's whistle. I suppose it's the name; there's a deal in the name of a tune."

But Solomon was already impatient to prelude again, and presently broke with much spirit into "Sir Roger de Coverley," at which there was a sound of chairs pushed back, and laughing voices.

"Ay, ay, Solomon, we know what that means," said the Squire, rising. "It's time to begin the dance, eh? Lead the way, then, and we'll all follow you."

So Solomon, holding his white head on one side, and playing vigorously, marched forward at the head of the gay procession into the White Parlor, where the mistletoe-bough was hung, and multitudinous tallow candles made rather a brilliant effect, gleaming from among the berried holly-boughs, and reflected in the old-fashioned oval mirrors fastened in the panels of the white wainscot. A quaint procession! Old Solomon, in his seedy clothes and long white locks, seemed to be luring that decent company by the magic scream of his fiddle—luring discreet matrons in turban-shaped caps, nay, Mrs. Crackenthorp herself, the summit of whose perpendicular feather was on a level with the Squire's shoulder—luring fair lasses complacently conscious of very short waists and skirts blameless of front-folds—luring burly fathers, in large variegated waistcoats, and ruddy sons, for the most part shy and sheepish, in short nether garments and very long coat-tails.

Already, Mr. Macey and a few other privileged villagers, who were allowed to be spectators on these great occasions, were seated on benches placed for them near the door; and great was the admiration and satisfaction in that quarter when the couples had formed themselves for the dance, and the Squire led off with Mrs. Crackenthorp, joining hands with the rector and Mrs. Osgood. That was as it should be—that was what everybody had been used to—and the charter of Raveloe seemed to be renewed by the ceremony.[11] It was not thought of as an unbecoming levity for the old and middle-aged people to dance a little before sitting down to cards, but rather as part of their social duties. For what were these if not to be merry at appropriate times, interchanging visits and poultry with due frequency, paying each other old-established compliments in sound traditional phrases, passing well-tried personal jokes, urging your guests to eat and drink too much out of hospitality, and eating and drinking too much in your neighbor's house to show that you liked your cheer? And the parson naturally set an example in these social duties. For it would not have been possible for the Raveloe mind, without a peculiar revelation, to know that a clergyman should be a pale-faced memento of solemnities, instead of a reasonably faulty man, whose exclusive authority to read prayers and preach, to christen, marry, and bury you, necessarily co-existed with the right to sell you the ground to be buried in, and to take tithe in kind;[12] on which last point, of course, there was a little grumbling, but not to the extent of irreligion—not of deeper significance than the grumbling at the rain, which was by no means accompanied with a spirit of impious defiance, but with a desire that the prayer for fine weather might be read forthwith.

There was no reason, then, why the rector's dancing should not be received as part of the fitness of things quite as much as the Squire's, or why, on the other hand, Mr. Macey's official respect should restrain him from subjecting the parson's performance to that criticism with which minds of extraordinary acuteness must necessarily contemplate the doings of their fallible fellow-men.

"The Squire's pretty springe,[13] considering his weight," said Mr. Macey, "and he stamps uncommon well. But Mr. Lammeter

---

[11] THE CHARTER . . . RENEWED BY THE CEREMONY—In the accomplishment of this annual rite the villagers of Raveloe renewed their sense of being faithful to the traditions of the town.

[12] IN KIND—In produce, such as grain and vegetables.

[13] SPRINGE—Colloquial for lively, active.

beats 'em all for shapes: you see, he holds his head like a sodger,[14] and he isn't so cushiony as most o' the oldish gentlefolks—they run fat in general; and he's got a fine leg. The parson's nimble enough, but he hasn't got much of a leg; it's a bit too thick down'ard, and his knees might be a bit nearer wi'out damage; but he might do worse, he might do worse. Though he hasn't that grand way o' waving his hand as the Squire has."

"Talk o' nimbleness, look at Mrs. Osgood," said Ben Winthrop, who was holding his son Aaron between his knees. "She trips along with her little steps, so as nobody can see how she goes—it's like as if she had little wheels to her feet. She doesn't look a day older nor last year: she's the finest-made woman as is, let the next be where she will."

"I don't heed how the women are made," said Mr. Macey, with some contempt. "They wear nayther coat nor breeches; you can't make much out o' their shapes."

"Fayder," said Aaron, whose feet were busy beating out the tune, "how does that big cock's-feather stick in Mrs. Crackenthorp's yead? Is there a little hole for it, like in my shuttlecock?"

"Hush, lad, hush; that's the way the ladies dress theirselves, that is," said the father; adding, however, in an undertone to Mr. Macey: "It does make her look funny, though—partly like a short-necked bottle wi' a long quill in it. Hey, by jingo, there's the young Squire leading off now, wi' Miss Nancy for partners. There's a lass for you!—like a pink-and-white posy—there's nobody 'ud think as anybody could be so pritty. I shouldn't wonder if she's Madam Cass some day, arter all—and nobody more rightfuller, for they'd make a fine match. You can find nothing against Master Godfrey's shapes, Macey, *I*'ll bet a penny."

Mr. Macey screwed up his mouth, leaned his head further on one side, and twirled his thumbs with a presto movement as his eyes followed Godfrey up the dance. At last he summed up his opinion.

"Pretty well down'ard, but a bit too round i' the shoulder-blades. And as for them coats as he gets from the Flitton tailor, they're a poor cut to pay double money for."

"Ah, Mr. Macey, you and me are two folks," said Ben, slightly indignant at this carping. "When I've got a pot o' good ale, I like

[14] SODGER—Soldier.

to swaller it, and do my inside good, i'stead o' smelling and staring at it to see if I can't find faut wi' the brewing. I should like you to pick me out a finer-limbed young fellow nor Master Godfrey—one as 'ud knock you down easier, or's more pleasanter-looksed when he's piert and merry."

"Tchuh!" said Mr. Macey, provoked to increased severity, "he isn't come to his right color yet: he's partly like a slack-baked pie. And I doubt he's got a soft place in his head, else why should he be turned round the finger by that offal Dunsey as nobody's seen o' late, and let him kill that fine hunting hoss as was the talk o' the country? And one while he was allays after Miss Nancy, and then it all went off again, like a smell o' hot porridge, as I may say. That wasn't my way when *I* went a-coorting."

"Ah, but mayhap Miss Nancy hung off, like, and your lass didn't," said Ben.

"I should say she didn't," said Mr. Macey, significantly. "Before I said 'sniff,' I took care to know as she'd say 'snaff,' and pretty quick, too. I wasn't a-going to open *my* mouth, like a dog at a fly, and snap it to again, wi' nothing to swaller."

"Well, I think Miss Nancy's a-coming round again," said Ben, "for Master Godfrey doesn't look so down-hearted to-night. And I see he's for taking her away to sit down, now they're at the end o' the dance: that looks like sweet-hearting, that does."

The reason why Godfrey and Nancy had left the dance was not so tender as Ben imagined. In the close press of couples a slight accident had happened to Nancy's dress, which, while it was short enough to show her neat ankle in front, was long enough behind to be caught under the stately stamp of the Squire's foot, so as to rend certain stitches at the waist, and cause much sisterly agitation in Priscilla's mind, as well as serious concern in Nancy's. One's thoughts may be much occupied with love-struggles, but hardly so as to be insensible to a disorder in the general framework of things. Nancy had no sooner completed her duty in the figure they were dancing than she said to Godfrey, with a deep blush, that she must go and sit down till Priscilla could come to her; for the sisters had already exchanged a short whisper and an open-eyed glance full of meaning. No reason less urgent than this could have prevailed on Nancy to give Godfrey this opportunity of sitting apart with her. As for Godfrey, he was feeling so happy and oblivious under the long charm of the country-dance with Nancy, that he got rather bold on the strength of her confusion, and was capable of leading her straight away, without leave asked, into the adjoining small parlor, where the card-tables were set.

"Oh, no, thank you," said Nancy coldly, as soon as she perceived where he was going, "not in there. I'll wait here till Priscilla's ready to come to me. I'm sorry to bring you out of the dance and make myself troublesome."

"Why, you'll be more comfortable here by yourself," said the artful Godfrey; "I'll leave you here till your sister can come." He spoke in an indifferent tone.

That was an agreeable proposition, and just what Nancy desired; why, then, was she a little hurt that Mr. Godfrey should make it? They entered, and she seated herself on a chair against one of the card-tables, as the stiffest and most unapproachable position she could choose.

"Thank you, sir," she said immediately. "I needn't give you any more trouble. I'm sorry you've had such an unlucky partner."

"That's very ill-natured of you," said Godfrey, standing by her without any sign of intended departure, "to be sorry you've danced with me."

"Oh, no, sir, I don't mean to say what's ill-natured at all," said Nancy, looking distractingly prim and pretty. "When gentlemen have so many pleasures, one dance can matter but very little."

"You know that isn't true. You know one dance with you matters more to me than all the other pleasures in the world."

It was a long, long while since Godfrey had said anything so direct as that, and Nancy was startled. But her instinctive dignity and repugnance to any show of emotion made her sit perfectly still, and only throw a little more decision into her voice as she said,—

"No, indeed, Mr. Godfrey, that's not known to me, and I have very good reasons for thinking different. But if it's true, I don't wish to hear it."

"Would you never forgive me, then, Nancy—never think well of me, let what would happen—would you never think the present made amends for the past? Not if I turned a good fellow, and gave up everything you didn't like?"

Godfrey was half conscious that this sudden opportunity of speaking to Nancy alone had driven him beside himself; but blind feeling had got the mastery of his tongue. Nancy really felt much agitated by the possibility Godfrey's words suggested, but this very pressure of emotion that she was in danger of finding too strong for her roused all her power of self-command.

"I should be glad to see a good change in anybody, Mr. Godfrey," she answered, with the slightest discernible difference of tone, "but it 'ud be better if no change was wanted."

"You're very hard-hearted, Nancy," said Godfrey pettishly. "You might encourage me to be a better fellow. I'm very miserable —but you've no feeling."

"I think those have the least feeling that act wrong to begin with," said Nancy, sending out a flash in spite of herself. Godfrey was delighted with that little flash, and would have liked to go on and make her quarrel with him; Nancy was so exasperatingly quiet and firm. But she was not indifferent to him *yet*.

The entrance of Priscilla, bustling forward and saying, "Dear heart alive, child, let us look at this gown," cut off Godfrey's hopes of a quarrel.

"I suppose I must go now," he said to Priscilla.

"It's no matter to me whether you go or stay," said that frank lady, searching for something in her pocket, with a preoccupied brow.

"Do *you* want me to go?" said Godfrey, looking at Nancy, who was now standing up by Priscilla's order.

"As you like," said Nancy, trying to recover all her former coldness, and looking down carefully at the hem of her gown.

"Then I like to stay," said Godfrey, with a reckless determination to get as much of this joy as he could to-night, and think nothing of the morrow.

## CHAPTER XII

While Godfrey Cass was taking draughts of forgetfulness from the sweet presence of Nancy, willingly losing all sense of that hidden bond which at other moments galled and fretted him so as to mingle irritation with the very sunshine, Godfrey's wife was walking with slow uncertain steps through the snow-covered Raveloe lanes, carrying her child in her arms.

This journey on New Year's Eve was a premeditated act of vengeance which she had kept in her heart ever since Godfrey, in a fit of passion, had told her he would sooner die than acknowledge her as his wife. There would be a great party at the Red House on New Year's Eve, she knew: her husband would be smiling and smiled upon, hiding *her* existence in the darkest corner of his heart. But she would mar his pleasure: she would go in her dingy rags, with her faded face, once as handsome as the best, with her little child that had its father's hair and eyes, and disclose herself to the Squire as his eldest son's wife. It is seldom that the miserable can help regarding their misery as a wrong inflicted by those who are less miserable. Molly knew that the cause of her dingy rags was not her husband's neglect, but the demon Opium to whom she was enslaved, body and soul, except in the lingering mother's tenderness that refused to give him her hungry child. She knew this well; and yet, in the moments of wretched unbenumbed consciousness, the sense of her want and degradation transformed itself continually into bitterness towards Godfrey. *He* was well off; and if she had her rights she would be well off, too. The belief that he repented his marriage, and suffered from it, only aggravated her vindictiveness. Just and self-reproving thoughts do not come to us too thickly, even in the purest air, and with the best lessons of heaven and earth; how should those white-winged delicate messengers make their way to Molly's poisoned chamber, inhabited by no higher memories than those of a barmaid's paradise of pink ribbons and gentlemen's jokes?

She had set out at an early hour, but had lingered on the road, inclined by her indolence to believe that if she waited under a warm shed the snow would cease to fall. She had waited longer than she knew, and now that she found herself belated in the snow-hidden ruggedness of the long lanes, even the animation of a vindictive purpose could not keep her spirit from failing. It was seven o'clock, and by this time she was not very far from Raveloe, but she was not familiar enough with those monotonous lanes to know how near she was to her journey's end. She needed comfort, and she knew but one comforter—the familiar demon in her bosom; but she hesitated a moment, after drawing out the black remnant,[1] before she raised it to her lips. In that moment the mother's love

[1] Black remnant—The remainder of the drug she had been taking.

pleaded for painful consciousness rather than oblivion—pleaded to be left in aching weariness, rather than to have the encircling arms benumbed so that they could not feel the dear burden. In another moment Molly had flung something away, but it was not the black remnant—it was an empty phial. And she walked on again under the breaking cloud, from which there came now and then the light of a quickly veiled star, for a freezing wind had sprung up since the snowing had ceased. But she walked always more and more drowsily, and clutched more and more automatically the sleeping child at her bosom.

Slowly the demon was working his will, and cold and weariness were his helpers. Soon she felt nothing but a supreme immediate longing that curtained off all futurity—the longing to lie down and sleep. She had arrived at a spot where her footsteps were no longer checked by a hedgerow, and she had wandered vaguely, unable to distinguish any objects, notwithstanding the wide whiteness around her, and the growing starlight. She sank down against a straggling furze bush, an easy pillow enough; and the bed of snow, too, was soft. She did not feel that the bed was cold, and did not heed whether the child would wake and cry for her. But her arms had not yet relaxed their instinctive clutch; and the little one slumbered on as gently as if it had been rocked in a lace-trimmed cradle.

But the complete torpor came at last: the fingers lost their tension, the arms unbent; then the little head fell away from the bosom, and the blue eyes opened wide on the cold starlight. At first there was a little peevish cry of "mammy," and an effort to regain the pillowing arm and bosom; but mammy's ear was deaf, and the pillow seemed to be slipping away backward. Suddenly, as the child rolled downward on its mother's knees, all wet with snow, its eyes were caught by a bright glancing light on the white ground, and, with the ready transition of infancy, it was immediately absorbed in watching the bright living thing running towards it, yet never arriving. That bright living thing must be caught; and in an instant the child had slipped on all fours, and held out one little hand to catch the gleam. But the gleam would not be caught in that way, and now the head was held up to see where the cunning gleam came from. It came from a very bright place; and the little one, rising on its legs, toddled through the snow, the old grimy

Brown Brothers

**Silas Finds Eppie**

**In the dim light of his cottage Silas thinks for a moment that his gold has miraculously returned, but finds instead something far more precious.**

shawl in which it was wrapped trailing behind it, and the queer little bonnet dangling at its back—toddled on to the open door of Silas Marner's cottage, and right up to the warm hearth, where there was a bright fire of logs and sticks, which had thoroughly warmed the old sack (Silas's greatcoat) spread out on the bricks to dry. The little one, accustomed to be left to itself for long hours without notice from its mother, squatted down on the sack, and spread its tiny hands towards the blaze, in perfect contentment, gurgling and making many inarticulate communications to the cheerful fire, like a new-hatched gosling beginning to find itself comfortable. But presently the warmth had a lulling effect, and the little golden head sank down on the old sack, and the blue eyes were veiled by their delicate half-transparent lids.

But where was Silas Marner while this strange visitor had come to his hearth? He was in the cottage, but he did not see the child. During the last few weeks, since he had lost his money, he had contracted the habit of opening his door and looking out from time to time, as if he thought that his money might be somehow coming back to him, or that some trace, some news of it, might be mysteriously on the road, and be caught by the listening ear or the straining eye. It was chiefly at night, when he was not occupied in his loom, that he fell into this repetition of an act for which he could have assigned no definite purpose, and which can hardly be understood except by those who have undergone a bewildering separation from a supremely loved object. In the evening twilight, and later whenever the night was not dark, Silas looked out on that narrow prospect around the Stone-pits, listening and gazing, not with hope, but with mere yearning and unrest.

This morning he had been told by some of his neighbors that it was New Year's Eve, and that he must sit up and hear the old year rung out and the new rung in, because that was good luck, and might bring his money back again. This was only a friendly Raveloe-way of jesting with the half-crazy oddities of a miser, but it had perhaps helped to throw Silas into a more than usually excited state. Since the on-coming of twilight he had opened his door again and again, though only to shut it immediately at seeing all distance veiled by the falling snow. But the last time he opened it the snow had ceased, and the clouds were parting here and there. He stood and listened, and gazed for a long while—there was really something on the road coming towards him then, but he caught no sign of it; and the stillness and the wide trackless snow seemed to narrow his solitude, and touched his yearning with the chill of despair. He went in again, and put his right hand on the latch of the door to close it—but he did not close it: he was arrested, as he had been already since his loss, by the invisible wand of catalepsy, and stood like a graven image, with wide but sightless eyes, holding open his door, powerless to resist either the good or evil that might enter there.

When Marner's sensibility returned, he continued the action which had been arrested, and closed his door, unaware of the chasm in his consciousness, unaware of any intermediate change, except that the light had grown dim, and that he was chilled and faint. He thought he had been too long standing at the door and looking out. Turning towards the hearth where the two logs had fallen apart, and sent forth only a red uncertain glimmer, he seated himself on his fireside chair, and was stooping to push his logs together, when, to his blurred vision, it seemed as if there were gold on the floor in front of the hearth. Gold!—his own gold—brought back to him as mysteriously as it had been taken away! He felt his heart begin to beat violently, and for a few moments he was unable to stretch out his hand and grasp the restored treasure. The heap of gold seemed to glow and get larger beneath his agitated gaze. He leaned forward at last, and stretched forth his hand; but instead of the hard coin with the familiar resisting outline, his fingers encountered soft warm curls. In utter amazement, Silas fell on his knees and bent his head low to examine the marvel: it was a sleeping child—a round, fair thing, with soft yellow rings all over its head. Could this be his little sister[2] come back to him in a dream—his little sister whom he had carried about in his arms for a year before she died, when he was a small boy without shoes or stockings? That was the first thought that darted across Silas's blank wonderment. *Was* it a dream? He rose to his feet again, pushed his logs together, and, throwing on some dried leaves and sticks, raised a flame; but the flame did not disperse the vision—it only lit up more distinctly the little round form of the child and its

[2] HIS LITTLE SISTER—George Eliot has given us the impression that all of Marner's memories are associated with some unfortunate consequence. The memory of his little sister, however, is pleasant. It suggests a period antedating anything we have heard about in the story.

shabby clothing. It was very much like his little sister. Silas sank into his chair powerless, under the double presence of an inexplicable surprise and a hurrying influx of memories. How and when had the child come in without his knowledge? He had never been beyond the door. But along with that question, and almost thrusting it away, there was a vision of the old home and the old streets leading to Lantern Yard—and within that vision another, of the thoughts which had been present with him in those far-off scenes. The thoughts were strange to him now, like old friendships impossible to revive; and yet he had a dreamy feeling that this child was somehow a message come to him from that far-off life: it stirred fibres that had never been moved in Raveloe—old quiverings of tenderness—old impressions of awe at the presentiment of some Power presiding over his life; for his imagination had not yet extricated itself from the sense of mystery in the child's sudden presence, and had formed no conjectures of ordinary natural means by which the event could have been brought about.

But there was a cry on the hearth: the child had awaked, and Marner stooped to lift it on his knee. It clung round his neck, and burst louder and louder into that mingling of inarticulate cries with "mammy" by which little children express the bewilderment of waking. Silas pressed it to him, and almost unconsciously uttered sounds of hushing tenderness, while he bethought himself that some of his porridge, which had got cool by the dying fire, would do to feed the child with if it were only warmed up a little.

He had plenty to do through the next hour. The porridge, sweetened with some dry brown sugar from an old store which he had refrained from using for himself, stopped the cries of the little one, and made her lift her blue eyes with a wide quiet gaze at Silas, as he put the spoon into her mouth. Presently she slipped from his knee and began to toddle about, but with a pretty stagger that made Silas jump up and follow her lest she should fall against anything that would hurt her. But she only fell in a sitting posture on the ground, and began to pull at her boots, looking up at him with a crying face as if the boots hurt her. He took her on his knee again, but it was some time before it occurred to Silas's dull bachelor mind that the wet boots were the grievance, pressing on her warm ankles. He got them off with difficulty, and baby was at once happily occupied with the primary mystery of her own toes, inviting Silas, with much chuckling, to consider the mystery too. But the wet boots had at last suggested to Silas that the child had been walking on the snow, and this roused him from his entire oblivion of any ordinary means by which it could have entered or been brought into his house. Under the prompting of this new idea, and without waiting to form conjectures, he raised the child in his arms, and went to the door. As soon as he had opened it, there was the cry of "mammy" again, which Silas had not heard since the child's first hungry waking. Bending forward, he could just discern the marks made by the little feet on the virgin snow, and he followed their track to the furze bushes. "Mammy!" the little one cried again and again, stretching itself forward so as almost to escape from Silas's arms, before he himself was aware that there was something more than the bush before him—that there was a human body, with the head sunk low in the furze, and half covered with the shaken snow.

## CHAPTER XIII

It was after the early supper-time at the Red House, and the entertainment was in that stage when bashfulness itself had passed into easy jollity, when gentlemen, conscious of unusual accomplishments, could at length be prevailed on to dance a hornpipe, and when the Squire preferred talking loudly, scattering snuff, and patting his visitors' backs, to sitting longer at the whist-table—a choice exasperating to Uncle Kimble, who, being always volatile in sober business hours, became intense and bitter over cards and brandy, shuffled before his adversary's deal with a glare of suspicion, and turned up a mean trump-card with an air of inexpressible disgust, as if in a world where such things could happen one might as well enter on a course of reckless profligacy. When the evening had advanced to this pitch of freedom and enjoyment, it was usual for the servants, the heavy duties of supper being well over, to get their share of amusement by coming to look on at the dancing; so that the back regions of the house were left in solitude.

There were two doors by which the White Parlor was entered from the hall, and they were both standing open for the sake of air; but the lower one was crowded with the servants and villagers, and only the upper doorway was left free. Bob Cass was figuring in a hornpipe, and his father, very proud of this lithe son, whom he repeatedly declared to be just like himself in his young days in a tone that implied this to be the very highest stamp of juvenile merit, was the centre of a group who had placed themselves opposite the performer, not far from the upper door. Godfrey was standing a little way off, not to admire his brother's dancing, but to keep sight of Nancy, who was seated in the group, near her father. He stood aloof, because he wished to avoid suggesting himself as a subject for the Squire's fatherly jokes in connection with matrimony and Miss Nancy Lammeter's beauty, which were likely to become more and more explicit. But he had the prospect of dancing with her again when the hornpipe was concluded, and in the meanwhile it was very pleasant to get long glances at her quite unobserved.

But when Godfrey was lifting his eyes from one of those long glances they encountered an object as startling to him at that moment as if it had been an apparition from the dead. It *was* an apparition from that hidden life which lies, like a dark by-street behind the goodly ornamented façade[1] that meets the sunlight and the gaze of respectable admirers. It was his own child, carried in Silas Marner's arms. That was his instantaneous impression, unaccompanied by doubt, though he had not seen the child for months past; and when the hope was rising that he might possibly be mistaken, Mr. Crackenthorp and Mr. Lammeter had already advanced to Silas in astonishment at this strange advent. Godfrey joined them immediately, unable to rest without hearing every word—trying to control himself, but conscious that if any one noticed him, they must see that he was white-lipped and trembling.

But now all eyes at that end of the room were bent on Silas Marner; the Squire himself had risen, and asked angrily, "How's this?—what's this?—what do you do coming in here in this way?"

"I'm come for the doctor—I want the doctor," Silas had said, in the first moment, to Mr. Crackenthorp.

"Why, what's the matter, Marner?" said the rector. "The doctor's here; but say quietly what you want him for."

"It's a woman," said Silas, speaking low, and half breathlessly, just as Godfrey came up. "She's dead, I think—dead in the snow at the Stone-pits—not far from my door."

[1] FAÇADE (fá-säd′)—Front.

Godfrey felt a great throb: there was one terror in his mind at that moment: it was, that the woman might *not* be dead. That was an evil terror—an ugly inmate to have found a nestling-place in Godfrey's kindly disposition; but no disposition is a security from evil wishes to a man whose happiness hangs on duplicity.

"Hush, hush!" said Mr. Crackenthorp. "Go out into the hall there. I'll fetch the doctor to you. Found a woman in the snow—and thinks she's dead," he added, speaking low to the Squire. "Better say as little about it as possible: it will shock the ladies. Just tell them a poor woman is ill from cold and hunger. I'll go and fetch Kimble."

By this time, however, the ladies had pressed forward, curious to know what could have brought the solitary linen-weaver there under such strange circumstances, and interested in the pretty child, who, half alarmed and half attracted by the brightness and the numerous company, now frowned and hid her face, now lifted up her head again and looked round placably, until a touch or a coaxing word brought back the frown, and made her bury her face with new determination.

"What child is it?" said several ladies at once, and, among the rest, Nancy Lammeter, addressing Godfrey.

"I don't know—some poor woman's who has been found in the snow, I believe," was the answer Godfrey wrung from himself with a terrible effort. ("After all, *am* I certain?" he hastened to add, in anticipation of his own conscience.)

"Why, you'd better leave the child here, then, Master Marner," said good-natured Mrs. Kimble, hesitating, however, to take those dingy clothes into contact with her own ornamented satin bodice. "I'll tell one o' the girls to fetch it."

"No—no—I can't part with it, I can't let it go," said Silas abruptly. "It's come to me—I've a right to keep it."

The proposition to take the child from him had come to Silas quite unexpectedly, and his speech, uttered under a strong sudden impulse, was almost like a revelation to himself: a minute before he had no distinct intention about the child.

"Did you ever hear the like?" said Mrs. Kimble, in mild surprise, to her neighbor.

"Now, ladies, I must trouble you to stand aside," said Mr. Kimble, coming from the card-room, in some bitterness at the interruption, but drilled by the long habit of his profession into obedience to unpleasant calls, even when he was hardly sober.

"It's a nasty business turning out now, eh, Kimble?" said the Squire. "He might ha' gone for your young fellow,—the 'prentice, there,—what's his name?"

"Might? ay,—what's the use of talking about might?" growled Uncle Kimble, hastening out with Marner, and followed by Mr. Crackenthorp and Godfrey. "Get me a pair of thick boots, Godfrey, will you? And stay, let somebody run to Winthrop's and fetch Dolly,—she's the best woman to get. Ben was here himself before supper; is he gone?"

"Yes, sir, I met him," said Marner; "but I couldn't stop to tell him anything, only I said I was going for the doctor, and he said the doctor was at the Squire's. And I made haste and ran, and there was nobody to be seen at the back o' the house, and so I went in to where the company was."

The child, no longer distracted by the bright light and the smiling women's faces, began to cry and call for "mammy," though always clinging to Marner, who had apparently won her thorough confidence.[2] Godfrey had come back with the boots, and felt the cry as if some fibre were drawn tight within him.

"I'll go," he said hastily, eager for some movement: "I'll go and fetch the woman,—Mrs. Winthrop."

"Oh, pooh,—send somebody else," said Uncle Kimble, hurrying away with Marner.

"You'll let me know if I can be of any use, Kimble," said Mr. Crackenthorp. But the doctor was out of hearing.

Godfrey, too, had disappeared: he was gone to snatch his hat and coat, having just reflection enough to remember that he must not look like a madman; but he rushed out of the house into the snow without heeding his thin shoes.

In a few minutes he was on his rapid way to the Stone-pits by the side of Dolly, who, though feeling that she was entirely in her place in encountering cold and snow on an errand of mercy, was much concerned at a young gentleman's getting his feet wet under a like impulse.

[2] Who had apparently won her thorough confidence—George Eliot is not a complete realist or she would let actions speak for themselves. When the child clings to Silas, we know without being told that he has won her confidence. Note also that the author repeatedly remarks on Godfrey's weakness, though it is already evident from his actions.

"You'd a deal better go back, sir," said Dolly, with respectful compassion. "You've no call to catch cold; and I'd ask you if you'd be so good as tell my husband to come, on your way back—he's at the Rainbow, I doubt—if you found him any way sober enough to be o' use. Or else, there's Mrs. Snell 'ud happen[3] send the boy up to fetch and carry, for there may be things wanted from the doctor's."

"No, I'll stay, now I'm once out—I'll stay outside here," said Godfrey, when they came opposite Marner's cottage. "You can come and tell me if I can do anything."

"Well, sir, you're very good: you've a tender heart," said Dolly, going to the door.

Godfrey was too painfully preoccupied to feel a twinge of self-reproach at this undeserved praise. He walked up and down, unconscious that he was plunging ankle-deep in snow, unconscious of everything but trembling suspense about what was going on in the cottage, and the effect of each alternative on his future lot. No, not quite unconscious of everything else. Deeper down, and half smothered by passionate desire and dread, there was the sense that he ought not to be waiting on these alternatives; that he ought to accept the consequences of his deeds, own the miserable wife, and fulfil the claims of the helpless child. But he had not moral courage enough to contemplate that active renunciation of Nancy as possible for him: he had only conscience and heart enough to make him forever uneasy under the weakness that forbade the renunciation. And at this moment his mind leaped away from all restraint toward the sudden prospect of deliverance from his long bondage.

"Is she dead?" said the voice that predominated over every other within him. "If she is, I may marry Nancy; and then I shall be a good fellow in future, and have no secrets, and the child—shall be taken care of somehow." But across that vision came the other possibility—"She may live, and then it's all up with me."

Godfrey never knew how long it was before the door of the cottage opened and Mr. Kimble came out. He went forward to meet his uncle, prepared to suppress the agitation he must feel, whatever news he was to hear.

"I waited for you, as I'd come so far," he said, speaking first.

"Pooh, it was nonsense for you to come out. Why didn't you

[3] HAPPEN—Perhaps.

send one of the men? There's nothing to be done. She's dead—has been dead for hours, I should say."

"What sort of woman is she?" said Godfrey, feeling the blood rush to his face.

"A young woman, but emaciated, with long black hair. Some vagrant—quite in rags. She's got a wedding-ring on, however. They must fetch her away to the workhouse[4] to-morrow. Come, come along."

"I want to look at her," said Godfrey. "I think I saw such a woman yesterday. I'll overtake you in a minute or two."

Mr. Kimble went on, and Godfrey turned back to the cottage. He cast only one glance at the dead face on the pillow, which Dolly had smoothed with decent care; but he remembered that last look at his unhappy hated wife so well, that at the end of sixteen years every line in the worn face was present to him when he told the full story[5] of this night.

He turned immediately towards the hearth where Silas Marner sat lulling the child. She was perfectly quiet now, but not asleep—only soothed by sweet porridge and warmth into that wide-gazing calm which makes us older human beings, with our inward turmoil, feel a certain awe in the presence of a little child, such as we feel before some quiet majesty or beauty in the earth or sky—before a steady-glowing planet, or a full-flowered eglantine, or the bending trees over a silent pathway. The wide-open blue eyes looked up at Godfrey's without any uneasiness or sign of recognition; the child could make no visible audible claim on its father; and the father felt a strange mixture of feelings, a conflict of regret and joy, that the pulse of that little heart had no response for the half-jealous yearning in his own, when the blue eyes turned away from him slowly, and fixed themselves on the weaver's queer face, which was bent low down to look at them, while the small hand began to pull Marner's withered cheek with loving disfiguration.

"You'll take the child to the parish[6] to-morrow?" asked Godfrey, speaking as indifferently as he could.

---

[4] Workhouse—Poorhouse.

[5] When he told the full story—Again the author anticipates her story, making no mystery of whether or not Godfrey will confess. Now our interest will be concentrated on the influences which lead to the confession.

[6] Take the child to the parish—Hand the child over to be cared for by the community.

"Who says so?" said Marner sharply. "Will they make me take her?"

"Why, you wouldn't like to keep her, should you—an old bachelor like you?"

"Till anybody shows they've a right to take her away from me," said Marner. "The mother's dead, and I reckon it's got no father; it's a lone thing—and I'm a lone thing. My money's gone, I don't know where—and this is come from I don't know where. I know nothing—I'm partly mazed."

"Poor little thing!" said Godfrey. "Let me give something towards finding[7] it clothes."

He had put his hand in his pocket and found half a guinea, and, thrusting it into Silas's hand, he hurried out of the cottage to overtake Mr. Kimble.

"Ah, I see it's not the same woman I saw," he said, as he came up. "It's a pretty little child; the old fellow seems to want to keep it; that's strange for a miser like him. But I gave him a trifle to help him out; the parish isn't likely to quarrel with him for the right to keep the child."

"No; but I've seen the time when I might have quarrelled with him for it myself. It's too late now, though. If the child ran into the fire, your aunt's too fat to overtake it; she could only sit and grunt like an alarmed sow. But what a fool you are, Godfrey, to come out in your dancing shoes and stockings in this way—and you one of the beaux of the evening, and at your own house! What do you mean by such freaks, young fellow? Has Miss Nancy been cruel, and do you want to spite her by spoiling your pumps?"

"Oh, everything has been disagreeable to-night. I was tired to death of jigging and gallanting, and that bother about the hornpipes. And I'd got to dance with the other Miss Gunn," said Godfrey, glad of the subterfuge his uncle had suggested to him.

The prevarication and white lies which a mind that keeps itself ambitiously pure is as uneasy under as a great artist under the false touches that no eye detects but his own, are worn as lightly as mere trimmings when once the actions have become a lie.

Godfrey reappeared in the White Parlor with dry feet, and, since the truth must be told, with a sense of relief and gladness that was too strong for painful thoughts to struggle with. For

[7] Finding—Providing.

could he not venture now, whenever opportunity offered, to say the tenderest things to Nancy Lammeter—to promise her and himself that he would always be just what she would desire to see him? There was no danger that his dead wife would be recognized: those were not days of active inquiry and wide report; and as for the registry of their marriage, that was a long way off, buried in unturned pages, away from every one's interest but his own. Dunsey might betray him if he came back; but Dunsey might be won to silence.

And when events turn out so much better for a man than he has had reason to dread, is it not a proof that his conduct has been less foolish and blameworthy than it might otherwise have appeared?[8] When we are treated well, we naturally begin to think that we are not altogether unmeritorious, and that it is only just we should treat ourselves well, and not mar our own good fortune. Where, after all, would be the use of his confessing the past to Nancy Lammeter, and throwing away his happiness?—nay, hers? for he felt some confidence that she loved him. As for the child, he would see that it was cared for; he would never forsake it; he would do everything but own it. Perhaps it would be just as happy in life without being owned by its father, seeing that nobody could tell how things would turn out, and that—is there any other reason wanted?—well, then, that the father would be much happier without owning the child.

## CHAPTER XIV

There was a pauper's burial that week in Raveloe, and up Kench Yard at Batherley it was known that the dark-haired woman with the fair child, who had lately come to lodge there, was gone away again. That was all the express note taken that Molly had disappeared from the eyes of men. But the unwept death which, to the general lot, seemed as trivial as the summer-shed leaf, was charged with the force of destiny to certain human lives that we know of, shaping their joys and sorrows even to the end.[1]

---

[8] AND WHEN EVENTS . . . HAVE APPEARED?—This is Godfrey's reasoning, not George Eliot's.

[1] CHARGED WITH . . . TO THE END—A statement of George Eliot's philosophical and literary creed. Every action, however trivial, has its consequences.

Silas Marner's determination to keep the "tramp's child" was matter of hardly less surprise and iterated talk in the village than the robbery of his money. That softening of feeling towards him which dated from his misfortune, that merging of suspicion and dislike in a rather contemptuous pity for him as lone and crazy, was now accompanied with a more active sympathy, especially amongst the women. Notable mothers, who knew what it was to keep children "whole and sweet;" lazy mothers, who knew what it was to be interrupted in folding their arms and scratching their elbows by the mischievous propensities of children just firm on their legs, were equally interested in conjecturing how a lone man would manage with a two-year-old child on his hands, and were equally ready with their suggestions: the notable chiefly telling him what he had better do, and the lazy ones being emphatic in telling him what he would never be able to do.

Among the notable mothers, Dolly Winthrop was the one whose neighborly offices were the most acceptable to Marner, for they were rendered without any show of bustling instruction. Silas had shown her the half-guinea given to him by Godfrey, and had asked her what he should do about getting some clothes for the child.

"Eh, Master Marner," said Dolly, "there's no call to buy, no more nor a pair o' shoes; for I've got the little petticoats as Aaron wore five years ago, and it's ill spending the money on them baby-clothes, for the child 'ull grow like grass i' May, bless it—that it will."

And the same day Dolly brought her bundle, and displayed to Marner, one by one, the tiny garments in their due order of succession, most of them patched and darned, but clean and neat as fresh-sprung herbs. This was the introduction to a great ceremony with soap and water, from which Baby came out in new beauty, and sat on Dolly's knee, handling her toes and chuckling and patting her palms together with an air of having made several discoveries about herself, which she communicated by alternate sounds of "gug-gug-gug," and "mammy." The "mammy" was not a cry of need or uneasiness; Baby had been used to utter it without expecting either tender sound or touch to follow.

"Anybody 'ud think the angils in heaven couldn't be prettier," said Dolly, rubbing the golden curls and kissing them. "And to think of its being covered wi' them dirty rags—and the poor mother— froze to death; but there's Them as took care of it, and brought it to your door, Master Marner. The door was open, and it walked in over the snow, like as if it had been a little starved robin. Didn't you say the door was open?"

"Yes," said Silas meditatively. "Yes—the door was open. The money's gone I don't know where, and this is come from I don't know where."

He had not mentioned to any one his unconsciousness of the child's entrance, shrinking from questions which might lead to the fact he himself suspected—namely, that he had been in one of his trances.

"Ah," said Dolly, with soothing gravity, "it's like the night and the morning, and the sleeping and the waking, and the rain and the harvest—one goes and the other comes, and we know nothing how nor where. We may strive and scrat and fend,[2] but it's little we can do arter all—the big things come and go wi' no striving o' our'n—they do, that they do; and I think you're in the right on it to keep the little un, Master Marner, seeing as it's been sent to you, though there's folks as thinks different. You'll happen be a bit moithered[3] with it while it's so little; but I'll come, and welcome, and see to it for you; I've a bit o' time to spare most days, for when one gets up betimes i' the morning, the clock seems to stan' still tow'rt ten, afore it's time to go about the victual. So, as I say, I'll come and see to the child for you, and welcome."

"Thank you . . . kindly," said Silas, hesitating a little. "I'll be glad if you'll tell me things. But," he added uneasily, leaning forward to look at Baby with some jealousy, as she was resting her head backward against Dolly's arm, and eyeing him contentedly from a distance, "but I want to do things for it myself, else it may get fond o' somebody else, and not fond o' me. I've been used to fending for myself in the house—I can learn, I can learn."

"Eh, to be sure," said Dolly gently. "I've seen men as are wonderful handy wi' children. The men are awk'ard and contrairy mostly, God help 'em—but when the drink's out of 'em, they aren't unsensible, though they're bad for leeching and bandaging—so fiery and unpatient. You see this goes first, next the skin," proceeded Dolly, taking up the little shirt, and putting it on.

---

[2] Scrat and fend—Colloquial for scratch and struggle.

[3] Moithered—Bothered.

"Yes," said Marner docilely, bringing his eyes very close, that they might be initiated in the mysteries; whereupon Baby seized his head with both her small arms, and put her lips against his face with purring noises.

"See there," said Dolly, with a woman's tender tact, "she's fondest o' you. She wants to go o' your lap, I'll be bound. Go, then; take her, Master Marner; you can put the things on, and then you can say as you've done for her from the first of her coming to you."

Marner took her on his lap, trembling, with an emotion mysterious to himself, at something unknown dawning on his life. Thought and feeling were so confused within him that if he had tried to give them utterance, he could only have said that the child was come instead of the gold—that the gold had turned into the child. He took the garments from Dolly, and put them on under her teaching, interrupted, of course, by Baby's gymnastics.

"There, then! why, you take to it quite easy, Master Marner," said Dolly; "but what shall you do when you're forced to sit in your loom? For she'll get busier and mischievouser every day—she will, bless her. It's lucky as you've got that high hearth i'stead of a grate, for that keeps the fire more out of her reach; but if you've got anything as can be spilt or broke, or as is fit to cut her fingers off, she'll be at it—and it is but right you should know."

Silas meditated a little while in some perplexity. "I'll tie her to the leg o' the loom," he said at last—"tie her with a good long strip o' something."

"Well, mayhap that'll do, as it's a little gell, for they're easier persuaded to sit i' one place nor the lads. I know what the lads are, for I've had four—four I've had, God knows—and if you was to take and tie 'em up, they'd make a fighting and a crying as if you was ringing the pigs.[4] But I'll bring you my little chair, and some bits o' red rag and things for her to play wi'; an' she'll sit and chatter to 'em as if they was alive. Eh, if it wasn't a sin to the lads to wish 'em made different, bless 'em, I should ha' been glad for one of 'em to be a little gell; and to think as I could ha' taught her to scour, and mend, and the knitting, and everything. But I can teach 'em this little un, Master Marner, when she gets old enough."

[4] RINGING THE PIGS—Putting rings in the pigs' noses.

"But she'll be *my* little un," said Marner, rather hastily. "She'll be nobody else's."

"No, to be sure; you'll have a right to her if you're a father to her, and bring her up according. But," added Dolly, coming to a point which she had determined beforehand to touch upon, "you must bring her up like christened folks's children, and take her to church, and let her learn her catechise, as my little Aaron can say off—the 'I believe,' and everything, and 'hurt nobody by word or deed,'—as well as if he was the clerk. That's what you must do, Master Marner, if you'd do the right thing by the orphin child."

Marner's pale face flushed suddenly under a new anxiety. His mind was too busy trying to give some definite bearing to Dolly's words for him to think of answering her.

"And it's my belief," she went on, "as the poor little creature has never been christened, and it's nothing but right as the parson should be spoke to; and if you was noways unwilling, I'd talk to Mr. Macey about it this very day. For if the child ever went anyways wrong, and you hadn't done your part by it, Master Marner—'noculation,[5] and everything to save it from harm—it 'ud be a thorn i' your bed forever o' this side of the grave; and I can't think as it 'ud be easy lying down for anybody when they'd got to another world, if they hadn't done their part by the helpless children as come wi'out their own asking."

Dolly herself was disposed to be silent for some time now, for she had spoken from the depths of her own simple belief, and was much concerned to know whether her words would produce the desired effect on Silas. He was puzzled and anxious, for Dolly's word "christened" conveyed no distinct meaning to him. He had only heard of baptism, and had only seen the baptism of grown-up men and women.

"What is it as you mean by 'christened'?" he said at last timidly. "Won't folks be good to her without it?"

"Dear, dear! Master Marner," said Dolly, with gentle distress and compassion. "Had you never no father nor mother as taught you to say your prayers, and as there's good words and good things to keep us from harm?"

"Yes," said Silas, in a low voice; "I know a deal about that—used to, used to. But your ways are different; my country was

[5] 'Noculation—Inoculation against smallpox.

a good way off." He paused a few moments, and then added, more decidedly, "But I want to do everything as can be done for the child. And whatever's right for it i' this country, and you think 'ull do it good, I'll act according, if you'll tell me."

"Well, then, Master Marner," said Dolly, inwardly rejoiced, "I'll ask Mr. Macey to speak to the parson about it; and you must fix on a name for it, because it must have a name giv' it when it's christened."

"My mother's name was Hephzibah," said Silas, "and my little sister was named after her."

"Eh, that's a hard name," said Dolly. "I partly think it isn't a christened name."

"It's a Bible name," said Silas, old ideas recurring.

"Then I've no call to speak again' it," said Dolly rather startled by Silas's knowledge on this head; "but you see I'm no scholard, and I'm slow at catching the words. My husband says I'm allays like as if I was putting the haft for the handle—that's what he says—for he's very sharp, God help him. But it was awk'ard calling your little sister by such a hard name, when you'd got nothing big to say, like—wasn't it, Master Marner?"

"We called her Eppie," said Silas.

"Well, if it was noways wrong to shorten the name, it 'ud be a deal handier. And so I'll go now, Master Marner, and I'll speak about the christening afore dark; and I wish you the best o' luck, and it's my belief as it'll come to you, if you do what's right by the orphin child;—and there's the 'noculation to be seen to; and as to washing its bits o' things, you need look to nobody but me, for I can do 'em wi' one hand when I've got my suds about. Eh, the blessed angil! You'll let me bring my Aaron one o' these days, and he'll show her his little cart as his father's made for him, and the black-and-white pup as he's got a-rearing."

Baby *was* christened, the rector deciding that a double baptism was the lesser risk to incur; and on this occasion Silas, making himself as clean and tidy as he could, appeared for the first time within the church, and shared in the observances held sacred by his neighbors. He was quite unable, by means of anything he heard or saw, to identify the Raveloe religion with his old faith; if he could at any time in his previous life have done so, it must have been by the aid of a strong feeling ready to vibrate with sympathy rather than by a comparison of phrases and ideas; and now for long years that feeling had been dormant. He had no distinct idea about the baptism and the church-going, except that Dolly had said it was for the good of the child; and in this way, as the weeks grew to months, the child created fresh and fresh links between his life and the lives from which he had hitherto shrunk continually into narrower isolation. Unlike the gold which needed nothing, and must be worshipped in close-locked solitude,—which was hidden away from the daylight, was deaf to the song of birds, and started to no human tones,—Eppie was a creature of endless claims and ever-growing desires, seeking and loving sunshine, and living sounds, and living movements; making trial of everything, with trust in new joy, and stirring the human kindness in all eyes that looked on her. The gold had kept his thoughts in an ever-repeated circle, leading to nothing beyond itself; but Eppie was an object compacted of changes and hopes that forced his thoughts onward, and carried them far away from their old eager pacing towards the same blank limit—carried them away to the new things that would come with the coming years, when Eppie would have learned to understand how her father Silas cared for her; and made him look for images of that time in the ties and charities that bound together the families of his neighbors. The gold had asked that he should sit weaving longer and longer, deafened and blinded more and more to all things except the monotony of his loom and the repetition of his web; but Eppie called him away from his weaving, and made him think all its pauses a holiday, reawakening his senses with her fresh life, even to the old winter-flies that came crawling forth in the early spring sunshine, and warming him into joy because *she* had joy.

And when the sunshine grew strong and lasting, so that the buttercups were thick in the meadows, Silas might be seen in the sunny mid-day, or in the late afternoon when the shadows were lengthening under the hedgerows, strolling out with uncovered head to carry Eppie beyond the Stone-pits to where the flowers grew, till they reached some favorite bank where he could sit down, while Eppie toddled to pluck the flowers, and make remarks to the winged things that murmured happily above the bright petals, calling "Dad-dad's" attention continually by bringing him the flowers. Then she would turn her ear to some sudden bird-note, and Silas learned to please her by making signs of hushed stillness, that they might listen for the note to come again: so that when it came, she set up her small back and laughed with gurgling triumph. Sitting on the banks in this way, Silas began to look for the once familiar herbs again; and as the leaves, with their unchanged outline and markings, lay on his palm, there was a sense of crowding remembrances from which he turned away timidly, taking refuge in Eppie's little world, that lay lightly on his enfeebled spirit.

As the child's mind was growing into knowledge, his mind was growing into memory; as her life unfolded, his soul, long stupefied in a cold, narrow prison, was unfolding too, and trembling gradually into full consciousness.

It was an influence which must gather force with every new year: the tones that stirred Silas's heart grew articulate, and called for more distinct answers; shapes and sounds grew clearer for Eppie's eyes and ears, and there was more that "Dad-dad" was imperatively required to notice and account for. Also, by the time Eppie was three years old, she developed a fine capacity for mischief, and for devising ingenious ways of being troublesome, which found much exercise, not only for Silas's patience, but for his watchfulness and penetration. Sorely was poor Silas puzzled on such occasions by the incompatible demands of love. Dolly Winthrop told him that punishment was good for Eppie, and that as for rearing a child without making it tingle a little in soft and safe places now and then, it was not to be done.

"To be sure, there's another thing you might do, Master Marner," added Dolly, meditatively; "you might shut her up once i' the coal-hole. That was what I did wi' Aaron; for I was that silly wi' the youngest lad as I could never bear to smack him. Not as I could find i' my heart to let him stay i' the coal-hole more nor a minute, but it was enough to colly[6] him all over, so as he must be new washed and dressed, and it was as good as a rod to him,—that was. But I put it upo' your conscience, Master Marner, as there's one of 'em you must choose,—ayther smacking or the coal-hole,—else she'll get so masterful, there'll be no holding her."

Silas was impressed with the melancholy truth of this last remark; but his force of mind failed before the only two penal methods open to him, not only because it was painful to him to hurt Eppie,

[6] Colly—Blacken.

but because he trembled at a moment's contention with her, lest she should love him the less for it. Let even an affectionate Goliath get himself tied to a small tender thing, dreading to hurt it by pulling, and dreading still more to snap the cord, and which of the two, pray, will be master? It was clear that Eppie, with her short toddling steps, must lead father Silas a pretty dance on any fine morning when circumstances favored mischief.

For example. He had wisely chosen a broad strip of linen as a means of fastening her to his loom when he was busy; it made a broad belt round her waist, and was long enough to allow of her reaching the truckle-bed and sitting down on it, but not long enough for her to attempt any dangerous climbing. One bright summer's morning Silas had been more engrossed than usual in "setting up" a new piece of work, an occasion on which his scissors were in requisition. These scissors, owing to an especial warning of Dolly's, had been kept carefully out of Eppie's reach; but the click of them had had a peculiar attraction for her ear, and, watching the results of that click, she had derived the philosophic lesson that the same cause would produce the same effect. Silas had seated himself in his loom, and the noise of weaving had begun; but he had left his scissors on a ledge which Eppie's arm was long enough to reach; and now, like a small mouse, watching her opportunity, she stole quietly from her corner, secured the scissors, and toddled to the bed again, setting up her back as a mode of concealing the fact. She had a distinct intention as to the use of the scissors; and having cut the linen strip in a jagged but effectual manner, in two moments she had run out at the open door where the sunshine was inviting her, while poor Silas believed her to be a better child than usual. It was not until he happened to need his scissors that the terrible fact burst upon him: Eppie had run out by herself,—had perhaps fallen into the Stone-pit. Silas, shaken by the worst fear that could have befallen him, rushed out, calling "Eppie!" and ran eagerly about the unenclosed space, exploring the dry cavities into which she might have fallen, and then gazing with questioning dread at the smooth red surface of the water. The cold drops stood on his brow. How long had she been out? There was one hope—that she had crept through the stile and got into the fields where he habitually took her to stroll. But the grass was high in the meadow, and there was no descrying her, if she were there, except by a close search that would be a trespass on Mr. Osgood's crop. Still, that misdemeanor must be committed; and poor Silas, after peering all round the hedgerows, traversed the grass, beginning with perturbed vision to see Eppie behind every group of red sorrel,[7] and to see her moving always farther off as he approached. The meadow was searched in vain; and he got over the stile into the next field, looking with dying hope towards a small pond which was now reduced to its summer shallowness, so as to leave a wide margin of good adhesive mud. Here, however, sat Eppie, discoursing cheerfully to her own small boot, which she was using as a bucket to convey the water into a deep hoof-mark, while her little naked foot was planted comfortably on a cushion of olive-green mud. A red-headed calf was observing her with alarmed doubt through the opposite hedge.

Here was clearly a case of aberration[8] in a christened child which demanded severe treatment; but Silas, overcome with convulsive joy at finding his treasure again, could do nothing but snatch her up, and cover her with half-sobbing kisses. It was not until he had carried her home, and had begun to think of the necessary washing, that he recollected the need that he should punish Eppie, and "make her remember." The idea that she might run away again and come to harm gave him unusual resolution, and for the first time he determined to try the coal-hole—a small closet near the hearth.

"Naughty, naughty Eppie," he suddenly began, holding her on his knee, and pointing to her muddy feet and clothes; "naughty to cut with the scissors, and run away. Eppie must go into the coal-hole for being naughty. Daddy must put her in the coal-hole."

He half expected that this would be shock enough, and that Eppie would begin to cry. But instead of that, she began to shake herself on his knee, as if the proposition opened a pleasing novelty. Seeing that he must proceed to extremities, he put her into the coal-hole, and held the door closed, with a trembling sense that he was using a strong measure. For a moment there was silence, but then came a little cry, "Opy, opy!" and Silas let her out again,

---

[7] Sorrel—An herb having a sour juice.

[8] Aberration—Departure from the normal or proper conduct that christening might be supposed to insure in a child.

saying, "Now Eppie 'ull never be naughty again, else she must go into the coal-hole—a black, naughty place."

The weaving must stand still a long while this morning, for now Eppie must be washed and have clean clothes on; but it was to be hoped that this punishment would have a lasting effect, and save time in future; though, perhaps, it would have been better if Eppie had cried more.

In half an hour she was clean again, and Silas, having turned his back to see what he could do with the linen band, threw it down again, with the reflection that Eppie would be good without fastening for the rest of the morning. He turned round again, and was going to place her in her little chair near the loom, when she peeped out at him with black face and hands again, and said, "Eppie in de toal-hole!"

This total failure of the coal-hole discipline shook Silas's belief in the efficacy of punishment. "She'd take it all for fun," he observed to Dolly, "if I didn't hurt her, and that I can't do, Mrs. Winthrop. If she makes me a bit o' trouble I can bear it. And she's got no tricks but what she'll grow out of."

"Well, that's partly true, Master Marner," said Dolly sympathetically; "and if you can't bring your mind to frighten her off touching things, you must do what you can to keep 'em out of her way. That's what I do wi' the pups as the lads are allays a-rearing. They *will* worry and gnaw—worry and gnaw they will, if it was one's Sunday cap as hung anywhere so as they could drag it. They know no difference, God help 'em; it's the pushing o' the teeth as sets 'em on, that's what it is."

So Eppie was reared without punishment, the burden of her misdeeds being borne vicariously[9] by father Silas. The stone hut was made a soft nest for her, lined with downy patience; and also in the world that lay beyond the stone hut she knew nothing of frowns and denials.

Notwithstanding the difficulty of carrying her and his yarn or linen at the same time, Silas took her with him in most of his journeys to the farm-houses, unwilling to leave her behind at Dolly Winthrop's, who was always ready to take care of her; and little curly-headed Eppie, the weaver's child, became an object of interest at several out-lying homesteads, as well as in the village. Hitherto

[9] VICARIOUSLY—In place of (Eppie).

he had been treated very much as if he had been a useful gnome or brownie,—a queer and unaccountable creature, who must necessarily be looked at with wondering curiosity and repulsion, and with whom one would be glad to make all greetings and bargains as brief as possible, but who must be dealt with in a propitiatory way, and occasionally have a present of pork or garden-stuff to carry home with him, seeing that without him there was no getting the yarn woven. But now Silas met with open, smiling faces and cheerful questioning, as a person whose satisfactions and difficulties could be understood. Everywhere he must sit a little and talk about the child, and words of interest were always ready for him: "Ah, Master Marner, you'll be lucky if she takes the measles soon and easy!"—or, "Why, there isn't many lone men 'ud ha' been wishing to take up with a little un like that; but I reckon the weaving makes you handier than men as do outdoor work; you're partly as handy as a woman, for weaving comes next to spinning." Elderly masters and mistresses, seated observantly in large kitchen armchairs, shook their heads over the difficulties attendant on rearing children, felt Eppie's round arms and legs, and pronounced them remarkably firm, and told Silas that, if she turned out well (which, however, there was no telling), it would be a fine thing for him to have a steady lass to do for him when he got helpless. Servant maidens were fond of carrying her out to look at the hens and chickens, or to see if any cherries could be shaken down in the orchard; and the small boys and girls approached her slowly, with cautious movement and steady gaze, like little dogs face to face with one of their own kind, till attraction had reached the point at which the soft lips were put out for a kiss. No child was afraid of approaching Silas when Eppie was near him: there was no repulsion around him now, either for young or old; for the little child had come to link him once more with the whole world. There was love between him and the child that blent them into one, and there was love between the child and the world—from men and women with parental looks and tones to the red lady-birds and the round pebbles.

Silas began now to think of Raveloe life entirely in relation to Eppie: she must have everything that was a good in Raveloe; and he listened docilely, that he might come to understand better what this life was, from which, for fifteen years, he had stood aloof as from a strange thing, wherewith he could have no communion; as some man who has a precious plant to which he would give a nurturing home in a new soil thinks of the rain, and the sunshine, and all influences, in relation to his nursling, and asks industriously for all knowledge that will help him to satisfy the wants of the searching roots, or to guard leaf and bud from invading harm. The disposition to hoard had been utterly crushed at the very first by the loss of his long-stored gold; the coins he earned afterwards seemed as irrelevant as stones brought to complete a house suddenly buried by an earthquake; the sense of bereavement was too heavy upon him for the old thrill of satisfaction to arise again at the touch of the newly earned coin. And now something had come to replace his hoard which gave a growing purpose to the earnings, drawing his hope and joy continually onward beyond the money.

In old days there were angels who came and took men by the hand and led them away from the city of destruction. We see no white-winged angels now. But yet men are led away from threatening destruction: a hand is put into theirs which leads them forth gently towards a calm and bright land, so that they look no more backward; and the hand may be a little child's.[10]

## CHAPTER XV

There was one person, as you will believe, who watched, with keener though more hidden interest than any other, the prosperous growth of Eppie under the weaver's care. He dared not do anything that would imply a stronger interest in a poor man's adopted child than could be expected from the kindliness of the young Squire, when a chance meeting suggested a little present to a simple old fellow whom others noticed with good-will; but he told himself that the time would come when he might do something towards furthering the welfare of his daughter without incurring suspicion. Was he very uneasy in the mean time at his inability to give his daughter her birthright? I cannot say that he was. The child was being taken care of, and would very likely be happy, as people in humble stations often were—happier, perhaps, than those brought up in luxury.

[10] In old days . . . a little child's—Here is the first statement of the central theme of *Silas Marner.* Compare with the Biblical phrasing: "A little child shall lead them."

That famous ring that pricked its owner when he forgot duty and followed desire—I wonder if it pricked very hard when he set out on the chase, or whether it pricked but lightly then, and only pierced to the quick when the chase had long been ended, and Hope, folding her wings, looked backward and became Regret?

Godfrey Cass's cheek and eye were brighter than ever now. He was so undivided in his aims that he seemed like a man of firmness. No Dunsey had come back; people had made up their minds that he was gone for a soldier, or gone "out of the country," and no one cared to be specific in their[1] inquiries on a subject delicate to a respectable family. Godfrey had ceased to see the shadow of Dunsey across his path; and the path now lay straight forward to the accomplishment of his best, longest-cherished wishes. Everybody said Mr. Godfrey had taken the right turn; and it was pretty clear what would be the end of things, for there were not many days in the week that he was not seen riding to the Warrens. Godfrey himself, when he was asked jocosely if the day had been fixed, smiled with the pleasant consciousness of a lover who could say "yes," if he liked. He felt a reformed man, delivered from temptation; and the vision of his future life seemed to him as a promised land for which he had no cause to fight. He saw himself with all his happiness centred on his own hearth, while Nancy would smile on him as he played with the children.

And that other child—not on the hearth—he would not forget it; he would see that it was well provided for. That was a father's duty.

---

[1] THEIR—Incorrect form of the pronoun. Singular form is required.

# Part II

## CHAPTER XVI

It was a bright autumn Sunday, sixteen years after Silas Marner had found his new treasure on the hearth. The bells of the old Raveloe church were ringing the cheerful peal which told that the morning service was ended; and out of the arched doorway in the tower came slowly, retarded by friendly greetings and questions, the richer parishioners who had chosen this bright Sunday morning as eligible for church-going. It was the rural fashion of that time for the more important members of the congregation to depart first, while their humbler neighbors waited and looked on, stroking their bent heads or dropping their curtsies to any large rate-payer[1] who turned to notice them.

Foremost among these advancing groups of well-clad people there are some whom we shall recognize, in spite of Time, who has laid his hand on them all. The tall blond man of forty is not much changed in feature from the Godfrey Cass of six and twenty; he is only fuller in flesh, and has only lost the indefinable look of youth,—a loss which is marked even when the eye is undulled and the wrinkles are not yet come. Perhaps the pretty woman, not much younger than he, who is leaning on his arm, is more changed than her husband; the lovely bloom that used to be always on her cheek now comes but fitfully, with the fresh morning air or with some strong surprise; yet to all who love human faces best for what they tell of human experience, Nancy's beauty has a heightened interest. Often the soul is ripened into fuller goodness while age has spread an ugly film, so that mere glances can never divine the preciousness of the fruit. But the years have not been so cruel to Nancy. The firm yet placid mouth, the clear veracious glance of the brown eyes, speak now of a nature that has been tested and has kept its highest qualities; and even the costume, with its dainty neatness and purity, has more significance now the coquetries of youth can have nothing to do with it.

Mr. and Mrs. Godfrey Cass (any higher title has died away from Raveloe lips since the old Squire was gathered to his fathers and his inheritance was divided) have turned round to look for

[1] Rate-payer—Taxpayer.

the tall aged man and the plainly dressed woman who are a little behind,—Nancy having observed that they must wait for "father and Priscilla,"—and now they all turn into a narrower path leading across the churchyard to a small gate opposite the Red House. We will not follow them now; for may there not be some others in this departing congregation whom we should like to see again, —some of those who are not likely to be handsomely clad, and whom we may not recognize so easily as the master and mistress of the Red House?

But it is impossible to mistake Silas Marner. His large brown eyes seem to have gathered a longer vision, as is the way with eyes that have been short-sighted in early life, and they have a less vague, a more answering gaze; but in everything else one sees signs of a frame much enfeebled by the lapse of the sixteen years. The weaver's bent shoulders and white hair give him almost the look of advanced age, though he is not more than five and fifty; but there is the freshest blossom of youth close by his side—a blond, dimpled girl of eighteen, who has vainly tried to chastise her curly auburn hair into smoothness under her brown bonnet; the hair ripples as obstinately as a brooklet under the March breeze, and the little ringlets burst away from the restraining comb behind and show themselves below the bonnet-crown. Eppie cannot help being rather vexed about her hair, for there is no other girl in Raveloe who has hair at all like it, and she thinks hair ought to be smooth. She does not like to be blameworthy even in small things: you see how neatly her prayer-book is folded in her spotted handkerchief.

That good-looking young fellow, in a new fustian suit, who walks behind her, is not quite sure upon the question of hair in the abstract when Eppie puts it to him, and thinks that perhaps straight hair is the best in general, but he doesn't want Eppie's hair to be different. She surely divines that there is some one behind her who is thinking about her very particularly, and mustering courage to come to her side as soon as they are out in the lane, else why should she look rather shy, and take care not to turn away her head from her father Silas, to whom she keeps murmuring little sentences as to who was at church, and who was not at church, and how pretty the red mountain-ash is over the Rectory wall!

"I wish *we* had a little garden, father, with double daisies in, like Mrs. Winthrop's," said Eppie, when they were out in the lane; "only they say it 'ud take a deal of digging and bringing fresh soil,—and you couldn't do that, could you, father? Anyhow, I shouldn't like you to do it, for it 'ud be too hard work for you."

"Yes, I could do it, child, if you want a bit o' garden: these long evenings I could work at taking in a little bit o' the waste, just enough for a root or two o' flowers for you; and again, i' the morning, I could have a turn wi' the spade before I sat down to the loom. Why didn't you tell me before as you wanted a bit o' garden?"

"*I* can dig it for you, Master Marner," said the young man in fustian, who was now by Eppie's side, entering into the conversation without the trouble of formalities. "It'll be play to me after I've done my day's work, or any odd bits o' time when the work's slack. And I'll bring you some soil from Mr. Cass's garden—he'll let me, and willing."

"Eh, Aaron, my lad, are you there?" said Silas. "I wasn't aware of you; for when Eppie's talking o' things, I see nothing but what she's a-saying. Well, if you could help me with the digging, we might get her a bit o' garden all the sooner."

"Then, if you think well and good," said Aaron, "I'll come to the Stone-pits this afternoon, and we'll settle what land's to be taken in, and I'll get up an hour earlier i' the morning, and begin on it."

"But not if you don't promise me not to work at the hard digging, father," said Eppie. "For I shouldn't ha' said anything about it," she added, half bashfully, half roguishly, "only Mrs. Winthrop said as Aaron 'ud be so good, and"—

"And you might ha' known it without mother telling you," said Aaron. "And Master Marner knows too, I hope, as I'm able and willing to do a turn o' work for him, and he won't do me the unkindness to anyways take it out o' my hands."

"There, now, father, you won't work in it till it's all easy," said Eppie; "and you and me can mark out the beds, and make holes and plant the roots. It'll be a deal livelier at the Stone-pits when we've got some flowers, for I always think the flowers can see us and know what we're talking about. And I'll have a bit o' rosemary, and bergamot, and thyme, because they're so sweet-smelling; but there's no lavender only in the gentlefolks' gardens, I think."

"That's no reason why you shouldn't have some," said Aaron, "for I can bring you slips of anything; I'm forced to cut no end of 'em when I'm gardening, and throw 'em away mostly. There's a big bed o' lavender at the Red House; the missis is very fond of it."

"Well," said Silas gravely, "so as you don't make free[2] for us, or ask for anything as is worth much at the Red House; for Mr. Cass's been so good to us and built us up the new end o' the cottage, and given us beds and things, as I couldn't abide to be imposin' for garden-stuff or anything else."

"No, no, there's no imposin'," said Aaron; "there's never a garden in all the parish but what there's endless waste in it for want o' somebody as could use everything up. It's what I think to myself sometimes, as there need nobody run short o' victuals if the land was made the most on, and there was never a morsel but what could find its way to a mouth. It sets one thinking o' that—gardening does. But I must go back now, else mother 'ull be in trouble as I aren't there."

"Bring her with you this afternoon, Aaron," said Eppie; "I shouldn't like to fix about the garden, and her not know everything from the first—should *you*, father?"

"Ay, bring her if you can, Aaron," said Silas; "she's sure to have a word to say as'll help us to set things on their right end."

Aaron turned back up the village, while Silas and Eppie went on up the lonely sheltered lane.

"O daddy!" she began, when they were in privacy, clasping and squeezing Silas's arm, and skipping round to give him an energetic kiss. "My little old daddy! I'm so glad. I don't think I shall want anything else when we've got a little garden; and I knew Aaron would dig it for us," she went on with roguish triumph; "I knew that very well."

"You're a deep little puss, you are," said Silas, with the mild, passive happiness of love-crowned age in his face; "but you'll make yourself fine and beholden[3] to Aaron."

"Oh, no, I shan't," said Eppie, laughing and frisking; "he likes it."

"Come, come, let me carry your prayer-book, else you'll be dropping it, jumping i' that way."

[2] Make free—Take too many liberties.

[3] Fine and beholden—Deeply indebted.

Eppie was now aware that her behavior was under observation, but it was only the observation of a friendly donkey, browsing with a log fastened to his foot,—a meek donkey, not scornfully critical of human trivialities, but thankful to share in them, if possible, by getting his nose scratched; and Eppie did not fail to gratify him with her usual notice, though it was attended with the inconvenience of his following them, painfully, up to the very door of their home.

But the sound of a sharp bark inside, as Eppie put the key in the door, modified the donkey's views, and he limped away again without bidding. The sharp bark was the sign of an excited welcome that was awaiting them from a knowing brown terrier, who, after dancing at their legs in a hysterical manner, rushed with a worrying noise at a tortoise-shell kitten under the loom, and then rushed back with a sharp bark again, as much as to say, "I have done my duty by this feeble creature, you perceive;" while the lady-mother of the kitten sat sunning her white bosom in the window, and looked round with a sleepy air of expecting caresses, though she was not going to take any trouble for them.

The presence of this happy animal life was not the only change which had come over the interior of the stone cottage. There was no bed now in the living-room, and the small space was well filled with decent furniture, all bright and clean enough to satisfy Dolly Winthrop's eye. The oaken table and three-cornered oaken chair were hardly what was likely to be seen in so poor a cottage; they had come, with the beds and other things, from the Red House; for Mr. Godfrey Cass, as every one said in the village, did very kindly by the weaver; and it was nothing but right a man should be looked on and helped by those who could afford it, when he had brought up an orphan child, and been father and mother to her,—and had lost his money, too, so as he had nothing but what he worked for week by week, and when the weaving was going down, too,—for there was less and less flax spun,—and Master Marner was none so young. Nobody was jealous of the weaver, for he was regarded as an exceptional person, whose claims on neighborly help were not to be matched in Raveloe. Any superstition that remained concerning him had taken an entirely new color; and Mr. Macey, now a very feeble old man of fourscore and six, never seen except in his chimney-corner or sitting in the sunshine at his door-sill, was of opinion that when a man had done what Silas had done by an orphan child, it was a sign that his money would come to light again,[4] or leastwise that the robber would be made to answer for it; for, as Mr. Macey observed of himself, his faculties were as strong as ever.

Silas sat down now and watched Eppie with a satisfied gaze as she spread the clean cloth, and set on it the potato-pie, warmed up slowly in a safe Sunday fashion, by being put into a dry pot over a slowly dying fire, as the best substitute for an oven. For Silas would not consent to have a grate and oven added to his conveniences: he loved the old brick hearth as he had loved his brown pot,—and was it not there when he had found Eppie? The gods of the hearth exist for us still; and let all new faith be tolerant of that fetishism,[5] lest it bruise its own roots.

Silas ate his dinner more silently than usual, soon laying down his knife and fork, and watching half abstractedly Eppie's play with Snap and the cat, by which her own dining was made rather a lengthy business. Yet it was a sight that might well arrest wandering thoughts: Eppie, with the rippling radiance of her hair and the whiteness of her rounded chin and throat set off by the dark blue cotton gown, laughing merrily as the kitten held on with her four claws to one shoulder, like a design for a jug-handle, while Snap on the right hand and Puss on the other put up their paws towards a morsel which she held out of the reach of both,—Snap occasionally desisting in order to remonstrate with the cat by a cogent worrying growl on the greediness and futility of her conduct; till Eppie relented, caressed them both, and divided the morsel between them.

But at last Eppie, glancing at the clock, checked the play and said, "O daddy, you're wanting to go into the sunshine to smoke your pipe. But I must clear away first, so as the house may be tidy when godmother comes. I'll make haste—I won't be long."

Silas had taken to smoking a pipe daily during the last two years, having been strongly urged to it by the sages of Raveloe, as a practice "good for the fits;" and this advice was sanctioned by Dr. Kimble, on the ground that it was as well to try what could

---

[4] Money would come to light again—George Eliot here erects a "sign post"; that is, plants in the reader's mind the possibility of the return of Silas's gold.

[5] Fetishism—Unreasoning devotion to an object or idea.

do no harm,—a principle which was made to answer for a great deal of work in that gentleman's medical practice. Silas did not highly enjoy smoking, and often wondered how his neighbors could be so fond of it; but a humble sort of acquiescence in what was held to be good had become a strong habit of that new self which had been developed in him since he had found Eppie on his hearth; it had been the only clue his bewildered mind could hold by in cherishing this young life that had been sent to him out of the darkness into which his gold had departed. By seeking what was needful for Eppie, by sharing the effect that everything produced on her, he had himself come to appropriate the forms of custom and belief which were the mould of Raveloe life; and as, with reawakening sensibilities, memory also reawakened, he had begun to ponder over the elements of his old faith, and blend them with his new impressions, till he recovered a consciousness of unity between his past and present. The sense of presiding goodness and the human trust which come with all pure peace and joy had given him a dim impression that there had been some error, some mistake, which had thrown that dark shadow over the days of his best years; and as it grew more and more easy to him to open his mind to Dolly Winthrop, he gradually communicated to her all he could describe of his early life. The communication was necessarily a slow and difficult process, for Silas's meagre power of explanation was not aided by any readiness of interpretation in Dolly, whose narrow outward experience gave her no key to strange customs, and made every novelty a source of wonder that arrested them at every step of the narrative. It was only by fragments, and at intervals which left Dolly time to revolve what she had heard till it acquired some familiarity for her, that Silas at last arrived at the climax of the sad story,—the drawing of lots, and its false testimony concerning him; and this had to be repeated in several interviews, under new questions on her part as to the nature of this plan for detecting the guilty and clearing the innocent.

"And yourn's the same Bible, you're sure o' that, Master Marner—the Bible as you brought wi' you from that country—it's the same as what they've got at church, and what Eppie's a-learning to read in?"

"Yes," said Silas, "every bit the same; and there's drawing o' lots in the Bible, mind you," he added in a lower tone.

"Oh, dear, dear," said Dolly, in a grieved voice, as if she were hearing an unfavorable report of a sick man's case. She was silent for some minutes; at last she said,—

"There's wise folks, happen, as know how it all is; the parson knows, I'll be bound; but it takes big words to tell them things, and such as poor folks can't make much out on. I can never rightly know the meaning o' what I hear at church, only a bit here and there, but I know it's good words—I do But what lies upo' your mind—it's this, Master Marner: as, if Them above had done the right thing by you, They'd never ha' let you be turned out for a wicked thief when you was innicent."

"Ah!" said Silas, who had now come to understand Dolly's phraseology, "that was what fell on me like as if it had been red-hot iron; because, you see, there was nobody as cared for me or clave to me above nor below. And him as I'd gone out and in wi' for ten year and more, since when we was lads and went halves—mine own familiar friend, in whom I trusted, had lifted up his heel again' me, and worked to ruin me."

"Eh, but he was a bad un—I can't think as there's another such," said Dolly. "But I'm o'ercome, Master Marner; I'm like as if I'd waked and didn't know whether it was night or morning. I feel somehow as sure as I do when I've laid something up though I can't justly put my hand on it, as there was a rights in what happened to you, if one could but make it out; and you'd no call to lose heart as you did. But we'll talk on it again; for sometimes things come into my head when I'm leeching or poulticing, or such, as I could never think on when I was sitting still."

Dolly was too useful a woman not to have many opportunities of illumination of the kind she alluded to, and she was not long before she recurred to the subject.

"Master Marner," she said, one day that she came to bring home Eppie's washing, "I've been sore puzzled for a good bit wi' that trouble o' yourn and the drawing o' lots; and it got twisted back'ards and for'ards, as I didn't know which end to lay hold on. But it come to me all clear like, that night when I was sitting up wi' poor Bessy Fawkes, as is dead and left her children behind, God help 'em—it come to me as clear as daylight; but whether I've got hold on it now, or can anyways bring it to my tongue's end, that I don't know. For I've often a deal inside me as 'll never come out; and for what you talk o' your folks in your old country niver saying prayers by heart nor saying 'em out of a book, they must be wonderful cliver; for if I didn't know 'Our Father,' and little bits o' good words as I can carry out o' church wi' me, I might down o' my knees every night, but nothing could I say."

"But you can mostly say something as I can make sense on, Mrs. Winthrop," said Silas.

"Well, then, Master Marner, it come to me summat like this: I can make nothing o' the drawing o' lots and the answer coming wrong; it 'ud mayhap take the parson to tell that, and he could only tell us i' big words. But what come to me as clear as the daylight, it was when I was troubling over poor Bessy Fawkes, and it allays comes into my head when I'm sorry for folks, and feel as I can't do a power to help 'em, not if I was to get up i' the middle o' the night—it comes into my head as Them above has got a deal tenderer heart nor what I've got—for I can't be anyways better nor Them as made me; and if anything looks hard to me, it's because there's things I don't know on; and for the matter o' that, there may be plenty o' things I don't know on, for it's little as I know—that it is. And so, while I was thinking o' that, you come into my mind, Master Marner, and it all come pouring in:—if *I* felt i' my inside what was the right and just thing by you, and them as prayed and drawed the lots, all but that wicked un, if *they*'d ha' done the right thing by you if they could, isn't there Them as was at the making on us, and knows better and has a better will? And that's all as ever I can be sure on, and everything else is a big puzzle to me when I think on it. For there was the fever come and took off them as were full-growed, and left the helpless children; and there's the breaking o' limbs; and them as 'ud do right and be sober have to suffer by them as are contrairy—eh, there's trouble i' this world, and there's things as we can niver make out the rights on. And all as we've got to do is to trusten, Master Marner—to do the right thing as fur as we know, and to trusten. For if us as knows so little can see a bit o' good and rights, we may be sure as there's a good and a rights bigger nor what we can know—I feel it i' my own inside as it must be so. And if you could but ha' gone on trustening, Master Marner, you wouldn't ha' run away from your fellow-creaturs and been so lone."

"Ah, but that 'ud ha' been hard," said Silas, in an undertone; "it 'ud ha' been hard to trusten then."

"And so it would," said Dolly, almost with compunction; "them things are easier said nor done; and I'm partly ashamed o' talking."

"Nay, nay," said Silas, "you're i' the right, Mrs. Winthrop—you're i' the right. There's good i' this world—I've a feeling o' that now; and it makes a man feel as there's a good more nor he can see, i' spite o' the trouble and the wickedness. That drawing o' the lots is dark; but the child was sent to me: there's dealings with us—there's dealings."

This dialogue took place in Eppie's earlier years when Silas had to part with her for two hours every day, that she might learn to read at the dame school,[6] after he had vainly tried himself to guide her in that first step to learning. Now that she was grown up, Silas had often been led, in those moments of quiet outpouring which come to people who live together in perfect love, to talk with *her,* too, of the past, and how and why he had lived a lonely man until she had been sent to him. For it would have been impossible for him to hide from Eppie that she was not his own child: even if the most delicate reticence on the point could have been expected from Raveloe gossips in her presence, her own questions about her mother could not have been parried, as she grew up, without that complete shrouding of the past which would have made a painful barrier between their minds. So Eppie had long known how her mother had died on the snowy ground, and how she herself had been found on the hearth by father Silas, who had taken her golden curls for his lost guineas brought back to him. The tender and peculiar love with which Silas had reared her in almost inseparable companionship with himself, aided by the seclusion of their dwelling, had preserved her from the lowering influences of the village talk and habits, and had kept her mind in that freshness which is sometimes falsely supposed to be an invariable attribute of rusticity. Perfect love has a breath of poetry which can exalt the relations of the least instructed human beings; and this breath of poetry had surrounded Eppie from the time when she had followed the bright gleam that beckoned her to Silas's hearth; so that it is not surprising if, in other things besides her delicate prettiness, she was not quite a common village maiden, but had a

[6] DAME SCHOOL—Private school for small children taught by a woman.

touch of refinement and fervor which came from no other teaching than that of tenderly nurtured unvitiated feeling. She was too childish and simple for her imagination to rove into questions about her unknown father; for a long while it did not even occur to her that she must have had a father; and the first time that the idea of her mother having had a husband presented itself to her was when Silas showed her the wedding-ring which had been taken from the wasted finger, and had been carefully preserved by him in a little lacquered box shaped like a shoe. He delivered this box into Eppie's charge when she had grown up, and she often opened it to look at the ring; but still she thought hardly at all about the father of whom it was the symbol. Had she not a father very close to her, who loved her better than any real fathers in the village seemed to love their daughters? On the contrary, who her mother was and how she came to die in that forlornness were questions that often pressed on Eppie's mind. Her knowledge of Mrs. Winthrop, who was her nearest friend next to Silas, made her feel that a mother must be very precious; and she had again and again asked Silas to tell her how her mother looked, whom she was like, and how he had found her against the furze bush, led towards it by the little footsteps and the outstretched arms. The furze bush was there still; and this afternoon, when Eppie came out with Silas into the sunshine, it was the first object that arrested her eyes and thoughts.

"Father," she said, in a tone of gentle gravity, which sometimes came like a sadder, slower cadence across her playfulness, "we shall take the furze bush into the garden; it'll come into the corner, and just against it I'll put snowdrops and crocuses, 'cause Aaron says they won't die out, but 'll always get more and more."

"Ah, child," said Silas, always ready to talk when he had his pipe in his hand, apparently enjoying the pauses more than the puffs, "it wouldn't do to leave out the furze bush; and there's nothing prettier, to my thinking, when it's yallow with flowers. But it's just come into my head what we're to do for a fence—mayhap Aaron can help us to a thought; but a fence we must have, else the donkeys and things 'ull come and trample everything down. And fencing's hard to be got at, by what I can make out."

"Oh, I'll tell you, daddy," said Eppie, clasping her hands suddenly, after a minute's thought. "There's lots o' loose stones about, some of 'em not big, and we might lay 'em atop of one another, and make a wall. You and me could carry the smallest, and Aaron 'ud carry the rest—I know he would."

"Eh, my precious un," said Silas, "there isn't enough stones to go all round; and as for you carrying, why, wi' your little arms you couldn't carry a stone no bigger than a turnip. You're dillicate made, my dear," he added, with a tender intonation—"that's what Mrs. Winthrop says."

"Oh, I'm stronger than you think, daddy," said Eppie; "and if there wasn't stones enough to go all round, why they'll go part o' the way, and then it'll be easier to get sticks and things for the rest. See here, round the big pit, what a many stones!"

She skipped forward to the pit, meaning to lift one of the stones and exhibit her strength, but she started back in surprise.

"Oh, father, just come and look here," she exclaimed—"come and see how the water's gone down since yesterday! Why, yesterday the pit was ever so full!"

"Well, to be sure," said Silas, coming to her side. "Why, that's the draining they've begun on, since harvest, i' Mr. Osgood's fields, I reckon. The foreman said to me the other day, when I passed by 'em, 'Master Marner,' he said, 'I shouldn't wonder if we lay your bit o' waste as dry as a bone.' It was Mr. Godfrey Cass, he said, had gone into the draining; he'd been taking these fields o' Mr. Osgood."

"How odd it'll seem to have the old pit dried up!" said Eppie, turning away, and stooping to lift rather a large stone. "See, daddy, I can carry this quite well," she said, going along with much energy for a few steps, but presently letting it fall.

"Ah, you're fine and strong, aren't you?" said Silas, while Eppie shook her aching arms and laughed. "Come, come, let us go and sit down on the bank against the stile there, and have no more lifting. You might hurt yourself, child. You'd need have somebody to work for you—and my arm isn't over strong."

Silas uttered the last sentence slowly, as if it implied more than met the ear; and Eppie, when they sat down on the bank, nestled close to his side, and, taking hold caressingly of the arm that was not over strong, held it on her lap, while Silas puffed again dutifully at the pipe, which occupied his other arm. An ash in the hedgerow behind made a fretted screen from the sun, and threw happy playful shadows all about them.

"Father," said Eppie, very gently, after they had been sitting in silence a little while, "if I was to be married, ought I to be married with my mother's ring?"

Silas gave an almost imperceptible start, though the question fell in with the under-current of thought in his own mind, and then said, in a subdued tone, "Why, Eppie, have you been a-thinking on it?"

"Only this last week, father," said Eppie, ingenuously, "since Aaron talked to me about it."

"And what did he say?" said Silas, still in the same subdued way, as if he were anxious lest he should fall into the slightest tone that was not for Eppie's good.

"He said he should like to be married, because he was a-going in four and twenty, and had got a deal of gardening work, now Mr. Mott's given up; and he goes twice a week regular to Mr. Cass's, and once to Mr. Osgood's, and they're going to take him on at the Rectory."

"And who is it as he's wanting to marry?" said Silas, with rather a sad smile.

"Why, me, to be sure, daddy," said Eppie, with dimpling laughter, kissing her father's cheek; "as if he'd want to marry anybody else!"

"And you mean to have him, do you?" said Silas.

"Yes, some time," said Eppie, "I don't know when. Everybody's married some time, Aaron says. But I told him that wasn't true; for, I said, look at father—he's never been married."

"No, child," said Silas, "your father was a lone man till you was sent to him."

"But you'll never be lone again, father," said Eppie tenderly. "That was what Aaron said—'I could never think o' taking you away from Master Marner, Eppie.' And I said, 'It 'ud be no use if you did, Aaron.' And he wants us all to live together, so as you needn't work a bit, father, only what's for your own pleasure; and he'd be as good as a son to you—that was what he said."

"And should you like that, Eppie?" said Silas, looking at her.

"I shouldn't mind it, father," said Eppie, quite simply. "And I should like things to be so as you needn't work much. But if it wasn't for that, I'd sooner things didn't change. I'm very happy: I like Aaron to be fond of me, and come and see us often, and behave pretty to you—he always *does* behave pretty to you, doesn't he, father?"

"Yes, child, nobody could behave better," said Silas emphatically. "He's his mother's lad."

"But I don't want any change," said Eppie. "I should like to go on a long, long while, just as we are. Only Aaron does want a change; and he made me cry a bit—only a bit—because he said I didn't care for him, for if I cared for him I should want us to be married, as he did."

"Eh, my blessed child," said Silas, laying down his pipe as if it were useless to pretend to smoke any longer, "you're o'er young to be married. We'll ask Mrs. Winthrop—we'll ask Aaron's mother what *she* thinks; if there's a right thing to do, she'll come at it. But there's this to be thought on, Eppie: things *will* change, whether we like it or not; things won't go on for a long while just as they are and no difference. I shall get older and helplesser, and be a burden on you, belike, if I don't go away from you altogether. Not as I mean you'd think me a burden—I know you wouldn't—but it 'ud be hard upon you; and when I look for'ard to that, I like to think as you'd have somebody else besides me—somebody young and strong, as 'll outlast your own life, and take care on you to the end." Silas paused, and, resting his wrists on his knees, lifted his hands up and down meditatively as he looked on the ground.

"Then, would you like me to be married, father?" said Eppie, with a little trembling in her voice.

"I'll not be the man to say no, Eppie," said Silas emphatically; "but we'll ask your godmother. She'll wish the right thing by you and her son, too."

"There they come then," said Eppie. "Let us go and meet 'em. Oh, the pipe! won't you have it lit again, father?" said Eppie, lifting that medicinal appliance from the ground.

"Nay, child," said Silas, "I've done enough for today. I think, mayhap, a little of it does me more good than so much at once."

## CHAPTER XVII

While Silas and Eppie were seated on the bank discoursing in the fleckered shade of the ash-tree, Miss Priscilla Lammeter was resisting her sister's arguments, that it would be better to take tea at the Red House, and let her father have a long nap, than drive home to the Warrens so soon after dinner. The family party (of four only) were seated round the table in the dark wainscoted parlor, with the Sunday dessert before them, of fresh filberts, apples, and pears, duly ornamented with leaves by Nancy's own hand before the bells had rung for church.

A great change has come over the dark wainscoted parlor since we saw it in Godfrey's bachelor days, and under the wifeless reign of the old Squire. Now all is polish, on which no yesterday's dust is ever allowed to rest, from the yard's width of oaken boards round the carpet to the old Squire's gun and whips and walking-sticks, ranged on the stag's antlers above the mantelpiece. All other signs of sporting and outdoor occupation Nancy has removed to another room; but she has brought into the Red House the habit of filial reverence, and preserves sacredly in a place of honor these relics of her husband's departed father. The tankards are on the side-table still, but the bossed silver is undimmed by handling, and there are no dregs to send forth unpleasant suggestions: the only prevailing scent is of the lavender and rose-leaves that fill the vases of Derbyshire spar. All is purity and order in this once dreary room, for, fifteen years ago, it was entered by a new presiding spirit.

"Now, father," said Nancy, "*is* there any call for you to go home to tea? Mayn't you just as well stay with us?—such a beautiful evening as it's likely to be."

The old gentleman had been talking with Godfrey about the increasing poor-rate[1] and the ruinous times, and had not heard the dialogue between his daughters.

"My dear, you must ask Priscilla," he said, in the once firm voice, now become rather broken. "She manages me and the farm too."

"And reason good as I should manage you, father," said Priscilla, "else you'd be giving yourself your death with rheumatism. And as for the farm, if anything turns out wrong, as it can't but do in these times, there's nothing kills a man so soon as having nobody to find fault with but himself. It's a deal the best way o' being master, to let somebody else do the ordering, and keep the blaming in your own hands. It 'ud save many a man a stroke, *I* believe."

[1] THE INCREASING POOR-RATE—To help the needy in the hard times following the Napoleonic Wars "poor taxes" were collected for relief purposes. So badly managed were the funds thus collected that it was necessary to keep increasing the tax to meet the need.

"Well, well, my dear," said her father, with a quiet laugh, "I didn't say you don't manage for everybody's good."

"Then manage so as you may stay tea, Priscilla," said Nancy, putting her hand on her sister's arm affectionately. "Come now; and we'll go round the garden while father has his nap."

"My dear child, he'll have a beautiful nap in the gig, for I shall drive. And as for staying tea, I can't hear of it; for there's this dairymaid, now she knows she's to be married, turned Michaelmas,[2] she'd as lieve pour the new milk into the pig-trough as into the pans. That's the way with 'em all: it's as if they thought the world 'ud be new-made because they're to be married. So come and let me put my bonnet on, and there'll be time for us to walk round the garden while the horse is being put in."

When the sisters were treading the neatly swept garden-walks, between the bright turf that contrasted pleasantly with the dark cones and arches and wall-like hedges of yew, Priscilla said,—

"I'm as glad as anything at your husband's making that exchange o' land with cousin Osgood, and beginning the dairying. It's a thousand pities you didn't do it before; for it'll give you something to fill your mind. There's nothing like a dairy if folks want a bit o' worrit to make the days pass. For as for rubbing furniture, when you can once see your face in a table there's nothing else to look for; but there's always something fresh with the dairy; for even in the depths o' winter there's some pleasure in conquering the butter, and making it come whether or no. My dear," added Priscilla, pressing her sister's hand affectionately as they walked side by side, "you'll never be low when you've got a dairy."

"Ah, Priscilla," said Nancy, returning the pressure with a grateful glance of her clear eyes, "but it won't make up to Godfrey: a dairy's not so much to a man. And it's only what he cares for that ever makes me low. I'm contented with the blessings we have, if he could be contented."

"It drives me past patience," said Priscilla impetuously, "that way o' the men—always wanting and wanting, and never easy with what they've got: they can't sit comfortable in their chairs when they've neither ache nor pain, but either they must stick a pipe in

[2] MICHAELMAS—Religious anniversary in commemoration of the Archangel Michael, celebrated Sept. 29.

their mouths, to make 'em better than well, or else they must be swallowing something strong, though they're forced to make haste before the next meal comes in. But joyful be it spoken, our father was never that sort o' man. And if it had pleased God to make you ugly, like me, so as the men wouldn't ha' run after you, we might have kept to our own family, and had nothing to do with folks as have got uneasy blood in their veins."

"Oh, don't say so, Priscilla," said Nancy, repenting that she had called forth this outburst; "nobody has any occasion to find fault with Godfrey. It's natural he should be disappointed at not having any children: every man likes to have somebody to work for and lay by for, and he always counted so on making a fuss with 'em when they were little. There's many another man 'ud hanker more than he does. He's the best of husbands."

"Oh, I know," said Priscilla, smiling sarcastically, "I know the way o' wives; they set one on to abuse their husbands, and then they turn round on one and praise 'em as if they wanted to sell 'em. But father'll be waiting for me; we must turn now."

The large gig with the steady old gray was at the front door, and Mr. Lammeter was already on the stone steps, passing the time in recalling to Godfrey what very fine points Speckle had when his master used to ride him.

"I always *would* have a good horse, you know," said the old gentleman, not liking that spirited time to be quite effaced from the memory of his juniors.

"Mind you bring Nancy to the Warrens before the week's out, Mr. Cass," was Priscilla's parting injunction, as she took the reins, and shook them gently, by way of friendly incitement to Speckle.

"I shall just take a turn to the fields against the Stone-pits, Nancy, and look at the draining," said Godfrey.

"You'll be in again by tea-time, dear?"

"Oh, yes, I shall be back in an hour."

It was Godfrey's custom on a Sunday afternoon to do a little contemplative farming in a leisurely walk. Nancy seldom accompanied him; for the women of her generation—unless, like Priscilla, they took to outdoor management—were not given to much walking beyond their own house and garden, finding sufficient exercise in domestic duties. So, when Priscilla was not with her, she usually sat with Mant's Bible[3] before her, and after following the text with her eyes for a little while, she would gradually permit them to wander as her thoughts had already insisted on wandering.

But Nancy's Sunday thoughts were rarely quite out of keeping with the devout and reverential intention implied by the book spread open before her. She was not theologically instructed enough to discern very clearly the relation between the sacred documents of the past which she opened without method, and her own obscure, simple life; but the spirit of rectitude, and the sense of responsibility for the effect of her conduct on others, which were strong elements in Nancy's character, had made it a habit with her to scrutinize her past feelings and actions with self-questioning solicitude. Her mind not being courted by a great variety of subjects, she filled the vacant moments by living inwardly, again and again, through all her remembered experience, especially through the fifteen years of her married time, in which her life and its significance had been doubled. She recalled the small details, the words, tones, and looks, in the critical scenes which had opened a new epoch for her by giving her a deeper insight into the relations and trials of life, or which had called on her for some little effort of forbearance, or of painful adherence to an imagined or real duty—asking herself continually whether she had been in any respect blamable. This excessive rumination and self-questioning is perhaps a morbid habit inevitable to a mind of much moral sensibility when shut out from its due share of outward activity and of practical claims on its affections—inevitable to a noble-hearted, childless woman, when her lot is narrow. "I can do so little—have I done it all well?" is the perpetually recurring thought; and there are no voices calling her away from that soliloquy, no peremptory demands to divert energy from vain regret or superfluous scruple.

There was one main thread of painful experience in Nancy's married life, and on it hung certain deeply felt scenes, which were the oftenest revived in retrospect. The short dialogue with Priscilla in the garden had determined the current of retrospect in that frequent direction this particular Sunday afternoon. The first wandering of her thought from the text, which she still attempted dutifully to follow with her eyes and silent lips, was into an

[3] MANT'S BIBLE—Richard Mant, an English prelate, published in 1817 a fully annotated version of the Bible that proved immensely popular.

imaginary enlargement of the defence she had set up for her husband against Priscilla's implied blame. The vindication of the loved object is the best balm affection can find for its wounds. "A man must have so much on his mind," is the belief by which a wife often supports a cheerful face under rough answers and unfeeling words. And Nancy's deepest wounds had all come from the perception that the absence of children from their hearth was dwelt on in her husband's mind as a privation to which he could not reconcile himself.

Yet sweet Nancy might have been expected to feel still more keenly the denial of a blessing to which she had looked forward with all the varied expectations and preparations, solemn and prettily trivial, which fill the mind of a loving woman when she expects to become a mother. Was there not a drawer filled with the neat work of her hands, all unworn and untouched, just as she had arranged it there fourteen years ago—just, but for one little dress, which had been made the burial-dress?[4] But under this immediate personal trial Nancy was so firmly unmurmuring, that years ago she had suddenly renounced the habit of visiting this drawer, lest she should in this way be cherishing a longing for what was not given.

Perhaps it was this very severity towards any indulgence of what she held to be sinful regret in herself that made her shrink from applying her own standard to her husband. "It is very different—it is much worse for a man to be disappointed in that way: a woman can always be satisfied with devoting herself to her husband, but a man wants something that will make him look forward more—and sitting by the fire is so much duller to him than to a woman." And always, when Nancy reached this point in her meditations—trying, with predetermined sympathy, to see everything as Godfrey saw it—there came a renewal of self-questioning. *Had* she done everything in her power to lighten Godfrey's privation? Had she really been right in the resistance which had cost her so much pain six years ago, and again four years ago—the resistance to her husband's wish that they should adopt a child? Adoption was more remote from the ideas and habits of that time than of our own; still Nancy had her opinion on it. It was as necessary

[4] BURIAL-DRESS—The author is telling us indirectly that Nancy's only baby had died at birth.

to her mind to have an opinion on all topics, not exclusively masculine, that had come under her notice, as for her to have a precisely marked place for every article of her personal property: and her opinions were always principles to be unwaveringly acted on. They were firm, not because of their basis, but because she held them with a tenacity inseparable from her mental action. On all the duties and proprieties of life, from filial behavior to the arrangements of the evening toilette, pretty Nancy Lammeter, by the time she was three and twenty, had her unalterable little code, and had formed every one of her habits in strict accordance with that code. She carried these decided judgments within her in the most unobtrusive way: they rooted themselves in her mind, and grew there as quietly as grass. Years ago, we know, she insisted on dressing like Priscilla, because "it was right for sisters to dress alike," and because "she would do what was right if she wore a gown dyed with cheese-coloring." That was a trivial but typical instance of the mode in which Nancy's life was regulated.

It was one of those rigid principles, and no petty egoistic feeling, which had been the ground of Nancy's difficult resistance to her husband's wish. To adopt a child, because children of your own had been denied you, was to try and choose your lot in spite of Providence: the adopted child, she was convinced, would never turn out well, and would be a curse to those who had wilfully and rebelliously sought what it was clear that, for some high reason, they were better without. When you saw a thing was not meant to be, said Nancy, it was a bounden duty to leave off so much as wishing for it. And so far, perhaps, the wisest of men could scarcely make more than a verbal improvement in her principle. But the conditions under which she held it apparent that a thing was not meant to be depended on a more peculiar mode of thinking. She would have given up making a purchase at a particular place if, on three successive times, rain, or some other cause of Heaven's sending, had formed an obstacle; and she would have anticipated a broken limb or other heavy misfortune to any one who persisted in spite of such indications.

"But why should you think the child would turn out ill?" said Godfrey, in his remonstrances. "She has thriven as well as child can do with the weaver; and *he* adopted her. There isn't such a pretty little girl anywhere else in the parish, or one fitter for the station we could give her. Where can be the likelihood of her being a curse to anybody?"

"Yes, my dear Godfrey," said Nancy, who was sitting with her hands tightly clasped together, and with yearning, regretful affection in her eyes. "The child may not turn out ill with the weaver. But, then, he didn't go to seek her, as we should be doing. It will be wrong; I feel sure it will. Don't you remember what that lady we met at the Royston Baths told us about the child her sister adopted? That was the only adopting I ever heard of: and the child was transported[5] when it was twenty-three. Dear Godfrey, don't ask me to do what I know is wrong: I should never be happy again. I know it's very hard for *you*—it's easier for me—but it's the will of Providence."

It might seem singular that Nancy—with her religious theory pieced together out of narrow social traditions, fragments of church doctrine imperfectly understood, and girlish reasonings on her small experience—should have arrived by herself at a way of thinking so nearly akin to that of many devout people, whose beliefs are held in the shape of a system quite remote from her knowledge—singular, if we did not know that human beliefs, like all other natural growths, elude the barriers of system.

Godfrey had from the first specified Eppie, then about twelve years old, as a child suitable for them to adopt. It had never occurred to him that Silas would rather part with his life than with Eppie. Surely the weaver would wish the best to the child he had taken so much trouble with, and would be glad that such good fortune should happen to her; she would always be very grateful to him, and he would be well provided for to the end of his life—provided for as the excellent part he had done by the child deserved. Was it not an appropriate thing for people in a higher station to take a charge off the hands of a man in a lower? It seemed an eminently appropriate thing to Godfrey, for reasons that were known only to himself; and by a common fallacy, he imagined the measure would be easy because he had private motives for desiring it. This was rather a coarse mode of estimating Silas's relation to Eppie; but we must remember that many of the impressions which Godfrey was likely to gather concerning the laboring people around him would favor the idea that deep affections can

[5] TRANSPORTED—Sentenced to exile.

hardly go along with callous palms and scant means; and he had not had the opportunity, even if he had had the power, of entering intimately into all that was exceptional in the weaver's experience. It was only the want of adequate knowledge that could have made it possible for Godfrey deliberately to entertain an unfeeling project: his natural kindness had outlived that blighting time of cruel wishes, and Nancy's praise of him as a husband was not founded entirely on a wilful illusion.

"I was right," she said to herself, when she had recalled all their scenes of discussion—"I feel I was right to say him nay, though it hurt me more than anything; but how good Godfrey has been about it! Many men would have been very angry with me for standing out against their wishes; and they might have thrown out that they'd had ill-luck in marrying me; but Godfrey has never been the man to say me an unkind word. It's only what he can't hide: everything seems so blank to him, I know; and the land—what a difference it 'ud make to him, when he goes to see after things, if he'd children growing up that he was doing it all for! But I won't murmur; and perhaps if he'd married a woman who'd have had children, she'd have vexed him in other ways."

This possibility was Nancy's chief comfort; and to give it greater strength, she labored to make it impossible that any other wife should have had more perfect tenderness. She had been *forced* to vex him by that one denial. Godfrey was not insensible to her loving effort, and did Nancy no injustice as to the motives of her obstinacy. It was impossible to have lived with her fifteen years and not be aware that an unselfish clinging to the right and a sincerity clear as the flower-born dew were her main characteristics; indeed, Godfrey felt this so strongly, that his own more wavering nature, too averse to facing difficulty to be unvaryingly simple and truthful, was kept in a certain awe of this gentle wife who watched his looks with a yearning to obey them. It seemed to him impossible that he should ever confess to her the truth about Eppie: she would never recover from the repulsion the story of his earlier marriage would create, told to her now, after that long concealment. And the child, too, he thought, must become an object of repulsion: the very sight of her would be painful. The shock to Nancy's mingled pride and ignorance of the world's evil might even be too much for her delicate frame. Since he had married her with that secret on his heart he must keep it there to the last. Whatever else he did, he could not make an irreparable breach between himself and this long-loved wife.

Meanwhile, why could he not make up his mind to the absence of children from a hearth brightened by such a wife? Why did his mind fly uneasily to that void, as if it were the sole reason why life was not thoroughly joyous to him? I suppose it is the way with all men and women who reach middle age without the clear perception that life never *can* be thoroughly joyous: under the vague dulness of the gray hours, dissatisfaction seeks a definite object, and finds it in the privation of an untried good. Dissatisfaction, seated musingly on a childless hearth, thinks with envy of the father whose return is greeted by young voices—seated at the meal where the little heads rise one above another like nursery plants, it sees a black care hovering behind every one of them, and thinks the impulses by which men abandon freedom, and seek for ties, are surely nothing but a brief madness. In Godfrey's case there were further reasons why his thoughts should be continually solicited by this one point in his lot: his conscience, never thoroughly easy about Eppie, now gave his childless home the aspect of a retribution; and as the time passed on, under Nancy's refusal to adopt her, any retrieval of his error became more and more difficult.

On this Sunday afternoon it was already four years since there had been any allusion to the subject between them, and Nancy supposed that it was forever buried.

"I wonder if he'll mind it less or more as he gets older," she thought; "I'm afraid more. Aged people feel the miss of children: what would father do without Priscilla? And if I die, Godfrey will be very lonely—not holding together with his brothers much. But I won't be over-anxious, and trying to make things out beforehand: I must do my best for the present."

With that last thought Nancy roused herself from her reverie, and turned her eyes again towards the forsaken page. It had been forsaken longer than she imagined, for she was presently surprised by the appearance of the servant with the tea-things. It was, in fact, a little before the usual time for tea; but Jane had her reasons.

"Is your master come into the yard, Jane?"

"No 'm, he isn't," said Jane, with a slight emphasis, of which, however, her mistress took no notice.

"I don't know whether you've seen 'em, 'm," continued Jane, after a pause, "but there's folks making haste all one way, afore the front window. I doubt something's happened. There's niver a man to be seen i' the yard, else I'd send and see. I've been up into the top attic, but there's no seeing anything for trees. I hope nobody's hurt, that's all."

"Oh, no, I daresay there's nothing much the matter," said Nancy. "It's perhaps Mr. Snell's bull got out again, as he did before."

"I wish he mayn't gore anybody, then, that's all," said Jane, not altogether despising a hypothesis which covered a few imaginary calamities.

"That girl is always terrifying me," thought Nancy; "I wish Godfrey would come in."

She went to the front window and looked as far as she could see along the road, with an uneasiness which she felt to be childish, for there were now no such signs of excitement as Jane had spoken of, and Godfrey would not be likely to return by the village road, but by the fields. She continued to stand, however, looking at the placid churchyard with the long shadows of the gravestones across the bright green hillocks, and at the glowing autumn colors of the Rectory trees beyond. Before such calm external beauty the presence of a vague fear is more distinctly felt—like a raven flapping its slow wing across the sunny air. Nancy wished more and more that Godfrey would come in.

## CHAPTER XVIII

Some one opened the door at the other end of the room, and Nancy felt that it was her husband. She turned from the window with gladness in her eyes, for the wife's chief dread was stilled.

"Dear, I'm so thankful you're come," she said, going towards him. "I began to get"—

She paused abruptly, for Godfrey was laying down his hat with trembling hands, and turned towards her with a pale face and a strange unanswering glance, as if he saw her indeed, but saw her as part of a scene invisible to herself. She laid her hand on his arm, not daring to speak again; but he left the touch unnoticed, and threw himself into his chair.

Jane was already at the door with the hissing urn. "Tell her to keep away, will you?" said Godfrey; and when the door was closed again he exerted himself to speak more distinctly.

"Sit down, Nancy—there," he said, pointing to a chair opposite him. "I came back as soon as I could, to hinder anybody's telling you but me. I've had a great shock—but I care most about the shock it'll be to you."

"It isn't father and Priscilla?" said Nancy, with quivering lips, clasping her hands together tightly on her lap.

"No, it's nobody living," said Godfrey, unequal to the considerate skill with which he would have wished to make his revelation. "It's Dunstan—my brother Dunstan, that we lost sight of sixteen years ago. We've found him—found his body—his skeleton."

The deep dread Godfrey's look had created in Nancy made her feel these words a relief. She sat in comparative calmness to hear what else he had to tell. He went on: "The Stone-pit has gone dry suddenly—from the draining, I suppose; and there he lies—has lain for sixteen years, wedged between two great stones. There's his watch and seals, and there's my gold-handled hunting-whip, with my name on: he took it away, without my knowing, the day he went hunting on Wildfire, the last time he was seen."

Godfrey paused: it was not so easy to say what came next. "Do you think he drowned himself?" said Nancy, almost wondering that her husband should be so deeply shaken by what had happened all those years ago to an unloved brother, of whom worse things had been augured.

"No, he fell in," said Godfrey, in a low but distinct voice, as if he felt some deep meaning in the fact. Presently he added: "Dunstan was the man that robbed Silas Marner."

The blood rushed to Nancy's face and neck at this surprise and shame, for she had been bred up to regard even a distant kinship with crime as a dishonor.

"O Godfrey!" she said, with compassion in her tone, for she had immediately reflected that the dishonor must be felt still more keenly by her husband.

"There was the money in the pit," he continued—"all the weaver's money. Everything's been gathered up, and they're taking the skeleton to the Rainbow. But I came back to tell you: there was no hindering it; you must know."

He was silent, looking on the ground for two long minutes. Nancy would have said some words of comfort under this disgrace, but she refrained, from an instinctive sense that there was something behind—that Godfrey had something else to tell her. Presently he lifted his eyes to her face, and kept them fixed on her, as he said,—

"Everything comes to light, Nancy, sooner or later. When God Almighty wills it, our secrets are found out. I've lived with a secret on my mind, but I'll keep it from you no longer. I wouldn't have you know it by somebody else, and not by me—I wouldn't have you find it out after I'm dead. I'll tell you now. It's been 'I will' and 'I won't' with me all my life—I'll make sure of myself now."

Nancy's utmost dread had returned. The eyes of the husband and wife met with awe in them, as at a crisis which suspended affection.

"Nancy," said Godfrey slowly, "when I married you, I hid something from you—something I ought to have told you. That woman Marner found dead in the snow—Eppie's mother—that wretched woman—was my wife: Eppie is my child."

He paused, dreading the effect of his confession. But Nancy sat quite still, only that her eyes dropped and ceased to meet his. She was pale and quiet as a meditative statue, clasping her hands on her lap.

"You'll never think the same of me again," said Godfrey, after a little while, with some tremor in his voice.

She was silent.

"I ought n't to have left the child unowned: I ought n't to have kept it from you. But I couldn't bear to give you up, Nancy. I was led away into marrying her—I suffered for it."

Still Nancy was silent, looking down; and he almost expected that she would presently get up and say she would go to her father's. How could she have any mercy for faults that must seem so black to her, with her simple, severe notions?

But at last she lifted up her eyes to his again and spoke. There was no indignation in her voice—only deep regret.

"Godfrey, if you had but told me this six years ago, we could have done some of our duty by the child. Do you think I'd have refused to take her in, if I'd known she was yours?"

At that moment Godfrey felt all the bitterness of an error that was not simply futile, but had defeated its own end. He had not measured this wife with whom he had lived so long. But she spoke again, with more agitation.

"And—O Godfrey—if we'd had her from the first, if you'd taken to her as you ought, she'd have loved me for her mother—and you'd have been happier with me: I could better have bore my little baby dying, and our life might have been more like what we used to think it 'ud be."

The tears fell, and Nancy ceased to speak.

"But you wouldn't have married me then, Nancy, if I'd told you," said Godfrey, urged, in the bitterness of his self-reproach, to prove to himself that his conduct had not been utter folly. "You may think you would now, but you wouldn't then. With your pride and your father's, you'd have hated having anything to do with me after the talk there'd have been."

"I can't say what I should have done about that, Godfrey. I should never have married anybody else. But I wasn't worth doing wrong for—nothing is in this world. Nothing is so good as it seems beforehand—not even our marrying wasn't, you see." There was a faint sad smile on Nancy's face as she said the last words.

"I'm a worse man than you thought I was, Nancy," said Godfrey, rather tremulously. "Can you forgive me ever?"

"The wrong to me is but little, Godfrey; you've made it up to me—you've been good to me for fifteen years. It's another you did the wrong to; and I doubt it can never be all made up for."

"But we can take Eppie now," said Godfrey. "I won't mind the world knowing at last. I'll be plain and open for the rest o' my life."

"It'll be different coming to us, now she's grown up," said Nancy, shaking her head sadly. "But it's your duty to acknowledge her and provide for her; and I'll do my part by her, and pray to God Almighty to make her love me."

"Then we'll go together to Silas Marner's this very night, as soon as everything's quiet at the Stone-pits."

## CHAPTER XIX

Between eight and nine o'clock that evening Eppie and Silas were seated alone in the cottage. After the great excitement the weaver had undergone from the events of the afternoon, he had felt a longing for this quietude, and had even begged Mrs. Winthrop and Aaron, who had naturally lingered behind every one else, to leave him alone with his child. The excitement had not passed away: it had only reached that stage when the keenness of the susceptibility makes external stimulus intolerable[1]—when there is no sense of weariness, but rather an intensity of inward life, under which sleep is an impossibility. Any one who has watched such moments in other men remembers the brightness of the eyes and the strange definiteness that comes over coarse features from that transient influence. It is as if a new fineness of ear for all spiritual voices had sent wonder-working vibrations through the heavy mortal frame—as if "beauty born of murmuring sound"[2] had passed into the face of the listener.

Silas's face showed that sort of transfiguration, as he sat in his armchair and looked at Eppie. She had drawn her own chair towards his knees, and leaned forward, holding both his hands, while she looked up at him. On the table near them, lit by a candle, lay the recovered gold—the old long-loved gold, ranged in orderly heaps, as Silas used to range it in the days when it was his only joy. He had been telling her how he used to count it every night, and how his soul was utterly desolate till she was sent to him.

"At first, I'd a sort o' feeling come across me now and then," he was saying in a subdued tone, "as if you might be changed into the gold again; for sometimes, turn my head which way I would, I seemed to see the gold; and I thought I should be glad if I could feel it, and find it was come back. But that didn't last long. After a bit, I should have thought it was a curse come again if it had drove you from me, for I'd got to feel the need o' your looks and your voice and the touch o' your little fingers.[3] You didn't know

---

[1] When the keenness . . . intolerable—When a person is so alive to one outstanding consideration that he can not endure contact with anything else.

[2] "Beauty born of murmuring sound"—From Wordsworth's *Three Years She Grew in Sun and Shower.*

[3] Touch o' your little fingers—This indicates how fully Silas has outgrown the need for his gold under Eppie's influence. There is in it, however, the threat that with the return of the gold, Eppie may be taken from him.

then, Eppie, when you were such a little un—you didn't know what your old father Silas felt for you."

"But I know now, father," said Eppie. "If it hadn't been for you, they'd have taken me to the workhouse, and there'd have been nobody to love me."

"Eh, my precious child, the blessing was mine. If you hadn't been sent to save me, I should ha' gone to the grave in my misery. The money was taken away from me in time; and you see it's been kept—kept till it was wanted for you. It's wonderful—our life is wonderful."

Silas sat in silence a few minutes, looking at the money. "It takes no hold of me now," he said, ponderingly—"the money doesn't. I wonder if it ever could again—I doubt it might if I lost you, Eppie. I might come to think I was forsaken again, and lose the feeling that God was good to me."

At that moment there was a knocking at the door,[4] and Eppie was obliged to rise without answering Silas. Beautiful she looked, with the tenderness of gathering tears in her eyes and a slight flush on her cheeks, as she stepped to open the door. The flush deepened when she saw Mr. and Mrs. Godfrey Cass. She made her little rustic curtsy, and held the door wide for them to enter.

"We're disturbing you very late, my dear," said Mrs. Cass, taking Eppie's hand, and looking in her face with an expression of anxious interest and admiration. Nancy herself was pale and tremulous.

Eppie, after placing chairs for Mr. and Mrs. Cass, went to stand against Silas, opposite to them.

"Well, Marner," said Godfrey, trying to speak with perfect firmness, "it's a great comfort to me to see you with your money again, that you've been deprived of so many years. It was one of my family did you the wrong,—the more grief to me,—and I feel bound to make up to you for it in every way. Whatever I can do for you will be nothing but paying a debt, even if I looked no further than the robbery. But there are other things I'm beholden—shall be beholden to you for, Marner."

Godfrey checked himself. It had been agreed between him and his wife that the subject of his fatherhood should be approached

---

[4] A KNOCKING AT THE DOOR—The framework of the plot sticks out a little here. After Silas's last words it is a little too pat to have Godfrey enter immediately to claim his child.

very carefully, and that, if possible, the disclosure should be reserved for the future, so that it might be made to Eppie gradually. Nancy had urged this, because she felt strongly the painful light in which Eppie must inevitably see the relation between her father and mother.

Silas, always ill at ease when he was being spoken to by "betters," such as Mr. Cass,—tall, powerful, florid men, seen chiefly on horseback—answered with some constraint,—

"Sir, I've a deal to thank you for a'ready. As for the robbery, I count it no loss to me. And if I did, you couldn't help it: you aren't answerable for it."

"You may look at it in that way, Marner, but I never can; and I hope you'll let me act according to my own feeling of what's just. I know you're easily contented: you've been a hard-working man all your life."

"Yes, sir, yes," said Marner meditatively. "I should ha' been bad off without my work: it was what I held by when everything else was gone from me."

"Ah," said Godfrey, applying Marner's words simply to his bodily wants, "it was a good trade for you in this country, because there's been a great deal of linen-weaving to be done. But you're getting rather past such close work, Marner: it's time you laid by and had some rest. You look a good deal pulled down, though you're not an old man, *are* you?"

"Fifty-five, as near as I can say, sir," said Silas.

"Oh, why, you may live thirty years longer—look at old Macey! And that money on the table, after all, is but little. It won't go far either way—whether it's put out to interest, or you were to live on it as long as it would last: it wouldn't go far if you'd nobody to keep but yourself, and you've had two to keep for a good many years now."

"Eh, sir," said Silas, unaffected by anything Godfrey was saying, "I'm in no fear o' want. We shall do very well—Eppie and me 'ull do well enough. There's few working-folks have got so much laid by as that. I don't know what it is to gentlefolks, but I look upon it as a deal—almost too much. And as for us, it's little we want."

"Only the garden, father," said Eppie, blushing up to the ears the moment after.

"You love a garden, do you, my dear?" said Nancy, thinking that this turn in the point of view might help her husband. "We should agree in that: I give a deal of time to the garden."

"Ah, there's plenty of gardening at the Red House," said Godfrey, surprised at the difficulty he found in approaching a proposition which had seemed so easy to him in the distance. "You've done a good part by Eppie, Marner, for sixteen years. It 'ud be a great comfort to you to see her well provided for, wouldn't it? She looks blooming and healthy, but not fit for any hardships: she doesn't look like a strapping girl come of working parents. You'd like to see her taken care of by those who can leave her well off, and make a lady of her; she's more fit for it than for a rough life, such as she might come to have in a few years' time."

A slight flush came over Marner's face, and disappeared, like a passing gleam. Eppie was simply wondering Mr. Cass should talk so about things that seemed to have nothing to do with reality; but Silas was hurt and uneasy.

"I don't take your meaning, sir," he answered, not having words at command to express the mingled feelings with which he had heard Mr. Cass's words.

"Well, my meaning is this, Marner," said Godfrey, determined to come to the point. "Mrs. Cass and I, you know, have no children—nobody to be the better for our good home and everything else we have—more than enough for ourselves. And we should like to have somebody in the place of a daughter to us—we should like to have Eppie, and treat her in every way as our own child. It'ud be a great comfort to you in your old age, I hope, to see her fortune made in that way, after you've been at the trouble of bringing her up so well. And it's right you should have every reward for that. And Eppie, I'm sure, will always love you and be grateful to you: she'd come and see you very often, and we should all be on the lookout to do everything we could towards making you comfortable."

A plain man like Godfrey Cass, speaking under some embarrassment, necessarily blunders on words that are coarser than his intentions, and that are likely to fall gratingly on susceptible feelings.[5] While he had been speaking, Eppie had quietly passed

---

[5] SUSCEPTIBLE FEELINGS—Recollect also that the finding of the gold has profoundly moved Silas, while the kind but indelicate words of Godfrey revive his superstitious fear that the recovery of the money may mean the loss of Eppie.

her arm behind Silas's head, and let her hand rest against it caressingly: she felt him trembling violently. He was silent for some moments when Mr. Cass had ended—powerless under the conflict of emotions, all alike painful. Eppie's heart was swelling at the sense that her father was in distress; and she was just going to lean down and speak to him, when one struggling dread at last gained the mastery over every other in Silas, and he said faintly,—

"Eppie, my child, speak. I won't stand in your way. Thank Mr. and Mrs. Cass."

Eppie took her hand from her father's head, and came forward a step. Her cheeks were flushed, but not with shyness this time: the sense that her father was in doubt and suffering banished that sort of self-consciousness. She dropped a low curtsy, first to Mrs. Cass and then to Mr. Cass, and said,—

"Thank you, ma'am—thank you, sir. But I can't leave my father, nor own anybody nearer than him. And I don't want to be a lady—thank you all the same" (here Eppie dropped another curtsy). "I couldn't give up the folks I've been used to."

Eppie's lip began to tremble a little at the last words. She retreated to her father's chair again, and held him round the neck; while Silas, with a subdued sob, put up his hand to grasp hers.

The tears were in Nancy's eyes, but her sympathy with Eppie was, naturally, divided with distress on her husband's account. She dared not speak, wondering what was going on in her husband's mind.

Godfrey felt an irritation inevitable to almost all of us when we encounter an unexpected obstacle. He had been full of his own penitence and resolution to retrieve his error as far as the time was left to him; he was possessed with all-important feelings, that were to lead to a predetermined course of action which he had fixed on as the right, and he was not prepared to enter with lively appreciation into other people's feelings counteracting his virtuous resolves. The agitation with which he spoke again was not quite unmixed with anger.

"But I've a claim on you, Eppie—the strongest of all claims. It's my duty, Marner, to own Eppie as my child, and provide for her. She's my own child: her mother was my wife. I've a natural claim on her that must stand before every other."

Eppie had given a violent start, and turned quite pale. Silas, on the contrary, who had been relieved, by Eppie's answer, from the dread lest his mind should be in opposition to hers, felt the spirit of resistance in him set free, not without a touch of parental fierceness. "Then, sir," he answered, with an accent of bitterness that had been silent in him since the memorable day when his youthful hope had perished—"then, sir, why didn't you say so sixteen years ago, and claim her before I'd come to love her, i'stead o' coming to take her from me now, when you might as well take the heart out o' my body? God gave her to me because you turned your back upon her, and He looks upon her as mine: you've no right to her! When a man turns a blessing from his door, it falls to them as take it in."

"I know that, Marner. I was wrong. I've repented of my conduct in that matter," said Godfrey, who could not help feeling the edge of Silas's words.

"I'm glad to hear it, sir," said Marner, with gathering excitement; "but repentance doesn't alter what's been going on for sixteen year. Your coming now and saying 'I'm her father,' doesn't alter the feelings inside us. It's me she's been calling her father ever since she could say the word."

"But I think you might look at the thing more reasonably, Marner," said Godfrey, unexpectedly awed by the weaver's direct truth-speaking. "It isn't as if she was to be taken quite away from you, so that you'd never see her again. She'll be very near you, and come to see you very often. She'll feel just the same towards you."

"Just the same?" said Marner, more bitterly than ever. "How'll she feel just the same for me as she does now, when we eat o' the same bit, and drink o' the same cup, and think o' the same things from one day's end to another? Just the same? That's idle talk. You'd cut us i' two."

Godfrey, unqualified by experience to discern the pregnancy of Marner's simple words, felt rather angry again. It seemed to him that the weaver was very selfish (a judgment readily passed by those who have never tested their own power of sacrifice) to oppose what was undoubtedly for Eppie's welfare; and he felt himself called upon, for her sake, to assert his authority.

"I should have thought, Marner," he said severely,—"I should have thought your affection for Eppie would make you rejoice in what was for her good, even if it did call upon you to give up something. You ought to remember your own life's uncertain, and she's at an age now when her lot may soon be fixed in a way very different from what it would be in her father's home: she may marry some low working-man, and then, whatever I might do for her, I couldn't make her well off. You're putting yourself in the way of her welfare; and though I'm sorry to hurt you after what you've done, and what I've left undone, I feel now it's my duty to insist on taking care of my own daughter. I want to do my duty."

It would be difficult to say whether it were Silas or Eppie that was most deeply stirred by this last speech of Godfrey's. Thought had been very busy in Eppie as she listened to the contest between her old long-loved father and this new unfamiliar father who had suddenly come to fill the place of that black featureless shadow which had held the ring and placed it on her mother's finger. Her imagination had darted backward in conjectures, and forward in previsions, of what this revealed fatherhood implied; and there were words in Godfrey's last speech which helped to make the previsions especially definite. Not that these thoughts, either of past or future, determined her resolution—*that* was determined by the feelings which vibrated to every word Silas had uttered; but they raised, even apart from these feelings, a repulsion towards the offered lot and the newly-revealed father.

Silas, on the other hand, was again stricken in conscience, and alarmed lest Godfrey's accusation should be true—lest he should be raising his own will as an obstacle to Eppie's good. For many moments he was mute, struggling for the self-conquest necessary to the uttering of the difficult words. They came out tremulously.

"I'll say no more. Let it be as you will. Speak to the child. I'll hinder nothing."

Even Nancy, with all the acute sensibility of her own affections, shared her husband's view, that Marner was not justifiable in his wish to retain Eppie, after her real father had avowed himself. She felt that it was a very hard trial for the poor weaver, but her code allowed no question that a father by blood must have a claim above that of any foster-father.[6] Besides, Nancy, used all her life to plenteous circumstances and the privileges of "respectability,"

[6] SHE FELT . . . FOSTER-FATHER—While Silas is moved by simple facts and realities, Nancy acts and argues in accordance with her own strict code of conduct and thought.

could not enter into the pleasures which early nurture and habit connect with all the little aims and efforts of the poor who are born poor: to her mind, Eppie, in being restored to her birthright, was entering on a too long withheld but unquestionable good. Hence she heard Silas's last words with relief, and thought, as Godfrey did, that their wish was achieved.

"Eppie, my dear," said Godfrey, looking at his daughter, not without some embarrassment, under the sense that she was old enough to judge him, "it'll always be our wish that you should show your love and gratitude to one who's been a father to you so many years, and we shall want to help you to make him comfortable in every way. But we hope you'll come to love us as well; and though I haven't been what a father should ha' been to you all these years, I wish to do the utmost in my power for you for the rest of my life, and provide for you as my only child. And you'll have the best of mothers in my wife—that'll be a blessing you haven't known since you were old enough to know it."

"My dear, you'll be a treasure to me," said Nancy, in her gentle voice. "We shall want for nothing when we have our daughter."

Eppie did not come forward and curtsy, as she had done before. She held Silas's hand in hers, and grasped it firmly—it was a weaver's hand, with a palm and finger-tips that were sensitive to such pressure—while she spoke with colder decision than before. "Thank you, ma'am—thank you, sir, for your offers—they're very great, and far above my wish. For I should have no delight i' life any more if I was forced to go away from my father, and knew he was sitting at home, a-thinking of me and feeling lone. We've been used to be happy together every day, and I can't think o' no happiness without him. And he says he'd nobody i' the world till I was sent to him, and he'd have nothing when I was gone. And he's took care of me and loved me from the first, and I'll cleave to him as long as he lives, and nobody shall ever come between him and me."

"But you must make sure, Eppie," said Silas, in a low voice —"you must make sure as you won't ever be sorry, because you've made your choice to stay among poor folks, and with poor clothes and things, when you might ha' had everything o' the best."

His sensitiveness on this point had increased as he listened to Eppie's words of faithful affection.

"I can never be sorry, father," said Eppie. "I shouldn't know what to think on or to wish for with fine things about me, as I haven't been used to. And it 'ud be poor work for me to put on things, and ride in a gig, and sit in a place at church, as 'ud make them as I'm fond of think me unfitting company for 'em. What could *I* care for then?"

Nancy looked at Godfrey with a pained, questioning glance. But his eyes were fixed on the floor, where he was moving the end of his stick, as if he were pondering on something absently. She thought there was a word which might perhaps come better from her lips than from his.

"What you say is natural, my dear child—it's natural you should cling to those who've brought you up," she said mildly; "but there's a duty you owe to your lawful father. There's perhaps something to be given up on more sides than one. When your father opens his home to you, I think it's right you shouldn't turn your back on it."

"I can't feel as I've got any father but one," said Eppie impetuously, while the tears gathered. "I've always thought of a little home where he'd sit i' the corner, and I should fend and do everything for him: I can't think o' no other home. I wasn't brought up to be a lady, and I can't turn my mind to it. I like the working-folks, and their victuals, and their ways. And," she ended passionately, while the tears fell, "I'm promised to marry a working-man, as 'll live with father, and help me to take care of him."

Godfrey looked up at Nancy with a flushed face and smarting, dilated eyes. This frustration of a purpose towards which he had set out under the exalted consciousness that he was about to compensate in some degree for the greatest demerit of his life, made him feel the air of the room stifling.

"Let us go," he said, in an undertone.

"We won't talk of this any longer now," said Nancy, rising. "We're your well-wishers, my dear—and yours too, Marner. We shall come and see you again. It's getting late now."

In this way she covered her husband's abrupt departure, for Godfrey had gone straight to the door, unable to say more.

## CHAPTER XX

Nancy and Godfrey walked home under the starlight in silence. When they entered the oaken parlor, Godfrey threw himself into his chair, while Nancy laid down her bonnet and shawl, and stood on the hearth near her husband, unwilling to leave him even for a few minutes, and yet fearing to utter any word lest it might jar on his feeling. At last Godfrey turned his head towards her, and their eyes met, dwelling in that meeting without any movement on either side. That quiet mutual gaze of a trusting husband and wife is like the first moment of rest or refuge from a great weariness or a great danger—not to be interfered with by speech or action which would distract the sensations from the fresh enjoyment of repose.

But presently he put out his hand, and as Nancy placed hers within it, he drew her towards him, and said, "That's ended!"

She bent to kiss him, and then said, as she stood by his side, "Yes, I'm afraid we must give up the hope of having her for a daughter. It wouldn't be right to want to force her to come to us against her will. We can't alter her bringing up and what's come of it."

"No," said Godfrey, with a keen decisiveness of tone, in contrast with his usually careless and unemphatic speech—"there's debts we can't pay like money debts, by paying extra for the years that have slipped by. While I've been putting off and putting off, the trees have been growing—it's too late now. Marner was in the right in what he said about a man's turning away a blessing from his door: it falls to somebody else. I wanted to pass for childless once, Nancy—I shall pass for childless now against my wish."

Nancy did not speak immediately, but after a little while she asked, "You won't make it known, then, about Eppie's being your daughter?"

"No—where would be the good to anybody?—only harm. I must do what I can for her in the state of life she chooses. I must see who it is she's thinking of marrying."

"If it won't do any good to make the thing known," said Nancy, who thought she might now allow herself the relief of entertaining a feeling which she had tried to silence before, "I should be very thankful for father and Priscilla never to be troubled with knowing what was done in the past, more than about Dunsey: it can't be helped, their knowing that."

"I shall put it in my will—I think I shall put it in my will. I shouldn't like to leave anything to be found out like this about Dunsey," said Godfrey meditatively. "But I can't see anything but difficulties that 'ud come from telling it now. I must do what I can to make her happy in her own way. I've a notion," he added, after a moment's pause, "it's Aaron Winthrop she meant she was engaged to. I remember seeing him with her and Marner going away from church."

"Well, he's very sober and industrious," said Nancy, trying to view the matter as cheerfully as possible.

Godfrey fell into thoughtfulness again. Presently he looked up at Nancy sorrowfully, and said,—

"She's a very pretty, nice girl, isn't she, Nancy?"

"Yes, dear; and with just your hair and eyes. I wondered it had never struck me before."

"I think she took a dislike to me at the thought of my being her father. I could see a change in her manner after that."

"She couldn't bear to think of not looking on Marner as her father," said Nancy, not wishing to confirm her husband's painful impression.

"She thinks I did wrong by her mother as well as by her. She thinks me worse than I am. But she *must* think it: she can never know all. It's part of my punishment, Nancy, for my daughter to dislike me. I should never have got into that trouble if I'd been true to you—if I hadn't been a fool. I'd no right to expect anything but evil could come of that marriage—and when I shirked doing a father's part too."

Nancy was silent: her spirit of rectitude would not let her try to soften the edge of what she felt to be a just compunction. He spoke again after a little while, but the tone was rather changed: there was tenderness mingled with the previous self-reproach.

"And I got *you,* Nancy, in spite of all; and yet I've been grumbling and uneasy because I hadn't something else—as if I deserved it."

"You've never been wanting to me, Godfrey," said Nancy, with quiet sincerity. "My only trouble would be gone if you resigned yourself to the lot that's been given us."

"Well, perhaps it isn't too late to mend a bit there. Though it *is* too late to mend some things, say what they will."

## CHAPTER XXI

The next morning, when Silas and Eppie were seated at their breakfast, he said to her,—

"Eppie, there's a thing I've had on my mind to do this two year, and now the money's been brought back to us, we can do it. I've been turning it over and over in the night, and I think we'll set out to-morrow, while the fine days last. We'll leave the house and everything for your godmother to take care on, and we'll make a little bundle o' things and set out."

"Where to go, daddy?" said Eppie, in much surprise.

"To my old country—to the town where I was born—up Lantern Yard. I want to see Mr. Paston, the minister: something may ha' come out to make 'em know I was innicent o' the robbery. And Mr. Paston was a man with a deal o' light—I want to speak to him about the drawing o' the lots. And I should like to talk to him about the religion o' this country-side, for I partly think he doesn't know on it."

Eppie was very joyful, for there was the prospect not only of wonder and delight at seeing a strange country, but also of coming back to tell Aaron all about it. Aaron was so much wiser than she was about most things—it would be rather pleasant to have this little advantage over him. Mrs. Winthrop, though possessed with a dim fear of dangers attendant on so long a journey, and requiring many assurances that it would not take them out of the region of carriers' carts and slow wagons, was nevertheless well pleased that Silas should revisit his own country, and find out if he had been cleared from that false accusation.

"You'd be easier in your mind for the rest o' your life, Master Marner," said Dolly—"that you would. And if there's any light to be got up the Yard as you talk on, we've need of it i' this world, and I'd be glad on it myself, if you could bring it back."

So, on the fourth day from that time, Silas and Eppie, in their Sunday clothes, with a small bundle tied in a blue linen handkerchief, were making their way through the streets of a great manufacturing town. Silas, bewildered by the changes thirty years had brought over his native place, had stopped several persons in succession to ask them the name of this town, that he might be sure he was not under a mistake about it.

"Ask for Lantern Yard, father—ask this gentleman with the tassels on his shoulders[1] a-standing at the shop door; he isn't in a hurry like the rest," said Eppie, in some distress at her father's bewilderment, and ill at ease, besides, amidst the noise, the movement, and the multitude of strange indifferent faces.

"Eh, my child, he won't know anything about it," said Silas; "gentlefolks didn't ever go up the Yard. But happen somebody can tell me which is the way to Prison Street, where the jail is. I know the way out o' that as if I'd seen it yesterday."

With some difficulty, after many turnings and new inquiries, they reached Prison Street; and the grim walls of the jail, the first object that answered to any image in Silas's memory, cheered him with the certitude, which no assurance of the town's name had hitherto given him, that he was in his native place.

"Ah," he said, drawing a long breath, "there's the jail, Eppie; that's just the same: I aren't afraid now. It's the third turning on the left hand from the jail doors—that's the way we must go."

"Oh, what a dark ugly place!" said Eppie. "How it hides the sky! It's worse than the workhouse. I'm glad you don't live in this town now, father. Is Lantern Yard like this street?"

"My precious child," said Silas, smiling, "it isn't a big street like this. I never was easy i' this street myself, but I was fond o' Lantern Yard. The shops here are all altered, I think—I can't make 'em out; but I shall know the turning, because it's the third."

"Here it is," he said, in a tone of satisfaction, as they came to a narrow alley. "And then we must go to the left again, and then straight for'ard for a bit, up Shoe Lane; and then we shall be at the entry next to the o'erhanging window, where there's the nick in the road for the water to run. Eh, I can see it all."

"O father, I'm like as if I was stifled," said Eppie. "I couldn't ha' thought as any folks lived i' this way, so close together. How pretty the Stone-pits 'ull look when we get back!"

"It looks comical to *me,* child, now—and smells bad. I can't think as it usened to smell so."

---

[1] **WITH THE TASSELS ON HIS SHOULDERS—Probably an officer with epaulettes, or shoulder ornaments, on his uniform.**

Here and there a sallow, begrimed face looked out from a gloomy doorway at the strangers, and increased Eppie's uneasiness, so that it was a longed-for relief when they issued from the alleys into Shoe Lane, where there was a broader strip of sky.

"Dear heart!" said Silas; "why, there's people coming out o' the Yard as if they'd been to chapel at this time o' day—a weekday noon!"

Suddenly he started and stood still with a look of distressed amazement, that alarmed Eppie. They were before an opening in front of a large factory, from which men and women were streaming for their midday meal.

"Father," said Eppie, clasping his arm, "what's the matter?"

But she had to speak again and again before Silas could answer her.

"It's gone, child," he said, at last, in strong agitation—"Lantern Yard's gone. It must ha' been here, because here's the house with the o'erhanging window—I know that—it's just the same; but they've made this new opening; and see that big factory! It's all gone—chapel and all."

"Come into that little brush-shop and sit down, father—they'll let you sit down," said Eppie, always on the watch lest one of her father's strange attacks should come on. "Perhaps the people can tell you all about it."

But neither from the brush-maker, who had come to Shoe Lane only ten years ago, when the factory was already built, nor from any other source within his reach, could Silas learn anything of the old Lantern Yard friends, or of Mr. Paston, the minister.

"The old place is all swep' away," Silas said to Dolly Winthrop on the night of his return—"the little graveyard and everything. The old home's gone; I've no home but this now. I shall never know whether they got at the truth o' the robbery, nor whether Mr. Paston could ha' given me any light about the drawing o' the lots. It's dark to me, Mrs. Winthrop, that is; I doubt it'll be dark to the last."

"Well, yes, Master Marner," said Dolly, who sat with a placid listening face, now bordered by gray hairs; "I doubt it may. It's the will o' Them above as a many things should be dark to us; but there's some things as I've never felt i' the dark about, and they're mostly what comes i' the day's work. You were hard done by that

Brown Brothers

**After the Wedding**

Through a crowd of admiring villagers the bride and groom, accompanied by old Silas, turn homeward to begin a new and happier life in Raveloe.

once, Master Marner, and it seems as you'll never know the rights of it; but that doesn't hinder there *being* a rights, Master Marner, for all it's dark to you and me."

"No," said Silas, "no; that doesn't hinder. Since the time the child was sent to me and I've come to love her as myself, I've had light enough to trusten by; and, now she says she'll never leave me, I think I shall trusten till I die."

## CONCLUSION

There was one time of the year which was held in Raveloe to be especially suitable for a wedding. It was when the great lilacs and laburnums in the old-fashioned gardens showed their golden and purple wealth above the lichen-tinted walls, and when there were calves still young enough to want bucketfuls of fragrant milk. People were not so busy then as they must become when the full cheese-making and the mowing had set in; and, besides, it was a time when a light bridal dress could be worn with comfort and seen to advantage.

Happily the sunshine fell more warmly than usual on the lilac tufts the morning that Eppie was married, for her dress was a very light one. She had often thought, though with a feeling of renunciation, that the perfection of a wedding-dress would be a white cotton, with the tiniest pink sprig at wide intervals; so that when Mrs. Godfrey Cass begged to provide one, and asked Eppie to choose what it should be, previous meditation had enabled her to give a decided answer at once.

Seen at a little distance as she walked across the churchyard and down the village, she seemed to be attired in pure white, and her hair looked like the dash of gold on a lily. One hand was on her husband's arm, and with the other she clasped the hand of her father Silas.

"You won't be giving me away, father," she had said before they went to church; "you'll only be taking Aaron to be a son to you."

Dolly Winthrop walked behind with her husband, and there ended the little bridal procession.

There were many eyes to look at it, and Miss Priscilla Lammeter was glad that she and her father had happened to drive up to the door of the Red House just in time to see this pretty sight. They had come to keep Nancy company to-day, because Mr. Cass had had to go away to Lytherly, for special reasons. That seemed to be a pity, for otherwise he might have gone, as Mr. Crackenthorp and Mr. Osgood certainly would, to look on at the wedding-feast which he had ordered at the Rainbow, naturally feeling a great interest in the weaver who had been wronged by one of his own family.

"I could ha' wished Nancy had had the luck to find a child like that and bring her up," said Priscilla to her father, as they sat in the gig; "I should ha' had something young to think of then, besides the lambs and the calves."

"Yes, my dear, yes," said Mr. Lammeter; "one feels that as one gets older. Things look dim to old folks: they'd need have some young eyes about 'em, to let 'em know the world's the same as it used to be."

Nancy came out now to welcome her father and sister; and the wedding-group had passed on beyond the Red House to the humbler part of the village.

Dolly Winthrop was the first to divine that old Mr. Macey, who had been set in his armchair outside his own door, would expect some special notice as they passed, since he was too old to be at the wedding-feast.

"Mr. Macey's looking for a word from us," said Dolly; "he'll be hurt if we pass him and say nothing—and him so racked with rheumatiz."

So they turned aside to shake hands with the old man. He had looked forward to the occasion, and had his premeditated speech.

"Well, Master Marner," he said, in a voice that quavered a good deal, "I've lived to see my words come true. I was the first to say there was no harm in you, though your looks might be again' you; and I was the first to say you'd get your money back. And it's nothing but rightful as you should. And I'd ha' said the 'Amens,' and willing, at the holy matrimony; but Tookey's done it a good while now, and I hope you'll have none the worse luck."

In the open yard before the Rainbow the party of guests were already assembled, though it was still nearly an hour before the appointed feast-time. But by this means they could not only enjoy the slow advent of their pleasure; they had also ample leisure to talk of Silas Marner's strange history, and arrive by due degrees at the conclusion that he had brought a blessing on himself by acting like a father to a lone, motherless child. Even the farrier did not negative this sentiment: on the contrary, he took it up as peculiarly his own, and invited any hardy person present to contradict him. But he met with no contradiction; and all differences among the company were merged in a general agreement with Mr. Snell's sentiment, that when a man had deserved his good luck, it was the part of his neighbors to wish him joy.

As the bridal group approached, a hearty cheer was raised in the Rainbow yard; and Ben Winthrop, whose jokes had retained their acceptable flavor, found it agreeable to turn in there and receive congratulations; not requiring the proposed interval of quiet at the Stone-pits before joining the company.

Eppie had a larger garden than she had ever expected there now; and in other ways there had been alterations at the expense of Mr. Cass, the landlord, to suit Silas's larger family. For he and Eppie had declared that they would rather stay at the Stone-pits than go to any new home. The garden was fenced with stones on two sides, but in front there was an open fence, through which the flowers shone with answering gladness, as the four united people came within sight of them.

"O father," said Eppie, "what a pretty home ours is! I think nobody could be happier than we are."

## QUESTIONS

### Chapters I–IV

In the first four chapters, the two sets of characters and the two series of incidents are presented, together with the first link between the two plot strands.

1. Some writers omit an introduction, beginning at once with the actions of the characters. Which method is preferable in a psychological novel?
2. What traces of Satanism, or belief in the activities of a personal devil, do you find among the inhabitants of Raveloe?
3. The term *Merry England* is a common one. What do you think is "merry" about the England of this period? Do you consider the United States merry in the same way?
4. Why do the villagers distrust Silas?
5. How does the author prepare the reader for William Dane's falseness? What is the significance of Dane's interpretation of Silas's fits?
6. What do you think of the incident of the robbery in which Dane throws suspicion on Silas? Is it clever? Would you accept it in a modern detective story? How does Dane get the money without being seen by Silas? What purpose in advancing the action does the robbery incident serve?
7. What sudden change comes over Silas when the lots declare him guilty? If they had declared him innocent, what would have happened to Silas? How would his later life in Lantern Yard have differed from his life in Raveloe? Why does George Eliot think it better for her purpose to shift the scene to Raveloe?
8. How does Silas try to forget the past? Is he successful?
9. What change in physical appearance does Marner's slaving for gold produce?
10. Why does the author emphasize Silas's reluctance to communicate his sorrows to his new neighbors? What explains his attitude?
11. What incident shows that Silas's capacity for affection is not wholly destroyed?
12. How does Silas's love for his gold differ from that of an ordinary miser?
13. Why do the English farmers consider the Napoleonic Wars a godsend? How would you characterize this attitude? Does it have its counterpart today?
14. From what point of view are the members of the Cass household presented: the author's or the villagers'? Which home sounds the more attractive, that of the Osgoods or of the Casses?
15. Do you think it is good literary taste for the author to have Snuff, the spaniel, crawl under a chair when Dunstan Cass enters the room? How does the dog act toward Godfrey? What is the purpose of these exhibitions?
16. Why does not Godfrey tell his father the whole story? What is Godfrey's greatest fault? What would happen if the Squire should find out Godfrey's secret by accident?
17. Why does Bryce infer that Dunstan wishes to sell Wildfire? Which of the two men is the keener?

18. What traits of Dunstan's character make him capable of conceiving and executing the robbery? Which character seems to you the more believable, Godfrey or Dunstan? Why?
19. After the robbery, Dunstan closes the door as he goes out. Who is the more anxious to get that door closed, Dunstan or the author? Note how little space George Eliot gives to the narration of physical action even at such dramatic points. Why does she hurry over them so quickly?

### Chapters V–X

In these chapters the effect of the robbery on Silas and on the villagers is revealed.

1. Does it strike you as remarkable that Silas should have left his house at the moment of Dunstan's arrival? He thinks he must do an errand; he has been given meat for his supper; it is impossible to lock the door; the weather is unusual; and Dunstan Cass is returning home afoot. How does this series of coincidences impress you? Would you say these factors belong to the tradition of romance or realism?
2. What makes Silas think it is Jem Rodney who has stolen his gold?
3. Why does Silas go to the Rainbow to announce his loss?
4. What effect on the reader's interest has the interlude of Chapter VI, in which the author leaves Silas running through the dark, and takes up the scene at the Rainbow?
5. Who are at the Rainbow? What are their respective occupations? Have any of these persons been introduced before?
6. Why does the author call the farrier, Mr. Dowlas, the "negative" spirit of the company?
7. What part does Mr. Snell, the Rainbow host, play in the conversation? On what principle are his arguments based?
8. What gives us a clue as to the age of the firm of *Macey, Tailor?*
9. Follow the discussion on ghosts through to the end of the chapter. Who, in your opinion, has the best of the argument?
10. Why does Marner's sudden appearance make such a profound impression on the company? Are you at all surprised when Mr. Snell seizes Silas and bids him talk sensibly? What makes the farrier think he has not been "quite on a par with himself"?
11. What memory is aroused in Silas when Mr. Macey declares against accusing the innocent?
12. Why do some of the villagers think that the robbery is not one to have much light cast upon it by "tinder-boxes"?
13. Why does no one associate the fact of Dunstan's absence with the loss of Marner's gold?
14. Why does Godfrey ride to Tarley? How does he quiet his fear that the Squire may find out his secret before very long?
15. Why does the Squire take a walk every morning? What do you think of the characterization of the Squire? Is he a type or a real person? Support your argument by evidence from the text.
16. The author states that the flower of courtesy does not bloom in such homes as Red House. Nevertheless we think of Godfrey as being much gentler and better-mannered than his father or Dunstan. Do you make any distinction between *courtesy* and *good manners?*

17. Why is the intention of Godfrey to pay the Squire a hundred pounds "an inversion of the paternal and filial relations"?
18. The reader is told that the Squire's memory consists of "certain strong impressions unmodified by detail." What does this mean? Does it coincide with other information about the Squire's character?
19. What would happen if the Squire were to speak to Mr. Lammeter for Godfrey?
20. In the last paragraph of Chapter IX, the author describes the place held by Chance in the minds of the careless. What do you think of the truth of these statements?
21. Silas Marner, according to George Eliot, had led an "eager life" and a "clinging life." How well do you think the words *eager* and *clinging* sound the keynotes of Marner's character?
22. "He filled the blank with grief." Would you go so far as to say that Silas's main grief is the fact that he has lost money? Explain the position the gold held in his life.
23. What effect on Silas does the loss of his gold have on his social sense? What is the effect on the villagers?
24. What do you think of Mr. Macey's efforts to console Silas? What is Silas's reaction to his comments?
25. What is the place of Dolly Winthrop in the community? What impression of Mrs. Winthrop's nature does the author wish to give when she reports that Dolly "did not lightly forsake a serviceable phrase"?
26. Why was Godfrey looking forward to the New Year's Eve party at Red House with particular pleasure?

### Chapters XI–XV

And now the coming of Eppie changes Silas's life, and the death of Molly changes Godfrey's fortunes.

1. Nancy has a very clear conception of what her attitude toward Godfrey should be. What do you think of this attitude? Does it occur to you that she lacks flexibility? Is that a fault or a virtue?
2. Why do the Lammeter sisters dress alike? Whose idea is it, and what characteristic does insistence upon it show?
3. What does the rector mean when he tells Nancy Lammeter he has seen roses blooming on New Year's Eve?
4. Why does Mr. Macey criticize Godfrey's coats, made by the worthy tailor of Flitton?
5. Why does George Eliot take pains to explain that the older people at the party, including Rector Crackenthorp, join in the dancing, when the facts speak for themselves?
6. While the New Year's Eve party is in progress at Red House, who is approaching Raveloe? What brings the stranger to the village?
7. To explain why Silas was standing by the open door on New Year's Eve, the author describes a habit contracted by him since the disappearance of his gold. Do you find this explanation satisfactory?
8. Notice that this is the second time the author has used the somewhat artificial trick of letting an important event in the life of Silas occur during one of his cataleptic fits. What do you think of this device?
9. What is Marner's first impression of the child? What is the influence of this impression on his instinctive sympathy?

10. Until Silas Marner breaks into the party at Red House we have seen Godfrey as vacillating before every problem. Why is he suddenly anxious to be present at a scene which may prove extremely painful for him? Do you attribute his decision to courage or cowardice?
11. Does the touching passage describing Marner lulling the babe to sleep strike you as realistic or colored with romantic sentimentality?
12. How does Godfrey justify to himself his intention not to own the child as his?
13. How do the villagers receive the news that Silas intends to keep the child? To what other event in Raveloe history does this compare in importance?
14. What is the difference between Marner's new treasure and his old one? How does the new one affect him differently?
15. How does Mrs. Winthrop propose that Silas discipline Eppie? How does the plan work out? What is your opinion of George Eliot's ability to portray children?
16. What is Godfrey's attitude toward his daughter? Has any change taken place in Godfrey? Has any change taken place in his relations with Nancy?

### Chapter XVI–Conclusion

The problem is solved, the rewards and penalties are meted out, and the moral is driven home.

1 How many years have elapsed since the end of Part I? Why has the author skipped so many years? Is the gap necessary?
2. Are you satisfied with Eppie's choice of a husband? Why, or why not?
3. What is Mr. Macey's theory about Marner's gold? On what does he base his prophecy?
4. What arguments does Nancy advance against Godfrey's proposal to adopt a child? Are they reasonable? From the point of view of characterization, Nancy is one of the best-drawn persons in *Silas Marner*. By what do you judge whether or not characterization is well done?
5. Why does Godfrey imagine that his own childless home is a measure of retribution? Is this in keeping with his intellectual make-up?
6. What effect on you has the discovery of Dunstan's body? Had you expected it? Why is it essential for George Eliot's purpose?
7. Prior to the discovery of Dunstan's body, has your interest in Part II been as keen as in Part I? If not, can you explain why?
8. What do you think of Godfrey's notion that deep feelings do not go with callous hands and scant means?
9. How would you characterize Nancy's reaction to Godfrey's confession? Is it what you expected of her?
10. What is your estimate of Godfrey's vow to be "plain and open" the rest of his life?
11. In the discussion which takes place at Marner's cottage, whose arguments are the most reasonable: Silas's, Godfrey's, or Nancy's? What is the first argument Godfrey uses to persuade Silas to let Eppie come to Red House?
12. Why does Godfrey decide against making it generally known that Eppie is his daughter? What is Nancy's attitude in this matter? In making this decision, of whose welfare are they thinking?

13. Why does the proposed journey to Lantern Yard appeal to Eppie? Why do you think George Eliot introduces Marner's useless visit to Lantern Yard, since his innocence can never be established? Do you feel that all the questions raised by a novelist should be answered? How would a realist answer this?
14. What has become of Lantern Yard? Is there anything significant, symbolic even, in its complete obliteration?
15. Is the Conclusion necessary to the story? What reader taste does it satisfy?
16. In Raveloe, what is considered the best time of year for a wedding? Why is this time the most suitable?
17. How many old friends appear in this short Conclusion?
18. Do you like the last sentence in the book? Which of the following adjectives would you apply to it: original, superfluous, pretty, trite, characteristic (of Eppie), satisfying (as a concluding speech for the novel)?

## GENERAL QUESTIONS

1. In the writing of *Silas Marner* what is the advantage of the point of view chosen by the author?
2. What is the theme of the story? Phrase it briefly.
3. What traces of the romantic school can you find in this novel? Where is the realism most noticeable?
4. What is the advantage of using two strands of plot instead of one? What is the first point where the two strands join?
5. What character, aside from Silas, do you think is the best drawn?
6. If you had been writing the story, at what point in Silas's life would you have chosen to begin the narrative? Why did not George Eliot begin with Silas Marner's childhood?
7. What factors in the novel—of incident, character, setting, manners, or point of view—are distinctly of George Eliot's own time?
8. To what extent do the author's own religious views get into the story?
9. Is there anything in the presentation or point of view to show that the author is a woman? If so, what?
10. What is the climax of the story; that is, at what point does Silas's problem begin to be solved and his fortunes take a turn for the better?
11. What is your opinion of George Eliot's style? Is it readable? Is it clear? Is it vivid? Is it original?
12. Can you find any flaws in the psychology of the characters? Have you any adverse criticism of the incidents invented by the author (not the actions of the characters) to prove her point?
13. What effect on your interest have the moral comments offered by George Eliot? Do you think they impede the action of the story?
14. What do you think of the choice of setting? How much "local color" does the author provide?
15. Is any character too near perfection to suit you? Is any one of them too wicked to be plausible?
16. Why does not George Eliot tell us how Godfrey came to marry such a woman as Molly, instead of merely suggesting that Dunstan maneuvered it? In the light of Godfrey's character, is this secret union difficult to believe?

17. An author, especially a realist, cannot rely too greatly on coincidence without making the reader skeptical. How many coincidences can you find in *Silas Marner?*
18. What can you say of George Eliot's observation of detail? What are a few of the best examples of such observations?
19. What is the great lesson George Eliot wishes to teach: honesty? faith in God? service to fellow-man? resignation? retribution?
20. Which do you like the better, a realistic novel or a romantic novel?

## EXERCISES

Exercises preceded by a star are designed for assignment at the discretion of the teacher, or for any student who volunteers.

### Chapters I–IV

1. Explain the value of the introductory paragraph of the novel, noting that it contains no reference to any definite individual or community.
2. Contrast the life of Silas Marner in Lantern Yard with his life in Raveloe.
3. Contrast the attitude of the residents of Lantern Yard toward Marner's cataleptic fits with that of the villagers of Raveloe.
4. Explain what great need in his life Marner's gold fills.

*5. Silas's knowledge of the healing power of herbs is the one thing that might lead him into normal relations with his neighbors. Show how it widens instead of bridges the gulf between him and the villagers.

6. Describe the Cass household, and contrast life at Red House with that at the weaver's cottage.
7. Make two lists of adjectives: the first descriptive of Godfrey; the second, of Dunstan.
8. Trace the unfolding of the idea of the theft in Dunstan's mind.

*9. Comment on George Eliot's treatment of the theft incident.

10. Essay topics: *Superstitions in Lantern Yard and Raveloe; The Miser; Riding to Hounds; Handwork and the Machine Age.*

### Chapters V–X

1. A man is most easily attacked through the thing he loves most. Suggest a reason to explain why George Eliot makes Silas a miser.
2. Describe Silas's reactions when he finds his gold has been stolen.

*3. Discuss George Eliot's method of revealing past happenings and present conditions as illustrated in Chapter VI.

4. Designating the speaker as in a printed play, rewrite in dialogue form the discussion on ghosts.
5. Comment on the significance of Marner's visit to the Rainbow.
6. Explain why Silas, as soon as he has come to his senses, takes back his charge of robbery against Jem Rodney.

*7. After re-reading the passage concerning the pedlar, write a brief narrative illustrating the spread of some unfounded suspicion.

8. Suggest what traits in Squire Cass's character have been inherited by Godfrey; by Dunstan.
9. Write brief character studies of Mr. Macey, Mr. Snell, and Mr. Dowlas.
10. Essay topics: *Breakfast at Red House; Neighborliness; Country Taverns.*

### Chapters XI–XV

*1. Imagine you are a reporter sent by a newspaper in one of the larger cities to "cover" the New Year's Eve party at Red House. Write an account of the party for your paper, keeping always the city man's point of view.

*2. Discuss the artistic purpose of the party, showing what place it occupies in George Eliot's scheme.

3. Contrast the characters of Nancy and Priscilla. Describe the "Miss Gunns."

*4. Rewrite the scene at the party between Godfrey and Nancy, adding conversation and action to build up the incident. Be sure to keep them both in character and to remember that each is in love with the other though Nancy will not admit it.

5. Silas Marner, having lost his faith in God and man through the verdict of the lots, atones by fifteen years of loneliness. Then his gold is taken from him. Finally Eppie comes to him from he knows not where. Comment on the principle of justice George Eliot professes to discern in this life.

6. We know absolutely nothing of Silas Marner's childhood. Point out one memory of that time which the author inserts in Chapter XII.

7. Explain the effect on Godfrey of his discovery of Molly's death. Also suggest the influence on his character of the concealment of his sin.

8. Write an account of Eppie's childhood as she might have related it years later, using the first person in your narrative.

9. Write character sketches of Doctor Kimble and Dolly Winthrop.

10. Essay topics: *"Breed is Stronger than Pasture"; A Guilty Conscience; Death in the Dusk at the Stone-pits; Youth and Age.*

### Chapters XVI–Conclusion

1. Write a description of the scene in front of the Raveloe church.

2. Show the changes that sixteen years have brought to the important characters in the story.

*3. Explain why George Eliot jumped sixteen years in her narrative, and show why it is easier for a novelist to permit such a gap than for a short story writer or even a dramatist.

4. Comment on Nancy's reproof of Godfrey: "But I wasn't worth doing wrong for—nothing is in this world."

5. In the discussion concerning Eppie's future, suggest the viewpoint of Godfrey, Nancy, Silas, and Eppie, listing the chief arguments each advances. Discuss the likelihood of Eppie's refusing to change her humble sphere for a life of luxury at Red House.

*6. Remembering that Silas Marner has won back to faith in spite of the unjust decree of the lots, suggest a reason to explain why George Eliot does not have his innocence established on that trip to Lantern Yard.

7. Comment on the significance of Silas's words: "I think I shall trusten till I die."

8. Give your opinion of the value of the chapter called *Conclusion.* Suggest another ending for the story.

9. Give your reasons for considering as satisfactory or unsatisfactory the solution of the problems presented in the novel.
10. Essay topics: *Squire and Weaver; Two Women* (Nancy and Eppie); *English Gardens; The Silver Lining; The Death of Silas Marner.*

## GENERAL EXERCISES

1. Report on the period and background of *Silas Marner.*
2. Separate the two plot strands by chapters, and show at what points the two sets of characters are drawn together.
3. Invent headings for each of the chapter divisions.
4. Trace through the novel the character development of Silas Marner, Godfrey Cass, and Nancy Lammeter. Which of the three shows the least change? Which the most?

*5. Comment on the realistic and the romantic phases of *Silas Marner.*

6. Indicate how large a part heredity and environment play in the story.

*7. Write an essay on *George Eliot and the Psychological Novel.*

8. Discuss, with frequent reference to the text, *George Eliot's* treatment of humor, pathos, and dramatic action.
9. Point out which events in the story are due to chance as distinguished from those growing out of character.
10. Make a synopsis of the plot of *Silas Marner.*
11. Discuss George Eliot's method of character analysis and presentation. For example, does she let actions speak for themselves, or does she explain as an author the qualities of the persons she has created?
12. Select one character from the novel and invent an episode that might have taken place in his or her life.

*13. Write a one-act play based on a scene in the story, borrowing freely from the novel for action and dialogue.

14. Debate the proposition that virtue is always rewarded.
15. Contrast *Silas Marner* with *Ivanhoe* or some other romantic novel you have read.

*16. Read the Book of *Job* and contrast its view of justice in this life with that of George Eliot as illustrated in *Silas Marner.*

*17. Write an essay on *Art and Morals,* with particular reference to the use of fiction to teach a lesson.

18. Write a book review of *Silas Marner.*
19. Using your library index and *Reader's Guide,* compile a bibliography of books and articles on George Eliot.
20. Report on one other novel by a Victorian author, discussing some of the general problems raised in the study of *Silas Marner.*

## SUGGESTED READING LIST

Other Novels:

*Pride and Prejudice,* Jane Austen
*Jane Eyre,* Charlotte Brontë
*A Tale of Two Cities,* Charles Dickens
*The Cloister and the Hearth,* Charles Reade
*The Mill on the Floss,* George Eliot
*The Ordeal of Richard Feverel,* George Meredith
*The Return of the Native,* Thomas Hardy
*The Little Minister,* Sir James M. Barrie
*Babbitt,* Sinclair Lewis
*The Plutocrat,* Booth Tarkington

Reference Books:

*The Life of George Eliot,* J. W. Cross
*George Eliot and Her Times,* E. S. Haldane
*Early Life of George Eliot,* M. H. Deakin
*George Eliot,* Mathilde Blind
*Life of George Eliot,* Oscar Browning
*Charlotte Brontë, George Eliot, Jane Austen,* Henry Houston Bonnell
*George Eliot,* Sir Leslie Stephen

# *Prose Pictures of English Life*

*from*

Charles II to George III

1660–1775

*Diary—Letters—Biography*

Keystone View Co. of N. Y., Inc.

CHARLES II, THE MERRY MONARCH

Tiring of the stern rule of the Puritans, the English people in 1660 called Charles II to the throne. His reign ushered in a gay glittering period which is reflected in the literature of those days.

# PROSE PICTURES OF ENGLISH LIFE FROM CHARLES II TO GEORGE III

## BACKGROUND OF THE PERIOD

The modern reader who turns back to the literature of the century between the Restoration and the reign of George III finds himself in a world altogether different from his own. The men who write and the men they write about appear in cocked hats, lace ruffles, and silver buckles, and carry snuff-boxes and swords and canes. Perfumed and powdered wigs of various styles are part of the wardrobe of every well-dressed man. The costumes of the women are as elaborate. It is the day of silks and stiff brocades, of hoop skirts, and of powdered hair often arranged in enormous head-dresses. Jewelled fans and ornamental face-patches set off the beauty of the society belles. The fair ladies are devoted to their lap-dogs. It is the period of coffee houses and clubs, of dueling, gambling, sedan chairs, and stage coaches. It is a period of bitter partisan activity, of bitter personal quarrels, of unusual lawlessness in spite of brutal punishments. For minor offenses there is flogging and public execution, or imprisonment in horrible prisons.

The late seventeenth century followed a stormy religious and political period in English history. In 1649 Charles I had been beheaded and the government seized by the Puritan leader, Oliver Cromwell. Charles' son, heir to the throne, fled to France, and Cromwell established a sort of democratic government known as the Commonwealth.

Under the Puritans English life underwent a marked change. The carefree, reckless habits of the reign of Charles gave way to stern discipline enforced by Cromwell and his followers. Luxury and extravagance were frowned upon. In their religious zeal, the Puritans destroyed beautiful churches and works of art, believing these things were sinful. Yet they were intensely sincere, and their earnestness influenced the nation long after they had lost political power. It was John Milton who expressed in prose and poetry the noblest sentiments of the Puritan age.

The Commonwealth was short-lived, for in 1660 Prince Charles returned from exile in France and with great rejoicing was crowned Charles II.

With the restoration of the monarchy begins the period we are to study. The Puritan age with its moral earnestness is over. Freed from the stern rule of Cromwell, the people go to the other extreme. They become a mad, pleasure-seeking lot, taking liberties of speech and conduct that are shocking even to our own worldly-wise generation. Only the *appearance* of propriety is demanded. The theaters, which the

Puritans closed, are re-opened. In the ranting tragedies of the day virtue is extolled; in the court and drawing room it is ridiculed. The real sentiments of the age find expression in the comedies, which, while sparkling with wit, are coarse. Here the villain becomes the hero, and virtue goes down to defeat amid the guffaws of the audience. Charles II has been well nicknamed "The Merry Monarch."

Notwithstanding the loose morals of the time, new social and political conditions demand expression. Pamphlets, magazines, and newspapers take an important place in English writing. Men are beginning to consider the rights of their fellow men. Factories are growing and are gradually taking the place of cottage industries. Cities are becoming crowded, and modern economic problems are developing. Men are finding it necessary to study the world they live in. Prose becomes more terse and readable instead of scholarly and involved. In spite of much that is unfamiliar to us, in some ways the spirit of the period seems modern.

The first part of the period which we are to study lies roughly between the years 1660 and 1700. During this time prose is confined chiefly to criticism, society comedies, and controversy which reached its height in the denunciations of preachers against the indecencies of the stage. Two isolated works stand out: John Bunyan's great allegory, *The Pilgrim's Progress,* and Pepy's *Diary,* which, though written in code and not intended for publication, was deciphered many years later.

The second part of our period (extending from 1700 to about 1775) sees the beginning of several great prose forms. In the early years of the century Addison and Steele are publishing their essays. Swift is shocking people out of their smugness with his bitter satires. Defoe, Richardson, Fielding, and later Smollet, Sterne, and Goldsmith are developing the novel as a literary form. And Dr. Samuel Johnson, in his heavy, lumbering way, is hammering at philosophical, moral, and literary problems with such force that he is recognized as a dictator among the writers of his time. Nor should one forget Johnson's satellite, the persistent Scot, James Boswell, who dogs his idol's every step and from his copious notes of incident and dialogue begins a new type of biography. Our best information concerning the period—customs, conversation, famous people—is derived from Boswell's *Life of Johnson.*

Because the age was interested in ideas and in the clear expression of them, it has been called an age of prose; and much of the poetry has the virtues of prose rather than those of poetry. The verse is remarkable for its neatness, its clearness, and its polish, rather than for its imagination. Fashions and ideals in literature change from age to age almost as much as do customs and dress. Perhaps at no time in English history are we better able to study a fashion in writing, to see its almost complete dominance over all important literary works, and finally to watch its gradual yielding to other ideals.

# THE DIARY OF SAMUEL PEPYS[1]

## THE MAN AND HIS DIARY

It is not extravagant to say that Samuel Pepys has taught us more about the reign of Charles II than any one else. But he has done a great deal more than that. He has turned his mind inside out and revealed a human being stripped of all pretense. If he had consciously intended to make this revelation, he could not possibly have been so successful; but because he wrote for his own eyes alone, jotting down in short-hand his thoughts, his every-day acts, his pleasures and follies and little triumphs, his *Diary* has become one of the famous classics of literature.

This frank recital of events, both private and public, is enlivened by Pepys' insatiable curiosity and his quick appreciation of beauty, irony, and tragedy. Pepys loved music almost as well as he loved a pretty woman. He enjoyed a ramble over the countryside and reported hearing the song of a blackbird with as much pleasure as he related the experiences of a jolly get-together at an inn. He was always vowing to turn over a new leaf and give up the pleasures in vogue at the time; but when temptation offered, his good resolutions vanished and he joined in lusty choruses with other gay blades of London-Town.

Judged by modern standards, Pepys' life was on the free and easy side; yet in comparison with most of the gentlemen of the time he conducted himself with considerable restraint. He hated bestiality and cruelty—and there was plenty of both in the reign of the Merry Monarch. He could find no excuse for the weakness and dissipation of his king. His comments on the political situation are shrewd enough, and his talk of the theater, dancing, bear-baiting, executions, court functions, and a hundred other things show a spontaneous joy in life tempered by an inborn sense of decency.

Pepys was born in February, 1633, and died in May, 1703. During his seventy years of life he saw Charles I ousted and beheaded by the Puritans under Cromwell; the establishment of the Commonwealth; the restoration of the Stuart dynasty under Charles II, followed by the short reign of James II, Charles' brother; the Revolution of 1688 which deposed James II and placed William and Mary of Orange on the throne; and finally the accession of Queen Anne. Bustling times, those—wars, political intrigues, the great plague, the London fire, pomp, gayety, love, and sudden death—all reflected in this fascinating, intimate diary of Samuel Pepys, a record that was not deciphered until more than a century after his death. In it we see a man, a likeable man, with enough talent to win a responsible place in the Navy office, but not quite

[1] PEPYS (pēēps).

enough strength of character to refuse a bribe. Yet he sticks at his job during the great fire when others are scampering to safety. If he quarrels with his pretty French wife, his conscience torments him and he patches up the differences. Each year he celebrates with a dinner the anniversary of the "cutting of his stone," an operation that brought him health and freedom from pain. More than a little vain, he enjoys the attentions of royalty and the nobility. Nevertheless, except for the assistance of his distant cousin, the Earl of Sandwich (referred to in the diary as "My Lord") it is through merit alone that he rises to a position of importance in the government.

Yet always it is the man, not the official, in whom we are interested. His days are filled with activity, both of business and pleasure; and at night, when he comes home to write in his diary, he leaves the reader with an agreeable sense of healthy tiredness in those familiar words—"And so to bed."

## DIARY OF SAMUEL PEPYS[1]

*1660.* Blessed be God, at the end of the last year I was in very good health, without any sense of my old pain, but upon taking a cold. I lived in Axe Yard, having my wife, and servant Jane, and no more in family than us three. My own private condition very handsome, and esteemed rich, but indeed very poor; besides my goods of my house, and my office, which at present is somewhat uncertain. Mr. Downing master of my office.

*Jan. 16th.* At noon, Harry Ethall came to me and went along with Mr. Maylard by coach as far as Salsbury Court, and there we set him down, and we went to the Clerks, where we came a little too late, but in a closet we had a very good dinner by Mr. Pinkney's courtesy, and after dinner we had pretty good singing, and one, Hazard, sung alone after the old fashion, which was very much cried up, but I did not like it. Thence we went to the Green Dragon, on Lambeth Hill, both the Mr. Pinkney's, Smith, Harrison, Morrice, that sang the bass, Sheply and I, and there we sang of all sorts of things, and I ventured with good success upon things at first sight, and after that I played on my flageolet, and staid there till nine o'clock, very merry and drawn on with one song after another till

[1] Diary of Samuel Pepys—The following excerpts, from the eight-volume edition of *Pepys' Diary* have been chosen for their vivid portrayal of life during the Restoration. As a great many names, important and unimportant, appear in these pages, notes have been confined to essential matters. You are urged to refer to a standard English history for whatever additional information you may require.

it came to be so late. After that Sheply, Harrison and myself, we went towards Westminster on foot, and at the Golden Lion, near Charing Cross we went in and drank a pint of wine, and so parted, and thence home, where I found my wife and maid a-washing. I staid up till the bell-man came by with his bell just under my window as I was writing of this very line, and cried, "Past one of the clock, and a cold, frosty, windy morning." I then went to bed, and left my wife and the maid a-washing still.

*March 6th.* (Shrove Tuesday.) I called Mr. Sheply and we both went up to my Lord's[2] lodgings at Mr. Crew's, where he bade us to go home again, and get a fire against an hour after. Which we did at White Hall, whither he came, and after talking with him and me about his going to sea, he called me by myself to go along with him into the garden, where he asked me how things were with me, and what he had endeavoured to do with my uncle to get him to do something for me, but he would say nothing too. He likewise bade me look out now some good place, and he would use all his own, and all the interest of his friends that he had in England, to do me good. And asked me whether I could, without too much inconvenience, go to sea as his secretary, and bid me think of it. He also began to talk things of State, and told me that he did believe the King would come in, and did discourse with me about it, and about the affection of the people and City, at which I was full glad. My Lord told me, that there was great endeavours to bring in the Protector[3] again; but he told me, too, that he did believe it would not last long if he were brought in; no, nor the King neither (though he seems to think that he will come in), unless he carry himself very soberly and well. Every body now drinks the King's health without any fear, whereas before it was very private that a man dare do it.

*March 16th.* No sooner out of bed but troubled with abundance of clients, seamen. Then to Westminster Hall, where I heard how the Parliament had this day dissolved themselves, and did pass very cheerfully through the Hall, and the Speaker without his mace. The whole Hall was joyful thereat, as well as themselves, and now

---

[2] My Lord's—Referring to the Earl of Sandwich, Pepys' cousin, who helped Pepys obtain appointment in the government.

[3] The Protector—Richard Cromwell, son of Oliver, whose inefficiency was partly responsible for the collapse of the Commonwealth.

they begin to talk loud of the King. To-night I am told, that yesterday, about five o'clock in the afternoon, one came with a ladder to the Great Exchange, and wiped with a brush the inscription that was upon King Charles, and that there was a great bonfire made in the Exchange, and people called out "God bless King Charles the Second!" From the Hall I went home to bed, very sad in mind to part with my wife, but God's will be done.

*March 23rd.* Up early, carried my Lord's will in a black box to Mr. William Montagu for him to keep for him. Then to the barber's and put on my cravat there. So to my Lord again, who was almost ready to be gone and had staid for me. Soon as my Lord on board, the guns went off bravely from the ships.[4] And a little while after come to the Vice-Admiral Lawson, and seemed very respectful to my Lord, and so did the rest of the Commanders of the frigates that were thereabouts. I to the cabin allotted for me, which was the best that any had that belonged to my Lord. I got out some things out of my chest for writing and to work presently, Mr. Burr and I both.

*May 14th.* In the morning when I woke and rose, I saw myself out of the scuttle close by the shore, which afterwards I was told to be the Dutch shore; the Hague was clearly to be seen by us. My Lord went up in his nightgown into the cuddy,[5] to see how to dispose thereof for himself and us that belong to him, to give order for our removal to-day. I got the Captain to ask leave for me to go [ashore,] which my Lord did give, and I taking my boy and Judge Advocate with me, went in company with them. The weather bad; we were sadly washed when we came near the shore, it being very hard to land there. The shore is, as all the country between that and the Hague, all sand. The rest of the company got a coach by themselves; Mr. Creed and I went in the fore part of a coach wherein were two very pretty ladies, very fashionable and with black patches, who very merrily sang all the way and that very well, and were very free to kiss the two blades that were with them. I took out my flageolet and piped. The Hague is a most neat place in all respects. The houses so neat in all places and things as is possible. Here we walked up and down a great while, the town being now very full of Englishmen.

[4] SHIPS—This is the fleet sent to the Hague to bring Charles II back to England.

[5] SCUTTLE . . . CUDDY—Nautical terms meaning, respectively, *hatchway* and *cabin.*

*May 21st.* So into my naked bed and slept till 9 o'clock, and then John Goods waked me, [by] and by the captain's boy brought me four barrels of Mallows oysters, which Captain Tatnell had sent me from Murlace. The weather foul all this day also. By letters that came hither in my absence, I understand that the Parliament had ordered all persons to be secured, in order to a trial, that did sit as judges in the late King's death,[6] and all the officers too attending the Court. News brought that the two Dukes are coming on board, which, by and by, they did, in a Dutch boat, the Duke of York in yellow trimmings, the Duke of Gloucester in grey and red. My Lord went in a boat to meet them, the captain, myself, and others, standing at the entering port. So soon as they were entered we shot the guns off round the fleet. After that they went to view the ship all over, and were most exceedingly pleased with it. They seem to be both very fine gentlemen. News is sent us that the King is on shore; so my Lord fired all his guns round twice, and all the fleet after him, which in the end fell into disorder, which seemed very handsome. The gun over against my cabin I fired myself to the King, which was the first time that he had been saluted by his own ships since this change; but holding my head too much over the gun, I had almost spoiled my right eye. Nothing in the world but going of guns almost all this day.

*May 23rd.* The Doctor and I waked very merry. In the morning came infinity of people on board from the King to go along with him. The King, with the two Dukes and Queen of Bohemia, Princess Royal, and Prince of Orange, came on board, where I in their coming in kissed the King's, Queen's, and Princess's hands, having done the other before. After dinner the King and Duke altered the name of some of the ships. Which done, we weighed anchor, and with a fresh gale and most happy weather we set sail for England. All the afternoon the King walked here and there, up and down (quite contrary to what I thought him to have been), very active and stirring. Upon the quarter-deck he fell into discourse of his escape from Worcester, where it made me ready to weep to hear the stories that he told of his difficulties that he had passed through, as his travelling four days and three nights on foot, every step up to his knees in dirt, with nothing but a green coat and a

---

[6] THE LATE KING'S DEATH—The execution of Charles I.

pair of country breeches on, and a pair of country shoes that made him so sore all over his feet, that he could scarce stir. Yet he was forced to run away from a miller and other company, that took them for rogues. His sitting at table at one place, where the master of the house, that had not seen him in eight years, did know him, but kept it private; when at the same table there was one that had been of his own regiment at Worcester, could not know him, but made him drink the King's health, and said that the King was at least four fingers higher than he. At another place he was by some servants of the house made to drink, that they might know him not to be a Roundhead,[7] which they swore he was. In another place at his inn, the master of the house, as the King was standing with his hands upon the back of a chair by the fireside, kneeled down and kissed his hand, privately, saying, that he would not ask who he was, but bid God bless him whither he was going. Then the difficulty of getting a boat to get into France, where he was fain to plot with the master thereof to keep his design from the four men and a boy (which was all his ship's company), and so go to Fécamp in France. At Rouin he looked so poorly, that the people went into the rooms before he went away to see whether he had not stolen something or other. Under sail all night, and most glorious weather.

*May 25th.* By the morning we were come close to the land, and every body made ready to get on shore. The King and the two Dukes did eat their breakfast before they went, and there being set some ship's diet before them, only to show them the manner of the ship's diet, they eat of nothing else but pease and pork, and boiled beef. I spoke with the Duke of York about business, who called me Pepys by name, and upon my desire did promise me his future favour. Great expectation of the King's making some Knights, but there was none. About noon (though the brigantine that Beale made was there ready to carry him) yet he would go in my Lord's barge with the two Dukes. Our Captain steered, and my Lord went along bare with him. I went, and Mr. Mansell, and one of the King's footmen, with a dog that the King loved in a boat by ourselves, and so got on shore when the King did. The Mayor

[7] ROUNDHEAD—One of the followers of Cromwell, so called because of the Puritan fashion of cutting the hair close to the head. Charles' followers, the Cavaliers, wore their hair long.

of the town came and gave him his white staff, the badge of his place, which the King did give him again. The Mayor also presented him from the town a very rich Bible, which he took and said it was the thing that he loved above all things in the world. A canopy was provided for him to stand under, which he did, and talked awhile with General Monk and others, and so into a stately coach there set for him, and so away through the town towards Canterbury, without making any stay at Dover. The shouting and joy expressed by all is past imagination.

*October 13th.* To my Lord's in the morning, where I met with Captain Cuttance, but my Lord not being up I went out to Charing Cross, to see Major-general Harrison hanged, drawn, and quartered; which was done there, he looking as cheerful as any man could do in that condition. He was presently cut down, and his head and heart shown to the people, at which there was great shouts of joy. It is said, that he said that he was sure to come shortly at the right hand of Christ to judge them that now had judged him; and that his wife do expect his coming again. Thus it was my chance to see the King beheaded at White Hall, and to see the first blood shed in revenge for the blood of the King at Charing Cross. From thence to my Lord's, and took Captain Cuttance and Mr. Sheply to the Sun Tavern, and did give them some oysters. After that I went by water home, where I was angry with my wife for her things lying about, and in my passion kicked the little fine basket which I bought her in Holland, and broke it, which troubled me after I had done it. Within all the afternoon setting up shelves in my study. At night to bed.

*1661.* At the end of the last and the beginning of this year, I do live in one of the houses belonging to the Navy Office, as one of the principal officers, and have done now about half a year. After much trouble with workmen I am now almost settled. Myself in constant good health, and in a most handsome and thriving condition. Blessed be Almighty God for it. I take myself now to be worth £300 clear in money, and all my goods and all manner of debts paid, which are none at all.

*January 3rd.* To Will's, where Spicer and I eat our dinner of a roasted leg of pork which Will did give us, and after that to the Theatre, where was acted "Beggars' Bush," it being very well done;

and here the first time that ever I saw women come upon the stage.[8]

*February 17th* (Lord's day). A most tedious, unreasonable, and impertinent sermon, by an Irish Doctor. His text was "Scatter them, O Lord, that delight in war." Sir Wm. Batten and I very much angry with the parson.

*March 11th.* At night home and found my wife come home, and among other things she hath got her teeth new done by La Roche, and are indeed now pretty handsome, and I was much pleased with it. So to bed.

*April 11th.* At 2 o'clock, with very great mirth, we went to our lodging and to bed, and lay till 7, and then called up by Sir W. Batten, so I arose and we did some business, and then came Captn. Allen, and he and I withdrew and sang a song or two, and among others took pleasure in "Goe and bee hanged, that's goodbye." The young ladies came too, and so I did again please myself with Mrs. Rebecca, and about 9 o'clock, after we had breakfasted, we set forth for London, and indeed I was a little troubled to part with Mrs. Rebecca, for which God forgive me. Thus we went away through Rochester. We baited[9] at Dartford, and thence to London, but of all the journeys that ever I made this was the merriest, and I was in a strange mood for mirth. Among other things, I got my Lady to let her maid, Mrs. Anne, to ride all the way on horseback, and she rides exceedingly well; and so I called her my clerk, that she went to wait upon me. I met two little schoolboys going with pitchers of ale to their schoolmaster, and I did drink of some of one of them and give him two pence. By and by we come to two little girls keeping cows, and I saw one of them very pretty, so I had a mind to make her ask my blessing, and telling her that I was her godfather, she asked me innocently whether I was not Ned Wooding, and I said that I was, so she kneeled down and very simply called, "Pray, godfather, pray to God to bless me," which made us very merry, and I gave her twopence. In several places, I asked women whether they would sell me their children, but they denied me all, but said they would give me one to keep for them, if I would. Mrs. Anne and I rode under the man that hangs upon

[8] WOMEN . . . UPON THE STAGE—Previously female rôles had been played by boys or young men.

[9] BAITED—Fed the horses.

Shooter's Hill, and a filthy sight it was to see how his flesh is shrunk to his bones. So home and I found all well.

*April 13th.* So to Whitehall again and met with my Lord above with the Duke; and after a little talk with him, I went to the Banquet-house, and there saw the King heal,[10] the first time that ever I saw him do it; which he did with great gravity, and it seemed to me to be an ugly office and a simple one.

*April 23rd* (Coronacon day). About 4 I rose and got to the Abbey, where I followed Sir J. Denham, the Surveyor, with some company that he was leading in. And with much ado, by the favour of Mr. Cooper, his man, did get up into a great scaffold across the North end of the Abbey, where with a great deal of patience I sat from past 4 till 11 before the King came in. And a great pleasure it was to see the Abbey raised in the middle, all covered with red, and a throne (that is a chair) and footstool on the top of it; and all the officers of all kinds, so much as the very fidlers, in red vests. At last comes in the Dean and Prebends of Westminster, with the Bishops (many of them in cloth of gold copes), and after them the Nobility, all in their Parliament robes, which was a most magnificent sight. Then the Duke, and the King with a scepter (carried by my Lord Sandwich) and sword and mond[11] before him, and the crown too. The King in his robes, bare-headed, which was very fine. And after all had placed themselves, there was a sermon and the service; and then in the Quire at the high altar, the King passed through all the ceremonies of the Coronacon, which to my great grief I and most in the Abbey could not see. The crown being put upon his head, a great shout begun, and he came forth to the throne, and there passed more ceremonies.

*September 7th.* At the office all the morning. So I having appointed the young ladies at the Wardrobe to go with them to a play today, my wife and I took them to the Theatre, where we seated ourselves close by the King, and the Duke of York and Madame Palmer, which was great content; and, indeed, I can never enough admire her beauty. And here was "Bartholomew Fayre," with the puppet-show, acted to-day, which had not been these forty years (it being so satyricall against Puritanism, they durst not till

---

[10] SAW THE KING HEAL—It was believed that scrofula, a tubercular condition of the glands, could be cured by the touch of a king.

[11] MOND—A globe as an emblem of sovereignty. Usually written *mound*.

now, which is strange they should already dare to do it, and the King do countenance it.)

*December 3rd.* To the Paynter's and sat and had more of my picture done; but it do not please me, for I fear it will not be like me. To my Lady, where my Lady Wright was at dinner with her, and all our talk about the great happiness that my Lady Wright says there is in being in the fashion and in variety of fashions, in scorn of others that are not so, as citizens' wives and country gentlewomen, which though it did displease me enough, yet I said nothing to it.

*March 26th, 1662.* Up early. This being, by God's great blessing, the fourth solemn day of my cutting for the stone this day four years, and am by God's mercy in very good health, and like to do well, the Lord's name be praised for it.

*May 15th.* At night, all the bells of the town rung, and bonfires made for the joy of the Queen's arrival,[12] who came and landed at Portsmouth last night. But I do not see much thorough joy, but only an indifferent one, in the hearts of people, who are much discontented at the pride and luxury of the Court, and running in debt.

*June 14th.* Up by four o'clock in the morning and up on business at my office. Then we sat down to business, and about 11 o'clock, having a room got ready for us, we all went out to the Tower-hill; and there, over against the scaffold, made on purpose this day, saw Sir Henry Vane[13] brought. A very great press of people. He made a long speech, many times interrupted by the Sheriff and others there; and they would have taken his paper out of his hand but he would not let it go. But they caused all the books of those that writ after him to be given the Sheriff; and the trumpets were brought under the scaffold that he might not be heard. Then he prayed, and so fitted himself, and received the blow; but the scaffold was so crowded that we could not see it done.

*June 30th.* Observations. This I take to be as bad a juncture as ever I observed. The King and his new Queen minding their

---

[12] THE QUEEN'S ARRIVAL—For reasons of state Charles married a Portuguese princess, Catherine of Braganza.

[13] SIR HENRY VANE—Former member of the Long Parliament, which had defied Charles I.

pleasures at Hampton Court. All people discontented; some that the King do not gratify them enough; and the others, Fanatiques of all sorts, that the King do take away their liberty of conscience; and the height of the Bishops, who I fear will ruin all again. They do much cry up the manner of Sir H. Vane's death, and he deserves it. They clamour against the chimney-money,[14] and say they will not pay it without force.

*August 23rd.* And so all along Thames-street, but could not get a boat: I offered eight shillings for a boat to attend me this afternoon, and they would not, it being the day of the Queen's coming to town from Hampton Court. Anon come the King and Queen in a barge under a canopy with 10,000 barges and boats, I think, for we could see no water for them, nor discern the King nor Queen. And so they landed at White Hall Bridge, and the great guns on the other side went off. But that which pleased me best was, that my Lady Castlemaine stood over against us upon a piece of White Hall, where I glutted myself with looking on her. One thing more; there happened a scaffold below to fall, and we feared some hurt, but there was none, but she of all the great ladies only run down among the common rabble to see what hurt was done, and did take care of a child that received some little hurt, which methought was so noble. Anon there came one there booted and spurred that she talked long with. And by and by, she being in her hair, she put on his hat, which was but an ordinary one, to keep the wind off. But methinks it became her mightily, as every thing else do. The show being over, I went away, not weary with looking on her.

*November 27th.* At my waking, I found the tops of the houses covered with snow, which is a rare sight, that I have not seen these three years. We all went to the next house upon Tower Hill, to see the coming by of the Russia Embassador; for whose reception all the City trained-bands[15] do attend in the streets, and the King's lifeguards, and most of the wealthy citizens in their black velvet coats, and gold chains. I could not see the Embassador in his coach; but his attendants in their habits and fur caps very handsome, comely men, and most of them with hawkes upon their fists to present to

[14] CHIMNEY-MONEY—Money the king received from a tax levied on each chimney of a house.

[15] TRAINED-BANDS—Bands or companies of citizens, like both militia and volunteers.

the King. But Lord! to see the absurd nature of Englishmen, that cannot forbear laughing and jeering at everything that looks strange.

*April 3rd, 1663.* Going out of White Hall, I met Captain Grove, who did give me a letter directed to myself from himself. I discerned money to be in it, and took it, knowing, as I found it to be, the proceed of the place I have got him to be, the taking up of vessels for Tangier. But I did not open it till I came home to my office, and there I broke it open, not looking into it till all the money was out, that I might say I saw no money in the paper, if ever I should be questioned. There was a piece in gold and 4£ in silver.

*April 19th* (Easter day). Up and this day put on my close-kneed coloured suit, which, with new stockings of the colour, with belt, and new gilt-handled sword, is very handsome.

*October 19th.* Waked with a very high wind, and said to my wife, "I pray God I hear not of the death of any great person, this wind is so high!" fearing that the Queen might be dead. So up; and going by coach with Sir W. Batten and Sir J. Minnes to St. James's, they tell me that Sir W. Compton died yesterday: at which I was most exceedingly surprised, he being, and so all the world saying that he was, one of the worthyest men and best officers of State now in England. Coming to St. James's, I hear that the Queen did sleep five hours pretty well tonight, and that she waked and gargled her mouth, and to sleep again; but that her pulse beats fast, beating twenty to the King's, or my Lady Suffolk's eleven; but not so strong as it was. It seems she was so ill as to be shaved and pidgeons put to her feet, and to have the extreme unction given her by the priests, who were so long about it that the doctors were angry. The King, they all say, is most fondly disconsolate for her, and weeps by her, which makes her weep; which one this day told me he reckons a good sign, for that it carries away some rheume from the head.

*March 14th, 1664.* So to the 'Change, and thence home, where my wife and I fell out about my not being willing to have her have her gowne laced, but would lay out the same money and more on a plain new one. At this she flounced away in a manner I never saw her, nor which I could ever endure. So I away to the office, though she had dressed herself to go see my Lady Sandwich. She by and by in a rage follows me, and coming to me tells me in a spiteful manner like a vixen and with a look full of rancor that she would go buy a new one and lace it and make me pay for it, and then let me burn it if I would after she had done it, and so went away in a fury.

*April 5th.* Home myself, where I find my wife dressed as if she had been abroad, but I think she was not, but she answering me some way that I did not like I pulled her by the nose, indeed to offend her, though afterwards to appease her I denied it, but only it was done in haste. The poor wretch took it mighty ill, and I believe besides wringing her nose she did feel pain, and so cried a great while, but by and by I made her friends, and so after supper to my office a while, and then home to bed.

*October 25th.* It seems the City did last night very freely lend the King £100,000 without any security but the King's word, which was very noble.

*August 31, 1665.* Up; and, after putting several things in order to my removal, to Woolwich; the plague having a great encrease this week, beyond all expectation of almost 2,000, making the general Bill 7,000, odd 100; and the plague over 6,000. Thus this month ends with great sadness upon the publick, through the greatness of the plague every where through the kingdom almost. Every day sadder and sadder news of its encrease. In the City died this week 7,496, and of them 6,102 of the plague. But it is feared that the true number of the dead this week is near 10,000; partly from the poor that cannot be taken notice of, through the greatness of the number, and partly from the Quakers and others that will not have any bell ring for them.[16] Our fleete gone out to find the Dutch, we having about 100 sail in our fleete, and in them the Soveraigne one; so that it is a better fleete than the former with the Duke was.

*September 2, 1666* (Lord's day). Some of our mayds sitting up last night to get things ready against our feast to-day, Jane called

[16] Bell ring for them—Deaths from the plague were so numerous that formal funerals became impracticable. Carts went through the city at night, the drivers ringing a bell and calling: "Bring out your dead!" Many people, among them the Quakers, rebelled at the lack of ceremony and would not comply with the regulations.

us up about three in the morning, to tell us of a great fire they saw in the City. So I rose and slipped on my night-gowne,[17] and went to her window, and thought it to be on the back-side of Marke-lane at the farthest; but, being unused to such fires as followed, I thought it far enough off; and so went to bed again and to sleep. About seven rose again to dress myself, and there looked out at the window, and saw the fire not so much as it was and further off. By and by Jane comes and tells me that she hears that above 300 houses have been burned down to-night by the fire we saw, and that it is now burning down all Fish-street, by London Bridge. So I made myself ready presently, and walked to the Tower, and there got up upon one of the high places, Sir J. Robinson's little son going up with me; and there I did see the houses at that end of the bridge all on fire, and an infinite great fire on this and the other side the end of the bridge; which, among other people, did trouble me for poor little Michell and our Sarah on the bridge. So down, with my heart full of trouble, to the Lieutenant of the Tower, who tells me that it begun this morning in the King's baker's house in Pudding-lane, and that it hath burned St. Magnus's Church and most part of Fish-street already. So I down to the water-side, and there got a boat and through bridge, and there saw a lamentable fire. Poor Michell's house, as far as the Old Swan, already burned that way, and the fire running further, that in a very little time it got as far as the Steele-yard, while I was there. Everybody endeavouring to remove their goods, and flinging into the river or bringing them into lighters[18] that lay off; poor people staying in their houses as long as till the very fire touched them, and then running into boats, or clambering from one pair of stairs by the water-side to another. And among other things, the poor pigeons, I perceive, were loth to leave their houses, but hovered about the windows and balconys till they were, some of them burned, their wings, and fell down. . . . To White Hall, and there up to the King's closett in the Chappell, where people come about me, and I did give them an account dismayed them all, and word was carried in to the King. So I was called for, and did tell the King and Duke of Yorke what I saw, and that unless his Majesty did command houses to be pulled down nothing could stop the fire. They seemed much troubled,

[17] NIGHT-GOWNE—Dressing gown.

[18] LIGHTERS—Vessels for transporting freight about a harbor.

and the King commanded me to go to my Lord Mayor from him, and command him to spare no houses, but to pull down before the fire every way. At last met my Lord Mayor in Canning-street, like a man spent, with a handkercher about his neck. To the King's message he cried, like a fainting woman, "Lord, what can I do? I am spent: people will not obey me. I have been pulling down houses; but the fire overtakes us faster than we can do it." People all almost distracted, and no manner of means used to quench the fire. The houses, too, so very thick thereabouts, and full of matter of burning, as pitch and tarr, in Thames-street; and warehouses of oyle, and wines, and brandy, and other things. And to see the churches all filling with goods by people who themselves should have been quietly there at this time. Met with the King and Duke of York in their barge, and with them to Queenhithe, and there called Sir Richard Browne to them. Their order was only to pull down houses apace, and so below bridge at the water-side; but little was or could be done, the fire coming upon them so fast. River full of lighters and boats taking in goods, and good goods swimming in the water, and only I observed that hardly one lighter or boat in three that had the goods of a house in, but there was a pair of Virginalls[19] in it. So near the fire as we could for smoke; and all over the Thames, with one's face in the wind, you were almost burned with a shower of fire-drops. This is very true; so as houses were burned by these drops and flakes of fire, three or four, nay five or six houses, one from another. When we could endure no more upon the water, we to a little ale-house on the Bankside, over against the Three Cranes, and there staid till it was dark almost, and saw the fire grow; and, as it grew darker, appeared more and more, and in corners and upon steeples, and between churches and houses, as far as we could see up the hill of the City, in a most horrid malicious bloody flame, not like the fine flame of an ordinary fire. We staid till, it being darkish, we saw the fire as only one entire arch of fire from this to the other side the bridge, and in a bow up the hill for an arch of above a mile long; it made me weep to see it. The churches, houses, and all on fire and flaming at once; and a horrid noise the flames made, and the cracking of houses at their ruine. So home with a sad heart, and there find every body

[19] A PAIR OF VIRGINALLS—A wire-stringed musical instrument that was the forerunner of the piano.

discoursing and lamenting the fire; and poor Tom Hater come with some few of his goods saved out of his house, which is burned upon Fish-streete Hill. I invited him to lie at my house, and did receive his goods, but was deceived in his lying there, the newes coming every moment of the growth of the fire; so as we were forced to begin to pack up our owne goods, and prepare for their removal; and did by moonshine (it being brave dry, and moonshine, and warm weather) carry much of my goods into the garden, and Mr. Hater and I did remove my money and iron chests into my cellar, as thinking that the safest place. And got my bags of gold into my office, ready to carry away, and my chief papers of accounts also there, and my tallys into a box by themselves.

*September 3rd.* About four o'clock in the morning, my Lady Batten sent me a cart to carry away all my money, and plate, and best things, to Sir W. Rider's at Bednall-greene. Which I did, riding myself in my night-gowne in the cart; and, Lord! to see how the streets and the highways are crowded with people running and riding, and getting of carts at any rate to fetch away things. At night lay down a little upon a quilt of W. Hewer's in the office, all my owne things being packed up or gone; and after me my poor wife did the like, we having fed upon the remains of yesterday's dinner, having no fire nor dishes, nor any opportunity of dressing any thing.

*September 4th.* Up by break of day to get away the remainder of my things. Sir W. Batten not knowing how to remove his wine, did dig a pit in the garden, and laid it in there; and I took the opportunity of laying all the papers of my office that I could not otherwise dispose of. And in the evening Sir W. Pen and I did dig another, and put our wine in it; and I my Parmazan cheese, as well as my wine and some other things. Only now and then walking into the garden, and saw how horridly the sky looks, all on a fire in the night, was enough to put us out of our wits; and, indeed, it was extremely dreadful, for it looks just as if it was at us, and the whole heaven on fire. I after supper walked in the darke down to Tower-streete, and there saw it all on fire, at the Trinity House on that side, and the Dolphin Taverne on this side, which was very near us; and the fire with extraordinary vehemence. Now begins the practice of blowing up of houses in Tower-streete, those next the Tower, which at first did frighten people more than any thing;

but it stopped the fire where it was done, it bringing down the houses to the ground in the same places they stood, and then it was easy to quench what little fire was in it, though it kindled nothing almost. Paul's[20] is burned, and all Cheapside. I wrote to my father this night, but the post-house being burned, the letter could not go.

*September 5th.* About two in the morning my wife calls me up and tells me of new cryes of fire, it being come to Barkeing Church, which is the bottom of our lane. I up, and finding it so, resolved presently to take her away, and did, and took my gold, which was about £2,350, W. Hewer, and Jane, down by Proundy's boat to Woolwich; but, Lord! what a sad sight it was by moone-light to see the whole City almost on fire, that you might see it plain at Woolwich, as if you were by it. There, when I come, I find the gates shut, but no guard kept at all, which troubled me, because of discourse now begun, that there is plot in it, and that the French had done it. I got the gates open, and to Mr. Shelden's, where I looked up my gold, and charged my wife and W. Hewer never to leave the room without one of them in it, night or day. So back again, by the Way seeing my goods well in the lighters at Deptford, and watched well by people. Home, and whereas I expected to have seen our house on fire, it being now about seven o'clock, it was not. I up to the top of Barking steeple, and there saw the saddest sight of desolation that I ever saw; every where great fires, oyle-cellars, and brimstone, and other things burning. I became afeard to stay there long, and therefore down again as fast as I could, the fire being spread as far as I could see it; and to Sir W. Pen's, and there eat a piece of cold meat, having eaten nothing since Sunday, but the remains of Sunday's dinner.

*September 7th.* Up by five o'clock; and, blessed be God! find all well; and by water to Paul's Wharfe. Walked thence, and saw all the towne burned, and a miserable sight of Paul's church, with all the roofs fallen, and the body of the quire fallen into St. Fayth's; Paul's school also, Ludgate, and Fleet-street, my father's house, and the church, and a good part of the Temple the like. This day our Merchants first met at Gresham College, which, by proclamation, is to be their Exchange. Strange to hear what is bid for houses all

---

[20] PAUL'S—St. Paul's Cathedral, later rebuilt by the famous architect, Sir Christopher Wren.

up and down here; a friend of Sir W. Rider's having £150 for what he used to let for £40 per annum. Much dispute where the Custom-house shall be; thereby the growth of the City again to be foreseen. I home late to Sir W. Pen's, who did give me a bed; but without curtains or hanging, all being down. So here I went the first time into a naked bed, only my drawers on; and did sleep pretty well: but still both sleep and waking had a fear of fire in my heart, that I took little rest. People do all the world over cry out of the simplicity of my Lord Mayor in generall, and more particularly in this business of the fire, laying it all upon him.

*September 13th.* And so home, having this day also got my wine out of the ground again, and set in my cellar; but with great pain to keep the porters that carried it in from observing the money-chests there.

*September 17th.* Up betimes, and shaved myself after a week's growth: but, Lord! how ugly I was yesterday and how fine to-day! By water, seeing the City all the way, a sad sight indeed, much fire being still in. I to finish my letters, and home to bed; and find to my infinite joy many rooms clean; and myself and wife lie in our own chamber again. But much terrified in the nights now-a-days with dreams of fire, and falling down of houses.

*May 27, 1667.* Up, and there comes Greeting my flagelette master, and I practised with him. There comes also Richardson, the bookbinder, with one of Ogilby's Bibles for me to see and buy. So to my chamber, and there did some little business, and then abroad, and stopped at the Bear-garden-stairs, there to see a prize fought. But the house was so full there was no getting in there, so forced to go through an alehouse into the pit, where the bears are baited; and upon a stool did see them fight, which they did very furiously, a butcher and a waterman. The former had the better all along, till by and by the latter dropped his sword out of his hand, and the butcher, whether not seeing his sword dropped I know not, but did give him a cut over the wrist, so as he was disabled to fight any longer. But, Lord! to see how in a minute the whole stage was full of watermen to revenge the foul play, and the butchers to defend their fellow, though most blamed him; and there they all fell to it knocking down and cutting many on each side. It was pleasant to see, but that I stood in the pit, and feared that in the tumult I might get some hurt. At last the rabble broke up, and so I away to White Hall and so to St. James's.

*July 14th* (Lord's day). Up, and my wife, a little before four, and to make us ready; and by and by Mrs. Turner come to us, by agreement, and she and I staid talking below, while my wife dressed herself, which vexed me that she was so long about it keeping us till past five o'clock before she was ready. She ready; and, taking some bottles of wine, and beer, and some cold fowle with us into the coach, we took coach and four horses, which I had provided last night, and so away. We got to Epsum by eight o'clock, to the well; where much company, and there we 'light, and I drank the water: they did not, but do go about and walk a little among the women, but I did drink four pints. So we took coach again and to the towne, to the King's Head, where our coachman carried us, and there had an ill room for us to go into, but the best in the house that was not taken up. Here we called for drink, and bespoke dinner. Then I carried them to see my cozen Pepy's house, and 'light, and walk round about it, and they like it, as indeed it deserves, very well, and is a pretty place; and then I walked them to the wood hard by, and there got them in the thickets till they had lost themselves and I could not find the way into any of the walks in the wood, which indeed are very pleasant, if I could have found them. At last got out of the wood again; and I, by leaping down the little bank coming out of the wood, did sprain my right foot, which brought me great present pain, but presently, with walking, it went away for the present, and so the women and W. Hewer and I walked upon the Downes, where a flock of sheep was; and the most pleasant and innocent sight that ever I saw in my life—we find a shepherd and his little boy reading, far from any houses or sight of people, the Bible to him; so I made the boy read to me, which he did, with the forced tone that children do usually read, that was mighty pretty, and then I did give him something, and went to the father, and talked with him; and I find he had been a servant in my cozen Pepy's house, and told me what was become of their old servants. He did content himself mightily in my liking his boy's reading, and did bless God for him, the most like one of the old patriarchs that ever I saw in my life, and it brought those thoughts of the old age of the world in my mind for two or three days after. So to our inne, and there had a dish of creame, but it was sour, and so had no pleasure in it; and so paid our reckoning, and took coach, it being about seven at night, and passed and saw the people walking with their wives and children to take the ayre, and we set out for home, the sun by and by going down, and we in the cool of the evening all the way with much pleasure home, talking and pleasing ourselves with the pleasure of this day's work. Anon it grew dark, and as it grew dark we had the pleasure to see several glow-wormes, which was mighty pretty, but my foot begins more and more to pain me, which Mrs. Turner, by keeping her warm hand upon it, did much ease.

*May 31, 1669.* And thus ends all that I doubt I shall ever be able to do with my own eyes in the keeping of my Journal, I being not able to do it any longer, having done now so long as to undo my eyes almost every time that I take a pen in my hand; and, therefore, whatever comes of it, I must forbear: and, therefore, resolve, from this time forward, to have it kept by my people in long-hand, and must therefore be contented to set down no more than is fit for them and all the world to know; or, if there be anything, which cannot be much, now my *amours* to Deb. are past, and my eyes hindering me in almost all other pleasures, I must endeavour to keep a margin in my book open, to add, here and there, a note in short-hand with my own hand.

And so I betake myself to that course, which is almost as much as to see myself go into my grave: for which, and all the discomforts that will accompany my being blind, the good God prepare me!

S. P.

## QUESTIONS AND EXERCISES

Exercises preceded by a star are designed for assignment at the discretion of the teacher, or for any student who volunteers.

1. Suggest what sort of man you think Samuel Pepys was. Would you like to have known him? What do you like best about him?
2. Which passage of the *Diary* is most dramatic? Most agreeable? Most brutal?
3. What differences between Pepys' time and our own have you noted? Have you discovered any similarities? What?
4. In your own words write a description of one of the following scenes: the coronation of Charles II, the London fire, the trip to the country.

*5. Consult an English history and study the chapter on the Restoration Period. Tell the class any new and interesting things you have learned.

# THE LETTERS OF THE EARL OF CHESTERFIELD TO HIS SON

## THE MAN AND HIS LETTERS

To appreciate the characteristics of an age one must know rather intimately a great many different persons who lived in that age—know them, that is, through the intimate personal records they have left. As Pepys has given us vivid pictures of the latter part of the seventeenth century, so Philip Dormer Stanhope, fourth Earl of Chesterfield, has reflected one phase of life in the next century.

He was born in 1694 during the reign of William and Mary. He lived through the reigns of Queen Anne, Georges I and II, and into the reign of George III, dying three years before the outbreak of the American Revolution. A graduate of Cambridge and a member of Parliament, he was noted as a statesman, a patron of the arts, and a man of fashion; yet it is as the man of fashion, the dictator of rules of etiquette, that he is best remembered.

Although Lord Chesterfield's *Letters to His Son* rank among the most famous letters in the world, the advice he offers is to be carefully considered before one adopts it as a guide for conduct. Chesterfield ranks *appearances* higher than we do in this century. Almost anything may be said or done, he suggests, if it is said or done with grace and an air of good breeding. Polite manners, a suave self-control, distinction in dress—these, he would have us believe, make the man, or at least the better part of the man.

Nevertheless, there is much practical wisdom in his advice to his son. If we can take the good and let the rest go, remembering that in his time superficial brilliance was the yardstick by which a man was measured, we can afford to be tolerant toward this model of eighteenth century decorum. Here is the wit, the shrewd negotiator of treaties the generous patron, and the ornament of milady's drawing room.

As you read a few of his letters, remember that they represent but one side of the picture. As we shall soon see, there is another.

*London, July 26, O.S.*[1] *1748.*

Dear Boy: There are two sorts of understandings; one of which hinders a man from ever being considerable, and the other commonly makes him ridiculous; I mean the lazy mind, and the

[1] O.S.—Old style; that is, according to the Julian calendar established by Julius Caesar. See page 14, note 11.

trifling frivolous mind. Yours, I hope, is neither. The lazy mind will not take the trouble of going to the bottom of anything; but, discouraged by the first difficulties (and everything worth knowing or having is attained with some), stops short, contents itself with easy, and consequently superficial knowledge, and prefers a great degree of ignorance to a small degree of trouble. These people either think, or represent, most things as impossible; whereas few things are so, to industry and activity. But difficulties seem to them impossibilities, or at least they pretend to think them so, by way of excuse for their laziness. An hour's attention to the same subject is too laborious for them; they take everything in the light in which it first presents itself, never consider it in all its different views; and, in short, never think it through. The consequence of this is, that when they come to speak upon these subjects before people who have considered them with attention, they only discover their own ignorance and laziness, and lay themselves open to answers that put them in confusion. Do not then be discouraged by the first difficulties, but resolve to go to the bottom of all those things which every gentleman ought to know well. . . . The trifling and frivolous mind is always busied, but to little purpose; it takes little objects for great ones, and throws away upon trifles that time and attention which only important things deserve. Knick-knacks, butterflies, shells, insects, etc., are the subjects of their most serious researches. They contemplate the dress, not the characters of the company they keep. They attend more to the decorations of a play than the sense of it; and to the ceremonies of a court more than to its politics. Such an employment of time is an absolute loss of it. You have now,[2] at most, three years to employ, either well or ill; for as I have often told you, you will be all your life what you shall be three years hence. For God's sake then reflect. Will you throw this time away either in laziness, or in trifles? Or will you not rather employ every moment of it in a manner that must so soon reward you with so much pleasure, figure, and character? I cannot, I will not doubt of your choice. Read only useful books; and never quit a subject till you are thoroughly master of it, but read and inquire on till then. . . . Never be ashamed nor afraid of asking questions; for if they lead to information, and if you

[2] Now—When this letter was written, Lord Chesterfield's son, Philip Stanhope, was sixteen years old.

accompany them with some excuse, you will never be reckoned an impertinent or rude questioner. All those things, in the common course of life, depend entirely upon the manner; and, in that respect, the vulgar saying is true, That one man may better steal a horse, than another look over the hedge. There are few things that may not be said, in some manner or other; either in a seeming confidence, or a genteel irony, or introduced with wit; and one great part of the knowledge of the world consists in knowing when and where to make use of these different manners.

*London, Dec. 30, O.S. 1748.*

Dear Boy: I direct this letter to Berlin,[3] where, I suppose, it will either find you, or at least wait but a very little time for you. I cannot help being anxious for your success, at this your first appearance upon the great stage of the world; for though the spectators are always candid enough to give great allowances, and to show great indulgence to a new actor; yet, from the first impressions which he makes upon them, they are apt to decide, in their own minds at least, whether he will ever be a good one, or not: if he seems to understand what he says, by speaking it properly; if he is attentive to his part, instead of staring negligently about him; and if, upon the whole, he seems ambitious to please, they willingly pass over little awkwardnesses and inaccuracies, which they ascribe to a commendable modesty in a young and inexperienced actor. They pronounce that he will be a good one in time; and by the encouragement which they give him, make him so the sooner. This, I hope, will be your case: you have sense enough to understand your part; a constant attention, and ambition to excel in it, with a careful observation of the best actors, will inevitably qualify you, if not for the first, at least for considerable parts.

Your dress (as significant a thing as dress is in itself) is now become an object worthy of some attention; for I confess, I cannot help forming some opinion of a man's sense and character from his dress; and I believe most people do as well as myself. Any affectation whatsover in dress implies, in my mind, a flaw in the understanding. Most of our young fellows here display some character or other by their dress; some affect the tremendous, and

[3] Berlin—Chesterfield had sent his son abroad with a tutor.

wear a great and fiercely cocked hat, an enormous sword, a short waistcoat and a black cravat; these I should be almost tempted to swear the peace against, in my own defence, if I were not convinced that they are but meek asses in lions' skins. Others go in brown frocks, leather breeches, great oaken cudgels in their hands, their hats uncocked, and their hair unpowdered; and imitate grooms, stage-coachmen, and country bumpkins so well, in their outsides, that I do not make the least doubt of their resembling them equally in their insides. A man of sense carefully avoids any particular character in his dress; he is accurately clean for his own sake; but all the rest is for other people's. He dresses as well, and in the same manner, as the people of sense and fashion of the place where he is. If he dresses better, as he thinks, that is, more than they, he is a fop; if he dresses worse, he is unpardonably negligent: but, of the two, I would rather have a young fellow too much than too little dressed; the excess on that side will wear off, with a little age and reflection; but if he is negligent at twenty, he will be a sloven at forty. . . . Dress yourself fine, where others are fine; and plain where others are plain; but take care always that your clothes are well made, and fit you, for otherwise they will give you a very awkward air. When you are once well dressed for the day think no more of it afterwards; and without any stiffness for fear of discomposing that dress, let all your motions be as easy and natural as if you had no clothes on at all. So much for dress, which I maintain to be a thing of consequence in the polite world.

*London, September 29, 1752.*

My dear Friend: There is nothing so necessary, but at the same time there is nothing more difficult (I know it by experience) for you young fellows, than to know how to behave yourselves prudently towards those whom you do not like. Your passions are warm, and your heads are light; you hate all those who oppose your views, either of ambition or love; and a rival, in either, is almost a synonymous term for an enemy. Whenever you meet such a man, you are awkwardly cold to him, at best; but often rude, and always desirous to give him some indirect slap. This is unreasonable; for one man has as good a right to pursue an employment as another. . . .

When I went to the Hague, in 1744, it was to engage the Dutch to come roundly into the war, and to stipulate their quotas of troops, &c.: your acquaintance, the Abbé de la Ville, was there on the part of France, to endeavour to hinder them from coming into the war at all. I was informed, and very sorry to hear it, that he had abilities, temper, and industry. We could not visit, our two masters being at war; but the first time I met him at a third place, I got somebody to present me to him; and I told him, that though we were to be national enemies, I flattered myself we might be, however, personal friends, with a good deal more of the same kind; which he returned in full as polite a manner. Two days afterwards, I went, early in the morning, to solicit the Deputies of Amsterdam, where I found l'Abbé de la Ville, who had been beforehand with me; upon which I addressed myself to the Deputies, and said, smilingly, I am very sorry, Gentlemen, to find my enemy with you; my knowledge of his capacity is already sufficient to make me fear him; we are not upon equal terms; but I trust to your own interests, against his talents. If I have not this day had the first word, I shall at least have the last. They smiled: the Abbé was pleased with the compliment, and the manner of it, staid about a quarter of an hour, and then left me to my Deputies, with whom I continued upon the same tone, though in a very serious manner, and told them, that I was only come to state their own true interests, to them, plainly and simply, without any of those arts, which it was very necessary for my friend to make use of to deceive them. I carried my point, and continued my *procédé*[4] with the Abbé; and by this easy and polite commerce with him I often found means to fish out from him whereabouts he was.

Remember, there are but two *procédés* in the world for a gentleman and a man of parts; either extreme politeness or knocking down. If a man notoriously and designedly insults and affronts you, knock him down; but if he only injures you, your best revenge is to be extremely civil to him in your outward behaviour, though at the same time you counterwork him, and return him the compliment, perhaps with interest. . . . The world judges from the appearances of things, and not from the reality, which few are able, and still fewer are inclined to fathom: and a man, who will take care always

[4] *Procédé*—Method of procedure.

to be in the right in those things, may afford to be sometimes a little in the wrong in more essential ones: there is a willingness, a desire to excuse him. With nine people in ten, good-breeding passes for good-nature, and they take attentions for good offices. At courts there will be always coldnesses, dislikes, jealousies, and hatred, the harvest being but small in proportion to the number of laborers; but then, as they arise often, they die soon, unless they are perpetuated by the manner in which they have been carried on, more than by the matter which occasioned them. The turns and vicissitudes of courts frequently make friends of enemies, and enemies of friends: you must labour, therefore, to acquire that great and uncommon talent, of hating with good-breeding, and loving with prudence; to make no quarrel irreconcilable, by silly and unnecessary indications of anger; and no friendship dangerous, in case it breaks, by a wanton, indiscreet, and unreserved confidence.

## QUESTIONS AND EXERCISES

Exercises preceded by a star are designed for assignment at the discretion of the teacher, or for any student who volunteers.

1. What habits does Lord Chesterfield believe a young man should cultivate? What does this advice indicate concerning his own character?
2. What is Chesterfield's idea of the importance of dress? Do you agree? If not, what is your opinion?
3. What picture of the times is given in the letters reprinted here? Do you note any differences between this period and the age in which Pepys lived?
4. For what purpose does Lord Chesterfield relate his experiences with the Abbé de la Ville?
5. Discuss Lord Chesterfield's statement: "The world judges from the appearances of things, and not from the reality . . . and a man, who will take care always to be in the right in those things, may afford to be sometimes a little in the wrong in more essential ones."

*6. In the rôle of the son, write Lord Chesterfield a letter refuting some of his arguments which in your opinion are not sound.

# THE LETTERS OF HORACE WALPOLE

## THE MAN AND HIS LETTERS

With the exception of a few poets who were beginning to discover the beauties of nature, nearly all the literary men of England during the first three-quarters of the eighteenth century were joined in one common enthusiasm: love of London. It was in this city with its teeming millions that they found inspiration; and not for another generation was country life to be celebrated in prose and poetry. Said Dr. Johnson: "To a man whose pleasure is intellectual, London is the place." "The chief advantage of London," remarked another, "is that a man is always *so near his burrow.*"

Horace Walpole, author and politician, was no exception to the rule. The son of Sir Robert Walpole, powerful Whig minister under George II, he had the advantages of a fine education, opportunity for travel, and friendships with the most distinguished men of the time. He was born in 1717 and died in 1797. While studying at Eton, he met the poet, Thomas Gray, and with him spent two years touring through France and Italy. Upon his return to England, Walpole entered Parliament and until his retirement in 1768 took an active part in political affairs. His house became a mecca for sightseers who came to view the collection of curiosities which he had acquired during his travels. He was a voluminous writer; he had the gout; and he died unmarried.

Among the many volumes which came from Walpole's pen are romantic novels, tragedies, diaries, and a wealth of correspondence with famous men. "The best letter writer in the English language" he has been called. If you read between the lines, however, you cannot fail to discern the note of cynicism which pervades much of his work. The too-too beautiful cloak of English culture is beginning to grow frayed and show shabby spots in the lining. Watch for signs of this disillusionment in the two letters which follow, written to Sir Horace Mann, British envoy to the court of Tuscany, Italy, with whom Walpole had recently spent a year in Florence.

*Arlington Street, Jan. 27, 1743.*

I could not write to you last Thursday, I was so much out of order with a cold; your brother came and found me in bed. To-night, that I can write, I have nothing to tell you; except that yesterday the welcome news (to the Ministry) came of the accession of the

Dutch[1] to the King's measures. They are in great triumph; but till it is clear what part his Prussian Uprightness[2] is acting, other people take the liberty to be still in suspense. So they are about all our domestic matters too. It is a general stare! . . .

You will wonder, perhaps be peevish, when I protest I have not another paragraph by me in the world. I want even common conversation; for I cannot persist, like the Royal Family, in asking people the same questions, "Do you love walking?" "Do you love music?" "Was you at the opera?" "When do you go into the country?" I have nothing else to say: nothing happens; scarce the common episodes of a newspaper, of a man falling off a ladder and breaking his leg; or of a countryman cheated out of his leather pouch, with fifty shillings in it. We are in such a state of sameness, that I shall begin to wonder at the change of seasons, and talk of the spring as a strange incident. Lord Tyrawley, who has been fifteen years in Portugal, is of my opinion; he says he finds nothing but a fog, whist, and the House of Commons.

In this lamentable state, when I know not what to write even to you, what can I do about my serene Princess Grifoni? Alas! I owe her two letters, and where to find a beau sentiment,[3] I cannot tell! I believe I may have some by me in an old chest of drawers, with some exploded red-heel shoes and full-bottom wigs; but they would come out so yellow and moth-eaten! Do vow to her, in every superlative degree in the language, that my eyes have been so bad, that as I wrote you word, over and over, I have not been able to write a line. That will move her, when she hears what melancholy descriptions I write, of my not being able to write—nay, indeed it will not be so ridiculous as you think; for it is ten times worse for the eyes to write in a language one don't much practise! I remember a tutor at Cambridge, who had been examining some lads in Latin, but in a little while excused himself, and said he must speak English, for his mouth was very sore.

[1] DUTCH—Holland was an ally of England and Austria against France, Prussia and Spain in the War of the Austrian Succession.

[2] PRUSSIAN UPRIGHTNESS—Ironic reference to Frederick the Great of Prussia. Walpole, as you will notice, is very skillful in his sarcastic thrusts. It was in his time considered a mark of the man of the world to be able to wound neatly.

[3] BEAU SENTIMENT—A pretty compliment. This art of the "pretty compliment" was much admired and much practiced in Walpole's time. In the "high society" of those days, an ability to say pretty nothings delightfully was just as necessary as the knack (which Walpole has shown) for clever, well-mannered, and biting sarcasm. The sarcasm was more likely to be sincere than the compliments.

*Newmarket, Oct. 3, 1743.*

I am writing to you in an inn on the road to London. What a paradise should I have thought this when I was in the Italian inns! in a wide barn with four ample windows, which had nothing more like glass than shutters and iron bars! no tester to the bed, and the saddles and portmanteaus heaped on me to keep off the cold. What a paradise did I think the inn at Dover when I came back! and what magnificence were twopenny prints, salt-sellers, and boxes to hold the knives; but the *summum bonum*[4] was small-beer and the newspaper.

"I bless'd my stars, and call'd it luxury!"[5]

Who was the Neapolitan ambassadress that could not live at Paris, because there was no maccaroni? Now am I relapsed into all the dissatisfied repinement of a true English grumbling voluptuary. I could find in my heart to write . . . against the Government, because I am not quite so much at my ease as on my own sofa. . . . How dismal, how solitary, how scrub does this town look; and yet it has actually a street of houses better than Parma or Modena. Nay, the houses of the people of fashion, who come hither for the races, are palaces to what houses in London itself were fifteen years ago. People do begin to live again now, and I suppose in a term we shall revert to York Houses, Clarendon Houses, &c. But from that grandeur all the nobility had contracted themselves to live in coops of a dining-room, a dark back-room, with one eye in a corner, and a closet. Think what London would be, if the chief houses were in it, as in the cities in other countries, and not dispersed like great rarity-plums in a vast pudding of country. Well, it is a tolerable place as it is! Were I a physician, I would prescribe nothing but recipe, CCCLXV drachm. Londin. Would you know why I like London so much? Why, if the world must consist of so many fools as it does, I choose to take them in the gross, and not made into separate pills, as they are prepared in the country. Besides there is no being alone but in a metropolis: the worst place in the world to find solitude is the country: questions grow there, and that unpleasant Christian commodity, neighbours. Oh! they are all good Samaritans, and do so pour balms and nostrums upon one, if one has but the tooth-

[4] *Summum bonum*—The best of all.

[5] "I BLESS'D . . . LUXURY!"—Paraphrase of a line in Joseph Addison's *Cato*.

ache, or a journey to take, that they break one's head. A journey to take—ay! they talk over the miles to you, and tell you, you will be late in. My Lord Lovel says, *John* always goes two hours in the dark in the morning, to avoid being one hour in the dark in the evening. I was pressed to set out to-day before seven: I did before nine; and here am I arrived at a quarter past five, for the rest of the night.

I am more convinced every day, that there is not only no knowledge of the world out of a great city, but no decency, no practicable society—I had almost said, not a virtue. I will only instance in modesty, which all *old Englishmen* are persuaded cannot exist within the atmosphere of Middlesex. Lady Mary has a remarkable taste and knowledge of music, and can sing; I don't say, like your sister, but I am sure she would be ready to die if obliged to sing before three people, or before one with whom she is not intimate. The other day there came to see her a Norfolk heiress; the young gentlewoman had not been three hours in the house, and that for the first time of her life, before she notified her talent for singing, and invited herself up-stairs, to Lady Mary's harpsichord; where, with a voice like thunder, and with as little harmony, she sang to nine or ten people for an hour. "Was ever nymph like Rossymonde?"—no, *d'honneur*.[6] We told her she had a very strong voice. "Lord, Sir! my master says it is nothing to what it was." My dear child, she brags abominably; if it had been a thousandth degree louder, you must have heard it at Florence.

I did not write to you last post, being overwhelmed with this sort of people: I will be more punctual in London. Patapan is in my lap; I had him wormed lately, which he took heinously; I made it up with him by tying a collar of rainbow riband about his neck, for a token that he is never to be wormed any more.

I had your long letter of two sheets of Sept. 17th, and wonder at your perseverance in telling me so much as you always do, when I, dull creature, find so little for you. I can only tell you that the more you write, the happier you make me; and I assure you, the more details the better. . . . Oh! I was struck the other day with a resemblance of mine hostess at Brandon to old Sarazin. You must know, the ladies of Norfolk universally wear periwigs, and affirm

[6] *D'honneur*—Upon my honor!

that it is the fashion at London. "Lord, Mrs. White, have you been ill, that you have shaved your head?" Mrs. White, in all the days of my acquaintance with her, had a professed head of red hair: to-day, she had no hair at all before, and at a distance above her ears, I descried a smart brown bob, from beneath which had escaped long strings of original scarlet—so like old Sarazin at two in the morning, when she has been losing at Pharaoh,[7] and clawed her wig aside, and her old trunk is shaded with the venerable white ivy of her own locks. . . .

The Duke of Argyle is dead—a death of how little moment, and of how much it would have been a year or two ago![8] It is provoking, if one must die, that one can't even die *à propos*![9]

How does your friend Dr. Cocchi? You never mention him: do only knaves and fools deserve to be spoken of? Adieu!

## QUESTIONS AND EXERCISES

1. A *bon mot* is a neat, brief phrasing of a humorous thought. Find at least two *bon mots* in the first Walpole letter reprinted here.
2. What does Walpole think of life in the country? How does it compare with Italian country life?
3. What touches of cynicism can you find in these letters?
4. Explain Walpole's remark that "there is no being alone but in a metropolis: the worst place in the world to find solitude is the country."
5. Would you like to have Walpole catch you in a social blunder? What seems to be his opinion of the human race in general?

---

[7] Pharaoh—Same as *faro*, a gambling card game.

[8] A year or two ago—When the Duke was a real power in the government.

[9] *À propos!*—Opportunely, at the right time.

# LIFE OF JOHNSON

## JAMES BOSWELL

1740–1795

### THE AUTHOR AND HIS HERO

When critics speak of literary dictators, they usually mean men whose principles of writing became the accepted fashion of their age; but when they call Dr. Samuel Johnson a dictator, they mean exactly what they say—a despot of literature whose word was law to his contemporaries, a man with thunder in his voice before whom lesser men quailed. When he shook his walking stick and shouted, "Sir!" the very rafters trembled. It took a brave fellow indeed to stand up against this ponderous, irascible, and yet strangely lovable Sam Johnson.

There was little happiness in Johnson's life. It was hard work and poverty from the very beginning, and it ended with pain and illness. He was born in Lichfield, England, in 1709. He took a degree at Oxford. He taught school and didn't like it. He did translations for the press, and was poorly paid. Deep in debt, he complicated matters by marrying. Then he went to London, walking the streets at night for want of money to buy lodging, dividing his few pennies with little waifs of the great city, learning what it means to be hungry and cold and homeless. Yet fame did come. It lifted him from obscurity to the topmost rung of the ladder and at last earned him a pension which helped to comfort his declining years. He died in 1784.

Though Johnson was the most important literary figure of his time, he left no important literary work. Some one has said that Johnson's best book is Boswell's life of him. Boswell, the son of a Scottish judge, met Johnson in 1763, and from that day followed him about with the cheerful devotion of a watchdog. He took notes of nearly everything interesting that Johnson said, and Johnson was always saying something interesting. When the Doctor discovered what his friend's purpose was, he said that if he thought Boswell really meant to *write his life* he would prevent it *by taking Boswell's!* Fortunately this facetious threat was never carried out; for the *Life* stands as the world's greatest biography of a man of letters. It is as intimate as an autobiography, filled with dialogue, which Boswell has recorded word for word, and with pictures of the early part of the reign of George III, just a century after Pepys wrote his *Diary.*

Like most men of his time Johnson loved London—but he did not love all the people in it. Lord Chesterfield, for instance. Of the latter's famous *Letters to His Son,* the good doctor said that they teach the morals of a libertine and the manners of a dancing master. "This man," he said at another time, "I thought had been a Lord among wits; but, I find, he is only a wit among Lords." Johnson had reason for his bitterness. Having been assured of Lord Chesterfield's patronage in his project for writing a dictionary, Johnson addressed a plan of the work to His Lordship. Nothing happened. He was completely ignored and had to struggle along without any assistance whatever. Just before publication every one became excited about the *Dictionary*. Its success was certain and Lord Chesterfield hastened to write two flattering papers for the weekly *World,* in the hope that the volume would be dedicated to him. This belated interest offended Johnson even more than the neglect had done, and he immediately wrote His Lordship a letter that is the most celebrated example of sarcasm and disciplined indignation in the language. That, with a typical passage of dialogue as reported by Boswell, gives another picture of the mid-eighteenth century, now known as the Age of Johnson.

To the Right Honourable The Earl of Chesterfield

*February 7, 1755.*

My Lord,

I have lately been informed by the proprietor of "The World," that two papers, in which my "Dictionary" is recommended to the public, were written by your lordship. To be so distinguished is an honour, which, being very little accustomed to favours from the great, I know not well how to receive, or in what terms to acknowledge.

When, upon some slight encouragement, I first visited your lordship, I was overpowered, like the rest of mankind, by the enchantment of your address, and could not forbear to wish that I might boast myself *Le vainqueur du vainqueur de la terre*;[1]—that I might attain that regard for which I saw the world contending; but I found my attendance so little encouraged, that neither pride nor modesty would suffer me to continue it. When I had once addressed your lordship in public, I had exhausted all the arts of pleasing which a retired and uncourtly scholar can possess. I had done all that I could; and no man is well pleased to have his all neglected, be it ever so little.

Seven years, my lord, have now passed since I waited in your outward rooms, or was repulsed from your door; during that time I

[1] *Le vainqueur . . . terre*—The conqueror of the conqueror of the world.

have been pushing on my work through difficulties, of which it is useless to complain, and have brought it, at last, to the verge of publication, without one act of assistance, one word of encouragement, or one smile of favour. Such treatment I did not expect, for I never had a patron before.

The shepherd in Virgil grew at last acquainted with Love, and found him a native of the rocks.

Is not a patron, my lord, one who looks with unconcern on a man struggling for life in the water, and when he has reached ground, encumbers him with help? The notice which you have been pleased to take of my labours, had it been early, had been kind; but it has been delayed till I am indifferent, and cannot enjoy it; till I am solitary,[2] and cannot impart it; till I am known, and do not want it. I hope it is no very cynical asperity not to confess obligations where no benefit has been received, or to be unwilling that the public should consider me as owing that to a patron, which Providence has enabled me to do for myself.

Having carried on my work thus far with so little obligation to any favourer of learning, I shall not be disappointed though I should conclude it, if less be possible, with less; for I have been long wakened from that dream of hope in which I once boasted myself with so much exultation, My Lord, your lordship's most humble, most obedient servant,

SAM. JOHNSON.

We talked of living in the country. JOHNSON: "No wise man will go to live in the country, unless he has something to do which can be better done in the country. For instance: if he is to shut himself up for a year to study a science, it is better to look out to the fields, than to an opposite wall. Then if a man walks out in the country, there is nobody to keep him from walking in again; but if a man walks out in London, he is not sure when he shall walk in again. A great city is, to be sure, the school for studying life; and 'The proper study of mankind is man,' as Pope observes." BOSWELL: "I fancy London is the best place for society; though I have heard that the very first society of Paris is still beyond any-

[2] SOLITARY—An allusion to the death of his wife.

thing that we have here." JOHNSON: "Sir, I question if in Paris such a company as is sitting around this table could be got together in less than half a year. They talk in France of the felicity of men and women living together: the truth is, that there the men are not higher than the women, they know no more than the women do, and they are not held down in their conversation by the presence of women." RAMSAY: "Literature is upon the growth, it is in its spring in France: here it is rather passée."[3] JOHNSON: "Literature was in France long before we had it. Paris was the second city for the revival of letters:[4] Italy had it first, to be sure. . . . Caxton[5] printed only two books, Chaucer and Gower,[6] that were not translations from the French; and Chaucer, we know, took much from the Italians. No, sir, if literature be in its spring in France, it is a second spring; it is after a winter. We are now before the French in literature; but we had it long after them. In England, any man who wears a sword and a powdered wig is ashamed to be illiterate. I believe it is not so in France. Yet there is, probably, a great deal of learning in France, because they have such a number of religious establishments; so many men who have nothing else to do but to study. I do not know this; but I take it upon the common principles of chance. Where there are many shooters, some will hit."

Talking of London he observed, "Sir, if you wish to have a just notion of the magnitude of this city, you must not be satisfied with seeing its great streets and squares, but must survey the innumerable little lanes and courts. It is not in the showy evolutions of buildings, but in the multiplicity of human habitations which are crowded together, that the wonderful immensity of London consists. I have often amused myself with thinking how different a place London is to different people. They, whose narrow minds are contracted to the consideration of some one particular pursuit, view it only through that medium. A politician thinks of it merely as the seat of government in its different departments; a grazier, as a vast market for cattle; a mercantile man, as a place where a prodigious deal of busi-

[3] PASSÉE—Past its prime; in a decline.

[4] REVIVAL OF LETTERS—The Renaissance, or the new birth of learning and art in Europe near the end of the Middle Ages.

[5] CAXTON—William Caxton, the first English printer, born about 1422.

[6] CHAUCER AND GOWER—English poets of the fourteenth century.

ness is done upon 'Change; a dramatic enthusiast, as the grand scene of theatrical entertainments; a man of pleasure, as an assemblage of taverns. . . . But the intellectual man is struck with it, as comprehending the whole of human life in all its variety, the contemplation of which is inexhaustible."

## QUESTIONS AND EXERCISES

Exercises preceded by a star are designed for assignment at the discretion of the teacher, or for any student who volunteers.

1. Describe the tone of Johnson's letter to Chesterfield. What adjective best describes it? If you had been in Chesterfield's place, how do you suppose you would have felt upon receipt of the letter?
*2. In the eighteenth century it was still difficult for a man to earn a living by writing alone. Usually he had to have a patron to assist him with money and influence. Suggest some disadvantages of this system. Mention at least one possible advantage. Is this today's way?
3. To what does Johnson compare a patron? Why is the sarcasm so biting? Find two other examples of sarcasm in the letter to Chesterfield.
4. Why does Johnson love London?
5. Often Johnson is severely critical of the literature of his own time. What is his general view of it, however, as indicated by the dialogue reprinted from Boswell's *Life of Johnson?*
6. What sort of man do you imagine Johnson was? How did he differ from Chesterfield?

## GENERAL QUESTIONS AND EXERCISES

Exercises preceded by a star are designed for assignment at the discretion of the teacher, or for any student who volunteers.

1. Why are diaries and letters valuable sources of information in studying the characteristics of a period? Why is such a biography as that of Boswell's *Life of Johnson* valuable?
2. Which of the four units in this section did you enjoy most? Which gives the best picture of its time?
3. Name one modern book you have read or heard about which you think gives an accurate picture of present-day life.
*4. Report to class on other types of prose literature in the period extending roughly from the Restoration to the outbreak of the American revolution.

# *English Poetry*

*from*

*Charles II to George III*

*1660–1775*

Publishers' Photo Service, N. Y.

ALEXANDER POPE

He made clearness of thought and perfection of form the two chief aims of poetry. Many of his fellow poets feared the ridicule of this little hunchback whose heroic couplets were like polished arrows tipped with venom.

# GENERAL INTRODUCTION TO POETRY

## 1. Form

"The rhythm of life" is a phrase that has been vaguely and often meaninglessly used; yet there *is* a beat, a rhythmic surge, in life that is difficult to explain. Perhaps it comes from the pulsing of the human heart, or it may arise from some power in the universe, such as the motion of the planets or the tides. Why have people loved music and dancing and poetry since the beginning of the race if there is not some mysterious incentive to rhythmical expression?

To many persons poetry means rime, yet rime is simply a method of ornamentation. The fundamentals of poetry are beat and accent. Primitive poetry is chiefly a matter of stress on certain words or syllables, these stresses recurring as regularly as the poet could devise. For example, *Beowulf,* the oldest English epic, has a four-stressed line with a pause in the middle. The following is a modern English translation of one of the Anglo-Saxon lines in *Beowulf*:

Oft Scýld the Scéfing // from squádroned fóes

We find here, however, the beginnings of a rime scheme; not the rime ending we are used to in modern poetry, but an initial rime in which several of the stressed syllables begin with the same sound. In the line above notice the repetition of the *sc* sound, pronounced as *sk*. Initial rime as used in modern poetry is called alliteration. Notice, however, that in the example given below, from one of Tennyson's poems, the *m* sound occurs in unaccented as well as in accented syllables.

The moán of doves in ímmemórial elḿs

Poets advanced from the simple practice of stressing a few syllables to a regular arrangement of stressed and unstressed syllables throughout the line. Each line is called a verse, and each verse is made up of feet, just as music is made up of measures. The arrangement of these feet in a line is called meter. The number of feet in a verse gives the line its name, the Greek numerical prefix being combined with the word meter. For example the six-foot line is called hexameter; the five-foot line, pentameter; the four-foot line, tetrameter; the three-foot line, trimeter; the two-foot line, dimeter. Dividing a line into feet and marking the stresses is called scanning.

There are different kinds of feet, but a foot usually has one or two unstressed syllables combined with a stressed syllable. In English the following four types of feet are most common:

1. The iambic foot, or iambus: one unstressed syllable followed by one stressed syllable.

Thy soul/ was like/ a star/ and dwelt/ apart//

2. The trochaic foot, or trochee: one stressed syllable followed by one unstressed syllable.

Once up/on a/ midnight/ dreary/ while I/ pondered/ weak and/ weary//

3. The anapestic foot, or anapest: two unstressed syllables followed by one stressed syllable.

For the moon/ never beams/ without bring/ing me dreams//

4. The dactylic foot, or dactyl: one stressed syllable followed by two unstressed syllables.

This is the/ forest prim/eval. The/ murmuring/ pines and the/ hemlocks//

The poet, however, does not always hold to one type of poetic foot. To avoid monotony he may use different types of feet in the same line. A frequent combination is the iambus and the anapest:

The day/ is done,/ and the dark/ness falls/ from the wings/ of Night//

For variation even iambics and trochees may be united. Note in the following iambic line what a leaping start the opening trochaic foot gives:

Gallop/ apace/ ye fi/ery-foot/ed steeds//

Each type of foot has a quality and a pace of its own. Anapests give the impression of speed. Dactyls have stateliness, though sustained use in English tends toward monotony. By far the greatest number of lines in English poetry are written in iambic meter. A poet must adapt his meter to the thought he wishes to express just as the composer must make the time of his music fit his theme. Indeed, poetry and music have much in common. Instead of scanning a line, one may express it in musical terms:

The day/ is done,/ and the dark/ ness falls/ from the wings/ of Night//

Although the feet and the measures are not uniform, the arrangement of syllables in the third and fifth feet differing from the other four, there is unity of time; that is, each foot requires the same time in reading. It is this variety of arrangement within definite time limits that prevents poetry from becoming a monotonous succession of accents. In reading poetry the student is urged to forget all about accent and meter. Read it naturally, and the rhythm and music will take care of themselves. The sing-song manner in which some persons read verse destroys all its beauty and emphasizes what is merely the framework for the poet's art.

### 2. Spirit

If form were the most important factor in poetry, any one could become a poet by learning the rules of meter and rime. But structure is subordinate to imagination and expression. If one were to judge the ancient ballads by their crude rimes and even cruder meters, they would be of importance only as historical evidence of the development of poetry. Instead, they still rank high as literary creations. Their dramatic brevity and picturesqueness are in the best tradition of poetry, for it is imagination and the faculty of hitting upon exactly the right word or figure that raises poetry above the level of prose. Skillful use of rime and meter are by no means enough. One must be able to see beauty and ugliness with a penetrating eye and discover a relationship between them and man's aspirations before he can hope to produce great poetry.

At its best poetry is specific. It deals with things that we know through the senses—things that we can see, hear, touch, taste, or smell: mountain vistas and city streets, battles and lovers' trysts, the freshness of the grass in the morning and the soft coming on of night. Some think that it is enough to recapture these in descriptive verse. Is not beauty all we know and all we need to know? Others believe there is a deep meaning in life which it is the poet's duty to discover. Where did we come from? Whither are we traveling? For what purpose have we been placed on this planet? If the first are in danger of becoming superficial, the latter may bring poetry out of the realm of fancy into the prosaic world of argument. The greatest poetry is that which reveals "sermons in stones" yet does not preach the sermon.

There are three great divisions of poetry: epic, dramatic, lyric. All other kinds are either dependent upon these or a combination of them. The epic is narrative poetry of great events concerned with the fortunes of some central figure. It is majestic in style and has usually a tragic ending.

Dramatic poetry is conversation or monologues in verse that reveal, through the speech and action of the characters, the development of a situation through a climax to a conclusion. Shakespeare is the supreme dramatic poet, combining in a high degree the playwright's craft with the poet's art.

These two types, epic and dramatic poetry, are distinctly objective; that is, the poet suppresses his own feelings and ideas, presenting without personal bias his characters and their story. This is particularly true of the drama, in which the actors must play their parts without comment from the author.

Lyric poetry, on the contrary, is extremely subjective. Written often in the first person, it gives expression to a personal emotion. It is the revelation of the poet's own feelings in a brief, melodious poem that deals with a single thought or emotion. All lyrics lend themselves naturally to musical accompaniment, while many are written expressly to be sung. In ancient times, this type of poetry was composed to be sung to the music of the lyre, a stringed instrument resembling the harp.

Two minor divisions of poetry may be mentioned. Satiric poetry ridicules and pokes fun at individuals or customs or institutions. Often it carries a sting, especially when used by poets of strong likes and dislikes. Didactic poetry aims to instruct through the medium of verse, and is, therefore, rarely inspiring.

The difference between prose and poetry is not simply a matter of form. Prose is the chief instrument for expressing ideas. It appeals to the intelligence. Poetry is the language of the feelings, and makes its appeal directly to the emotions. Although both thought and feeling overlap in prose and poetry, there are some subjects which demand poetic treatment just as there are others which find best presentation through the medium of prose. He who would win fame in either medium must first determine the effect he wishes to produce and then bring the form of his work into harmony with its spirit.

# ENGLISH POETRY
# FROM CHARLES II TO GEORGE III

## THE AGE OF CLASSICISM AND THE BEGINNINGS OF ROMANTICISM

During the period which we have designated roughly as extending from 1660 to 1775, prose flourished in new and attractive forms. In addition to interesting memoirs, collections of letters, and biographies, the rise of the periodical essay and the beginning of the novel show that the prose writers of this century and more, were experimenters in literature and in ideas. Unfortunately the principles of sound sense, wit, and genteel restraint which were the keynotes of the time are ill adapted to poetry. Poetry lives by the imagination, not by logic. The story of the years we are to study is really the story of poetry's struggle to unfold her wings and soar aloft as she had done in the past and as, later, she would do again.

A number of factors are important in explaining the fashion of poetry which developed in the first part of this period. Many of the literary men had been driven out of England with Charles and his court when the Puritans came into power in 1649. Most of them went to France, where they came under the influence of the most brilliant group of writers in French history. When they returned to England after the Restoration they brought back the teachings they had learned, especially a tendency to follow established rules of writing, to emphasize close reasoning rather than romantic fancy, and to use short, clean-cut sentences without an unnecessary word.

As a natural result of this influence, many of the writers of the period were dissatisfied with the English literature of the past. The Elizabethan poets and dramatists had been led by patriotism, by enthusiasm, and in general by romantic emotions. They wrote in a natural style, without regard to rules, and though they exaggerated and used too many words, their works are delightful because of their vigor and freshness and fine feeling. But after Elizabeth's death, patriotism largely disappeared from politics and enthusiasm from literature. The leading writers of the Restoration and for half a century after rebelled against the exaggerations and loose form of the Elizabethans. In place of a natural, spontaneous expression they cultivated an artificial style, beautiful but cold.

Like many followers of fashion, these men went to extremes. We learn with amazement that even Shakespeare failed to please them. It is astonishing to read in the diary of Samuel Pepys (1660–1669) that he has been to see a play called *A Midsummer Night's Dream,* but that he will never go again to hear Shakespeare, "for it is the most insipid, ridiculous play that ever I saw in my life." And again we read in the diary of John Evelyn, another writer who reflects the spirit of the time: "I have seen *Hamlet,* but now these old plays begin to disgust this refined century, since their majesties have been so long abroad." To bring Shakespeare's plays up to date, dramatists of the period set to work to rewrite them. *Romeo and Juliet, Antony and Cleopatra*—play after play was reworked on the basis of the new rules.

It is important to remember that this was a period dominated by an elaborate social code. Rules of etiquette played an unbelievably large part in the life of the upper classes. A gentleman might not act naturally but had to follow exact rules in doffing his hat, in entering a room, in wearing a wig. Rules in literature were in keeping with formality in conduct. Writers lost individuality and became formal and artificial because life was formal and artificial.

One may well ask where the poets of this age obtained the rules of writing that seemed to them so important. They professed to look to the works of genius in past ages—to the classics. We sometimes call a "classic" any book that has stood the test of time, but in the minds of the poets and critics of that age the term was limited to the works of ancient Greeks and Romans. The attempt to write English poetry in the style of the classics has led students of literature to call this the Classical, or Pseudo-Classical, Period of English literature. Though the Elizabethans had exhibited an interest in the classics, no one ever thinks of applying the term classical to them. Their works were too intensely English at the core. The writers of the period we are about to study, however, were slavish imitators of models they thought were classical. Strangely, few of them were great students of the classics. They were content to take their rules second-hand from the French, who professed to have discovered the rules from the Greeks. Theirs was, therefore, really a pseudo-classicism—that is, a false or sham classicism.

Literary lawgivers of this period held that a rigid following of certain rules was more important than native genius in producing a masterpiece. It was supposed that almost any one who stuck to the formula could write a fine poem or play. No style that did not follow the rules as they understood them was considered good. In their anxiety to catch the loftiness of the classics, these imitators sought for precise and elegant methods of expression. Consequently, the form of their poetry often received more attention than the content.

> "True wit is nature to advantage dressed;
> What oft was thought, but ne'er so well expressed,"

wrote Pope, who shared with Dryden the chief literary honors of the classical period.

The form of the above quotation is called the heroic couplet. The heroic couplet consists of two riming lines, each of five iambic feet. Almost all the best poetry of the age was written in this form. As in this case, there is usually a pause at the end of each line and at the end of each couplet so that, when taken from the poem, the couplet makes complete sense. The classicists developed this form in their effort to find the smoothest possible medium of expression. The heroic couplet allows the poet to polish and prune until each part of his poem becomes almost perfect in its pointedness, its compression, its clarity. But of course many ideas cannot well be compressed into such a small unit as the couplet. Such a form cramps the reason and the imagination. We know, for example, that many of the greatest passages in Shakespeare and Milton do not even rime, and that often there is no pause at the end of the line.

In excluding emotion, these classicists restricted the range of their poetry. This is not a period of exuberant verse, delicate love lyrics, great heroic epics, or sincere nature poems. The classicists were a town-loving group who cared little for the fields and flowers and birds. They despised enthusiasm and passion. The larger part of their poetry was intellectual. The spirit was critical. Satire, philosophy, criticism, and translation occupied the attention of most of the poets of the period, and their lyric poetry confined itself chiefly to hymns, elegies, and odes. Both odes and elegies are poems expressing some noble sentiment in a dignified style, but an elegy always treats of death. (See Gray's *Elegy Written in a Country Churchyard.*)

In writing satires, essays, and criticism in verse, the classical poets were thus using poetry for the same practical ends as prose. One can enjoy the smooth-flowing lines, grasp the meaning of the witty comments on life, and visualize the scenes that are painted, without being deeply moved or believing that the poet himself was deeply moved. The brain responds, but not the heart. Such poetry plays decoratively along the surface but rarely touches the inner feelings. There is no catch at the throat for some sorrow common to all mankind. There is no suspension of breath before a scene of surpassing beauty. Fire and enthusiasm are lost in the poet's self-conscious attitudes.

To the student of poetry it is interesting to see that such poetry and such views of poetry could not long remain dominant. True poets cannot resist the romantic appeal of nature, the inspiration of noble character however humble, and the enthusiasm inspired by great events. Even before the middle of the eighteenth century the expression of individual emotion began to creep back into English literature. Our study of this period will reveal to us a poet like Pope who is dominantly classical. It will reveal others who, like Gray, Cowper, and Goldsmith, use generally the forms of poetry perfected by the classicists but who at the same time show a tendency to be interested in romantic subjects. And lastly, we shall see in the work of Blake the blazing forth of true lyrical poetry again.

# ALEXANDER POPE

## 1688–1744

Alexander Pope tells us that as a child he "lisped in numbers, for the numbers came." At the age of twelve he had tried writing odes and had persuaded his friends to take him to Will's Coffee House to gaze upon the great Dryden, whom, in another dozen years, he was to succeed as the most important poet of the age.

Few great men in literature have struggled against greater odds than did Pope. A severe illness as a child left him a cripple for life. He was a hunch-back, and he suffered from intensely severe headaches. Scarcely four and a half feet high, his rickety frame was supported by spindle legs which not even three pairs of stockings could make look substantial. Bright eyes peered out of a sharp-featured, pinched little face. "A lively little creature, with long legs and arms—a spider is no ill emblem of him; he has been taken at a distance for a windmill."

At this time of intense religious feeling his Roman Catholic faith prevented him from rising politically and under the strict eighteenth century laws even forbade him the privilege of education in a public school or university. Because of his sickly, deformed body, he could not enter the usual professions of English gentlemen; yet he became the most important literary man of his day. His genius won the friendship of many eminent men and women, and he associated on terms of equality with the proudest of the nobility.

Alexander Pope was born in London in 1688, the year of the bloodless revolution which brought William and Mary to the throne. His father was a linen merchant who, shortly after the poet's birth, retired with a small fortune to an estate in Windsor Forest. Pope secured his education in a haphazard fashion from tutors and from his own wide reading. Though he acquired the rudiments of Latin and Greek, his studies were not orderly and he was never a scholar in the strict sense of the word. Notwithstanding the gaps in his education, his active mind led him into philosophy, theology, history, and literary criticism.

Pope early resolved to devote himself to poetry. He showed a remarkable talent for rime and even as a boy spent long hours imitating various writers. Among the English poets, Dryden was his model. As early as 1708, when he was but twenty years of age, he won instant recognition by the publication of his *Pastorals.* Then came a period of great productivity. His *Essay on Criticism,* 1711, *The Rape of the Lock,* 1712, and *Windsor Forest,* 1713, were sufficient to make him recognized as the greatest living poet.

So complete was the recognition of his importance that when in 1713 he proposed a translation of Homer's *Iliad,* it was regarded as a great national event. Every one of importance subscribed in advance for copies of the work. The *Iliad* appeared in six volumes and was published at intervals between 1715 and 1720. The profits of the translation were over £5000, an amazing amount in that day. It was followed by the *Odyssey* (1725–6), which brought him three or four thousand pounds more. Though artificial in character, his translation is a great work. Gibbon, the historian, has well said that it has every merit except faithfulness to the original. Homer is simple and direct, and Pope, who likes the polished line, is not able to achieve the Greek simplicity.

These translations made him rich. Indeed, he was the first English man of letters to make a fortune directly by his writings. Other writers depended on patrons or politics or pensions for fame and livelihood. The profits of his translations provided money to buy a small estate at Twickenham, on the Thames, near London. There he indulged his fancy for landscape gardening, filling his grounds with formal statuary, and building among other curiosities his famous grotto ornamented with mirrors. At Twickenham he lived for the rest of his life, entertaining his friends, writing, and taking an important part in the literary life of the time. Among his intimates were a group of men who formed the Scriblerus Club, a famous literary association.

Pope's later years were devoted entirely to didactic and satiric poetry. The *Dunciad* (1728) is a mock-heroic epic directed against false pretenders to wit and learning, many of them the literary enemies of the Scriblerus Club. The *Essay on Man* (1732–4), *Moral Essays* (1731–5), and the *Epistle to Dr. Arbuthnot* (1735), are his most important later works.

His most widely read poems are the *Essay on Criticism,* the *Essay on Man,* and *The Rape of the Lock.* The *Essay on Criticism,* written when the poet was only twenty-three, contains literary opinions which had long been current but which Pope expressed in pointed heroic couplets. Besides showing a critical soundness and judgment that usually belong only to age and experience, it is remarkable for a large number of quotable lines. We find such old favorites as the following:

"For fools rush in where angels fear to tread."

"To err is human, to forgive divine."

"A little learning is a dangerous thing."

The *Essay on Man* is a philosophical poem with the object of vindicating the ways of God to man. In keeping with the emphasis on intellect so characteristic of his time, Pope found satisfactory grounds for belief in God by the exercise of reason. He aimed to present society with a rational, practical philosophy that men of his age could understand and accept. Like all his works, it includes many polished, quotable lines.

*The Rape of the Lock* is generally considered Pope's masterpiece. It is a mock epic, and has the supernatural elements supposed to be necessary for the epic. He takes a trifling subject and builds around it a delightfully satirical picture of the society of his time.

Pope gives us a remarkably clear reflection of the spirit of the age in which he lived. There is hardly an ideal, a belief, doubt, fashion, or whim not neatly expressed. Like so many of his age, however, he lacked sympathy with nature and humanity. Though he pretended to follow nature, it was a nature made pretty and artificial to suit the taste of the ladies of the court. Pope and his readers believed that there was nothing new under the sun. They strove to give their commonplace ideas the most apt, the most perfectly chiseled form possible. Correctness was Pope's aim, and few have come closer to attaining it than he. In his poetry we find exactness of meter, compression, and epigrammatic force. He has brilliance of diction, and keenness of wit and phrasing. He brings the heroic couplet to perfection.

There is little doubt that bodily ailments checked the growth of great character in Pope. He was naturally secretive and given to double dealing. One of his friends said he could not even drink tea without a stratagem. His sensitiveness and taste for intrigue involved him in many quarrels, and his biography is largely a history of these quarrels and intrigues. His vanity prompted him to have his letters to various friends published. Lest he be criticized for doing it, he pretended to have them stolen and published against his will. As a result, he was involved in net after net of falsehood.

For his friends, Jonathan Swift, John Gay, and John Arbuthnot, he had the greatest regard, but few of the other writers of the time escaped the poisoned darts of his pen. Some of the personal insults he put in his *Dunciad* are almost incredible. With the playwright Cibber he had a violent and historic feud. Even the gentle Addison, most graceful essayist of the period, was not spared. In lines that have just enough truth to make them remembered, and more than enough jealousy to turn them against their author, Pope pictured Addison as delighting to

"Damn with faint praise, assent with civil leer,
And without sneering teach the rest to sneer."

But though Pope may have had, as some of his critics say, a "crooked body with a crooked mind," we like better to remember that he loved his art—that in it is elegance, ease, irony, and pungent wit that will always delight the reader. He is wittier but less profound than Dryden. Only Shakespeare among English writers has been able to perfect more quotable lines. By sheer force of ambition he won a place and held it. The most famous poet of his age, he had no serious rival for thirty years. So supreme was he in the first half of the eighteenth century that the period is often known as the Age of Pope.

## THE RAPE OF THE LOCK

It is one evening in the early years of the eighteenth century. A group of high-spirited ladies and gentlemen are gathered together, outwardly decorous according to the code of the period, yet beneath the wigs and head-dresses just as full of fun and mischief as young people today. Here is a pretty miss sipping her coffee so politely and all unaware that behind her stands one of the beaux enchanted with her beauty. Suddenly she screams. A white arm flies to a lovely neck. Another scream. That bold, bad man has snipped off a lock of her hair, a precious lock whose power to charm she knows only too well!

Though it was done in a frolicsome mood, the escapade led to a quarrel between the families of the two young people. A friend of Pope's suggested that a humorous poem on the subject might remove the bad feeling. The result was *The Rape of the Lock,* written in 1712 and elaborated two years later with the addition of the sylphs and gnomes.

Delightful as the poem is to the ordinary reader, it is doubly so to one who remembers the form of the *Odyssey* and of other epics; for this is a mock-epic, the most brilliant one ever written. Epics deal with great, heroic actions. This poem deals with the most insignificant subject imaginable. Instead of the gods and goddesses of the great epic, the fairy-like sylphs help to guide the action. William Hazlitt, the critic, has called it a "triumph of insignificance." Pope deliberately elaborates all the details of fashionable life, the lady's toilet table, making coffee, and playing cards. Everything is handled with mock solemnity. Even the verse form is treated humorously, especially in its tendency toward anticlimax, as in the line:

"When husbands, or when lap-dogs breathe their last"

Yet for all the delightful mockery, Pope has an earnest purpose in the poem. He levels the dart of his satire against the weaknesses of social life where dress, manners, and conventions are so exaggerated. The first three cantos level their satire particularly against the lack of good sense; the remainder against the lack of good humor. Nor is the poem only a satire on society. It is a witty parody of the heroic style employed by the tragic dramatists of the day. Indeed, the comic effect of the poem is achieved through the treatment of a trivial subject in a grand manner. Selections from the first three cantos follow:

### CANTO I

What dire offense from amorous causes springs,
What mighty contests rise from trivial things,
I sing—This verse to Caryll,[1] Muse! is due:

[1] Caryll—John Caryll, a close friend of Pope's.

This, even Belinda[2] may vouchsafe to view:
Slight is the subject, but not so the praise,
If she inspire, and he approve my lays.

Say what strange motive, goddess![3] could compel
A well-bred lord[4] to assault a gentle belle?
Oh, say what stranger cause, yet unexplored,
Could make a gentle belle reject a lord?
In tasks so bold, can little men engage,
And in soft bosoms dwells such mighty rage?

Sol through white curtains shot a timorous ray,
And oped those eyes that must eclipse the day:
Now lap-dogs give themselves the rousing shake,
And sleepless lovers, just at twelve, awake:
Thrice rung the bell, the slipper knocked the ground,[5]
And the pressed watch[6] returned a silver sound.
Belinda still her downy pillow pressed,
Her guardian sylph prolonged the balmy rest:
'T was he had summoned to her silent bed
The morning dream that hovered o'er her head;
A youth more glittering than a birth-night beau[7]
(That e'en in slumber caused her cheek to glow),
Seemed to her ear his winning lips to lay,
And thus in whispers said, or seemed to say:

'Fairest of mortals, thou distinguished care
Of thousand bright inhabitants of air!
Know, then, unnumbered spirits round thee fly,
The light militia of the lower sky:
These, though unseen, are ever on the wing,
Hang o'er the box, and hover round the ring.[8]

---

[2] Belinda—Miss Arabella Fermor, a belle of the period, from whom the lock celebrated in the poem was stolen.

[3] Say . . . goddess—Pope is parodying the opening lines of Virgil's epic, the *Æneid.*

[4] A well-bred lord—Lord Petre, who had stolen the curl.

[5] The slipper knocked the ground—Rapping for the servant.

[6] Pressed watch—A watch which, when pressed, strikes the nearest hour.

[7] A birth-night beau—A fine gentleman dressed for a celebration of the king's birthday.

[8] Box . . . ring—Theater boxes and the circular drive in Hyde Park in London were fashionable meeting places for the society of the period.

Think what an equipage thou hast in air,
And view with scorn two pages and a chair.[9]

'Of these am I, who thy protection claim,
A watchful sprite, and Ariel is my name.
Late, as I ranged the crystal wilds of air,
In the clear mirror of thy ruling star
I saw, alas! some dread event impend,
Ere to the main this morning sun descend,
But Heaven reveals not what, or how, or where:
Warned by the sylph, O pious maid, beware!
This to disclose is all thy guardian can:
Beware of all, but most beware of man!'

He said; when Shock, who thought she slept too long,
Leaped up, and waked his mistress with his tongue.
'T was then, Belinda, if report say true,
Thy eyes first opened on a billet-doux;[10]
Wounds, charms, and ardors were no sooner read,
But all the vision vanished from thy head.

And now, unveiled, the toilet stands displayed,
Each silver vase in mystic order laid.
First, robed in white, the nymph intent adores,
With head uncovered, the cosmetic powers.
A heavenly image in the glass appears.
To that she bends, to that her eyes she rears;
The inferior priestess,[11] at her altar's side,
Trembling begins the sacred rites of pride.
Unnumbered treasures ope at once, and here
The various offerings of the world appear;
From each she nicely culls with curious toil,
And decks the goddess with the glittering spoil.
This casket India's glowing gems unlocks,
And all Arabia breathes from yonder box.
The tortoise here and elephant unite,
Transformed to combs, the speckled, and the white.

---

[9] CHAIR—A sedan chair.
[10] BILLET-DOUX—Love letter or note.
[11] INFERIOR PRIESTESS—The maid, Betty. (See line 78.)

Here files of pins extend their shining rows,
Puffs, powders, patches, bibles, billet-doux.
Now awful beauty puts on all its arms;
The fair each moment rises in her charms,
Repairs her smiles, awakens every grace,
And calls forth all the wonders of her face;
Sees by degrees a purer blush arise,
And keener lightnings quicken in her eyes.
The busy sylphs surround their darling care,
These set the head, and those divide the hair,
Some fold the sleeve, whilst others plait the gown;
And Betty's praised for labors not her own.

Not with more glories, in the ethereal plain,
The sun first rises o'er the purpled main,
Than, issuing forth, the rival of his beams[12]
Launched on the bosom of the silver Thames.
Fair nymphs, and well-dressed youths around her shone,
But every eye was fixed on her alone.
On her white breast a sparkling cross she wore,
Which Jews might kiss, and infidels adore.
Her lively looks a sprightly mind disclose,
Quick as her eyes, and as unfixed as those;
Favors to none, to all she smiles extends;
Oft she rejects, but never once offends.
Bright as the sun, her eyes the gazers strike,
And, like the sun, they shine on all alike.
Yet graceful ease, and sweetness void of pride,
Might hide her faults, if belles had faults to hide;
If to her share some female errors fall,
Look on her face, and you'll forget 'em all.

This nymph, to the destruction of mankind,
Nourished two locks, which graceful hung behind
In equal curls, and well conspired to deck
With shining ringlets the smooth ivory neck.

[12] THE RIVAL OF HIS BEAMS—Belinda.

Love in these labyrinths his slaves detains,
And mighty hearts are held in slender chains.
With hairy springes,[13] we the birds betray,
Slight lines of hair surprise the finny prey,
Fair tresses man's imperial race ensnare,
And beauty draws us with a single hair.

The adventurous baron the bright locks admired;
He saw, he wished, and to the prize aspired.
Resolved to win, he meditates the way,
By force to ravish, or by fraud betray;
For when success a lover's toil attends,
Few ask, if fraud or force attained his ends.

But when to mischief mortals bend their will,
How soon they find fit instruments of ill!
Just then Clarissa[14] drew with tempting grace
A two-edged weapon from her shining case:
So ladies in romance assist their knight,
Present the spear, and arm him for the fight.
He takes the gift with reverence, and extends
The little engine on his finger's ends;
This just behind Belinda's neck he spread,
As o'er the fragrant steams she bends her head.
Swift to the lock a thousand sprites repair,
A thousand wings, by turns, blow back the hair;
And thrice they twitched the diamond in her ear;
Thrice she looked back, and thrice the foe drew near.
Just in that instant, anxious Ariel sought
The close recesses of the virgin's thought;
As on the nosegay in her breast reclined,
He watched the ideas rising in her mind,
Sudden he viewed, in spite of all her art,
An earthly lover lurking at her heart.
Amazed, confused, he found his power expired,
Resigned to fate, and with a sigh retired.

[13] SPRINGES—Snares.
[14] CLARISSA—Another belle.

The peer now spreads the glittering forfex[15] wide,
To inclose the lock; now joins it, to divide.
Even then, before the fatal engine closed,
A wretched sylph too fondly interposed;
Fate urged the shears, and cut the sylph in twain,
(But airy substance soon unites again)
The meeting points the sacred hair dissever
From the fair head, for ever, and for ever!

Then flashed the living lightning from her eyes,
And screams of horror rend the affrighted skies.
Not louder shrieks to pitying Heaven are cast,
When husbands, or when lapdogs breathe their last;
Or when rich China vessels, fallen from high,
In glittering dust and painted fragments lie!

'Let wreaths of triumph now my temples twine,'
(The victor cried), 'the glorious prize is mine!
While fish in streams, or birds delight in air,
Or in a coach and six the British fair,
As long as Atalantis[16] shall be read,
Or the small pillow[17] grace a lady's bed,
While visits shall be paid on solemn days,
When numerous wax-lights in bright order blaze,
While nymphs take treats, or assignations give,
So long my honor, name, and praise shall live!
What Time would spare, from steel receives its date,[18]
And monuments, like men, submit to fate!
Steel could the labor of the gods destroy,
And strike to dust the imperial towers of Troy;
Steel could the works of mortal pride confound,
And hew triumphal arches to the ground.
What wonder then, fair nymph! thy hairs should feel
The conquering force of unresisted steel?'

---

[15] FORFEX—A pair of shears.

[16] ATALANTIS—*The New Atalantis* (1709), a popular romance by Mrs. Manley based on contemporary scandal.

[17] SMALL PILLOW—Used when ladies of fashion received their friends in their bedchambers according to the French custom.

[18] DATE—Ending.

## QUESTIONS AND EXERCISES

**Exercises preceded by a star are designed for assignment at the discretion of the teacher, or for any student who volunteers.**

1. What dream does Belinda have before she awakes? Who is responsible for the dream? What warning does he give her?
*2. From the *Odyssey* or from some other epic you have read, give instances of characters who are warned in dreams.
3. How was Belinda awakened? What caused her to forget the dream?
4. Contrast Belinda's ideas of making herself beautiful with those of a girl of today.
5. How does Belinda compare in beauty with the other belles of society? Describe her behavior. Memorize your favorite couplet in this description.
6. Why should the baron desire the curl?
7. How does the baron manage to effect the theft?
8. Why should Pope call a pair of scissors a two-edged weapon, a little engine, and a forfex?
9. Why is Ariel not able to warn Belinda of the danger? What happens to the sylph that tries to protect the curl?
10. What does the poem show us about the society of Pope's day?
11. Make a list of big words used for little things and explain why Pope should use them.
*12. Write a pantomime in several scenes based on *The Rape of the Lock.*
13. Find at least six couplets which you feel are neatly enough written and compressed enough to justify Swift's criticism of Pope as "Paper-sparing Pope." Memorize them.
14. What reasons can you give to explain why Pope's lines are so often quoted?
15. Select one couplet from the poem, and mark the scansion.
16. Topics for classroom report: *Characteristics of the Classical Period; Prose in the Age of Pope; The Man Pope.*

# THOMAS GRAY

## 1716–1771

Thomas Gray, the author of the famous *Elegy Written in a Country Churchyard,* was the most scholarly poet of his age.

There are few incidents to record in his life. Though as a child he was a weakling, he was the only one of twelve children to survive to manhood. He spent an unhappy childhood, partly because of his ill health and partly because of the tyranny of his father, who appears to have been a selfish, extravagant, violent man. This unhappy childhood gave Gray's whole life a tinge of melancholy noticeable in his poems.

Later he went to Eton School where his uncle was assistant master. From Eton he went to the University of Cambridge, where he became fast friends with Horace Walpole, the son of the Prime Minister, and of Richard West, whose father was Lord Chancellor. Gray's letters to these friends are among the best in literature. They reveal to us his shy retiring nature and his sly humor as well as his deep scholarship. At Cambridge Gray did not take a degree, for he disliked mathematics, which was required. He occupied himself with classical literature, history, and modern languages. Several of his translations and Latin poems were written during this time. He intended to study law, but after college Walpole took him abroad for a three year's tour of the Continent, an experience which Gray made the most of. He was keenly sensitive to beauty, especially that of nature, and was delighted by each new vista that unfolded before him. Unfortunately, the two friends quarreled, and Gray had to go back to England. After his return, Gray lived for a short time (1741–42) with his mother at Stoke Poges, a little village near Windsor and the scene of his famous *Elegy.* Here he wrote his *Ode on a Distant Prospect of Eton College* and probably sketched his *Elegy,* which was finished eight years later.

In 1742 he went to live at Peterhouse College, Cambridge, moving in 1756 to Pembroke Hall in the same college. He lived in scholarly seclusion the rest of his life, taking no part in the affairs of the university, seeing little company, but reading and studying and prowling among the books and manuscripts of the library. His interests took him into nearly every subject. A friend says of him, "Mr. Gray was perhaps the most learned man in Europe. He knew every branch of history both natural and civil; had read all the original historians of England, France, and Italy; and was a great antiquarian. Criticism, metaphysics, morals, politics, made up a principal part of his study. Voyages and travels of all sorts were his favourite amusements; and he had a fine taste in painting, prints, architecture and gardening." He was widely and accurately versed in botany and zoology, in ancient and modern literature, and in geography; and he was an excellent musician.

But the melancholy which had characterized him from childhood grew upon him. His depression of spirits prevented him from writing as his friends urged him to write. Only an occasional poem came from his pen. His reputation was such, however, that in 1757 he was offered the poet laureateship. Modest as ever, he refused it. In 1768 he was appointed Professor of Modern History and Languages at Cambridge. He talked of giving lectures, but because of ill health and chronic low spirits, no lectures were given. Indulging his love for traveling, he made short journeys to Scotland, Wales, and the English Lakes, and shortly before his death was even planning a visit to Switzerland. In 1771, he died and was buried in Stoke Poges Churchyard.

A summary of Gray's poetic development is really a summary of the history of eighteenth century lyric poetry. In form it was confined almost entirely to classical models, the ode and the elegy. We can mark three periods in his development: a classical period, a transitional period, and a romantic period. His early work reflects the conventions of the usual eighteenth century verse. In it we find elevated diction and emphasis upon good sense. His first published poem appeared in 1747, an *Ode on a Distant Prospect of Eton College.* It, as well as several other minor poems such as his *Hymn to Adversity* and his ode *To Spring,* shows the melancholy which characterizes much of the poetry of the mid-eighteenth century. It indicates also that Gray was not so much interested in the beauties of nature for their own sake as for a suitable background for the play of the human emotions he wished to express.

In his second or transitional period he clung to the general reflective type of elegy popular in his day but applied it directly to English life. The *Elegy Written in a Country Churchyard* is the most significant poem of this period. It shows the classical love for concise and quotable thoughts, but it includes much genuine personal emotion. In it he turns, as do the later romanticists, to speak of humble humanity. Dr. Samuel Johnson, the literary dictator of the middle of the century, says that it "abounds in images which find a mirror in every mind, and with sentiments to which every bosom returns an echo."

To his transitional period also belong two of his best known odes. *The Progress of Poesy* is strongly suggestive of Dryden's *Alexander's Feast,* but it contains more melody and a much greater variety of expression. The second, *The Bard,* thrills with the fire of an ancient and noble race of men. The bard is an old minstrel, the last of the Welsh singers, who stops King Edward and his army in a wild mountain pass to prophesy with poetic frenzy the doom of the tyrant. In this ode, the poet is going back to the early history of the nation.

In his third period Gray turned to a new field of romantic interest in two Norse poems, *The Fatal Sisters* and *The Descent of Odin* (1761). These odes are classical in form, but in content they represent his readings of Norse and early English sagas, favorite sources for the Romantic poets who followed him.

In most respects, Gray was a man of his century. He was a scholar, familiar with the intellectual interests of his age. His work has much of the polish and precision of the poets of his generation. While it is dominantly classical in its fastidious workmanship, it shows also the awakened interest in nature, in common man, and in medieval culture, sure signs of the approach of romanticism.

Critics have tried in many ways to account for the small volume of Gray's work. His importance is much in contrast with the slender volume of his poems. Though his *Letters* and his *Journal* are excellent reading, his fame rests on a few poems. The poet and critic, Matthew Arnold, believes that Gray suffered because he was one of the few true poets living in an age of prose. It is truly a fact that "he never spoke out" to the full extent of his powers. A few pages hold all his verse, yet in those few pages are to be found some of the greatest poetry between Milton and Wordsworth. The immense vogue of Pope and his style at first prevented Gray's reception. Except for the *Elegy,* which became popular at once, his poetry was of a type unfamiliar to his contemporaries. Pope and Dryden had conceived and composed poetry in the mind; genuine poetry is conceived in the soul. The sensitive soul of a reserved, delicate, serious poet like Gray is apt to be unhappy in such an age.

## ELEGY WRITTEN IN A COUNTRY CHURCHYARD

From the North Terrace of Windsor Castle, for centuries the chief residence of English sovereigns, you can see in the distance the spire of Stoke Poges Church. If you are tired of the pomp of kings, a visit to this peaceful churchyard where ancient trees cast shadows on the tombs will be a refreshing experience.

Let us suppose it is sunset time. Except for the sexton smoking his pipe in the cool of the evening, you are alone. As you sit on the bench beside a humble grave, the scene that meets your eyes is the same, with the exception of a few details, as that which Gray beheld nearly two hundred years ago. The yew tree still gives its grateful shade. From a neighboring field the tinkle of a bell is heard, and a little later from Windsor Castle come the deeper tones of the curfew.

At such a time and in such a rural seclusion, it is not difficult to conjure up the mood that inspired Gray to write his *Elegy.* The very stones with their fading inscriptions induce reflection; and if that reflection is of death, the melancholy has no tinge of bitterness or of horror. Millions have passed that way before; all paths lead but to the grave. No wonder that an experience so common, yet so filled with mystery, should awake the poetic instinct. Gray responded with a poem that still evokes a sad wonder at the riddle of life and death.

An elegy is a stately, dignified poem about death. Though it is usually written about the death of some definite person, Gray chose to deal with the theme in a general way. It is the common experience that interests him. The *Elegy Written in a Country Churchyard* (published 1751) is composed of three parts. The first three stanzas describe the quiet landscape at nightfall. Stanzas four to twenty-three inclusive make up the main body of the elegy and contain Gray's reflections on the lives of the humble men who rest in the churchyard, "each in his narrow cell for ever laid." The remainder of the poem is about Gray himself, his daily life and moods, and it concludes with the epitaph written for himself.

In the very first stanza of the *Elegy* the student can find three traces of the romantic spirit that will soon dominate poetry. The parting day, the lowing herd, and darkness suggest that feeling for nature which is part of the poetic awakening. The plowman indicates how far from the city and court life the characters of poetry have strayed. A humble rustic has crowded out the nobles, ladies of fashion, and the wits of Pope's day. And finally, the last word of the stanza, *me,* gives that intimate personal touch which is perhaps the most striking note of the romantic bards. Such literature, reflecting the thoughts and moods of the writer himself, we call subjective. It is the effect of the churchyard scene on Gray that is the interesting feature of the *Elegy.*

For a poem of such length as the *Elegy,* Gray has been amazingly successful in sustaining the mood. Not once is the tone of "intimate and sad sincerity" broken. The poem has the beautiful consistency of a true work of art. It is reported that General Wolfe recited the *Elegy* before the battle of Quebec and declared he had rather be the author of the poem than the conqueror of the city.

The Curfew[1] tolls the knell of parting day,
  The lowing herd wind slowly o'er the lea,
The plowman homeward plods his weary way,
  And leaves the world to darkness and to me.

Now fades the glimmering landscape on the sight,
  And all the air a solemn stillness holds,
Save where the beetle wheels his droning flight,
  And drowsy tinklings lull the distant folds;

Save that, from yonder ivy-mantled tower,
  The moping owl does to the moon complain
Of such, as wandering near her secret bower,
  Molest her ancient solitary reign.

[1] CURFEW—The regulation, dating from the Middle Ages, requiring that fires be covered or put out on the ringing of a bell at a fixed hour in the evening, was still in effect in Gray's time.

Ewing Galloway, N. Y.

THE CHURCHYARD AT STOKE POGES

Here Gray composed his famous *Elegy*. Even today, when evening falls, the visitor to this quiet country churchyard may feel the atmosphere that inspired the poet.

Beneath those rugged elms, that yew-tree's shade,
  Where heaves the turf in many a mouldering heap,
Each in his narrow cell for ever laid,
  The rude forefathers of the hamlet sleep.

The breezy call of incense-breathing Morn,
  The swallow twittering from the straw-built shed,
The cock's shrill clarion, or the echoing horn,
  No more shall rouse them from their lowly bed.

For them no more the blazing hearth shall burn,
  Or busy housewife ply her evening care:
No children run to lisp their sire's return,
  Or climb his knees the envied kiss to share.

Oft did the harvest to their sickle yield,
  Their furrow oft the stubborn glebe[2] has broke;
How jocund did they drive their team afield:
  How bowed the woods beneath their sturdy stroke!

Let not Ambition mock their useful toil,
  Their homely joys, and destiny obscure;
Nor Grandeur hear with a disdainful smile
  The short and simple annals of the poor.

The boast of heraldry,[3] the pomp of power,
  And all that beauty, all that wealth e'er gave,
Awaits alike the inevitable hour.
  The paths of glory lead but to the grave.

Nor you, ye Proud, impute to These the fault,
  If Memory o'er their Tomb no Trophies raise,
Where through the long-drawn aisle and fretted vault[4]
  The pealing anthem swells the note of praise.

---

[2] GLEBE—Farm soil.
[3] BOAST OF HERALDRY—Pride in high descent and noble family.
[4] FRETTED VAULT—The ornamented arched roof of the church.

Can storied urn[5] or animated bust
  Back to its mansion call the fleeting breath?
Can Honor's voice provoke[6] the silent dust,
  Or Flattery soothe the dull cold ear of Death?

Perhaps in this neglected spot is laid
  Some heart once pregnant with celestial fire;
Hands, that the rod of empire might have swayed,
  Or waked to ecstasy the living lyre.

But Knowledge to their eyes her ample page
  Rich with the spoils of time[7] did ne'er unroll;[8]
Chill Penury repressed their noble rage,[9]
  And froze the genial current of the soul.

Full many a gem of purest ray serene,
  The dark unfathomed caves of ocean bear:
Full many a flower is born to blush unseen,
  And waste its sweetness on the desert air.

Some village Hampden,[10] that with dauntless breast
  The little Tyrant of his fields withstood;
Some mute inglorious Milton here may rest,
  Some Cromwell[11] guiltless of his country's blood.

The applause of listening senates to command,
  The threats of pain and ruin to despise,
To scatter plenty o'er a smiling land,
  And read their history in a nation's eyes,

---

[5] STORIED URN—A burial urn on which is an inscription telling of the deeds of the dead.

[6] PROVOKE—Wake to life.

[7] SPOILS OF TIME—Treasures of knowledge accumulated through the ages.

[8] UNROLL—Before the invention of printing, books were long parchment rolls.

[9] RAGE—Poetical genius or enthusiasm.

[10] HAMPDEN—John Hampden (1594–1643), one of the chief heroes of tht Puritan Revolution; a statesman who resisted Charles the First's tax of "ship money" and stood with Oliver Cromwell in opposition to despotic government.

[11] CROMWELL—Oliver Cromwell (1599–1658), the leader of the Puritan Revolution. Gray like many men of his century believed that Cromwell was guilty of having sacrificed the blood of his country to his own ambitions.

Their lot forbade: nor circumscribed alone
  Their growing virtues, but their crimes confin'd;
Forbade to wade through slaughter to a throne,
  And shut the gates of mercy on mankind,

The struggling pangs of conscious truth to hide,
  To quench the blushes of ingenuous shame,
Or heap the shrine of Luxury and Pride
  With incense kindled at the Muse's flame.[12]

Far from the madding[13] crowd's ignoble strife,
  Their sober wishes never learned to stray;
Along the cool sequestered vale of life
  They kept the noiseless tenor of their way.

Yet even these bones from insult to protect,
  Some frail memorial[14] still erected nigh,
With uncouth rhymes and shapeless sculpture decked,
  Implores the passing tribute of a sigh.

Their name, their years, spelt by the unlettered muse,[15]
  The place of fame and elegy supply;
And many a holy text around she strews,
  That teach the rustic moralist to die.

For who to dumb Forgetfulness a prey,
  This pleasing anxious being e'er resigned,
Left the warm precincts of the cheerful day,
  Nor cast one longing lingering look behind?

On some fond breast the parting soul relies,
  Some pious drops the closing eye requires;
Ev'n from the tomb the voice of Nature cries,[16]
  Ev'n in our Ashes live their wonted Fires.

---

[12] OR HEAP THE SHRINE . . . FLAME—Gray refers to the practice of writing to flatter the rich and great as a means of securing position and wealth.

[13] MADDING—Mad, or frenzied.

[14] MEMORIAL—Headstone.

[15] SPELT BY THE UNLETTERED MUSE—Written by an uneducated poet. Some of the headstones have misspelled inscriptions.

[16] THE VOICE OF NATURE CRIES—That is, our natural affections and desire to be remembered are still alive after our bodies are buried.

For thee,[17] who mindful of the unhonored Dead
  Dost in these lines their artless tale relate,
If chance,[18] by lonely contemplation led,
  Some kindred Spirit shall inquire thy fate,

Haply some hoary-headed Swain may say,
  'Oft have we seen him at the peep of dawn
Brushing with hasty steps the dews away
  To meet the sun upon the upland lawn.

'There at the foot of yonder nodding beech
  That wreathes its old fantastic roots so high,
His listless length at noontide would he stretch,
  And pore upon the brook that babbles by.

'Hard by yon wood, now smiling as in scorn,
  Muttering his wayward fancies he would rove,
Now drooping, woeful wan, like one forlorn,
  Or crazed with care, or crossed in hopeless love.

'One morn I missed him on the customed hill,
  Along the heath and near his favorite tree;
Another came; nor yet beside the rill,
  Nor up the lawn, nor at the wood was he;

'The next with dirges due in sad array
  Slow through the church-way path we saw him borne.
Approach and read (for thou can'st read) the lay,
  Graved on the stone beneath yon agèd thorn.'

### THE EPITAPH

*Here rests his head upon the lap of Earth*
  *A Youth to Fortune and to Fame unknown.*
*Fair Science frowned not on his humble birth,*
  *And Melancholy marked him for her own.*

---

[17] THEE—Gray, who is writing this poem.
[18] CHANCE—Perchance.

*Large was his bounty, and his soul sincere,*
*Heav'n did a recompense as largely send:*
*He gave to Misery all he had, a tear,*
*He gained from Heaven ('t was all he wished) a friend.*

*No farther seek his merits to disclose,*
*Or draw his frailties from their dread abode*
*(There they alike in trembling hope repose),*
*The bosom of his Father and his God.*

## QUESTIONS AND EXERCISES

**Exercises preceded by a star are designed for assignment at the discretion of the teacher, or for any student who volunteers.**

1. What signs of approaching nightfall does the poet note in the opening stanzas? How does the atmosphere of twilight musing which Gray establishes in these lines prepare the reader for the reflections on life and death?
2. Why is the churchyard a fitting setting for the poem?
3. Describe the life, as the poet suggests it to you, of the men who sleep in the churchyard.
4. Why are they as worthy of a poet's lines as men of fame? What may have prevented them from winning fame?
5. What references does Gray make in this poem to his own stay in the neighborhood (at Stoke Poges)?

*6. Some critics think the epitaph more artificial in diction than the rest of the poem. Do you agree or disagree? Why?

7. What is the rime scheme used in the poem? What is the length of the lines? This stanza form is often called the "elegiac stanza."

*8. Note in this poem the careful choice of words. For example, note the quiet, subdued impression which the mellow *o's* give to the opening stanza. Find other passages where you feel that the sound helps the sense.

9. Search for examples of diction which seem to you to show Gray's classical leanings.
10. What in the poem shows Gray's romantic leanings? What word in the first stanza gives the subjective, or intimately personal, touch that is characteristic of romanticism?
11. In the fifteenth stanza, the original form of the poem contained the names of Cato, Tully (Cicero), and Cæsar instead of the English names of Hampden, Milton, and Cromwell. How is the change indicative of Gray's departure from the poetic fashions of classicism?
12. Memorize your favorite passages from this poem.

# WILLIAM COWPER[1]

## 1731–1800

William Cowper records his own thoughts and feelings with an intimate sincerity and self-revelation wholly unlike the writing of most of the eighteenth century poets. Cowper wrote some verse as a young man, but he is remembered for the work he did after he was fifty years old. It was at about that age that he turned to poetry as a means of escape for his distressed mind and spirit. For Cowper was shy and timid, and he found life filled with terrors for him.

He was born in 1731 in Hertfordshire, where his father was an English clergyman. Cowper was a delicate, sensitive child, whose life was saddened by the early death of his mother and by his neglect at home. When six years old he was sent away to a private school for boys where he was made miserable by his schoolmates. Even their well-meaning fun distressed him. One, more of a bully than the rest, terrified him so much that he never dared look at his face, but recognized his enemy by his shoe-buckles and shivered at his approach. These school experiences affected his mind and health. After attending Westminster School for a short time, he became a member of the Middle Temple where he studied and practiced law for about ten years. During this period he fell in love with his cousin, Theodora Cowper, but their marriage was prevented by her father. This disappointment seems to have prepared the way for his first attack of insanity in 1763. The immediate cause, however, was the necessity of taking a public law examination to qualify for a clerkship in the House of Lords which his uncle had secured for him. He became so terrified at the thoughts of the examination that he attempted to take his own life. The experience unsettled his mind, and for over a year he remained in an asylum.

Since Cowper at the death of his father had received sufficient money to make it unnecessary for him to struggle for his daily bread, he now was enabled to give up his law work in London and go to live at Huntingdon. There he met the Reverend Morley Unwin and his wife, Mary Unwin. They were cultured, kindly people who recognized the genius of this shy, melancholy man. They took him into their household, watched over him, protected his sensitive mind from the shocks to which it was still subject. After her husband's death, Mrs. Unwin continued to care for Cowper as a mother or elder sister. She and Cowper moved to the little village of Olney, attracted there by the fame of an evangelical clergyman.

Here Cowper lived a simple, deeply religious life. He was never happy for very long at a time. He was sometimes thrown into madness

[1] Cowper (kōō'pẽr).

by the terrible thought of God's wrath. "My mind has always a melancholy cast," he once wrote, "and is like some pools I have seen, which, though filled with a black and putrid water, will nevertheless in a bright day reflect the sunbeams from their surface." Through all these fits of depression Mrs. Unwin's care made his life on the whole a quiet one. He was loved in the village. Most of his time he spent in the simple pursuits of gardening, carpentering, visiting the sick, caring for his numerous pets, and rambling through the lanes.

It was at Olney that Cowper turned to writing poetry. His first volume was a collection of hymns, the *Olney Hymns,* published in 1779. Among them are the well-known ones beginning with the lines, "Oh! for a closer walk with God," and "There is a fountain filled with blood." These were followed by a volume of didactic poems written in the heroic couplet on such themes as "The Progress of Error," but sweetened by his gentle devout nature. His third volume, 1785, contains his greatest work, including as it does, *The Task,* and the humorous ballad, *The Diverting History of John Gilpin. The Task* is his greatest work. The title was given it humorously because his friend, Lady Austen, had asked him to write a poem in blank verse upon some subject or other, for instance, the sofa. He called the first book of this long poem *The Sofa.* In *The Task* Cowper turns from the artificial and conventional subjects which had been popular and describes the simple beauties of nature and the joys of country life. "God made the country, and man the town," he writes.

Cowper says that he described no spot which he had not seen, and expressed no emotion which he had not felt. Sincerity rings through all his poems. Though love of rural scenes was not common in his day, his interest in didactic subjects made him one of the popular poets of his time. Besides being a poet interested in nature scenes, a hymn writer, and a writer of humorous verse, he was also a translator of Homer and, like Gray, an excellent letter writer. These letters reveal the source of his poetic gifts, his gentle mischievousness, and his familiarity with the common things of life. He despises nothing as too homely or too trivial for his pen. From him we have received some of the loveliest pictures of the simple country life of his day.

## THE DIVERTING HISTORY OF JOHN GILPIN[1]

A ballad such as this famous one is a far cry from the didactic and satirical poetry of the classicists. In 1765, Percy had published his *Reliques,* a collection of early English ballads. *John Gilpin* is one of the earliest of the literary ballads, a type which was to be perfected by the romantic poet Coleridge in *The Rime of the Ancient Mariner.* It

[1] THE DIVERTING HISTORY OF JOHN GILPIN—The story of John Gilpin's ride was told to Cowper by his friend, Lady Austen, who had heard it as a child. It caused the poet a sleepless night, we are told, as he was kept awake by laughter at it. During these restless hours he turned it into the famous ballad.

became immediately so popular that it was printed everywhere in newspapers and magazines. It was even sung as a common ballad in the streets. In it Cowper throws all literary fashions aside and spontaneously sings this rollicking tale. In this very spontaneity he shows himself a worthy predecessor of the romanticists.

John Gilpin was a citizen
Of credit and renown,
A trainband[2] captain eke was he
Of famous London town.

John Gilpin's spouse said to her dear,
"Though wedded we have been
These twice ten tedious years, yet we
No holiday have seen.

To-morrow is our wedding day,
And we will then repair
Unto the Bell at Edmonton,[3]
All in a chaise and pair.[4]

My sister, and my sister's child,
Myself, and children three,
Will fill the chaise; so you must ride
On horseback after we."

He soon replied,—"I do admire
Of womankind but one,
And you are she, my dearest dear,
Therefore it shall be done.

I am a linendraper bold,
As all the world doth know,
And my good friend the calender[5]
Will lend his horse to go."

---

[2] Trainband—A band or company of citizens, partaking of the nature both of militia and volunteers.

[3] Bell at Edmonton—An inn. Edmonton and the other places named in the poem are north of London.

[4] Chaise and pair—A chaise was a two- or four-wheeled carriage, usually drawn by one horse. For this special occasion, Mrs. Gilpin will have a pair of horses.

[5] Calender—A man who operated a calender machine which was used for pressing and finishing cloth.

Quoth Mrs. Gilpin,—"That's well said;
And for that wine is dear,
We will be furnished with our own,
Which is both bright and clear."

John Gilpin kissed his loving wife;
O'erjoyed was he to find,
That, though on pleasure she was bent,
She had a frugal mind.

The morning came, the chaise was brought,
But yet was not allowed
To drive up to the door, lest all
Should say that she was proud.

So three doors off the chaise was stayed,
Where they did all get in;
Six precious souls, and all agog
To dash through thick and thin.

Smack went the whip, round went the wheels,
Were never folk so glad,
The stones did rattle underneath,
As if Cheapside[6] were mad.

John Gilpin at his horse's side
Seized fast the flowing mane,
And up he got, in haste to ride,
But soon came down again;

For saddletree scarce reached had he,
His journey to begin,
When turning round his head, he saw
Three customers come in.

So down he came; for loss of time,
Although it grieved him sore,
Yet loss of pence, full well he knew,
Would trouble him much more.

[6] CHEAPSIDE—A section of London.

'Twas long before the customers
  Were suited to their mind,
When Betty screaming came down stairs,
  "The wine is left behind!"

"Good lack!" quoth he, "yet bring it me
  My leathern belt likewise,
In which I bear my trusty sword
  When I do exercise."

Now Mistress Gilpin (careful soul!)
  Had two stone bottles found,
To hold the liquor that she loved,
  And keep it safe and sound.

Each bottle had a curling ear,
  Through which the belt he drew,
And hung a bottle on each side
  To make his balance true.

Then over all, that he might be
  Equipped from top to toe,
His long red cloak, well brushed and neat,
  He manfully did throw.

Now see him mounted once again
  Upon his nimble steed,
Full slowly pacing o'er the stones,
  With caution and good heed.

But finding soon a smoother road
  Beneath his well-shod feet,
The snorting beast began to trot,
  Which galled him in his seat.

So "Fair and softly," John he cried,
  But John he cried in vain;
That trot became a gallop soon,
  In spite of curb and rein.

So stooping down, as needs he must
Who cannot sit upright,
He grasped the mane with both his hands
And eke with all his might.

His horse, who never in that sort
Had handled been before,
What thing upon his back had got
Did wonder more and more.

Away went Gilpin, neck or nought;
Away went hat and wig;
He little dreamt, when he set out,
Of running such a rig.

The wind did blow, the cloak did fly,
Like streamer long and gay,
Till, loop and button failing both,
At last it flew away.

Then might all people well discern
The bottles he had slung;
A bottle swinging at each side
As hath been said or sung.

The dogs did bark, the children screamed,
Up flew the windows all;
And every soul cried out, "Well done!"
As loud as he could bawl.

Away went Gilpin—who but he?
His fame soon spread around;
"He carries weight!" "He rides a race!"
" 'Tis for a thousand pound!"

And still as fast as he drew near,
'Twas wonderful to view,
How in a trice the turnpike men[7]
Their gates wide open threw.

---

[7] TURNPIKE MEN—Men who kept toll-gates where according to law a small charge was made to all travelers passing through.

And now, as he went bowing down,
His reeking head full low,
The bottles twain behind his back
Were shattered at a blow.

Down ran the wine into the road,
Most piteous to be seen,
Which made his horse's flanks to smoke
As they had basted been.

But still he seemed to carry weight,
With leathern girdle braced;
For all might see the bottle necks
Still dangling at his waist.

Thus all through merry Islington,
These gambols he did play,
Until he came unto the Wash
Of Edmonton so gay;

And there he threw the Wash about,
On both sides of the way,
Just like unto a trundling mop,
Or a wild goose at play.

At Edmonton, his loving wife
From the balcony spied
Her tender husband, wondering much
To see how he did ride.

"Stop, stop, John Gilpin!—Here's the house!"
They all at once did cry;
"The dinner waits, and we are tired:"—
Said Gilpin—"So am I!"

But yet his horse was not a whit
Inclined to tarry there;
For why?—his owner had a house
Full ten miles off, at Ware.

So like an arrow swift he flew
  Shot by an archer strong;
So did he fly—which brings me to
  The middle of my song.

Away went Gilpin, out of breath,
  And sore against his will,
Till, at his friend the calender's,
  His horse at last stood still.

The calender, amazed to see
  His neighbor in such trim,
Laid down his pipe, flew to the gate,
  And thus accosted him:

"What news? what news? your tidings tell!
  Tell me you must and shall—
Say why bareheaded you are come,
  Or why you come at all?"

Now Gilpin had a pleasant wit,
  And loved a timely joke;
And thus unto the calender,
  In merry guise, he spoke:

"I came because your horse would come;
  And, if I well forebode,
My hat and wig will soon be here,—
  They are upon the road."

The calender, right glad to find
  His friend in merry pin,
Returned him not a single word,
  But to the house went in;

Whence straight he came with hat and wig;
  A wig that flowed behind,
A hat not much the worse for wear,
  Each comely in its kind.

He held them up, and in his turn,
  Thus showed his ready wit:
"My head is twice as big as yours,
  They therefore needs must fit.

But let me scrape the dirt away
  That hangs upon your face;
And stop and eat, for well you may
  Be in a hungry case."

Said John,—"It is my wedding day,
  And all the world would stare,
If wife should dine at Edmonton,
  And I should dine at Ware."

So turning to his horse, he said,
  "I am in haste to dine;
'Twas for your pleasure you came here,
  You shall go back for mine."

Ah! luckless speech, and bootless boast,
  For which he paid full dear;
For while he spake, a braying ass
  Did sing most loud and clear;

Whereat his horse did snort, as he
  Had heard a lion roar,
And galloped off with all his might,
  As he had done before.

Away went Gilpin, and away
  Went Gilpin's hat and wig:
He lost them sooner than at first,
  For why?—they were too big.

Now Mistress Gilpin, when she saw
  Her husband posting down
Into the country far away,
  She pulled out half a crown;

And thus unto the youth she said,
  That drove them to the Bell,
"This shall be yours, when you bring back
  My husband safe and well."

The youth did ride, and soon did meet
  John coming back amain;
Whom in a trice he tried to stop
  By catching at his rein;

But not performing what he meant,
  And gladly would have done,
The frighted steed he frighted more
  And made him faster run.

Away went Gilpin, and away
  Went postboy at his heels,
The postboy's horse right glad to miss
  The lumbering of the wheels.

Six gentlemen upon the road,
  Thus seeing Gilpin fly,
With postboy scampering in the rear,
  They raised the hue and cry:—

"Stop thief! stop thief!—a highwayman!"
  Not one of them was mute;
And all and each that passed that way
  Did join in the pursuit.

And now the turnpike-gates again
  Flew open in short space;
The toll-men thinking as before,
  That Gilpin rode a race.

And so he did, and won it too,
  For he got first to town;
Nor stopped till where he had got up
  He did again get down.

Now let us sing long live the King,
And Gilpin, long live he;
And when he next doth ride abroad,
May I be there to see!

## QUESTIONS AND EXERCISES

Exercises preceded by a star are designed for assignment at the discretion of the teacher, or for any student who volunteers.

1. Which lines in the description of John Gilpin and Mistress Gilpin did you find the most delightfully revealing of their characters?
2. What parts of the description show you their place in society?
3. Tell the story of the poem.
4. Write an imaginary dialogue representing what took place when Mistress Gilpin returned that evening.

*5. Review the characteristics of the ballad type of poetry and determine how well Cowper succeeds in following the form of the ancient ballad. Compare it with the literary ballads you know.

## TO MRS. UNWIN

Cowper's most intimate friends were the Reverend Morley Unwin and his wife Mary. Cowper began to live with them as a boarder in 1765. He and the lovers of literature owe a debt to Mrs. Unwin who cared for the poet until her death in 1796. That Cowper felt deep gratitude to her is shown in this sincere tribute, as well as in another moving poem entitled *To Mary.*

This poem has a form not used by the classicists. It is a sonnet, a form extremely popular among the Elizabethan writers. This sonnet is written in the form perfected by Shakespeare, being made up of three four-line groups called quatrains, and a couplet. It is one of the most difficult of poetic forms, and Cowper deserves credit for being one of the few poets of his age to write it artistically. As a personal expression of the poet's emotions, it registers another mile-post passed in the trend toward romanticism.

Mary! I want a lyre with other strings;
Such aid from Heaven as some have feigned they drew!
An eloquence scarce given to mortals, new,
And undebased by praise of meaner things!

That, ere through age or woe I shed my wings,[1]
I may record thy worth, with honor due,

---

[1] Ere . . . I shed my wings—That is, of song. Before I lose the power to write poetry.

In verse as musical as thou art true,—
Verse, that immortalizes whom it sings!

But thou hast little need: there is a book,
By seraphs writ with beams of heavenly light,
On which the eyes of God not rarely look;
A chronicle of actions just and bright!

There all thy deeds, my faithful Mary, shine,
And since thou own'st that praise, I spare thee mine.

## QUESTIONS AND EXERCISES

1. Explain the fifth line in the light of what you know of Cowper's life.
2. How can verse immortalize whom it sings?

Rudolph Lesch from Publishers' Photo Service, N. Y.

OLIVER GOLDSMITH

**Though known to his friends as an irresponsible, lovable ne'er-do-well, Oliver Goldsmith proved to be a literary genius. He gave new life to three types of literature—poetry, drama, and the novel.**

# OLIVER GOLDSMITH

## 1728–1774

When Oliver Goldsmith, the lovable, irresponsible poet, essayist, novelist, and dramatist, remarks that " no person ever had a better knack of hoping than I," he gives us the real key to his character. Dr. Johnson, speaking of him, says: "No man was more foolish when he had not a pen in his hand, or more wise when he had." "Poor Noll," as he was sometimes called, surprised every one by contributing something of lasting worth to almost every branch of literature.

One vivid picture of him as a lad is preserved for us. A boy, just turned sixteen and freed at last from the discipline of a school in a town some miles from his home in Ireland, is riding a broken-down nag through the growing dusk. He is thinking that soon he will be going up to college in Dublin—provided his father can spare the money. Or maybe he will have to earn his own way. His sister has recently married a wealthy young fellow, and his father, with the pride of a poor man, has insisted on giving her a dowry of £400. That gesture well-nigh emptied the family purse. Oh well, there's no use worrying. Something will turn up.

Take a good look at this young man. He is an ungainly youth, snub-nosed, pock-marked. His expression is almost stupid, but a look of imperishable good humor enlivens the face. A happy-go-lucky fellow, you would say, but lacking in self confidence, easily taken in, suffering from a sense of inferiority. Possibly it is this very feeling of inferiority that explains the airs he sometimes puts on. Just now the single gold guinea in his pocket is giving him an exaggerated sense of wealth. When darkness overtakes him at a little town, he asks a villager in a quite superior manner where he can find "the best house in town," meaning of course the best inn. But the villager is a wag. He sizes up the stranger and directs him, not to the tavern, but to the private home of the village squire.

The scene that follows would be painful if it were not so comic. Oliver Goldsmith, for it is he, putting on the airs of a gentleman, ordering his host about as if he were but an innkeeper, never once aware that the squire is enjoying the joke to the top of his bent. Poor Noll! He even condescends to invite the squire, the squire's wife, and the pretty daughter to join him in a glass of wine at supper. One can imagine his embarrassment when the misunderstanding is explained. It made such an impression on young Goldsmith that years later he built a play on the episode, a play that still holds a charm for modern audiences—*She Stoops to Conquer.*

Oliver Goldsmith was born in 1728 at the little village of Pallas, Ireland. His father was a humble Irish curate, poorly paid, yet as the poet was later to describe him, "passing rich with forty pounds a year." A year or two after Oliver's birth, the family moved to the neighborhood of Lissoy, a quiet country town resembling the "sweet Auburn" of *The Deserted Village*. Most of Goldsmith's early teachers agreed that he was a "blockhead"; but he wasn't really stupid, only lazy and irresponsible. One among them, however, caught the boy's fancy. That was Thomas (Paddy) Byrne, who had been a soldier in the Queen Anne Wars and loved to talk about his experiences as a vagabond. Paddy was romantic like most Irishmen, believed in fairies and pixies, and filled Goldsmith's head with folklore and Irish rogue tales.

There is a tradition that at an early age Oliver began to write verses. This is scarcely significant, for many a youngster who turns out to be a hard-headed business man later in life has had his period of scribbling rimes. Besides, Goldsmith's true talents did not manifest themselves until he was nearly forty. Unless we can say that mischievousness and lack of thrift are evidences of genius, there is little in his youth to suggest the great literary artist.

At the age of sixteen Goldsmith went up to Trinity College, Dublin, not as a pensioner, whose expenses are paid, but as a sizar, who performs menial labor about the college to pay for his tuition. Neither in school nor college were his student days particularly happy. He continually got into scrapes, seldom had any money and if he had, made haste to spend it. His unprepossessing appearance made him the butt of jokes and pranks. Once he narrowly missed being expelled from college after engaging in a riot whose purpose was the rescue of a fellow student from the clutches of a bailiff. Another time, having brought down the wrath of his tutor by staging a wild party in his room, he sold all his books and ran away. Penniless, he nearly starved before he made his way to Lissoy. To make matters worse, his father died, leaving him without funds to continue his studies.

In this extremity, as in many others, his Uncle Contarine stood by him, helping with advice and money. Though Oliver seldom took the advice, he had no scruples about spending the money. Back at college, he continued his old ways. He was always in debt, always in trouble, always coming home cheerfully impenitent. The best begging-letter-writer in the world, some one has called him.

When Goldsmith took his degree at Trinity College, last on the list as he had been lowest in the entrance examinations, he started out in the world apparently without the slightest idea of what he should do for a living. He studied for the ministry, but failed to qualify. He tried teaching without success. Once, he set forth to make his fortune equipped with a good horse and with gold coins jingling in his pocket. Some time later he returned, his money gone, his good horse traded for a sorry nag, and told a flimsy tale about having missed his ship to America. In that ship were all his possessions. At least, that was his story, and he stuck to it; but some of us will join Thackeray in being surprised that his mother and Uncle Contarine believed it. It has all the earmarks of a piece of fiction.

Law study in London was his next venture, but he lost money at cards and returned to his relatives as good-natured and helpless as ever. Then he took up medicine at Edinburgh, gambled as usual, but somehow convinced his family that schools on the Continent offered better opportunities in medical instruction for such genius as his. At any rate, we next see him wandering through Europe, singing and playing his flute for supper and lodging for all the world like the minstrels of old. Sometimes he lined his pockets with gambling winnings, only to send Uncle Contarine some rare tulip bulbs or to squander it all on a merry feast. He may have studied a little, however, for he finally turned up in London with what purported to be a medical degree. Unfortunately, it failed to obtain him an appointment as a physician.

Goldsmith never saw Ireland again. Until he was thirty he did hack-writing in London, turning out reviews, occasional essays, anything that would bring in a pound or two. Here and there some of the sly humor and delicious turns of phrase that mark his later work crop up in these early pieces, but there is nothing to indicate he will presently be hailed as the greatest poet since Pope. His first attempt at ambitious writing, *An Inquiry into the State of Polite Learning in Europe,* published anonymously as was all his early work, won him an offer to become a contributor to *The Bee,* a weekly magazine similar to the *Spectator* of Addison's day. Some of his essays in *The Bee* are delightfully whimsical. By a series of papers, called *The Citizen of the World,* purporting to be letters from a Chinaman to a London friend, and by a life of Beau Nash, famous fop and gambler of the time, Goldsmith succeeded in pulling himself up one more rung of the literary ladder. Dr. Johnson took an interest in him and included him in the original group that formed the renowned Literary Club, among whose members were such men as Sir Joshua Reynolds, the painter, and Edmund Burke, later famous for his eloquent defense of the American Colonies.

Goldsmith's great period began in 1764 with the publication of his long poem, *The Traveller.* Even his intimates of the Literary Club could not believe that Poor Noll had written such magnificent verse, and many, including Boswell, whispered that Johnson was the real author. For the first time Goldsmith affixed his signature to a major work, and his fame increased. When *The Vicar of Wakefield* appeared two years later, it was readily admitted that a most charming, versatile author had arisen, for this work rescued the novel from the coarseness into which it had fallen and gave new life to that form. Having contributed something original to the fields of poetry and the novel, Goldsmith then tried his hand at drama. His *Good Natured Man* and *She Stoops to Conquer* are as historically important in this branch of literature as are *The Traveller* and *The Deserted Village* in poetry, or *The Vicar of Wakefield* in prose. These two plays brought back real side-splitting comedy to the stage, which for fifty years had seen little but the insipid "genteel comedies" which we now call "sentimental drama."

In the light of these varied accomplishments, it is no wonder that Johnson, who wrote Goldsmith's epitaph, should record that he "touched nothing that he did not adorn." How tragic that in 1774, at the age of forty-six, at the height of his powers, Goldsmith should succumb to a fever aggravated by worries! He died as he had lived—in debt. The discovery that he owed £2,000 nipped in the bud his friends' plan to give him a public funeral and a tomb in Westminster Abbey. Later, however, the Literary Club raised a fund by public subscription and placed a bust of Goldsmith in the Poets' Corner. Johnson wrote the inscription, in Latin as one might expect, saying in his dictatorial way that "he would never consent to disgrace the walls of Westminster Abbey with an English inscription." And so one of the most English of writers, a rebel against many classical traditions, is honored by an epitaph in a dead language. Goldsmith himself would enjoy the irony of it.

## THE DESERTED VILLAGE

As a poet, Goldsmith partly conformed to, partly rebelled against, the tradition of Dryden and Pope. Though he rejected blank verse and the ode form developed by Gray, his use of the heroic couplet is different from Pope's. The sense flows more freely from one couplet to the next. He felt that poetry should be addressed to the heart. In him we see again a poet at first dominated by the classical standards of his age, but turning to romantic interests in his greatest work. *The Traveller* made Goldsmith's reputation with his contemporaries, who hailed it as the greatest poem of the age. Though a masterpiece of reflective and descriptive poetry, it is interesting to us principally as showing Goldsmith under the influence of the classical ideals. It is a long poem in heroic couplets, giving a survey of the social life of the various countries of Europe and reflecting many of Goldsmith's wanderings and impressions. *The Deserted Village* (1770), though written in the same couplet form, reveals to us the love of human nature which is so outstanding a characteristic of Goldsmith. Here is honest human sympathy for the humble. Here is revolt against institutions in favor of the individual. It is a pastoral lyric that possesses in its finest lines no artifice but the genuine emotion which grows poetical at beholding the joys of the peasantry or takes fire at seeing those joys pass into sorrows. No other poet of his age expresses with such tender pathos his sympathy for the poor, and with such hot indignation his feelings against a government that has made laws to grind the poor and elevate the rich. The naturalness and ease of his poetry show him an accomplished artist. Like the classicists, he gives us exquisitely chiseled imagery and elegance of diction; but there is a softness of music in his poetry that we look for in vain among them.

The greatness of *The Deserted Village* lies in its descriptions of village life and in its characters of the village preacher and the village schoolmaster. There are hardly any lines in English literature more familiar than some of these. Outside of Shakespeare and Pope there are few lines more often quoted.

But the reader of the poem is interested too in Goldsmith's attitude toward economic problems. Goldsmith held that the permanent strength of a nation must rest upon its small independent land-holders and that the life of such people is the happiest and freest. He believed that the accumulation of great landed estates, with its accompanying luxury, was a bad thing for the country. He deplored laws and customs which made it possible for powerful lords and squires to crush out the small land-holders and convert the land into parks and hunting grounds, thus making it necessary for the peasants to flock to the cities or emigrate to America.

Here then, in spite of the use of the heroic couplet, we feel the imminence of the romantic period. The love of nature and simple country life, the democratic sentiments that foreshadow political changes, the faithful descriptions of landscape, the creation of individual characters, and finally the sincerity of the emotions—these herald a new poetry that is to sweep away the old forms and themes and give freer rein to poetic feeling.

Sweet Auburn![1] loveliest village of the plain;
Where health and plenty cheered the laboring swain,
Where smiling spring its earliest visit paid,
And parting summer's lingering blooms delayed:
Dear lovely bowers of innocence and ease,
Seats of my youth, when every sport could please,
How often have I loitered o'er thy green,
Where humble happiness endeared each scene!
How often have I paused on every charm,
The sheltered cot, the cultivated farm,
The never-failing brook, the busy mill,
The decent church that topped the neighboring hill,
The hawthorn bush, with seats beneath the shade,
For talking age and whispering lovers made!
How often have I blest the coming day,
When toil remitting lent its turn to play,
And all the village train, from labor free,
Led up their sports beneath the spreading tree,
While many a pastime circled in the shade,

[1] Auburn—Goldsmith is probably referring to no special town, though the poem includes many descriptions based on memories of Lissoy, Ireland.

The young contending as the old surveyed;
And many a gambol frolicked o'er the ground,
And sleights of art and feats of strength went round.
And still, as each repeated pleasure tired,
Succeeding sports the mirthful band inspired;
The dancing pair that simply sought renown,
By holding out to tire each other down;
The swain mistrustless of his smutted face,
While secret laughter tittered round the place;
The bashful virgin's side-long looks of love,
The matron's glance that would those looks reprove:
These were thy charms, sweet village! sports like these,
With sweet succession, taught even toil to please:
These round thy bowers their cheerful influence shed:
These were thy charms—but all these charms are fled.

Sweet smiling village, loveliest of the lawn,
Thy sports are fled, and all thy charms withdrawn;
Amidst thy bowers the tyrant's hand[2] is seen,
And desolation saddens all thy green:
One only master grasps the whole domain,
And half a tillage[3] stints thy smiling plain.
No more thy glassy brook reflects the day,
But, choked with sedges, works its weedy way;
Along thy glades, a solitary guest,
The hollow sounding bittern guards its nest:
Amidst thy desert walks the lapwing flies,
And tires their echoes with unvaried cries;
Sunk are thy bowers in shapeless ruin all,
And the long grass o'er tops the moldering wall;
And trembling, shrinking from the spoiler's hand,
Far, far away thy children leave the land.

Ill fares the land, to hastening ills a prey,
Where wealth accumulates, and men decay:
Princes and lords may flourish, or may fade;

---

[2] Tyrant's hand—A wealthy landholder has increased his holdings until he is master of the whole countryside.

[3] Half a tillage—The wealthy landowner reserves half of the land for hunting purposes.

A breath[4] can make them, as a breath has made:
But a bold peasantry, their country's pride,
When once destroyed, can never be supplied.

A time[5] there was, ere England's griefs began,
When every rood of ground maintained its man;
For him light labor spread her wholesome store,
Just gave what life required, but gave no more:
His best companions, innocence and health;
And his best riches, ignorance of wealth.

But times are altered; trade's unfeeling train
Usurp the land and dispossess the swain;
Along the lawn, where scattered hamlets rose,
Unwieldy wealth and cumbrous pomp repose,
And every want to opulence allied,
And every pang that folly pays to pride.
These gentle hours that plenty bade to bloom,
Those calm desires that asked but little room,
Those healthful sports that graced the peaceful scene,
Lived in each look, and brightened all the green;
These, far departing, seek a kinder shore,
And rural mirth and manners are no more.[6]

Sweet Auburn! parent of the blissful hour,
Thy glades forlorn confess the tyrant's power.
Here, as I take my solitary rounds
Amidst thy tangling walks and ruined grounds,
And, many a year elapsed, return to view
Where once the cottage stood, the hawthorn grew,
Remembrance wakes with all her busy train,
Swells at my breast, and turns the past to pain.

In all my wanderings round this world of care,
In all my griefs—and God has given my share—
I still had hopes, my latest hours to crown,

---

[4] BREATH—The word of the king who confers the title of nobility.

[5] A TIME—The poet pictures a time not found in history.

[6] RURAL . . . MORE—Note the alliteration of this line, the repetition of consonants, which is so common in the poem.

Amidst these humble bowers to lay me down;
To husband out life's taper at the close,
And keep the flame from wasting by repose:
I still had hopes, for pride attends us still,
Amidst the swains to show my book-learned skill,
Around my fire an evening group to draw,
And tell of all I felt, and all I saw;
And, as an hare whom hounds and horns pursue,
Pants to the place from whence at first she flew,
I still had hopes, my long vexations past,
Here to return—and die at home at last.

O, blest retirement, friend to life's decline,
Retreats from care, that never must be mine,
How happy he who crowns in shades like these,
A youth of labor with an age of ease;
Who quits a world where strong temptations try,
And, since 't is hard to combat, learns to fly!
For him no wretches, born to work and weep,
Explore the mine, or tempt the dangerous deep;
No surly porter stands in guilty state,
To spurn imploring famine from the gate;
But on he moves to meet his latter end,
Angels around befriending Virtue's friend;
Bends to the grave with unperceived decay,
While resignation gently slopes the way;
And, all his prospects brightening to the last,
His heaven commences ere the world be past!

Sweet was the sound, when oft at evening's close
Up yonder hill the village murmur rose.
There, as I passed with careless steps and slow,
The mingling notes came softened from below;
The swain responsive as the milk-maid sung,
The sober herd that lowed to meet their young,
The noisy geese that gabbled o'er the pool,
The playful children just let loose from school,
The watch-dog's voice that bayed the whispering wind,

And the loud laugh that spoke the vacant mind;—[7]
These all in sweet confusion sought the shade,
And filled each pause the nightingale had made.
But now the sounds of population fail,
No cheerful murmurs fluctuate in the gale,
No busy steps the grass-grown foot-way tread,
For all the bloomy flush of life is fled.
All but yon widowed, solitary thing,
That feebly bends beside the plashy spring:
She, wretched matron, forced in age, for bread,
To strip the brook with mantling cresses spread,
To pick her wintry faggot from the thorn,
To seek her nightly shed, and weep till morn;
She only left of all the harmless train,
The sad historian of the pensive plain.

Near yonder copse, where once the garden smiled,
And still where many a garden flower grows wild;
There, where a few torn shrubs the place disclose,
The village preacher's modest mansion rose.
A man he was to all the country dear,
And passing rich with forty pounds a year;
Remote from towns he ran his godly race,
Nor e'er had changed, nor wished to change his place;
Unpracticed he to fawn, or seek for power,
By doctrines fashioned to the varying hour;
Far other aims his heart had learned to prize,
More skilled to raise the wretched than to rise.
His house was known to all the vagrant train;
He chid their wanderings but relieved their pain:
The long-remembered beggar was his guest,
Whose beard descending swept his aged breast;
The ruined spendthrift, now no longer proud,
Claimed kindred there, and had his claims allowed;
The broken soldier, kindly bade to stay,
Sat by the fire, and talked the night away,
Wept o'er his wounds or, tales of sorrow done,
Shouldered his crutch and showed how fields were won.

[7] VACANT MIND—A mind free from care.

Pleased with his guests, the good man learned to glow,
And quite forgot their vices in their woe;
Careless their merits or their faults to scan
His pity gave ere charity began.

Thus to relieve the wretched was his pride,
And e'en his failings leaned to Virtue's side;
But in his duty prompt at every call,
He watched and wept, he prayed and felt for all;
And, as a bird each fond endearment tries
To tempt its new-fledged offspring to the skies,
He tried each art, reproved each dull delay,
Allured to brighter worlds, and led the way.[8]

Beside the bed where parting life was laid,
And sorrow, guilt, and pain by turns dismayed,
The reverend champion stood. At his control
Despair and anguish fled the struggling soul;
Comfort came down the trembling wretch to raise,
And his last faltering accents whispered praise.

At church, with meek and unaffected grace,
His looks adorned the venerable place;
Truth from his lips prevailed with double sway,
And fools, who came to scoff, remained to pray.
The service past, around the pious man,
With steady zeal, each honest rustic ran;
Even children followed with endearing wile,
And plucked his gown to share the good man's smile.
His ready smile a parent's warmth exprest;
Their welfare pleased him, and their cares distrest:
To them his heart, his love, his griefs were given,
But all his serious thoughts had rest in heaven.
As some tall cliff that lifts its awful form,
Swells from the vale, and midway leaves the storm,

---

8 Led the way—Compare this description with the following famous description of the poor parson by our early English poet, Chaucer, in his *Canterbury Tales.*

"But Cristes lore, and his Apostles twelve
He taughte, but first he folwed it himselve."

Though round its breast the rolling clouds are spread,
Eternal sunshine settles on its head.

Beside yon straggling fence that skirts the way,
With blossomed furze unprofitably gay,
There, in his noisy mansion, skilled to rule,
The village master taught his little school.
A man severe he was, and stern to view;
I knew him well, and every truant knew;
Well had the boding tremblers learned to trace
The day's disasters in his morning face;
Full well they laughed with counterfeited glee
At all his jokes, for many a joke had he;
Full well the busy whisper circling round
Conveyed the dismal tidings when he frowned.
Yet he was kind, or, if severe in aught,
The love he bore to learning was in fault;
The village all declared how much he knew:
'T was certain he could write, and cipher too;
Lands he could measure, terms[9] and tides presage,
And even the story ran that he could gauge;[10]
In arguing, too, the parson owned his skill,
For, even though vanquished, he could argue still;
While words of learned length and thundering sound
Amazed the gazing rustics ranged around;
And still they gazed, and still the wonder grew,
That one small head could carry all he knew.

But past is all his fame. The very spot
Where many a time he triumphed, is forgot.
Near yonder thorn, that lifts its head on high,
Where once the sign-post caught the passing eye,
Low lies that house where nut-brown draughts inspired,
Where graybeard mirth and smiling toil retired,
Where village statesmen talked with looks profound,
And news much older than their ale went round.

---

[9] Terms—The sessions of the law courts, some of which were determined by the dates of certain days such as Easter, that fall at different times in successive years.

[10] Gauge—Estimate the capacity of barrels and casks.

Imagination fondly stoops to trace
The parlor splendors of that festive place:
The white-washed wall, the nicely sanded floor,
The varnished clock that clicked behind the door;
The chest contrived a double debt to pay,
A bed by night, a chest of drawers by day;
The pictures placed for ornament and use,
The twelve good rules,[11] the royal game of goose;[12]
The hearth, except when winter chilled the day,
With aspen boughs and flowers and fennel gay;
While broken tea-cups, wisely kept for show,
Ranged o'er the chimney, glistened in a row.

Vain transitory splendors! could not all
Reprieve the tottering mansion from its fall?
Obscure it sinks, nor shall it more impart
An hour's importance to the poor man's heart.
Thither no more the peasant shall repair
To sweet oblivion of his daily care;
No more the farmer's news, the barber's tale;
No more the woodman's ballad shall prevail;
No more the smith his dusky brow shall clear,
Relax his ponderous strength, and lean to hear;
The host himself no longer shall be found
Careful to see the mantling bliss[13] go round;
Nor the coy maid, half willing to be prest,
Shall kiss the cup to pass it to the rest.

Yes! let the rich deride, the proud disdain,
These simple blessings of the lowly train;
To me more dear, congenial to my heart,
One native charm, than all the gloss of art.
Spontaneous joys, where Nature has its play,
The soul adopts, and owns their first born sway;
Lightly they frolic o'er the vacant mind,
Unenvied, unmolested, unconfined.

---

[11] Twelve good rules—Rules of conduct attributed to Charles I.
[12] Game of goose—A game somewhat similar to checkers.
[13] Mantling bliss—Foaming cups of ale.

But the long pomp, the midnight masquerade,
With all the freaks of wanton wealth arrayed—
In these, ere triflers half their wish obtain,
The toiling pleasure sickens into pain;
And, even while fashion's brightest arts decoy,
The heart distrusting asks if this be joy.

Ye friends to truth, ye statesmen who survey
The rich man's joy increase, the poor's decay,
'T is yours to judge, how wide the limits stand
Between a splendid and a happy land.
Proud swells the tide with loads of freighted ore,
And shouting Folly hails them from her shore;
Hoards even beyond the miser's wish abound,
And rich men flock from all the world around.
Yet count our gains! This wealth is but a name
That leaves our useful products still the same.
Not so the loss. The man of wealth and pride
Takes up a space that many poor supplied;
Space for his lake, his park's extended bounds,
Space for his horses, equipage, and hounds:
The robe that wraps his limbs in silken sloth
Has robbed the neighboring fields of half their growth;
His seat, where solitary sports are seen,
Indignant spurns the cottage from the green:
Around the world each needful product flies,
For all the luxuries the world supplies;
While thus the land adorned for pleasure all
In barren splendor feebly waits the fall.
As some fair female unadorned and plain,[14]
Secure to please while youth confirms her reign,
Slights every borrowed charm that dress supplies,
Nor shares with art the triumph of her eyes;
But when those charms are past, for charms are frail,
When time advances, and when lovers fail,
She then shines forth, solicitous to bless,
In all the glaring impotence of dress.
Thus fares the land by luxury betrayed:

[14] PLAIN—Beautiful by nature.

In nature's simplest charms at first arrayed,
But verging to decline, its splendors rise,
Its vistas strike, its palaces surprise;
While, scourged by famine from the smiling land
The mournful peasant leads his humble band,
And while he sinks, without one arm to save,
The country blooms—a garden and a grave.

Where then, ah! where, shall poverty reside,
To 'scape the pressure of contiguous pride?
If to some common's fenceless limits strayed,
He drives his flock to pick the scanty blade,
Those fenceless fields the sons of wealth divide,
And even the bare-worn common is denied.

If to the city sped—what waits him there?
To see profusion that he must not share;
To see ten thousand baneful arts combined
To pamper luxury, and thin mankind;
To see those joys the sons of pleasure know
Extorted from his fellow-creature's woe.
Here while the courtier glitters in brocade,
There the pale artist plies the sickly trade;
Here while the proud their long-drawn pomps display,
There the black gibbet[15] glooms beside the way.
The dome where pleasure holds her midnight reign,
Here, richly decked, admits the gorgeous train:
Tumultuous grandeur crowds the blazing square,
The rattling chariots clash, the torches glare.
Sure scenes like these no troubles e'er annoy!
Sure these denote one universal joy!
Are these thy serious thoughts?—Ah, turn thine eyes
Where the poor, houseless, shivering female lies.
She once, perhaps, in village plenty blest,
Has wept at tales of innocence distrest;
Her modest looks the cottage might adorn,
Sweet as the primrose peeps beneath the thorn;

[15] BLACK GIBBET—Hanging was the common punishment for a great number of even minor crimes.

Now lost to all; her friends, her virtue fled,
Near her betrayer's door she lays her head,
And, pinched with cold, and shrinking from the shower,
With heavy heart deplores that luckless hour,
When idly first, ambitious of the town,
She left her wheel and robes of country brown.

Do thine, sweet Auburn, thine, the loveliest train,
Do thy fair tribes participate her pain?
Even now, perhaps, by cold and hunger led,
At proud men's doors they ask a little bread!

Ah, no! To distant climes, a dreary scene,
Where half the convex world intrudes between,
Through torrid tracts with fainting steps they go,
Where wild Altama[16] murmurs to their woe.
Far different there from all that charmed before
The various terrors of that horrid shore;
Those blazing suns that dart a downward ray,
And fiercely shed intolerable day;
Those matted woods, where birds forget to sing,
But silent bats in drowsy clusters cling;
Those poisonous fields with rank luxuriance crowned,
Where the dark scorpion gathers death around;
Where at each step the stranger fears to wake
The rattling terrors of the vengeful snake;
Where crouching tigers wait their hapless prey,
And savage men more murderous still than they;
While oft in whirls the mad tornado flies,
Mingling the ravaged landscape with the skies.
Far different these from every former scene,
The cooling brook, the grassy vested green,
The breezy covert of the warbling grove,
That only sheltered thefts of harmless love.

Good Heaven! what sorrows gloomed that parting day,
That called them from their native walks away;
When the poor exiles, every pleasure past,

[16] ALTAMA—The Altamaha River in Georgia. In 1733 a colony had been founded on its banks as a refuge for debtors.

Hung round the bowers, and fondly looked their last,
And took a long farewell, and wished in vain
For seats like these beyond the western main,
And shuddering still to face the distant deep,
Returned and wept, and still returned to weep.
The good old sire, the first prepared to go
To new found worlds, and wept for others' woe;
But for himself, in conscious virtue brave,
He only wished for worlds beyond the grave.
His lovely daughter, lovelier in her tears,
The fond companion of his helpless years,
Silent went next, neglectful of her charms,
And left a lover's for a father's arms.
With louder plaints the mother spoke her woes,
And blest the cot where every pleasure rose,
And kist her thoughtless babes with many a tear
And claspt them close, in sorrow doubly dear,
Whilst her fond husband strove to lend relief,
In all the silent manliness of grief.

O luxury! thou curst by Heaven's decree,
How ill exchanged are things like these for thee!
How do thy potions, with insidious joy,
Diffuse their pleasure only to destroy!
Kingdoms by thee, to sickly greatness grown,
Boast of a florid vigor not their own.
At every draught more large and large they grow,
A bloated mass of rank, unwieldly woe;
Till sapped their strength, and every part unsound,
Down, down, they sink, and spread a ruin round.

Even now the devastation is begun,
And half the business of destruction done;
Even now, methinks, as pondering here I stand,
I see the rural virtues leave the land.
Down where yon anchoring vessel spreads the sail,
That idly waiting flaps with every gale,
Downward they[17] move, a melancholy band,

[17] THEY—That is, the rural virtues.

Pass from the shore, and darken all the strand.
Contented toil, and hospitable care,
And kind connubial tenderness, are there;
And piety with wishes placed above,
And steady loyalty, and faithful love.
And thou, sweet Poetry, thou loveliest maid,
Still first to fly where sensual joys invade;
Unfit in these degenerate times of shame
To catch the heart,[18] or strike for honest fame;
Dear charming nymph, neglected and decried,
My shame in crowds, my solitary pride;
Thou source of all my bliss, and all my woe,
That found'st me poor at first, and keep'st me so;
Thou guide by which the nobler arts excel,
Thou nurse of every virtue, fare thee well!
Farewell, and oh! where'er thy voice be tried,
On Torno's cliffs,[19] or Pambamarca's[20] side,
Whether where equinoctial fervors glow,
Or winter wraps the polar world in snow,
Still let thy voice, .prevailing over time,
Redress the rigors of the inclement clime;
Aid slighted truth with thy persuasive strain;
Teach erring man to spurn the rage of gain:
Teach him, that states of native strength possest,
Though very poor, may still be very blest;
That trade's proud empire hastes to swift decay,
As ocean sweeps the labored mole[21] away;
While self-dependent power can time defy,
As rocks resist the billows and the sky.

## QUESTIONS AND EXERCISES

Exercises preceded by a star are designed for assignment at the discretion of the teacher, or for any student who volunteers.

1. What lines used in describing the village of Auburn most convinced you of its former charm?
2. Describe the village sports at evening.
3. What changed the village? Describe it in its changed condition.

[18] CATCH THE HEART—Consider how much more nearly Goldsmith's poetry succeeds in doing this than does the poetry of the more classical poets.

[19] TORNO'S CLIFFS—The cliffs of Lake Tornea in northern Sweden.

[20] PAMBAMARCA'S—Pambamarca is a mountain in Ecuador.

[21] MOLE—Dike.

4. In Goldsmith's opinion, what is the effect of wealth on a land?
5. In lines 57–62 the poet describes a perfect England, which of course existed only in his mind. Discuss the advantages and disadvantages of such a state of society as he pictures. Explain line 62 in which he states that ignorance of wealth is the peasant's best riches.
6. Describe the old age the poet had planned to enjoy before the destruction of Auburn. What pleasures and joys had he hoped for there?
7. Explain line 87, "To husband out life's taper at the close."
8. Describe the character of the preacher, his guests, and his care of his flock. Describe him at church.
9. Explain line 162, "His pity gave ere charity began."
10. What sort of man was the schoolmaster? What was his standing in the little community? Describe the attitude of the pupils toward him.
11. Describe the village tavern. What does line 224 suggest concerning the people and their contact with the outside world?
*12. What ideas in common with later romantic writers does Goldsmith show in lines 251–254? How does he differ from the usual classical poets in the next few lines?
13. Explain the poet's meaning in line 274 when he says that all the wealth, or goods, brought in "leaves our useful products still the same."
14. How, according to Goldsmith, does the man of wealth rob the poor?
15. What is meant by the *wheel* in line 336?
16. What is the position of the peasant in the city?
17. The Altama mentioned in line 344 is in Georgia. What parts of the description in the following lines show that the poet was not attempting to describe actual conditions there? How does the passage gain in effectiveness by the imaginary horrors he describes?
18. What, according to Goldsmith, is the state of poetry in an age like the one he has described? Why?
19. With what charge to poetry does the poem end? Name other services which poetry performs for mankind.
*20. In an essay compare, with respect to human interest, the pastor and the schoolmaster with some other character in a poem you have read.
21. Choose the passage in the poem which you enjoyed most and point out its merits.
22. What traces of the Pseudo-Classical Period are still to be found in *The Deserted Village?* What characteristics of the poem reveal the romantic spirit that is beginning to influence literature?
*23. Read Longfellow's *Evangeline* and contrast his picture of homeless peasants with the one given by Goldsmith.
*24. Memory passages for assignment: lines 1–14, 35–56, 113–128, 137–162, 193–216, 251–258, 295–302.

# WILLIAM BLAKE

## 1757–1827

What would you think if a friend should say to you in all seriousness: "I saw God putting his head out of a window this morning." Before you had recovered from the shock, suppose he added: "Yesterday I met the Devil coming down-stairs." If some time later he reported that he had had a familiar conversation with Jesus Christ and had argued at length with Moses, Dante, and Milton, your worst fears would be confirmed. "He's crazy," you would say, and there would be few to dispute you.

Yet William Blake insisted he saw and did all these things. He was very earnest about it. There was nothing of the impostor in him. The visions he saw were so real that they became more important than material things. Nor did he feel there was anything sacrilegious in saying that he talked with Christ or saw God looking out of a window. Instinctively he was a religious man, not in any formal way that had to do with doctrines, but in the sense of spiritual things. Before his eyes the forces of evil and of good took on shapes: horrible things with horns and gigantic fishes devouring corpses; or sweet and beautiful creatures that inspired him to flights of poetry that have the simplicity and vividness of childhood.

Impostor he was not, but was he a madman? The question has long been disputed. In many ways he was perfectly sane, and even in the sphere of grotesque fancy there is a logic that makes one wonder whether we can say where genius leaves off and insanity begins. The relation of eccentric genius to madness has puzzled the psychologists for years.

Curiously enough, as Lafcadio Hearn points out, the only other eighteenth century poet who can compare with Blake in originality—Christopher Smart—was also mad. Though a modern alienist would undoubtedly declare William Blake the victim of some form of mania, a study of his art makes one rebel at the word insanity. He was a real though abnormal genius. An artist at ten and a poet at twelve, he has been called. These arts he was to unite in after years, like William Morris a century later, in the writing, printing, and illustrating of his own books.

William Blake was the son of a London tradesman. He was a strange imaginative child whose soul was at home in the fields and along the brooks where he could dream of fairies. As a child he told his parents that he had visions of God and the angels. He saw elves, fairies, devils looking at him out of flowers. As a man he thought he received visits from the souls of the great dead. He seems never to have considered the possibility that some of these visions may have been illusions. Instead, he believed and trusted them fully. To him all nature was alive with spiritual significance.

Though he received little schooling, he began as a child to write verses and to copy prints. His father, seeing the imaginative nature of his son's mind, resolved to make a painter of him; but Blake, realizing how much it would cost, decided it would be unfair to his brothers and asked to be set to engraving instead. He attended a drawing school, went for a time to the Royal Academy, and became an engraver's apprentice. For over forty years he worked at book engraving, and while busy with his trade wrote his poems and curious mystical prophecies that reflect his visions.

As a man he lived a simple and devout life, isolated and content, happy in his home and at his work. Though the simple servant girl whom he married could not even write her own name, she proved a loving, faithful companion, interested in her husband's work and in sympathy with his ideals. Very early Blake had begun to bridge the gap in his own education with reading and meditation. He wandered among the country lanes and stored his memory with sights and sounds. Sometimes he had moments of ecstasy during which he wrote as under a spell, for he was a mystic, influenced by that great mystic teacher, Swedenborg. A mystic believes that he can free himself from the physical world and leave behind material things to come directly in touch with the infinite—that is, with the spiritual world.

Perhaps because of this absorption in things unseen, there are few important events to record in his life. One curious incident occurred while he was living at Felpham whither he had gone to do some art work. An old soldier whom Blake found in the garden and tried to eject for trespassing accused him of sedition. Blake was actually tried in court, but the testimony of his friends concerning his quiet and unoffending character soon freed him. He died in 1827 as obscurely as he had lived, still happily seeing visions.

Blake's poetry is amazingly unlike the verse that was being written in his day. In sympathy it belongs to a later generation though it is so original that there is difficulty in placing it anywhere. His work divides in three stages. His earliest lyrics (*Poetical Sketches,* 1783) show the influence of Elizabethan poets. *Songs of Innocence* (1789) and *Songs of Experience* (1794) represent his best work, while the prose and poetry of his later years exhibits such a weird strain of the supernatural that it is too obscure for enjoyment.

Being a painter and an engraver as well as a poet, Blake often combined all his arts in a single production. Nearly all his books were published by himself. He engraved his poem on a copper plate by a process he had invented, drew illustrations or designs to fit it, and did the printing himself. Sometimes he hand-colored the pictures later.

His best-known poems are noted for their originality and simple directness of expression. They are childlike in their phrasing and filled with a spiritual and mystic emotion, a quality that increased as he grew older. The other-world quality in his poems, the unearthiness, is even more pronounced than in Coleridge or Poe, both of whom he directly influenced. Blake did much to make popular the rebirth of wonder and the supernatural in poetry.

Most delightful of all his poems are the *Songs of Innocence* and *Songs of Experience.* The former are pictures of childhood in its days of placid acceptance of life, before trouble and doubts have come. The latter, while still retaining their simple charm, have moments of premonition that understanding will bring shadows and even terror. Childhood had had no attention from the classicists. Blake, with his lyric gift, wrote some of the most musical nursery songs in the language. On the surface he seems only a poet with a simple child-like mind, but underneath there are hidden meanings that strike deep into the heart of human experience.

When Blake died, he left, according to tradition, nearly a hundred volumes of poetry and prose, illustrated with his own engravings, which he believed to have been inspired by holy spirits. Upon the death of his wife a short time after, all these priceless manuscripts came into the hands of a clergyman belonging to a mystic sect. One look at the books and pictures convinced this superstitious man that only the Devil could have inspired such things, and he forthwith threw them all into the fire. What remains of Blake's original work is now among the most treasured possessions of museums and collectors.

## TO THE MUSES[1]

Like Goldsmith in the closing lines of his *Deserted Village,* Blake here gives expression to his belief that the art of poetry has fallen into decay. "The languid strings do scarcely move." He shows in his poetry that he has within himself much of the true genius for which he is searching.

Whether on Ida's[2] shady brow,
  Or in the chambers of the East,
The chambers of the Sun, that now
  From ancient melody have ceased;

Whether in Heaven ye wander fair,
  Or the green corners of the earth,
Or the blue regions of the air
  Where the melodious winds have birth;

---

[1] Muses—The nine daughters of Zeus, goddesses of the arts. Each was a patron of some particular branch of literature, the fine arts, or science.

[2] Ida's—Ida, a mountain in Crete, was one of the haunts of the Greek Muses.

Whether on crystal rocks ye rove,
Beneath the bosom of the sea
Wandering in many a coral grove,
Fair Nine,[3] forsaking poetry!

How have you left the ancient love
That bards of old enjoyed in you!
The languid strings do scarcely move,
The sound is forced, the notes are few!

## QUESTIONS AND EXERCISES

Exercises preceded by a star are designed for assignment at the discretion of the teacher, or for any student who volunteers.

1. What was the state of English poetry when Blake published this poem in his volume entitled *Poetical Sketches?*
2. What does Blake mean when he says "the notes are few"?

*3. Point out the chief differences between *To the Muses* and the closing lines of *The Deserted Village.*

## THE PIPER

*The Piper* is the introductory song in Blake's volume *Songs of Innocence.* No introduction could have been more fitting, for he indeed sings songs of pleasant glee, songs of happy cheer, that every child may joy to hear—songs that older lovers of poetry are happier for having read.

Piping down the valleys wild,
Piping songs of pleasant glee,
On a cloud I saw a child,
And he laughing said to me:

'Pipe a song about a Lamb!'
So I piped with merry cheer.
'Piper, pipe that song again;'
So I piped: he wept to hear.

'Drop thy pipe, thy happy pipe;
Sing thy songs of happy cheer:'
So I sang the same again,
While he wept with joy to hear.

---

[3] Fair Nine—The Muses.

'Piper, sit thee down and write
In a book, that all may read.'
So he vanished from my sight,
And I plucked a hollow reed,

And I made a rural pen,
And I stained the water clear,
And I wrote my happy songs
Every child may joy to hear.

QUESTIONS AND EXERCISES

1. Tell in what meter this poem is written. Does the rhythm fit the subject? What can you say of the diction?
2. Do you feel that there is any significance in the kind of pen and ink Blake chooses for his poems? Does the fancy add anything to the poem?

## THE LITTLE BLACK BOY

Blake's sympathy often extended to individuals born under less happy circumstances than are most of us. Only a poet with a simple, kindly nature can take our minds away from our own affairs and open our hearts to the longings of others, as Blake does in this little poem from *Songs of Innocence.*

My mother bore me in the southern wild,
And I am black, but O my soul is white!
White as an angel is the English child,
But I am black, as if bereaved of light.

My mother taught me underneath a tree,
And, sitting down before the heat of day,
She took me on her lap and kissed me,
And, pointing to the East, began to say:

"Look on the rising sun: there God does live,
And gives His light, and gives His heat away,
And flowers and trees and beasts and men receive
Comfort in morning, joy in the noonday.

"And we are put on earth a little space
That we may learn to bear the beams of love;

And these black bodies and this sunburnt face
  Are but a cloud, and like a shady grove.

"For, when our souls have learned the heat to bear,
  The cloud will vanish, we shall hear His voice,
Saying, 'Come out from the grove, my love and care,
  And round my golden tent like lambs rejoice.'"

Thus did my mother say, and kissed me,
  And thus I say to little English boy.
When I from black, and he from white cloud free,
  And round the tent of God like lambs we joy,

I'll shade him from the heat till he can bear
  To lean in joy upon our Father's knee;
And then I'll stand and stroke his silver hair,
  And be like him, and he will then love me.

### QUESTIONS AND EXERCISES

Exercises preceded by a star are designed for assignment at the discretion of the teacher, or for any student who volunteers.

1. Tell in your own words what the mother teaches the little black boy. To what does she compare the black bodies and the sunburnt face? Do you consider the comparison a beautiful one?
2. Explain line 23.
3. What idea in the poem do you like best?
*4. Make a list of the characteristics of the poem which are lacking in the work of Pope, Gray, Cowper, and Goldsmith.

## THE TIGER

*The Tiger,* taken from *Songs of Experience,* is Blake's best-known poem. Written simply as are his other poems, it expresses wonder and amazement at the perfection of this creature of the wilds. Apparently it is with the simplicity of a child that Blake asks, "Did he who made the Lamb make thee?" Yet is there something else in the poet's mind? Terror lurks in these stanzas . . .

"Tiger! Tiger! burning bright . . ."

Is this just colorful imagery? What is that power that could twist the sinews of such a heart, forge that fearful brain?

"What dread grasp
Dare its deadly terrors clasp?"

And why did the stars weep while "he" who made the Tiger "smiled"? Is there some terrible irony, some great questioning as to the source of good and evil? Could it be the same source for both? Did he who made the gentle Lamb also make the dreadful Tiger?

Perhaps it is just the simple poem it seems. Perhaps not. One can never tell with Blake. What impression does it leave with you?

Tiger! Tiger! burning bright
In the forests of the night,
What immortal hand or eye
Could frame thy fearful symmetry?

In what distant deeps or skies
Burnt the fire of thine eyes?
On what wings dare he aspire?
What the hand dare seize the fire?

And what shoulder, and what art,
Could twist the sinews of thy heart?
And when thy heart began to beat,
What dread hand and what dread feet?

What the hammer? what the chain?
In what furnace was thy brain?
What the anvil? what dread grasp
Dare its deadly terrors clasp?

When the stars threw down their spears,
And watered heaven with their tears,
Did he smile his work to see?
Did he who made the Lamb make thee?

Tiger! Tiger! burning bright
In the forests of the night,
What immortal hand or eye
Dare frame thy fearful symmetry?

## QUESTIONS AND EXERCISES

**Exercises preceded by a star are designed for assignment at the discretion of the teacher, or for any student who volunteers.**

1. What is meant by the "fearful symmetry" of the tiger?
2. Do you consider this a poem for children or for grown-up readers? Why?
3. What is the emotion this poem arouses?

*4. Comment on the meaning of the stanza beginning, "When the stars threw down their spears."

## GENERAL QUESTIONS

1. What are the limitations of the heroic couplet? Why did it fail to remain as a standard verse form?
2. How do the later poets included in this section show a broader human sympathy than their immediate predecessors?
3. How does the poetry of Pope reflect the customs and manners of the society of his time?
4. What changes in society can you infer from the changes evident in the poetry of the mid-eighteenth century?
5. Which poet in this section did you enjoy the most, and why?

## GENERAL EXERCISES

1. Describe the characteristics of Pseudo-Classical poetry.
2. In the work of the poets Gray, Cowper, and Goldsmith note what changes in form, subject matter, style, and point of view occur. Illustrate by definite passages.
3. Show in what ways Blake represents the goal toward which the poets of the transitional period have been striving.
4. Scan one line from the work of each author in this section.
5. Which did you like the better: the prose section representing this period, or the poetry section? Why?

## SUGGESTED READING LIST

Other poems that are similar in theme or atmosphere to the poems studied in this section.

*The Rape of the Lock:*
*Epistle to Dr. Arbuthnot,* Alexander Pope
*Alexander's Feast: A Song in Honor of St. Cecilia's Day,* John Dryden
*The Furniture of a Woman's Mind,* Jonathan Swift
*The Battle of the Kegs,* Francis Hopkinson
*The Battle of Blenheim,* Robert Southey
*The Akhound of Swat,* George Thomas Lanigan

*Elegy Written in a Country Churchyard:*
*Ode to Evening,* William Collins
*Winter* (from *The Seasons*), James Thomson
*Thanatopsis,* William Cullen Bryant
*The Loss of the Royal George,* William Cowper
*Break, Break, Break,* Alfred Tennyson
*Requiem,* Robert Louis Stevenson
*Annabel Lee,* Edgar Allan Poe
*Hymn to Night,* Henry Wadsworth Longfellow
*When Lilacs Last in the Dooryard Bloom'd,* Walt Whitman

*The Diverting History of John Gilpin:*
*The Deacon's Masterpiece,* Oliver Wendell Holmes
*The Glory Trail,* Badger Clark
*The Yarn of the Nancy Bell,* Sir William Schwenk Gilbert
*The Ballad of the Billycock,* Anthony C. Deane
*The Well of St. Keyne,* Robert Southey

*To Mrs. Unwin:*
*To Helen,* Edgar Allan Poe
*To Alison Cunningham—From Her Boy,* Robert Louis Stevenson
*To My Mother,* William Ernest Henley
*To My Brother,* Corinne Roosevelt Robinson

*The Deserted Village:*
*Evangeline,* Henry Wadsworth Longfellow
*The Cotter's Saturday Night,* Robert Burns
*Character of the Poor Parson* (From *Prologue to the Canterbury Tales*) Geoffrey Chaucer
*The Man with the Hoe,* Edwin Markham
*Ploughman at the Plough,* Louis Golding
*In School-Days,* John Greenleaf Whittier
*"Night is on the Downland,"* John Masefield

*To the Muses:*
*Prologue* to *The Lady of the Lake,* Sir Walter Scott
*The Harp That Once Through Tara's Halls,* Thomas Moore

*The Piper:*
*The Fiddler of Dooney,* William Butler Yeats
*A Song of the Road,* Robert Louis Stevenson
*Sea Shell,* Amy Lowell
*A Musical Instrument,* Elizabeth Barrett Browning
*Laughing Song,* William Blake

*The Little Black Boy:*
*Da Leetla Boy,* Thomas Augustine Daly
*Blessing on Little Boys,* Arthur Guiterman
*A Phantasy of Heaven,* Harry Kemp

*The Tiger:*
*The Lamb,* William Blake
*Miracles,* Walt Whitman
*To a Snowflake,* Francis Thompson

# *The Story-Essay*

P. F. Collier and Sons

WASHINGTON IRVING

Ambassador, man of letters, a cultured American gentleman, Irving was popular at home and abroad. The story-essay form which he developed in *The Sketch Book* was an ancestor of the short story.

# THE STORY-ESSAY

In regard to form, *The Sketch Book* of Washington Irving looks both backward and forward: backward to the periodical essays made famous in the *Spectator* of Addison and Steele in the eighteenth century; and forward to the short story which as an independent form was to find its first great expression in Poe's tales not many years later. It is a link between the two literary types. For convenience and clarity, let us call this combination The Story-Essay.

Some of Irving's sketches are almost wholly in the essay tradition, containing even less narrative than the *Sir Roger de Coverley Papers,* most famous of the *Spectator* numbers. Others, notably *Rip Van Winkle* and *The Legend of Sleepy Hollow,* are reaching out toward the short story form. Though rambling and lacking in compactness and unity, they nevertheless bear the same relation to Poe's short story as Defoe's *Robinson Crusoe* bears to the real novel developed by Richardson and Fielding. Without these forerunners, the establishment of both the novel and the short story as recognized types might have been delayed.

The true essay form is mainly expositive; that is, it explains. It shows the relation between certain ideas. It gives the reaction of the author to certain conditions, events, or scenes. The essay may be chiefly intellectual, as in discussions of science, morals, politics, literary criticism; or it may be familiar, with the emphasis on the style and mood of the writer. The purpose of the intellectual essay is to give information; in fact, it is often called the Informative Essay. The purpose of the Familiar Essay is to give entertainment by appealing to imagination and emotion.

Although Irving's style is not so intimate as that of the essayists who followed him, such as Oliver Wendell Holmes, or even as that of his own English contemporary, Charles Lamb, most of his essays are familiar in spirit. We are not so much interested in learning the exact details of English rural life or the architecture of Westminster Abbey as we are in discovering the effect of these things on Irving himself. Only in such an essay as *English Writers on America* does the argument become as important as the mood of the author or the style of the writing.

This is not the place for an exhaustive analysis of either the short story or the essay. Books I and II of the *Beacon Lights of Literature* series include discussions of the development and the characteristics of the short story. Book III contains a chronological survey of the essay, with an introduction treating of that form. As a connecting link between the two types, *The Sketch Book* is historically interesting, but, while keeping this in mind, the student will find greater enjoyment in reading the essays for their own sake.

# THE SKETCH BOOK

## WASHINGTON IRVING

1783–1859

### THE AUTHOR

Washington Irving, the foremost American author of the early days of the new Republic, has been called, "the first ambassador of letters from the New World to the Old." By the polished charm and gentle humor of his pen he brought American prose to its first excellence. In his unaffected poise and simple nobility he gave Europe, during his extensive travels, its first picture of an American gentleman and wrought a closer bond of sympathy between the United States and England. With Irving American national literature is born.

The greatness of Irving is more keenly realized after a survey of the meagre period of colonial literature, especially prose. Except for Cotton Mather's church history of New England, a few of Jonathan Edward's sermons, and Benjamin Franklin's *Poor Richard's Almanack,* little of worth was written in America before the muskets blazed at Lexington. The colonists were too actively engaged in the business of living to relax and produce authors and books. After the Revolutionary War the creative leadership of America was occupied in the welding of the new Republic, and literature again suffered. *The Autobiography of Benjamin Franklin* stands as the lone piece of representative prose in those anxious years before the turn of the century, and even that was not published until long after its author's death. On the whole, American literature was in the raw. Though it had great possibilities, it was yet crude.

Once the security of the Republic was assured and there was time for people to reflect on what had happened and what was happening, literature had a chance to develop. Although Irving was the first American author to gain wide recognition, two other original geniuses soon followed him. He had made his first bow to fame at the close of the first decade of the nineteenth century. Shortly after the beginning of the second decade, the publication of *The Spy* heralded the arrival of the American novelist, James Fenimore Cooper. Another ten or a dozen years and Edgar Allan Poe began to write those grotesque tales and eerie poems that set him apart from all other writers in our history.

Irving was the serene gentleman, with genial humor and a pride in careful craftsmanship. Cooper was a turbulent spirit who in spite of his massacre of the English language and lack of humor gripped millions of readers with the rugged vividness of his story-telling. Both these writers, especially Cooper, chose American themes. Poe, perhaps a greater artist than either of them, wandered off by himself to brood alone in a world where ghosts have a melancholy loveliness and men are hideous. Possibly Nathaniel Hawthorne should be mentioned, for he was nearly five years older than Poe. His genius, however, did not ripen until close to the middle of the century, and since he belongs to that amazing group which sprang up in New England—among them Emerson, Longfellow, Thoreau, Holmes, Lowell—it will be sufficient to forecast the great flowering of American literature that is to astonish even England before Irving is in his grave.

In 1783, the year of the peace treaty with England, Washington Irving was born in New York, a city which he was later to nickname unforgettably in his *Knickerbocker History.* Because Irving, like his friend, Sir Walter Scott, had a delicate body which made him unfit for a life of action, he turned to writing—first as a literary pastime, later as a necessary means of livelihood. Throughout his life Irving alternated between periods of feverish literary activity and of absolute laziness. Sometimes he would not touch a pen for months. Fortunately in youth he had a well-to-do merchant father, and several brothers who sacrificed not a little to give their talented younger brother his chance at success.

If it is true that early environment plays an important role in determining what a child is to become, it is not hard to understand why Irving in manhood was tolerant and gentle even as his mild Episcopalian mother. He revolted against the over-strict religious training of a Scotch-Presbyterian father who, like the Puritans, believed all pleasures wicked. Always a dreamer, the lad escaped as often as possible from home and the boredom of school to the quays of "old New York," where he could watch tall clipper ships, their "trucks aloft in sun-glow red as blood," and dream of lands beyond the sea. Once he tried to run away as a sailor.

Consumption threatened Irving at twenty-one, and his brothers sent him on a two-year European voyage. This incident was of great significance in the author's life—not only restoring his health, but giving him that love of travel and deepening capacity for friendships that, later, so distinguished Irving from his countrymen. He became a "cosmopolitan" figure known and loved on both sides of the Atlantic. His easy charm immediately attracted such men as Scott, Dickens, Thackeray and gained him audience with royalty.

Social life engrossed Irving on his return. Incidentally he contributed to a series of humorous articles, *Salmagundi Papers,* poking fun at his fellow-townsmen. Very incidentally he became a law clerk. We are interested in his legal career only as it serves as a background for his ill-fated romance with Matilda Hoffman, his senior partner's daughter. Their love was broken by her death from consumption at seventeen. Though he had other love-affairs in later life, Irving never married, and he cherished Matilda's miniature, Prayer Book, and Bible till his death.

Under the spur of this first sorrow Irving set to work in real earnest. His first work of note, *The Knickerbocker History of New York* (1809), was a burlesque history of New Amsterdam, recounting with quaint humor the picturesque oddities of Governor Wouter Van Twiller and the old Dutch settlers. It is the first genuine piece of American humor, and brings a smile even now with its quiet, rippling satire that amuses but never stings.

Yet dark days were ahead. Irving's trip to Liverpool in 1815 to manage his brothers' foreign interests resulted in bankruptcy, and for years Irving floundered financially. Almost as a last resource he turned to his pen, sending to his brother in America story-essays, mostly of English setting, under the general title of *The Sketch Book*. Such masterpieces as *Rip Van Winkle* and *The Legend of Sleepy Hollow* were highly praised in the United States. In 1820 the numbers of *The Sketch Book* were collected and printed in England, where they were welcomed with equal cordiality. Irving's fame was established.

Several years were to pass before Washington Irving saw America again. For some time he idled: traveling; writing a few scattered tales like *Bracebridge Hall* in the manner of *The Sketch Book;* spending a gay season with royalty at Dresden, where he seems to have fallen in love with an English lass, Emily Foster; and, curiously enough, collaborating with John Howard Payne, the author of *Home Sweet Home,* in the writing of several plays which were produced in London with fair success. In 1826 money matters came up again and Irving became an attaché at the American Legation in Madrid, Spain.

Spain opened a new chapter in Irving's life. Under the spell of its romantic past he wrote *The Life of Columbus* and *The Conquest of Granada,* which placed him among the first historians of the day. In these creations Irving not only showed his versatility in changing from the essay to history, but struck a new note—"accurate, romantic, fictionized history."

His homecoming in 1832 after seventeen years in Europe, the last three years of which were spent as Secretary of the American Legation in London, brought enthusiastic reception. Fêted, offered Congressional distinction, and a Tammany nomination for the mayoralty of New York—Irving preferred to settle down at Sunnyside, his charming estate on the Hudson near Tarrytown, and devote himself to publishing his *Alhambra,* the vivid account of the famous castle of the Moors in Spain. By special permission of the Spanish government Irving had lived for some time in this picturesque Moorish ruin.

Irving added to his reputation in Spain when in 1841 he returned as American ambassador under appointment from President Tyler. The greatness of Irving as a diplomat has been too often slighted. At a time when Spain was in the throes of revolution, Irving maintained the respect and honor of the United States at court. Later he was instrumental in settling the English-American dispute over the "54° 40′" boundary between the United States and Canada, when war seemed inevitable. Irving's early efforts for international good-will and honesty rank him among our first able ambassadors.

After his term as Ambassador to Spain, the author spent his remaining years at Sunnyside, the acknowledged dean of American letters. In 1849 he published his *Life of Goldsmith,* the great eighteenth century essayist, whose graceful style had so influenced Irving in *The Sketch Book.* A monumental work on *The Life of Washington* closed Irving's literary efforts and he died in the year of its publication, 1859. He was buried at Sleepy Hollow, where, Irving tells us in one of his stories, Ichabod Crane had clattered past, pursued by the headless horseman.

In his writing, as in his life, Washington Irving taught the philosophy of kindness and generosity. Yet he never preached. His message was himself—genial, modest, lovable. Very much like the essayists Steele and Goldsmith, he wrote flowing, perfectly polished prose, punctuated with dashes of humor and sentiment, tinged with romantic imagination. The lack of punch and excitement in Irving's writing lessens its popularity today. In his own time his pleasant story-essays, his vivid historical work, his gentle humor came as an enjoyable refreshment to folk who had tasted enough of the battle and scuffle of life.

Few writers have so unstained a literary reputation as Irving. He is one of the rare artists who never held a literary grudge or had an author's quarrel. On one occasion at personal sacrifice, he voluntarily gave up writing a history of Mexico because Prescott, a fellow-historian, had planned to write one. Not many would have been so charitable.

Withal he was a shy, dignified gentleman with a roguish twinkle in his eye, whose love for his brothers and sisters ran like a golden thread through his life. He often fell asleep at dinner. He wore a wig. He walked with kings and crowds and lost not his virtue or the common touch. He wrote pleasantly on many subjects. Had there been a Nobel Prize for distinction in the field of literature Washington Irving would probably have won it.

## THE SKETCHES

*The Sketch Book,* product of necessity, born out of discouragement, made Washington Irving famous. *The Knickerbocker History* had gained its author recognition, but the appearance of the first *Sketches,* in 1819, including the immortal story of *Rip Van Winkle,* brought Irving international favor. Almost in desperation he had turned to his pen after the failure of his brother's firm—the first American author to write for a living—and forwarded the first installment of his semi-narrative essays on English life to his brother Ebenezer in New York. He attached the cryptic note: "Should it not succeed—should my writings not acquire critical applause, I am content to throw up the pen and take to any commonplace employment." And he added in a sentence indicative of his true patriotism: " . . . My greatest desire is to make myself worthy of the good will of my countrymen."

It is interesting that the successful publication of the English edition of *The Sketch Book* was largely due to the fine-spirited efforts of Sir Walter Scott who was then at the height of his fame. Irving had unsuccessfully asked Murray, the prince of English booksellers, to publish his work. An attempt to bring out an edition by a lesser known publisher failed. Discouraged, Irving sought out Scott who, ever generous and chivalrous, prevailed upon the great Murray to publish *The Sketch Book.* In gratitude and appreciation Irving dedicated the English edition of the *Sketches* to Sir Walter. The fortunes of literature are strange. In 1826 Scott himself crashed to financial ruin and six years later died bravely trying to pay his debts.

The title, *The Sketch Book—of Geoffrey Crayon, Gent.,* indicates Irving's usual modesty by the use of a "nom de plume" and fittingly suggests the sweep of the work. It is a rambling sort of book, having no particular aim, much like an artist's sketch book with its happy abandonment to whatever subject pops up. Under the influence of one of his dearest friends, Washington Allston, the noted American painter, Irving had once thought of becoming an artist, and the nature of *The Sketch Book* suggests that it is an attempt to paint in prose what he would have liked to execute with brush and palette. So the sketches group themselves loosely, ranging from a character study of an American Indian chief to a description of Westminster Abbey. Now he talks about a village lass; next, in whimsical mood, he strikes off the weird story of a spectre bridegroom. He wanders through an English countryside, observes a rural church, celebrates an old-fashioned Christmas at Bracebridge Hall, runs over to Stratford-on-Avon to see where Will Shakespeare grew up, pays a visit to an old tavern. Turning to criticism Irving comments on the attitude of English writers toward America, pokes good natured fun at "John Bull," defends the American Indian. In such a many-shifting collection the only unity lies in the pensive, leisurely mood of the author. Geoffrey Crayon is not in a hurry; his essays move along with pleasant pace; he does not mind sitting down for a bit of a smoke and an honest enjoyment of nature.

This quietly modest note in the essays constitutes probably the chief difficulty to modern students, who in their first reading in *The Sketch Book* find Irving's writing stiff and formal. Though writing in the Romantic period Irving clung to the essay style of Addison and Steele which is distinguished by its polished form, flowing periodic sentences, abstract and rather long words, arranged in balanced, unhurried paragraphs.

There is a noticeable difference between Irving's *Sketches* and the essays of our time. The tempo of writing has changed as fashions change. Shorter, simple, concrete words, sentences looser in structure, and language brought closer to the everyday speech of people, mark the general tenor of prose today. Essay writing will probably never go back to the stately, decorous style of Irving and the earlier models of Steele, Addison, and Goldsmith, but just as convention and revolt, classicism and romanticism, have alternated in poetry, so it is probable that in some degree formalism will return to the essay. Washington Irving's essays are characterized by—

(1) Flowing, well-rounded sentences
(2) Romantic imagination (delight in romantic past)
(3) Quiet, subtle humor
(4) Admirable sense of form
(5) No attempt at moralizing
(6) Semi-narrative, semi-expositive method ("story-essay")
(7) "Delicately refined romantic sentiment . . . set forth in delicately refined classic style."

The *Sketches* must be read slowly for an appreciation of their real charm. Try to throw yourself back into the days of eighteenth century England where stage-coaches still lumbered merrily over the turnpikes . . . where Bracebridge Hall still held forth in old-fashioned jollity at Christmas-tide . . . where life moved leisurely and gracefully . . . where, too, the embers of anger at a new United States had not completely died down. Go with a warm-spirited Irving along the by-paths of old England from quaint Little Britain in London where Ben Franklin stayed—to the ruddy kitchen-fire of a genuine Devonshire inn. You have a good guide, genial Washington Irving.

A travel-jaunt is always more interesting when one has an itinerary. Accordingly the *Sketches* have been arranged arbitrarily by the editor under five headings: rambles along English lanes and hedgerows are grouped under *The Broad Highway;* the second group tells its own magic story, *London Town;* a holiday retreat at Bracebridge Hall comes as *A Christmas Interlude;* the author's thoughts and criticisms of literature and life appear as reflections on *Men and Books;* and, as shadows fall, and pipes come out, Irving tells some stories *By an Inn Fire.* Bon Voyage, Reader!

# THE SKETCH BOOK

## *THE BROAD HIGHWAY*

### THE AUTHOR'S ACCOUNT OF HIMSELF

In his early years Irving dreamed the dreams of youth and felt the magic of the sea. With refreshing simplicity he confesses in this first sketch his boyhood desire for new lands and new faces. Irving in spirit was a romanticist. He knew the secret of Longfellow's lines:

> "A boy's will is the wind's will,
> And the thoughts of youth are long, long thoughts."

It is pleasing to remember that these youthful yearnings were gratified and that when the time came to settle down at Sunnyside on the banks of the Hudson he had seen many of the quaint and beautiful places of the earth.

I was always fond of visiting new scenes, and observing strange characters and manners. Even when a mere child I began my travels, and made many tours of discovery into foreign parts and unknown regions of my native city, to the frequent alarm of my parents, and the emolument of the town crier. As I grew into boyhood, I extended the range of my observations. My holiday afternoons were spent in rambles about the surrounding country. I made myself familiar with all its places famous in history or fable. I knew every spot where a murder or robbery had been committed, or a ghost seen. I visited the neighboring villages, and added greatly to my stock of knowledge, by noting their habits and customs, and conversing with their sages and great men. I even journeyed one long summer's day to the summit of the most distant hill, whence I stretched my eye over many a mile of terra incognita,[1] and was astonished to find how vast a globe I inhabited.

This rambling propensity strengthened with my years. Books of voyages and travels became my passion, and in devouring their contents I neglected the regular exercises of the school. How wistfully would I wander about the pier heads in fine weather, and watch the parting ships, bound to distant climes—with what longing eyes would I gaze after their lessening sails, and waft myself in imagination to the ends of the earth!

[1] TERRA INCOGNITA—Unknown country.

Further reading and thinking, though they brought this vague inclination into more reasonable bounds, only served to make it more decided. I visited various parts of my own country; and had I been merely a lover of fine scenery, I should have felt little desire to seek elsewhere its gratification: for on no country have the charms of nature been more prodigally lavished. Her mighty lakes, like oceans of liquid silver; her mountains, with their bright aërial tints; her valleys, teeming with wild fertility; her tremendous cataracts, thundering in their solitudes; her boundless plains, waving with spontaneous verdure; her broad deep rivers, rolling in solemn silence to the ocean; her trackless forests, where vegetation puts forth all its magnificence; her skies, kindling with the magic of summer clouds and glorious sunshine:—no, never need an American look beyond his own country for the sublime and beautiful of natural scenery.

But Europe held forth the charms of storied and poetical association. There were to be seen the masterpieces of art, the refinements of highly cultivated society, the quaint peculiarities of ancient and local custom. My native country was full of youthful promise; Europe was rich in the accumulated treasures of age. Her very ruins told the history of times gone by, and every mouldering stone was a chronicle. I longed to wander over the scenes of renowned achievement—to tread, as it were, in the footsteps of antiquity—to loiter about the ruined castle—to meditate on the falling tower—to escape, in short, from the commonplace realities of the present, and lose myself among the shadowy grandeurs of the past.

I had, beside all this, an earnest desire to see the great men of the earth. We have, it is true, our great men in America: not a city but has an ample share of them. I have mingled among them in my time, and been almost withered by the shade into which they cast me; for there is nothing so baleful to a small man as the shade of a great one, particularly the great man of a city. But I was anxious to see the great men of Europe; for I had read in the works of various philosophers, that all animals degenerated in America, and man among the number. A great man of Europe, thought I, must therefore be as superior to a great man of America as a peak of the Alps to a highland of the Hudson; and in this idea I was confirmed, by observing the comparative importance and swelling magnitude of many English travellers among us, who, I was assured, were very little people in their own country. I will visit this land of wonders, thought I, and see the gigantic race from which I am degenerated.

It has been either my good or evil lot to have my roving passion gratified. I have wandered through different countries, and witnessed many of the shifting scenes of life. I cannot say that I have studied them with the eye of a philosopher, but rather with the sauntering gaze with which humble lovers of the picturesque stroll from the window of one print-shop to another; caught sometimes by the delineations of beauty, sometimes by the distortions of caricature, and sometimes by the loveliness of landscape. As it is the fashion for modern tourists to travel pencil in hand, and bring home their portfolios filled with sketches, I am disposed to get up a few for the entertainment of my friends. When, however, I look over the hints and memorandums I have taken down for the purpose, my heart almost fails me, at finding how my idle humor has led me aside from the great objects studied by every regular traveller who would make a book. I fear I shall give equal disappointment with an unlucky landscape-painter, who had travelled on the Continent, but, following the bent of his vagrant inclination, had sketched in nooks, and corners, and by-places. His sketch-book was accordingly crowded with cottages, and landscapes, and obscure ruins; but he had neglected to paint St. Peter's, or the Coliseum; the Cascade of Terni,[2] or the Bay of Naples; and had not a single glacier or volcano in his whole collection.

## QUESTIONS AND EXERCISES

Exercises preceded by a star are designed for assignment at the discretion of the teacher, or for any student who volunteers.

1. What traits of the author's personality do you learn at the outset of this first sketch?
2. Bearing in mind the general introduction to the *Sketches,* criticize Irving's style in the paragraph on natural beauty in America beginning, "Further reading and thinking . . ."
3. What are Irving's reasons for going to Europe? Would they be your reasons?
4 Write an "account of yourself" prior to a dreamed-of voyage.

*5. Read No. 1 Paper of *The Spectator Papers* for Addison's account of himself. Compare it with this first essay of Irving's in purpose; manner of writing.

[2] CASCADE OF TERNI—Beautiful Italian falls north of Rome.

## THE VOYAGE

Although Irving did not feel the mystical lure of the sea that inspired many of the poems of Masefield and the novels of Conrad, he was sensitive to its pictorial majesty—the lone sail on the horizon, the tumult of cloud and ocean in the storm, the unexpected emergence of a headland that had been hidden in mist, and the vastness of the waters under the dome of sky. These things he described with more awe than sympathy, but one must remember that in his day a voyage across the Atlantic was an undertaking of considerable hazard. Passengers were more concerned in reaching their destination than in philosophizing about the mysteries of the deep. While "The Voyage" has a certain superficiality, it is typical of the literary fashion in Irving's day of describing the sea.

To an American visiting Europe, the long[1] voyage he has to make is an excellent preparative. The temporary absence of worldly scenes and employments produces a state of mind peculiarly fitted to receive new and vivid impressions. The vast space of waters that separates the hemispheres is like a blank page in existence. There is no gradual transition by which, as in Europe, the features and population of one country blend almost imperceptibly with those of another. From the moment you lose sight of the land you have left, all is vacancy, until you step on the opposite shore, and are launched at once into the bustle and novelties of another world.

In travelling by land there is a continuity of scene, and a connected succession of persons and incidents, that carry on the story of life, and lessen the effect of absence and separation. We drag, it is true, "a lengthening chain" at each remove of our pilgrimage; but the chain is unbroken; we can trace it back link by link; and we feel that the last still grapples us to home. But a wide sea voyage severs us at once. It makes us conscious of being cast loose from the secure anchorage of settled life, and sent adrift upon a doubtful world. It interposes a gulf, not merely imaginary, but real, between us and our homes—a gulf subject to tempest, and fear, and uncertainty, rendering distance palpable, and return precarious.

Such, at least, was the case with myself. As I saw the last blue line of my native land fade away like a cloud in the horizon, it seemed as if I had closed one volume of the world and its concerns, and had time for meditation, before I opened another. That land,

---

[1] LONG—Irving's voyage from New York to Bordeaux in 1804 took forty-two days.

too, now vanishing from my view, which contained all most dear to me in life; what vicissitudes might occur in it—what changes might take place in me, before I should visit it again! Who can tell, when he sets forth to wander, whither he may be driven by the uncertain currents of existence; or when he may return; or whether it may ever be his lot to revisit the scenes of his childhood?

I said that at sea all is vacancy: I should correct the expression. To one given to day dreaming, and fond of losing himself in reveries, a sea voyage is full of subjects for meditation; but then they are the wonders of the deep and of the air, and rather tend to abstract the mind from worldly themes. I delighted to loll over the quarter-railing, or climb to the main-top, of a calm day, and muse for hours together on the tranquil bosom of a summer's sea;—to gaze upon the piles of golden clouds just peering above the horizon; fancy them some fairy realms, and people them with a creation of my own;—to watch the gentle undulating billows, rolling their silver volumes, as if to die away on those happy shores.

There was a delicious sensation of mingled security and awe with which I looked down, from my giddy height, on the monsters of the deep at their uncouth gambols: shoals of porpoises tumbling about the bow of the ship; the grampus[2] slowly heaving his huge form above the surface; or the ravenous shark, darting, like a spectre, through the blue waters. My imagination would conjure up all that I had heard or read of the watery world beneath me: of the finny herds that roam its fathomless valleys; of the shapeless monsters that lurk among the very foundations of the earth, and of those wild phantasms that swell the tales of fishermen and sailors.

Sometimes a distant sail, gliding along the edge of the ocean, would be another theme of idle speculation. How interesting this fragment of a world, hastening to rejoin the great mass of existence! What a glorious monument of human invention; which has in a manner triumphed over wind and wave; has brought the ends of the world into communion; has established an interchange of blessings, pouring into the sterile regions of the north all the luxuries of the south; has diffused the light of knowledge and the charities of cultivated life; and has thus bound together those scattered portions of the human race, between which nature seemed to have thrown an insurmountable barrier.

[2] Grampus—A "killer" whale.

We one day descried some shapeless object drifting at a distance. At sea everything that breaks the monotony of the surrounding expanse attracts attention. It proved to be the mast of a ship that must have been completely wrecked; for there were the remains of handkerchiefs, by which some of the crew had fastened themselves to this spar, to prevent their being washed off by the waves. There was no trace by which the name of the ship could be ascertained. The wreck had evidently drifted about for many months; clusters of shell-fish had fastened about it, and long sea-weeds flaunted at its sides. But where, thought I, is the crew? Their struggle has long been over—they have gone down amidst the roar of the tempest—their bones lie whitening among the caverns of the deep. Silence, oblivion, like the waves, have closed over them, and no one can tell the story of their end. What sighs have been wafted after that ship; what prayers offered up at the deserted fireside of home! How often has the mistress, the wife, the mother, pored over the daily news, to catch some casual intelligence of this rover of the deep! How has expectation darkened into anxiety—anxiety into dread—and dread into despair! Alas! not one memento may ever return for love to cherish. All that may ever be known, is, that she sailed from her port, "and was never heard of more!"

The sight of this wreck, as usual, gave rise to many dismal anecdotes. This was particularly the case in the evening, when the weather, which had hitherto been fair, began to look wild and threatening, and gave indications of one of those sudden storms which will sometimes break in upon the serenity of a summer voyage. As we sat round the dull light of a lamp, in the cabin, that made the gloom more ghastly, every one had his tale of shipwreck and disaster. I was particularly struck with a short one related by the captain.

"As I was once sailing," said he, "in a fine, stout ship, across the banks of Newfoundland, one of those heavy fogs which prevail in those parts rendered it impossible for us to see far ahead, even in the daytime; but at night, the weather was so thick that we could not distinguish any object at twice the length of the ship. I kept lights at the mast-head, and a constant watch forward to look out for fishing smacks, which are accustomed to lie at anchor on the banks. The wind was blowing a smacking breeze, and we were going at a great rate through the water. Suddenly the watch gave the alarm of a 'sail ahead!'—it was scarcely uttered before we were upon her. She was a small schooner, at anchor, with her broadside towards us. The crew were all asleep, and had neglected to hoist a light. We struck her just amid-ships. The force, the size, and weight of our vessel bore her down below the waves; we passed over her and were hurried on our course. As the crashing wreck was sinking beneath us, I had a glimpse of two or three half-naked wretches, rushing from her cabin; they just started from their beds to be swallowed shrieking by the waves. I heard their drowning cry mingling with the wind. The blast that bore it to our ears, swept us out of all farther hearing. I shall never forget that cry! It was some time before we could put the ship about, she was under such headway. We returned, as nearly as we could guess, to the place where the smack had anchored. We cruised about for several hours in the dense fog. We fired signal-guns, and listened if we might hear the halloo of any survivors: but all was silent—we never saw or heard any thing of them more."

I confess these stories, for a time, put an end to all my fine fancies. The storm increased with the night. The sea was lashed into tremendous confusion. There was a fearful, sullen sound of rushing waves and broken surges. Deep called unto deep.[3] At times the black column of clouds overhead seemed rent asunder by flashes of lightning which quivered along the foaming billows, and made the succeeding darkness doubly terrible. The thunders bellowed over the wild waste of waters, and were echoed and prolonged by the mountain waves. As I saw the ship staggering and plunging among these roaring caverns, it seemed miraculous that she regained her balance, or preserved her buoyancy. Her yards[4] would dip into the water; her bow was almost buried beneath the waves. Sometimes an impending surge appeared ready to overwhelm her, and nothing but a dexterous movement of the helm preserved her from the shock.

When I retired to my cabin, the awful scene still followed me. The whistling of the wind through the rigging sounded like funereal wailings. The creaking of the masts; the straining and groaning of bulk heads, as the ship labored in the weltering sea, were frightful. As I heard the waves rushing along the sides of the ship, and

[3] DEEP . . . DEEP—See Psalm 42:7.

[4] YARDS—Spars or cross-arms to support square sails.

roaring in my very ear, it seemed as if Death were raging round this floating prison, seeking for his prey: the mere starting of a nail, the yawning of a seam, might give him entrance.

A fine day, however, with a tranquil sea and favoring breeze, soon put all these dismal reflections to flight. It is impossible to resist the gladdening influence of fine weather and fair wind at sea. When the ship is decked out in all her canvas, every sail swelled, and careering gayly over the curling waves, how lofty, how gallant she appears—how she seems to lord it over the deep!

I might fill a volume with the reveries of a sea voyage; for with me it is almost a continual reverie—but it is time to get to shore.

It was a fine sunny morning when the thrilling cry of "land!" was given from the mast-head. None but those who have experienced it can form an idea of the delicious throng of sensations which rush into an American's bosom when he first comes in sight of Europe. There is a volume of associations with the very name. It is the land of promise, teeming with everything of which his childhood has heard, or on which his studious years have pondered.

From that time, until the moment of arrival, it was all feverish excitement. The ships of war that prowled like guardian giants along the coast; the headlands of Ireland, stretching out into the channel, the Welsh mountains towering into the clouds; all were objects of intense interest. As we sailed up the Mersey,[5] I reconnoitred the shores with a telescope. My eye dwelt with delight on neat cottages, with their trim shrubberies and green grass-plots. I saw the mouldering ruin of an abbey overrun with ivy, and the taper spire of a village church rising from the brow of a neighboring hill—all were characteristic of England.

The tide and wind were so favorable, that the ship was enabled to come at once to the pier. It was thronged with people; some idle lookers-on, others eager expectants of friends or relatives. I could distinguish the merchant to whom the ship was consigned. I knew him by his calculating brow and restless air. His hands were thrust into his pockets, he was whistling thoughtfully, and walking to and fro, a small space having been accorded him by the crowd, in deference to his temporary importance. There were

---

[5] MERSEY—Important river on the northwest coast of England, forming a harbor for the great port of Liverpool.

repeated cheerings and salutations interchanged between the shore and the ship, as friends happened to recognize each other. I particularly noticed one young woman of humble dress, but interesting demeanor. She was leaning forward from among the crowd; her eye hurried over the ship as it neared the shore, to catch some wished-for countenance. She seemed disappointed and agitated; when I heard a faint voice call her name. It was from a poor sailor who had been ill all the voyage, and had excited the sympathy of every one on board. When the weather was fine, his messmates had spread a mattress for him on deck in the shade, but of late his illness had so increased that he had taken to his hammock, and only breathed a wish that he might see his wife before he died. He had been helped on deck as we came up the river, and was now leaning against the shrouds, with a countenance so wasted, so pale, so ghastly, that it was no wonder even the eye of affection did not recognize him. But at the sound of his voice, her eye darted on his features; it read, at once, a whole volume of sorrow; she clasped her hands, uttered a faint shriek, and stood wringing them in silent agony.

All now was hurry and bustle. The meetings of acquaintances—the greetings of friends—the consultations of men of business. I alone was solitary and idle. I had no friend to meet, no cheering to receive. I stepped upon the land of my forefathers—but felt that I was a stranger in the land.

## QUESTIONS AND EXERCISES

Exercises preceded by a star are designed for assignment at the discretion of the teacher, or for any student who volunteers.

1. What makes the first sentence of the essay lack interest as a beginning? Suggest a better.
2. Outline the steps by which Irving develops the sketch.
3. What interests Irving most at sea?
4. Does Irving make you feel the power of what a modern American dramatist has called "dat ole davil, sea"?

*5. Conrad is one of the masters of sea-story writing. Read his *Youth,* a tale steeped in the weird fascination of the sea, and report on it to the class.

*6. To realize, as Irving did not, how strong for some people is the call of the sea, read Masefield's poem, *Sea-Fever.*

## RURAL LIFE IN ENGLAND

When an American visits England he inevitably makes contrasts. Irving was no exception, and in this essay an early nineteenth century American comments on early nineteenth century England. His observations and reflections, interspersed with pleasant descriptive passages, combine to paint an England of old lanes, hedgerows, Tudor manors, sturdy cottages, silver lakes, simple farm-folk, and genteel country squires. This sketch admirably illustrates Irving's formal style.

The stranger who would form a correct opinion of the English character, must not confine his observations to the metropolis. He must go forth into the country; he must sojourn in villages and hamlets; he must visit castles, villas, farm-houses, cottages; he must wander through parks and gardens; along hedges and green lanes; he must loiter about country churches; attend wakes and fairs, and other rural festivals; and cope with the people in all their conditions, and all their habits and humors.

In some countries the large cities absorb the wealth and fashion of the nation; they are the only fixed abodes of elegant and intelligent society, and the country is inhabited almost entirely by boorish peasantry. In England, on the contrary, the metropolis is a mere gathering-place, or general rendezvous, of the polite classes, where they devote a small portion of the year to a hurry of gayety and dissipation, and, having indulged this kind of carnival, return again to the apparently more congenial habits of rural life. The various orders of society are therefore diffused over the whole surface of the kingdom, and the most retired neighborhoods afford specimens of the different ranks.

The English, in fact, are strongly gifted with the rural feeling. They possess a quick sensibility to the beauties of nature, and a keen relish for the pleasures and employments of the country. This passion seems inherent in them. Even the inhabitants of cities, born and brought up among brick walls and bustling streets, enter with facility into rural habits, and evince a tact for rural occupation. The merchant has his snug retreat in the vicinity of the metropolis, where he often displays as much pride and zeal in the cultivation of his flower-garden, and the maturing of his fruits, as he does in the conduct of his business, and the success of a commercial enterprise. Even those less fortunate individuals, who are doomed to pass their lives in the midst of din and traffic, contrive to have something that shall remind them of the green aspect of nature. In the most dark and dingy quarters of the city, the drawing-room window resembles frequently a bank of flowers; every spot capable of vegetation has its grass-plot and flower-bed; and every square its mimic park, laid out with picturesque taste, and gleaming with refreshing verdure.

Those who see the Englishman only in town, are apt to form an unfavorable opinion of his social character. He is either absorbed in business, or distracted by the thousand engagements that dissipate time, thought, and feeling, in this huge metropolis. He has, therefore, too commonly, a look of hurry and abstraction. Wherever he happens to be, he is on the point of going somewhere else; at the moment he is talking on one subject, his mind is wandering to another; and while paying a friendly visit, he is calculating how he shall economize time so as to pay the other visits allotted in the morning. An immense metropolis, like London, is calculated to make men selfish and uninteresting. In their casual and transient meetings, they can but deal briefly in commonplaces. They present but the cold superficies[1] of character—its rich and genial qualities have no time to be warmed into a flow.

It is in the country that the Englishman gives scope to his natural feelings. He breaks loose gladly from the cold formalities and negative civilities of town, throws off his habits of shy reserve, and becomes joyous and free-hearted. He manages to collect round him all the conveniences and elegancies of polite life, and to banish its restraints. His country-seat abounds with every requisite, either for studious retirement, tasteful gratification, or rural exercise. Books, paintings, music, horses, dogs, and sporting implements of all kinds, are at hand. He puts no constraint, either upon his guests or himself, but, in the true spirit of hospitality, provides the means of enjoyment, and leaves every one to partake according to his inclination.

The taste of the English in the cultivation of land, and in what is called landscape gardening, is unrivalled. They have studied Nature intently, and discover an exquisite sense of her beautiful forms and harmonious combinations. Those charms, which in other countries, she lavishes in wild solitudes, are here assembled round the haunts of domestic life. They seem to have caught her coy and

[1] SUPERFICIES—Surface, or exterior.

furtive graces, and spread them, like witchery, about their rural abodes.

Nothing can be more imposing than the magnificence of English park scenery. Vast lawns that extend like sheets of vivid green, with here and there clumps of gigantic trees, heaping up rich piles of foliage. The solemn pomp of groves and woodland glades, with the deer trooping in silent herds across them; the hare bounding away to the covert; or the pheasant, suddenly bursting upon the wing. The brook, taught to wind in natural meanderings, or expand into a glassy lake—the sequestered pool, reflecting the quivering trees, with the yellow leaf sleeping on its bosom, and the trout roaming fearlessly about its limpid waters: while some rustic temple, or sylvan statue, grown green and dank with age, gives an air of classic sanctity to the seclusion.

These are but a few of the features of park scenery; but what most delights me, is the creative talent with which the English decorate the unostentatious abodes of middle life. The rudest habitation, the most unpromising and scanty portion of land, in the hands of an Englishman of taste, becomes a little paradise. With a nicely discriminating eye, he seizes at once upon its capabilities, and pictures in his mind the future landscape. The sterile spot grows into loveliness under his hand; and yet the operations of art which produce the effect are scarcely to be perceived. The cherishing and training of some trees; the cautious pruning of others; the nice distribution of flowers and plants of tender and graceful foliage; the introduction of a green slope of velvet turf; the partial opening to a peep of blue distance, or silver gleam of water—all these are managed with a delicate tact, a pervading yet quiet assiduity, like the magic touchings with which a painter finishes up a favorite picture.

The residence of people of fortune and refinement in the country has diffused a degree of taste and elegance in rural economy, that descends to the lowest class. The very laborer, with his thatched cottage and narrow slip of ground, attends to their embellishment. The trim hedge, the grass-plot before the door, the little flower-bed bordered with snug box, the woodbine trained up against the wall, and hanging its blossoms about the lattice; the pot of flowers in the window; the holly, providently planted about the house, to cheat winter of its dreariness, and to throw in a semblance of green summer to cheer the fireside:—all these bespeak the influence of taste, flowing down from high sources, and pervading the lowest levels of the public mind. If ever Love, as poets sing, delights to visit a cottage, it must be the cottage of an English peasant.

The fondness for rural life among the higher classes of the English has had a great and salutary effect upon the national character. I do not know a finer race of men than the English gentlemen. Instead of the softness and effeminacy which characterize the men of rank in most countries, they exhibit a union of elegance and strength, a robustness of frame and freshness of complexion, which I am inclined to attribute to their living so much in the open air, and pursuing so eagerly the invigorating recreations of the country. These hardy exercises produce also a healthful tone of mind and spirits, and a manliness and simplicity of manners, which even the follies and dissipations of the town cannot easily pervert, and can never entirely destroy. In the country, too, the different orders of society seem to approach more freely, to be more disposed to blend and operate favorably upon each other. The distinctions between them do not appear to be so marked and impassable, as in the cities. The manner in which property has been distributed into small estates and farms, has established a regular gradation from the nobleman, through the classes of gentry, small landed proprietors, and substantial farmers, down to the laboring peasantry; and while it has thus banded the extremes of society together, has infused into each intermediate rank a spirit of independence. This, it must be confessed, is not so universally the case at present as it was formerly; the larger estates having, in late years of distress, absorbed the smaller, and, in some parts of the country, almost annihilated the sturdy race of small farmers. These, however, I believe, are but casual breaks in the general system I have mentioned.

In rural occupation there is nothing mean and debasing. It leads a man forth among scenes of natural grandeur and beauty; it leaves him to the workings of his own mind, operated upon by the purest and most elevating of external influences. Such a man may be simple and rough, but he cannot be vulgar. The man of refinement, therefore, finds nothing revolting in an intercourse with the lower orders in rural life, as he does when he casually mingles with the lower orders of cities. He lays aside his distance and reserve, and is glad to waive the distinctions of rank, and to enter into the honest, heart-felt enjoyments of common life. Indeed, the very amusements of the country bring men more and more together; and the sound of hound and horn blend all feelings into harmony. I believe this is one great reason why the nobility and gentry are more popular among the inferior orders in England than they are in any other country; and why the latter have endured so many excessive pressures and extremities, without repining more generally at the unequal distribution of fortune and privilege.

To this mingling of cultivated and rustic society, may also be attributed the rural feeling that runs through British literature; the frequent use of illustrations from rural life; those incomparable descriptions of Nature, that abound in the British poets—that have continued down from *The Flower and the Leaf* of Chaucer,[2] and have brought into our closets all the freshness and fragrance of the dewy landscape. The pastoral writers of other countries appear as if they had paid Nature an occasional visit, and become acquainted with her general charms; but the British poets have lived and revelled with her—they have wooed her in her most secret haunts—they have watched her minutest caprices. A spray could not tremble in the breeze—a leaf could not rustle to the ground—a diamond drop could not patter in the stream—a fragrance could not exhale from the humble violet, nor a daisy unfold its crimson tints to the morning, but it has been noticed by these impassioned and delicate observers, and wrought up into some beautiful morality.

The effect of this devotion of elegant minds to rural occupations has been wonderful on the face of the country. A great part of the island is rather level, and would be monotonous, were it not for the charms of culture; but it is studded and gemmed, as it were, with castles and palaces, and embroidered with parks and gardens. It does not abound in grand and sublime prospects, but rather in little home scenes of rural repose and sheltered quiet. Every antique farm-house and moss-grown cottage is a picture; and as the roads are continually winding, and the view is shut in by groves and hedges, the eye is delighted by a continual succession of small landscapes of captivating loveliness.

The great charm, however, of English scenery, is the moral feeling that seems to pervade it. It is associated in the mind with

---

[2] CHAUCER—Geoffrey Chaucer (1340–1400) was the first great poet of England. His most famous work is a collection of story-poems, *The Canterbury Tales*.

ideas of order, of quiet, of sober well-established principles, of hoary usage and reverend custom. Everything seems to be the growth of ages of regular and peaceful existence. The old church of remote architecture, with its low massive portal; its Gothic[3] tower; its windows, rich with tracery and painted glass, in scrupulous preservation—its stately monuments of warriors and worthies of the olden time, ancestors of the present lords of the soil—its tombstones, recording successive generations of sturdy yeomanry, whose progeny still plough the same fields, and kneel at the same altar—the parsonage, a quaint irregular pile, partly antiquated, but repaired and altered in the tastes of various ages and occupants—the stile and footpath leading from the church-yard across pleasant fields, and along shady hedgerows, according to an immemorable right of way—the neighboring village, with its venerable cottages, its public green, sheltered by trees, under which the forefathers of the present race have sported—the antique family mansion, standing apart in some little rural domain, but looking down with a protecting air on the surrounding scene—all these common features of English landscape evince a calm and settled security, and hereditary transmission of home-bred virtues and local attachments, that speak deeply and touchingly for the moral character of the nation.

It is a pleasing sight, of a Sunday morning, when the bell is sending its sober melody across the quiet fields, to behold the peasantry in their best finery, with ruddy faces, and modest cheerfulness, thronging tranquilly along the green lanes to church; but it is still more pleasing to see them in the evenings, gathering about their cottage doors, and appearing to exult in the humble comforts and embellishments which their own hands have spread around them.

It is this sweet home feeling, this settled repose of affection in the domestic scene, that is, after all, the parent of the steadiest virtues and purest enjoyments; and I cannot close these desultory remarks better than by quoting the words of a modern English poet,[4] who has depicted it with remarkable felicity.

> Through each gradation, from the castled hall,
> The city dome, the villa crown'd with shade,

[3] Gothic—Originally, pertaining to the Goths, barbarians who invaded Italy in the third century; now applied to medieval church architecture which is marked by pointed arches, stone tracery, flying buttresses, lofty columns. English churches were built on a modified Gothic plan.

[4] A modern English poet—Rev. Rand Kennedy, A.M.

But chief from modest mansions numberless,
In town or hamlet, shelt'ring middle life,
Down to the cottaged vale and straw-roof'd shed;
This western isle hath long been famed for scenes
Where bliss domestic finds a dwelling-place;
Domestic bliss, that, like a harmless dove,
(Honor and sweet endearment keeping guard,)
Can centre in a little quiet nest
All that desire would fly for through the earth;
That can, the world eluding, be itself
A world enjoy'd; that wants no witnesses
But its own sharers and approving heaven;
That, like a flower deep hid in rocky cleft,
Smiles, though 'tis looking only at the sky.

## QUESTIONS AND EXERCISES

Exercises preceded by a star are designed for assignment at the discretion of the teacher, or for any student who volunteers.

1. Do you like Irving's description? Why?
2. What is your impression of the English country gentleman presented by Irving?
3. How does the Englishman's love of nature show itself?
4. Compare the rural life of England, as seen in this sketch, with rural life as we are familiar with it in our country.

*5. Read a modern essay and contrast it with "Rural Life in England."

## THE COUNTRY CHURCH

The first line of this sketch sounds its keynote—"There are few places more favorable to the study of character than an English country church." Irving's interest was in human nature rather than in the service itself, and by a clever comparison of two families present he suggests the true and false types of English nobility. Churches have not changed much, nor the people in them; and the truth in this essay strikes home today.

There are few places more favorable to the study of character than an English country church. I was once passing a few weeks at the seat of a friend, who resided in the vicinity of one, the appearance of which particularly struck my fancy. It was one of those rich morsels of quaint antiquity, which give such a peculiar charm to English landscape. It stood in the midst of a country filled with ancient families, and contained, within its cold and silent aisles, the congregated dust of many noble generations. The interior walls were incrusted with monuments of every age and style. The light streamed through windows dimmed with armorial bearings, richly emblazoned in stained glass. In various parts of the church were tombs of knights, and high-born dames, of gorgeous workmanship, with their effigies in colored marble. On every side the eye was struck with some instance of aspiring mortality; some haughty memorial which human pride had erected over its kindred dust, in this temple of the most humble of all religions.

The congregation was composed of the neighboring people of rank, who sat in pews sumptuously lined and cushioned, furnished with richly gilded prayer-books, and decorated with their arms upon the pew doors; of the villagers and peasantry, who filled the back seats, and a small gallery beside the organ; and of the poor of the parish, who were ranged on benches in the aisles.

The service was performed by a snuffling, well-fed vicar, who had a snug dwelling near the church. He was a privileged guest at all the tables of the neighborhood, and had been the keenest fox-hunter in the country, until age and good living had disabled him from doing anything more than ride to see the hounds throw off,[1] and make one at the hunting dinner.

Under the ministry of such a pastor, I found it impossible to get into the train of thought suitable to the time and place: so, having like many other feeble Christians, compromised with my conscience, by laying the sin of my own delinquency at another person's threshold, I occupied myself by making observations on my neighbors.

I was as yet a stranger in England, and curious to notice the manners of its fashionable classes. I found, as usual, that there was the least pretension where there was the most acknowledged title to respect. I was particularly struck, for instance, with the family of a nobleman of high rank, consisting of several sons and daughters. Nothing could be more simple and unassuming than their appearance. They generally came to church in the plainest equipage, and often on foot. The young ladies would stop and converse in the kindest manner with the peasantry, caress the children, and listen to the stories of the humble cottagers. Their countenances were open and beautifully fair, with an expression of high refinement, but at the same time, a frank cheerfulness, and

[1] HOUNDS . . . OFF—Start of a hunt.

an engaging affability. Their brothers were tall, and elegantly formed. They were dressed fashionably, but simply; with strict neatness and propriety, but without any mannerism or foppishness. Their whole demeanor was easy and natural, with that lofty grace, and noble frankness, which bespeak free-born souls that have never been checked in their growth by feelings of inferiority. There is a healthful hardiness about real dignity, that never dreads contact and communion with others, however humble. It is only spurious pride that is morbid and sensitive, and shrinks from every touch. I was pleased to see the manner in which they would converse with the peasantry about those rural concerns and field sports in which the gentlemen of this country so much delight. In these conversations there was neither haughtiness on the one part, nor servility on the other; and you were only reminded of the difference of rank by the habitual respect of the peasant.

In contrast to these, was the family of a wealthy citizen, who had amassed a vast fortune, and having purchased the estate and mansion of a ruined nobleman in the neighborhood, was endeavoring to assume all the style and dignity of an hereditary lord of the soil. The family always came to church *en prince*.[2] They were rolled majestically along in a carriage emblazoned with arms. The crest glittered in silver radiance from every part of the harness where a crest could possibly be placed. A fat coachman in a three-cornered hat, richly laced, and a flaxen wig, curling close round his rosy face, was seated on the box, with a sleek Danish dog beside him. Two footmen in gorgeous liveries, with huge bouquets and gold-headed canes, lolled behind. The carriage rose and sunk on its long springs with peculiar stateliness of motion. The very horses champed their bits, arched their necks, and glanced their eyes more proudly than common horses; either because they had caught a little of the family feeling, or were reined up more tightly than ordinary.

I could not but admire the style with which this splendid pageant was brought up to the gate of the church-yard. There was a vast effect produced at the turning of an angle of the wall;—a great smacking of the whip; straining and scrambling of horses; glistening of harness, and flashing of wheels through gravel. This was the moment of triumph and vainglory to the coachman. The horses were urged and checked, until they were fretted into a foam. They

[2] EN PRINCE—Like a prince.

threw out their feet in a prancing trot, dashing about pebbles at every step. The crowd of villagers sauntering quietly to church, opened precipitately to the right and left, gaping in vacant admiration. On reaching the gate, the horses were pulled up with a suddenness that produced an immediate stop, and almost threw them on their haunches.

There was an extraordinary hurry of the footmen to alight, pull down the steps, and prepare everything for the descent on earth of this august family. The old citizen first emerged his round red face from out the door, looking about him with the pompous air of a man accustomed to rule on 'change,[3] and shake the stock market with a nod. His consort, a fine, fleshy, comfortable dame, followed him. There seemed, I must confess, but little pride in her composition. She was the picture of broad, honest, vulgar enjoyment. The world went well with her; and she liked the world. She had fine clothes, a fine house, a fine carriage, fine children, everything was fine about her: it was nothing but driving about, and visiting and feasting. Life was to her a perpetual revel; it was one long Lord Mayor's Day.[4]

Two daughters succeeded to this goodly couple. They certainly were handsome; but had a supercilious air that chilled admiration, and disposed the spectator to be critical. They were ultra-fashionable in dress, and, though no one could deny the richness of their decorations, yet their appropriateness might be questioned amidst the simplicity of a country church. They descended loftily from the carriage, and moved up the line of peasantry with a step that seemed dainty of the soil it trod on. They cast an excursive glance around, that passed coldly over the burly faces of the peasantry, until they met the eyes of the nobleman's family, when their countenances immediately brightened into smiles, and they made the most profound and elegant courtesies, which were returned in a manner that showed they were but slight acquaintances.

I must not forget the two sons of this aspiring citizen, who came to church in a dashing curricle,[5] with outriders.[6] They were arrayed in the extremity of the mode, with all that pedantry of dress which

---

[3] 'Change—London Stock Exchange.

[4] Lord Mayor's Day—The people of London celebrate November 9, the day on which the newly-elected mayor takes the oath of office.

[5] Curricle—Light two-wheeled carriage.

[6] Outriders—Servants on horseback.

marks the man of questionable pretensions to style. They kept entirely by themselves, eyeing every one askance that came near them as if measuring his claims to respectability; yet they were without conversation, except the exchange of an occasional cant phrase. They even moved artificially, for their bodies, in compliance with the caprice of the day, had been disciplined into the absence of all ease and freedom. Art had done everything to accomplish them as men of fashion, but Nature had denied them the nameless grace. They were vulgarly shaped, like men formed for the common purposes of life, and had that air of supercilious assumption which is never seen in the true gentleman.

I have been rather minute in drawing the pictures of these two families, because I considered them specimens of what is often to be met with in this country—the unpretending great and the arrogant little. I have no respect for titled rank, unless it be accompanied with true nobility of soul; but I have remarked, in all countries where artificial distinctions exist, that the very highest classes are always the most courteous and unassuming. Those who are well assured of their own standing, are least apt to trespass on that of others: whereas nothing is so offensive as the aspirings of vulgarity, which thinks to elevate itself by humiliating its neighbor.

As I have brought these families into contrast, I must notice their behavior in church. That of the nobleman's family was quiet, serious, and attentive. Not that they appeared to have any fervor of devotion, but rather a respect for sacred things, and sacred places, inseparable from good-breeding. The others, on the contrary, were in perpetual flutter and whisper; they betrayed a continual consciousness of finery, and a sorry ambition of being the wonders of a rural congregation.

The old gentleman was the only one really attentive to the service. He took the whole burden of family devotion upon himself; standing bolt upright, and uttering the responses with a loud voice that might be heard all over the church. It was evident that he was one of those thorough church and king men, who connect the idea of devotion and loyalty; who consider the Deity, somehow or other, of the government party, and religion "a very excellent sort of thing that ought to be countenanced and kept up."

When he joined so loudly in the service, it seemed more by way of example to the lower orders, to show them, that though so great and wealthy, he was not above being religious; as I have seen a turtle-fed alderman swallow publicly a basin of charity soup, smacking his lips at every mouthful, and pronouncing it "excellent food for the poor."

When the service was at an end, I was curious to witness the several exits of my groups. The young noblemen and their sisters, as the day was fine, preferred strolling home across the fields, chatting with the country people as they went. The others departed as they came, in grand parade. Again were the equipages wheeled up to the gate. There was again the smacking of whips, the clattering of hoofs, and the glittering of harness. The horses started off almost at a bound; the villagers again hurried to right and left; the wheels threw up a cloud of dust, and the aspiring family was rapt out of sight in a whirlwind.

## QUESTIONS AND EXERCISES

**Exercises preceded by a star are designed for assignment at the discretion of the teacher, or for any student who volunteers.**

1. Contrast the two families. Is social rank as important today? Do you feel it should be? Why?
2. How does Irving paint the parson? What excuse does Irving give for not listening to the sermon?
3. Write a description of a church that you have attended, describing the people as well as the building.

*4. In *Tom Sawyer* read the description of Tom's "funeral service." Compare Mark Twain's treatment of this scene with Irving's picture of the country church.

## STRATFORD-ON-AVON

Perhaps it was May and the hawthorn in bloom along the hedgerows when Irving journeyed to Will Shakespeare's birthplace and put up at the Red Horse Inn. More than the mere recounting of a sightseeing trip to a famous literary shrine, Irving's sketch becomes a fascinating pilgrimage with a true lover of the great Elizabethan. You linger in the bare whitewashed room where they say the poet was born. A voluble landlady shows you the *original* splintered musketstock used by young Will on his poaching expeditions through Sir Thomas Lucy's estate. Later, wandering through that estate where tradition says Lucy caught and tried Shakespeare for killing deer, you go down by the quiet Avon. Of course there is a trip to the church under whose chancel the poet is buried, and, although he does not mention it, Irving probably walked over to Shottery by the same lane Shakespeare trod after seeing Anne Hathaway home in the blue of the evening.

Quaint reminiscences and literary allusions give to this longest of Irving's sketches some of the whimsical charm of the early nineteenth century English essayist, Charles Lamb, in his liking for old things: old houses, old books, old wine.

Irving was so taken by his pilgrimage to Stratford-on-Avon that, six years later, he wrote these four lines of poetry about it. This brief verse is now preserved at Stratford-on-Avon:

"Of mighty Shakespeare's birth the room we see;
That where he died, in vain to find we try.
Useless the search:—for all Immortal He,
And those who are Immortal never die."

To a homeless man, who has no spot on this wide world which he can truly call his own, there is a momentary feeling of something like independence and territorial consequence, when, after a weary day's travel, he kicks off his boots, thrusts his feet into slippers, and stretches himself before an inn fire. Let the world without go as it may; let kingdoms rise or fall, so long as he has the wherewithal to pay his bill, he is, for the time being, the very monarch of all he surveys. The arm-chair is his throne, the poker his sceptre, and the little parlor, some twelve feet square, his undisputed empire. It is a morsel of certainty, snatched from the midst of the uncertainties of life; it is a sunny moment gleaming out kindly on a cloudy day; and he who has advanced some way on the pilgrimage of existence, knows the importance of husbanding even morsels and moments of enjoyment. "Shall I not take mine ease in mine inn?" thought I, as I gave the fire a stir, lolled back in my elbow-chair, and cast a complacent look about the little parlor of the Red Horse, at Stratford-on-Avon.

The words of sweet Shakespeare were just passing through my mind as the clock struck midnight from the tower of the church in which he lies buried. There was a gentle tap at the door, and a pretty chambermaid, putting in her smiling face, inquired with a hesitating air, whether I had rung. I understood it as a modest hint that it was time to retire. My dream of absolute dominion was at an end; so abdicating my throne, like a prudent potentate, to avoid being deposed, and putting the Stratford Guide-Book under my arm, as a pillow companion, I went to bed, and dreamt all night of Shakespeare, the Jubilee, and David Garrick.[1]

---

[1] JUBILEE . . . GARRICK—In 1769 at Stratford-on-Avon, David Garrick, famous Shakespearean actor, gave a series of entertainments in honor of Shakespeare.

The next morning was one of those quickening mornings which we sometimes have in early spring, for it was about the middle of March. The chills of a long winter had suddenly given way; the north wind had spent its last gasp; and a mild air came stealing from the west, breathing the breath of life into nature, and wooing every bud and flower to burst forth into fragrance and beauty.

I had come to Stratford on a poetical pilgrimage. My first visit was to the house where Shakespeare was born,[2] and where, according to tradition, he was brought up to his father's craft of wool-combing. It is a small, mean-looking edifice of wood and plaster, a true nestling-place of genius, which seems to delight in hatching its offspring in by-corners. The walls of its squalid chambers are covered with names and inscriptions in every language, by pilgrims of all nations, ranks, and conditions, from the prince to the peasant; and present a simple, but striking instance of the spontaneous and universal homage of mankind to the great poet of nature.

The house is shown by a garrulous old lady, in a frosty red face, lighted up by a cold blue anxious eye, and garnished with artificial locks of flaxen hair, curling from under an exceedingly dirty cap. She was peculiarly assiduous in exhibiting the relics with which this, like all other celebrated shrines, abounds. There was the shattered stock of the very matchlock with which Shakespeare shot the deer on his poaching exploits. There, too, was his tobacco-box; which proves that he was a rival smoker of Sir Walter Raleigh; the sword also with which he played Hamlet; and the identical lantern with which Friar Laurence discovered Romeo and Juliet at the tomb! There was an ample supply also of Shakespeare's mulberry tree,[3] which seems to have as extraordinary powers of self-multiplication as the wood of the true cross; of which there is enough extant to build a ship of the line.

The most favorite object of curiosity, however, is Shakespeare's chair. It stands in the chimney-nook of a small gloomy chamber, just behind what was his father's shop. Here he may many a time have sat when a boy, watching the slowly-revolving spit, with all the longing of an urchin; or of an evening, listening to the cronies and gossips of Stratford, dealing forth churchyard tales and

[2] HOUSE . . . BORN—In Henley street are the remains of the house supposed to have been the poet's birthplace.

[3] MULBERRY TREE—According to tradition a certain mulberry tree in the orchard at Stratford was planted by Shakespeare's own hands.

legendary anecdotes of the troublesome times of England. In this chair it is the custom of every one that visits the house to sit: whether this be done with the hope of imbibing any of the inspiration of the bard, I am at a loss to say; I merely mention the fact; and mine hostess privately assured me, that, though built of solid oak, such was the fervent zeal of devotees, that the chair had to be new-bottomed at least once in three years. It is worthy of notice also, in the history of this extraordinary chair, that it partakes something of the volatile nature of the Santa Casa of Loretto,[4] or the flying chair of the Arabian enchanter; for though sold some few years since to a northern princess, yet, strange to tell, it has found its way back again to the old chimney-corner.

I am always of easy faith in such matters, and am ever willing to be deceived where the deceit is pleasant and costs nothing. I am therefore a ready believer in relics, legends, and local anecdotes of goblins and great men; and would advise all travellers who travel for their gratification to be the same. What is it to us whether these stories be true or false so long as we can persuade ourselves into the belief of them, and enjoy all the charm of the reality? There is nothing like resolute, good-humored credulity in these matters; and on this occasion I went even so far as willingly to believe the claims of mine hostess to a lineal descent from the poet, when, unluckily for my faith, she put into my hands a play of her own composition which set all belief in her consanguinity at defiance.

From the birthplace of Shakespeare a few paces brought me to his grave. He lies buried in the chancel of the parish church, a large and venerable pile, mouldering with age, but richly ornamented. It stands on the banks of the Avon, on an embowered point, and separated by adjoining gardens from the suburbs of the town. Its situation is quiet and retired: the river runs murmuring at the foot of the churchyard, and the elms which grow upon its banks droop their branches into its clear bosom. An avenue of limes, the boughs of which are curiously interlaced, so as to form in summer an arched way of foliage, leads up from the gate of the yard to the church porch. The graves are overgrown with grass; the gray tombstones, some of them nearly sunk into the earth, are

---

[4] Santa Casa of Loretto—House in which the Virgin Mary lived before the birth of Christ, and supposed to have been miraculously transported to Loretto, Italy, in 1295, where it is now a shrine.

half-covered with moss, which has likewise tinted the reverend old building. Small birds have built their nests among the cornices and fissures of the walls, and keep up a continual flutter and chirping; and rooks are sailing and cawing about its lofty gray spire.

In the course of my rambles I met with the gray-headed sexton, Edmonds, and accompanied him home to get the key of the church. He had lived in Stratford, man and boy, for eighty years, and seemed still to consider himself a vigorous man, with the trivial exception that he had nearly lost the use of his legs for a few years past. His dwelling was a cottage, looking out upon the Avon and its bordering meadows; and was a picture of that neatness, order, and comfort which pervade the humblest dwellings in this country. A low white-washed room, with a stone floor, carefully scrubbed, served for parlor, kitchen, and hall. Rows of pewter and earthen dishes glittered along the dresser. On an old oaken table, well rubbed and polished, lay the family Bible and prayer-book, and the drawer contained the family library, composed of about half a score of well-thumbed volumes. An ancient clock, that important article of cottage furniture, ticked on the opposite side of the room; with a bright warming-pan hanging on one side of it, and the old man's horn-handled Sunday cane on the other. The fireplace, as usual, was wide and deep enough to admit a gossip knot within its jambs. In one corner sat the old man's grand-daughter sewing, a pretty blue-eyed girl,—and in the opposite corner was a superannuated crony, whom he addressed by the name of John Ange, and who, I found, had been his companion from childhood. They had played together in infancy; they had worked together in manhood; they were now tottering about and gossiping away the evening of life; and in a short time they will probably be buried together in the neighboring churchyard. It is not often that we see two streams of existence running thus evenly and tranquilly side by side; it is only in such quiet "bosom scenes" of life that they are to be met with.

I had hoped to gather some traditionary anecdotes of the bard from these ancient chroniclers; but they had nothing new to impart. The long interval, during which Shakespeare's writings lay in comparative neglect, has spread its shadow over his history; and it is his good or evil lot, that scarcely anything remains to his biographers but a scanty handful of conjectures.

The sexton and his companion had been employed as carpenters, on the preparations for the celebrated Stratford Jubilee, and they remembered Garrick, the prime mover of the fête, who superintended the arrangements, and who, according to the sexton, was "a short punch man, very lively and bustling." John Ange had assisted also in cutting down Shakespeare's mulberry tree, of which he had a morsel in his pocket for sale; no doubt a sovereign quickener of literary conception.

I was grieved to hear these two worthy wights speak very dubiously of the eloquent dame who shows the Shakespeare house. John Ange shook his head when I mentioned her valuable collection of relics, particularly her remains of the mulberry tree; and the old sexton even expressed a doubt as to Shakespeare having been born in her house. I soon discovered that he looked upon her mansion with an evil eye, as a rival to the poet's tomb; the latter having comparatively but few visitors. Thus it is that historians differ at the very outset, and mere pebbles make the stream of truth diverge into different channels, even at the fountain head.

We approached the church through the avenue of limes, and entered by a Gothic porch, highly ornamented, with carved doors of massive oak. The interior is spacious, and the architecture and embellishments superior to those of most country churches. There are several ancient monuments of nobility and gentry, over some of which hang funeral escutcheons,[5] and banners dropping piecemeal from the walls. The tomb of Shakespeare is in the chancel. The place is solemn and sepulchral. Tall elms wave before the pointed windows, and the Avon, which runs at a short distance from the walls, keeps up a low perpetual murmur. A flat stone marks the spot where the bard is buried. There are four lines inscribed on it, said to have been written by himself, and which have in them something extremely awful. If they are indeed his own, they show that solicitude about the quiet of the grave, which seems natural to fine sensibilities and thoughtful minds:

Good friend, for Jesus' sake forbeare
To dig the dust enclosed here.
Blessed be he that spares these stones,
And curst be he that moves my bones.

---

[5] Escutcheons—Shields bearing coats-of-arms.

Just over the grave, in a niche of the wall, is a bust of Shakespeare, put up shortly after his death, and considered as a resemblance. The aspect is pleasant and serene, with a finely arched forehead; and I thought I could read in it clear indications of that cheerful, social disposition, by which he was as much characterized among his contemporaries as by the vastness of his genius. The inscription mentions his age at the time of his decease—fifty-three years; an untimely death for the world: for what fruit might not have been expected from the golden autumn of such a mind, sheltered as it was from the stormy vicissitudes of life, and flourishing in the sunshine of popular and royal favor!

The inscription on the tombstone has not been without its effect. It has prevented the removal of his remains from the bosom of his native place to Westminster Abbey, which was at one time contemplated. A few years since also, as some laborers were digging to make an adjoining vault, the earth caved in so as to leave a vacant space almost like an arch, through which one might have reached into his grave. No one, however, presumed to meddle with his remains so awfully guarded by a malediction, and lest any of the idle or the curious, or any collector of relics, should be tempted to commit depredations, the old sexton kept watch over the place for two days, until the vault was finished, and the aperture closed again. He told me that he had made bold to look in at the hole, but could see neither coffin nor bones; nothing but dust. It was something, I thought, to have seen the dust of Shakespeare.

Next to this grave are those of his wife, his favorite daughter, Mrs. Hall, and others of his family. On a tomb close by, also, is a full-length effigy of his old friend, John Combe,[6] of usurious memory, on whom he is said to have written a ludicrous epitaph. There are other monuments around, but the mind refuses to dwell on anything that is not connected with Shakespeare. His idea pervades the place—the whole pile seems but as his mausoleum. The feelings, no longer checked and thwarted by doubt, here indulge in perfect confidence: other traces of him may be false or dubious, but here is palpable evidence and absolute certainty. As I trod the sounding pavement, there was something intense and thrilling in the idea, that, in very truth, the remains of Shakespeare were

[6] John Combe—Rich man of Stratford who left Shakespeare five pounds in his will. Tradition says the poet wrote doggerel rimes satirizing his sharpness in business.

mouldering beneath my feet. It was a long time before I could prevail upon myself to leave the place; and as I passed through the churchyard, I plucked a branch from one of the yew trees, the only relic that I have brought from Stratford.

I had now visited the usual objects of a pilgrim's devotion, but I had a desire to see the old family seat of the Lucy's, at Charlecot, and to ramble through the park where Shakespeare, in company with some of the roysters of Stratford, committed his youthful offence of deer-stealing. In this hairbrained exploit we are told that he was taken prisoner, and carried to the keeper's lodge, where he remained all night in doleful captivity. When brought into the presence of Sir Thomas Lucy, his treatment must have been galling and humiliating; for it so wrought upon his spirit as to produce a rough pasquinade,[7] which was affixed to the park gate at Charlecot.*

This flagitious[8] attack upon the dignity of the Knight so incensed him, that he applied to a lawyer at Warwick to put the severity of the laws in force against the rhyming deer-stalker. Shakespeare did not wait to brave the united puissance of a Knight of the Shire and a country attorney. He forthwith abandoned the pleasant banks of the Avon, and his paternal trade; wandered away to London; became a hanger-on to the theatres; then an actor; and, finally, wrote for the stage; and thus, through the persecution of Sir Thomas Lucy, Stratford lost an indifferent wool-comber, and the world gained an immortal poet. He retained, however, for a long time, a sense of the harsh treatment of the Lord of Charlecot, and revenged himself in his writings; but in the sportive way of a good-natured mind. Sir Thomas is said to be the original Justice Shallow,[9] and the satire is slyly fixed upon him by the Justice's armorial

* The following is the only stanza extant of this lampoon:

A parliament member, a justice of peace,
At home a poor scarecrow, at London an asse,
If lowsie is Lucy, as some volke miscalle it,
Then Lucy is lowsie, whatever befall it.
    He thinks himself great,
    Yet an asse in his state,
We allow by his ears but with asses to mate,
If Lucy is lowsie, as some volke miscalle it,
Then sing lowsie Lucy whatever befall it.

[7] PASQUINADE—A lampoon or satirical writing.

[8] FLAGITIOUS—Scandalous.

[9] JUSTICE SHALLOW—A comedy character in Shakespeare's *Henry IV,* Part II.

Brown Brothers

**Sunnyside**

Washington Irving's residence at Tarrytown, New York, where lofty trees cast their shadows on lawns that slope gently to the Hudson River. After serving as Ambassador to Spain, Irving returned to this quiet spot to devote himself to his writing.

bearings, which, like those of the Knight, had white luces[10] in the quarterings.

Various attempts have been made by his biographers to soften and explain away this early transgression of the poet; but I look upon it as one of those thoughtless exploits natural to his situation and turn of mind. Shakespeare, when young, had doubtless all the wildness and irregularity of an ardent, undisciplined, and undirected genius. The poetic temperament has naturally something in it of the vagabond. When left to itself, it runs loosely and wildly, and delights in everything eccentric and licentious. It is often a turn-up of a die, in the gambling freaks of fate, whether a natural genius shall turn out a great rogue or a great poet; and had not Shakespeare's mind fortunately taken a literary bias, he might have as daringly transcended all civil, as he has all dramatic laws.

I have little doubt, that in early life, when running, like an unbroken colt, about the neighborhood of Stratford, he was to be found in the company of all kinds of odd anomalous characters; that he associated with all the madcaps of the place, and was one of those unlucky urchins, at mention of whom old men shake their heads, and predict that they will one day come to the gallows. To him the poaching in Sir Thomas Lucy's park was doubtless like a foray to a Scottish Knight, and struck his eager, and as yet untamed, imagination as something delightfully adventurous.

The old mansion of Charlecot and its surrounding park still remain in the possession of the Lucy family, and are peculiarly interesting from being connected with this whimsical but eventful circumstance in the scanty history of the bard. . . .

On returning to my inn, I could not but reflect on the singular gift of the poet; to be able thus to spread the magic of his mind over the very face of nature; to give to things and places a charm and character not their own, and to turn this "working-day world" into a perfect fairyland. He is indeed the true enchanter, whose spell operates, not upon the senses, but upon the imagination and the heart. Under the wizard influence of Shakespeare I had been walking all day in a complete delusion. I had surveyed the landscape through the prism of poetry, which tinged every object with the hues of the rainbow. I had been surrounded with fancied beings; with mere airy nothings, conjured up by poetic power; yet

[10] LUCES—Fish found in the river Avon.

which, to me, had all the charm of reality. I had heard Jaques soliloquize beneath his oak; had beheld the fair Rosalind and her companion adventuring through the woodlands: and, above all, had been once more present in spirit with fat Jack Falstaff, and his contemporaries, from the august Justice Shallow, down to the gentle Master Slender, and the sweet Anne Page.[11] Ten thousand honors and blessings on the bard who has thus gilded the dull realities of life with innocent illusions; who has spread exquisite and unbought pleasures in my chequered path; and beguiled my spirit in many a lonely hour, with all the cordial and cheerful sympathies of social life!

As I crossed the bridge over the Avon on my return, I paused to contemplate the distant church in which the poet lies buried, and could not but exult in the malediction which has kept his ashes undisturbed in its quiet and hallowed vaults. What honor could his name have derived from being mingled in dusty companionship with the epitaphs and escutcheons and venal eulogiums of a titled multitude? What would a crowded corner in Westminster Abbey have been, compared with this reverend pile, which seems to stand in beautiful loneliness as his sole mausoleum! The solicitude about the grave may be but the offspring of an overwrought sensibility; but human nature is made up of foibles and prejudices; and its best and tenderest affections are mingled with these factitious feelings. He who has sought renown about the world, and has reaped a full harvest of worldly favor, will find, after all, that there is no love, no admiration, no applause, so sweet to the soul as that which springs up in his native place. It is there that he seeks to be gathered in peace and honor, among his kindred and his early friends. And when the weary heart and failing head begin to warn him that the evening of life is drawing on, he turns as fondly as does the infant to the mother's arms, to sink to sleep in the bosom of the scene of his childhood.

How would it have cheered the spirit of the youthful bard, when, wandering forth in disgrace upon a doubtful world, he cast back a heavy look upon his paternal home, could he have foreseen that, before many years, he should return to it covered with renown; that his name should become the boast and glory of his native place; that his ashes should be religiously guarded as its most precious

[11] Jaques . . . Anne Page—Characters made famous in Shakespeare's plays.

treasure; and that its lessening spire, on which his eyes were fixed in tearful contemplation, should one day become the beacon, towering amidst the gentle landscape, to guide the literary pilgrim of every nation to his tomb!

## QUESTIONS AND EXERCISES

Exercises preceded by a star are designed for assignment at the discretion of the teacher, or for any student who volunteers.

1. Outline the essay, bearing in mind such points as: place and general description, reason for visiting Stratford, special points of interest, Irving's reflections and opinions.
2. From the background suggested in this essay write an imaginary sketch on "Shakespeare As I Knew Him As a Boy at Stratford-on-Avon."
3. What makes *Stratford-on-Avon* more than a mere guide–book account of Shakespeare's birthplace? Why would you like to visit Stratford?

*4. What elements typical of Irving's style do you find in this *Sketch?* Cite passages.

5. Do you think the last paragraph is essential to the essay?

*6. Read in Sydney Lee's *Stratford-on-Avon* one of the following chapters for a glimpse of Shakespeare's home-town: 12, 13, 17, 18, or 19.

# *LONDON TOWN*

## THE BOAR'S HEAD TAVERN, EASTCHEAP

### A SHAKESPEAREAN RESEARCH

With this *Sketch,* Irving leaves "The Broad Highway" and swings up to "London Town." There is something about the road to London that has always drawn traveler and adventurer like a magnet. Dick Whittington tramped it long ago with his beloved cat. The legend goes that he turned away from that great town but the bells of Bow Church seemed to call out to him "Turn again, Whittington, Lord Mayor of London." Years later that prophecy came true.

Irving appears in his London *Sketches* as an "antiquarian," a seeker of old things and places. A cathedral attracts him, an old cobbled lane suggests adventure at the end of it, old customs from the days of Queen Elizabeth and before interest him, a place made famous by a book compels his curiosity. It is that quality of Irving which has been referred to as his "delight in a romantic past." He was especially drawn by the halo of Shakespeare. This sketch describes another literary pilgrimage to a spot made unforgettable in the dramatist's great historical play, *King Henry IV,* the Boar's Head Tavern, where a jolly old rascal named Falstaff had spent many a roaring evening with "merry Prince Hal."

The Boar's Head Tavern that Shakespeare knew, and probably supped in, had been torn down long before Irving's time. However, there were traces—ancient buildings near the old tavern, the legends and anecdotes of neighborhood idlers, essays that had been written before by such authors as Goldsmith—and out of all these Irving weaves an enjoyable adventure.

It is a pious custom in some Catholic countries, to honor the memory of saints by votive lights burnt before their pictures. The popularity of a saint, therefore, may be known by the number of these offerings. One perhaps is left to moulder in the darkness of his little chapel; another may have a solitary lamp to throw its blinking rays athwart his effigy; while the whole blaze of adoration is lavished at the shrine of some beatified father of renown. The wealthy devotee brings his huge luminary of wax; the eager zealot his seven-branched candlestick, and even the mendicant pilgrim is by no means satisfied that sufficient light is thrown upon the deceased, unless he hangs up his little lamp of smoking oil. The consequence is, that in the eagerness to enlighten, they are often apt to obscure; and I have occasionally seen an unlucky saint almost smoked out of countenance by the officiousness of his followers.

In like manner has it fared with the immortal Shakespeare. Every writer considers it his bounden duty, to light up some portion of his character or works, and to rescue some merit from oblivion. The commentator, opulent in words, produces vast tomes of dissertations; the common herd of editors send up mists of obscurity from their notes at the bottom of each page; and every casual scribbler brings his farthing[1] rush-light of eulogy or research, to swell the cloud of incense and of smoke.

As I honor all established usages of my brethren of the quill, I thought it but proper to contribute my mite of homage to the memory of the illustrious bard. I was for some time, however, sorely puzzled in what way I should discharge this duty. I found myself anticipated in every attempt at a new reading; every doubtful line had been explained a dozen different ways, and perplexed beyond the reach of elucidation; and as to fine passages, they had all been amply praised by previous admirers: nay, so completely had the bard, of late, been overlarded with panegyric by a great German critic, that it was difficult now to find even a fault that had not been argued into a beauty.

[1] FARTHING—Coin equal to half a cent, U. S. currency.

In this perplexity I was one morning turning over his pages, when I casually opened upon the comic scenes of *Henry IV.*, and was, in a moment, completely lost in the madcap revelry of the Boar's Head Tavern. So vividly and naturally are these scenes of humor depicted, and with such force and consistency are the characters sustained, that they become mingled up in the mind with the facts and personages of real life. To few readers does it occur, that these are all ideal creations of a poet's brain, and that, in sober truth, no such knot of merry roysters ever enlivened the dull neighborhood of Eastcheap.

For my part I love to give myself up to the illusions of poetry. A hero of fiction that never existed, is just as valuable to me as a hero of history that existed a thousand years since; and, if I may be excused such an insensibility to the common ties of human nature, I would not give up fat Jack for half the great men of ancient chronicle. What have the heroes of yore done for me, or men like me? They have conquered countries of which I do not enjoy an acre; or they have gained laurels of which I do not inherit a leaf; or they have furnished examples of hair-brained prowess, which I have neither the opportunity nor the inclination to follow. But old Jack Falstaff!—kind Jack Falstaff!—sweet Jack Falstaff!—has enlarged the boundaries of human enjoyment; he has added vast regions of wit and good humor, in which the poorest man may revel; and has bequeathed a never-failing inheritance of jolly laughter, to make mankind merrier and better to the latest posterity.

A thought suddenly struck me: "I will make a pilgrimage to Eastcheap," said I, closing the book, "and see if the old Boar's Head Tavern still exists. Who knows but I may light upon some legendary traces of Dame Quickly[2] and her guests; at any rate there will be a kindred pleasure, in treading the halls once vocal with their mirth, to that the toper enjoys in smelling to the empty cask once filled with generous wine."

The resolution was no sooner formed than put in execution. I forbear to treat of the various adventures and wonders I encountered in my travels, of the haunted regions of Cock-Lane;[3] of the

---

[2] Dame Quickly—The hostess of the Boar's Head Tavern, in Shakespeare's play.

[3] Haunted . . . Cock-Lane—A fake ghost caused great excitement in this London lane in 1762. The ghost proved to be a money-making device.

faded glories of Little Britain, and the parts adjacent; what perils I ran in Cateaton-Street and old Jewry; of the renowned Guildhall and its two stunted giants,[4] the pride and wonder of the city, and the terror of all unlucky urchins; and how I visited London Stone[5] and struck my staff upon it, in imitation of that arch-rebel, Jack Cade.[6]

Let it suffice to say, that I at length arrived in merry Eastcheap, that ancient region of wit and wassail,[7] where the very names of the streets relished of good cheer, as Pudding-Lane bears testimony even at the present day. For Eastcheap, says old Stowe,[8] "was always famous for its convivial doings. The cookes cried hot ribbes of beef roasted, pies well baked, and other victuals: there was clattering of pewter pots, harpe, pipe, and sawtrie."[9] Alas! how sadly is the scene changed since the roaring days of Falstaff and old Stowe! The madcap royster has given place to the plodding tradesman; the clattering of pots and the sound of "harpe and sawtrie" to the din of carts and the accursed dinging of the dustman's[10] bell; and no song is heard, save, haply, the strain of some siren from Billingsgate,[11] chanting the eulogy of deceased mackerel.

I sought, in vain, for the ancient abode of Dame Quickly. The only relic of it is a boar's head carved in relief in stone, which formerly served as the sign, but, at present is built into the parting line of two houses which stand on the site of the renowned old tavern.

For the history of this little abode of good fellowship, I was referred to a tallow-chandler's widow, opposite, who had been born and brought up on the spot, and was looked up to, as the indisputable chronicler of the neighborhood. I found her seated in a little back parlor, the window of which looked out upon a yard about eight feet square, laid out as a flower-garden; while a glass

---

[4] GUILDHALL . . . GIANTS—London's City Hall. It was built in the year 1411, and restored after the fire of 1666. In the Guildhall were two gigantic wooden figures called Gog and Magog.

[5] LONDON STONE—A famous Roman mile-stone over 1,000 years old, now in the wall of St. Swithin's Church. It was believed that all roads in England radiated from this stone.

[6] JACK CADE—Leader of an ill-fated rebellion in 1450, who entered London, struck his sword on London Stone, crying that he was "Lord of this city." He was executed, and his followers dispersed.

[7] WASSAIL—Good cheer, expressed by drinking healths.

[8] STOWE—John Stowe, or Stow, an historian, published a history of London in 1598.

[9] SAWTRIE—Old form for *psaltery,* a Hebrew stringed instrument.

[10] DUSTMAN'S—Street cleaner's.

[11] BILLINGSGATE—Famous London fishmarket.

door opposite afforded a distant peep of the street, through a vista of soap and tallow candles; the two views, which comprised, in all probability, her prospects in life, and the little world in which she had lived, and moved, and had her being, for the better part of a century.

To be versed in the history of Eastcheap, great and little, from London Stone even unto the Monument,[12] was, doubtless, in her opinion, to be acquainted with the history of the universe. Yet, with all this, she possessed the simplicity of true wisdom, and that liberal, communicative disposition, which I have generally remarked in intelligent old ladies, knowing in the concerns of their neighborhood.

Her information, however, did not extend far back into antiquity. She could throw no light upon the history of the Boar's Head, from the time that Dame Quickly espoused the valiant Pistol,[13] until the great fire of London, when it was unfortunately burnt down. It was soon rebuilt, and continued to flourish under the old name and sign, until a dying landlord, struck with remorse for double scores, bad measures, and other iniquities which are incident to the sinful race of publicans,[14] endeavored to make his peace with Heaven, by bequeathing the tavern to St. Michael's Church, Crooked-Lane, towards the supporting of a chaplain. For some time the vestry meetings were regularly held there; but it was observed that the old Boar never held up his head under church government. He gradually declined, and finally gave his last gasp about thirty years since. The tavern was then turned into shops; but she informed me that a picture of it was still preserved in St. Michael's Church, which stood just in the rear. To get a sight of this picture was now my determination; so, having informed myself of the abode of the sexton, I took my leave of the venerable chronicler of Eastcheap, my visit having doubtless raised greatly her opinion of her legendary lore, and furnished an important incident in the history of her life.

It cost me some difficulty and much curious inquiry, to ferret out the humble hanger-on to the church. I had to explore Crooked-Lane, and diverse little alleys, and elbows, and dark passages, with

[12] Monument—Stone column, 202 feet high, erected on Fish Street Hill by Sir Christopher Wren to commemorate the great fire of 1666.

[13] Pistol—A character in *King Henry IV*, Part II.

[14] Publicans—English term for tavern-keepers.

which this old city is perforated, like an ancient cheese, or a worm-eaten chest of drawers. At length I traced him to a corner of a small court surrounded by lofty houses, where the inhabitants enjoy about as much of the face of heaven as a community of frogs at the bottom of a well. The sexton was a meek, acquiescing little man, of a bowing, lowly habit; yet he had a pleasant twinkling in his eye, and if encouraged, would now and then hazard a small pleasantry; such as a man of his low estate might venture to make in the company of high churchwardens, and other mighty men of the earth. I found him in company with the deputy organist, seated apart, like Milton's angels; discoursing, no doubt, on high doctrinal points, and settling the affairs of the church over a friendly pot of ale; for the lower classes of English seldom deliberate on any weighty matter without the assistance of a cool tankard to clear their understandings. I arrived at the moment when they had finished their ale and their argument, and were about to repair to the church to put it in order; so, having made known my wishes, I received their gracious permission to accompany them.

The church of St. Michael's, Crooked-Lane, standing a short distance from Billingsgate, is enriched with the tombs of many fishmongers of renown; and as every profession has its galaxy of glory, and its constellation of great men, I presume the monument of a mighty fishmonger of the olden time is regarded with as much reverence by succeeding generations of the craft, as poets feel on contemplating the tomb of Virgil, or soldiers the monument of a Marlborough or Turenne.

I cannot but turn aside, while thus speaking of illustrious men, to observe that St. Michael's, Crooked-Lane, contains also the ashes of that doughty champion, William Walworth, Knight, who so manfully clove down the sturdy wight, Wat Tyler, in Smithfield; a hero worthy of honorable blazon, as almost the only Lord Mayor on record famous for deeds of arms; the sovereigns of Cockney[15] being generally renowned as the most pacific of all potentates.

Adjoining the church, in a small cemetery, immediately under the back window of what was once the Boar's Head, stands the tombstone of Robert Preston, whilom drawer at the tavern. It is

---

[15] Cockney—Generally speaking, London as a whole, but applied particularly to the East End of the city.

now nearly a century since this trusty drawer of good liquor closed his bustling career, and was thus quietly deposited within call of his customers. As I was clearing away the weeds from his epitaph, the little sexton drew me on one side with a mysterious air, and informed me, in a low voice, that once upon a time, on a dark wintry night, when the wind was unruly, howling and whistling, banging about doors and windows, and twirling weathercocks, so that the living were frightened out of their beds, and even the dead could not sleep quietly in their graves, the ghost of honest Preston, which happened to be airing itself in the churchyard, was attracted by the well-known call of "waiter," from the Boar's Head, and made its sudden appearance in the midst of a roaring club, just as the parish clerk was singing a stave from the "mirre garland of Captain Death;" to the discomfiture of sundry train-band captains, and the conversion of an infidel attorney, who became a zealous Christian on the spot, and was never known to twist the truth afterwards, except in the way of business.

I beg it may be remembered, that I do not pledge myself for the authenticity of this anecdote; though it is well known that the churchyards and by-corners of this old metropolis are very much infested with perturbed spirits; and every one must have heard of the Cock-Lane ghost, and the apparition that guards the regalia in the Tower,[16] which has frightened so many bold sentinels almost out of their wits.

Be all this as it may, this Robert Preston seems to have been a worthy successor to the nimble-tongued Francis, who attended upon the revels of Prince Hal; to have been equally prompt with his "anon, anon, sir," and to have transcended his predecessor in honesty; for Falstaff, the veracity of whose taste no man will venture to impeach, flatly accuses Francis of putting lime in his sack; whereas, honest Preston's epitaph lauds him for the sobriety of his conduct, the soundness of his wine, and the fairness of his measure. The worthy dignitaries of the church, however, did not appear much captivated by the sober virtues of the tapster: the deputy organist, who had a moist look out of the eye, made some shrewd remark on the abstemiousness of a man brought up among full hogsheads; and the little sexton corroborated his opinion by a significant wink, and a dubious shake of the head.

[16] TOWER—The Tower of London.

Thus far my researches, though they threw much light on the history of tapsters, fishmongers, and Lord Mayors, yet disappointed me in the great object of my quest, the picture of the Boar's Head Tavern. No such painting was to be found in the church of St. Michael's. "Marry and amen!" said I, "here endeth my research!" So I was giving the matter up, with the air of a baffled antiquary, when my friend the sexton, perceiving me to be curious in everything relative to the old tavern, offered to show me the choice vessels of the vestry, which had been handed down from remote times, when the parish meetings were held at the Boar's Head. These were deposited in the parish club-room, which had been transferred, on the decline of the ancient establishment, to a tavern in the neighborhood.

A few steps brought us to the house, which stands No. 12, Miles-Lane, bearing the title of The Mason's Arms, and is kept by Master Edward Honeyball, the "bully-rook"[17] of the establishment. It is one of those little taverns, which abound in the heart of the city, and form the centre of gossip and intelligence of the neighborhood. We entered the bar-room, which was narrow and darkling; for in these close lanes but few rays of reflected light are enabled to struggle down to the inhabitants, whose broad day is at best but a tolerable twilight. The room was partitioned into boxes, each containing a table spread with a clean white cloth, ready for dinner. This showed that the guests were of the good old stamp, and divided their day equally, for it was but just one o'clock. At the lower end of the room was a clear coal fire, before which a breast of lamb was roasting. A row of bright brass candlesticks and pewter mugs glistened along the mantelpiece, and an old-fashioned clock ticked in one corner. There was something primitive in this medley of kitchen, parlor, and hall, that carried me back to earlier times, and pleased me. The place, indeed, was humble, but every thing had that look of order and neatness which bespeaks the superintendence of a notable English housewife. A group of amphibious-looking beings, who might be either fishermen or sailors, were regaling themselves in one of the boxes. As I was a visitor of rather high pretensions, I was ushered into a little misshapen back room, having at least nine corners. It was lighted by a skylight, furnished with antiquated leathern chairs, and ornamented with the

[17] BULLY-ROOK—The hearty host.

portrait of a fat pig. It was evidently appropriated to particular customers, and I found a shabby gentleman, in a red nose, and oil-cloth hat, seated in one corner, meditating on a half-empty pot of porter.

The old sexton had taken the landlady aside, and with an air of profound importance imparted to her my errand. Dame Honeyball was a likely, plump, bustling little woman, and no bad substitute for that paragon of hostesses, Dame Quickly. She seemed delighted with an opportunity to oblige; and hurrying upstairs to the archives of her house, where the precious vessels of the parish club were deposited, she returned, smiling and courtesying with them in her hands.

The first she presented me was a japanned iron tobacco-box of gigantic size, out of which, I was told, the vestry had smoked at their stated meetings, since time immemorial; and which was never suffered to be profaned by vulgar hands, or used on common occasions. I received it with becoming reverence; but what was my delight, at beholding on its cover the identical painting of which I was in quest! There was displayed the outside of the Boar's Head Tavern, and before the door was to be seen the whole convivial group, at table, in full revel, pictured with that wonderful fidelity and force with which the portraits of renowned generals and commodores are illustrated on tobacco-boxes, for the benefit of posterity. Lest, however, there should be any mistake, the cunning limner had warily inscribed the names of Prince Hal and Falstaff on the bottoms of their chairs.

On the inside of the cover was an inscription, nearly obliterated, recording that this box was the gift of Sir Richard Gore, for the use of the vestry meetings at the Boar's Head Tavern, and that it was "repaired and beautified by his successor, Mr. John Packard, 1767." Such is a faithful description of this august and venerable relic, and I question whether the learned Scriblerius[18] contemplated his Roman shield, or the Knights of the Round Table the long-sought Sangreal,[19] with more exultation.

While I was meditating on it with enraptured gaze, Dame Honeyball, who was highly gratified by the interest it excited, put in my hands a drinking cup or goblet, which also belonged to the

---

[18] SCRIBLERIUS—A character in one of Pope's satires.

[19] SANGREAL—Holy Grail. The cup from which Christ drank at the Last Supper. King Arthur's knights went in quest of it.

vestry, and was descended from the old Boar's Head. It bore the inscription of having been the gift of Francis Wythers, Knight, and was held, she told me, in exceeding great value, being considered very "antyke." This last opinion was strengthened by the shabby gentleman in the red nose, and oil-cloth hat, and whom I strongly suspected of being a lineal descendant from the valiant Bardolph.[20] He suddenly roused from his meditation on the pot of porter, and casting a knowing look at the goblet, exclaimed, "Ay, ay! the head don't ache now that made that there article!"

The great importance attached to this memento of ancient revelry by modern churchwardens, at first puzzled me; but there is nothing sharpens the apprehension so much as antiquarian research; for I immediately perceived that this could be no other than the identical "parcel-gilt goblet" on which Falstaff made his loving but faithless vow to Dame Quickly; and which would, of course, be treasured up with care among the regalia of her domains, as a testimony of that solemn contract.*

Mine hostess, indeed, gave me a long history how the goblet had been handed down from generation to generation. She also entertained me with many particulars concerning the worthy vestrymen who have seated themselves thus quietly on the stools of the ancient roysters of Eastcheap, and like so many commentators, utter clouds of smoke in honor of Shakespeare. These I forbear to relate, lest my readers should not be as curious in these matters as myself. Suffice it to say, the neighbors, one and all, about Eastcheap believe that Falstaff and his merry crew actually lived and revelled there. Nay, there are several legendary anecdotes concerning him still extant among the oldest frequenters of the Mason's Arms, which they give as transmitted down from their forefathers; and Mr. M'Kash, an Irish hair-dresser, whose shop stands on the site of the old Boar's Head, has several dry jokes of Fat Jack's not laid down in the books, with which he makes his customers ready to die of laughter.

* Thou didst swear to me upon a *parcel-gilt goblet,* sitting in my Dolphin chamber, at the round table, by a sea-coal fire, on Wednesday, in Whitsunweek, when the prince broke thy head for likening his father to a singing man at Windsor; thou didst swear to me then, as I was washing thy wound, to marry me, and make me my lady, thy wife. Canst thou deny it?—*Henry IV., Part II.*

---

[20] Bardolph—Character in *King Henry IV,* Parts I and II, with a prominent red nose inflamed by drinking.

I now turned to my friend the sexton to make some further inquiries, but I found him sunk in pensive meditation. His head had declined a little on one side; a deep sigh heaved from the very bottom of his stomach, and, though I could not see a tear trembling in his eye, yet a moisture was evidently stealing from a corner of his mouth. I followed the direction of his eye through the door which stood open, and found it fixed wistfully on the savory breast of lamb, roasting in dripping richness before the fire.

I now called to mind, that in the eagerness of my recondite investigation, I was keeping the poor man from his dinner. My bowels yearned with sympathy, and putting in his hand a small token of my gratitude and good-will, I departed, with a hearty benediction on him, Dame Honeyball, and the Parish Club of Crooked-Lane—not forgetting my shabby, but sententious friend, in the oil-cloth hat and copper nose.

Thus have I given a "tedious brief" account of this interesting research; for which, if it prove too short and unsatisfactory, I can only plead my inexperience in this branch of literature, so deservedly popular at the present day. I am aware that a more skilful illustrator of the immortal bard would have swelled the materials I have touched upon, to a good merchantable bulk, comprising the biographies of William Walworth, Jack Straw, and Robert Preston; some notice of the eminent fishmongers of St. Michael's; the history of Eastcheap, great and little; private anecdotes of Dame Honeyball and her pretty daughter, whom I have not even mentioned: to say nothing of a damsel tending the breast of lamb, (and whom, by the way, I remarked to be a comely lass, with a neat foot and ankle); the whole enlivened by the riots of Wat Tyler, and illuminated by the great fire of London.

All this I leave as a rich mine to be worked by future commentators; nor do I despair of seeing the tobacco-box, and the "parcel-gilt goblet," which I have thus brought to light, the subjects of future engravings, and almost as fruitful of voluminous dissertations and disputes as the shield of Achilles,[21] or the far-famed Portland vase.[22]

---

[21] Shield of Achilles—Gorgeously decorated shield of the famous Greek warrior of the *Iliad*. See Book XVIII of the *Iliad* for its description.

[22] Portland vase—Rare Roman vase of the first century, A. D., now in the British Museum. The vase, of carved dark blue glass, formerly belonged to the Duchess of Portland.

## QUESTIONS AND EXERCISES

**Exercises preceded by a star are designed for assignment at the discretion of the teacher, or for any student who volunteers.**

1. Locate "Eastcheap" on a large map of London; also, Little Britain, Guildhall, Billingsgate, Cock-Lane, Pudding-Lane, Fish Hill. Trace Irving's journey.
2. Do you like this sketch better than Stratford-on-Avon? Why?
3. What bits of "local color" freshen the description of The Mason's Arms kept by Master Edward Honeyball?
4. What is meant by the term "antiquarian" as applied to Washington Irving?

*5. Read *Henry IV,* Part I, Acts II and III, for your own enjoyment and to enter into the spirit of this *Sketch.* In the light of your reading of Shakespeare's play, comment on *The Boar's Head Tavern, Eastcheap.*

## LITTLE BRITAIN

In 1724 an eighteen-year-old youth came to London from America, and found a job in a printing shop. The lad was Benjamin Franklin and the place in which he stayed was Little Britain, a faded quarter of London in the shadow of the dome of St. Paul's Cathedral. To this place almost a hundred years later came a gentleman who rented quarters in an old wainscoted room on the second floor of "one of the smallest but oldest edifices" in the district. It is not hard to guess that this latter gentleman was Washington Irving.

Little Britain was of a nature to appeal immediately to the antiquarian in Irving. It was a queer little stronghold of stout tradesmen who believed in keeping up the customs of the good old days when the now rather shabby mansions were alive with lords and ladies, the rustle of silks, the clang of swords. In the role of spectator Irving observes and reflects on this "heart's core of old London," a bit saddened by its remnants of former splendor, mildly amused at its stubborn way of clinging to old customs: eating pancakes religiously on Shrove Tuesday . . . hot cross buns on Good Friday . . . sending letters on Valentine's Day (not antiquated yet) . . . kissing the girls under the mistletoe at Christmas . . . sticking to roast beef and plum pudding as a true Englishman's bill-of-fare.

In the centre of the great city of London lies a small neighborhood, consisting of a cluster of narrow streets and courts, of very venerable and debilitated houses, which goes by the name of LITTLE BRITAIN. Christ Church School and St. Bartholomew's Hospital bound it on the west; Smithfield and Long Lane on the north; Aldersgate-Street, like an arm of the sea, divides it from the eastern part of the city; whilst the yawning gulf of Bull-and-Mouth-Street separates it from Butcher Lane and the regions of

New-gate. Over this little territory, thus bounded and designated, the great dome of St. Paul's,[1] swelling above the intervening houses of Paternoster Row, Amen Corner, and Ave-Maria Lane, looks down with an air of motherly protection.

This quarter derives its appellation from having been, in ancient times, the residence of the Dukes of Brittany. As London increased, however, rank and fashion rolled off to the west, and trade creeping on at their heels, took possession of their deserted abodes. For some time, Little Britain became the great mart of learning, and was peopled by the busy and prolific race of booksellers: these also gradually deserted it, and, emigrating beyond the great strait of Newgate-Street, settled down in Paternoster Row and St. Paul's Church-yard, where they continue to increase and multiply, even at the present day.

But though thus fallen into decline, Little Britain still bears traces of its former splendor. There are several houses, ready to tumble down, the fronts of which are magnificently enriched with old oaken carvings of hideous faces, unknown birds, beasts, and fishes; and fruits and flowers which it would perplex a naturalist to classify. There are also, in Aldersgate-Street, certain remains of what were once spacious and lordly family mansions, but which have in latter days been subdivided into several tenements. Here may often be found the family of a petty tradesman, with its trumpery furniture, burrowing among the relics of antiquated finery, in great rambling time-stained apartments, with fretted[2] ceilings, gilded cornices, and enormous marble fireplaces. The lanes and courts also contain many smaller houses, not on so grand a scale; but like your small ancient gentry, sturdily maintaining their claims to equal antiquity. These have their gable-ends to the street; great bow-windows, with diamond panes set in lead; grotesque carvings; and low-arched doorways.

In this most venerable and sheltered little nest have I passed several quiet years of existence, comfortably lodged in the second floor of one of the smallest, but oldest edifices. My sitting-room is an old wainscoted chamber, with small panels, and set off with a miscellaneous array of furniture. I have a particular respect for

---

[1] St. Paul's—Noted London cathedral, having one of the most impressive domes in existence.

[2] Fretted—Ornamented with interlaced designs.

three or four high-backed, claw-footed chairs, covered with tarnished brocade, which bear the marks of having seen better days, and have doubtless figured in some of the old palaces of Little Britain. They seem to me to keep together, and to look down with sovereign contempt upon their leathern-bottomed neighbors; as I have seen decayed gentry carry a high head among the plebeian society with which they were reduced to associate. The whole front of my sitting-room is taken up with a bow-window, on the panes of which are recorded the names of previous occupants for many generations; mingled with scraps of very indifferent gentleman-like poetry, written in characters which I can scarcely decipher; and which extol the charms of many a beauty of Little Britain, who has long, long since bloomed, faded, and passed away. As I am an idle personage, with no apparent occupation, and pay my bill regularly every week, I am looked upon as the only independent gentleman of the neighborhood; and being curious to learn the internal state of a community so apparently shut up within itself, I have managed to work my way into all the concerns and secrets of the place.

Little Britain may truly be called the heart's-core of the city; the stronghold of true John Bullism. It is a fragment of London as it was in its better days, with its antiquated folks and fashions. Here flourish in great preservation many of the holiday games and customs of yore. The inhabitants most religiously eat pancakes on Shrove-Tuesday, hot-cross-buns on Good-Friday, and roast goose at Michaelmas; they send love-letters on Valentine's Day; "burn the Pope"[3] on the fifth of November, and kiss all the girls under the mistletoe at Christmas. Roast beef and plum-pudding are also held in superstitious veneration, and port and sherry maintain their grounds as the only true English wines—all others being considered vile outlandish beverages.

Little Britain has its long catalogue of city wonders, which its inhabitants consider the wonders of the world; such as the great bell of St. Paul's, which sours all the beer when it tolls: the figures that strike the hours at St. Dunstan's clock;[4] the Monument;[5] the

[3] Burn the Pope—Reference to the yearly Protestant celebration on November 5, "Guy Fawkes Day," over the discovery of the famous "Gunpowder Plot" of November 5, 1605, when it was alleged Catholics tried to blow up the King and Parliament.

[4] St. Dunstan's clock—Church clock distinguished by two projecting savage-like figures which struck the hours with their clubs. Their removal brought tears to the eyes of the essayist Charles Lamb.

[5] Monument—See Note 12 on *The Boar's Head Tavern, Eastcheap,* page 539.

lions in the Tower;[6] and the wooden giants in Guildhall.[7] They still believe in dreams and fortune-telling; and an old woman that lives in Bull-and-Mouth Street makes a tolerable subsistence by detecting stolen goods, and promising the girls good husbands. They are apt to be rendered uncomfortable by comets and eclipses; and if a dog howls dolefully at night, it is looked upon as a sure sign of a death in the place. There are even many ghost stories current, particularly concerning the old mansion-houses; in several of which it is said strange sights are sometimes seen. Lords and ladies, the former in full-bottomed wigs, hanging sleeves, and swords, the latter in lappets, stays, hoops, and brocade, have been seen walking up and down the great waste chambers on moonlight nights; and are supposed to be the shades of the ancient proprietors in their court-dresses.

Little Britain has likewise its sages and great men. One of the most important of the former is a tall, dry old gentleman, of the name of Skryme, who keeps a small apothecary's shop. He has a cadaverous countenance, full of cavities and projections; with a brown circle round each eye, like a pair of horn spectacles. He is much thought of by the old women, who consider him as a kind of conjurer, because he has two or three stuffed alligators hanging up in his shop, and several snakes in bottles. He is a great reader of almanacs and newspapers, and is much given to pore over alarming accounts of plots, conspiracies, fires, earthquakes, and volcanic eruptions; which last phenomena he considers as signs of the times. He has always some dismal tale of the kind to deal out to his customers, with their doses, and thus at the same time puts both soul and body into an uproar. He is a great believer in omens and predictions, and has the prophecies of Robert Nixon and Mother Shipton[8] by heart. No man can make so much out of an eclipse, or even an unusually dark day; and he shook the tail of the last comet over the heads of his customers and disciples until they were nearly frightened out of their wits. He has lately got hold of a popular legend or prophecy, on which he has been unusually eloquent. There

[6] Lions . . . Tower—The group of castle-like buildings known as the Tower of London served as the state prison for many distinguished prisoners, among them Sir Thomas More and Lady Jane Grey. From the time of Henry III to 1834 wild beasts were actually kept in a portion of the Tower.

[7] Giants . . . Guildhall—See Note 4 on *The Boar's Head Tavern, Eastcheap,* page 538.

[8] Nixon and Mother Shipton—Both of these people belonged to early English times and were believed capable of foretelling important events.

has been a saying current among the ancient Sibyls, who treasure up these things, that when the grasshopper on the top of the Exchange shook hands with the dragon on the top of Bow Church steeple, fearful events would take place. This strange conjunction, it seems, has as strangely come to pass. The same architect has been engaged lately on the repairs of the cupola of the Exchange and the steeple of Bow Church; and, fearful to relate, the dragon and the grasshopper actually lie, cheek by jole, in the yard of his workshop.

"Others," as Mr. Skryme is accustomed to say, "may go star-gazing and look for conjunctions in the heavens, but here is a conjunction on the earth, near at home, and under our own eyes, which surpasses all the signs and calculations of astrologers." Since these portentous weathercocks have thus laid their heads together, wonderful events[9] had already occurred. The good old king, notwithstanding that he had lived eighty-two years, had all at once given up the ghost; another king had mounted the throne; a royal duke had died suddenly—another, in France, had been murdered; there had been radical meetings in all parts of the kingdom; the bloody scenes at Manchester—the great plot in Cato Street:—and, above all, the Queen had returned to England! All these sinister events are recounted by Mr. Skryme with a mysterious look, and a dismal shake of the head; and being taken with his drugs, and associated in the minds of his auditors with stuffed sea-monsters, bottled serpents, and his own visage, which is a title-page of tribulation, they have spread great gloom through the minds of the people of Little Britain. They shake their heads whenever they go by Bow Church, and observe, that they never expected any good to come of taking down that steeple, which, in old times told nothing but glad tidings, as the history of Whittington and his cat bears witness.

The rival oracle of Little Britain is a substantial cheesemonger, who lives in a fragment of one of the old family mansions, and is as magnificently lodged as a round-bellied mite in the midst of one of his own Cheshires. Indeed, he is a man of no little standing and importance; and his renown extends through Huggin Lane, and

[9] Wonderful events—In 1816, a riot at Spa Fields; in August 1819, the Manchester massacre; in 1820, the death of George III, the murder of a nephew of Louis XVIII, and the discovery of the Cato Street conspiracy against the lives of King George IV's ministers.

Lad Lane, and even unto Aldermanbury. His opinion is very much taken in affairs of state, having read the Sunday papers for the last half century, together with the *Gentleman's Magazine,* Rapin's *History of England,* and the *Naval Chronicle.* His head is stored with invaluable maxims, which have borne the test of time and use for centuries. It is his firm opinion that "it is a moral impossible," so long as England is true to herself, that anything can shake her: and he has much to say on the subject of the national debt; which, somehow or other, he proves to be a great national bulwark and blessing. He passed the greater part of his life in the purlieus[10] of Little Britain, until of late years, when, having become rich, and grown into the dignity of a Sunday cane, he begins to take his pleasure and see the world. He has therefore made several excursions to Hampstead, Highgate, and other neighboring towns, where he has passed whole afternoons in looking back upon the metropolis through a telescope, and endeavoring to descry the steeple of St. Bartholomew's. Not a stage-coachman of Bull-and-Mouth Street but touches his hat as he passes; and he is considered quite a patron at the coach office of the Goose and Gridiron, St. Paul's Church-yard. His family have been very urgent for him to make an expedition to Margate, but he has great doubts of those new gimcracks, the steamboats, and indeed thinks himself too advanced in life to undertake sea-voyages.

Little Britain has occasionally its factions and divisions, and party spirit ran very high at one time in consequence of two rival "Burial Societies"[11] being set up in the place. One held its meeting at the Swan and Horseshoe, and was patronized by the cheesemonger; the other at the Cock and Crown, under the auspices of the apothecary: it is needless to say that the latter was the most flourishing. I have passed an evening or two at each, and have acquired much valuable information as to the best mode of being buried, the comparative merits of churchyards; together with divers hints on the subject of patent iron coffins. I have heard the question discussed in all its bearings, as to the legality of prohibiting the latter on account of their durability. The feuds occasioned by these societies have happily died of late; but they were for a long time

---

[10] PURLIEUS—Neighborhood.

[11] BURIAL SOCIETIES—Associations whose members pay dues which assure them proper burial at the expense of the society.

prevailing themes of controversy, the people of Little Britain being extremely solicitous of funereal honors, and of lying comfortably in their graves.

Besides these two funeral societies, there is a third of quite a different cast, which tends to throw the sunshine of good humor over the whole neighborhood. It meets once a week at a little old-fashioned house kept by a jolly publican of the name of Wagstaff, and bearing for insignia a resplendent half-moon, with a most seductive bunch of grapes. The old edifice is covered with inscriptions to catch the eye of the thirsty wayfarer; such as "Truman, Hanbury and Co.'s Entire," "Wine, Rum, and Brandy Vaults," "Old Tom, Rum, and Compounds, etc." This indeed has been a temple of Bacchus and Momus,[12] from time immemorial. It has always been in the family of the Wagstaffs, so that its history is tolerably preserved by the present landlord. It was much frequented by the gallants and cavalieros of the reign of Elizabeth, and was looked into now and then by the wits of Charles the Second's day. But what Wagstaff principally prides himself upon, is, that Henry the Eighth, in one of his nocturnal rambles, broke the head of one of his ancestors with his famous walking-staff. This, however, is considered as rather a dubious and vainglorious boast of the landlord.

The club which now holds its weekly sessions here goes by the name of "The Roaring Lads of Little Britain." They abound in old catches, glees, and choice stories, that are traditional in the place, and not to be met with in any other part of the metropolis. There is a madcap undertaker, who is inimitable at a merry song; but the life of the club, and indeed the prime wit of Little Britain, is bully Wagstaff himself. His ancestors were all wags before him, and he has inherited with the inn a large stock of songs and jokes, which go with it from generation to generation as heirlooms. He is a dapper little fellow with bandy legs and pot belly, a red face with a moist merry eye, and a little shock of gray hair behind. At the opening of every club night he is called in to sing his "Confession of Faith," which is the famous old drinking troll from *Gammer Gurton's Needle*.[13] He sings it, to be sure, with many

---

[12] Bacchus and Momus—Greek gods; Bacchus of wine, Momus of scorn and censure.

[13] *Gammer Gurton's Needle*—Early English comedy. Author unknown. Possibly John Still (1543–1608).

variations, as he received it from his father's lips, for it has been a standing favorite at the Half-Moon and Bunch of Grapes ever since it was written; nay, he affirms that his predecessors have often had the honor of singing it before the nobility and gentry at Christmas mummeries, when Little Britain was in all its glory.

It would do one's heart good to hear, on a club night, the shouts of merriment, the snatches of song, and now and then the choral bursts of half a dozen discordant voices, which issue from this jovial mansion. At such times the street is lined with listeners, who enjoy a delight equal to that of gazing into a confectioner's window, or snuffing up the steams of a cookshop.

There are two annual events which produce great stir and sensation in Little Britain; these are St. Bartholomew's Fair, and the Lord Mayor's Day. During the time of the Fair, which is held in the adjoining regions of Smithfield, there is nothing going on but gossiping and gadding about. The late quiet streets of Little Britain are overrun with an irruption of strange figures and faces;—every tavern is a scene of rout and revel. The fiddle and the song are heard from the taproom, morning, noon, and night; and at each window may be seen some group of boon companions, with half-shut eyes, hats on one side, pipe in mouth, and tankard in hand, fondling and prosing, and singing maudlin songs over their liquor. Even the sober decorum of private families, which I must say is rigidly kept up at other times among my neighbors, is no proof against this Saturnalia.[14] There is no such thing as keeping maid servants within doors. Their brains are absolutely set madding with Punch and the Puppet Show; the Flying Horses; Signior Polito; the Fire-Eater; the celebrated Mr. Paap; and the Irish Giant. The children, too, lavish all their holiday money in toys and gilt gingerbread, and fill the house with the Lilliputian[15] din of drums, trumpets, and penny whistles.

But the Lord Mayor's Day is the great anniversary. The Lord Mayor is looked up to by the inhabitants of Little Britain, as the greatest potentate upon earth; his gilt coach with six horses, as the summit of human splendor; and his procession, with all the Sheriffs and Aldermen in his train, as the grandest of earthly pageants.

---

[14] SATURNALIA—At the festival of Saturn the ancients indulged in riotous merriment.
[15] LILLIPUTIAN—Tiny. Reference to Swift's *Gulliver's Travels.*

How they exult in the idea that the King himself dare not enter the city without first knocking at the gate of Temple Bar, and asking permission of the Lord Mayor; for if he did, heaven and earth! there is no knowing what might be the consequence. The man in armor who rides before the Lord Mayor, and is the city champion, has orders to cut down everybody that offends against the dignity of the city; and then there is the little man with a velvet porringer[16] on his head, who sits at the window of the state coach and holds the city sword, as long as a pike-staff—Od's blood! if he once draws that sword, Majesty itself is not safe!

Under the protection of this mighty potentate, therefore, the good people of Little Britain sleep in peace. Temple Bar is an effectual barrier against all interior foes; and as to foreign invasion, the Lord Mayor has but to throw himself into the Tower, call in the train bands,[17] and put the standing army of Beef-eaters[18] under arms, and he may bid defiance to the world!

Thus wrapped up in its own concerns, its own habits, and its own opinions, Little Britain has long flourished as a sound heart to this great fungous metropolis. I have pleased myself with considering it as a chosen spot, where the principles of sturdy John Bullism were garnered up, like seed-corn, to renew the national character when it had run to waste and degeneracy. I have rejoiced also in the general spirit of harmony that prevailed throughout it; for though there might now and then be a few clashes of opinion between the adherents of the cheesemonger and the apothecary, and an occasional feud between the burial societies, yet these were but transient clouds, and soon passed away. The neighbors met with good-will, parted with a shake of the hand, and never abused each other except behind their backs.

I could give rare descriptions of snug junketing parties at which I have been present; where we played at All-Fours, Pope-Joan, Tom-come-tickle-me, and other choice old games: and where we sometimes had a good old English country dance to the tune of Sir Roger de Coverley. Once a year also the neighbors would gather together, and go on a gipsy party to Epping Forest. It would have done any man's heart good to see the merriment that took place

---

[16] Porringer—Saucer-shaped hat.

[17] Train bands—Citizen soldiery of London.

[18] Beef-eaters—Nickname for the guards of the Tower of London.

here as we banqueted on the grass under the trees. How we made the woods ring with bursts of laughter at the songs of little Wagstaff and the merry undertaker! After dinner, too, the young folks would play at blind-man's-buff and hide-and-seek; and it was amusing to see them tangled among the briers, and to hear a fine romping girl now and then squeak from among the bushes. The elder folks would gather round the cheesemonger and the apothecary, to hear them talk politics, for they generally brought out a newspaper in their pockets to pass away time in the country. They would now and then, to be sure, get a little warm in argument; but their disputes were always adjusted by reference to a worthy old umbrella-maker in a double chin, who, never exactly comprehending the subject, managed somehow or other to decide in favor of both parties.

All empires, however, says some philosopher or historian, are doomed to changes and revolutions. Luxury and innovation creep in; factions arise; and families now and then spring up, whose ambition and intrigues throw the whole system into confusion. Thus in latter days has the tranquility of Little Britain been grievously disturbed, and its golden simplicity of manners threatened with total subversion, by the aspiring family of a retired butcher.

The family of the Lambs had long been among the most thriving and popular in the neighborhood: the Miss Lambs were the belles of Little Britain, and everybody was pleased when old Lamb had made money enough to shut up shop, and put his name on a brass plate on his door. In an evil hour, however, one of the Miss Lambs had the honor of being a lady in attendance on the Lady Mayoress, at her grand annual ball, on which occasion she wore three towering ostrich feathers on her head. The family never got over it; they were immediately smitten with a passion for high life; set up a one-horse carriage, put a bit of gold lace round the errand-boy's hat, and have been the talk and detestation of the whole neighborhood ever since. They could no longer be induced to play at Pope-Joan or blind-man's-buff: they could endure no dances but quadrilles,[19] which nobody had ever heard of in Little Britain; and they took to reading novels, talking bad French, and playing upon the piano. Their brother, too, who had been articled to an attorney, set up for a dandy and a critic, characters hitherto unknown in these parts;

[19] QUADRILLES—A quadrille is an elaborately complex dance.

and he confounded the worthy folks exceedingly by talking about Kean,[20] the Opera, and the *Edinburgh Review*.[21]

What was still worse the Lambs gave a grand ball, to which they neglected to invite any of their old neighbors, but they had a great deal of genteel company from Theobald's Road, Red-Lion Square, and other parts towards the west. There were several beaux of their brother's acquaintance from Gray's Inn Lane and Hatton Garden, and not less than three Aldermen's ladies with their daughters. This was not to be forgotten or forgiven. All Little Britain was in an uproar with the smacking of whips, the lashing of miserable horses, and the rattling and the jingling of hackney-coaches. The gossips of the neighborhood might be seen popping their nightcaps out at every window, watching the crazy vehicles rumble by; and there was a knot of virulent old cronies, that kept a look-out from a house just opposite the retired butcher's, and scanned and criticized every one that knocked at the door.

This dance was a cause of almost open war, and the whole neighborhood declared they would have nothing more to say to the Lambs. It is true that Mrs. Lamb, when she had no engagements with her quality acquaintance, would give little humdrum tea junketings to some of her old cronies, "quite," as she would say, "in a friendly way"; and it is equally true that her invitations were always accepted, in spite of all previous vows to the contrary. Nay, the good ladies would sit and be delighted with the music of the Miss Lambs, who would condescend to strum an Irish melody for them on the piano; and they would listen with wonderful interest to Mrs. Lamb's anecdotes of Alderman Plunket's family, of Portsokenward, and the Miss Timberlakes, the rich heiresses of Crutched-Friars; but then they relieved their consciences, and averted the reproaches of their confederates, by canvassing at the next gossiping convocation everything that had passed, and pulling the Lambs and their rout all to pieces.

The only one of the family that could not be made fashionable, was the retired butcher himself. Honest Lamb, in spite of the meekness of his name, was a rough, hearty old fellow, with the voice of a lion, a head of black hair like a shoe-brush, and a broad face

---

[20] KEAN—Edmund Kean, the leading actor of the day.

[21] *Edinburgh Review*—One of the leading literary magazines of England, founded in 1802.

mottled like his own beef. It was in vain that the daughters always spoke of him as "the old gentleman," addressed him as "papa," in tones of infinite softness, and endeavored to coax him into a dressing-gown and slippers, and other gentlemanly habits. Do what they might, there was no keeping down the butcher. His sturdy nature would break through all their glozings. He had a hearty, vulgar good-humor that was irrepressible. His very jokes made his sensitive daughters shudder; and he persisted in wearing his blue cotton coat of a morning, dining at two o'clock, and having a "bit of sausage with his tea."

He was doomed, however, to share the unpopularity of his family. He found his old comrades gradually growing cold and civil to him; no longer laughing at his jokes, and now and then throwing out a fling at "some people," and a hint about "quality binding." This both nettled and perplexed the honest butcher; and his wife and daughters, with the consummate policy of the shrewder sex, taking advantage of the circumstance, at length prevailed upon him to give up his afternoon's pipe and tankard at Wagstaff's, to sit after dinner by himself and take his pint of port—a liquor he detested, and to nod in his chair in solitary and dismal gentility.

The Miss Lambs might now be seen flaunting along the streets in French bonnets, with unknown beaux; and talking and laughing so loud that it distressed the nerves of every good lady within hearing. They even went so far as to attempt patronage, and actually induced a French dancing-master to set up in the neighborhood; but the worthy folks of Little Britain took fire at it, and did so persecute the poor Gaul that he was fain to pack up fiddle and dancing-pumps, and decamp with such precipitation, that he absolutely forgot to pay for his lodgings.

I had flattered myself, at first, with the idea that all this fiery indignation on the part of the community was merely the overflowing of their zeal for good old English manners, and their horror of innovation; and I applauded the silent contempt they were so vociferous in expressing for upstart pride, French fashions, and the Miss Lambs. But I grieve to say, that I soon perceived the infection had taken hold; and that my neighbors, after condemning, were beginning to follow their example. I overheard my landlady importuning her husband to let their daughters have one quarter at French and music, and that they might take a few lessons in quadrille; I even saw, in the course of a few Sundays, no less than five French bonnets, precisely like those of the Miss Lambs, parading about Little Britain.

I still had my hopes that all this folly would gradually die away; that the Lambs might move out of the neighborhood; might die, or might run away with attorneys' apprentices; and that quiet and simplicity might be again restored to the community. But unluckily a rival power arose. An opulent oilman died, and left a widow with a large jointure,[22] and a family of buxom daughters. The young ladies had long been repining in secret at the parsimony of a prudent father, which kept down all their elegant aspirings. Their ambition, being now no longer restrained, broke out into a blaze, and they openly took the field against the family of the butcher. It is true that the Lambs, having had the first start, had naturally an advantage of them in the fashionable career. They could speak a little bad French, play the piano, dance quadrilles, and had formed high acquaintances; but the Trotters were not to be distanced. When the Lambs appeared with two feathers in their hats, the Miss Trotters mounted four, and of twice as fine colors. If the Lambs gave a dance, the Trotters were sure not to be behindhand; and though they might not boast of as good company, yet they had double the number and were twice as merry.

The whole community has at length divided itself into fashionable factions, under the banners of these two families. The old games of Pope-Joan and Tom-come-tickle-me are entirely discarded; there is no such thing as getting up an honest country dance; and on my attempting to kiss a young lady under the mistletoe last Christmas, I was indignantly repulsed; the Miss Lambs having pronounced it "shocking vulgar." Bitter rivalry has also broken out as to the most fashionable part of Little Britain; the Lambs standing up for the dignity of Cross-Keys Square, and the Trotters for the vicinity of St. Bartholomew's.

Thus is this little territory torn by factions and internal dissensions, like the great empire whose name it bears; and what will be the result would puzzle the apothecary himself, with all his talent at prognostics, to determine; though I apprehend that it will terminate in the total downfall of genuine John Bullism.

The immediate effects are extremely unpleasant to me. Being a single man, and, as I observed before, rather an idle good-for-

[22] JOINTURE—Estate settled on a wife.

nothing personage, I have been considered the only gentleman by profession in the place. I stand therefore in high favor with both parties, and have to hear all their cabinet councils and mutual back-bitings. As I am too civil not to agree with the ladies on all occasions, I have committed myself most horribly with both parties, by abusing their opponents. I might manage to reconcile this to my conscience, which is a truly accommodating one, but I cannot to my apprehension—if the Lambs and Trotters ever come to a reconciliation, and compare notes, I am ruined!

I have determined, therefore, to beat a retreat in time, and am actually looking out for some other nest in this great city where old English manners are still kept up; where French is neither eaten, drunk, danced, nor spoken; and where there are no fashionable families of retired tradesmen. This found, I will, like a veteran rat, hasten away before I have an old house about my ears—bid a long though a sorrowful adieu to my present abode—and leave the rival factions of the Lambs and the Trotters, to divide the distracted empire of LITTLE BRITAIN.

## QUESTIONS AND EXERCISES

Exercises preceded by a star are designed for assignment at the discretion of the teacher, or for any student who volunteers.

1. Is Irving's method of rambling description and observation effective? Explain.
2. Look up the following: Shrove Tuesday, Michaelmas, Dick Whittington, Temple Bar.
3. In what ways did Little Britain preserve the traditions and customs of John Bull?
4. Describe the feud between the Lambs and the Trotters. Is the account too generalized? What purpose does it serve in closing the essay?

*5. Imagine Washington Irving and Benjamin Franklin meeting in Little Britain. Write a brief dialogue between the two, showing their impressions of the district.

## WESTMINSTER ABBEY

The majestic gloom of Westminster, the swelling thunder of its organ, the dust and pomp of kings—these form the unforgettable background for this noblest example of Washington Irving's prose in *The Sketch Book*. In some parts of this essay Irving's diction has the quality of organ-music suggesting that of the greatest master of stately prose in the English language, Sir Thomas Browne, a contemporary of the great Milton.

The whole atmosphere of the sketch is clothed in a majestic melancholy. Purple shadows relieved by rare shafts of sunlight call forth words that catch the very spirit of this hallowed spot. Irving's romantic imagination is arrested, kindled by the "awful nature of the abbey."

Irving attempts to give in some logical order the noteworthy features of the famous cathedral, but more important is the "emotional reflection" inspired by each object, the reverence which sweeps over him when he thinks on men and kings and fruitless paths of glory. The *personal* note dominates this essay, bringing the "London Town" sketches to a fitting climax.

On one of those sober and rather melancholy days, in the latter part of autumn, when the shadows of morning and evening almost mingle together, and throw a gloom over the decline of the year, I passed several hours in rambling about Westminster Abbey. There was something congenial to the season in the mournful magnificence of the old pile; and as I passed its threshold, it seemed like stepping back into the regions of antiquity, and losing myself among the shades of former ages.

I entered from the inner court of Westminster school, through a long, low, vaulted passage that had an almost subterranean look, being dimly lighted in one part by circular perforations in the massive walls. Through this dark avenue I had a distant view of the cloisters, with the figure of an old verger,[1] in his black gown, moving along their shadowy vaults, and seeming like a spectre from one of the neighboring tombs. The approach to the abbey through these gloomy monastic remains, prepares the mind for its solemn contemplation. The cloisters still retain something of the quiet and seclusion of former days. The gray walls are discolored by damps, and crumbling with age; a coat of hoary moss has gathered over the inscriptions of the mural monuments, and obscured the death's heads, and other funereal emblems. The sharp touches of the chisel are gone from the rich tracery of the arches; the roses which adorned the keystones[2] have lost their leafy beauty; everything bears marks of the gradual dilapidations of time, which yet has something touching and pleasing in its very decay.

The sun was pouring down a yellow autumnal ray into the square of the cloisters; beaming upon a scanty plot of grass in the centre,

---

[1] VERGER—Guide, or caretaker in a cathedral.

[2] KEYSTONES—A keystone is the central stone in an arch.

and lighting up an angle of the vaulted passage with a kind of dusky splendor. From between the arcades, the eye glanced up to a bit of blue sky, or a passing cloud; and beheld the sun-gilt pinnacles of the abbey towering into the azure heaven.

As I paced the cloisters, sometimes contemplating this mingled picture of glory and decay, and sometimes endeavoring to decipher the inscriptions on the tombstones, which formed the pavement beneath my feet, my eye was attracted to three figures, rudely carved in relief, but nearly worn away by the footsteps of many generations. They were the effigies of three of the early abbots; the epitaphs were entirely effaced; the names alone remained, having no doubt been renewed in later times; (Vitalis. Abbas. 1082, and Gislebertus Crispinus. Abbas. 1114, and Laurentius. Abbas. 1176). I remained some little while, musing over these casual relics of antiquity, thus left like wrecks upon this distant shore of time, telling no tale but that such beings had been, and had perished; teaching no moral but the futility of that pride which hopes still to exact homage in its ashes, and to live in an inscription. A little longer, and even these faint records will be obliterated, and the monument will cease to be a memorial. Whilst I was yet looking down upon these gravestones, I was roused by the sound of the abbey clock, reverberating from buttress to buttress, and echoing among the cloisters. It is almost startling to hear this warning of departed time sounding among the tombs, and telling the lapse of the hour, which, like a billow, has rolled us onward towards the grave.

I pursued my walk to an arched door opening to the interior of the abbey. On entering here, the magnitude of the building breaks fully upon the mind, contrasted with the vaults of the cloisters. The eyes gaze with wonder at clustered columns of gigantic dimensions, with arches springing from them to such an amazing height; and man wandering about their bases, shrunk into insignificance in comparison with his own handiwork. The spaciousness and gloom of this vast edifice produce a profound and mysterious awe. We step cautiously and softly about, as if fearful of disturbing the hallowed silence of the tomb; while every footfall whispers along the walls, and chatters among the sepulchres, making us more sensible of the quiet we have interrupted.

It seems as if the awful nature of the place presses down upon the soul, and hushes the beholder into noiseless reverence. We feel that we are surrounded by the congregated bones of the great men of past times, who have filled history with their deeds, and the earth with their renown. And yet it almost provokes a smile at the vanity of human ambition, to see how they are crowded together, and jostled in the dust; what parsimony is observed in doling out a scanty nook—a gloomy corner—a little portion of earth, to those whom, when alive, kingdoms could not satisfy; and how many shapes, and forms, and artifices, are devised to catch the casual notice of the passenger, and save from forgetfulness, for a few short years, a name which once aspired to occupy ages of the world's thought and admiration.

I passed some time in Poet's Corner, which occupies an end of one of the transepts or cross aisles of the abbey. The monuments are generally simple; for the lives of literary men afford no striking themes for the sculptor. Shakespeare and Addison have statues erected to their memories; but the greater part have busts, medallions,[3] and sometimes mere inscriptions. Notwithstanding the simplicity of these memorials, I have always observed that the visitors to the abbey remained longest about them. A kinder and fonder feeling takes place of that cold curiosity or vague admiration with which they gaze on the splendid monuments of the great and the heroic. They linger about these as about the tombs of friends and companions; for indeed there is something of companionship between the author and the reader. Other men are known to posterity only through the medium of history, which is continually growing faint and obscure; but the intercourse between the author and his fellow-men is ever new, active, and immediate. He has lived for them more than for himself; he has sacrificed surrounding enjoyments, and shut himself up from the delights of social life, that he might the more intimately commune with distant minds and distant ages. Well may the world cherish his renown; for it has been purchased, not by deeds of violence and blood, but by the diligent dispensation of pleasure. Well may posterity be grateful to his memory; for he has left it an inheritance, not of empty names and sounding actions, but whole treasures of wisdom, bright gems of thought, and golden veins of language.

From Poet's Corner I continued my stroll towards that part of the abbey which contains the sepulchres of the kings. I wandered

[3] MEDALLIONS—Stone tablets, bearing sculptured designs in relief.

among what once were chapels, but which are now occupied by the tombs and monuments of the great. At every turn, I met with some illustrious name, or the cognizance of some powerful house renowned in history. As the eye darts into these dusky chambers of death, it catches glimpses of quaint effigies: some kneeling in niches, as if in devotion; others stretched upon the tombs, with hands piously pressed together; warriors in armor, as if reposing after battle; prelates with crosiers and mitres;[4] and nobles in robes and coronets,[5] lying as it were in state. In glancing over this scene, so strangely populous, yet where every form is so still and silent, it seems almost as if we were treading a mansion of that fabled city, where every being had been suddenly transmuted into stone.

I paused to contemplate a tomb on which lay the effigy of a knight in complete armor. A large buckler was on one arm; the hands were pressed together in supplication upon the breast; the face was almost covered by the morion;[6] the legs were crossed, in token of the warrior's having been engaged in the holy war. It was the tomb of a crusader; one of those military enthusiasts, who so strangely mingled religion and romance, and whose exploits form the connecting link between fact and fiction—between the history and the fairy tale. There is something extremely picturesque in the tombs of these adventurers, decorated as they are with rude armorial bearings and Gothic sculpture. They comport with the antiquated chapels in which they are generally found; and in considering them, the imagination is apt to kindle with the legendary associations, the romantic fiction, the chivalrous pomp and pageantry, which poetry has spread over the wars for the Sepulchre of Christ. They are the relics of time utterly gone by; of beings passed from recollection; of customs and manners with which ours have no affinity. They are like objects from some strange and distant land, of which we have no certain knowledge, and about which all our conceptions are vague and visionary. There is something extremely solemn and awful in those effigies on Gothic tombs, extended as if in the sleep of death, or in the supplication of the dying hour. They have an effect infinitely more impressive on my feelings than the fanciful attitudes, the overwrought conceits, and allegorical groups,

[4] CROSIERS AND MITRES—Symbols of a bishop's office, the former a shepherd's crook, the latter a peculiarly made tall hat.

[5] CORONETS—Small crowns.

[6] MORION—Type of open helmet.

which abound on modern monuments. I have been struck, also, with the superiority of many of the old sepulchral inscriptions. There was a noble way, in former times, of saying things simply, and yet saying them proudly: and I do not know an epitaph that breathes a loftier consciousness of family worth and honorable lineage, than one which affirms of a noble house, that "all the brothers were brave, and all the sisters virtuous."

In the opposite transept to Poet's Corner, stands a monument which is among the most renowned achievements of modern art; but which, to me, appears horrible rather than sublime. It is the tomb of Mrs. Nightingale, by Roubiliac.[7] The bottom of the monument is represented as throwing open its marble doors, and a sheeted skeleton is starting forth. The shroud is falling from his fleshless frame as he launches his dart at his victim. She is sinking into her affrighted husband's arms, who strives, with vain and frantic effort, to avert the blow. The whole is executed with terrible truth and spirit; we almost fancy we hear the gibbering yell of triumph, bursting from the distended jaws of the spectre. But why should we thus seek to clothe death with unnecessary terrors, and to spread horrors round the tomb of those we love? The grave should be surrounded by everything that might inspire tenderness and veneration for the dead; or that might win the living to virtue. It is the place, not of disgust and dismay, but of sorrow and meditation.

While wandering about these gloomy vaults and silent aisles, studying the records of the dead, the sound of busy existence from without occasionally reaches the ear:—the rumbling of the passing equipage; the murmur of the multitude; or perhaps the light laugh of pleasure. The contrast is striking with the deathlike repose around; and it has a strange effect upon the feelings, thus to hear the surges of active life hurrying along and beating against the very walls of the sepulchre.

I continued in this way to move from tomb to tomb, and from chapel to chapel. The day was gradually wearing away; the distant tread of loiterers about the abbey grew less and less frequent; the sweet-tongued bell was summoning to evening prayers; and I saw at a distance the choristers, in their white surplices, crossing the aisle and entering the choir. I stood before the entrance to Henry the

[7] Roubiliac—Louis Francois Roubiliac (1695–1762). French sculptor who was a master of technical skill.

Seventh's Chapel. A flight of steps lead up to it, through a deep and gloomy, but magnificent arch. Great gates of brass, richly and delicately wrought, turn heavily upon their hinges, as if proudly reluctant to admit the feet of common mortals into this most gorgeous of sepulchres.

On entering, the eye is astonished by the pomp of architecture, and the elaborate beauty of sculptured detail. The very walls are wrought into universal ornament, encrusted with tracery, and scooped into niches, crowded with the statues of saints and martyrs. Stone seems, by the cunning labor of the chisel, to have been robbed of its weight and density, suspended aloft, as if by magic, and the fretted roof achieved with the wonderful minuteness and airy security of a cobweb.

Along the sides of the chapel are the lofty stalls of the Knights of the Bath,[8] richly carved of oak, though with the grotesque decorations of Gothic architecture. On the pinnacles of the stalls are affixed the helmets and crests of the knights, with their scarfs and swords; and above them are suspended their banners, emblazoned with armorial bearings, and contrasting the splendor of gold and purple and crimson, with the cold gray fretwork of the roof. In the midst of this grand mausoleum stands the sepulchre of its founder,—his effigy, with that of his queen, extended on a sumptuous tomb, and the whole surrounded by a superbly wrought brazen railing.

There is a sad dreariness in this magnificence; this strange mixture of tombs and trophies; these emblems of living and aspiring ambition, close beside mementos which show the dust and oblivion in which all must sooner or later terminate. Nothing impresses the mind with a deeper feeling of loneliness, than to tread the silent and deserted scene of former throng and pageant. On looking round on the vacant stalls of the knights and their esquires, and on the rows of dusty but gorgeous banners that were once borne before them, my imagination conjured up the scene when this hall was bright with the valor and beauty of the land; glittering with the splendor of jewelled rank and military array; alive with the tread of many feet, and the hum of an admiring multitude. All had passed away; the silence of death had settled again upon the place, interrupted only by the casual chirping of birds, which had found

[8] Knights of the Bath—Honorary order formed by George I of England in 1725, rewarding military and civil achievement.

their way into the chapel, and built their nests among its friezes[9] and pendants[10]—sure signs of solitariness and desertion. When I read the names inscribed on the banners, they were those of men scattered far and wide about the world; some tossing upon distant seas; some under arms in distant lands; some mingling in the busy intrigues of courts and cabinets: all seeking to deserve one more distinction in this mansion of shadowy honors—the melancholy reward of a monument.

Two small aisles on each side of this chapel present a touching instance of the equality of the grave, which brings down the oppressor to a level with the oppressed, and mingles the dust of the bitterest enemies together. In one is the sepulchre of the haughty Elizabeth; in the other is that of her victim, the lovely and unfortunate Mary.[11] Not an hour in the day, but some ejaculation of pity is uttered over the fate of the latter, mingled with indignation at her oppressor. The walls of Elizabeth's sepulchre continually echo with the sighs of sympathy heaved at the grave of her rival.

A peculiar melancholy reigns over the aisle where Mary lies buried. The light struggles dimly through windows darkened by dust. The greater part of the place is in deep shadow, and the walls are stained and tinted by time and weather. A marble figure of Mary is stretched upon the tomb, round which is an iron railing, much corroded, bearing her national emblem—the thistle. I was weary with wandering, and sat down to rest myself by the monument, revolving in my mind the chequered and disastrous story of poor Mary.

The sound of casual footsteps had ceased from the abbey. I could only hear, now and then, the distant voice of the priest repeating the evening service, and the faint responses of the choir; these paused for a time, and all was hushed. The stillness, the desertion and obscurity that were gradually prevailing around, gave a deeper and more solemn interest to the place:

> For in the silent grave no conversation,
> No joyful tread of friends, no voice of lovers,
> No careful father's counsel—nothing's heard,
> For nothing is, but all oblivion,
> Dust, and an endless darkness.

---

[9] FRIEZES—Ornamented bands or strips set horizontally in a wall.

[10] PENDANTS—Hanging architectural ornaments.

[11] ELIZABETH . . . MARY—Mary, Queen of Scots, was beheaded by order of Queen Elizabeth in 1587.

Suddenly the notes of the deep-laboring organ burst upon the ear, falling with doubled and redoubled intensity and rolling as it were, huge billows of sound. How well do their volume and grandeur accord with this mighty building! With what pomp do they swell through its vast vaults, and breathe their awful harmony through these caves of death, and make the silent sepulchre vocal!—And now they rise in triumph and acclamation, heaving higher and higher their accordant notes, and piling sound on sound. And now they pause, and the soft voices of the choir break out into sweet gushes of melody; they soar aloft and warble along the roof, and seem to play about these lofty vaults like the pure airs of heaven. Again the pealing organ heaves its thrilling thunders, compressing air into music, and rolling it forth upon the soul. What long-drawn cadences! What solemn sweeping concords! It grows more and more dense and powerful—it fills the vast pile, and seems to jar the very walls—the ear is stunned—the senses are overwhelmed. And now it is winding up in full jubilee—it is rising from the earth to heaven—the very soul seems rapt away and floated upwards on this swelling tide of harmony!

I sat for some time lost in that kind of reverie which a strain of music is apt sometimes to inspire: the shadows of evening were gradually thickening round me; the monuments began to cast deeper and deeper gloom; and the distant clock again gave token of the slowly waning day.

I rose, and prepared to leave the abbey. As I descended the flight of steps which lead into the body of the building, my eye was caught by the shrine of Edward the Confessor, and I ascended the small staircase that conducts to it, to take from thence a general survey of this wilderness of tombs. The shrine is elevated upon a kind of platform, and close around it are the sepulchres of various kings and queens. From this eminence the eye looks down between pillars and funeral trophies to the chapels and chambers below, crowded with tombs; where warriors, prelates, courtiers, and statesmen lie mouldering in their "beds of darkness." Close by me stood the great chair of coronation, rudely carved of oak, in the barbarous taste of a remote and Gothic age. The scene seemed almost as if contrived, with theatrical artifice, to produce an effect upon the beholder. Here was a type of the beginning and the end of human pomp and power; here it was literally but a step from the throne to the sepulchre. Would not one think that these incongruous mementos had been gathered together as a lesson to living greatness?—to show it, even in the moment of its proudest exaltation, the neglect and dishonor to which it must soon arrive? how soon that crown which encircles its brow must pass away; and it must lie down in the dust and disgraces of the tomb, and be trampled upon by the feet of the meanest of the multitude? For, strange to tell, even the grave is here no longer a sanctuary. There is a shocking levity in some natures, which leads them to sport with awful and hallowed things; and there are base minds, which delight to revenge on the illustrious dead the abject homage and grovelling servility which they pay to the living. The coffin of Edward the Confessor has been broken open, and his remains despoiled of their funeral ornaments; the sceptre has been stolen from the hand of the imperious Elizabeth, and the effigy of Henry the Fifth lies headless. Not a royal monument but bears some proof how false and fugitive is the homage of mankind. Some are plundered; some mutilated; some covered with ribaldry and insult—all more or less outraged and dishonored!

The last beams of day were now faintly streaming through the painted windows in the high vaults above me; the lower parts of the abbey were already wrapped in the obscurity of twilight. The chapels and aisles grew darker and darker. The effigies of the kings faded into shadows; the marble figures of the monuments assumed strange shapes in the uncertain light; the evening breeze crept through the aisles like the cold breath of the grave; and even the distant footfall of a verger, traversing the Poet's Corner, had something strange and dreary in its sound. I slowly retraced my morning's walk, and as I passed out at the portal of the cloisters, the door closing with a jarring noise behind me, filled the whole building with echoes.

I endeavored to form some arrangement in my mind of the objects I had been contemplating, but found they were already fallen into indistinctness and confusion. Names, inscriptions, trophies, had all become confounded in my recollection, though I had scarcely taken my foot from off the threshold. What, thought I, is this vast assemblage of sepulchres but a treasury of humiliation; a huge pile of reiterated homilies on the emptiness of renown, and the certainty of oblivion? It is indeed the empire of Death; his great shadowy palace; where he sits in state, mocking at the relics of human glory, and spreading dust and forgetfulness on the monuments of princes. How idle a boast, after all, is the immortality of a name! Time is ever silently turning over his pages; we are too much engrossed by the story of the present, to think of the characters and anecdotes that gave interest to the past; and each age is a volume thrown aside to be speedily forgotten. The idol of to-day pushes the hero of yesterday out of our recollection; and will, in turn, be supplanted by his successor of to-morrow. "Our fathers," says Sir Thomas Browne, "find their graves in our short memories, and sadly tell us how we may be buried in our survivors." History fades into fable; fact becomes clouded with doubt and controversy; the inscription moulders from the tablet; the statue falls from the pedestal. Columns, arches, pyramids—what are they but heaps of sand—and their epitaphs, but characters written in the dust? What is the security of a tomb, or the perpetuity of an embalmment? The remains of Alexander the Great have been scattered to the wind, and his empty sarcophagus[12] is now the mere curiosity of a museum. "The Egyptian mummies, which Cambyses or time hath spared, avarice now consumeth; Mizraim cures wounds, and Pharaoh is sold for balsams."[13]

What then is to insure this pile, which now towers above me, from sharing the fate of mightier mausoleums? The time must come when its gilded vaults, which now spring so loftily, shall lie in rubbish beneath the feet; when, instead of the sound of melody and praise, the wind shall whistle through the broken arches, and the owl hoot from the shattered tower—when the garish sunbeam shall break into these gloomy mansions of death; and the ivy twine round the fallen column; and the foxglove hang its blossoms about the nameless urn, as if in mockery of the dead. Thus man passes away; his name perishes from record and recollection; his history is as a tale that is told, and his very monument becomes a ruin.

---

[12] SARCOPHAGUS—Stone coffin. The elaborately carved sarcophagus of Alexander the Great is now in the British Museum.

[13] THE EGYPTIAN . . . BALSAMS—Passage from Sir Thomas Browne's *Urn-Burial.*
CAMBYSES—King of the Medes and Persians in 6th century B. C.
MIZRAIM—The Biblical name of Egypt.
PHARAOH—Title given rulers of Egypt.

## QUESTIONS AND EXERCISES

Exercises preceded by a star are designed for assignment at the discretion of the teacher, or for any student who volunteers.

*1. Bring to class a report on Westminster Abbey, giving its history, lay-out, points and objects of special interest. Consult *The Encyclopædia Britannica,* and other reference works in a library.
2. What is the atmosphere struck by the author in this sketch? Does he make you feel it? If so, in what ways?
3. Outline Irving's journey through the Abbey, giving briefly the author's reaction to the various relics and historical objects.
4. Why in the third paragraph does Irving mention "a bit of blue sky . . . and the sun-gilt pinnacles of the Abbey"?
5. Irving's style is marked here by long words. Make a list of 12 such words used in the essay and define them.
*6. Read Sir Thomas Browne's *Urn-Burial* and give your opinion as to whether Irving is influenced by it in *Westminster Abbey.*
7. In your opinion what is the most eloquent paragraph in the essay?

# *A CHRISTMAS INTERLUDE*

## CHRISTMAS

Rib roast of beef and Yorkshire pudding are the earmarks of a really old-fashioned English Christmas dinner. Whenever you sit down to this hearty dish it is pleasant to recall the scene in Bracebridge Hall in Yorkshire with the merry company at the sturdy, old Squire's gathered around the Yule-fire in the great hall. . . . Sit back in the shadows with Washington Irving and let the spell of a Christmas in the old-English tradition weave itself about you.

This first paper in "A Christmas Interlude" is nothing more than an introductory essay setting forth the general significance of the English Christmas-tide and preparing the reader for the sketches of Christmas customs that are to follow.

*But is old, old, good old Christmas gone? Nothing but the hair of his good, gray old head and beard left? Well, I will have that, seeing I cannot have more of him.*—Hue and Cry after Christmas.

Nothing in England exercises a more delightful spell over my imagination than the lingerings of the holiday customs and rural games of former times. They recall the pictures my fancy used to draw in the May morning of life, when as yet I only knew the world through books, and believed it to be all that poets had painted it; and they bring with them the flavor of those honest days of yore, in which, perhaps with equal fallacy, I am apt to think the world was more home-bred, social, and joyous than at present.

I regret to say that they are daily growing more and more faint, being gradually worn away by time, but still more obliterated by modern fashion. They resemble those picturesque morsels of Gothic architecture, which we see crumbling in various parts of the country, partly dilapidated by the waste of ages, and partly lost in the additions and alterations of later days. Poetry, however, clings with cherishing fondness about the rural game and holiday revel, from which it has derived so many of its themes—as the ivy winds its rich foliage about the Gothic arch and mouldering tower, gratefully repaying their support, by clasping together their tottering remains, and, as it were, embalming them in verdure.

Of all the old festivals, however, that of Christmas awakens the strongest and most heartfelt associations. There is a tone of solemn and sacred feeling that blends with our conviviality, and lifts the spirit to a state of hallowed and elevated enjoyment. The services of the Church about this season are extremely tender and inspiring: they dwell on the beautiful story of the origin of our faith, and the pastoral scenes that accompanied its announcement: they gradually increase in fervor and pathos during the season of Advent,[1] until they break forth in full jubilee on the morning that brought peace and good-will to men. I do not know a grander effect of music on the moral feelings than to hear the full choir and the pealing organ performing a Christmas anthem in a cathedral, and filling every part of the vast pile with triumphant harmony.

It is a beautiful arrangement, also, derived from days of yore, that this festival, which commemorates the announcement of the religion of peace and love, has been made the season for gathering together of family connections, and drawing closer again those bands of kindred hearts, which the cares and pleasures and sorrows of the world are continually operating to cast loose; of calling back the children of a family, who have launched forth in life, and wandered widely asunder, once more to assemble about the paternal hearth, that rallying-place of the affections, there to grow young and loving again among the endearing mementos of childhood.

There is something in the very season of the year that gives a charm to the festivity of Christmas. At other times, we derive a great portion of our pleasures from the mere beauties of Nature. Our feelings sally forth and dissipate themselves over the sunny

[1] Advent—Period including the four Sundays before Christmas.

landscape, and we "live abroad and everywhere." The song of the bird, the murmur of the stream, the breathing fragrance of spring, the soft voluptuousness of summer, the golden pomp of autumn, earth with its mantle of refreshing green, and heaven with its deep delicious blue and its cloudy magnificence,—all fill us with mute but exquisite delight, and we revel in the luxury of mere sensation. But in the depth of winter, when Nature lies despoiled of every charm, and wrapped in her shroud of sheeted snow, we turn for our gratifications to moral sources. The dreariness and desolation of the landscape, the short gloomy days and darksome nights, while they circumscribe our wanderings, shut in our feelings also from rambling abroad, and make us more keenly disposed for the pleasures of the social circle. Our thoughts are more concentrated; our friendly sympathies more aroused. We feel more sensibly the charm of each other's society, and are brought more closely together by dependence on each other for enjoyment. Heart calleth unto heart, and we draw our pleasures from the deep wells of loving-kindness which lie in the quiet recesses of our bosoms; and which, when resorted to, furnish forth the pure element of domestic felicity.

The pitchy gloom without makes the heart dilate on entering the room filled with the glow and warmth of the evening fire. The ruddy blaze diffuses an artificial summer and sunshine through the room, and lights up each countenance into a kindlier welcome. Where does the honest face of hospitality expand into a broader and more cordial smile—where is the shy glance of love more sweetly eloquent—than by the winter fireside? and as the hollow blast of wintry wind rushes through the hall, claps the distant door, whistles about the casement, and rumbles down the chimney, what can be more grateful than that feeling of sober and sheltered security, with which we look round upon the comfortable chamber, and the scene of domestic hilarity?

The English, from the great prevalence of rural habit throughout every class of society, have always been fond of those festivals and holidays which agreeably interrupt the stillness of country life; and they were in former days particularly observant of the religious and social rites of Christmas. It is inspiring to read even the dry details which some antiquaries have given of the quaint humors, the burlesque pageants, the complete abandonment to mirth and good-fellowship, with which this festival was celebrated. It seemed to throw open every door, and unlock every heart. It brought the peasant and the peer together, and blended all ranks in one warm generous flow of joy and kindness. The old halls of castles and manor-houses resounded with the harp and the Christmas carol, and their ample boards groaned under the weight of hospitality. Even the poorest cottage welcomed the festive season with green decorations of bay and holly—the cheerful fire glanced its rays through the lattice, inviting the passengers to raise the latch, and join the gossip knot huddled round the hearth, beguiling the long evening with legendary jokes, and oft-told Christmas tales.

One of the least pleasing effects of modern refinement is the havoc it has made among the hearty old holiday customs. It has completely taken off the sharp touchings and spirited reliefs of these embellishments of life, and has worn down society into a more smooth and polished, but certainly a less characteristic surface. Many of the games and ceremonials of Christmas have entirely disappeared, and, like the sherris sack[2] of old Falstaff, are become matters of speculation and dispute among commentators. They flourished in times full of spirit and lustihood, when men enjoyed life roughly, but heartily and vigorously: times wild and picturesque, which have furnished poetry with its richest materials, and the drama with its most attractive variety of characters and manners. The world has become more worldly. There is more of dissipation and less of enjoyment. Pleasure has expanded into a broader, but a shallower stream, and has forsaken many of those deep and quiet channels, where it flowed sweetly through the calm bosom of domestic life. Society has acquired a more enlightened and elegant tone; but it has lost many of its strong local peculiarities, its home bred feelings, its honest fireside delights. The traditionary customs of golden-hearted antiquity, its feudal hospitalities, and lordly wassailings,[3] have passed away with the baronial castles and stately manor-houses in which they were celebrated. They comported with the shadowy hall, the great oaken gallery, and the tapestried parlor, but are unfitted to the light showy saloons and gay drawing-rooms of the modern villa.

---

[2] SHERRIS SACK—Sherry, a light wine.

[3] WASSAILINGS—Drinking healths from a huge punch bowl.

Shorn, however, as it is, of its ancient and festive honors, Christmas is still a period of delightful excitement in England. It is gratifying to see that home feeling completely aroused which holds so powerful a place in every English bosom. The preparations making on every side for the social board that is again to unite friends and kindred—the presents of good cheer passing and repassing, those tokens of regard and quickeners of kind feelings—the evergreens distributed about houses and churches, emblems of peace and gladness—all these have the most pleasing effect in producing fond associations, and kindling benevolent sympathies. Even the sound of the waits,[4] rude as may be their minstrelsy, breaks upon the mid-watches of a winter night with the effect of perfect harmony. As I have been awakened by them in that still and solemn hour, "when deep sleep falleth upon man," I have listened with a hushed delight, and connecting them with the sacred and joyous occasion, have almost fancied them into another celestial choir, announcing peace and good-will to mankind. How delightfully the imagination when wrought upon by these moral influences turns everything to melody and beauty! The very crowing of the cock, heard sometimes in the profound repose of the country, "telling the night watches to his feathery dames," was thought by the common people to announce the approach of this sacred festival:

> "Some say that ever 'gainst that season comes
> Wherein our Saviour's birth is celebrated,
> This bird of dawning singeth all night long;
> And then, they say, no spirit dares stir abroad;
> The nights are wholesome—then no planets strike,
> No fairy takes, no witch hath power to charm,
> So hallow'd and so gracious is the time."[5]

Amidst the general call to happiness, the bustle of the spirits, and stir of the affections, which prevail at this period, what bosom can remain insensible? It is, indeed, the season of regenerated feeling—the season for kindling not merely the fire of hospitality in the hall, but the genial flame of charity in the heart. The scene of early love again rises green to memory beyond the sterile waste of years, and the idea of home, fraught with the fragrance of home-dwelling joys, reanimates the drooping spirit—as the Arabian

[4] WAITS—Carolers who sang before homes on Christmas eve.

[5] SOME SAY . . . TIME—See Shakespeare's *Hamlet:* Act I, Scene 1.

breeze will sometimes waft the freshness of the distant fields to the weary pilgrim of the desert.

Stranger and sojourner as I am in the land—though for me no social hearth may blaze, no hospitable roof throw open its doors, nor the warm grasp of friendship welcome me at the threshold—yet I feel the influence of the season beaming into my soul from the happy looks of those around me. Surely happiness is reflective, like the light of heaven; and every countenance bright with smiles, and glowing with innocent enjoyment, is a mirror transmitting to others the rays of a supreme and ever-shining benevolence. He who can turn churlishly away from contemplating the felicity of his fellow-beings, and can sit down darkling and repining in his loneliness when all around is joyful, may have his moments of strong excitement and selfish gratification, but he wants the genial and social sympathies which constitute the charm of a merry Christmas.

### QUESTIONS AND EXERCISES

1. Does the essay seem to you to strike an artificial note?
2. Look up in a dictionary the difference between *sentiment* and *sentimentality*. Which does Irving employ here?
3. Give the essence of the essay in your own words.

## THE STAGE COACH

In addition to being an excellent pen-picture of early nineteenth century traveling in England with its lumbering stage-coaches and the ruddy fire-glows of Yorkshire inns, this sketch sets the stage for Irving's *imaginary* stay at Bracebridge Hall for a season of Christmastide festivity. Notice particularly the portrait of "ye coachman"—he is one of the finest of the author's pen-children.

This and the following two *Sketches* form a continuous narrative which should be read at one sitting. It is the only instance in *The Sketch Book* where several *Sketches* dovetail into one story.

In the preceding paper I have made some general observations on the Christmas festivities of England, and am tempted to illustrate them by some anecdotes of a Christmas passed in the country; in perusing which, I would most courteously invite my reader to lay aside the austerity of wisdom, and to put on that genuine holiday spirit, which is tolerant of folly and anxious only for amusement.

In the course of a December tour in Yorkshire, I rode for a long distance in one of the public coaches, on the day preceding Christmas. The coach was crowded, both inside and out, with passengers, who, by their talk, seemed principally bound to the mansions of relations or friends, to eat the Christmas dinner. It was loaded also with hampers of game, and baskets and boxes of delicacies; and hares hung dangling their long ears about the coachman's box, presents from distant friends for the impending feast. I had three fine rosy-cheeked boys for my fellow-passengers inside, full of the buxom health and manly spirit which I have observed in the children of this country. They were returning home for the holidays, in high glee, and promising themselves a world of enjoyment. It was delightful to hear the gigantic plans of the little rogues, and the impracticable feats they were to perform during their six weeks' emancipation from the abhorred thraldom of book, birch, and pedagogue. They were full of anticipations of the meeting with the family and household, down to the very cat and dog; and of the joy they were to give their little sisters, by the presents with which their pockets were crammed; but the meeting to which they seemed to look forward with the greatest impatience was with Bantam, which I found to be a pony, and according to their talk, possessed of more virtues than any steed since the days of Bucephalus.[1] How he could trot! how he could run! and then such leaps as he would take—there was not a hedge in the whole country that he could not clear.

They were under the particular guardianship of the coachman, to whom whenever an opportunity presented they addressed a host of questions, and pronounced him one of the best fellows in the world. Indeed, I could not but notice the more than ordinary air of bustle and importance of the coachman, who wore his hat a little on one side, and had a large bunch of Christmas greens stuck in the button-hole of his coat. He is always a personage full of mighty care and business; but he is particularly so during this season, having so many commissions to execute in consequence of the great interchange of presents. And here, perhaps, it may not be unacceptable to my untravelled readers, to have a sketch that may serve as a general representation of this very numerous and important class

[1] Bucephalus—The celebrated war horse of Alexander the Great. He allowed no one but his master to ride him.

of functionaries, who have a dress, a manner, a language, an air, peculiar to themselves, and prevalent throughout the fraternity; so that, wherever an English stage-coachman may be seen, he cannot be mistaken for one of any other craft or mystery.

He has commonly a broad, full face, curiously mottled with red, as if the blood had been forced by hard feeding into every vessel of the skin; he is swelled into jolly dimensions by frequent potations of malt liquors, and his bulk is still further increased by a multiplicity of coats, in which he is buried like a cauliflower, the upper one reaching to his heels. He wears a broad-brimmed low-crowned hat, a huge roll of colored handkerchief about his neck, knowingly knotted and tucked in at the bosom; and has in summer-time a large bouquet of flowers in his button-hole—the present, most probably, of some enamoured country lass. His waistcoat is commonly of some bright color, striped, and his small-clothes[2] extend far below the knees, to meet a pair of jockey boots which reach about half-way up his legs.

All this costume is maintained with much precision; he has a pride in having his clothes of excellent materials, and notwithstanding the seeming grossness of his appearance, there is still discernible that neatness and propriety of person, which is almost inherent in an Englishman. He enjoys great consequence and consideration along the road; has frequent conferences with the village housewives, who look upon him as a man of great trust and dependence; and he seems to have a good understanding with every bright-eyed country lass. The moment he arrives where the horses are to be changed, he throws down the reins with something of an air, and abandons the cattle to the care of the hostler, his duty being merely to drive from one stage to another. When off the box, his hands are thrust into the pockets of his great-coat, and he rolls about the inn-yard with an air of the most absolute lordliness. Here he is generally surrounded by an admiring throng of hostlers, stable-boys, shoeblacks, and those nameless hangers-on that infest inns and taverns, and run errands, and do all kind of odd jobs, for the privilege of battening on the drippings of the kitchen and the leakage of the tap-room. These all look up to him as to an oracle; treasure up his cant phrases; echo his opinions about horses and other topics of jockey lore; and, above all, endeavor to imitate his air and

[2] SMALL-CLOTHES—Knee breeches.

carriage. Every ragamuffin that has a coat to his back, thrusts his hands in the pockets, rolls in his gait, talks slang, and is an embryo "Coachey."

Perhaps it might be owing to the pleasing serenity that reigned in my own mind, that I fancied I saw cheerfulness in every countenance throughout the journey. A Stage-Coach, however, carries animation always with it, and puts the world in motion as it whirls along. The horn, sounded at the entrance of a village, produces a general bustle. Some hasten forth to meet friends; some with bundles and band-boxes to secure places, and in the hurry of the moment can hardly take leave of the group that accompanies them. In the mean time, the coachman has a world of small commissions to execute. Sometimes he delivers a hare or pheasant; sometimes jerks a small parcel or newspaper to the door of a public house; and sometimes, with knowing leer and words of sly import, hands to some half-blushing, half-laughing housemaid, an odd-shaped billet-doux from some rustic admirer. As the coach rattles through the village, every one runs to the window, and you have glances on every side of fresh country faces, and blooming, giggling girls. At the corners are assembled juntos[3] of village idlers and wise men, who take their stations there for the important purpose of seeing company pass: but the sagest knot is generally at the blacksmith's, to whom the passing of the coach is an event fruitful of much speculation. The smith, with the horse's heel in his lap, pauses as the vehicle whirls by; the cyclops[4] round the anvil suspend their ringing hammers, and suffer the iron to grow cool; and the sooty spectre in brown paper cap, laboring at the bellows, leans on the handle for a moment, and permits the asthmatic engine to heave a long-drawn sigh, while he glares through the murky smoke and sulphureous gleams of the smithy.

Perhaps the impending holiday might have given a more than usual animation to the country, for it seemed to me as if everybody was in good looks and good spirits. Game, poultry, and other luxuries of the table, were in brisk circulation in the villages; the grocers', butchers', and fruiterers' shops were thronged with customers. The housewives were stirring briskly about, putting their dwellings in order; and the glossy branches of holly, with their

[3] JUNTOS—Groups. The term originally meant "secret councils."
[4] CYCLOPS—In classical mythology, forgers of thunderbolts.

bright-red berries began to appear at the windows. The scene brought to mind an old writer's account of Christmas preparations: "Now capons and hens, beside turkeys, geese, and ducks, with beef and mutton—must all die—for in twelve days a multitude of people will not be fed with a little. Now plums and spice, sugar and honey, square it among pies and broth. Now or never must music be in tune, for the youth must dance and sing to get them a heat, while the aged sit by the fire. The country maid leaves half her market, and must be sent again if she forgets a pack of cards on Christmas eve. Great is the contention of Holly and Ivy, whether master or dame wears the breeches. Dice and cards benefit the butler; and if the cook do not lack wit, he will sweetly lick his fingers."

I was roused from this fit of luxurious meditation, by a shout from my little travelling companions. They had been looking out of the coach-windows for the last few miles, recognizing every tree and cottage as they approached home, and now there was a general burst of joy—"There's John! and there's old Carlo! and there's Bantam!" cried the happy little rogues, clapping their hands.

At the end of the lane, there was an old sober-looking servant in livery waiting for them; he was accompanied by a superannuated pointer, and by the redoubtable Bantam, a little old rat of a pony, with a shaggy mane and long rusty tail, who stood dozing quietly by the road-side, little dreaming of the bustling times that awaited him.

I was pleased to see the fondness with which the little fellows leaped about the steady old footman, and hugged the pointer, who wriggled his whole body for joy. But Bantam was the great object of interest; all wanted to mount at once, and it was with some difficulty that John arranged that they should ride by turns, and the eldest should ride first.

Off they set at last; one on the pony, with the dog bounding and barking before him, and the others holding John's hands; both talking at once, and overpowering him with questions about home, and with school anecdotes. I looked after them with a feeling in which I do not know whether pleasure or melancholy predominated; for I was reminded of those days when, like them, I had neither known care nor sorrow, and a holiday was the summit of earthly felicity. We stopped a few moments afterwards to water the horses; and on resuming our route, a turn of the road brought us in sight of a neat country-seat. I could just distinguish the forms of a lady and two young girls in the portico, and I saw my little comrades, with Bantam, Carlo, and old John, trooping along the carriage road. I leaned out of the coach-window, in hopes of witnessing the happy meeting, but a grove of trees shut it from my sight.

In the evening we reached a village where I had determined to pass the night. As we drove into the great gateway of the inn, I saw, on one side, the light of a rousing kitchen fire beaming through a window. I entered, and admired, for the hundredth time that picture of convenience, neatness, and broad honest enjoyment—the kitchen of an English inn. It was of spacious dimensions, hung round with copper and tin vessels highly polished, and decorated here and there with a Christmas green. Hams, tongues, and flitches of bacon were suspended from the ceiling; a smoke-jack[5] made its ceaseless clanking beside the fire-place, and a clock ticked in one corner.

A well-scoured deal table extended along one side of the kitchen, with a cold round of beef, and other hearty viands, upon it, over which two foaming tankards of ale seemed mounting guard. Travellers of inferior order were preparing to attack this stout repast, while others sat smoking and gossiping over their ale on two high-backed oaken settles beside the fire. Trim housemaids were hurrying backwards and forwards under the directions of a fresh, bustling landlady; but still seizing an occasional moment to exchange a flippant word, and have a rallying laugh, with the group round the fire. The scene completely realized Poor Robin's humble idea of the comforts of midwinter:

> Now trees their leafy hats do bare
> To reverence Winter's silver hair;
> A handsome hostess, merry host,
> A pot of ale now and a toast,
> Tobacco and a good coal fire,
> Are things this season doth require.*

I had not been long at the inn, when a post-chaise[6] drove up to the door. A young gentleman stept out, and by the light of the lamps I caught a glimpse of a countenance which I thought I knew.

* *Poor Robin's Almanac,* 1684.

---

[5] Smoke-jack—Contrivance for turning a spit, or roasting rod.

[6] Post-chaise—Four-wheeled public carriage making regular stops along a fixed route.

I moved forward to get a nearer view, when his eye caught mine. I was not mistaken; it was Frank Bracebridge, a sprightly, good-humored young fellow with whom I had once travelled on the continent. Our meeting was extremely cordial, for the countenance of an old fellow-traveller always brings up the recollection of a thousand pleasant scenes, odd adventures, and excellent jokes. To discuss all these in a transient interview at an inn, was impossible; and finding that I was not pressed for time, and was merely making a tour of observation, he insisted that I should give him a day or two at his father's country-seat, to which he was going to pass the holidays, and which lay at a few miles' distance. "It is better than eating a solitary Christmas dinner at an inn," said he, "and I can assure you of a hearty welcome, in something of the old-fashioned style." His reasoning was cogent, and I must confess the preparation I had seen for universal festivity and social enjoyment, had made me feel a little impatient of my loneliness. I closed, therefore, at once with his invitation; the chaise drove up to the door, and in a few moments I was on my way to the family mansion of the Bracebridges.

## QUESTIONS AND EXERCISES

Exercises preceded by a star are designed for assignment at the discretion of the teacher, or for any student who volunteers.

1. What gives this essay the snap and dash lacking in the preceding sketch, *Christmas?*
2. Give a word-picture of "ye coachman."
*3. With the paragraph beginning "In the evening we entered a village . . ." as a guide, write a description of a stage-set for a play supposed to take place in the Yorkshire Inn.
*4. Read Charles Dickens' description of an English stage-coach driver in Chapter XXIII of *Pickwick Papers.* Does he resemble the one described by Irving? Which seems the better description?
5. Describe the method of traveling in Washington Irving's time.

## CHRISTMAS EVE

It was a brilliant moonlight night, but extremely cold; our chaise whirled rapidly over the frozen ground; the post-boy smacked his whip incessantly, and a part of the time his horses were on a gallop. "He knows where he is going," said my companion, laughing, "and is eager to arrive in time for some of the merriment and good cheer of the servants' hall. My father, you must know, is a bigoted devotee of the old school, and prides himself upon keeping up something of old English hospitality. He is a tolerable specimen of what you will rarely meet with nowadays in its purity,—the old English country gentleman; for our men of fortune spend so much of their time in town, and fashion is carried so much into the country, that the strong rich peculiarities of ancient rural life are almost polished away. My father, however, from early years, took honest Peacham* for his text-book instead of Chesterfield;[1] he determined in his own mind, that there was no condition more truly honorable and enviable than that of a country gentleman on his paternal lands, and, therefore, passes the whole of his time on his estate. He is a strenuous advocate for the revival of the old rural games and holiday observances, and is deeply read in the writers, ancient and modern, who have treated on the subject. Indeed, his favorite range of reading is among the authors who flourished at least two centuries since; who, he insists, wrote and thought more like true Englishmen than any of their successors. He even regrets sometimes that he had not been born a few centuries earlier, when England was itself, and had its peculiar manners and customs. As he lives at some distance from the main road, in rather a lonely part of the country, without any rival gentry near him, he has that most enviable of all blessings to an Englishman, an opportunity of indulging the bent of his own humor without molestation. Being representative of the oldest family in the neighborhood, and a great part of the peasantry being his tenants, he is much looked up to, and, in general, is known simply by the appellation of 'The Squire,' a title which has been accorded to the head of the family since time immemorial. I think it best to give you these hints about my worthy old father, to prepare you for any eccentricities that might otherwise appear absurd."

We had passed for some time along the wall of a park, and at length the chaise stopped at the gate. It was in a heavy magnificent old style, of iron bars, fancifully wrought at top into flourishes and flowers. The huge square columns that supported the gate were

* Peacham's *Complete Gentleman*, 1622.

[1] Chesterfield—Philip Dormer Stanhope (Earl of Chesterfield) is famous for the letters written to his son advising him on social matters. The letters, written in the middle of the eighteenth century, were important contributions to the growth of the English essay.

surmounted by the family crest. Close adjoining was the porter's lodge, sheltered under dark fir trees, and almost buried in shrubbery.

The post boy rang a large porter's bell, which resounded through the still frosty air, and was answered by the distant barking of dogs, with which the mansion-house seemed garrisoned. An old woman immediately appeared at the gate. As the moonlight fell strongly upon her, I had a full view of a little primitive dame, dressed very much in the antique taste, with a neat kerchief and stomacher, and her silver hair peeping from under a cap of snowy whiteness. She came courtesying forth with many expressions of simple joy at seeing her young master. Her husband, it seemed, was up at the house, keeping Christmas eve in the servants' hall; they could not do without him, as he was the best hand at a song and story in the household.

My friend proposed that we should alight and walk through the park to the Hall, which was at no great distance, while the chaise should follow on. Our road wound through a noble avenue of trees, among the naked branches of which the moon glittered as she rolled through the deep vault of a cloudless sky. The lawn beyond was sheeted with a slight covering of snow, which here and there sparkled as the moonbeams caught a frosty crystal; and at a distance might be seen a thin transparent vapor, stealing up from the low grounds, and threatening gradually to shroud the landscape.

My companion looked around him with transport:—"How often," said he, "have I scampered up this avenue, on returning home on school vacations! How often have I played under these trees when a boy! I feel a degree of filial reverence for them, as we look up to those who have cherished us in childhood. My father was always scrupulous in exacting our holidays, and having us around him on family festivals. He used to direct and superintend our games with the strictness that some parents do the studies of their children. He was very particular that we should play the old English games according to their original form; and consulted old books for precedent and authority for every 'merrie disport'; yet, I assure you, there never was pedantry so delightful. It was the policy of the good old gentleman to make his children feel that home was the happiest place in the world, and I value this delicious home-feeling as one of the choicest gifts a parent could bestow."

We were interrupted by the clamor of a troop of dogs of all sorts and sizes, "mongrel, puppy, whelp, and hound, and curs of low degree," that, disturbed by the ring of the porter's bell and the rattling of the chaise, came bounding open-mouthed across the lawn.

> "——The little dogs and all,
> Tray, Blanch, and Sweetheart, see, they bark at me!"[2]

cried Bracebridge, laughing. At the sound of his voice the bark was changed into a yelp of delight, and in a moment he was surrounded and almost overpowered by the caresses of the faithful animals.

We had now come in full view of the old family mansion, partly thrown in deep shadow, and partly lit up by the cold moonshine. It was an irregular building of some magnitude, and seemed to be of the architecture of different periods. One wing was evidently very ancient, with heavy stone-shafted bow-windows jutting out and overrun with ivy, from among the foliage of which the small diamond-shaped panes of glass glittered with the moon-beams. The rest of the house was in the French taste of Charles the Second's time, having been repaired and altered, as my friend told me, by one of his ancestors, who returned with that monarch at the Restoration.[3] The grounds about the house were laid out in the old formal manner of artificial flower-beds, clipped shrubberies, raised terraces, and heavy stone balustrades, ornamented with urns, a leaden statue or two, and a jet of water. The old gentleman, I was told, was extremely careful to preserve this obsolete finery in all its original state. He admired this fashion in gardening; it had an air of magnificence, was courtly and noble, and befitting good old family style. The boasted imitation of nature in modern gardening had sprung up with modern republican notions, but did not suit a monarchical government—it smacked of the levelling system. I could not help smiling at this introduction of politics into gardening, though I expressed some apprehension that I should find the old gentleman rather intolerant in his creed. Frank assured me, however, that it was almost the only instance in which he had ever heard his father meddle with politics; and he believed that he had got this notion from a member of Parliament,

---

[2] THE LITTLE DOGS . . . ME—See Shakespeare's *King Lear;* Act III, Scene 6.

[3] RESTORATION—The crowning of Charles II in 1660 put an end to the Puritan Revolution and brought back monarchy to England.

who once passed a few weeks with him. The Squire was glad of any argument to defend his clipped yew trees and formal terraces, which had been occasionally attacked by modern landscape gardeners.

As we approached the house we heard the sound of music, and now and then a burst of laughter, from one end of the building. This, Bracebridge said, must proceed from the servants' hall, where a great deal of revelry was permitted, and even encouraged by the Squire throughout the twelve days of Christmas, provided everything was done conformably to ancient usage. Here were kept up the old games of hoodman blind, shoe the wild mare, hot cockles, steal the white loaf, bob-apple, and snap-dragon; the Yule clog, and Christmas candle, were regularly burnt, and the mistletoe, with its white berries, hung up, to the imminent peril of all the pretty housemaids.

So intent were the servants upon their sports, that we had to ring repeatedly before we could make ourselves heard. On our arrival being announced, the Squire came out to receive us, accompanied by his two other sons; one a young officer in the army, home on leave of absence; the other an Oxonian,[4] just from the university. The Squire was a fine, healthy-looking old gentleman, with silver hair curling lightly round an open florid countenance; in which the physiognomist,[5] with the advantage, like myself, of a previous hint or two, might discover a singular mixture of whim and benevolence.

The family meeting was warm and affectionate; as the evening was far advanced, the Squire would not permit us to change our travelling dresses, but ushered us at once to the company, which was assembled in a large old-fashioned hall. It was composed of different branches of a numerous family connection, where there were the usual proportion of old uncles and aunts, comfortable married dames, superannuated spinsters, blooming country cousins, half-fledged striplings, and bright-eyed boarding-school hoydens. They were variously occupied: some at a round game of cards; others conversing around the fireplace; at one end of the hall was a group of the young folks, some nearly grown up, others of a more tender and budding age, fully engrossed by a merry game; and a profusion of wooden horses, penny trumpets, and tattered dolls about the floor showed traces of a troop of little fairy beings, who, having

---

[4] OXONIAN—Oxford undergraduate. Also applies to Oxford graduates.

[5] PHYSIOGNOMIST—One skilled in reading character from the face.

frolicked through a happy day, had been carried off to slumber through a peaceful night.

While the mutual greetings were going on between young Bracebridge and his relatives, I had time to scan the apartment. I have called it a hall, for so it had certainly been in old times, and the Squire had evidently endeavored to restore it to something of its primitive state. Over the heavy projecting fireplace was suspended a picture of a warrior in armor, standing by a white horse, and on the opposite wall hung a helmet, buckler, and lance. At one end an enormous pair of antlers were inserted in the wall, the branches serving as hooks on which to suspend hats, whips, and spurs; and in the corners of the apartment were fowling-pieces, fishing-rods, and other sporting implements. The furniture was of the cumbrous workmanship of former days, though some articles of modern convenience had been added, and the oaken floor had been carpeted; so that the whole presented an odd mixture of parlor and hall.

The grate had been removed from the wide overwhelming fireplace, to make way for a fire of wood, in the midst of which was an enormous log, glowing and blazing, and sending forth a vast volume of light and heat: this I understood was the Yule clog, which the Squire was particular in having brought in and illumined on a Christmas eve, according to ancient custom.*

It was really delightful to see the old Squire, seated in his hereditary elbow chair, by the hospitable fireside of his ancestors, and looking around him like the sun of a system, beaming warmth and gladness to every heart. Even the very dog that lay stretched at his feet, as he lazily shifted his position and yawned, would look fondly up in his master's face, wag his tail against the floor, and stretch himself again to sleep, confident of kindness and protection. There is an emanation from the heart in genuine hospitality, which cannot be described, but is immediately felt, and puts the stranger at once at his ease. I had not been seated many minutes by the comfortable hearth of the worthy old cavalier, before I found myself as much at home as if I had been one of the family.

* The *Yule clog* is a great log of wood, sometimes the root of a tree, brought into the house with great ceremony on Christmas eve, laid in the fireplace, and lighted with the brand of last year's clog. While it lasted, there was great drinking, singing, and telling of tales. Sometimes it was accompanied by Christmas candles; but in the cottages the only light was from the ruddy blaze of the great wood fire. The Yule clog was to burn all night; if it went out, it was considered a sign of ill luck. . . .

Supper was announced shortly after our arrival. It was served up in a spacious oaken chamber, the panels of which shone with wax, and around which were several family portraits decorated with holly and ivy. Besides the accustomed lights, two great wax tapers, called Christmas candles, wreathed with greens, were placed on a highly polished beaufet among the family plate. The table was abundantly spread with substantial fare; but the Squire made his supper of frumenty, a dish made of wheat cakes boiled in milk, with rich spices, being a standing dish in old times for Christmas eve. I was happy to find my old friend, minced pie, in the retinue of the feast; and finding him to be perfectly orthodox, and that I need not be ashamed of my predilection, I greeted him with all the warmth wherewith we usually greet an old and very genteel acquaintance.

The mirth of the company was greatly promoted by the humors of an eccentric personage, whom Mr. Bracebridge always addressed with the quaint appellation of Master Simon. He was a tight brisk little man, with the air of an arrant old bachelor. His nose was shaped like the bill of a parrot, his face slightly pitted with the small-pox, with a dry perpetual bloom on it, like a frost-bitten leaf in autumn. He had an eye of great quickness and vivacity, with a drollery and lurking waggery of expression that was irresistible. He was evidently the wit of the family, dealing very much in sly jokes and innuendoes with the ladies; and making infinite merriment by harping upon old themes, which, unfortunately, my ignorance of the family chronicles did not permit me to enjoy. It seemed to be his great delight, during supper, to keep a young girl next to him in a continual agony of stifled laughter, in spite of her awe of the reproving looks of her mother, who sat opposite. Indeed, he was the idol of the younger part of the company, who laughed at everything he said or did, and at every turn of his countenance. I could not wonder at it, for he must have been a miracle of accomplishments in their eyes. He could imitate Punch and Judy; make an old woman of his hand, with the assistance of a burnt cork and pocket handkerchief; and cut an orange into such a ludicrous caricature, that the young folks were ready to die with laughing.

I was let briefly into his history by Frank Bracebridge. He was an old bachelor, of a small independent income, which by careful management was sufficient for all his wants. He revolved through the family system like a vagrant comet in its orbit; sometimes visiting one branch, and sometimes another quite remote; as is often the case with gentlemen of extensive connections and small fortunes in England. He had a chirping, buoyant disposition, always enjoying the present moment; and his frequent change of scene and company prevented his acquiring those rusty, unaccommodating habits, with which old bachelors are so uncharitably charged. He was a complete family chronicle, being versed in the genealogy, history, and intermarriages of the whole house of Bracebridge, which made him a great favorite with the old folks; he was a beau of all the elder ladies and superannuated spinsters, among whom he was habitually considered rather a young fellow; and he was master of the revels among the children; so that there was not a more popular being in the sphere in which he moved, than Mr. Simon Bracebridge. Of late years, he had resided almost entirely with the Squire, to whom he had become a factotum,[6] and whom he particularly delighted by jumping with his humor in respect to old times, and by having a scrap of an old song to suit every occasion. We had presently a specimen of his last-mentioned talent; for no sooner was supper removed, and spiced wines and other beverages peculiar to the season introduced, than Master Simon was called on for a good old Christmas song. He bethought himself for a moment, and then, with a sparkle of the eye, and a voice that was by no means bad, excepting that it ran occasionally into a falsetto, like the notes of a split reed, he quavered forth a quaint old ditty:

Now Christmas is come,
Let us beat up the drum,
And call all our neighbors together,
And when they appear,
Let us make them such cheer,
As will keep out the wind and the weather, etc.

The supper had disposed every one to gayety, and an old harper was summoned from the servants' hall, where he had been strumming all the evening, and to all appearance comforting himself with some of the Squire's home-brewed. He was a kind of hanger-on, I was told, of the establishment, and, though ostensibly a resident of the village, was oftener to be found in the Squire's kitchen than

[6] Factotum—General assistant.

his own home, the old gentleman being fond of the sound of "Harp in hall."

The dance, like most dances after supper, was a merry one; some of the older folks joined in it, and the Squire himself figured down several couple with a partner with whom he affirmed he had danced at every Christmas for nearly half a century. Master Simon, who seemed to be a kind of connecting link between the old times and the new, and to be withal a little antiquated in the taste of his accomplishments, evidently piqued himself on his dancing, and was endeavoring to gain credit by the heel and toe, rigadoon,[7] and other graces of the ancient school; but he had unluckily assorted himself with a little romping girl from boarding-school, who, by her wild vivacity, kept him continually on the stretch, and defeated all his sober attempts at elegance:—such are the ill-assorted matches to which antique gentlemen are unfortunately prone!

The young Oxonian, on the contrary, had led out one of his maiden aunts, on whom the rogue played a thousand little knaveries with impunity; he was full of practical jokes, and his delight was to tease his aunts and cousins; yet, like all madcap youngsters, he was a universal favorite among the women. The most interesting couple in the dance was the young officer, and a ward of the Squire's, a beautiful blushing girl of seventeen. From several shy glances which I had noticed in the course of the evening, I suspected there was a little kindness growing up between them; and, indeed, the young soldier was just the hero to captivate a romantic girl. He was tall, slender, and handsome; and, like most young British officers of late years, had picked up various small accomplishments on the continent—he could talk French and Italian—draw landscapes—sing very tolerably—dance divinely; but above all, he had been wounded at Waterloo:—what girl of seventeen, well read in poetry and romance, could resist such a mirror of chivalry and perfection?

The moment the dance was over, he caught up a guitar, and lolling against the old marble fireplace, in an attitude which I am half inclined to suspect was studied, began the little French air of the Troubadour.[8] The Squire, however, exclaimed against having anything on Christmas eve but good old English; upon which the young minstrel, casting up his eye for a moment, as if in an effort

[7] RIGADOON—A spirited dance executed by one couple.

[8] TROUBADOUR—One of the wandering minstrel poets of southern France.

of memory, struck into another strain, and with a charming air of gallantry, gave Herrick's[9] *Night-Piece to Julia:*

Her eyes the glow-worm lend thee,
The shooting stars attend thee,
    And the elves also,
    Whose little eyes glow
Like the sparks of fire, befriend thee.

No Will o' the Wisp mislight thee;
Nor snake nor slow-worm bite thee;
    But on, on thy way,
    Not making a stay,
Since ghost there is none to affright thee.

Then let not the dark thee cumber;
What though the moon does slumber,
    The stars of the night
    Will lend thee their light,
Like tapers clear without number.

Then, Julia, let me woo thee,
Thus, thus to come unto me,
    And when I shall meet
    Thy silvery feet,
My soul I'll pour into thee.

The song might or might not have been intended in compliment to the fair Julia, for so I found his partner was called; she, however, was certainly unconscious of any such application; for she never looked at the singer, but kept her eyes cast upon the floor: her face was suffused, it is true, with a beautiful blush, and there was a gentle heaving of the bosom, but all that was doubtless caused by the exercise of the dance; indeed, so great was her indifference, that she amused herself with plucking to pieces a choice bouquet of hot-house flowers, and by the time the song was concluded the nosegay lay in ruins on the floor.

The party now broke up for the night, with the kind hearted old custom of shaking hands. As I passed through the hall on my way to my chamber, the dying embers of the Yule clog still sent forth a dusky glow; and had it not been the season when "no spirit

---

[9] Herrick's—Robert Herrick, a clergyman, was one of the noted poets of the seventeenth century. His poetry is remarkable for its grace.

dares stir abroad," I should have been half tempted to steal from my room at midnight, and peep whether the fairies might not be at their revels about the hearth.

My chamber was in the old part of the mansion, the ponderous furniture of which might have been fabricated in the days of the giants. The room was panelled with cornices of heavy carved work, in which flowers and grotesque faces were strangely intermingled, and a row of black-looking portraits stared mournfully at me from the walls. The bed was of rich, though faded, damask, with a lofty tester,[10] and stood in a niche opposite a bow-window. I had scarcely got into bed when a strain of music seemed to break forth in the air just below the window: I listened, and found it proceeded from a band, which I concluded to be the waits from some neighboring village. They went round the house, playing under the windows. I drew aside the curtains, to hear them more distinctly. The moonbeams fell through the upper part of the casement, partially lighting up the antiquated apartment. The sounds, as they receded, became more soft and aerial, and seemed to accord with quiet and moonlight. I listened and listened—they became more and more tender and remote, and as they gradually died away, my head sunk upon the pillow, and I fell asleep.

## QUESTIONS AND EXERCISES

Exercises preceded by a star are designed for assignment at the discretion of the teacher, or for any student who volunteers.

1. Is your first impression of Bracebridge Hall a favorable one? Describe the night view of the Hall.
2. What kind of gentleman does Squire Bracebridge seem? What hints does the author give you?
3. Tell the history of Master Simon. Is he a likable character? What is the rest of the company at the Hall like?

*4. Compare this Christmas Eve with the one described in Charles Dickens' *Christmas Carol.*

## CHRISTMAS DAY

When I woke the next morning, it seemed as if all the events of the preceding evening had been a dream, and nothing but the identity of the ancient chamber convinced me of their reality. While I lay musing on my pillow, I heard the sound of little feet pattering outside of the door, and a whispering consultation. Presently a

[10] TESTER—Canopy over a four-posted bed.

choir of small voices chanted forth an old Christmas carol, the burden of which was—

> Rejoice, our Saviour he was born
> On Christmas day in the morning.

I rose softly, slipt on my clothes, opened the door suddenly, and beheld one of the most beautiful little fairy groups that a painter could imagine. It consisted of a boy and two girls, the eldest not more than six, and lovely as seraphs. They were going the rounds of the house, and singing at every chamber door, but my sudden appearance frightened them into mute bashfulness. They remained for a moment playing on their lips with their fingers, and now and then stealing a shy glance from under their eyebrows, until, as if by one impulse, they scampered away, and as they turned an angle of the gallery, I heard them laughing in triumph at their escape.

Everything conspired to produce kind and happy feelings, in this stronghold of old-fashioned hospitality. The window of my chamber looked out upon what in summer would have been a beautiful landscape. There was a sloping lawn, a fine stream winding at the foot of it, and a track of park beyond, with noble clumps of trees and herds of deer. At a distance was a neat hamlet, with the smoke from the cottage chimneys hanging over it; and a church, with its dark spire in strong relief against the clear, cold sky. The house was surrounded with evergreens, according to the English custom, which would have given almost an appearance of summer; but the morning was extremely frosty; the light vapor of the preceding evening had been precipitated by the cold, and covered all the trees and every blade of grass with its fine crystallizations. The rays of a bright morning sun had a dazzling effect among the glittering foliage. A robin perched upon the top of a mountain ash, that hung its clusters of red berries just before my window, was basking himself in the sunshine, and piping a few querulous notes; and a peacock was displaying all the glories of his train, and strutting with the pride and gravity of a Spanish grandee on the terrace-walk below.

I had scarcely dressed myself, when a servant appeared to invite me to family prayers. He showed me the way to a small chapel in the old wing of the house, where I found the principal part of the family already assembled in a kind of gallery, furnished with cushions, hassocks, and large prayer-books; the servants were seated on benches below. The old gentleman read prayers from a desk in front of the gallery, and Master Simon acted as clerk and made the responses; and I must do him the justice to say that he acquitted himself with great gravity and decorum.

The service was followed by a Christmas carol which Mr. Bracebridge himself had constructed from a poem of his favorite author, Herrick; and it had been adapted to an old church melody by Master Simon. As there were several good voices among the household, the effect was extremely pleasing; but I was particularly gratified by the exaltation of heart, and sudden sally of grateful feeling, with which the worthy Squire delivered one stanza; his eye glistening, and his voice rambling out of all the bounds of time and tune:

> 'Tis thou that crown'st my glittering hearth
> With guiltlesse mirth,
> And giv'st me Wassaile bowles[1] to drink
> Spiced to the brink:
>
> Lord, 'tis thy plenty-dropping hand
> That soiles my land:
> And giv'st me for my bushell sowne,
> Twice ten for one.

I afterwards understood that early morning service was read on every Sunday and saints' day throughout the year, either by Mr. Bracebridge or by some member of the family. It was once almost universally the case at the seats of the nobility and gentry of England, and it is much to be regretted that the custom is falling into neglect; for the dullest observer must be sensible of the order and serenity prevalent in those households where the occasional exercise of a beautiful form of worship in the morning gives, as it were, the key-note to every temper for the day, and attunes every spirit to harmony.

Our breakfast consisted of what the Squire denominated true old English fare. He indulged in some bitter lamentations over modern breakfasts of tea and toast, which he censured as among the causes of modern effeminacy and weak nerves, and the decline of old English heartiness: and though he admitted them to his table

---

[1] WASSAILE BOWLES—Bowls containing punch with which to pledge one another's health.

to suit the palates of his guests, yet there was a brave display of cold meats, wine, and ale, on the sideboard.

After breakfast I walked about the grounds with Frank Bracebridge and Master Simon, or Mr. Simon, as he was called by everybody but the Squire. We were escorted by a number of gentleman-like dogs that seemed loungers about the establishment; from the frisking spaniel to the steady old stag-hound—the last of which was of a race that had been in the family time out of mind—they were all obedient to a dog-whistle which hung to Master Simon's button-hole, and in the midst of their gambols would glance an eye occasionally upon a small switch he carried in his hand.

The old mansion had a still more venerable look in the yellow sunshine than by pale moonlight; and I could not but feel the force of the Squire's idea, that the formal terraces, heavily moulded balustrades, and clipped yew trees carried with them an air of proud aristocracy.

There appeared to be an unusual number of peacocks about the place, and I was making some remarks upon what I termed a flock of them that were basking under a sunny wall, when I was gently corrected in my phraseology by Master Simon, who told me that according to the most ancient and approved treatise on hunting, I must say a *muster* of peacocks. "In the same way," added he, with a slight air of pedantry, "we say a flight of doves or swallows, a bevy of quails, a herd of deer, of wrens, or cranes, a skulk of foxes, or a building of rooks." He went on to inform me that according to Sir Anthony Fitzherbert[2] we ought to ascribe to this bird "both understanding and glory; for being praised he will presently set up his tail, chiefly against the sun, to the intent you may the better behold the beauty thereof. But at the fall of the leaf, when his tail falleth, he will mourn and hide himself in corners till his tail come again as it was."

I could not help smiling at this display of small erudition on so whimsical a subject; but I found that the peacocks were birds of some consequence at the Hall; for Frank Bracebridge informed me that they were great favorites with his father, who was extremely careful to keep up the breed, partly because they belonged to

[2] Sir Anthony Fitzherbert—Some writer of little known merit. There are several authors mentioned in this sketch, but, with the exception of Izaak Walton, they are of secondary value.

chivalry, and were in great request at the stately banquets of the olden time; and partly because they had a pomp and magnificence about them highly becoming an old family mansion. Nothing, he was accustomed to say, had an air of greater state and dignity than a peacock perched upon an antique stone balustrade.

Master Simon had now to hurry off, having an appointment at the parish church with the village choristers, who were to perform some music of his selection. There was something extremely agreeable in the cheerful flow of animal spirits of the little man; and I confess I had been somewhat surprised at his apt quotations from authors who certainly were not in the range of everyday reading. I mentioned this last circumstance to Frank Bracebridge, who told me with a smile that Master Simon's whole stock of erudition was confined to some half a dozen old authors, which the Squire had put into his hands, and which he read over and over, whenever he had a studious fit; as he sometimes had on a rainy day or a long winter evening. Sir Anthony Fitzherbert's *Book of Husbandry,* Markham's *Country Contentments,* the *Tretyse of Hunting,* by Sir Thomas Cockayne, Knight, Izaak Walton's *Angler,* and two or three more such ancient worthies of the pen, were his standard authorities; and like all men who know but a few books, he looked up to them with a kind of idolatry, and quoted them on all occasions. As to his songs, they were chiefly picked out of old books in the Squire's library, and adapted to tunes that were popular among the choice spirits of the last century. His practical application of scraps of literature, however, had caused him to be looked upon as a prodigy of book-knowledge by all the grooms, huntsmen, and small sportsmen of the neighborhood.

While we were talking we heard the distant tolling of the village bell, and I was told that the Squire was a little particular in having his household at church on a Christmas morning; considering it a day of pouring out of thanks and rejoicing; for, as old Tusser[3] observed—

At Christmas be merry, *and thankful withal,*
And feast thy poor neighbors, the great with the small.

"If you are disposed to go to church," said Frank Bracebridge, "I can promise you a specimen of my cousin Simon's musical

[3] TUSSER—Thomas Tusser, English agricultural poet of the 16th century.

achievements. As the church is destitute of an organ, he has formed a band from the village amateurs, and established a musical club for their improvement; he has also sorted a choir, as he sorted my father's pack of hounds, according to the directions of Jervaise Markham, in his *Country Contentments;* for the bass he has sought out all the 'deep, solemn mouths,' and for the tenor the 'loud-ringing mouths,' among the country bumpkins; and for 'sweet mouths,' he has culled with curious taste among the prettiest lasses in the neighborhood; though these last, he affirms, are the most difficult to keep in tune; your pretty female singer being exceedingly wayward and capricious, and very liable to accident."

As the morning, though frosty, was remarkably fine and clear, the most of the family walked to the church, which was a very old building of gray stone, and stood near a village, about half a mile from the park gate. Adjoining it was a low snug parsonage, which seemed coeval with the church. The front of it was perfectly matted with a yew tree, that had been trained against its walls, through the dense foliage of which, apertures had been formed to admit light into the small antique lattices. As we passed this sheltered nest, the parson issued forth and preceded us.

I had expected to see a sleek, well-conditioned pastor, such as is often found in a snug living in the vicinity of a rich patron's table, but I was disappointed. The parson was a little, meagre, black-looking man, with a grizzled wig that was too wide and stood off from each ear; so that his head seemed to have shrunk away within it, like a dried filbert in its shell. He wore a rusty coat, with great skirts, and pockets that would have held the church Bible and prayer-book: and his small legs seemed still smaller, from being planted in large shoes, decorated with enormous buckles.

I was informed by Frank Bracebridge that the parson had been a chum of his father's at Oxford, and had received this living shortly after the latter had come to his estate. He was a complete black-letter[4] hunter, and would scarcely read a work printed in the Roman character. The editions of Caxton and Wynkyn de Worde[5] were his delight; and he was indefatigable in his researches after such old English writers as have fallen into oblivion from their

---

[4] BLACK-LETTER—Old English or Gothic lettering used in earliest English books.

[5] CAXTON . . . WYNKYN DE WORDE—William Caxton introduced printing into England in 1476. Wynkyn de Worde was his assistant.

worthlessness. In deference, perhaps, to the notions of Mr. Bracebridge, he had made diligent investigations into the festive rites and holiday customs of former times; and had been as zealous in the inquiry, as if he had been a boon companion; but it was merely with that plodding spirit with which men of adust[6] temperament follow up any track of study, merely because it is denominated learning; indifferent to its intrinsic nature, whether it be the illustration of the wisdom, or of the ribaldry and obscenity of antiquity. He had pored over these old volumes so intensely, that they seemed to have been reflected in his countenance; which, if the face be indeed an index of the mind, might be compared to a title page of black-letter.

On reaching the church-porch we found the parson rebuking the gray-headed sexton for having used mistletoe among the greens with which the church was decorated. It was, he observed, an unholy plant, profaned by having been used by the Druids[7] in their mystic ceremonies; and though it might be innocently employed in the festive ornamenting of halls and kitchens, yet it had been deemed by the Fathers of the Church as unhallowed, and totally unfit for sacred purposes. So tenacious was he on this point, that the poor sexton was obliged to strip down a great part of the humble trophies of his taste, before the parson would consent to enter upon the service of the day.

The interior of the church was venerable, but simple; on the walls were several mural monuments of the Bracebridges, and just beside the altar, was a tomb of ancient workmanship, on which lay the effigy of a warrior in armor, with his legs crossed, a sign of his having been a crusader. I was told it was one of the family who had signalized himself in the Holy Land, and the same whose picture hung over the fireplace in the hall.

During service, Master Simon stood up in the pew, and repeated the responses very audibly; evincing that kind of ceremonious devotion punctually observed by a gentleman of the old school, and a man of old family connections. I observed, too, that he turned over the leaves of a folio prayer-book with something of a flourish, possibly to show off an enormous seal ring which enriched one of his

---

[6] ADUST—Fiery.

[7] DRUIDS—Ancient Celtic priests who used mistletoe as a symbol in their weird nature worship.

P. F. Collier and Sons

THE CHURCH CHOIR AND ORCHESTRA

Sometimes the fiddler lagged a little and had to travel a passage uncommon fast to catch up; or a singer, having lingered too long on a familiar note, would render a nasal solo several bars behind the rest of the choir.

fingers, and which had the look of a family relic. But he was evidently most solicitous about the musical part of the service, keeping his eye fixed intently on the choir, and beating time with much gesticulation and emphasis.

The orchestra was in a small gallery, and presented a most whimsical grouping of heads piled one above the other, among which I particularly noticed that of the village tailor, a pale fellow with a retreating forehead and chin, who played on the clarionet, and seemed to have blown his face to a point: and there was another, a short pursy man, stooping and laboring at a bass viol, so as to show nothing but the top of a round bald head, like the egg of an ostrich. There were two or three pretty faces among the female singers, to which the keen air of a frosty morning had given a bright rosy tint: but the gentlemen choristers had evidently been chosen, like old Cremona fiddles, more for tone than looks; and as several had to sing from the same book, there were clusterings of odd physiognomies, not unlike those groups of cherubs we sometimes see on country tombstones.

The usual services of the choir were managed tolerably well, the vocal parts generally lagging a little behind the instrumental, and some loitering fiddler now and then making up for lost time by travelling over a passage with prodigious celerity, and clearing more bars than the keenest fox-hunter, to be in at the death. But the great trial was an anthem that had been prepared and arranged by Master Simon, and on which he had founded great expectation. Unluckily there was a blunder at the very outset—the musicians became flurried; Master Simon was in a fever; everything went on lamely and irregularly, until they came to a chorus beginning, "Now let us sing with one accord," which seemed to be a signal for parting company: all became discord and confusion; each shifted for himself, and got to the end as well, or, rather, as soon as he could; excepting one old chorister, in a pair of horn spectacles, bestriding and pinching a long sonorous nose; who happened to stand a little apart, and being wrapped up in his own melody, kept on a quavering course, wriggling his head, ogling his book, and winding all up by a nasal solo of at least three bars' duration.

The parson gave us a most erudite sermon on the rites and ceremonies of Christmas, and the propriety of observing it, not merely as a day of thanksgiving, but of rejoicing; supporting the correctness of his opinions by the earliest usages of the church, and enforcing them by the authorities of Theophilus of Cesarea, St. Cyprian, St. Chrysostom, St. Augustine,[8] and a cloud more of saints and fathers from whom he made copious quotations. I was a little at a loss to perceive the necessity of such a mighty array of forces to maintain a point which no one present seemed inclined to dispute; but I soon found that the good man had a legion of ideal adversaries to contend with; having, in the course of his researches on the subject of Christmas, got completely embroiled in the sectarian controversies of the Revolution,[9] when the Puritans made such a fierce assault upon the ceremonies of the church, and poor old Christmas was driven out of the land by proclamation of Parliament. The worthy parson lived but with times past, and knew but little of the present.

Shut up among worm-eaten tomes in the retirement of his antiquated little study, the pages of old times were to him as the gazettes of the day; while the era of the Revolution was mere modern history. He forgot that nearly two centuries had elapsed since the fiery persecution of poor mince-pie throughout the land; when plum porridge was denounced as "mere popery," and roast-beef as anti-Christian; and that Christmas had been brought in again triumphantly with the merry court of King Charles at the Restoration. He kindled into warmth with the ardor of his contest, and the host of imaginary foes with whom he had to combat; he had a stubborn conflict with old Prynne and two or three other forgotten champions of the Roundheads,[10] on the subject of Christmas festivity; and concluded by urging his hearers, in the most solemn and affecting manner, to stand to the traditional customs of their fathers, and feast and make merry on this joyful anniversary of the Church.

I have seldom known a sermon attended apparently with more immediate effects; for on leaving the church, the congregation seemed one and all possessed with the gayety of spirit so earnestly enjoined by their pastor. The elder folks gathered in knots in the churchyard, greeting and shaking hands; and the children ran about crying "Ule! Ule!" and repeating some uncouth rhymes, which the parson, who had joined us, informed me had been handed down

[8] THEOPHILUS . . . ST. AUGUSTINE—Famous Christians of the Early Church.

[9] REVOLUTION—Oliver Cromwell's overthrow of Charles I.

[10] ROUNDHEADS—Nickname given by the followers of Charles I to the Puritans who wore their hair cut close instead of in ringlets.

from days of yore. The villagers doffed their hats to the Squire as he passed, giving him the good wishes of the season with every appearance of heartfelt sincerity, and were invited by him to the hall, to take something to keep out the cold of the weather; and I heard blessings uttered by several of the poor, which convinced me that in the midst of his enjoyments, the worthy old cavalier had not forgotten the true Christmas virtue of charity.

On our way homeward, his heart seemed overflowed with generous and happy feelings. As we passed over a rising ground which commanded something of a prospect, the sounds of rustic merriment now and then reached our ears: the Squire paused for a few moments, and looked around with an air of inexpressible benignity. The beauty of the day was of itself sufficient to inspire philanthropy. Notwithstanding the frostiness of the morning, the sun in his cloudless journey had acquired sufficient power to melt away the thin covering of snow from every southern declivity, and to bring out the living green which adorns an English landscape even in mid-winter. Large tracts of smiling verdure contrasted with the dazzling whiteness of the shaded slopes and hollows. Every sheltered bank on which the broad rays rested, yielded its silver rill of cold and limpid water, glittering through the dripping grass; and sent up slight exhalations to contribute to the thin haze that hung just above the surface of the earth. There was something truly cheering in this triumph of warmth and verdure over the frosty thraldom of winter; it was, as the Squire observed, an emblem of Christmas hospitality breaking through the chills of ceremony and selfishness and thawing every heart into a flow. He pointed with pleasure to the indications of good cheer reeking from the chimneys of the comfortable farm-houses and low thatched cottages. "I love," said he, "to see this day well kept by rich and poor; it is a great thing to have one day in the year, at least, when you are sure of being welcome wherever you go, and of having, as it were, the world thrown all open to you; and I am almost disposed to join with Poor Robin, in his malediction on every churlish enemy to this honest festival:

Those who at Christmas do repine
  And would fain hence dispatch him,
May they with old Duke Humphry dine,
  Or else may Squire Ketch catch 'em.

The Squire went on to lament the deplorable decay of the games and amusements which were once prevalent at this season among the lower orders, and countenanced by the higher; when the old halls of the castles and manor-houses were thrown open at daylight; when the tables were covered with brawn,[11] and beef, and humming ale; when the harp and the carol resounded all day long, and when rich and poor were alike welcome to enter and make merry. "Our old games and local customs," said he, "had a great effect in making the peasant fond of his home, and the promotion of them by the gentry made him fond of his lord. They made the times merrier, and kinder, and better, and I can truly say with one of our old poets,

> 'I like them well—the curious preciseness
> And all-pretended gravity of those
> That seek to banish hence these harmless sports,
> Have thrust away much ancient honesty.'

"The nation," continued he, "is altered; we have almost lost our simple true-hearted peasantry. They have broken asunder from the higher classes, and seem to think their interests are separate. They have become too knowing, and begin to read newspapers, listen to ale house politicians, and talk of reform. I think one mode to keep them in good-humor in these hard times, would be for the nobility and gentry to pass more time on their estates, mingle more among the country people, and set the merry old English games going again."

Such was the good Squire's project for mitigating public discontent: and, indeed, he had once attempted to put his doctrine in practice, and a few years before had kept open house during the holidays in the old style. The country people, however, did not understand how to play their parts in the scene of hospitality; many uncouth circumstances occurred; the manor was overrun by all the vagrants of the country, and more beggars drawn into the neighborhood in one week than the parish officers could get rid of in a year. Since then he had contented himself with inviting the decent part of the neighboring peasantry to call at the Hall on Christmas day, and with distributing beef, and bread, and ale among the poor, that they might make merry in their own dwellings.

[11] BRAWN—Boar's meat.

We had not been long home, when the sound of music was heard from a distance. A band of country lads, without coats, their shirt sleeves fancifully tied with ribbons, their hats decorated with greens, and clubs in their hands, were seen advancing up the avenue, followed by a large number of villagers and peasantry. They stopped before the hall door, where the music struck up a peculiar air, and the lads performed a curious and intricate dance,[12] advancing, retreating, and striking their clubs together, keeping exact time to the music; while one, whimsically crowned with a fox's skin, the tail of which flaunted down his back, kept capering round the skirts of the dance, and rattling a Christmas-box[13] with many antic[14] gesticulations.

The Squire eyed this fanciful exhibition with great interest and delight, and gave me a full account of its origin, which he traced to the times when the Romans held possession of the island; plainly proving that this was a lineal descendant of the sword dance of the ancients. "It was now," he said, "nearly extinct, but he had accidentally met with traces of it in the neighborhood, and had encouraged its revival; though, to tell the truth, it was too apt to be followed up by the rough cudgel play, and broken heads, in the evening."

After the dance was concluded, the whole party was entertained with brawn and beef, and stout home-brewed. The Squire himself mingled among the rustics, and was received with awkward demonstrations of deference and regard. It is true, I perceived two or three of the younger peasants, as they were raising their tankards to their mouths, when the Squire's back was turned, making something of a grimace, and giving each other the wink; but the moment they caught my eye they pulled grave faces, and were exceedingly demure. With Master Simon, however, they all seemed more at their ease. His varied occupations and amusements had made him well known throughout the neighborhood. He was a visitor at every farm, house and cottage; gossiped with the farmers and their wives; romped with their daughters; and like that type of a vagrant bachelor, the humblebee, tolled the sweets from all the rosy lips of the country round.

---

[12] DANCE—In imitation of the old-fashioned "Morris" or May-day dancers.

[13] CHRISTMAS-BOX—A closed box with a slit in which the entertainers collected money.

[14] ANTIC—Literally, antique; here, fantastic or grotesque.

The bashfulness of the guests soon gave way before good cheer and affability. There is something genuine and affectionate in the gayety of the lower orders, when it is excited by the bounty and familiarity of those above them; the warm glow of gratitude enters into their mirth, and a kind word or a small pleasantry frankly uttered by a patron, gladdens the heart of the dependant more than oil and wine. When the Squire had retired, the merriment increased, and there was much joking and laughter, particularly between Master Simon and a hale, ruddy-faced, white-headed farmer, who appeared to be the wit of the village; for I observed all his companions to wait with open mouths for his retorts, and burst into a gratuitous laugh before they could well understand them.

The whole house indeed seemed abandoned to merriment: as I passed to my room to dress for dinner, I heard the sound of music in a small court, and looking through a window that commanded it, I perceived a band of wandering musicians, with pandean pipes and tambourine; a pretty coquettish housemaid was dancing a jig with a smart country lad, while several of the other servants were looking on. In the midst of her sport, the girl caught a glimpse of my face at the window, and, coloring up, ran off with an air of roguish affected confusion.

## QUESTIONS AND EXERCISES

Exercises preceded by a star are designed for assignment at the discretion of the teacher, or for any student who volunteers.

1. What was the scene from Irving's window early Christmas morning?
2. Describe the village church service. Would you have enjoyed meeting the village parson?
3. Why did the Squire wish to keep up the old customs and traditions? Name some of them.
4. Do people today care as much about cherishing such traditions? Is there any value in maintaining such customs? If so, what?

*5. Draw an imaginary map of the Bracebridge estate from the description furnished in this essay.

6. What glimpses do you get in this sketch of the author's likes and dislikes?
7. What incident closes the sketch?

## GENERAL QUESTIONS AND EXERCISES

1. Retell briefly the story of Irving's Christmas at Bracebridge Hall. In a similar vein describe the happiest Christmas you ever spent.

*2. Read a few passages from *The Sir Roger de Coverley Papers* in the *Spectator.* Does Irving's manner of writing in the Christmas *Sketches* appear to be modeled after Addison?

3. Which of the Christmas *Sketches* did you most enjoy? Give reasons for your choice.
4. List, with references to particular passages, points of Irving's style in these essays. (See General Introduction to the *Sketches*.)

*5. Irving continued his experiences at Bracebridge Hall in a later volume of sketches, *Bracebridge Hall.* Read *one* of the following three *Sketches* taken from it: *The Hall, The Busy Man, The Stout Gentleman.* Do you prefer it to the Christmas *Sketches?* In what ways?

## *MEN AND BOOKS*

### PHILIP OF POKANOKET[1]

#### AN INDIAN MEMOIR

Almost thirty years before the birth of "Buffalo Bill" and nearly three score years before Custer fell in a rain of Sioux arrows, Washington Irving published two essays in defense of the American Indian. Coming at a time when Indian hostility was very strong, Irving's defense in *Traits of Indian Character,* and *Philip of Pokanoket,* was remarkable for its fair-mindedness, vigor and force. The two sketches, first printed in the *Analectic Magazine,* New York, were reprinted in the English edition of *The Sketch Book* in 1820. With the exception of the stories of Rip Van Winkle and Ichabod Crane, they are the only *Sketches* purely American in color and background. *Philip of Pokanoket* has been chosen for this section because of its historical value. The figure of a great warrior stalks through these pages, a brave chief driven to his last stand, back to his last sunset.

It is to be regretted that those early writers who treated of the discovery and settlement of America have not given us more particular and candid accounts of the remarkable characters that flourished in savage life. The scanty anecdotes which have reached us are full of peculiarity and interest; they furnish us with nearer glimpses of human nature, and show what man is in a comparatively primitive state, and what he owes to civilization. There is something of the charm of discovery in lighting upon these wild and unexplored tracts of human nature: in witnessing, as it were, the native growth of moral sentiment; and perceiving those generous and romantic qualities which have been artificially cultivated by society, vegetating in spontaneous hardihood and rude magnificence.

In civilized life, where the happiness, and indeed almost the existence, of man depends so much upon the opinion of his fellowmen, he is constantly acting a studied part. The bold and peculiar

[1] POKANOKET (pō-kăn'ō-kĕt)

traits of native character are refined away, or softened down by the levelling influence of what is termed good breeding; and he practises so many petty deceptions, and affects so many generous sentiments, for the purposes of popularity, that it is difficult to distinguish his real from his artificial character. The Indian, on the contrary, free from the restraints and refinements of polished life, and, in a great degree, a solitary and independent being, obeys the impulses of his inclination or the dictates of his judgment; and thus the attributes of his nature, being freely indulged, grow singly great and striking. Society is like a lawn, where every roughness is smoothed, every bramble eradicated, and where the eye is delighted by the smiling verdure of a velvet surface; he, however, who would study Nature in its wildness and variety, must plunge into the forest, must explore the glen, must stem the torrent, and dare the precipice.

These reflections arose on casually looking through a volume of early colonial history, wherein are recorded, with great bitterness, the outrages of the Indians, and their wars with the settlers of New England. It is painful to perceive, even from these partial narratives, how the footsteps of civilization may be traced in the blood of the aborigines; how easily the colonists were moved to hostility by the lust of conquest; how merciless and exterminating was their warfare. The imagination shrinks at the idea, how many intellectual beings were hunted from the earth—how many brave and noble hearts, of Nature's sterling coinage, were broken down and trampled in the dust!

Such was the fate of PHILIP OF POKANOKET, an Indian warrior whose name was once a terror throughout Massachusetts and Connecticut. He was the most distinguished of a number of contemporary Sachems, who reigned over the Pequods, the Narragansetts, the Wampanoags, and the other eastern tribes, at the time of the first settlement of New England: a band of native untaught heroes; who made the most generous struggle of which human nature is capable; fighting to the last gasp in the cause of their country, without a hope of victory or a thought of renown. Worthy of an age of poetry, and fit subjects for local story and romantic fiction, they have left scarcely any authentic traces on the page of history, but stalk, like gigantic shadows in the dim twilight of tradition.

When the Pilgrims, as the Plymouth settlers are called by their descendants, first took refuge on the shores of the New World, from the religious persecutions of the Old, their situation was to the last degree gloomy and disheartening. Few in number, and that number rapidly perishing away through sickness and hardships; surrounded by a howling wilderness and savage tribes; exposed to the rigors of an almost arctic winter, and the vicissitudes of an ever-shifting climate; their minds were filled with doleful forebodings, and nothing preserved them from sinking into despondency but the strong excitement of religious enthusiasm. In this forlorn situation, they were visited by Massasoit, chief Sagamore[2] of the Wampanoags, a powerful chief, who reigned over a great extent of country. Instead of taking advantage of the scanty number of the strangers, and expelling them from his territories, into which they had intruded, he seemed at once to conceive for them a generous friendship, and extended towards them the rites of primitive hospitality. He came early in the spring to their settlement of New Plymouth, attended by a mere handful of followers; entered into a solemn league of peace and amity, sold them a portion of the soil, and promised to secure for them the good-will of his savage allies. Whatever may be said of Indian perfidy, it is certain that the integrity and good faith of Massasoit have never been impeached. He continued a firm and magnanimous friend of the white men; suffering them to extend their possessions, and to strengthen themselves in the land; and betraying no jealousy of their increasing power and prosperity. Shortly before his death, he came once more to New Plymouth, with his son Alexander, for the purpose of renewing the covenant of peace, and of securing it to his posterity.

At this conference, he endeavored to protect the religion of his forefathers from the encroaching zeal of the missionaries; and stipulated that no further attempt should be made to draw off his people from their ancient faith; but, finding the English obstinately opposed to any such condition, he mildly relinquished the demand. Almost the last act of his life was to bring his two sons, Alexander and Philip (as they had been named by the English), to the residence of a principal settler, recommending mutual kindness and confidence; and entreating that the same love and amity which had existed between the white men and himself, might be continued afterwards with his children. The good old Sachem died in peace, and was happily gathered to his fathers before sorrow came upon his tribe;

[2] Sagamore—Generally means *sachem,* or chief.

his children remained behind to experience the ingratitude of white men.

His eldest son, Alexander, succeeded him. He was of a quick and impetuous temper, and proudly tenacious of his hereditary rights and dignity. The intrusive policy and dictatorial conduct of the strangers excited his indignation; and he beheld with uneasiness their exterminating wars with the neighboring tribes. He was doomed soon to incur their hostility, being accused of plotting with the Narragansetts to rise against the English and drive them from the land. It is impossible to say whether this accusation was warranted by facts, or was grounded on mere suspicion. It is evident, however, by the violent and overbearing measures of the settlers, that they had by this time begun to feel conscious of the rapid increase of their power, and to grow harsh and inconsiderate in their treatment of the natives. They despatched an armed force to seize upon Alexander, and to bring him before their courts. He was traced to his woodland haunts, and surprised at a hunting house, where he was reposing with a band of his followers, unarmed, after the toils of the chase. The suddenness of his arrest, and the outrage offered to his sovereign dignity, so preyed upon the irascible feelings of this proud savage, as to throw him into a raging fever; he was permitted to return home on condition of sending his son as a pledge for his reappearance; but the blow he had received was fatal, and before he had reached his home he fell a victim to the agonies of a wounded spirit.

The successor of Alexander was Metacomet, or King Philip, as he was called by the settlers on account of his lofty spirit and ambitious temper. These, together with his well-known energy and enterprise, had rendered him an object of great jealousy and apprehension, and he was accused of having always cherished a secret and implacable hostility towards the whites. Such may very probably, and very naturally, have been the case. He considered them as originally but mere intruders into the country, who had presumed upon indulgence, and were extending an influence baneful to savage life. He saw the whole race of his countrymen melting before them from the face of the earth; their territories slipping from their hands, and their tribes becoming feeble, scattered, and dependent. It may be said that the soil was originally purchased by the settlers; but who does not know the nature of Indian purchases, in the early periods of colonization? The Europeans always made thrifty bargains, through their superior adroitness in traffic; and they gained vast accessions of territory by easily-provoked hostilities. An uncultivated savage is never a nice inquirer into the refinements of law, by which an injury may be gradually and legally inflicted. Leading facts are all by which he judges; and it was enough for Philip to know, that before the intrusion of the Europeans his countrymen were lords of the soil, and that now they were becoming vagabonds in the land of their fathers.

But whatever may have been his feelings of general hostility, and his particular indignation at the treatment of his brother, he suppressed them for the present; renewed the contract with the settlers, and resided peaceably for many years at Pokanoket, or, as it was called by the English, Mount Hope,* the ancient seat of dominion of his tribe. Suspicions, however, which were at first but vague and indefinite, began to acquire form and substance; and he was at length charged with attempting to instigate the various Eastern tribes to rise at once, and by a simultaneous effort to throw off the yoke of their oppressors. It is difficult at this distant period to assign the proper credit due to these early accusations against the Indians. There was a proneness to suspicion, and an aptness to acts of violence on the part of the whites, that gave weight and importance to every idle tale. Informers abounded where talebearing met with countenance and reward; and the sword was readily unsheathed, when its success was certain, and it carved out empire.

The only positive evidence on record against Philip is the accusation of one Sausaman, a renegado[3] Indian, whose natural cunning had been quickened by a partial education which he had received among the settlers. He changed his faith and his allegiance two or three times, with a facility that evinced the looseness of his principles. He had acted for some time as Philip's confidential secretary and counsellor, and had enjoyed his bounty and protection. Finding, however, that the clouds of adversity were gathering round his patron, he abandoned his service and went over to the whites; and in order to gain their favor charged his former benefactor with plotting against their safety. A rigorous investigation took place. Philip and several of his subjects submitted to be examined, but

* Now Bristol, Rhode Island.

[3] RENEGADO—Traitorous.

nothing was proved against them. The settlers, however, had now gone too far to retract; they had previously determined that Philip was a dangerous neighbor; they had publicly evinced their distrust; and had done enough to insure his hostility; according, therefore, to the usual mode of reasoning in these cases, his destruction had become necessary to their security. Sausaman, the treacherous informer, was shortly afterwards found dead in a pond, having fallen a victim to the vengeance of his tribe. Three Indians, one of whom was a friend and counsellor of Philip, were apprehended and tried, and, on the testimony of one very questionable witness, were condemned and executed as murderers.

This treatment of his subjects and ignominious punishment of his friend, outraged the pride and exasperated the passions of Philip. The bolt which had fallen thus at his very feet, awakened him to the gathering storm, and he determined to trust himself no longer in the power of the white men. The fate of his insulted and broken-hearted brother still rankled in his mind; and he had a further warning in the tragical story of Miantonimo, a great sachem of the Narragansetts, who, after manfully facing his accusers before a tribunal of the colonists, exculpating himself from a charge of conspiracy, and receiving assurances of amity, had been perfidiously despatched at their instigation. Philip, therefore, gathered his fighting men about him; persuaded all strangers that he could, to join his cause, sent the women and children to the Narragansetts for safety; and wherever he appeared, was continually surrounded by armed warriors.

When the two parties were thus in a state of distrust and irritation, the least spark was sufficient to set them in a flame. The Indians, having weapons in their hands, grew mischievous, and committed various petty depredations. In one of their maraudings, a warrior was fired on and killed by a settler. This was the signal for open hostilities; the Indians pressed to revenge the death of their comrade, and the alarm of war resounded through the Plymouth colony.

In the early chronicles of these dark and melancholy times, we meet with many indications of the diseased state of the public mind. The gloom of religious abstraction, and the wildness of their situation, among trackless forests and savage tribes, had disposed the colonists to superstitious fancies, and had filled their imaginations with the frightful chimeras[4] of witchcraft and spectrology.[5] They were much given also to a belief in omens. The troubles with Philip and his Indians were preceded, we are told, by a variety of those awful warnings which forerun great and public calamities. The perfect form of an Indian bow appeared in the air at New Plymouth, which was looked upon by the inhabitants as a "prodigious apparition." At Hadley, Northampton, and other towns in their neighborhood "was heard the report of a great piece of ordnance,[6] with a shaking of the earth and a considerable echo."* Others were alarmed on a still sunshiny morning, by the discharge of guns and muskets; bullets seemed to whistle past them, and the noise of drums resounded in the air, seeming to pass away to the westward; others fancied that they heard the galloping of horses over their head; and certain monstrous births which took place about the time, filled the superstitious in some towns with doleful forebodings. Many of these portentous sights and sounds may be ascribed to natural phenomena; to the northern lights which occur vividly in those latitudes; the meteors which explode in the air; the casual rushing of a blast through the top branches of the forest; the crash of fallen trees or disrupted rocks; and to those other uncouth sounds and echoes, which will sometimes strike the ear so strangely amidst the profound stillness of woodland solitudes. These may have startled some melancholy imaginations, may have been exaggerated by the love of the marvellous, and listened to with that avidity with which we devour whatever is fearful and mysterious. The universal currency of these superstitious fancies, and the grave record made of them by one of the learned men of the day, are strongly characteristic of the times.

The nature of the contest that ensued was such as too often distinguishes the warfare between civilized men and savages. On the part of the whites, it was conducted with superior skill and success, but with a wastefulness of the blood and a disregard of the natural rights of their antagonists: on the part of the Indians, it was waged with the desperation of men fearless of death, and who had nothing to expect from peace, but humiliation, dependence, and decay.

* The Rev. Increase Mather's *History*.

[4] Chimeras—Nightmares or frightful dreams.
[5] Spectrology—The "science" which treats of spectres, or ghosts.
[6] Ordnance—Artillery.

The events of the war are transmitted to us by a worthy clergyman of the time, who dwells with horror and indignation on every hostile act of the Indians, however justifiable, whilst he mentions with applause the most sanguinary atrocities of the whites. Philip is reviled as a murderer and a traitor; without considering that he was a true-born prince, gallantly fighting at the head of his subjects to avenge the wrongs of his family; to retrieve the tottering power of his line; and to deliver his native land from the oppression of usurping strangers.

The project of a wide and simultaneous revolt, if such had really been formed, was worthy of a capacious mind, and, had it not been prematurely discovered, might have been overwhelming in its consequences. The war that actually broke out was but a war of detail; a mere succession of casual exploits and unconnected enterprises. Still it sets forth the military genius and daring prowess of Philip; and wherever, in the prejudiced and passionate narrations that have been given of it, we can arrive at simple facts, we find him displaying a vigorous mind; a fertility of expedients; a contempt of suffering and hardship; and an unconquerable resolution, that command our sympathy and applause.

Driven from his paternal domains at Mount Hope, he threw himself into the depths of those vast and trackless forests that skirted the settlements, and were almost impervious to anything but a wild beast or an Indian. Here he gathered together his forces, like the storm accumulating its stores of mischief in the bosom of the thunder-cloud, and would suddenly emerge at a time and place least expected, carrying havoc and dismay into the villages. There were now and then indications of these impending ravages, that filled the minds of the colonists with awe and apprehension. The report of a distant gun would perhaps be heard from the solitary woodland, where there was known to be no white man; the cattle which had been wandering in the woods would sometimes return home wounded; or an Indian or two would be seen lurking about the skirts of the forests, and suddenly disappearing; as the lightning will sometimes be seen playing silently about the edge of the cloud that is brewing up the tempest.

Though sometimes pursued, and even surrounded by the settlers, yet Philip as often escaped almost miraculously from their toils; and, plunging into the wilderness, would be lost to all search or inquiry until he again emerged at some far-distant quarter, laying the country desolate. Among his strongholds were the great swamps or morasses, which extend in some parts of New England; composed of loose bogs of deep black mud; perplexed with thickets, brambles, rank weeds, the shattered and mouldering trunks of fallen trees, overshadowed by lugubrious hemlocks. The uncertain footing and the tangled mazes of these shaggy wilds, rendered them almost impracticable to the white man, though the Indian could thrid[7] their labyrinths with the agility of a deer. Into one of these, the great swamp of Pocasset Neck, was Philip once driven with a band of his followers. The English did not dare to pursue him, fearing to venture into these dark and frightful recesses, where they might perish in fens and miry pits, or be shot down by lurking foes. They therefore invested[8] the entrance to the neck and began to build a fort, with the thought of starving out the foe; but Philip and his warriors wafted themselves on a raft over an arm of the sea, in the dead of the night, leaving the women and children behind; and escaped away to the westward, kindling the flames of war among the tribes of Massachusetts and the Nipmuck country, and threatening the colony of Connecticut.

In this way Philip became a theme of universal apprehension. The mystery in which he was enveloped exaggerated his real terrors. He was an evil that walked in darkness; whose coming none could foresee, and against which none knew when to be on the alert. The whole country abounded with rumors and alarms. Philip seemed almost possessed of ubiquity;[9] for, in whatever part of the widely extended frontier an irruption from the forest took place, Philip was said to be its leader. Many superstitious notions also were circulated concerning him. He was said to deal in necromancy, and to be attended by an old Indian witch or prophetess, whom he consulted, and who assisted him by her charms and incantations. This indeed was frequently the case with Indian chiefs; either through their own credulity, or to act upon that of their followers: and the influence of the prophet and dreamer over Indian superstition has been fully evidenced in recent instances of savage warfare.

---

[7] THRID—Thread, or find a passage through.
[8] INVESTED—Occupied.
[9] UBIQUITY—Ability to be everywhere at once.

At the time that Philip effected his escape from Pocasset, his fortunes were in a desperate condition. His forces had been thinned by repeated fights, and he had lost almost the whole of his resources. In this time of adversity he found a faithful friend in Canonchet, Chief Sachem of all the Narragansetts. He was the son and heir of Miantonimo, the great Sachem who, as already mentioned, after an honorable acquittal of the charge of conspiracy, had been privately put to death at the perfidious instigations of the settlers. "He was the heir," says the old chronicler, "of all his father's pride and insolence, as well as of his malice towards the English"—he certainly was the heir of his insults and injuries, and the legitimate avenger of his murder. Though he had forborne to take an active part in this hopeless war, yet he received Philip and his broken forces with open arms; and gave them the most generous countenance and support. This at once drew upon him the hostility of the English; and it was determined to strike a signal blow, that should involve both the Sachems in one common ruin. A great force was, therefore, gathered together from Massachusetts, Plymouth, and Connecticut, and was sent into the Narragansett country in the depth of winter, when the swamps, being frozen and leafless, could be traversed with comparative facility and would no longer afford dark and impenetrable fastnesses to the Indians.

Apprehensive of attack, Canonchet had conveyed the greater part of his stores, together with the old, the infirm, the women and children of his tribe, to a strong fortress; where he and Philip had likewise drawn up the flower of their forces. This fortress, deemed by the Indians impregnable, was situated upon a rising mound, or kind of island, of five or six acres, in the midst of a swamp; it was constructed with a degree of judgment and skill vastly superior to what is usually displayed in Indian fortification, and indicative of the martial genius of these two chieftains.

Guided by a renegado Indian, the English penetrated through December snows, to this stronghold, and came upon the garrison by surprise. The fight was fierce and tumultuous. The assailants were repulsed in their first attack, and several of their bravest officers were shot down in the act of storming the fortress, sword in hand. The assault was renewed with greater success. A lodgment was effected. The Indians were driven from one post to another. They disputed their ground inch by inch, fighting with the fury of despair. Most of their veterans were cut to pieces; and after a long and bloody battle, Philip and Canonchet, with a handful of surviving warriors, retreated from the fort, and took refuge in the thickets of the surrounding forest.

The victors set fire to the wigwams and the fort; the whole was soon in a blaze; many of the old men, the women, and the children perished in the flames. This last outrage overcame even the stoicism of the savage. The neighboring woods resounded with the yells of rage and despair, uttered by the fugitive warriors as they beheld the destruction of their dwellings, and heard the agonizing cries of their wives and offspring. "The burning of the wigwams," says a contemporary writer, "the shrieks and cries of the women and children, and the yelling of the warriors, exhibited a most horrible and affecting scene, so that it greatly moved some of the soldiers." The same writer cautiously adds: "They were in *much doubt* then, and afterwards seriously inquired, whether burning their enemies alive could be consistent with humanity and the benevolent principles of the Gospel."*

The fate of the brave and generous Canonchet is worthy of particular mention: the last scene of his life is one of the noblest instances on record of Indian magnanimity.

Broken down in his power and resources by this signal defeat, yet faithful to his ally and to the hapless cause which he had espoused, he rejected all overtures of peace, offered on condition of betraying Philip and his followers, and declared that "he would fight it out to the last man, rather than become a servant to the English." His home being destroyed; his country harassed and laid waste by the incursions of the conquerors; he was obliged to wander away to the banks of the Connecticut; where he formed a rallying point to the whole body of western Indians and laid waste several of the English settlements.

Early in the spring, he departed on a hazardous expedition, with only thirty chosen men, to penetrate to Seaconck, in the vicinity of Mount Hope, and to procure seed-corn to plant for the sustenance of his troops. This little band of adventurers had passed safely through the Pequod country, and were in the centre of the Narragansett, resting at some wigwams near Pawtucket River, when an alarm was given of an approaching enemy. Having but seven

* MS. of the Rev. W. Ruggles.

men by him at the time, Canonchet despatched two of them to the top of a neighboring hill, to bring intelligence of the foe.

Panic-struck by the appearance of a troop of English and Indians rapidly advancing, they fled in breathless terror past their chieftain, without stopping to inform him of the danger. Canonchet sent another scout, who did the same. He then sent two more, one of whom, hurrying back in confusion and affright, told him that the whole British army was at hand. Canonchet saw there was no choice but immediate flight. He attempted to escape round the hill, but was perceived and hotly pursued by the hostile Indians, and a few of the fleetest of the English. Finding the swiftest pursuer close upon his heels, he threw off, first his blanket, then his silver-laced coat and belt of peag,[10] by which his enemies knew him to be Canonchet, and redoubled the eagerness of pursuit.

At length, in dashing through the river, his foot slipped upon a stone, and he fell so deep as to wet his gun. This accident so struck him with despair that, as he afterwards confessed, "his heart and his bowels turned within him, and he became like a rotten stick, void of strength."

To such a degree was he unnerved that, being seized by a Pequod Indian within a short distance of the river, he made no resistance, though a man of great vigor of body and boldness of heart. But on being made prisoner, the whole pride of his spirit arose within him; and from that moment, we find, in the anecdotes given by his enemies, nothing but repeated flashes of elevated and prince-like heroism. Being questioned by one of the English who first came up with him, and who had not attained his twenty-second year, the proud-hearted warrior, looking with lofty contempt upon his youthful countenance, replied, "You are a child—you cannot understand matters of war—let your brother or your chief come—him will I answer."

Though repeated offers were made to him of his life, on condition of submitting with his nation to the English, yet he rejected them with disdain, and refused to send any proposals of the kind to the great body of his subjects; saying that he knew none of them would comply. Being reproached with his breach of faith towards the whites; his boast that he would not deliver up a Wampanoag, nor the paring of a Wampanoag's nail; and his threat that he would

[10] Peag—Small shell beads used for wampum belts and as money.

burn the English alive in their houses, he disdained to justify himself, haughtily answering that others were as forward for the war as himself, "and he desired to hear no more thereof."

So noble and unshaken a spirit, so true a fidelity to his cause and his friend, might have touched the feelings of the generous and the brave; but Canonchet was an Indian; a being towards whom war had no courtesy, humanity no law, religion no compassion—he was condemned to die. The last words of him that are recorded, are worthy the greatness of his soul. When sentence of death was passed upon him, he observed, "that he liked it well, for he should die before his heart was soft or he had spoken anything unworthy of himself." His enemies gave him the death of a soldier, for he was shot at Stoningham, by three young sachems of his own rank.

The defeat at the Narragansett fortress, and the death of Canonchet, were fatal blows to the fortunes of King Philip. He made an ineffectual attempt to raise a head of war, by stirring up the Mohawks to take arms; but though possessed of the native talents of a statesman, his arts were counteracted by the superior arts of his enlightened enemies, and the terror of their warlike skill began to subdue the resolution of the neighboring tribes. The unfortunate chieftain saw himself daily stripped of power, and his ranks rapidly thinning around him. Some were suborned by the whites; others fell victims to hunger and fatigue, and to the frequent attacks by which they were harassed. His stores were all captured; his chosen friends were swept away from before his eyes; his uncle was shot down by his side; his sister was carried into captivity; and in one of his narrow escapes he was compelled to leave his beloved wife and only son to the mercy of the enemy. "His ruin," says the historian, "being thus gradually carried on, his misery was not prevented, but augmented thereby; being himself made acquainted with the sense and experimental feeling of the captivity of his children, loss of friends, slaughter of his subjects, bereavement of all family relations, and being stripped of all outward comforts, before his own life should be taken away."

To fill up the measure of his misfortunes, his own followers began to plot against his life, that by sacrificing him they might purchase dishonorable safety. Through treachery, a number of his faithful adherents, the subjects of Wetamoe, an Indian princess of Pocasset, a near kinswoman and confederate of Philip, were betrayed into the hands of the enemy. Wetamoe was among them at the time, and attempted to make her escape by crossing a neighboring river; either exhausted by swimming, or starved by cold and hunger, she was found dead and naked near the water side. But persecution ceased not at the grave: even death, the refuge of the wretched, where the wicked commonly cease from troubling, was no protection to this outcast female, whose great crime was affectionate fidelity to her kinsman and her friend. Her corpse was the object of unmanly and dastardly vengeance; the head was severed from the body and set upon a pole, and was thus exposed, at Taunton, to the view of her captive subjects. They immediately recognized the features of their unfortunate queen, and were so affected at this barbarous spectacle, that we are told they broke forth into the "most horrible and diabolical lamentations."

However Philip had borne up against the complicated miseries and misfortunes that surrounded him, the treachery of his followers seemed to wring his heart and reduce him to despondency. It is said that "he never rejoiced afterwards, nor had success in any of his designs." The spring of hope was broken—the ardor of enterprise was extinguished: he looked around, and all was danger and darkness; there was no eye to pity, nor any arm that could bring deliverance. With a scanty band of followers, who still remained true to his desperate fortunes, the unhappy Philip wandered back to the vicinity of Mount Hope, the ancient dwelling of his fathers. Here he lurked about, like a spectre, among the scenes of former power and prosperity, now bereft of home, of family, and friend. There needs no better picture of his destitute and piteous situation, than that furnished by the homely pen of the chronicler, who is unwarily enlisting the feelings of the reader in favor of the hapless warrior whom he reviles. "Philip," he says, "like a savage wild beast, having been hunted by the English forces through the woods above a hundred miles backward and forward, at last was driven to his own den upon Mount Hope, where he retired, with a few of his best friends into a swamp, which proved but a prison to keep him fast till the messengers of death came by divine permission to execute vengeance upon him."

Even in this last refuge of desperation and despair, a sullen grandeur gathers round his memory. We picture him to ourselves seated among his care-worn followers, brooding in silence over his blasted fortunes, and acquiring a savage sublimity from the wildness and dreariness of his lurking-place. Defeated, but not dismayed—crushed to the earth, but not humiliated—he seemed to grow more haughty beneath disaster, and to experience a fierce satisfaction in draining the last dregs of bitterness. Little minds are tamed and subdued by misfortune; but great minds rise above it. The very idea of submission awakened the fury of Philip, and he smote to death one of his followers, who proposed an expedient of peace. The brother of the victim made his escape, and in revenge betrayed the retreat of his chieftain. A body of white men and Indians were immediately despatched to the swamp where Philip lay crouched, glaring with fury and despair. Before he was aware of their approach, they had begun to surround him. In a little while he saw five of his trustiest followers laid dead at his feet; all resistance was vain; he rushed forth from his covert, and made a headlong attempt to escape, but was shot through the heart by a renegado Indian of his own nation.

Such is the scanty story of the brave, but unfortunate King Philip; persecuted while living, slandered and dishonored when dead. If, however, we consider even the prejudiced anecdotes furnished us by his enemies, we may perceive in them traces of amiable and lofty character, sufficient to awaken sympathy for his fate and respect for his memory. We find, that amidst all the harassing cares and ferocious passions of constant warfare, he was alive to the softer feelings of connubial love and paternal tenderness, and to the generous sentiment of friendship. The captivity of his "beloved wife and only son" are mentioned with exultation, as causing him poignant misery; the death of any near friend is triumphantly recorded as a new blow on his sensibilities; but the treachery and desertion of many of his followers, in whose affections he had confided, is said to have desolated his heart, and to have bereaved him of all further comfort. He was a patriot, attached to his native soil—a prince true to his subjects, and indignant of their wrongs—a soldier, daring in battle, firm in adversity, patient of fatigue, of hunger, of every variety of bodily suffering, and ready to perish in the cause he had espoused. Proud of heart, and with an untamable love of natural liberty, he preferred to enjoy it among the beasts of the forests, or in the dismal and famished recesses of swamps and morasses, rather than bow his haughty spirit to submission, and live dependent and despised in the ease and luxury of the settlements. With heroic qualities and bold achievements that would have graced a civilized warrior, and have rendered him the theme of the poet and historian, he lived a wanderer and a fugitive in his native land, and went down like a lonely bark, foundering amid darkness and tempest—without a pitying eye to weep his fall, or a friendly hand to record his struggle.

## QUESTIONS AND EXERCISES

Exercises preceded by a star are designed for assignment at the discretion of the teacher, or for any student who volunteers.

1. Does the author make the character of Philip real to you? Describe Philip.
*2. Check Irving's account with the history of Philip of Pokanoket in an encyclopædia.
3. What was the fate of Canonchet?
4. Does the paragraph on pages 610–611 beginning "In the early chronicles . . ." add anything of value to the *Sketch?*

## JOHN BULL

From a cartooned page he has smiled broadly at you many a time, this "sturdy, corpulent old fellow, with a three-cornered hat, red waistcoat, leather breeches, and stout oaken cudgel"—John Bull. Irving pokes mild fun at the peculiarities of the Englishman's character. But his caricature is much more than of the individual Britisher. It becomes a personification of the whole English nation—even the British Empire. The author's analysis has a keener relish the more one knows of English history. There is quick satire, or ridicule, in this essay, but its edge is tempered with courtesy, its justice by mercy. *John Bull* shares honors with the next essay, *English Writers on America,* as the best of Irving's "critical" writing in *The Sketch Book.*

There is no species of humor in which the English more excel, than that which consists in caricaturing and giving ludicrous appellations or nicknames. In this way they have whimsically designated, not merely individuals, but nations; and in their fondness for pushing a joke, they have not spared even themselves. One would think that, in personifying itself, a nation would be apt to picture something grand, heroic, and imposing; but it is characteristic of the peculiar humor of the English, and of their love for what is blunt, comic, and familiar, that they have embodied their national oddities in the figure of a sturdy, corpulent old fellow, with a three-cornered hat, red waistcoat, leather breeches, and stout oaken cudgel. Thus they have taken a singular delight in exhibiting their most private foibles in a laughable point of view; and have been so successful in their delineations, that there is scarcely a being in actual existence more absolutely present to the public mind, than that eccentric personage, John Bull.

Perhaps the continual contemplation of the character thus drawn of them, has contributed to fix it upon the nation; and thus to give reality to what at first may have been painted in a great measure from the imagination. Men are apt to acquire peculiarities that are continually ascribed to them. The common orders of English seem wonderfully captivated with the *beau ideal*[1] which they have formed of John Bull, and endeavor to act up to the broad caricature that is perpetually before their eyes. Unluckily, they sometimes make their boasted Bull-ism an apology for their prejudice or grossness; and this I have especially noticed among those truly home-bred and genuine sons of the soil who have never migrated beyond the sound of Bow-bells.[2] If one of these should be a little uncouth in speech, and apt to utter impertinent truths, he confesses that he is a real John Bull, and always speaks his mind. If he now and then flies into an unreasonable burst of passion about trifles, he observes that John Bull is a choleric old blade, but then his passion is over in a moment, and he bears no malice. If he betrays a coarseness of taste, and an insensibility to foreign refinements, he thanks Heaven for his ignorance—he is a plain John Bull, and has no relish for frippery and knick-knacks. His very proneness to be gulled by strangers, and to pay extravagantly for absurdities, is excused under the plea of munificence—for John is always more generous than wise.

Thus, under the name of John Bull, he will contrive to argue every fault into a merit, and will frankly convict himself of being the honestest fellow in existence.

However little, therefore, the character may have suited in the first instance, it has gradually adapted itself to the nation, or rather they have adapted themselves to each other; and a stranger who wishes to study English peculiarities, may gather much valuable

---

[1] *Beau ideal*—Ideal picture.

[2] SOUND . . . BOW-BELLS—All Londoners living within sound of the bells of St. Mary's in Bow Street were called "Cockney."

information from the innumerable portraits of John Bull, as exhibited in the windows of the caricature-shops. Still, however, he is one of those fertile humorists, that are continually throwing out new portraits, and presenting different aspects from different points of view; and, often as he has been described, I cannot resist the temptation to give a slight sketch of him, such as he has met my eye.

John Bull, to all appearance, is a plain, downright, matter-of-fact fellow, with much less of poetry about him than rich prose. There is little of romance in his nature, but a vast deal of strong natural feeling. He excels in humor more than in wit; is jolly rather than gay; melancholy rather than morose; can easily be moved to a sudden tear, or surprised into a broad laugh; but he loathes sentiment, and has no turn for light pleasantry. He is a boon companion, if you allow him to have his humor and to talk about himself; and he will stand by a friend in a quarrel, with life and purse, however soundly he may be cudgelled.

In this last respect, to tell the truth, he has a propensity to be somewhat too ready. He is a busy-minded personage, who thinks not merely for himself and family, but for all the country round, and is most generously disposed to be everybody's champion. He is continually volunteering his services to settle his neighbors' affairs, and takes it in great dudgeon if they engage in any matter of consequence without asking his advice; though he seldom engages in any friendly office of the kind without finishing by getting into a squabble with all parties, and then railing bitterly at their ingratitude. He unluckily took lessons in his youth in the noble science of defence, and having accomplished himself in the use of his limbs and his weapons, and become a perfect master at boxing and cudgel-play, he has had a troublesome life of it ever since. He cannot hear of a quarrel between the most distant of his neighbors, but he begins incontinently to fumble with the head of his cudgel, and consider whether his interest or honor does not require that he should meddle in the broil. Indeed, he has extended his relations of pride and policy so completely over the whole country, that no event can take place, without infringing some of his finely-spun rights and dignities. Couched in his little domain, with these filaments stretching forth in every direction, he is like some choleric, bottle-bellied old spider, who has woven his web over a whole chamber, so that a fly cannot buzz, nor a breeze blow, without startling his repose, and causing him to sally forth wrathfully from his den.

Though really a good-hearted, good-tempered old fellow at bottom, yet he is singularly fond of being in the midst of contention. It is one of his peculiarities, however, that he only relishes the beginning of an affray; he always goes into a fight with alacrity, but comes out of it grumbling even when victorious; and though no one fights with more obstinacy to carry a contested point, yet, when the battle is over and he comes to the reconciliation, he is so much taken up with the mere shaking of hands, that he is apt to let his antagonist pocket all that they have been quarrelling about. It is not, therefore, fighting that he ought so much to be on his guard against, as making friends. It is difficult to cudgel him out of a farthing; but, put him in good humor, and you may bargain him out of all the money in his pocket. He is like a stout ship, which will weather the roughest storm uninjured, but roll its masts overboard in the succeeding calm.

He is a little fond of playing the magnifico[3] abroad; of pulling out a long purse; flinging his money bravely about at boxing-matches, horse-races, cock-fights, and carrying a high head among "gentlemen of the fancy"; but immediately after one of these fits of extravagance, he will be taken with violent qualms of economy; stop short at the most trivial expenditure; talk desperately of being ruined and brought upon the parish; and in such moods will not pay the smallest tradesman's bill without violent altercation. He is, in fact, the most punctual and discontented paymaster in the world; drawing his coin out of his breeches pocket with infinite reluctance; paying to the uttermost farthing, but accompanying every guinea with a growl.

With all his talk of economy, however, he is a bountiful provider and a hospitable housekeeper. His economy is a whimsical kind, its chief object being to devise how he may afford to be extravagant; for he will begrudge himself a beefsteak and a pint of port one day, that he may roast an ox whole, broach a hogshead of ale, and treat all his neighbors on the next.

His domestic establishment is enormously expensive; not so much from any great outward parade, as from the great consumption of solid beef and pudding, the vast number of followers he

[3] PLAYING THE MAGNIFICO—Posing as a grand gentleman.

feeds and clothes, and his singular disposition to pay hugely for small services. He is a most kind and indulgent master, and, provided his servants humor his peculiarities, flatter his vanity a little now and then, and do not peculate[4] grossly on him before his face, they may manage him to perfection. Everything that lives on him seems to thrive and grow fat. His house-servants are well paid, and pampered, and have little to do. His horses are sleek and lazy, and prance slowly before his state carriage; and his house-dogs sleep quietly about the door, and will hardly bark at a house breaker.

His family mansion is an old castellated[5] manor-house, gray with age, and of a most venerable, though weather-beaten, appearance. It has been built upon no regular plan, but is a vast accumulation of parts, erected in various tastes and ages. The centre bears evident traces of Saxon architecture, and is as solid as ponderous stone and old English oak can make it. Like all the relics of that style, it is full of obscure passages, intricate mazes, and dusky chambers; and though these have been partially lighted up in modern days, yet there are many places where you must still grope in the dark. Additions have been made to the original edifice from time to time, and great alterations have taken place; towers and battlements have been erected during wars and tumults; wings built in time of peace; and out-houses, lodges, and offices, run up according to the whim or convenience of different generations, until it has become one of the most spacious, rambling tenements imaginable. An entire wing is taken up with the family chapel; a reverend pile, that must have been exceedingly sumptuous, and indeed, in spite of having been altered and simplified at various periods, has still a look of solemn religious pomp. Its walls within are stored with the monuments of John's ancestors; and it is snugly fitted up with soft cushions and well-lined chairs, where such of his family as are inclined to church services, may doze comfortably in the discharge of their duties.

To keep up this chapel has cost John much money; but he is staunch in his religion, and piqued in his zeal, from the circumstance that many dissenting chapels[6] have been erected in his

---

[4] PECULATE—Steal.
[5] CASTELLATED—Castle-like, having towers, etc.
[6] DISSENTING CHAPELS—Denominations which broke away from the Church of England.

vicinity, and several of his neighbors, with whom he has had quarrels, are strong Papists.[7]

To do the duties of the chapel, he maintains at a large expense, a pious and portly family chaplain. He is a most learned and decorous personage, and a truly well-bred Christian, who always backs the old gentleman in his opinions, winks discreetly at his little peccadilloes, rebukes the children when refractory, and is of great use in exhorting the tenants to read their Bibles, say their prayers, and, above all, to pay their rents punctually, and without grumbling.

The family apartments are in a very antiquated taste, somewhat heavy, and often inconvenient, but full of the solemn magnificence of former times; fitted up with rich, though faded tapestry, unwieldy furniture, and loads of massy, gorgeous old plate. The vast fire-places, ample kitchens, extensive cellars, and sumptuous banqueting halls,—all speak of the roaring hospitality of days of yore, of which the modern festivity at the manor-house is but a shadow. There are, however, complete suites of rooms apparently deserted and time-worn; and towers and turrets that are tottering to decay; so that in high winds there is danger of their tumbling about the ears of the household.

John has frequently been advised to have the old edifice thoroughly overhauled,[8] and to have some of the useless parts pulled down, and the others strengthened with their materials; but the old gentleman always grows testy on this subject. He swears the house is an excellent house—that it is tight and weather-proof, and not to be shaken by tempests—that it has stood for several hundred years, and therefore, is not likely to tumble down now—that as to its being inconvenient, his family is accustomed to the inconveniences, and would not be comfortable without them—that as to its unwieldy size and irregular construction, these result from its being the growth of centuries, and being improved by the wisdom of every generation—that an old family, like his, requires a large house to dwell in; new, upstart families may live in modern cottages and

---

[7] Papists—Roman Catholics. Irving is referring to France and Spain among other nations.

[8] To have . . . overhauled—Plans leading to the Reform Bill of 1832, which improved social conditions in England, were being formed at the time of the writing of *The Sketch Book.* The Reform Bill changed the method of electing members of Parliament, and gave fairer representation to all parts of the country.

snug boxes, but an old English family should inhabit an old English manor-house. If you point out any part of the building as superfluous, he insists that it is material to the strength or decoration of the rest, and the harmony of the whole; and swears that the parts are so built into each other; that, if you pull down one, you run the risk of having the whole about your ears.

The secret of the matter is, that John has a great disposition to protect and patronize. He thinks it indispensable to the dignity of an ancient and honorable family, to be bounteous in its appointments, and to be eaten up by dependents; and so, partly from pride, and partly from kind-heartedness, he makes it a rule always to give shelter and maintenance to his superannuated servants.

The consequence is, that like many other venerable family establishments, his manor is encumbered by old retainers whom he cannot turn off, and an old style which he cannot lay down. His mansion is like a great hospital of invalids, and with all its magnitude, is not a whit too large for its inhabitants. Not a nook or corner but is of use in housing some useless personage. Groups of veteran beef-eaters, gouty pensioners, and retired heroes of the buttery and the larder, are seen lolling about its walls, crawling over its lawns, dozing under its trees, or sunning themselves upon the benches at its doors. Every office and out-house is garrisoned by these supernumeraries and their families; for they are amazingly prolific, and when they die off are sure to leave John a legacy of hungry mouths to be provided for. A mattock cannot be struck against the most mouldering tumble-down tower, but out pops, from some cranny or loophole, the gray pate of some superannuated hanger-on, who has lived at John's expense all his life, and makes the most grievous outcry, at their pulling down the roof from over the head of a worn-out servant of the family. This is an appeal that John's honest heart never can withstand; so that a man who has faithfully eaten his beef and pudding all his life, is sure to be rewarded with a pipe and tankard in his old days.

A great part of his park, also, is turned into paddocks, where his broken-down chargers are turned loose to graze undisturbed for the remainder of their existence—a worthy example of grateful recollection, which, if some of his neighbors were to imitate, would not be to their discredit. Indeed, it is one of his great pleasures to point out these old steeds to his visitors, to dwell on their good qualities, extol their past services, and boast with some little vain-glory, of the perilous adventures and hardy exploits through which they have carried him.

He is given, however, to indulge his veneration for family usages, and family incumbrances, to a whimsical extent. His manor is infested by gangs of gypsies; yet he will not suffer them to be driven off, because they have infested the place time out of mind, and been regular poachers upon every generation of the family. He will scarcely permit a dry branch to be lopped from the great trees that surround the house, lest it should molest the rooks, that have bred there for centuries. Owls have taken possession of the dove-cote, but they are hereditary owls, and must not be disturbed. Swallows have nearly choked up every chimney with their nests; martins[9] build in every frieze and cornice; crows flutter about the towers, and perch on every weather-cock; and old gray-headed rats may be seen in every quarter of the house, running in and out of their holes undauntedly in broad daylight. In short, John has such a reverence for everything that has been long in the family, that he will not hear even of abuses being reformed, because they are good old family abuses.

All those whims and habits have concurred wofully to drain the old gentleman's purse; and as he prides himself on punctuality in money matters, and wishes to maintain his credit in the neighborhood, they have caused him great perplexity in meeting his engagements. This, too, has been increased by the altercations and heart-burnings which are continually taking place in his family. His children have been brought up to different callings, and are of different ways of thinking; and as they have always been allowed to speak their minds freely, they do not fail to exercise the privilege most clamorously in the present posture of his affairs. Some stand up for the honor of the race, and are clear that the old establishment should be kept up in all its state, whatever may be the cost; others, who are more prudent and considerate, entreat the old gentleman to retrench his expenses, and to put his whole system of housekeeping on a more moderate footing. He has, indeed, at times, seemed inclined to listen to their opinions, but their wholesome advice has been completely defeated by the obstreperous conduct of one of his sons. This is a noisy rattle-pated fellow, of rather low

[9] MARTINS—Small birds of the swallow family.

habits, who neglects his business to frequent ale-houses—is the orator of village clubs, and a complete oracle among the poorest of his father's tenants. No sooner does he hear any of his brothers mention reform or retrenchment, than up he jumps, takes the words out of their mouths, and roars out for an overturn. When his tongue is once going, nothing can stop it. He rants about the room; hectors the old man about his spendthrift practices; ridicules his tastes and pursuits; insists that he shall turn the old servants out of doors; give the broken-down horses to the hounds; send the fat chaplain packing and take a field-preacher in his place; nay, that the whole family mansion shall be levelled with the ground, and a plain one of brick and mortar built in its place. He rails at every social entertainment and family festivity, and skulks away growling to the ale-house whenever an equipage drives up to the door. Though constantly complaining of the emptiness of his purse, yet he scruples not to spend all his pocket-money in these tavern convocations, and even runs up scores for the liquor over which he preaches about his father's extravagance.

It may readily be imagined how little such thwarting agrees with the old cavalier's fiery temperament. He has become so irritable, from repeated crossings, that the mere mention of retrenchment or reform is a signal for a brawl between him and the tavern oracle. As the latter is too sturdy and refractory for paternal discipline, having grown out of all fear of the cudgel, they have frequent scenes of wordy warfare, which at times run so high, that John is fain to call in the aid of his son Tom, an officer who has served abroad, but is at present living at home, on half-pay. This last is sure to stand by the old gentleman, right or wrong; likes nothing so much as a racketing roystering life; and is ready, at a wink or nod, to out sabre, and flourish it over the orator's head, if he dares to array himself against paternal authority.

These family dissensions, as usual, have got abroad, and are rare food for scandal in John's neighborhood. People begin to look wise, and shake their heads, whenever his affairs are mentioned. They all "hope that matters are not so bad with him as represented; but when a man's own children begin to rail at his extravagance, things must be badly managed. They understand he is mortgaged over head and ears, and is continually dabbling with money lenders. He is certainly an open-handed old gentleman, but they fear he has lived too fast; indeed, they never knew any good come of this fondness for hunting, racing, revelling, and prize-fighting. In short, Mr. Bull's estate is a very fine one, and has been in the family a long while; but for all that, they have known many finer estates come to the hammer."

What is worst of all, is the effect which these pecuniary embarrassments and domestic feuds have had on the poor man himself. Instead of that jolly round corporation, and smug rosy face, which he used to present, he has of late become as shrivelled and shrunk as a frost-bitten apple. His scarlet gold-laced waistcoat, which bellied out so bravely in those prosperous days when he sailed before the wind, now hangs loosely about him like a mainsail in a calm. His leather breeches are all in folds and wrinkles; and apparently have much ado to hold up the boots that yawn on both sides of his once sturdy legs.

Instead of strutting about, as formerly, with his three-cornered hat on one side; flourishing his cudgel, and bringing it down every moment with a hearty thump upon the ground; looking every one sturdily in the face, and trolling out a stave of a catch or a drinking song; he now goes about whistling thoughtfully to himself, with his head drooping down, his cudgel tucked under his arm, and his hands thrust to the bottom of his breeches pockets, which are evidently empty.

Such is the plight of honest John Bull at present; yet for all this, the old fellow's spirit is as tall and as gallant as ever. If you drop the least expression of sympathy or concern, he takes fire in an instant; swears that he is the richest and stoutest fellow in the country; talks of laying out large sums to adorn his house or buy another estate; and, with a valiant swagger and grasping of his cudgel, longs exceedingly to have another bout at quarter staff.[10]

Though there may be something rather whimsical in all this, yet I confess I cannot look upon John's situation without strong feelings of interest. With all his odd humors and obstinate prejudices, he is a sterling-hearted old blade. He may not be so wonderfully fine a fellow as he thinks himself, but he is at least twice as good as his neighbors represent him. His virtues are all his own; all plain, homebred, and unaffected. His very faults smack

---

[10] Bout . . . quarter staff—Form of duel with long staffs. The staff was grasped with one hand in the middle, the other hand a quarter of the way from the end.

of the raciness of his good qualities. His extravagance savors of his generosity; his quarrelsomeness, of his courage; his credulity, of his open faith; his vanity, of his pride; and his bluntness, of his sincerity. They are all the redundancies of a rich and liberal character. He is like his own oak; rough without, but sound and solid within; whose bark abounds with excrescences in proportion to the growth and grandeur of the timber; and whose branches make a fearful groaning and murmuring in the least storm, from their very magnitude and luxuriance. There is something, too, in the appearance of his old family mansion, that is extremely poetical and picturesque; and, as long as it can be rendered comfortably habitable, I should almost tremble to see it meddled with during the present conflict of tastes and opinions. Some of his advisers are no doubt good architects, that might be of service; but many, I fear, are mere levellers, who, when they had once got to work with their mattocks on this venerable edifice, would never stop until they had brought it to the ground, and perhaps buried themselves among the ruins. All that I wish is, that John's present troubles may teach him more prudence in future; that he may cease to distress his mind about other people's affairs; that he may give up the fruitless attempt to promote the good of his neighbors, and the peace and happiness of the world, by dint of the cudgel; that he may remain quietly at home; gradually get his house into repair; cultivate his rich estate according to his fancy; husband his income—if he thinks proper; bring his unruly children into order—if he can; renew the jovial scenes of ancient prosperity; and long enjoy, on his paternal lands, a green, an honorable, and a merry old age.

## QUESTIONS AND EXERCISES

Exercises preceded by a star are designed for assignment at the discretion of the teacher, or for any student who volunteers.

1. Define "caricature." Do you think Irving has drawn a good caricature?
2. What are the peculiarities of John Bull suggested by Irving?
3. Write a brief caricature of "Uncle Sam" imagining yourself as an English writer of today.

*4. Name the English institutions or phases of English history indicated by the following phrases (Look up a history of England in the library): *took lessons in his youth in the noble science of defence, his family mansion, the family chapel, singularly fond of being in the midst of contention, John has a great disposition to protect and patronize, reverence for every thing that has been long in the family, these family dissensions.* Suggest some more.

## ENGLISH WRITERS ON AMERICA

Someone has called this essay "The American Declaration of Literary Independence" and, as a document of literary history, it deserves the title. At the time of its writing, the tone of English literary criticism was, in general, ill-natured, and toward America especially bitter. British writers seemed to enjoy encouraging prejudice against anything American, and, as Irving expresses it, "I would place implicit confidence in an Englishman's descriptions of the regions beyond the cataracts of the Nile; of unknown islands in the Yellow Sea. . . . But I would cautiously receive his account of his immediate neighbors . . . However I might be disposed to trust his probity, I dare not trust his prejudices."

The essay is a courteous rebuke to narrow English critics—it is an equal warning to American authors who would sully their country and pens by retaliation. He adds in a note of prophecy that England will find it advisable to stop such practice; not only for its own lack of charity, but because it will sever two nations bound together by ties of blood and sympathy, and lose England "a friend, whose possible alienation may prove dangerous."

It is with feelings of deep regret that I observe the literary animosity daily growing up between England and America. Great curiosity has been awakened of late with respect to the United States, and the London press has teemed with volumes of travels through the Republic; but they seem intended to diffuse error rather than knowledge; and so successful have they been, that, notwithstanding the constant intercourse between the nations, there is no people concerning whom the great mass of the British public have less pure information, or entertain more numerous prejudices.

English travellers are the best and the worst in the world. Where no motives of pride or interest intervene, none can equal them for profound and philosophical views of society, or faithful and graphical descriptions of external objects; but when either the interest or reputation of their own country comes in collision with that of another, they go to the opposite extreme, and forget their usual probity and candor, in the indulgence of splenetic remark, and an illiberal spirit of ridicule.

Hence, their travels are more honest and accurate, the more remote the country described. I would place implicit confidence in an Englishman's descriptions of the regions beyond the cataracts of the Nile; of unknown islands in the Yellow Sea; of the interior of India; or of any other tract which other travellers might be apt to picture out with the illusions of their fancies. But I would cautiously receive his account of his immediate neighbors, and of those nations with which he is in habits of most frequent intercourse. However I might be disposed to trust his probity, I dare not trust his prejudices.

It has also been the particular lot of our country to be visited by the worst kind of English travellers. While men of philosophical spirit and cultivated minds have been sent from England to ransack the poles, to penetrate the deserts, and to study the manners and customs of barbarous nations, with which she can have no permanent intercourse of profit or pleasure; it has been left to the broken-down tradesman, the scheming adventurer, the wandering mechanic, the Manchester and Birmingham agent, to be her oracles respecting America. From such sources she is content to receive her information respecting a country in a singular state of moral and physical development; a country in which one of the greatest political experiments in the history of the world is now performing, and which presents the most profound and momentous studies to the statesman and the philosopher.

That such men should give prejudicial accounts of America is not a matter of surprise. The themes it offers for contemplation are too vast and elevated for their capacities. The national character is yet in a state of fermentation: it may have its frothiness and sediment, but its ingredients are sound and wholesome: it has already given proofs of powerful and generous qualities; and the whole promises to settle down into something substantially excellent. But the causes which are operating to strengthen and ennoble it, and its daily indications of admirable properties, are all lost upon these purblind[1] observers; who are only affected by the little asperities incident to its present situation. They are capable of judging only of the surface of things; of those matters which come in contact with their private interests and personal gratifications. They miss some of the snug conveniences and petty comforts which belong to an old, highly-finished, and over-populous state of society; where the ranks of useful labor are crowded, and many earn a painful and servile subsistence, by studying the very caprices of appetite and self-indulgence. These minor comforts, however, are all-important in the estimation of narrow minds; which either do not

[1] PURBLIND—Almost totally blind.

perceive, or will not acknowledge, that they are more than counterbalanced among us, by great and generally diffused blessings.

They may, perhaps, have been disappointed in some unreasonable expectation of sudden gain. They may have pictured America to themselves an El Dorado,[2] where gold and silver abounded, and the natives were lacking in sagacity; and where they were to become strangely and suddenly rich, in some unforeseen but easy manner. The same weakness of mind that indulges absurd expectations, produces petulance in disappointment. Such persons become embittered against the country on finding that there, as everywhere else, a man must sow before he can reap; must win wealth by industry and talent; and must contend with the common difficulties of nature, and the shrewdness of an intelligent and enterprising people.

Perhaps, through mistaken or ill-directed hospitality, or from the prompt disposition to cheer and countenance the stranger, prevalent among my countrymen, they may have been treated with unwonted respect in America; and, having been accustomed all their lives to consider themselves below the surface of good society, and brought up in a servile feeling of inferiority, they become arrogant on the common boon of civility; they attribute to the lowliness of others their own elevation; and underrate a society where there are no artificial distinctions, and where by any chance such individuals as themselves can rise to consequence.

One would suppose, however, that information coming from such sources, on a subject where the truth is so desirable, would be received with caution by the censors of the press; that the motives of these men, their veracity, their opportunities of inquiry and observation, and their capacities for judging correctly, would be rigorously scrutinized, before their evidence was admitted, in such sweeping extent against a kindred nation. The very reverse, however, is the case, and it furnishes a striking instance of human inconsistency. Nothing can surpass the vigilance with which English critics will examine the credibility of the traveller who publishes an account of some distant, and comparatively unimportant, country. How warily will they compare the measurements of a pyramid, or the descriptions of a ruin; and how sternly will they censure any inaccuracy in these contributions of merely curious knowledge:

---

[2] El Dorado—The gilded. Refers to a fabulous country or city of gold in the New World. It was sought by Spanish explorers and Sir Walter Raleigh.

while they will receive, with eagerness and unhesitating faith, the gross misrepresentations of coarse and obscure writers, concerning a country with which their own is placed in the most important and delicate relations. Nay, they will even make these apocryphal[3] volumes text-books, on which to enlarge, with a zeal and an ability worthy of a more generous cause.

I shall not, however, dwell on this irksome and hackneyed topic; nor should I have adverted to it, but for the undue interest apparently taken in it by my countrymen, and certain injurious effects which I apprehend it might produce upon the national feeling. We attach too much consequence to these attacks. They cannot do us any essential injury. The tissue of misrepresentations attempted to be woven round us, are like cobwebs woven round the limbs of an infant giant. Our country continually outgrows them. One falsehood after another falls off of itself. We have but to live on, and every day we live a whole volume of refutation. All the writers of England united, if we could for a moment suppose their great minds stooping to so unworthy a combination, could not conceal our rapidly growing importance and matchless prosperity. They could not conceal that these are owing, not merely to physical and local, but also to moral causes;—to the political liberty, the general diffusion of knowledge, the prevalence of sound, moral, and religious principles, which give force and sustained energy to the character of a people; and which, in fact, have been the acknowledged and wonderful supporters of their own national power and glory.

But why are we so exquisitely alive to the aspersions of England? Why do we suffer ourselves to be so affected by the contumely she has endeavored to cast upon us? It is not in the opinion of England alone that honor lives, and reputation has its being. The world at large is the arbiter of a nation's fame: with its thousand eyes it witnesses a nation's deeds, and from their collective testimony is national glory or national disgrace established.

For ourselves, therefore, it is comparatively of but little importance whether England does us justice or not; it is, perhaps, of far more importance to herself. She is instilling anger and resentment into the bosom of a youthful nation, to grow with its growth, and strengthen with its strength. If in America, as some

---

[3] APOCRYPHAL—Doubtful, or fictitious. Originally applied to certain books not included in the Protestant Bible because of doubtful authorship.

of her writers are laboring to convince her, she is hereafter to find an invidious rival and a gigantic foe, she may thank those very writers for having provoked rivalship, and irritated hostility. Every one knows the all-pervading influence of literature at the present day, and how much the opinions and passions of mankind are under its control. The mere contests of the sword are temporary; their wounds are but in the flesh, and it is the pride of the generous to forgive and forget them; but the slanders of the pen pierce to the heart; they rankle longest in the noblest spirits; they dwell ever present in the mind, and render it morbidly sensitive to the most trifling collision. It is but seldom that any one overt act produces hostilities between two nations; there exists, most commonly, a previous jealousy and ill-will, a predisposition to take offence. Trace these to their cause, and how often will they be found to originate in the mischievous effusions of mercenary writers; who, secure in their closets, and for ignominious bread, concoct and circulate the venom that is to inflame the generous and the brave.

I am not laying too much stress upon this point; for it applies most emphatically to our particular case. Over no nation does the press hold a more absolute control than over the people of America; for the universal education of the poorest classes makes every individual a reader. There is nothing published in England on the subject of our country, that does not circulate through every part of it. There is not a calumny dropped from English pen, nor an unworthy sarcasm uttered by an English statesman, that does not go to blight good-will, and add to the mass of latent resentment. Possessing then, as England does, the fountain-head whence the literature of the language flows, how completely is it in her power, and how truly is it her duty, to make it the medium of amiable and magnanimous feeling—a stream where the two nations might meet together, and drink in peace and kindness. Should she, however, persist in turning it to waters of bitterness, the time may come when she may repent her folly. The present friendship of America may be of but little moment to her; but the future destinies of that country do not admit of a doubt: over those of England, there lower some shadows of uncertainty. Should, then, a day of gloom arrive—should these reverses overtake her from which the proudest empires have not been exempt—she may look back with regret at her infatuation, in repulsing from her side a nation she might have grappled to her bosom, and thus destroying her only chance for real friendship beyond the boundaries of her own dominions.

There is a general impression in England, that the people of the United States are inimical to the parent country. It is one of the errors which have been diligently propagated by designing writers. There is, doubtless, considerable political hostility, and a general soreness at the illiberality of the English press; but, generally speaking, the prepossessions of the people are strongly in favor of England. Indeed, at one time they amounted, in many parts of the Union, to an absurd degree of bigotry. The bare name of Englishman was a passport to the confidence and hospitality of every family, and too often gave a transient currency to the worthless and the ungrateful. Throughout the country, there was something of enthusiasm connected with the idea of England. We looked to it with a hallowed feeling of tenderness and veneration, as the land of our forefathers—the august repository of the monuments and antiquities of our race—the birth-place and mausoleum of the sages and heroes of our paternal history. After our own country, there was none in whose glory we more delighted—none whose good opinion we were more anxious to possess—none towards which our hearts yearned with such throbbings of warm consanguinity. Even during the late war,[4] whenever there was the least opportunity for kind feelings to spring forth, it was the delight of the generous spirits of our country to show, that in the midst of hostilities, they still kept alive the sparks of future friendship.

Is all this to be at an end? Is this golden band of kindred sympathies, so rare between nations, to be broken forever?—Perhaps it is for the best—it may dispel an illusion which might have kept us in mental vassalage; which might have interfered occasionally with our true interests, and prevented the growth of proper national pride. But it is hard to give up the kindred tie!—and there are feelings dearer than interest—closer to the heart than pride—that will still make us cast back a look of regret, as we wander farther and farther from the paternal roof, and lament the waywardness of the parent that would repel the affections of the child.

Short-sighted and injudicious, however, as the conduct of England may be in this system of aspersion, recrimination on our

[4] Late war—War of 1812.

part would be equally ill-judged. I speak not of a prompt and spirited vindication of our country, nor the keenest castigation of her slanderers—but I allude to a disposition to retaliate in kind, to retort sarcasm and inspire prejudice, which seems to be spreading widely among our writers. Let us guard particularly against such a temper; for it would double the evil, instead of redressing the wrong. Nothing is so easy and inviting as the retort of abuse and sarcasm; but it is a paltry and an unprofitable contest. It is the alternative of a morbid mind, fretted into petulance, rather than warmed into indignation. If England is willing to permit the mean jealousies of trade, or the rancorous animosities of politics, to deprave the integrity of her press, and poison the fountain of public opinion, let us beware of her example. She may deem it her interest to diffuse error, and engender antipathy, for the purpose of checking emigration; we have no purpose of the kind to serve. Neither have we any spirit of national jealousy to gratify; for as yet, in all our rivalships with England, we are the rising and the gaining party. There can be no end to answer, therefore, but the gratification of resentment—a mere spirit of retaliation; and even that is impotent. Our retorts are never republished in England; they fall short, therefore, of their aim; but they foster a querulous and peevish temper among our writers; they sour the sweet flow of our early literature, and sow thorns and brambles among its blossoms. What is still worse, they circulate through our own country, and, as far as they have effect, excite virulent national prejudices. This last is the evil most especially to be deprecated. Governed, as we are, entirely by public opinion, the utmost care should be taken to preserve the purity of the public mind. Knowledge is power, and truth is knowledge; whoever, therefore, knowingly propagates a prejudice, wilfully saps the foundation of his country's strength.

The members of a republic, above all other men, should be candid and dispassionate. They are, individually, portions of the sovereign mind and sovereign will, and should be enabled to come to all questions of national concern with calm and unbiased judgments. From the peculiar nature of our relations with England, we must have more frequent questions of a difficult and delicate character with her, than with any other nation; questions that affect the most acute and excitable feelings: and as, in the adjusting of these, our national measures must ultimately be determined by popular sentiment, we cannot be too anxiously attentive to purify it from all latent passion or prepossession.

Opening too, as we do, an asylum for strangers from every portion of the earth, we should receive all with impartiality. It should be our pride to exhibit an example of one nation, at least, destitute of national antipathies, and exercising, not merely the overt acts of hospitality, but those more rare and noble courtesies which spring from liberality of opinion.

What have we to do with national prejudices? They are the inveterate diseases of old countries, contracted in rude and ignorant ages, when nations knew but little of each other, and looked beyond their own boundaries with distrust and hostility. We, on the contrary, have sprung into national existence in an enlightened and philosophic age, when the different parts of the habitable world, and the various branches of the human family, have been indefatigably studied and made known to each other; and we forego the advantages of our birth, if we do not shake off the national prejudices, as we would the local superstitions, of the old world.

But above all, let us not be influenced by any angry feelings, so far as to shut our eyes to the perception of what is really excellent and amiable in the English character. We are a young people, necessarily an imitative one, and must take our examples and models, in a great degree, from the existing nations of Europe. There is no country more worthy of our study than England. The spirit of her constitution is most analogous to ours. The manners of her people—their intellectual activity—their freedom of opinion—their habits of thinking on those subjects which concern the dearest interests and most sacred charities of private life, are all congenial to the American character; and, in fact, are all intrinsically excellent: for it is in the moral feeling of the people that the deep foundations of British prosperity are laid; and however the superstructure may be time-worn, or overrun by abuses, there must be something solid in the basis, admirable in the materials, and stable in the structure of an edifice that so long has towered unshaken amidst the tempests of the world.

Let it be the pride of our writers, therefore, discarding all feelings of irritation, and disdaining to retaliate the illiberality of British authors, to speak of the English nation without prejudice, and with determined candor. While they rebuke the indiscriminating bigotry with which some of our countrymen admire and imitate everything English, merely because it is English, let them frankly point out what is really worthy of approbation. We may thus place England before us as a perpetual volume of reference, wherein are recorded sound deductions from ages of experience; and while we avoid the errors and absurdities which may have crept into the page, we may draw thence golden maxims of practical wisdom, wherewith to strengthen and to embellish our national character.

## QUESTIONS AND EXERCISES

Exercises preceded by a star are designed for assignment at the discretion of the teacher, or for any student who volunteers.

1. Summarize the main thought of the essay.
2. What are the chief criticisms of America made by English writers? Are they just?
3. Has Irving's prophecy in regard to the necessity of a closer bond of sympathy between England and the United States been increasingly true? Illustrate.

*4. To realize the historical significance of Irving's essay in its bearing on the relation of Great Britain to the United States, read *America and the English Tradition,* an essay by Harry Morgan Ayres, or any other article or book on the subject to be found in your library.

# *BY AN INN FIRE*

## THE PRIDE OF THE VILLAGE

The first tale by the inn fire is the "sentimental" romance of the belle of the village, "blushing and smiling in all the beautiful confusion of girlish diffidence and delight," and her soldier lover.

It has been selected to illustrate Irving's one marked fault—"sentimentalism." Today we would call such phrases as *blushing and smiling . . . beautiful confusion . . . girlish diffidence and delight . . .* "mushy." Such writing has a goody-goody, artificial note about it that repulses the reader. It must be remembered, however, that sentimentalism was characteristic of the period, and Irving but followed a tendency which gave unrestrained expression to the finer emotions of love, honor, sorrow, and reverence by a flood of sighs—blushes—swoons—tears.

In the course of an excursion through one of the remote counties of England, I had struck into one of those cross-roads that lead through the more secluded parts of the country, and stopped one afternoon at a village, the situation of which was beautifully rural and retired. There was an air of primitive simplicity about its inhabitants not to be found in the villages which lie on the great coach-roads. I determined to pass the night there, and having taken an early dinner, strolled out to enjoy the neighboring scenery.

My ramble, as is usually the case with travellers, soon led me to the church, which stood at a little distance from the village. Indeed, it was an object of some curiosity, its old tower being completely overrun with ivy, so that only here and there a jutting buttress, an angle of gray wall, or a fantastically carved ornament, peered through the verdant covering. It was a lovely evening. The early part of the day had been dark and showery, but in the afternoon it had cleared up; and though sullen clouds still hung overhead, yet there was a broad tract of golden sky in the west, from which the setting sun gleamed through the dripping leaves, and lit up all nature with a melancholy smile. It seemed like the parting hour of a good Christian, smiling on the sins and sorrows of the world, and giving, in the serenity of his decline, an assurance that he will rise again in glory.

I had seated myself on a half-sunken tombstone, and was musing, as one is apt to do at this sober-thoughted hour, on past scenes, and early friends,—on those who were distant, and those who were dead,—and indulging in that kind of melancholy fancying, which has in it something sweeter even than pleasure. Every now and then, the stroke of a bell from the neighboring tower fell on my ear; its tones were in unison with the scene, and, instead of jarring, chimed in with my feelings; and it was some time before I recollected that it must be tolling the knell of some new tenant of the tomb.

Presently I saw a funeral train moving across the village green; it wound slowly along a lane; was lost, and reappeared through the breaks of the hedges, until it passed the place where I was sitting. The pall was supported by young girls, dressed in white; and another, about the age of seventeen, walked before, bearing a chaplet[1] of white flowers: a token that the deceased was a young and unmarried female. The corpse was followed by the parents. They were a venerable couple, of the better order of peasantry. The father seemed to repress his feelings; but his fixed eye, contracted brow,

[1] CHAPLET—Garland or wreath.

and deeply furrowed face, showed the struggle that was passing within. His wife hung on his arm, and wept aloud with the convulsive bursts of a mother's sorrow.

I followed the funeral into the church. The bier was placed in the centre aisle, and the chaplet of white flowers, with a pair of white gloves, was hung over the seat which the deceased had occupied.

Every one knows the soul-subduing pathos of the funeral service; for who is so fortunate as never to have followed some one he has loved to the tomb? but when performed over the remains of innocence and beauty, thus laid low in the bloom of existence—what can be more affecting? At that simple, but most solemn consignment of the body to the grave,—"Earth to earth—ashes to ashes—dust to dust,"[2] the tears of the youthful companions of the deceased flowed unrestrained. The father still seemed to struggle with his feelings, and to comfort himself with the assurance, that the dead are blessed which die in the Lord: but the mother only thought of her child as a flower of the field cut down and withered in the midst of its sweetness; she was like Rachel,[3] "mourning over her children, and would not be comforted."

On returning to the inn, I learned the whole story of the deceased. It was a simple one, and such as has often been told. She had been the beauty and pride of the village. Her father had once been an opulent farmer, but was reduced in circumstances. This was an only child, and brought up entirely at home, in the simplicity of rural life. She had been the pupil of the village pastor, the favorite lamb of his little flock. The good man watched over her education with paternal care; it was limited, and suitable to the sphere in which she was to move; for he only sought to make her an ornament to her station in life, not to raise her above it. The tenderness and indulgence of her parents, and the exemption from all ordinary occupations, had fostered a natural grace and delicacy of character that accorded with the fragile loveliness of her form. She appeared like some tender plant of the garden, blooming accidentally amid the hardier natives of the fields.

The superiority of her charms was felt and acknowledged by her companions, but without envy; for it was surpassed by the

---

[2] EARTH . . . DUST—From the funeral service of the Church of England.
[3] RACHEL—See Mathew II, 16–18.

unassuming gentleness and winning kindness of her manners. It might be truly said of her,—

> This is the prettiest low-born lass that ever
> Ran on the green-sward; nothing she does or seems
> But smacks of something greater than herself,
> Too noble for this place.[4]

The village was one of those sequestered spots which still retain some vestiges of old English customs. It had its rural festivals and holiday pastimes, and still kept up some faint observance of the once popular rites of May. These, indeed, had been promoted by its present pastor; who was a lover of old customs, and one of those simple Christians that think their mission fulfilled by promoting joy on earth and good-will among mankind. Under his auspices the May-pole stood from year to year in the centre of the village green; on May-day it was decorated with garlands and streamers; and a queen or lady of the May was appointed, as in former times, to preside at the sports, and distribute the prizes and rewards. The picturesque situation of the village, and the fancifulness of its rustic fêtes, would often attract the notice of casual visitors. Among these, on one May-day, was a young officer, whose regiment had been recently quartered in the neighborhood. He was charmed with the native taste that pervaded this village pageant; but, above all, with the dawning loveliness of the queen of May. It was the village favorite, who was crowned with flowers, and blushing and smiling in all the beautiful confusion of girlish diffidence and delight. The artlessness of rural habits enabled him readily to make her acquaintance; he gradually won his way into her intimacy; and paid his court to her in that unthinking way in which young officers are too apt to trifle with rustic simplicity.

There was nothing in his advances to startle or alarm. He never even talked of love; but there are modes of making it more eloquent than language, and which convey it subtilely and irresistibly to the heart. The beam of the eye, the tone of voice, the thousand tendernesses which emanate from every word, and look, and action—these form the true eloquence of love, and can always be felt and understood, but never described. Can we wonder that they should readily win a heart, young, guileless, and susceptible? As to her,

[4] THIS IS . . . PLACE—See Shakespeare's *The Winter's Tale:* Act IV, Scene 3.

she loved almost unconsciously; she scarcely inquired what was the growing passion that was absorbing every thought and feeling, or what were to be its consequences. She, indeed, looked not to the future. When present, his looks and words occupied her whole attention; when absent, she thought but of what had passed at their recent interview. She would wander with him through the green lanes and rural scenes of the vicinity. He taught her to see new beauties in nature; he talked in the language of polite and cultivated life, and breathed into her ear the witcheries of romance and poetry.

Perhaps there could not have been a passion between the sexes more pure than this innocent girl's. The gallant figure of her youthful admirer, and the splendor of his military attire, might at first have charmed her eye; but it was not these that had captivated her heart. Her attachment had something in it of idolatry; she looked up to him as to a being of a superior order. She felt in his society the enthusiasm of a mind naturally delicate and poetical, and now first awakened to a keen perception of the beautiful and grand. Of the sordid distinctions of rank and fortune, she thought nothing; it was the difference of intellect, of demeanor, of manners, from those of the rustic society to which she had been accustomed, that elevated him in her opinion. She would listen to him with charmed ear and downcast look of mute delight, and her cheek would mantle with enthusiasm: or if ever she ventured a shy glance of timid admiration, it was as quickly withdrawn, and she would sigh and blush at the idea of her comparative unworthiness.

Her lover was equally impassioned; but his passion was mingled with feelings of a coarser nature. He had begun the connection in levity; for he had often heard his brother officers boast of their village conquests, and thought some triumph of the kind necessary to his reputation as a man of spirit. But he was too full of youthful fervor. His heart had not yet been rendered sufficiently cold and selfish by a wandering and a dissipated life; it caught fire from the very flame it sought to kindle; and before he was aware of the nature of his situation he became really in love.

What was he to do? There were the old obstacles which so incessantly occur in these heedless attachments. His rank in life—the prejudices of titled connections—his dependence upon a proud and unyielding father—all forbade him to think of matrimony:—but when he looked down upon this innocent being, so tender and confiding, there was a purity in her manners, a blamelessness in her life, and a beseeching modesty in her looks, that awed down every licentious feeling. In vain did he try to fortify himself, by a thousand heartless examples of men of fashion, and to chill the glow of generous sentiment, with that cold, derisive levity with which he had heard them talk of female virtue; whenever he came into her presence, she was still surrounded by that mysterious, but impassive charm of virgin purity, in whose hallowed sphere no guilty thought can live.

The sudden arrival of orders for the regiment to repair to the continent completed the confusion of his mind. He remained for a short time in a state of the most painful irresolution; he hesitated to communicate the tidings, until the day for marching was at hand; when he gave her the intelligence in the course of an evening ramble.

The idea of parting had never before occurred to her. It broke in at once upon her dream of felicity; she looked upon it as a sudden and insurmountable evil, and wept with the guileless simplicity of a child. He drew her to his bosom and kissed the tears from her soft cheek, nor did he meet with a repulse, for there are moments of mingled sorrow and tenderness which hallow the caresses of affection. He was naturally impetuous, and the sight of beauty apparently yielding in his arms, the confidence of his power over her, and the dread of losing her forever, all conspired to overwhelm his better feelings—he ventured to propose that she should leave her home, and be the companion of his fortunes.

He was quite a novice in seduction, and blushed and faltered at his own baseness; but so innocent of mind was his intended victim, that she was at first at a loss to comprehend his meaning;—and why she should leave her native village and the humble roof of her parents. When at last the nature of his proposal flashed upon her pure mind, the effect was withering. She did not weep—she did not break forth into reproaches—she said not a word—but she shrunk back aghast as from a viper, gave him a look of anguish that pierced to his very soul, and, clasping her hands in agony, fled as if for refuge to her father's cottage.[5]

The officer retired, confounded, humiliated, and repentant. It is uncertain what might have been the result of the conflict of his

[5] This whole page reflects the rank sentimentality of the times.

feelings, had not his thoughts been diverted by the bustle of departure. New scenes, new pleasures, and new companions, soon dissipated his self-reproach, and stifled his tenderness. Yet amidst the stir of camps, the revelries of garrisons, the array of armies, and even the din of battles, his thoughts would sometimes steal back to the scenes of rural quiet and village simplicity—the white cottage—the footpath along the silver brook and up the hawthorn hedge, and the little village maid loitering along it, leaning on his arm and listening to him with eyes beaming with unconscious affection.

The shock which the poor girl had received, in the destruction of all her ideal world, had indeed been cruel. Faintings and hysterics had at first shaken her tender frame, and were succeeded by a settled and pining melancholy. She had beheld from her window the march of the departing troops. She had seen her faithless lover borne off, as if in triumph, amidst the sound of drum and trumpet, and the pomp of arms. She strained a last aching gaze after him, as the morning sun glittered about his figure, and his plume waved in the breeze; he passed away like a bright vision from her sight, and left her all in darkness.

It would be trite to dwell on the particulars of her after story. It was, like other tales of love, melancholy. She avoided society, and wandered out alone in the walks she had most frequented with her lover. She sought, like the stricken deer, to weep in silence and loneliness, and brood over the barbed sorrow that rankled in her soul. Sometimes she would be seen late of an evening sitting in the porch of the village church; and the milkmaids, returning from the fields, would now and then overhear her, singing some plaintive ditty in the hawthorn walk. She became fervent in her devotions at church; and as the old people saw her approach, so wasted away, yet with a hectic bloom, and that hallowed air which melancholy diffuses round the form, they would make way for her, as for something spiritual, and looking after her would shake their heads in gloomy foreboding.

She felt a conviction that she was hastening to the tomb, but looked forward to it as a place of rest. The silver cord that had bound her to existence was loosed, and there seemed to be no more pleasure under the sun. If ever her gentle bosom had entertained resentment against her lover, it was extinguished. She was incapable of angry passions, and in a moment of saddened tenderness she penned him a farewell letter. It was couched in the simplest language, but touching from its very simplicity. She told him that she was dying, and did not conceal from him that his conduct was the cause. She even depicted the sufferings which she had experienced; but concluded with saying that she could not die in peace, until she had sent him her forgiveness and her blessing.

By degrees her strength declined, she could no longer leave the cottage. She could only totter to the window, where, propped up in her chair, it was her enjoyment to sit all day and look out upon the landscape. Still she uttered no complaint, nor imparted to any one the malady that was preying on her heart. She never even mentioned her lover's name; but would lay her head on her mother's bosom and weep in silence. Her poor parents hung, in mute anxiety, over this fading blossom of their hopes, still flattering themselves that it might again revive to freshness, and that the bright unearthly bloom which sometimes flushed her cheek, might be the promise of returning health.

In this way she was seated between them one Sunday afternoon; her hands were clasped in theirs, the lattice was thrown open, and the soft air that stole in, brought with it the fragrance of the clustering honeysuckle, which her own hands had trained round the window.

Her father had just been reading a chapter in the Bible; it spoke of the vanity of worldly things and of the joys of heaven; it seemed to have diffused comfort and serenity through her bosom. Her eye was fixed on the distant village church—the bell had tolled for the evening service—the last villager was lagging into the porch—and everything had sunk into that hallowed stillness peculiar to the day of rest. Her parents were gazing on her with yearning hearts. Sickness and sorrow, which pass so roughly over some faces, had given to hers the expression of a seraph's.[6] A tear trembled in her soft blue eye. Was she thinking of her faithless lover?—or were her thoughts wandering to that distant churchyard, into whose bosom she might soon be gathered?

Suddenly the clang of hoofs was heard—a horseman galloped to the cottage—he dismounted before the window—the poor girl gave a faint exclamation and sunk back in her chair:—it was her repentant lover! He rushed into the house and flew to clasp her to his bosom; but her wasted form—her deathlike countenance—so wan,

[6] SERAPH'S—Angel's.

and yet so lovely in its desolation—smote him to the soul, and he threw himself in agony at her feet. She was too faint to rise—she attempted to extend her trembling hand—her lips moved as if she spoke, but no word was articulated—she looked down upon him with a smile of unutterable tenderness, and closed her eyes forever!

Such are the particulars which I gathered of this village story. They are but scanty, and I am conscious have little novelty to recommend them. In the present rage also for strange incident and high-seasoned narrative, they may appear trite and insignificant, but they interested me strongly at the time; and, taken in connection with the affecting ceremony which I had just witnessed, left a deeper impression on my mind than many circumstances of a more striking nature. I have passed through the place since, and visited the church again from a better motive than mere curiosity. It was a wintry evening; the trees were stripped of their foliage; the churchyard looked naked and mournful, and the wind rustled coldly through the dry grass. Evergreens, however, had been planted about the grave of the village favorite, and osiers were bent over it to keep the turf uninjured. The church door was open and I stepped in. There hung the chaplet of flowers and the gloves, as on the day of the funeral: the flowers were withered, it is true, but care seemed to have been taken that no dust should soil their whiteness. I have seen many monuments, where art has exhausted its powers to awaken the sympathy of the spectator; but I have met with none that spoke more touchingly to my heart, than this simple, but delicate memento of departed innocence.

## QUESTIONS AND EXERCISES

Exercises preceded by a star are designed for assignment at the discretion of the teacher, or for any student who volunteers.

1. From your reading of the story give your own definition of *sentiment* as opposed to *sentimentalism*.
2. Comment on the following passage telling of the lover's arrival: "She was too faint to rise—she attempted to extend her trembling hand—her lips moved as if she spoke . . . etc."
3. Could the story be told in such a way as to arouse the true emotion of "sorrow"?
4. What current short-story magazines and books come under the classification of "sentimental"? What danger results from reading them? How do you explain their popularity today? Do you or do you not enjoy this style of reading? Why?

*5. Write an imaginary incident which in your opinion has true pathos.

## THE INN KITCHEN

There are two places in the world best for story-telling: a campfire and a hearthside. The magic of flames . . . the fantastic leap of shadows . . . the play of half-light over the faces of the listeners . . . create a scene at once familiar and unforgettable.

Irving uses this *Sketch* to set the atmosphere for his story of *The Spectre Bridegroom.* In itself this very brief sketch is a charming half-tone of a cheery inn kitchen on a night of storm in the Netherlands.

*Shall I not take mine ease in mine inn?*

*Falstaff.*[1]

During a journey that I once made through the Netherlands, I arrived one evening at the *Pomme d'Or,*[2] the principal inn of a small Flemish village. It was after the hour of the *table d'hôte,*[3] so that I was obliged to make a solitary supper from the relics of its ampler board. The weather was chilly; I was seated alone in one end of a great gloomy dining-room, and my repast being over, I had the prospect before me of a long dull evening, without any visible means of enlivening it. I summoned mine host, and requested something to read; he brought me the whole literary stock of his household, a Dutch family Bible, an almanac in the same language, and a number of old Paris newspapers. As I sat dozing over one of the latter, reading old news and stale criticisms, my ear was now and then struck with bursts of laughter which seemed to proceed from the kitchen. Every one that has travelled on the Continent must know how favorite a resort the kitchen of a country inn is to the middle and inferior order of travellers; particularly in that equivocal kind of weather when a fire becomes agreeable toward evening. I threw aside the newspaper, and explored my way to the kitchen, to take a peep at the group that appeared to be so merry. It was composed partly of travellers who had arrived some hours before in a diligence,[4] and partly of the usual attendants and hangers-on of inns. They were seated round a great burnished stove, that might have been mistaken for an altar, at which they were worshipping. It was covered with various kitchen vessels of resplendent brightness; among which steamed and hissed a huge

[1] Falstaff—This is a quotation from Shakespeare's *King Henry IV,* Part I, Act III, Scene 3.

[2] *Pomme d'Or* (pôm d'ôr)—Golden Apple.

[3] *Table d'hôte* (tȧ-blĕ-dō't)—A regular meal served at a fixed price.

[4] Diligence—Stage-coach.

copper tea-kettle. A large lamp threw a strong mass of light upon the group, bringing out many odd features in strong relief. Its yellow rays partially illumined the spacious kitchen, dying duskily away into remote corners except where they settled in mellow radiance on the broad side of a flitch of bacon, or were reflected back from well-scoured utensils that gleamed from the midst of obscurity. A strapping Flemish lass, with long golden pendants in her ears and a necklace with a golden heart suspended to it, was the presiding priestess of the temple.

Many of the company were furnished with pipes, and most of them with some kind of evening potation. I found their mirth was occasioned by anecdotes which a little swarthy Frenchman, with a dry weazen face and large whiskers, was giving of his love adventures; at the end of each of which there was one of those bursts of honest unceremonious laughter, in which a man indulges in that temple of true liberty, an inn.

As I had no better mode of getting through a tedious blustering evening, I took my seat near the stove, and listened to a variety of traveller's tales, some very extravagant, and most very dull. All of them, however, have faded from my treacherous memory, except one, which I will endeavor to relate. I fear, however, it derived its chief zest from the manner in which it was told, and the peculiar air and appearance of the narrator. He was a corpulent old Swiss, who had the look of a veteran traveller. He was dressed in a tarnished green travelling-jacket, with a broad belt round his waist, and a pair of overalls with buttons from the hips to the ankles. He was of a full, rubicund countenance, with a double chin, aquiline nose, and a pleasant, twinkling eye. His hair was light, and curled from under an old green velvet travelling-cap, stuck on one side of his head. He was interrupted more than once by the arrival of guests, or the remarks of his auditors; and paused, now and then, to replenish his pipe; at which times he had generally a roguish leer, and a sly joke, for the buxom kitchen maid.

I wish my readers could imagine the old fellow lolling in a huge arm-chair, one arm a-kimbo,[5] the other holding a curiously twisted tobacco-pipe, formed of genuine *écume de mer,*[6] decorated with

---

[5] A-KIMBO—Hand on hip, elbow outward.

[6] *Écume de mer* (ā-küm-dĕ-mâr)—Meerschaum, a clay-like mineral light enough to float on water, and hence "sea foam," the German of which is *Meer-Schaum.*

silver chain and silken tassel—his head cocked on one side, and a whimsical cut of the eye occasionally, as he related the following story.

### QUESTIONS AND EXERCISES

1. Give a "bird's-eye" view of the inn kitchen.
2. Picture the story-teller.
3. What anticipation of the story to follow does this sketch give? Where have you seen this introductory "device" used before in *The Sketch Book?*

## THE SPECTRE BRIDEGROOM[1]

### A Traveller's Tale

On the summit of one of the heights of the Odenwald, a wild and romantic tract of Upper Germany, that lies not far from the confluence of the Main and the Rhine, there stood, many, many years since, the castle of the Baron Von Landshort. It is now quite fallen to decay, and almost buried among beech trees and dark firs; above which, however, its old watch-tower may still be seen struggling, like the former possessor I have mentioned, to carry a high head, and look down upon the neighboring country.

The Baron was a dry branch of the great family of Katzenellenbogen,* and inherited the relics of the property, and all the pride of his ancestors. Though the warlike disposition of his predecessors had much impaired the family possessions, yet the Baron still endeavored to keep up some show of former state. The times were peaceable, and the German nobles, in general, had abandoned their inconvenient old castles, perched like eagles' nests among the mountains, and had built more convenient residences in the valleys; still the Baron remained proudly drawn up in his little fortress, cherishing with hereditary inveteracy all the old family feuds; so that he was on ill terms with some of his nearest neighbors, on account of disputes that had happened between their great-great-grandfathers.

The Baron had but one child, a daughter; but Nature, when she grants but one child, always compensates by making it a prodigy;

* *I.e.,* Cat's-Elbow. The name of a family of those parts very powerful in former times. The appellation, we are told, was given in compliment to a peerless dame of the family, celebrated for her fine arm.

---

[1] *The Spectre Bridegroom*—This is the third tale of Irving's that closely approaches the short story form. *Rip Van Winkle* and *The Legend of Sleepy Hollow* have been omitted because they are so often read in the elementary grades.

and so it was with the daughter of the Baron. All the nurses, gossips, and country cousins assured her father that she had not her equal for beauty in all Germany; and who should know better than they? She had, moreover, been brought up with great care, under the superintendence of two maiden aunts, who had spent some years of their early life at one of the little German courts, and were skilled in all the branches of knowledge necessary to the education of a fine lady. Under their instructions, she became a miracle of accomplishments. By the time she was eighteen she could embroider to admiration, and had worked whole histories of the saints in tapestry, with such strength of expression in their countenances, that they looked like so many souls in purgatory. She could read without great difficulty, and had spelled her way through several church legends, and almost all the chivalric wonders of the *Heldenbuch.*[2] She had even made considerable proficiency in writing, could sign her own name without missing a letter, and so legibly, that her aunts could read it without spectacles. She excelled in making little elegant good-for-nothing lady-like knickknacks of all kinds; was versed in the most abstruse dancing of the day; played a number of airs on the harp and guitar; and knew all the tender ballads of the Minne-lieders[3] by heart.

Her aunts, too, having been great flirts and coquettes in their younger days, were admirably calculated to be vigilant guardians and strict censors of the conduct of their niece; for there is no duenna[4] so rigidly prudent, and inexorably decorous, as a superannuated coquette. She was rarely suffered out of their sight; never went beyond the domains of the castle, unless well attended, or rather well watched; had continual lectures read to her about strict decorum and implicit obedience; and as to the men—pah! she was taught to hold them at such a distance and in such absolute distrust, that, unless properly authorized, she would not have cast a glance upon the handsomest cavalier in the world—no, not if he were even dying at her feet.

The good effects of this system were wonderfully apparent. The young lady was a pattern of docility and correctness. While others

[2] *Heldenbuch*—Book of Heroes. Collection of 13th and 14th century poems, including the famous *Niebelungen* epic.

[3] MINNE-LIEDERS—Love songs. Irving probably means *Minnesingers,* the wandering minstrels of Germany in the Middle Ages.

[4] DUENNA—Chaperon.

were wasting their sweetness in the glare of the world, and liable to be plucked and thrown aside by every hand, she was coyly blooming into fresh and lovely womanhood under the protection of those immaculate spinsters, like a rose-bud blushing forth among guardian thorns. Her aunts looked upon her with pride and exultation, and vaunted that though all the other young ladies in the world might go astray, yet, thank Heaven, nothing of the kind could happen to the heiress of Katzenellenbogen.

But, however scantily the Baron Von Landshort might be provided with children, his household was by no means a small one, for Providence had enriched him with abundance of poor relations. They, one and all, possessed the affectionate disposition common to humble relatives; were wonderfully attached to the Baron, and took every possible occasion to come in swarms and enliven the castle. All family festivals were commemorated by these good people at the Baron's expense; and when they were filled with good cheer, they would declare that there was nothing on earth so delightful as these family meetings, these jubilees of the heart.

The Baron, though a small man, had a large soul, and it swelled with satisfaction at the consciousness of being the greatest man in the little world about him. He loved to tell long stories about the dark old warriors whose portraits looked grimly down from the walls around, and he found no listeners equal to those that fed at his expense. He was much given to the marvellous, and a firm believer in all those supernatural tales with which every mountain and valley in Germany abounds. The faith of his guests exceeded even his own: they listened to every tale of wonder with open eyes and mouth, and never failed to be astonished, even though repeated for the hundredth time. Thus lived the Baron Von Landshort, the oracle of his table, the absolute monarch of his little territory, and happy, above all things, in the persuasion that he was the wisest man of the age.

At the time of which my story treats, there was a great family-gathering at the castle, on an affair of the utmost importance:—it was to receive the destined bridegroom of the Baron's daughter. A negotiation had been carried on between the father and an old nobleman of Bavaria, to unite the dignity of their houses by the marriage of their children. The preliminaries had been conducted with proper punctilio. The young people were betrothed without seeing each other, and the time was appointed for the marriage ceremony. The young Count Von Altenburg had been recalled from the army for the purpose, and was actually on his way to the Baron's to receive his bride. Missives had even been received from him, from Würtzburg, where he was accidentally detained, mentioning the day and hour when he might be expected to arrive.

The castle was in a tumult of preparation to give him a suitable welcome. The fair bride had been decked out with uncommon care. The two aunts had superintended her toilet, and quarreled the whole morning about every article of her dress. The young lady had taken advantage of their contest to follow the bent of her own taste; and fortunately it was a good one. She looked as lovely as youthful bridegroom could desire; and the flutter of expectation heightened the lustre of her charms.

The suffusions that mantled her face and neck, the gentle heaving of the bosom, the eye now and then lost in reverie, all betrayed the soft tumult that was going on in her little heart. The aunts were continually hovering around her; for maiden aunts are apt to take great interest in affairs of this nature; they were giving her a world of staid counsel how to deport herself, what to say, and in what manner to receive the expected lover.

The Baron was no less busied in preparations. He had in truth nothing exactly to do; but he was naturally a fuming, bustling little man, and could not remain passive when all the world was in a hurry. He worried from top to bottom of the castle with an air of infinite anxiety; he continually called the servants from their work to exhort them to be diligent, and buzzed about every hall and chamber, as idly restless and importunate as a blue-bottle fly of a warm summer's day.

In the mean time, the fatted calf had been killed; the forests had rung with the clamor of the huntsmen; the kitchen was crowded with good cheer; the cellars had yielded up whole oceans of *Rhein-wein* and *Ferne-wein*,[5] and even the great Heidelberg tun[6] had been laid under contribution. Everything was ready to receive the distinguished guest with *Saus und Braus*[7] in the true spirit of German

---

[5] *Rhein-wein . . . Ferne-wein* (rīn′vīn . . . fĕr′nĕ-vīn)—Rhine wine and old wine.
[6] Heidelberg tun—Famous cask in Heidelberg Castle holding 800 hogsheads.
[7] *Saus . . . Braus* (sous . . . brous)—Mirth and revelry.

hospitality—but the guest delayed to make his appearance. Hour rolled after hour. The sun, that had poured his downward rays upon the rich forest of the Odenwald, now just gleamed along the summits of the mountains. The Baron mounted the highest tower, and strained his eyes in hope of catching a distant sight of the Count and his attendants. Once he thought he beheld them; the sound of horns came floating from the valley, prolonged by the mountain echoes: a number of horsemen were seen far below, slowly advancing along the road; but when they had nearly reached the foot of the mountain, they suddenly struck off in a different direction. The last ray of sunshine departed—the bats began to flit by in the twilight—the road grew dimmer and dimmer to the view: and nothing appeared stirring in it but now and then a peasant lagging homeward from his labor.

While the old castle of Landshort was in this state of perplexity, a very interesting scene was transacting in a different part of the Odenwald.

The young Count Von Altenburg was tranquilly pursuing his route in that sober jog-trot way in which a man travels toward matrimony when his friends have taken all the trouble and uncertainty of courtship off his hands, and a bride is waiting for him, as certainly as a dinner, at the end of his journey. He had encountered at Würtzburg a youthful companion in arms, with whom he had seen some service on the frontiers; Hermann Von Starkenfaust, one of the stoutest hands and worthiest hearts of German chivalry, who was now returning from the army. His father's castle was not far distant from the old fortress of Landshort, although an hereditary feud rendered the families hostile, and strangers to each other.

In the warm-hearted moment of recognition the young friends related all their past adventures and fortunes, and the Count gave the whole history of his intended nuptials with a young lady whom he had never seen, but of whose charms he had received the most enrapturing descriptions.

As the route of the friends lay in the same direction, they agreed to perform the rest of their journey together; and that they might do it the more leisurely, set off from Würtzburg at an early hour, the Count having given directions for his retinue to follow and overtake him.

They beguiled their wayfaring with recollections of their military scenes and adventures; but the Count was apt to be a little tedious, now and then, about the reputed charms of his bride, and the felicity that awaited him.

In this way they had entered among the mountains of the Odenwald, and were traversing one of its most lonely and thickly wooded passes. It is well known that the forests of Germany have always been as much infested by robbers as its castles by spectres; and at this time, the former were particularly numerous, from the hordes of disbanded soldiers wandering about the country. It will not appear extraordinary, therefore, that the cavaliers were attacked by a gang of these stragglers, in the midst of the forest. They defended themselves with bravery, but were nearly overpowered when the Count's retinue arrived to their assistance. At sight of them the robbers fled, but not until the Count had received a mortal wound. He was slowly and carefully conveyed back to the city of Würtzburg, and a friar summoned from a neighboring convent, who was famous for his skill in administering to both soul and body. But half of his skill was superfluous; the moments of the unfortunate Count were numbered.

With his dying breath he entreated his friend to repair instantly to the castle of Landshort, and explain the fatal cause of his not keeping his appointment with his bride. Though not the most ardent of lovers, he was one of the most punctilious of men, and appeared earnestly solicitous that his mission should be speedily and courteously executed. "Unless this is done," said he, "I shall not sleep quietly in my grave!" He repeated these last words with peculiar solemnity. A request, at a moment so impressive, admitted no hesitation. Starkenfaust endeavored to soothe him to calmness; promised faithfully to execute his wish, and gave him his hand in solemn pledge. The dying man pressed it in acknowledgment, but soon lapsed into delirium—raved about his bride—his engagements—his plighted word; ordered his horse, that he might ride to the castle of Landshort, and expired in the fancied act of vaulting into the saddle.

Starkenfaust bestowed a sigh and a soldier's tear on the untimely fate of his comrade; and then pondered on the awkward mission he had undertaken. His heart was heavy, and his head perplexed; for he was to present himself an unbidden guest among hostile people, and to damp their festivity with tidings fatal to their hopes.

Still there were certain whisperings of curiosity in his bosom to see this far-famed beauty of Katzenellenbogen, so cautiously shut up from the world; for he was a passionate admirer of the sex, and there was a dash of eccentricity and enterprise in his character, that made him fond of all singular adventure.

Previous to his departure, he made all due arrangements with the holy fraternity of the convent for the funeral solemnities of his friend, who was to be buried in the cathedral of Würtzburg, near some of his illustrious relatives; and the mourning retinue of the Count took charge of his remains.

It is now high time that we should return to the ancient family of Katzenellenbogen, who were impatient for their guest, and still more for their dinner; and to the worthy little Baron, whom we left airing himself on the watch-tower.

Night closed in, but still no guest arrived. The Baron descended from the tower in despair. The banquet, which had been delayed from hour to hour, could no longer be postponed. The meats were already overdone; the cook in an agony; and the whole household had the look of a garrison that had been reduced by famine. The Baron was obliged reluctantly to give orders for the feast without the presence of the guest. All were seated at table, and just on the point of commencing, when the sound of a horn from without the gate gave notice of the approach of a stranger. Another long blast filled the old courts of the castle with its echoes, and was answered by the warder from the walls. The Baron hastened to receive his future son-in-law.

The drawbridge had been let down, and the stranger was before the gate. He was a tall, gallant cavalier, mounted on a black steed. His countenance was pale, but he had a beaming, romantic eye, and an air of stately melancholy. The Baron was a little mortified that he should have come in this simple, solitary style. His dignity for a moment was ruffled, and he felt disposed to consider it a want of proper respect for the important occasion, and the important family with which he was to be connected. He pacified himself, however, with the conclusion that it must have been youthful impatience which had induced him thus to spur on sooner than his attendants.

"I am sorry," said the stranger, "to break in upon you thus unseasonably—"

Here the Baron interrupted him with a world of compliments and greetings; for, to tell the truth, he prided himself upon his courtesy and eloquence. The stranger attempted, once or twice, to stem the torrent of words, but in vain; so he bowed his head and suffered it to flow on. By the time the Baron had come to a pause, they had reached the inner court of the castle; and the stranger was again about to speak, when he was once more interrupted by the appearance of the female part of the family, leading forth the shrinking and blushing bride. He gazed on her for a moment as one entranced; it seemed as if his whole soul beamed forth in the gaze, and rested upon that lovely form. One of the maiden aunts whispered something in her ear; she made an effort to speak; her moist blue eye was timidly raised, gave a shy glance of inquiry on the stranger, and was cast again to the ground. The words died away; but there was a sweet smile playing about her lips, and a soft dimpling of the cheek, that showed her glance had not been unsatisfactory. It was impossible for a girl of the fond age of eighteen, highly predisposed for love and matrimony, not to be pleased with so gallant a cavalier.

The late hour at which the guest had arrived left no time for parley. The Baron was peremptory, and deferred all particular conversation until the morning, and led the way to the untasted banquet.

It was served up in the great hall of the castle. Around the walls hung the hard-favored portraits of the heroes of the house of Katzenellenbogen, and the trophies which they had gained in the field and in the chase. Hacked corselets,[8] splintered jousting spears, and tattered banners were mingled with the spoils of sylvan warfare: the jaws of the wolf, and the tusks of the boar, grinned horribly among cross-bows and battle-axes, and a huge pair of antlers branched immediately over the head of the youthful bridegroom.

The cavalier took but little notice of the company or the entertainment. He scarcely tasted the banquet, but seemed absorbed in admiration of his bride. He conversed in a low tone, that could not be overheard—for the language of love is never loud; but where is the female ear so dull that it cannot catch the softest whisper of the lover? There was a mingled tenderness and gravity in his

[8] Corselets—Chain armor.

manner, that appeared to have a powerful effect upon the young lady. Her color came and went, as she listened with deep attention. Now and then she made some blushing reply, and when his eye was turned away, she would steal a sidelong glance at his romantic countenance, and heave a gentle sigh of tender happiness. It was evident that the young couple were completely enamored. The aunts, who were deeply versed in the mysteries of the heart, declared that they had fallen in love with each other at first sight.

The feast went on merrily, or at least noisily, for the guests were all blessed with those keen appetites that attend upon light purses and mountain air. The Baron told his best and longest stories, and never had he told them so well or with such great effect. If there was any thing marvellous, his auditors were lost in astonishment; and if any thing facetious, they were sure to laugh exactly in the right place. The Baron, it is true, like most great men, was too dignified to utter any joke but a dull one; it was always enforced, however, by a bumper of excellent Hochheimer;[9] and even a dull joke, at one's own table, served up with jolly old wine, is irresistible. Many good things were said by poorer and keener wits, that would not bear repeating, except on similar occasions; many sly speeches whispered in ladies' ears that almost convulsed them with suppressed laughter; and a song or two roared out by a poor, but merry and broad-faced cousin of the Baron that absolutely made the maiden aunts hold up their fans.

Amidst all this revelry, the stranger guest maintained a most singular and unseasonable gravity. His countenance assumed a deeper cast of dejection as the evening advanced, and, strange as it may appear, even the Baron's jokes seemed only to render him the more melancholy. At times he was lost in thought, and at times there was a perturbed and restless wandering of the eye that bespoke a mind but ill at ease. His conversations with the bride became more and more earnest and mysterious. Lowering clouds began to steal over the fair serenity of her brow, and tremors to run through her tender frame.

All this could not escape the notice of the company. Their gayety was chilled by the unaccountable gloom of the bridegroom; their spirits were infected; whispers and glances were interchanged,

[9] HOCHHEIMER—A famous Rhine wine.

accompanied by shrugs and dubious shakes of the head. The song and the laugh grew less and less frequent; there were dreary pauses in the conversation, which were at length succeeded by wild tales, and supernatural legends. One dismal story produced another still more dismal, and the Baron nearly frightened some of the ladies into hysterics with the history of the goblin horseman that carried away the fair Leonora[10]—a dreadful story, which has since been put into excellent verse, and is read and believed by all the world.

The bridegroom listened to this tale with profound attention. He kept his eyes steadily fixed on the Baron, and as the story drew to a close, began gradually to rise from his seat, growing taller and taller, until, in the Baron's entranced eye, he seemed almost to tower into a giant. The moment the tale was finished, he heaved a deep sigh, and took a solemn farewell of the company. They were all amazement. The Baron was perfectly thunderstruck.

"What! going to leave the castle at midnight? why, every thing was prepared for his reception; a chamber was ready for him if he wished to retire."

The stranger shook his head mournfully and mysteriously; "I must lay my head in a different chamber to-night!"

There was something in this reply, and the tone in which it was uttered, that made the Baron's heart misgive him; but he rallied his forces, and repeated his hospitable entreaties.

The stranger shook his head silently, but positively, at every offer; and, waving his farewell to the company, stalked slowly out of the hall. The maiden aunts were absolutely petrified—the bride hung her head, and a tear stole to her eye.

The Baron followed the stranger to the great court of the castle, where the black charger stood pawing the earth, and snorting with impatience. When they had reached the portal, whose deep archway was dimly lighted by a cresset,[11] the stranger paused, and addressed the Baron in a hollow tone of voice which the vaulted roof rendered still more sepulchral. "Now that we are alone," said he, "I will impart to you the reason of my going. I have a solemn, an indispensable engagement—"

---

[10] LEONORA—Heroine of a popular ballad. Her dead lover appeared to her as a goblin horseman and carried her off.

[11] CRESSET—Ancient lantern made by burning a coil of tarred rope in an iron cup.

"Why," said the Baron, "cannot you send some one in your place?"

"It admits of no substitute—I must attend it in person—I must away to Würtzburg cathedral—"

"Ay," said the Baron, plucking up spirit, "but not until to-morrow—to-morrow you shall take your bride there."

"No! no!" replied the stranger, with ten-fold solemnity, "my engagement is with no bride—the worms! the worms expect me! I am a dead man—I have been slain by robbers—my body lies at Würtzburg—at midnight I am to be buried—the grave is waiting for me—I must keep my appointment!"

He sprang on his black charger, dashed over the drawbridge, and the clattering of his horse's hoofs was lost in the whistling of the night-blast.

The Baron returned to the hall in the utmost consternation, and related what had passed. Two ladies fainted outright; others sickened at the idea of having banqueted with a spectre. It was the opinion of some, that this might be the wild huntsman famous in German legend. Some talked of mountain sprites, of wood-demons, and of other supernatural beings, with which the good people of Germany have been so grievously harassed since time immemorial. One of the poor relations ventured to suggest that it might be some sportive evasion of the young cavalier, and that the very gloominess of the caprice seemed to accord with so melancholy a personage. This, however, drew on him the indignation of the whole company, and especially of the Baron, who looked upon him as little better than an infidel; so that he was fain to abjure his heresy as speedily as possible, and come into the faith of the true believers.

But whatever may have been the doubts entertained, they were completely put to an end by the arrival, next day, of regular missives, confirming the intelligence of the young Count's murder, and his interment in Würtzburg cathedral.

The dismay at the castle may well be imagined. The Baron shut himself up in his chamber. The guests, who had come to rejoice with him could not think of abandoning him in his distress. They wandered about the courts, or collected in groups in the hall, shaking their heads and shrugging their shoulders at the troubles of so good a man; and sat longer than ever at table, and ate and drank more stoutly than ever, by way of keeping up their spirits. But the situation of the widowed bride was the most pitiable. To have lost a husband before she had even embraced him—and such a husband! if the very spectre could be so gracious and noble, what must have been the living man! She filled the house with lamentations.

On the night of the second day of her widowhood, she had retired to her chamber, accompanied by one of her aunts, who insisted on sleeping with her. The aunt, who was one of the best tellers of ghost stories in all Germany, had just been recounting one of her longest, and had fallen asleep in the very midst of it. The chamber was remote, and overlooked a small garden. The niece lay pensively gazing at the beams of the rising moon, as they trembled on the leaves of an aspen tree before the lattice. The castle clock had just tolled midnight, when a soft strain of music stole up from the garden. She rose hastily from her bed, and stepped lightly to the window. A tall figure stood among the shadows of the trees. As it raised its head, a beam of moonlight fell upon the countenance. Heaven and earth! she beheld the Spectre Bridegroom! A loud shriek at that moment burst upon her ear, and her aunt, who had been awakened by the music, and had followed her silently to the window, fell into her arms. When she looked again, the spectre had disappeared.

Of the two females, the aunt now required the most soothing, for she was perfectly beside herself with terror. As to the young lady, there was something, even in the spectre of her lover, that seemed endearing. There was still the semblance of manly beauty; and though the shadow of a man is but little calculated to satisfy the affections of a love-sick girl, yet, where the substance is not to be had, even that is consoling. The aunt declared she would never sleep in that chamber again; the niece, for once, was refractory, and declared as strongly that she would sleep in no other in the castle: the consequence was, that she had to sleep in it alone; but she drew a promise from her aunt not to relate the story of the spectre, lest she should be denied the only melancholy pleasure left her on earth—that of inhabiting the chamber over which the guardian shade of her lover kept its nightly vigils.

How long the good old lady would have observed this promise is uncertain, for she dearly loved to talk of the marvellous, and there is a triumph in being the first to tell a frightful story; it is, however, still quoted in the neighborhood, as a memorable instance of female secrecy, that she kept it to herself for a whole week; when she was suddenly absolved from all further restraint, by intelligence brought to the breakfast table one morning that the young lady was not to be found. Her room was empty—the bed had not been slept in—the window was open—and the bird had flown!

The astonishment and concern with which the intelligence was received, can only be imagined by those who have witnessed the agitation which the mishaps of a great man cause among his friends. Even the poor relations paused for a moment from the indefatigable labors of the trencher; when the aunt, who had at first been struck speechless, wrung her hands and shrieked out, "The goblin! the goblin! she's carried away by the goblin."

In a few words she related the fearful scene of the garden, and concluded that the spectre must have carried off his bride. Two of the domestics corroborated the opinion, for they had heard the clattering of a horse's hoofs down the mountain about midnight, and had no doubt that it was the spectre on his black charger, bearing her away to the tomb. All present were struck with the direful probability; for events of the kind are extremely common in Germany, as many well-authenticated histories bear witness.

What a lamentable situation was that of the poor Baron! What a heart-rending dilemma for a fond father, and a member of the great family of Katzenellenbogen! His only daughter had either been rapt away to the grave, or he was to have some wood-demon for a son-in-law, and perchance, a troop of goblin grand-children. As usual, he was completely bewildered, and all the castle in an uproar. The men were ordered to take horse, and scour every road and path and glen of the Odenwald. The Baron himself had just drawn on his jack-boots, girded on his sword, and was about to mount his steed to sally forth on the doubtful quest, when he was brought to a pause by a new apparition. A lady was seen approaching the castle, mounted on a palfrey, attended by a cavalier on horseback. She galloped up to the gate, sprang from her horse, and falling at the Baron's feet embraced his knees. It was his lost daughter and her companion—the Spectre Bridegroom! The Baron was astounded. He looked at his daughter, then at the Spectre, and almost doubted the evidence of his senses. The latter, too, was wonderfully improved in his appearance since his visit to the world of spirits. His dress was splendid, and set off a noble figure of manly symmetry. He was no longer pale and melancholy. His fine countenance was flushed with the glow of youth, and joy rioted in his large dark eye.

The mystery was soon cleared up. The cavalier (for in truth as you must have known all the while, he was no goblin) announced himself as Sir Hermann Von Starkenfaust. He related his adventure with the young Count. He told how he had hastened to the castle to deliver the unwelcome tidings, but that the eloquence of the Baron had interrupted him in every attempt to tell his tale. How the sight of the bride had completely captivated him, and that to pass a few hours near her, he had tacitly suffered the mistake to continue. How he had been sorely perplexed in what way to make a decent retreat, until the Baron's goblin stories had suggested his eccentric exit. How, fearing the feudal hostility of the family, he had repeated his visits by stealth—had haunted the garden beneath the young lady's window—had wooed—had won—had borne away in triumph—and, in a word, had wedded the fair.

Under any other circumstances the Baron would have been inflexible, for he was tenacious of paternal authority, and devoutly obstinate in all family feuds; but he loved his daughter; he had lamented her as lost; he rejoiced to find her still alive; and, though her husband was of a hostile house, yet, thank Heaven, he was not a goblin. There was something, it must be acknowledged, that did not exactly accord with his notions of strict veracity, in the joke the knight had passed upon him of his being a dead man; but several old friends present, who had served in the wars, assured him that every stratagem was excusable in love, and that the cavalier was entitled to especial privilege, having lately served as a trooper.

Matters, therefore, were happily arranged. The Baron pardoned the young couple on the spot. The revels at the castle were resumed. The poor relations overwhelmed this new member of the family with loving kindness; he was so gallant, so generous—and so rich. The aunts, it is true, were somewhat scandalized that their system of strict seclusion and passive obedience should be so badly exemplified, but attributed it all to their negligence in not having the windows grated. One of them was particularly mortified at having her marvellous story marred, and that the only spectre she had ever seen should turn out a counterfeit; but the niece seemed perfectly happy at having found him substantial flesh and blood—and so the story ends.

## QUESTIONS AND EXERCISES

Exercises preceded by a star are designed for assignment at the discretion of the teacher, or for any student who volunteers.

1. Do you like the story? Give your reasons.
2. On a map of Germany locate the following places mentioned in this story: junction of *Main* and *Rhine Rivers, Bavaria, Würtzburg, Heidelberg.*
3. How successful is Irving in building up atmosphere for *The Spectre Bridegroom?* Contrast the atmosphere of this story with that developed in the Christmas *Sketches.*

*4. Report on *Rip Van Winkle,* or *The Legend of Sleepy Hollow,* comparing it with *The Spectre Bridegroom.* Which do you consider the better story?

## L'ENVOY

In conclusion, Irving sums it up: there will be some *Sketches* here you will like, some you will reject. He has written for your enjoyment. The fire has glimmered low, the genial gentleman in the armchair, Washington Irving, must depart. Remember—he tried to entertain you. *Auf Wiedersehen!*[1] Good-bye till we meet again.

In concluding a second volume of the *Sketch Book,* the Author cannot but express his deep sense of the indulgence with which his first has been received, and of the liberal disposition that has been evinced to treat him with kindness as a stranger. Even the critics, whatever may be said of them by others, he has found to be a singularly gentle and good-natured race; it is true that each has in turn objected to some one or two articles, and that these individual exceptions, taken in the aggregate, would amount almost to a total condemnation of his work; but then he has been consoled by observing, that what one has particularly censured, another has as particularly praised: and thus, the encomiums being set off against the objections, he finds his work, upon the whole, commended far beyond its deserts.

He is aware that he runs a risk of forfeiting much of this kind favor by not following the counsel that has been liberally bestowed upon him; for where abundance of valuable advice is given gratis, it may seem a man's own fault if he should go astray. He can only say, in his vindication, that he faithfully determined, for a time,

[1] *Auf Wiedersehen* (ouf vē'dĕr-zā-ĕn)

to govern himself in his second volume by the opinions passed upon his first; but he was soon brought to a stand by the contrariety of excellent counsel. One kindly advised him to avoid the ludicrous; another to shun the pathetic; a third assured him that he was tolerable at description, but cautioned him to leave narrative alone; while a fourth declared that he had a very pretty knack at turning a story, and was really entertaining when in a pensive mood, but was grievously mistaken if he imagined himself to possess a spirit of humor.

Thus perplexed by the advice of his friends, who each in turn closed some particular path, but left him all the world beside to range in, he found that to follow all their counsels would, in fact, be to stand still. He remained for a time sadly embarrassed; when all at once the thought struck him to ramble on as he had begun; that his work being miscellaneous, and written for different humors, it could not be expected that any one would be pleased with the whole; but that if it should contain something to suit each reader, his end would be completely answered. Few guests sit down to a varied table with an equal appetite for every dish. One has an elegant horror of a roasted pig; another holds a curry or a devil in utter abomination; a third cannot tolerate the ancient flavor of venison and wild fowl; and a fourth, of truly masculine stomach, looks with sovereign contempt on those knickknacks, here and there dished up for the ladies. Thus each article is condemned in its turn; and yet, amidst this variety of appetites, seldom does a dish go away from the table without being tasted and relished by some one or other of the guests.

With these considerations he ventures to serve up this second volume in the same heterogeneous way with his first; simply requesting the reader, if he should find here and there something to please him, to rest assured that it was written expressly for intelligent readers like himself, but entreating him, should he find anything to dislike, to tolerate it as one of those articles which the Author has been obliged to write for readers of a less refined taste.

To be serious—the Author is conscious of the numerous faults and imperfections of his work; and well aware how little he is disciplined and accomplished in the arts of authorship. His deficiencies are also increased by a diffidence arising from his peculiar situation. He finds himself writing in a strange land, and appearing before a public which he has been accustomed, from childhood, to regard with the highest feelings of awe and reverence. He is full of solicitude to deserve their approbation, yet finds that very solicitude continually embarrassing his powers, and depriving him of that ease and confidence which are necessary to successful exertion. Still the kindness with which he is treated encourages him to go on, hoping that in time he may acquire a steadier footing; and thus he proceeds, half-venturing, half-shrinking, surprised at his own good fortune and wondering at his own temerity.

## QUESTIONS AND EXERCISES

1. What makes this a good "farewell"?
2. What does *L'Envoy* illustrate in the author's character?

## GENERAL QUESTIONS

1. What is your general opinion of Washington Irving from your reading of his life-story in the Introduction to *The Sketch Book?*
2. What interesting glimpses do you get of the author's personality in the various *Sketches?*
3. Do you enjoy *The Sketch Book* as a whole? Why?
4. What particular Section of the *Sketches* appeals most to you? In what ways?
5. Do you think Irving would have altered *The Sketch Book* if he were living today? How?
6. Is the author a good describer of country life? Of city life?
7. How does Irving impress you as a literary critic?
8. What importance has Washington Irving in the development of the short story?
9. What is meant by referring to the author as an "antiquarian"?
10. What brief definition of the *essay* can you give after this study of *The Sketch Book?* What famous essayists and essays did Irving use as models?
11. Do you agree with the statement that the sketch, *Westminster Abbey,* represents "Irving's art at its noblest height"? Can you defend your answer by *particular* passages from the essay?
12. Would you class Irving as a "romanticist" or a "realist" in his writing? Why?
13. What traits of Washington Irving, revealed in *The Sketch Book,* indicate that he must have been an able ambassador?
14. In what great ways have the England and America of Irving's day changed? Are these changes for the better? Explain.
15. What has been the most valuable thing derived from your reading of *The Sketch Book* of Washington Irving?

## GENERAL EXERCISES

**Exercises preceded by a star are designed for assignment at the discretion of the teacher, or for any student who volunteers.**

1. Write a brief essay on "Washington Irving, Ambassador, Man of Letters."
2. Retell how *The Sketch Book* came to be written.
3. Illustrate with specific references to *The Sketch Book,* the following characteristics of Irving's style:
(1) Flowing, well-rounded sentences; (2) Romantic imagination (delight in "romantic past"); (3) Quiet, subtle humor; (4) Admirable sense of form; (5) Sentimentalism; (6) Narrative power; (7) Antiquarianism.

*4. Review General Introduction to *The Sketch Book.* Select a passage from one of the *Sketches* and compare it with a passage of equal length from some modern essayist on the following four points:
(1) Length of words; (2) Type of words; (3) Style; (4) General impression.

5. Select the essay you most enjoyed. Explain your choice.
6. List the following references and name the essay, or *Sketch,* to which it belongs; *a wreck at sea, a broken-hearted maid, features of English estates, Izaak Walton, a great chief, a tavern made famous in a play, Poet's Corner, Master Simon, true and false nobility, a birthplace, unjust criticism, an English inn kitchen, Katzenellenbogen, Ben Franklin.*

*7. Pick out the three *Sketches* containing the greatest amount of narration and show how they differ from modern short stories. Define the term *Story-Essay.*

*8. Read Irving's "The Golden Reign of Wouter Van Twiller" (*Knickerbocker History of New York;* Book III, Chapters 1–4) and make a class report.

## SUGGESTED READING LIST

*"The Broad Highway":*

*Au Large,* Henry Van Dyke (*Little Rivers*)
*On Going a Journey,* William Hazlitt (*Table-Talk*)
*Travels with a Donkey* (Ch. I and IX), Robert Louis Stevenson
*To Stratford-on-Avon to see Sarah Bernhardt,* Richard Le Gallienne (*Travels in England*)

*"London-Town":*

*Impressions of London,* Stephen Leacock (*My Discovery of England*)
*House-Hunting in London,* A. E. Newton (*A Tourist in Spite of Himself*)
*Street Music,* William Bolitho (*Camera Obscura*)
*Christ's Hospital Five and Thirty Years Ago,* Charles Lamb (*Essays of Elia*)

*"A Christmas Interlude":*

*A Christmas Sermon,* Robert Louis Stevenson (*Across the Plains*)
*Christmas Eve and Christmas Day,* Leigh Hunt (*Day by the Fire*)
*Round About the Christmas Tree,* William Makepeace Thackeray (*Roundabout Papers*)

*"Men and Books":*

*On a Certain Condescension in Foreigners,* James Russell Lowell (*My Study Windows*)
*American and Briton,* John Galsworthy (*Another Sheaf*)
*Woodrow Wilson,* William Allen White (*Masks in a Pageant*)

*"By an Inn Fire":*

*Dream Children: A Reverie,* Charles Lamb (*Essays of Elia*)
*The Fifty-First Dragon,* Heywood Broun (*The Copeland Reader*)
*The Legend of Sleepy Hollow,* Washington Irving
*Rip Van Winkle,* Washington Irving

Collections of Essays:

*Bracebridge Hall,* Washington Irving
*Sketch Books,* William Makepeace Thackeray
*An Inland Voyage,* Robert Louis Stevenson
*Creole Sketches,* Lafcadio Hearn
*Back Log Studies,* Charles Dudley Warner
*Modern Essays,* Christopher Morley
*Oxford Book of American Essays,* Brander Matthews

Reference Books on Washington Irving and *The Sketch Book:*

*Life and Letters of Washington Irving,* Pierre M. Irving
*Washington Irving,* G. W. Hellman
*Washington Irving,* Charles Dudley Warner (*American Men of Letters*)
*London in the Eighteenth Century,* Walter Besant
*Stratford-on-Avon,* Sydney Lee
*Among English Hedgerows,* Clifton Johnson (*Chautauqua Home Reading*)

# *Modern Short Stories*

Brown Brothers

RUDYARD KIPLING

The youthful vitality which inspired his early writings can be seen in this older Kipling. Much of his rugged prose and rhythmic poetry celebrates the glory of the British Empire and the courage of the British soldier.

# MODERN SHORT STORIES

## 1. Nature and Origin of the Short Story

The Short Story is, in a sense, typical of the modern spirit. In the stress of our swiftly-moving life, many people find it wearying to concentrate attention on the long, leisurely novels popular in our grandfathers' day. Americans in particular like the swift, telling strokes of the Short Story. While riding on the train or waiting for luncheon or passing an hour before retiring, one has time to begin and finish a short story. It is a complete emotional experience in a tabloid dose.

This popular demand has produced hundreds of short story magazines, each catering to a particular section of the reading public. Besides, there are year-books containing the best short stories of the preceding twelve months—best, at least, in the opinion of the editors. There is nothing new in this universal liking for brief fiction. The story-telling impulse is as old as the race; but the literary form which we are to study is of comparatively recent origin. It is important to fix in mind its place in the scheme of world literature.

Drama, history, argumentation, most of the poetic forms, and several of the fiction types go back centuries, many of them to that dim period when there was no written language and when memory alone kept alive the songs and stories from one generation to the next. The Homeric epics date back nine or ten centuries before the birth of Christ. Æschylus, the Greek dramatist, was writing his great tragedies of fate in the fifth century B. C. Minstrels were singing their ballads from court to court and from castle to castle before there were any scribes to copy the words and preserve them for posterity. We can say roughly that the basic forms of literature have existed for at least two or three thousand years.

When we contemplate this vast stretch of time, how strange to think that the most popular form of reading today came into being little more than one hundred years ago! There are people still living who were born about the time the Short Story, as we know it, was being developed. The founders of our republic—Washington, Franklin, Jefferson, and the rest—never forgot their worries of an evening by reading a short story in front of the fire, for the simple reason that there were no short stories to read. Not until a third of the nineteenth century had slipped away did Edgar Allan Poe lay down the principles upon which his own short stories and those of later writers are based.

There is a great difference between the modern Short Story and the short fiction of the previous centuries. Æsop's fables, the parables of the Scriptures, the racy tales of the Middle Ages—these were short narratives, but rarely short stories in the modern sense. For the most part they were anecdotes presenting a single episode. Even when a writer combined several episodes, there was seldom any attempt at a logical development toward a climax. The events simply followed one another in a natural time order, and the narrative could be brought to an end at the conclusion of any one of the episodes without materially injuring the effect. In the modern Short Story every incident the author makes use of must in some way advance the action toward a conclusion that, when it comes, seems inevitable.

Of course, this notion of perfect building, of careful organization of material, was not conceived all at once. A few of the tales in Boccaccio's *Decameron,* written in the fourteenth century, approach the model of a genuine Short Story. In the early eighteenth century the rise of the periodical essay foreshadowed the later story form. Many of the *Spectator Papers* of Addison and Steele were character sketches built up through narration. Though their chief purpose was to offer comment on the customs and manners of the time, the narrative touch, the economy of detail, and the presentation make them distinctly a link between the pure expository essay and the Short Story. Because they have elements of both types, it has been convenient to call them Story-Essays.

It was in this story-essay form that Washington Irving cast most of the articles in his *Sketch Book.* Indeed, a few of them are closer to the Short Story than to the essay. Though *Rip Van Winkle* and *The Legend of Sleepy Hollow* are sometimes called short stories, they lack the condensation, the compactness, that Poe asserted is a basic feature of the true type. They are too leisurely and too rambling to fit our definition. They lack that technical art which eliminates irrelevant material and, to obtain a single effect, reduces the number of characters and incidents to a minimum.

All this points to the fact that the true Short Story is a distinct literary type in itself. It is *not* a short or condensed novelette. It is *not* a narrative that started out to be a novel and fell short of the desired length. It is built upon its own principles; it has its own technique; it is as individual as any other type of fiction. True, the Short Story is shorter than the novel and, usually, the novelette; yet it may run anywhere from a few hundred words to ten or fifteen thousand. It is the author's purpose and the narrative's structure that make the difference. In other words, a Short Story differs chiefly in quality or kind, not in quantity or length, from the novel. Brander Matthews, teacher and critic, once suggested that the term *Short-story* be written with the hyphen to distinguish it from a story that just happens to be short.

## 2. Definitions

Before discussing principles of short story writing, it is advisable to have a clear understanding of some of the more common terms used in literary criticism.

Technique—the general plan or method according to which a work of art—in this case, a short story—is constructed. It may also apply to an author's particular method of execution; that is, his treatment of his materials.

Plot—the plan of the action in a narrative. It is composed of a series of connected and interrelated incidents by which the story moves to its conclusion.

Situation—the state of affairs at a given moment.

Character development—the unfolding and growth of character. Because of its brevity, the short story offers less opportunity for character development than the novel.

Setting—the place where the action of the story is supposed to occur. Two types of narrative grow out of setting: atmosphere stories and local color stories.

Atmosphere—a term denoting the mood or tone of a story. It depends chiefly on setting, but may be heightened by factors of style, incident, and character. Atmosphere appeals directly to the emotions, as in Poe's stories.

Local color—the presentation of descriptive details from some actual locality. It appeals directly to the eye. Local color stories are those in which the characters and plot grow out of the nature of the surroundings, as in Kipling's tales of India.

Theme—the general topic of the story It can usually be stated in a word or simple sentence.

Climax—the high point of the story, both as to construction and the emotion aroused. In a short story, the climax is very near the end.

Opposition of forces—those "furtherances and hindrances" encountered by the chief character in his effort to achieve a certain goal; the conflict upon which all fiction depends for dramatic interest.

Suspense—the feeling of tense expectation experienced by the reader as he awaits the outcome of a situation. It is distinguished from surprise.

Surprise—the effect gained by some totally unexpected development.

Exposition—the process of revealing to the reader essential information concerning events which have occurred before the story opens. When the narrative is interrupted in order to relate past events in detail, the usual term is *cut-back* or *flash-back*.

### 3. Principles of the Short Story

From whatever angle the student approaches the Short Story, he comes sooner or later to Edgar Allan Poe. Though Prosper Mérimée, a Frenchman, wrote what may be called the first modern short story (*Mateo Falcone,* 1829), it was Poe who a few years later developed and established the type. He not only wrote many stories characterized by their sure technique, but he also analyzed the form and laid down principles of short story construction which, with some modification, are accepted today. Since his writings became popular in Europe as well as in America, he has had an influence on short story development that is second to none.

Poe had not only imagination but a genius for craftsmanship. He studied every possible device of word, structure, setting, and detail to produce the effect he desired. For inspiration, or the careless outpouring of words in a moment of emotion, he had little use. A writer was a workman, failing or succeeding in proportion to his skill in construction. Even Poe's poems were written according to a formula. As a result of his study and experimentation with the tale of earlier writers, Poe drafted the following rules of short story construction:

1. A short story writer must conceive a *unique* or *single* effect which he wishes to create, and make everything in the story work toward that effect. That is, the author must decide first what the conclusion of the story is to be; he must then invent incidents and characters that will lead toward this conclusion.

2. Everything that does not advance the action toward the conclusion which has been decided upon must be rigidly excluded. However exciting, or beautiful, or generally significant it may be, unless it has a direct bearing on the story, the writer must discard it. He may not, like the novelist, digress from the theme or introduce characters picturesque but not essential to the story. Economy of detail, of incident, of persons, must be the rule. Some one has wisely said that the essence of art is omission.

3. When a writer has decided what material to use to produce his effect, he must then work out the proper order for the parts. Each part must lead naturally and logically to the next until the conclusion is reached. Poe believed there is only one right arrangement of parts and that this must be discovered if the full value of the story is to be realized.

4. A short story must be brief enough to be read at a single sitting. Otherwise, that unique, single effect is lost by interruption. A novel we may dip into now and again, taking up the thread of the story where we left off; but a short story depends for its effect upon concentrated and continuous attention.

5. So far these principles have had to do with construction, with technique. Poe has one observation regarding the subject matter itself. It must have striking originality. We may ask ourselves how it is possible nowadays, with thousands of stories being written each year, to turn out one that has striking originality. The answer is that originality does not necessarily mean the choice of some extraordinary subject. A story may be fresh in treatment, style, and point of view, yet deal with scenes and people with which we are familiar. Even old situations which have been used many times before can be transformed into absorbing narrative by a different approach.

Although modern writers observe the spirit of these rules, they are inclined to interpret them more liberally than did Poe. For example, in a short story of today one may find both tears and laughter, horror and comedy; but it is to be noted that one always prevails over the other, with the tone or mood established at the very beginning. Whatever elements enter in, the author has written with a view to what the complete effect will be. Though some of the concentration of Poe's method is lost, the story comes closer to human life. In life emotions are seldom single. They are mingled, as joy and sorrow so often are.

Recent writers and critics have added to Poe's principles of technique. They have, for instance, pointed out the similarity between the Short Story and the Drama. Both forms advance through a series of crises to the final solution. These crises have been reached through another series of struggles, often called *opposition of forces* or *furtherances and hindrances.* In every story and drama there is a chief actor who is trying to achieve some goal. If he should reach that goal without opposition, there would be no story and no drama. Each advance made by the chief actor toward his goal is usually followed by a setback or disappointment, so that the reader is held in suspense until the last few paragraphs. Because the majority of readers like happy endings, the heroes of most stories emerge from the struggles victorious. Yet many powerful narratives have been written in which the hero finally succumbs to the forces against which he has been fighting.

It has already been indicated that the mood is established very early in the narrative. A story that is to have a tragic ending cannot be written in the vein of light comedy. The writer who disappoints his readers destroys the value of his work both as art and entertainment. Often the mood is fixed by style and choice of words. Study two of Poe's opening sentences:

> "I was sick—sick unto death with that long agony . . ."
>
> —*The Pit and the Pendulum*

> "During the whole of a dull, dark, and soundless day in the autumn of the year, when the clouds hung oppressively low in the heavens, I had been passing alone, on horseback, through a singularly dreary tract of country . . ."
>
> —*The Fall of the House of Usher*

In the first example the horrors that are to follow are foreshadowed in a single compact statement. In the second, every important word, even to the mention of the season, strikes a sombre note that prepares the reader for the fate that hangs over the house of Usher. In both instances, the remainder of the opening paragraph emphasizes the mood suggested in the first sentence.

The student will find it worth while to observe the method an author employs to open his story. He may have an introductory paragraph to set the scene and atmosphere; or he may use dialogue; or, to excite immediate interest, he may start with a vivid bit of action, later giving the information necessary to an understanding of the situation. But whatever method of approach he uses, he must lead from that beginning through a series of minor crises to the grand climax.

The short story writer, however, rarely starts his narrative at the very beginning of the events to be related. For the sake of economy and compactness, he usually chooses a point from which the interest rises rapidly. He must, therefore, give the reader information necessary to an understanding of what has previously occurred. He may interrupt his story with a paragraph of explanation. He may let one of the characters tell the reader about it. Or he may reveal it gradually through dialogue and action. This process of providing the reader with a knowledge of events which have taken place before the story opens is called Exposition. The most successful method of Exposition is that which reveals necessary information about the past during the progress of present action. In this manner the reader absorbs what knowledge is necessary without losing interest in the main thread of the story—often without even realizing that the author is carefully preparing him for an understanding of the situation.

It is possible to classify short stories in several different ways. They may be grouped according to theme: love triumphant, self-sacrifice, heroism, and the like; or according to the emotion they arouse: pity, fear, humor, love, etc.

One of the most common classifications is that based on the three elements of a story: plot, character, setting. In a story of plot, the interest centers in the action. In a story of character, the personality of the chief actor is of greater importance than either plot or background. Sometimes, however, the setting or background is of such a nature that both the characters and their actions grow out of their surroundings, as in tales of the gold-mining days in the West or of life in the tenement districts of great cities. A fourth type, though rare, may be added to this grouping. The Thesis Story has a purpose; that is, the author manipulates his characters, plot, and background to teach some lesson. There are but a few really great stories of this type, because the author is inclined to force his characters into actions that prove his thesis or lesson instead of allowing the actions to grow naturally out of the characters he has invented. In all fiction, one of the most important principles is this: each person created by the author must act only as his character and mentality dictate. The villain who in a moment turns into a saint is a favorite with second-rate writers, but it is not good art because it is not true to life.

There is another classification that is worth noting. Short stories may be divided into narratives of accomplishment and narratives of decision. In other words, the interest in some stories lies in the effort of the chief character to accomplish in fact a purpose he has already resolved upon. In that case, much of the action is external, a struggle between the actor and outside forces. In other stories, the struggle is chiefly mental or internal, and the reader's interest hinges on some all-important decision which the chief character must make, just as the dramatic suspense in *Hamlet* hangs upon the Prince's delayed decision to avenge his father's death. The action of such stories is psychological rather than physical.

Stories differ also as to the point of view in the narration. If the story is told in the first person, with the use of "I," then all the events must be portrayed through the eyes and mind of that character, whether he is the chief character or a subordinate actor in the plot. On the other hand, the story may be written from the point of view of an all-knowing author who assumes knowledge of what is going on in several places at once and of what is passing through the minds of the various characters. Even in this case, it is essential to select one of the characters through whom most of the reader's impressions come. This concentrates attention and helps give unity to the story.

There remains the fundamental distinction between the realistic and the romantic—the portrayal of life as accurately as possible or the refashioning of it to suit one's own ideas. The realist tries to tell the truth about the common things of this workaday world. The romanticist seeks to reveal a deeper, spiritual truth in the uncommon, often the strange and remote. To explain this in relation to the Short Story is peculiarly difficult, because, while most modern stories are realistic in detail, they are usually romantic in method. Writers nowadays incline to treat of familiar people and scenes, the material of life as we know it, but the molding of this material is still largely in the romantic manner. Problems are happily solved, lovers are reunited in spite of seemingly insurmountable obstacles, and the dragons of the twentieth century are slain as heroically as in our fondest dreams.

Because the brevity of the Short Story demands the unfolding and emphasizing of an idea in a short space, it is far easier to choose a theme and show how it works out in a particular case (the romantic method) than to present a number of cases from which the reader finally comprehends the theme (the realistic method). This is also the difference between deduction and induction in reasoning. One of the few brilliant and truly realistic short stories, both in detail and method, is Katherine Brush's *Night Club,* in which snatches of conversation heard in the women's dressing room give an idea of the drama in the lives of tired, pleasure-hunting girls of today. Under a strict interpretation of Poe's principles, *Night Club* could not be classed as a short story. This fact indicates that the Short Story is outgrowing some of its earlier restrictions without losing its status as an independent form of literature.

Perhaps the most successful attempt at defining the Short Story was made by Clayton Hamilton:

"The aim of a short story is to produce a single narrative effect with the greatest economy of means that is consistent with the utmost emphasis."

## 4. Study Outline

This outline will help you analyze stories. After each general topic several subheads are suggested. When the subhead contains two or more items, choose the one which applies to the story you are studying.

| TOPIC | SUBHEAD |
|---|---|
| Title: | Commonplace, or exciting interest. |
| | Application to the story. |
| Theme: | Brief statement of the main idea. |
| Type: | Plot, character, setting, or thesis. |
| | Love, adventure, mystery, etc. |
| | Story of accomplishment or of decision. |
| | Romantic or realistic: in detail or in method. |
| Point of view: | That of chief actor, subordinate actor, or all-knowing author. |
| Opening: | Mood established. |
| | Method: incident, dialogue, or author's introduction. |
| Time scheme: | Continuous, or interrupted (cut-back). |
| Technique: | Single definite impression. |
| | Exclusion of irrelevant material. |
| | Logical order of events. |
| | Length (Could it be told in shorter space without loss of effect?) |
| Interest: | Treatment original or hackneyed. |
| | Conflict strong or weak. |
| | Achieved by surprise or suspense. |
| Style: | Literary, or in language of common speech. |
| | Vivid, or colorless. |
| Action: | Physical, or mental. |
| | Violent, or leisurely. |
| | Advanced through simple narration or through dialogue. |
| Plot: | Plausible, or unbelievable. |
| | Intricate, or simple. |
| Characters: | True to life, or exaggerated. |
| | Few, or many (Could one or more be eliminated?) |
| | Character development, if any. |
| Setting: | Imagined, or real (local color). |
| | Important for the story, or unimportant. |
| Period: | Accurate reflection of the times, or not. |
| | Relation to author's own life, if any. |
| Climax: | Logical, or inconsistent. |
| | Method employed to lead to it. |
| | Dramatic, or quiet. |
| | Happy, or tragic. |
| Effect: | Entertaining, instructive, boring. |
| | Uplifting, or depressing. |

# THE MAN WHO WAS

## RUDYARD KIPLING

## 1865–

### THE AUTHOR

One day in 1889 a stranger entered the office of the *San Francisco Examiner,* the newspaper which young William Randolph Hearst had just acquired. He was rather shabbily dressed and wore huge spectacles which gave him an owlish look. His skin was tanned to a deep brown. Under his arm he carried a bulky manuscript.

The Negro doorman, accustomed to the visits of would-be authors, was not surprised when the caller asked to see the literary editor. With that assumption of authority which seems to be a mark of all doormen, he told the young man to leave his package and call later. For a week or so the manuscript cluttered the desk of some assistant editor. No one bothered with it. When its owner returned, the doorman fished it out of a stack of copy and handed it back. Looking at it sadly, the stranger tucked it under his arm and departed. At that moment Hearst, now one of the most powerful influences in American journalism, lost the chance of a lifetime.

The stranger was Rudyard Kipling, within a year to be hailed as a new star on the literary horizon. The manuscript was a sheaf of stories of India, entitled, *Plain Tales from the Hills,* now one of the most popular of all his volumes. Kipling was on a trip that took him from India across the Pacific to America and thence to London. Although he had already made a name for himself in India, he was little known in the United States and was looking for a publisher. To get himself before the American public he would have sold his stories at almost any price. Yet no publisher, either in San Francisco or New York, cared to take a chance on this young man's work.

It is possible that this disappointment accounts in part for the streak of bitterness that runs through Kipling's writings on America. In *American Notes,* a series of letters contributed to a paper in India, he gave satiric pictures of this American tour. They are clever sketches, somewhat superficial and marred by too much journalistic smartness. Probably no other writer since Dickens has been so widely read as Kipling, and it is a curious coincidence that Dickens too was a severe critic of the United States.

So much a product of his early environment are most of Kipling's works that any approach to a study of his writing must be prefaced with an account of his life in India. Born in Bombay in 1865, of British parents, he grew up in the atmosphere of mystery that in the Orient seems to hover just beyond the hard and often brutal facts of existence. His father was an artist of some repute and was curator of the Lahore Museum of India. His mother, a woman noted for her beauty and wit, came of a distinguished family. Both ancestry and surroundings, therefore, can be drawn upon to explain the talent which so early developed in Kipling.

When he was six years old, Kipling was sent to England to be educated. Of his school days there is a highly colored account in the stories collected under the title, *Stalky and Co.* While not malicious, Kipling was apparently a difficult youth to manage. His near-sightedness kept him from many of the sports of his comrades, but he was always ready to join them in a prank. Flogging seemed to have little effect. He had a talent for cleverness rather than scholarship, and for two years he edited his school paper, contributing poems and articles something above the usual schoolboy product.

Back in India at the age of seventeen, he became sub-editor of the *Lahore Civil and Military Gazette,* and five years later he took over the assistant editorship of the important *Pioneer* of Allahabad. This journalistic experience had a lasting influence on his literary work. His first major effort, a volume of poetry called *Departmental Ditties,* was published in 1886. The following year saw the appearance of *Plain Tales from the Hills.* For the next decade he wrote rapidly, often unevenly, but always with vigor. Famous at twenty-five, most of his best work was done before he was forty. After that there was a decline in power that not even the most loyal Kipling lover can explain away.

His early period has two outstanding characteristics: vigor and cynicism. While the vigor remained, maturity brought a more sympathetic understanding of character. Undoubtedly influenced by what Bret Harte was doing with local color stories of the American West, Kipling undertook to interpret the soul of India. There were stories of British officialdom; of the Secret Service and things in the native world that no white man can understand; and, sometimes, an idyll of that borderland of romance between the white and the brown peoples in which there is beauty and tenderness as well as strength.

To the cool, well-groomed people who made polite conversation in British drawing-rooms in the eighties and nineties, Kipling was like a thunderclap in a blue sky. He was a new experience in letters. He was practically the first great English writer since the Elizabethans who dared call a spade a spade. *Vulgar* and *brutal* were adjectives applied to him before the full power of his work was appreciated. At times, it is true, he mistook mere coarseness for strength, especially in his early writings, and he frequently assumed the cynical air of a young man who knew life too well. He wrote frothy tales and verse of society in India that, while clever, have a world-weary pose that does not quite fit the youthful author. Nevertheless, the work of those first years will be read long after some of his more mature compositions have been forgotten.

Kipling was both imperialistic and democratic at once, on the one hand glorifying the Empire and on the other championing the common man against a short-sighted government. His favorite theme was the British soldier, *Tommy Atkins,* who fought and sweat and died far from Queen Victoria's comfortable palace at Windsor with no one to sing his requiem. No one except Kipling. Kipling immortalized him in such characters as Private Mulvaney, who was "a corpril wanst but was rejuced aftherwards"; and in ballads that have the language of the barrack-room and the swing of a march.

As Kipling grew older, the imperialist in him grew stronger. He harped continually on the superiority of the white people, especially the English, and celebrated in verse and prose the greatness of the British Empire, "the map that is half unrolled." By the end of the Boer War (1902), it was difficult to believe that this singer of the Anglo-Saxon saga was the same who had penned *The Recessional,* as clear a warning to ambitious nations as ever was written.

The scope of Kipling's work is too great to consider here in detail. In the *Jungle Books* and *Just-So Stories* he tapped a new source of enjoyment for child and adult alike. His novels are less successful than his stories and poems, though *Kim* stands out as a fine, original creation. Perhaps one explanation is to be found in the fact that character drawing is Kipling's weakest point. He paints pictures, gives vigorous action, builds up a vivid background; but the novel demands something more. While his method is admirably suited to the Short Story, in which there is little space for character development, the reader feels a lack of depth in most of his longer narratives.

About the turn of the century, there was a change in Kipling's outlook. He suddenly became mechanical-minded, writing stories of ships and locomotives and bridges. They were not commonplace stories. He gave machinery a soul and showed how the various parts learned to forget themselves and work as a whole. Again, the comparison with the British Empire is inescapable. The dominions must sink their identity in the larger Empire of which they are a part. In union there is strength. Hopes that Kipling would be the great inspiration behind the British in the World War soon faded. If he had not exactly "written himself out," at least he could not recapture the majesty and masculinity of his earlier work, or give Tommy Atkins the marching songs that made the last long mile a bit easier. Much of his later work, though showing sympathy in place of youthful cynicism, lacks the dynamic energy that makes *Soldiers Three* and *Mine Own People* so effective.

Early in 1892 Kipling had married Caroline Balestier, an American, and for about four years lived in Brattleboro, Vermont. Here many of his finest poems were written, as well as that Gloucester fishing tale. *Captains Courageous.* After 1896 the Kiplings made their home in England. It was during a visit to America in 1899 that Kipling was stricken with a nearly fatal attack of pneumonia. Forgetting his thrusts at America, the entire nation joined in a deep and spontaneous sympathy. Few persons, especially foreigners, have been accorded such a demonstration of good will and reverence.

A reading of such a poem as *The Widow at Windsor* will explain why Kipling was never chosen the official poet laureate to celebrate in verse England's grand occasions. Though by far the greatest poet writing in English, he had been too forthright in his treatment of royalty. In 1896 and in 1913, when laureates were chosen, Kipling was passed by for lesser men more respectful to majesty. He has, however, been unofficially designated "the laureate of the Empire," and the award of the Nobel Prize in literature in 1907 helped to compensate for his sovereigns' neglect. But that, as Kipling is wont to say, is another story.

## THE STORY

Like Bismarck, the German statesman, Kipling feared Russia; not feared exactly, but mistrusted. Again and again he warned his country to watch out for Russia, "the bear that walks like a man." About the time of the first Hague Conference, called in 1899 by the Czar for the promotion of international peace, he wrote a poem, *The Truce of the Bear,* in which his suspicions of the Czar's motives were bitterly phrased.

*The Man Who Was,* published in 1890, expresses the same thought in prose that *The Truce of the Bear* does in poetry. It is a story filled with forebodings of conflict to come. Khyber Pass is the sole gateway between India and Afghanistan. It is a little over thirty miles in length, and in one spot is only about ten feet wide. If Russia should ever be tempted to dispute British sovereignty over India, the key to the invasion would be Khyber Pass. It has figured in many campaigns since the days of Alexander the Great. During the Afghan Wars of 1839–42, the British army twice fought its way through against stiff resistance from the natives.

There is little subtlety in *The Man Who Was.* It needs little. It is a story of dramatic incident told with bold strokes, and the message it brings is underlined in red. The brotherhood of British officers. Polo games. The old ritual of toasting the Queen. The painful courtesy accorded an enemy who hates and is hated. Dirkovitch, Little Mildred, Hira Singh, and the Man Who Was—characters drawn in clean-cut outline but with little depth. Yet their story will grip you as it has gripped millions, and your throat will be constricted as Limmason snaps the shank of a wine glass between his fingers, as they used to do when they pledged the Queen.

It is a curious thing that when the World War broke out, Russia was aligned with England and the Allies against the Central Powers. Many a critic had a good laugh at Kipling's expense, but in view of what has since happened only the years can tell whether Kipling was right or wrong.

## THE MAN WHO WAS[1]

Let it be clearly understood that the Russian is a delightful person till he tucks his shirt in. As an Oriental he is charming. It is only when he insists upon being treated as the most easterly of western peoples, instead of the most westerly of easterns, that he becomes a racial anomaly extremely difficult to handle. The host never knows which side of his nature is going to turn up next.

Dirkovitch was a Russian—a Russian of the Russians, as he said—who appeared to get his bread by serving the Czar as an officer in a Cossack[2] regiment, and corresponding for a Russian newspaper with a name that was never twice the same. He was a handsome young Oriental, with a taste for wandering through unexplored portions of the earth, and he arrived in India from nowhere in particular. At least no living man could ascertain whether it was by way of Balkh, Budukhshan, Chitral, Beloochistan, Nepaul,[3] or anywhere else. The Indian Government, being in an unusually affable mood, gave orders that he was to be civilly treated, and shown everything that was to be seen; so he drifted, talking bad English and worse French, from one city to another till he forgathered with her Majesty's White Hussars in the city of Peshawur, which stands at the mouth of that narrow sword-cut in the hills that men call the Khyber Pass. He was undoubtedly an officer, and he was decorated, after the manner of the Russians, with little enamelled crosses, and he could talk, and (though this has nothing to do with his merits) he had been given up as a hopeless task or case by the Black Tyrones, who, individually and collectively, with hot whiskey and honey, mulled brandy and mixed spirits of all kinds, had striven in all hospitality to make him drunk. And when the Black Tyrones, who are exclusively Irish, fail to disturb the peace of head of a foreigner, that foreigner is certain to be a superior man. This was the argument of the Black Tyrones, but they were ever an unruly and self-opinionated regiment, and they allowed junior subalterns of four years' service to choose their wines. The spirits were always purchased by the colonel and a committee of majors. And a regiment that would so behave may be respected but cannot be loved.

[1] Reprinted from the original story in *Harper's Weekly* for April 5, 1890.
[2] Cossack—A bold warlike people of Russia noted for their remarkable horsemanship.
[3] Balkh . . Nepaul—Districts near, or bordering on, Northwest India.

The White Hussars were as conscientious in choosing their wine as in charging the enemy. There was a brandy that had been purchased by a cultured colonel a few years after the battle of Waterloo. It has been maturing ever since, and it was a marvellous brandy at the purchasing. The memory of that liquor would cause men to weep as they lay dying in the teak forests of upper Burmah or the slime of the Irrawaddy.[4] And there was a port which was notable; and there was a champagne of an obscure brand, which always came to mess without any labels, because the White Hussars wished none to know where the source of supply might be found. The officer on whose head the champagne-choosing lay was forbidden the use of tobacco for six weeks previous to sampling.

This particularity of detail is necessary to emphasize the fact that that champagne, that port, and, above all, that brandy—the green and yellow and white liqueurs did not count—was placed at the absolute disposition of Dirkovitch, and he enjoyed himself hugely—even more than among the Black Tyrones.

But he remained distressingly European through it all. The White Hussars were "My dear true friends," "Fellow-soldiers glorious," and "Brothers inseparable." He would unburden himself by the hour on the glorious future that awaited the combined arms of England and Russia when their hearts and their territories should run side by side, and the great mission of civilizing Asia should begin. That was unsatisfactory, because Asia is not going to be civilized after the methods of the West. There is too much Asia, and she is too old. You cannot reform a lady of many lovers, and Asia has been insatiable in her flirtations aforetime. She will never attend Sunday-school, or learn to vote save with swords for tickets.

Dirkovitch knew this as well as any one else, but it suited him to talk special correspondently[5] and to make himself as genial as he could. Now and then he volunteered a little, a very little, information about his own Sotnia[6] of Cossacks, left apparently to look after themselves somewhere at the back of beyond. He had done rough work in Central Asia, and had seen rather more help-yourself fighting than most men of his years. But he was careful never to betray his superiority, and more than careful to praise on all

[4] IRRAWADDY—Large river in Burma, a province of India.

[5] SPECIAL CORRESPONDENTLY—Like a special correspondent, or reporter, writing to his newspaper.

[6] SOTNIA—A Cossack cavalry squadron.

occasions the appearance, drill, uniform, and organization of her Majesty's White Hussars. And, indeed, they were a regiment to be admired. When Mrs. Durgan, widow of the late Sir John Durgan, arrived in their station, and after a short time had been proposed to by every single man at mess, she put the public sentiment very neatly when she explained that they were all so nice that unless she could marry them all, including the colonel and some majors who were already married, she was not going to content herself with one of them. Wherefore she wedded a little man in a rifle regiment—being by nature contradictious—and the White Hussars were going to wear crape on their arms, but compromised by attending the wedding in full force, and lining the aisle with unutterable reproach. She had jilted them all—from Basset-Holmer, the senior captain, to Little Mildred, the last subaltern, and he could have given her four thousand a year and a title. He was a viscount, and on his arrival the mess had said he had better go into the Guards, because they were all sons of large grocers and small clothiers in the Hussars, but Mildred begged very hard to be allowed to stay, and behaved so prettily that he was forgiven, and became a man, which is much more important than being any sort of viscount.

The only persons who did not share the general regard for the White Hussars were a few thousand gentlemen of Jewish extraction who lived across the border, and answered to the name of Pathan.[7] They had only met the regiment officially, and for something less than twenty minutes, but the interview, which was complicated with many casualties, had filled them with prejudice. They even called the White Hussars "children of the devil," and sons of persons whom it would be perfectly impossible to meet in decent society. Yet they were not above making their aversion fill their money belts. The regiment possessed carbines, beautiful Martini-Henri carbines, that would cob a bullet into an enemy's camp at one thousand yards, and were even handier than the long rifle. Therefore they were coveted all along the border, and, since demand inevitably breeds supply, they were supplied at the risk of life and limb for exactly their weight in coined silver—seven and one-half pounds of rupees,[8] or sixteen pounds and a few shillings each, reckoning the rupee at

---

[7] PATHAN—The principal race of Afghanistan.

[8] RUPEES—Coin of India worth about 32 cents.

par. They were stolen at night by snaky-haired thieves that crawled on their stomachs under the nose of the sentries; they disappeared mysteriously from arm racks; and in the hot weather, when all the doors and windows were open, they vanished like puffs of their own smoke. The border people desired them first for their own family vendettas,[9] and then for contingencies. But in the long cold nights of the northern Indian winter they were stolen most extensively. The traffic of murder was liveliest among the hills at that season, and prices ruled high. The regimental guards were first doubled and then trebled. A trooper does not much care if he loses a weapon—Government must make it good—but he deeply resents the loss of his sleep. The regiment grew very angry, and one night-thief who managed to limp away bears the visible marks of their anger upon him to this hour. That incident stopped the burglaries for a time, and the guards were reduced accordingly, and the regiment devoted itself to polo with unexpected results, for it beat by two goals to one that very terrible polo corps the Lushkar Light Horse, though the latter had four ponies apiece for a short hour's fight, as well as a native officer who played like a lambent flame across the ground.

Then they gave a dinner to celebrate the event. The Lushkar team came, and Dirkovitch came, in the fullest full uniform of a Cossack officer, which is as full as a dressing-gown, and was introduced to the Lushkars, and opened his eyes as he regarded them. They were lighter men than the Hussars, and they carried themselves with the swing that is the peculiar right of the Punjab[10] frontier force and all irregular horse. Like everything else in the service, it has to be learned; but, unlike many things, it is never forgotten, and remains on the body till death.

The great beam-roofed mess-room of the White Hussars was a sight to be remembered. All the mess plate was on the long table—the same table that had served up the bodies of five dead officers in a forgotten fight long and long ago—the dingy, battered standards faced the door of entrance, clumps of winter roses lay between the silver candlesticks, the portraits of eminent officers deceased looked down on their successors from between the heads of sambhur,[11]

[9] VENDETTAS—Feuds.
[10] PUNJAB—Province of Northwest British India.
[11] SAMBHUR, ETC.—Animals of the deer and antelope species.

nilghai, markhor, and, pride of all the mess, two grinning snow-leopards that had cost Basset-Holmer four months' leave that he might have spent in England instead of on the road to Thibet, and the daily risk of his life on ledge, snow-slide, and glassy grass slope.

The servants, in spotless white muslin and the crest of their regiments on the brow of their turbans, waited behind their masters, who were clad in the scarlet and gold of the White Hussars and the cream and silver of the Lushkar Light Horse. Dirkovitch's dull green uniform was the only dark spot at the board, but his big onyx eyes made up for it. He was fraternizing effusively with the captain of the Lushkar team, who was wondering how many of Dirkovitch's Cossacks his own long lathy down-countrymen could account for in a fair charge. But one does not speak of these things openly.

The talk rose higher and higher, and the regimental band played between the courses, as is the immemorial custom, till all tongues ceased for a moment with the removal of the dinner slips and the First Toast of Obligation, when the colonel rising said, "Mr. Vice,[12] the Queen," and Little Mildred from the bottom of the table answered, "The Queen, God bless her!" and the big spurs clanked as the big men heaved themselves up and drank the Queen, upon whose pay they were falsely supposed to pay their mess bills. That sacrament of the mess never grows old, and never ceases to bring a lump into the throat of the listener wherever he be by land or by sea. Dirkovitch rose with his "brothers glorious," but he could not understand. No one but an officer can understand what the toast means; and the bulk have more sentiment than comprehension. It all comes to the same in the end, as the enemy said when he was wriggling on a lance point. Immediately after the little silence that follows on the ceremony there entered the native officer who had played for the Lushkar team. He could not of course eat with the alien, but he came in at dessert, all six feet of him, with the blue and silver turban atop, and the big black top-boots below. The mess rose joyously as he thrust forward the hilt of his sabre, in token of fealty, for the colonel of the White Hussars to touch, and dropped into a vacant chair amid shouts of "*Rung ho!* Hira Singh!" (which being translated means "Go in and win!"). "Did

---

[12] Mr. Vice—Equivalent to our "Mr. Toastmaster."

I whack you over the knee, old man?" "Ressaidar[13] Sahib,[14] what the devil made you play that kicking pig of a pony in the last ten minutes?" "Shabash,[15] Ressaidar Sahib!" Then the voice of the colonel, "The health of Ressaidar Hira Singh!"

After the shouting had died away Hira Singh rose to reply, for he was the cadet[16] of a royal house, the son of a king's son, and knew what was due on these occasions. Thus he spoke in the vernacular: "Colonel Sahib and officers of this regiment, much honor have you done me. This will I remember. We came down from afar to play you; but we were beaten." ("No fault of yours, Ressaidar Sahib. Played on our own ground, y'know. Your ponies were cramped from the railway. Don't apologize"). "Therefore perhaps we will come again if it be so ordained." ("Hear! Hear, Hear, indeed! Bravo! Hsh!"). "Then we will play you afresh" ("Happy to meet you"), "till there are left no feet upon our ponies. Thus far for sport." He dropped one hand on his sword-hilt and his eye wandered to Dirkovitch lolling back in his chair. "But if by the will of God there arises any other game which is not the polo game, then be assured, Colonel Sahib and officers, that we shall play it out side by side, though *they*"—again his eye sought Dirkovitch—"though *they,* I say, have fifty ponies to our one horse." And with a deep-mouthed *Rung ho!* that rang like a musket butt on flag-stones, he sat down amid shoutings.

Dirkovitch, who had devoted himself steadily to the brandy—the terrible brandy aforementioned—did not understand, nor did the expurgated translations offered to him at all convey the point. Decidedly the native officer's was the speech of the evening, and the clamor might have continued to the dawn had it not been broken by the noise of a shot without that sent every man feeling at his defenceless left side. It is notable that Dirkovitch "reached back," after the American fashion—a gesture that set the captain of the Lushkar team wondering how Cossack officers were armed at mess. Then there was a scuffle, and a yell of pain.

"Carbine stealing again!" said the adjutant, calmly sinking back in his chair. "This comes of reducing the guards. I hope the sentries have killed him."

---

13 Ressaidar—Title of a native captain.

14 Sahib—Title of respect, equivalent to "Sir" or "Master."

15 Shabash—Cry of approval, as "Good work!" or, in American slang, "Atta boy!"

16 Cadet—A younger son.

The feet of armed men pounded on the veranda flags, and it sounded as though something was being dragged.

"Why don't they put him in the cells till the morning?" said the colonel, testily. "See if they've damaged him, sergeant."

The mess sergeant fled out into the darkness, and returned with two troopers and a corporal, all very much perplexed.

"Caught a man stealin' carbines, sir," said the corporal. "Leastways 'e was crawlin' towards the barricks, sir, past the main-road sentries; an' the sentry 'e says, sir—"

The limp heap of rags upheld by the three men groaned. Never was seen so destitute and demoralized an Afghan. He was turbanless, shoeless, caked with dirt, and all but dead with rough handling. Hira Singh started slightly at the sound of the man's pain. Dirkovitch took another liqueur glass of brandy.

"*What* does the sentry say?" said the colonel.

"Sez he speaks English, sir," said the corporal.

"So you brought him into mess instead of handing him over to the sergeant! If he spoke all the tongues of the Pentecost[17] you've no business—"

Again the bundle groaned and muttered. Little Mildred had risen from his place to inspect. He jumped back as though he had been shot.

"Perhaps it would be better, sir, to send the men away," said he to the colonel, for he was a much-privileged subaltern. He put his arms round the rag-bound horror as he spoke, and dropped him into a chair. It may not have been explained that the littleness of Mildred lay in his being six feet four, and big in proportion. The corporal, seeing that an officer was disposed to look after the capture, and that the colonel's eye was beginning to blaze, promptly removed himself and his men. The mess was left alone with the carbine thief, who laid his head on the table and wept bitterly, hopelessly, and inconsolably, as little children weep.

Hira Singh leaped to his feet with a long-drawn vernacular oath. "Colonel Sahib," said he, "that man is no Afghan, for they weep *'Ai! Ai!'* Nor is he of Hindustan, for they weep *'Oh! Ho!'* He weeps after the fashion of the white men, who say *'Ow! Ow!'* "

"Now where the dickens did you get that knowledge, Hira Singh?" said the captain of the Lushkar team.

---

[17] PENTECOST—See Acts II, 1–4: "And they . . . began to speak with other tongues."

"Hear him!" said Hira Singh, simply, pointing at the crumpled figure that wept as though it would never cease.

"He said, 'My God!' " said Little Mildred. "I heard him say it."

The colonel and the mess-room looked at the man in silence. It is a horrible thing to hear a man cry. A woman can sob from the top of her palate, or her lips, or anywhere else, but a man cries from his diaphragm, and it rends him to pieces. Also, the exhibition causes the throat of the on-looker to close at the top.

"Poor devil!" said the colonel, coughing tremendously. "We ought to send him to hospital. He's been man-handled."

Now the adjutant loved his rifles. They were to him as his grandchildren—the men standing in the first place. He grunted rebelliously: "I can understand an Afghan stealing, because he's made that way. But I can't understand his crying. That makes it worse."

The brandy must have affected Dirkovitch, for he lay back in his chair and stared at the ceiling. There was nothing special in the ceiling beyond a shadow as of a huge black coffin. Owing to some peculiarity in the construction of the mess-room this shadow was always thrown when the candles were lighted. It never disturbed the digestion of the White Hussars. They were, in fact, rather proud of it.

"Is he going to cry all night?" said the colonel, "or are we supposed to sit up with Little Mildred's guest until he feels better?"

The man in the chair threw up his head and stared at the mess. Outside, the wheels of the first of those bidden to the festivities crunched the roadway.

"Oh, my God!" said the man in the chair, and every soul in the mess rose to his feet. Then the Lushkar captain did a deed for which he ought to have been given the Victoria Cross[18]—distinguished gallantry in a fight against overwhelming curiosity. He picked up his team with his eyes as the hostess picks up the ladies at the opportune moment, and pausing only by the colonel's chair to say, "This isn't *our* affair, you know, sir," led the team into the veranda and the gardens. Hira Singh was the last, and he looked at Dirkovitch as he moved. But Dirkovitch had departed into a brandy paradise of his own. His lips moved without sound, and he was studying the coffin on the ceiling.

[18] Victoria Cross—British medal for distinguished bravery.

"White—white all over," said Basset-Holmer, the adjutant. "What a pernicious renegade he must be! I wonder where he came from?"

The colonel shook the man gently by the arm, and "Who are you?" said he.

There was no answer. The man stared round the mess-room and smiled in the colonel's face. Little Mildred, who was always more of a woman than a man till "Boot and saddle" was sounded, repeated the question in a voice that would have drawn confidences from a geyser. The man only smiled. Dirkovitch, at the far end of the table, slid gently from his chair to the floor. No son of Adam, in this present imperfect world, can mix the Hussars' champagne with the Hussars' brandy by five and eight glasses of each without remembering the pit whence he has been digged and descending thither. The band began to play the tune with which the White Hussars, from the date of their formation, preface all their functions. They would sooner be disbanded than abandon that tune. It is a part of their system. The man straightened himself in his chair and drummed on the table with his fingers.

"I don't see why we should entertain lunatics," said the colonel; "call a guard and send him off to the cells. We'll look into the business in the morning. Give him a glass of wine first, though."

Little Mildred filled a sherry glass with the brandy and thrust it over to the man. He drank, and the tune rose louder, and he straightened himself yet more. Then he put out his long-taloned hands to a piece of plate opposite and fingered it lovingly. There was a mystery connected with that piece of plate in the shape of a spring, which converted what was a seven-branched candlestick, three springs each side and one in the middle, into a sort of wheel-spoke candelabrum. He found the spring, pressed it, and laughed weakly. He rose from his chair and inspected a picture on the wall, then moved on to another picture, the mess watching him without a word. When he came to the mantel-piece he shook his head and seemed distressed. A piece of plate representing a mounted hussar in full uniform caught his eye. He pointed to it, and then to the mantel-piece, with inquiry in his eyes.

"What is it—oh, what is it?" said Little Mildred. Then, as a mother might speak to a child, "That is a horse—yes, a horse."

Very slowly came the answer, in a thick, passionless guttural: "Yes, I—have seen. But—where is *the* horse?"

You could have heard the hearts of the mess beating as the men drew back to give the stranger full room in his wanderings. There was no question of calling the guard.

Again he spoke, very slowly, "Where is *our* horse?"

There is no saying what happened after that. There is but one horse in the White Hussars, and his portrait hangs outside the door of the mess-room. He is the piebald drum-horse, the king of the regimental band, that served the regiment for seven-and-thirty years, and in the end was shot for old age. Half the mess tore the thing down from its place and thrust it into the man's hands. He placed it above the mantel-piece; it clattered on the ledge, as his poor hands dropped it, and he staggered toward the bottom of the table, falling into Mildred's chair. The band began to play the *River of Years* waltz, and the laughter from the gardens came into the tobacco-scented mess-room. But nobody, even the youngest, was thinking of waltzes. They all spoke to one another something after this fashion: "The drum-horse hasn't hung over the mantel-piece since '67." "How does he know?" "Mildred, go and speak to him again." "Colonel, what are you going to do?" "Oh, dry up, and give the poor devil a chance to pull himself together!" "It isn't possible, anyhow. The man's a lunatic."

Little Mildred stood at the colonel's side talking into his ear. "Will you be good enough to take your seats, please, gentlemen?" he said, and the mess dropped into the chairs.

Only Dirkovitch's seat, next to Little Mildred's, was blank, and Little Mildred himself had found Hira Singh's place. The wide-eyed mess-sergeant filled the glasses in dead silence. Once more the colonel rose, but his hand shook, and the port spilled on the table as he looked straight at the man in Little Mildred's chair and said, hoarsely, "Mr. Vice, the Queen." There was a little pause, but the man sprung to his feet and answered, without hesitation, "The Queen, God bless her!" and as he emptied the thin glass he snapped the shank between his fingers.

Long and long ago, when the Empress of India was a young woman, and there were no unclean ideals in the land, it was the custom in a few messes to drink the Queen's toast in broken glass, to the huge delight of the mess contractors.[19] The custom is now dead, because there is nothing to break anything for, except now and again the word of a Government, and that has been broken already.

"That settles it," said the colonel, with a gasp. "He's not a sergeant. What in the world is he?"

The entire mess echoed the word, and the volley of questions would have scared any man. Small wonder that the ragged, filthy invader could only smile and shake his head.

From under the table, calm and smiling urbanely, rose Dirkovitch, who had been roused from healthful slumber by feet upon his body. By the side of the man he rose, and the man shrieked and grovelled at his feet. It was a horrible sight, coming so swiftly upon the pride and glory of the toast that had brought the strayed wits together.

Dirkovitch made no offer to raise him, but Little Mildred heaved him up in an instant. It is not good that a gentleman who can answer to the Queen's toast should lie at the feet of a subaltern of Cossacks.

The hasty action tore the wretch's upper clothing nearly to the waist, and his body was seamed with dry black scars. There is only one weapon in the world that cuts in parallel lines, and it is neither the cane nor the cat.[20] Dirkovitch saw the marks, and the pupils of his eyes dilated—also, his face changed. He said something that sounded like "Shto ve takete,"[21] and the man, fawning, answered "chetyre."

"What's that?" said everybody together.

"His number. That is number four, you know." Dirkovitch spoke very thickly.

"What has a Queen's officer to do with a qualified number?" said the colonel, and there rose an unpleasant growl round the table.

"How can I tell?" said the affable Oriental, with a sweet smile. "He is a—how you have it?—escape—runaway, from over there." He nodded toward the darkness of the night.

"Speak to him, if he'll answer you, and speak to him gently," said Little Mildred, settling the man in a chair. It seemed most

---

19 Mess contractors—Those who sold supplies to the regiment.

20 Cat—Cat-o'-nine-tails, a whip with a knotted lash.

21 Shto ve takete—Who are you?

improper to all present that Dirkovitch should sip brandy as he talked in purring, spitting Russian to the creature who answered so feebly and with such evident dread. But since Dirkovitch appeared to understand, no man said a word. They breathed heavily, leaning forward, in the long gaps of the conversation. The next time that they have no engagements on hand the White Hussars intend to go to St. Petersburg and learn Russian.

"He does not know how many years ago," said Dirkovitch, facing the mess, "but he says it was very long ago, in a war.[22] I think that there was an accident. He says he was of this glorious and distinguished regiment in the war."

"The rolls! The rolls! Holmer get the rolls!" said Little Mildred, and the adjutant dashed off bareheaded to the orderly-room where the rolls of the regiment were kept. He returned just in time to hear Dirkovitch conclude, "Therefore I am most sorry to say there was an accident, which would have been reparable if he had apologized to that our colonel, which he had insulted."

Another growl, which the colonel tried to beat down. The mess was in no mood to weigh insults to Russian colonels just then.

"He does not remember, but I think that there was an accident, and so he was not exchanged among the prisoners, but he was sent to another place—how do you say?—the country. *So,* he says, he came here. He does not know how he came. Eh? He was at Chepany"—the man caught the word, nodded, and shivered—"at Zhigansk and Irkutsk.[23] I cannot understand how he escaped. He says, too, that he was in the forests for many years, but how many years he has forgotten—that with many things. It was an accident; done because he did not apologize to that our colonel. Ah!"

Instead of echoing Dirkovitch's sigh of regret, it is sad to record that the White Hussars livelily exhibited unchristian delight and other emotions, hardly restrained by their sense of hospitality. Holmer flung the frayed and yellow regimental rolls on the table, and the men flung themselves atop of these.

"Steady! Fifty-six—fifty-five—fifty-four," said Holmer. "Here we are. 'Lieutenant Austin Limmason—*missing.*' That was before

[22] In a war—The Crimean War (1853-56), in which England and France supported Turkey against Russia.

[23] Chepany . . . Zhigansk . . . Irkutsk—Towns in Siberia where under the Czar political prisoners were exiled at hard labor.

Sebastopol.[24] What an infernal shame! Insulted one of their colonels, and was quietly shipped off. Thirty years of his life wiped out."

"But he never apologized. Said he'd see him—first," chorussed the mess.

"Poor devil! I suppose he never had the chance afterwards. How did he come here?" said the colonel.

The dingy heap in the chair could give no answer.

"Do you know who you are?"

It laughed weakly.

"Do you know that you are Limmason—Lieutenant Limmason, of the White Hussars?"

Swift as a shot came the answer, in a slightly surprised tone, "Yes, I'm Limmason, of course." The light died out in his eyes, and he collapsed afresh, watching every motion of Dirkovitch with terror. A flight from Siberia may fix a few elementary facts in the mind, but it does not lead to continuity of thought. The man could not explain how, like a homing pigeon, he had found his way to his own old mess again. Of what he had suffered or seen he knew nothing. He cringed before Dirkovitch as instinctively as he had pressed the spring of the candlestick, sought the picture of the drum-horse, and answered to the Queen's toast. The rest was a blank that the dreaded Russian tongue could only in part remove. His head bowed on his breast, and he giggled and cowered alternately.

The devil that lived in the brandy prompted Dirkovitch at this extremely inopportune moment to make a speech. He rose, swaying slightly, gripped the table edge, while his eyes glowed like opals, and began:

"Fellow-soldiers glorious—true friends and hospitables. It was an accident, and deplorable—most deplorable." Here he smiled sweetly all round the mess. "But you will think of this little, little thing. So little, is it not? The Czar! Posh! I slap my fingers—I snap my fingers at him. Do I believe in him? No! But the Slav[25] who has done nothing, *him* I believe. Seventy—how much?

[24] Sebastopol—Russian fortified port which in 1855 surrendered to the allies after a long siege.

[25] The Slav—A curiously prophetic utterance. It indicates that it was not so much the Czar that Kipling mistrusted as the Slavic peoples—the Russians, Poles, Serbs. Today the nations of the world are fighting Communism inspired from Moscow.

—millions that have done nothing—not one thing. Napoleon was an episode."[26] He banged a hand on the table. "Hear you, old peoples, we have done nothing in the world—out here. All our work is to do; and it shall be done, old peoples. Get a-way!" He waved his hand imperiously, and pointed to the man. "You see him. He is not good to see. He was just one little—oh, so little—accident, that no one remembered. Now he is *That*. So will you be, brother soldiers so brave—so will you be. But you will never come back. You will all go where he is gone, or"—he pointed to the great coffin shadow on the ceiling, and muttering, "Seventy millions—get away, you old peoples," fell asleep.

"Sweet, and to the point," said Little Mildred. "What's the use of getting wrath? Let's make the poor devil comfortable."

But that was a matter suddenly and swiftly taken from the loving hands of the White Hussars. The lieutenant had returned only to go away again three days later, when the wail of the "Dead March" and the tramp of the squadrons told the wondering station, that saw no gap in the table, an officer of the regiment had resigned his new-found commission.

And Dirkovitch—bland, supple and always genial—went away too by a night train. Little Mildred and another saw him off, for he was the guest of the mess, and even had he smitten the colonel with the open hand the law of the mess allowed no relaxation of hospitality.

"Good-by, Dirkovitch, and a pleasant journey," said Little Mildred.

"*Au revoir*,[27] my true friends," said the Russian.

"Indeed! But we thought you were going home?"

"Yes; but I will come again. My friends, is that road shut?" He pointed to where the north-star burned over the Khyber Pass.

"By Jove! I forgot. Of course. Happy to meet you, old man, any time you like. Got everything you want—cheroots, ice, bedding? That's all right. Well, *au revoir*, Dirkovitch."

"Um," said the other man, as the tail-lights of the train grew small. "Of—all—the—unmitigated—"

---

[26] NAPOLEON WAS AN EPISODE—Napoleon's retreat from Moscow in 1812 was so disastrous that it put an end to his ambition to bring Russia under his power.

[27] *Au revoir*—A French form of farewell which implies another meeting soon.

Little Mildred answered nothing, but watched the north-star, and hummed a selection from a recent burlesque that had much delighted the White Hussars. It ran:

"I'm sorry for Mister Bluebeard,
I'm sorry to cause him pain;
But a terrible spree there's sure to be
When he comes back again."

## QUESTIONS

1. What does the opening sentence of the story mean? Can it be taken as a statement of the theme?
2. What do you suspect was Dirkovitch's real business in India? What does Kipling reveal of his activities?
3. What does Kipling mean when he says the Pathans once met the White Hussars "officially"?
4. Of what value is the account of the polo game?
5. What is "the other game" to which Hira Singh refers in his speech?
6. What incidents does Kipling use to demonstrate the fact that Limmason was once an officer of the White Hussars?
7. How many characters in the story stand out? Which one do you most admire? Why?
8. What information does the story give concerning the relations between the British and the natives?
9. When Dirkovitch calls Limmason's case just "a little accident," what is the effect on the officers? On you?
10. In his description of the room where the banquet is being held, how does Kipling suggest the threat that hangs over them all?
11. What is the significance of Dirkovitch's speech about "the old peoples"?
12. How does the song with which the story concludes apply to the situation?

## EXERCISES

Exercises preceded by a star are designed for assignment at the discretion of the teacher, or for any student who volunteers.

1. In *The Man Who Was* point out passages that support Kipling's assertion (*Ballad of East and West*) that "East is East, and West is West, and never the twain shall meet."
2. Point out a passage that suggests why Queen Victoria was not always an admirer of Kipling.

*3. Obtain a volume of Kipling's poetry and read *The Truce of the Bear.* Comment on its relation to *The Man Who Was.*

4. Explain the force of Kipling's line describing Limmason: "It laughed weakly."

*5. Write a book review of one of Kipling's other works.

*6. Report on one of the following subjects: *The British in India, Kipling the Imperialist, Russia Yesterday and Today.*

# THE PIECE OF STRING

## GUY DE MAUPASSANT[1]

## 1850–1893

### THE AUTHOR

About the time Kipling was making a name for himself in English literature, a Frenchman was achieving fame in his country as the greatest French master of the short story form. Yet they had almost nothing in common. Their work represented the two extremes of technique: Kipling, full of surging action, vivid color, and enthusiasms and antagonisms that were reflected in everything he wrote; the Frenchman, cold, precise, trimming his narrative to the very minimum of language and never letting his own feelings disturb the metallic smoothness of his art.

It is not often that a man's name strikes the keynote of his life, but it was tragically so in the case of Henri René Albert Guy de Maupassant. Maupassant means "unfortunate passerby"—and if ever a man fared through life under an evil sign it was this strong-bodied, reckless-living Norman whose life was as bitter as his stories were great.

He was born in a rambling old chateau in sunny Normandy in 1850, the same year that witnessed the deaths of Balzac, a great French novelist, and Wordsworth, England's poet-laureate. Madame Maupassant, to whom Guy was passionately devoted, prophesied that her son would be an author. She lived to see that dream come true. A few years in a boys' seminary proved distasteful to the precocious young Maupassant, who managed to get himself expelled by writing sarcastic verses about his teachers. He finally won a degree and at twenty-three entered government work in Paris. Here he spent much of his time rowing on the river Seine—a river which he loved—and attending literary meetings at the home of the great French novelist, Gustave Flaubert, where he met the literary celebrities of the day. For seven years Maupassant studied under Flaubert the art of writing. He had a hard literary taskmaster but a good one. Maupassant learned the secret of art—hard work and patience.

From the publication of his first short stories in 1880 to later successful works like *Mademoiselle Fifi* (1883), *Clair de Lune* (1884), and such a novel as *Pierre et Jean* (1888) Guy de Maupassant was in the forefront of French writers. That much for literary success. Always along with that went the evil in Maupassant's life. The end of the nineteenth century saw much immorality in France, and the author drifted with it. Wild living and extreme dissipation made terrific ravages

[1] Guy de Maupassant (gē dē mō-pá-sä).

upon him. His health undermined, his body diseased, Maupassant began to lose his great writing power. Blindness threatened him. His mind began to fail. In 1892 he attempted to kill himself with a razor. At the age of forty-three he died in a straight-jacket, insane. Maupassant "went out like a lamp that has no more oil."

Though he "burned his candle at both ends," Maupassant lived long enough to link his name unforgettably with the short story form. In addition he was a poet and a novelist. A realist, Maupassant looked at life—its slums, peasants, princes, boors, wine, beauty, and evil—and refused to argue about the good and the bad. He simply put it down in the thirty volumes of his work in ten brief years of writing. One quarter of the work would have made him famous. Tolstoi, the famous Russian writer, said with some exaggeration, "Next to Victor Hugo, Maupassant is the best writer of our time. I am very fond of him and rank him above all his contemporaries."

Maupassant lived too furiously. Sinning, he had no regrets; yet toward the end of his life he kept a volume of *The Imitation of Christ* by his bedside. A man of extremes and contrasts, he mingled virtue with vice. Often kind and lovable, he never quite escaped from the cloud of evil that encompassed him. He was indeed the "unfortunate passerby."

## THE STORY

Maupassant is one of the greatest masters of the Short Story. He lived for his art, and his art was to see life, to observe its minutest details and place them, without comment, on paper. Trained under the great Flaubert he learned to look at life impartially, to be swayed neither by good nor evil, and to write without wasting words. Flaubert was a perfect master. He would send Guy out on tours of observation with some such command as—"Go a walk, my lad, look about you and tell me in a hundred lines what you have seen"; or, "Walk along until you see a janitor doing something outside his lodge, watch him, and then write out all you have noticed." And when Maupassant came back Flaubert would roar out instructions to his pupil, and correct his manuscripts like a schoolmaster, cutting out all unnecessary words, ruthlessly chopping away all superlatives and poor-sounding sentences. Under all this Maupassant was patient, diligent. When his short stories began to appear they swept the nation by storm. Today Maupassant is one of the most popular of the great short story writers.

It is this genius of accurate observation, of writing with economy, telling the story simply and with strength, that makes Guy de Maupassant what he is. Above all else, he is a realist. He honestly puts down what he sees. It is the hardest thing in the world to describe without betraying your own attitude or opinion in your description. Maupassant did just that. He refrained from commenting on his characters or his theme. In the words of John Macy, the critic, ". . . Maupassant within his range of observation has that faculty which Dumas has in another way, of letting life tell itself through action, of keeping his hand off and not seeming to manipulate human affairs." If you read much of Maupassant you will notice him betray himself in only one way—cynicism. Such a life as he lived could not help being reflected in some measure in his work.

*The Piece of String* shows fully the author's skill. It is a character-study revealing itself in the unfolding of the story. A character-study is one of the most difficult types of short story, for it has a purpose far deeper than the mere entertainment from the plot. All the mechanism of the story—introduction, setting, plot, dialogue, ending—must be so woven together, that we *unconsciously* learn the truth about the inner nature of the characters while we are enjoying the progress of the story.

Beginning with a trivial detail, "a piece of string," Maupassant unfolds a compelling story in a few pages of simple words and creates an unforgettable character. So magical is Maupassant's art that you have reached the last line of the story before you have grasped the whole kernel of the character-study. *The Piece of String* is one of the great short stories of the world. When you finish it you will find yourself saying—"This story is true . . . it is life."

## THE PIECE OF STRING[1]

It was market-day, and over all the roads round Goderville the peasants and their wives were coming towards the town. The men walked easily, lurching the whole body forward at every step. Their long legs were twisted and deformed by the slow, painful labors of the country:—by bending over to plough, which is what also makes their left shoulders too high and their figures crooked; and by reaping corn, which obliges them for steadiness' sake to spread their knees too wide. Their starched blue blouses, shining as though varnished, ornamented at collar and cuffs with little patterns of white stitch-work, and blown up big around their bony bodies, seemed exactly like balloons about to soar, but putting forth a head, two arms, and two feet.[2]

Some of these fellows dragged a cow or a calf at the end of a rope. And just behind the animal, beating it over the back with a leaf-covered branch to hasten its pace, went their wives, carrying large baskets from which came forth the heads of chickens or the heads of ducks. These women walked with steps far shorter and quicker than the men; their figures, withered and upright, were

[1] Reprinted by permission from Bigelow, Brown & Co. complete edition of de Maupassant.

[2] THE MEN . . . FEET—An excellent example of Maupassant's "minute observation."

adorned with scanty little shawls pinned over their flat bosoms; and they enveloped their heads each in a white cloth, close fastened round the hair and surmounted by a cap.

Now a char-à-banc passed by, drawn by a jerky-paced nag. It shook up strangely the two men on the seat. And the woman at the bottom of the cart held fast to its sides to lessen the hard joltings.

In the market-place at Goderville was a great crowd, a mingled multitude of men and beasts. The horns of cattle, the high and long-napped hats of wealthy peasants, the head-dress of the women, came to the surface of that sea. And voices, clamorous, sharp, shrill, made a continuous and savage din. Above it a huge burst of laughter from the sturdy lungs of a merry yokel would sometimes sound, and sometimes a long bellow from a cow tied fast to the wall of a house.

It all smelled of the stable, of milk, of hay, and of perspiration, giving off that half-human, half-animal odor which is peculiar to the men of the fields.

Maître Hauchecorne, of Bréauté,[3] had just arrived at Goderville, and was taking his way towards the square, when he perceived on the ground a little piece of string. Maître Hauchecorne, economical, like all true Normans,[4] reflected that everything was worth picking up which could be of any use; and he stooped down—but painfully, because he suffered from rheumatism. He took the bit of thin cord from the ground, and was carefully preparing to roll it up when he saw Maître Malandain, the harness-maker, on his doorstep, looking at him. They had once had a quarrel about a halter, and they had remained angry, bearing malice on both sides. Maître Hauchecorne was overcome with a sort of shame at being seen by his enemy looking in the dirt so for a bit of string. He quickly hid his find beneath his blouse; then in the pocket of his breeches; then pretended to be still looking for something on the ground which he did not discover; and at last went off towards the market-place, with his head bent forward, and a body almost doubled in two by rheumatic pains.

He lost himself immediately in the crowd, which was clamorous, slow, and agitated by interminable bargains. The peasants examined

---

[3] Maitre Hauchecorne, of Bréauté (mâ'trẽ ōsh-kôr'n brā-ō-tā)—Mr. Hauchecorne of Bréauté, a town in Normandy in northeastern France.

[4] Like . . . Normans—Normans had the reputation of being tricky and thrifty.

the cows, went off, came back, always in great perplexity and fear of being cheated, never quite daring to decide, spying at the eye of the seller, trying ceaselessly to discover the tricks of the man and the defect in the beast.

The women, having placed their great baskets at their feet, had pulled out the poultry, which lay upon the ground, tied by the legs, with eyes scared, with combs scarlet.

They listened to propositions, maintaining their prices, with a dry manner, with an impassible face; or, suddenly, perhaps, deciding to take the lower price which was offered, they cried out to the customer, who was departing slowly:

"All right, I'll let you have them, Maît'[5] Anthime."

Then, little by little, the square became empty, and when the *Angelus*[6] struck midday those who lived at a distance poured into the inns.

At Jourdain's[7] the great room was filled with eaters, just as the vast court was filled with vehicles of every sort—wagons, gigs, char-à-bancs, tilburys, tilt-carts which have no name, yellow with mud, misshapen, pieced together, raising their shafts to heaven like two arms, or it may be with their nose in the dirt and their rear in the air.

Just opposite to where the diners were at table the huge fireplace, full of clear flame, threw a lively heat on the backs of those who sat along the right. Three spits[8] were turning, loaded with chickens, with pigeons, and with joints of mutton; and a delectable odor of roast meat, and of gravy gushing over crisp brown skin, took wing from the hearth, kindled merriment, caused mouths to water.

All the aristocracy of the plough were eating there at Maît' Jourdain's, the innkeeper's, a dealer in horses also, and a sharp fellow who had made a pretty penny in his day.

The dishes were passed round, were emptied, with jugs of yellow cider. Every one told of his affairs, of his purchases and his sales. They asked news about the crops. The weather was good for green stuffs, but a little wet for wheat.

---

[5] MAÎT'—Abbreviation of Maitre.

[6] *Angelus*—Angelus bell. At 6 a. m., noon, and 6 p. m. prayers were said regularly in many countries of Europe. A bell announced these prayers to the people. The Angelus is still rung in Europe. It was the inspiration for a famous painting by Millet.

[7] JOURDAIN'S (zhōōr-dă).

[8] SPITS—Pointed rods for roasting meat over fire.

All of a sudden the drum rolled in the court before the house. Every one, except some of the most indifferent, was on his feet at once, and ran to the door, to the windows, with his mouth still full and his napkin in his hand.

When the public crier had finished his tattoo he called forth in a jerky voice, making his pauses out of time:

"Be it known to the inhabitants of Goderville, and in general to all—persons present at the market, that there has been lost this morning, on the Beuzeville[9] road, between—nine and ten o'clock, a pocket-book of black leather, containing five hundred francs[10] and business papers. You are requested to return it—to the mayor's office, at once or to Maître Fortuné Houlbrèque,[11] of Manneville. There will be twenty francs reward."

Then the man departed. They heard once more at a distance the dull beatings on the drum and the faint voice of the crier.

Then they began to talk of this event, reckoning up the chances which Maître Houlbrèque had of finding or of not finding his pocket-book again.

And the meal went on.

They were finishing their coffee when the corporal of gendarmes[12] appeared on the threshold.

He asked:

"Is Maître Hauchecorne, of Bréauté, here?"

Maître Hauchecorne, seated at the other end of the table, answered:

"Here I am."

And the corporal resumed:

"Maître Hauchecorne, will you have the kindness to come with me to the mayor's office? M. le Maire[13] would like to speak to you."

The peasant, surprised and uneasy, gulped down his little glass of cognac, got up, and, even worse bent over than in the morning, since the first steps after a rest were always particularly difficult, started off, repeating:

"Here I am, here I am."

---

[9] BEUZEVILLE (bûz-vēl).

[10] FRANCS—French coins worth about $.20 in normal times.

[11] FORTUNÉ HOULBRÈQUE (fôr-tü-nā o͞ol-brâ'k).

[12] GENDARMES (zhän-därm)—Policemen.

[13] M. LE MAIRE—Monsieur le Maire (mẽ-syû lẽ mâ'r), his Honor the Mayor.

And he followed the corporal.

The mayor was waiting for him, seated in an armchair. He was the notary of the place, a tall, grave man of pompous speech.

"Maître Hauchecorne," said he, "this morning, on the Beuzeville road, you were seen to pick up the pocket-book lost by Maître Houlbrèque, of Manneville."

The countryman, speechless, regarded the mayor, frightened already by this suspicion which rested on him he knew not why.

"I, I picked up that pocket-book?"

"Yes, you."

"I swear I didn't even know nothing about it at all."

"You were seen."

"They saw me, me? Who is that who saw me?"

"M. Malandain, the harness-maker."

Then the old man remembered, understood, and, reddening with anger: "Ah! he saw me, did he, the rascal? He saw me picking up this string here, M'sieu' le Maire."

And, fumbling at the bottom of his pocket, he pulled out of it the little end of string.

But the mayor incredulously shook his head:

"You will not make me believe, Maître Hauchecorne, that M. Malandain, who is a man worthy of credit, has mistaken this string for a pocket-book."

The peasant, furious, raised his hand and spit as if to attest his good faith, repeating:

"For all that, it is the truth of the good God, the blessed truth, M'sieu' le Maire. There! on my soul and my salvation I repeat it."

The mayor continued:

"After having picked up the thing in question, you even looked for some time in the mud to see if a piece of money had not dropped out of it."

The good man was suffocated with indignation and with fear:

"If they can say—if they can say . . . such lies as that to slander an honest man! If they can say!—"

He might protest, he was not believed.

He was confronted with M. Malandain, who repeated and sustained his testimony. They abused one another for an hour. At his own request Maître Hauchecorne was searched. Nothing was found upon him.

At last, the mayor, much perplexed, sent him away, warning him that he would inform the public prosecutor, and ask for orders.

The news had spread. When he left the mayor's office, the old man was surrounded, interrogated with a curiosity which was serious or mocking as the case might be, but into which no indignation entered. And he began to tell the story of the string. They did not believe him. They laughed.

He passed on, button-holed by every one, himself button-holing his acquaintances, beginning over and over again his tale and his protestations, showing his pockets turned inside out to prove that he had nothing.

They said to him:

"You old rogue, *va!*"

And he grew angry, exasperated, feverish, in despair at not being believed, and always telling his story.

The night came.[14] It was time to go home. He set out with three of his neighbors, to whom he pointed out the place where he had picked up the end of the string; and all the way he talked of his adventure.

That evening he made the round in the village of Bréauté, so as to tell every one. He met only unbelievers.

He was ill of it all night long.

The next day, about one in the afternoon, Marius Paumelle, a farm hand of Maître Breton, the market-gardener at Ymauville,[15] returned the pocket-book and its contents to Maître Houlbrèque, of Manneville.

This man said, indeed, that he had found it on the road; but not knowing how to read, he had carried it home and given it to his master.[16]

The news spread to the environs. Maître Hauchecorne was informed. He put himself at once upon the go, and began to relate his story as completed by the *dénouement*.[17] He triumphed.

"What grieved me," said he, "was not the thing itself, do you understand; but it was the lies. There's nothing does you so much harm as being in disgrace for lying."

---

[14] THE NIGHT CAME—An instance of the author's amazing simplicity and condensation of expression.

[15] YMAUVILLE (ē-mō-vēl).

[16] THIS MAN . . . MASTER—Apparently the story is over.

[17] *Dénouement*—Solution.

All day he talked of his adventure, he told it on the roads to the people who passed; at the cabaret to the people who drank; and the next Sunday, when they came out of church. He even stopped strangers to tell them about it. He was easy, now, and yet something worried him without his knowing exactly what it was. People had a joking manner while they listened. They did not seem convinced. He seemed to feel their tittle-tattle behind his back.

On Tuesday of the next week he went to market at Goderville, prompted entirely by the need of telling his story.

Malandain, standing on his door-step, began to laugh as he saw him pass. Why?

He accosted a farmer of Criquetot,[18] who did not let him finish, and, giving him a punch in the pit of his stomach, cried in his face: "Oh you great rogue, *va!*" Then turned his heel upon him.

Maître Hauchecorne remained speechless, and grew more and more uneasy. Why had they called him "great rogue"?

When seated at table in Jourdain's tavern he began again to explain the whole affair.

A horse-dealer of Montivilliers[19] shouted at him:

"Get out, get out, you old scamp; I know all about your string!"

Hauchecorne stammered:

"But since they found it again, the pocket-book!"

But the other continued:

"Hold your tongue, daddy; there's one who finds it and there's another who returns it. And no one the wiser."

The peasant was choked. He understood at last. They accused him of having had the pocket-book brought back by an accomplice, by a confederate.

He tried to protest. The whole table began to laugh. He could not finish his dinner, and went away amid a chorus of jeers.

He went home, ashamed and indignant, choked with rage, with confusion, the more cast-down since from his Norman cunning, he was, perhaps, capable of having done what they accused him of, and even of boasting of it as a good trick. His innocence dimly seemed to him impossible to prove, his craftiness being so well known. And he felt himself struck to the heart by the injustice of the suspicion.

---

18 Criquetot (krēk'tō).

19 Montivilliers (mô-tē-vē-lēyā).

Then he began anew to tell of his adventure, lengthening his recital every day, each time adding new proofs, more energetic protestations, and more solemn oaths which he thought of, which he prepared in his hours of solitude, his mind being entirely occupied by the story of the string. The more complicated his defence, the more artful his arguments, the less he was believed.

"Those are liars' proofs," they said behind his back.

He felt this; it preyed upon his heart. He exhausted himself in useless efforts.

He was visibly wasting away.

The jokers now made him tell the story of "The Piece of String" to amuse them, just as you make a soldier who has been on a campaign tell his story of the battle. His mind, struck at the root, grew weak.

About the end of December he took to his bed.

He died early in January, and, in the delirium of the death-agony, he protested his innocence, repeating:

"A little bit of string—a little bit of string—see, here it is, M'sieu' le Maire."

## QUESTIONS

1. Who is the chief actor? What is the flaw in his character that makes the story possible?
2. What is the setting of the story? How much local color does Maupassant create for you at the opening of the story?
3. Are the characters in *The Piece of String* idealized or life-like? Which would you prefer them to be? Why?
4. Master Hauchecorne pretends to be searching for something when Malandain sees him pick up the piece of string. Why should he do this? What important part does this play as evidence later in the story?
5. Who accused Hauchecorne of picking up the pocket-book? What was his motive in making the accusation? Was it justifiable?
6. How does Maupassant create suspense in the story? Can you find the particular paragraph which he uses for this purpose?
7. What apparently settles the innocence of Hauchecorne? Why will not the people believe his story?
8. Are there any weak points in the plot? In the dialogue? In the description?
9. What kind of feeling does the end of the story leave with you?
10. Is *The Piece of String* a successful character-study? Why? Is the title in keeping with the story? Can you suggest a different one?
11. It has been stated that Maupassant was impartial and objective in his writing. Does he betray his own views or intrude his own personality in any way during the course of the story?

## EXERCISES

**Exercises preceded by a star are designed for assignment at the discretion of the teacher, or for any student who volunteers.**

1. Write a brief character-sketch of Master Hauchecorne.
2. Outline the plot of the story, including in it: opening situation, chief complication, preparation for crisis, the crisis, suspense, final complication, climax.
3. Select three passages of "minute observation."
4. Write an essay of about 100 words on Maupassant as a master of the Short Story as revealed in *The Piece of String.*
5. Show that Maupassant is realistic in plot, action, setting, and dialogue. Refer to specific passages.
6. Flaubert made his pupil observe and write about small happenings in the life about him. Write an observation of 50 lines of some person or incident in the everyday life about you.

*7. Contrast *The Piece of String* with *The Man Who Was,* with special reference to style, purpose, plot, characterization, and general effect.

*8. Select a modern character-study from some magazine or book and briefly discuss it.

9. Try to find some description or detail which could be omitted without detracting from the story. Report on the result of your search.

# THE LITTLE REGIMENT

## STEPHEN CRANE

### 1871–1900

### THE AUTHOR

Someone has said—"A poet should die before thirty." But history casts doubt on such an assertion. Too many geniuses have died before realizing the full extent of their powers. Stephen Crane was one of them. He was barely thirty when tuberculosis cut him down. The famed novelist, Joseph Conrad, who loved Crane deeply, wrote at the ill-timed passing of his young American friend, ". . . his passage on this earth was like that of a horseman riding swiftly in the dawn of a day fated to be short and without sunshine."

Stephen Crane's position among American authors is important, and his work is considered by many critics to mark the beginning of modern American literature. A passionate realism, a desire to see and represent life colorfully but naturally, dominates the fourteen volumes of his collected novels, verses, and short stories. Crane hated sentimentality. Unflinchingly he told the truth, often with deep irony, as in his novel, *Maggie* (1896), an honest study of poverty and crime in New York City. His most famous work, *The Red Badge of Courage* (1895), is a novel of the Civil War, describing the experiences of an ordinary private. It is written with such vividness and flaming reality that it is hard to realize the author had never seen a battle or served under gunfire before writing it. In two volumes of unusual poetry, *The Black Riders* (1895), and *War Is Kind* (1899), he became one of the forerunners of unrimed "free verse." Crane's short stories like *The Open Boat, Wounds in the Rain,* and *The Little Regiment* grip with their naturalism. H. G. Wells thought *The Open Boat,* "the finest short story in the English language."

Stephen Crane was born at Newark, New Jersey, November 1, 1871, the fourteenth child of a Methodist minister. At sixteen he was trying his hand at newspaper writing. Crane entered Lafayette College only to transfer to Syracuse University where he played varsity baseball, smoked, dreamed, did a little writing. At the end of his freshman year he left, drifting to New York City to enter journalism. He never finished his college course.

The year 1898 saw him as a newspaper correspondent in the Spanish-American War. The next year he went with his wife to live in Sussex, England, where he formed a close friendship with Conrad. We see him in those days as "a young man of medium stature, slender build, with very steady, penetrating blue eyes, the eyes of a man who not only sees visions but can brood on them to some purpose."

The feverish energy with which Crane wrote, and the success of his *Red Badge of Courage,* resulted in his being sent as a special correspondent to cover the Græco-Turkish War in 1897. On the return trip he was shipwrecked and suffered privations which paved the way for his death. In 1900 while on a trip to the Black Forest, Germany, in the vain hope of curing his fatal malady, he died. It is not an exaggeration to say of this slim, volcanic genius, who was the eternal youth in his love for horses and the sea, that he was one of the most gifted American writers of his day.

## THE STORY

War—with its blood-trampled trenches, whine of shells, moans of wounded, and the red horror of death—gleams in unforgettable pictures in this short story, *The Little Regiment,* which has been called "one of the world's few perfect short stories." Ambrose Bierce, probably the greatest American writer of war stories, significantly praised Stephen Crane when he said—"This young man has the power to feel. He knows nothing of war, yet he is drenched in blood. Most beginners who deal with this subject spatter themselves merely with ink."

It is Crane's ability to drench his war scenes in blood while knowing nothing of war that spells his unique success. Out of the accurate wealth of his fertile imagination, he depicted battles which never were, and upon whose scenes no eyes had ever gazed, with such convincing reality, such vivid, burning detail, that old veterans reproached him for divulging too much of the battles they had been through. It is an interesting contrast to point out that as an actual war correspondent in the Spanish-American War, Crane was practically a failure. His imagination simply refused to stay within bounds.

It is as a realist that Crane is famous. Here, in a story which can be read at one sitting, he takes you into the living heart of the Civil War. There are no spangles and tinsel. It is stark truth. The realism in *The Little Regiment* is achieved by the author's power of "direct expression." He has a knack of saying things abruptly and straight-forwardly. His sentences ring out crisply, clearly. The images are sharp as cameos. There is no display of sentimentality—Crane despised it.

The strength of the story does not lie in its plot—which turns on the relationship between two jealous brothers—but in its powerful description and keen characterization. Crane seldom refers to his two main characters except by their first names. So strong is his character analysis that names are not needed to etch the individuals on the reader's mind.

The author's greatest force, however, rests in his descriptions. He has a natural vividness, an instinctive power of using tiny details to build up a complete atmosphere and picture. Everything he writes is revealed with the uncanny brilliance of a lightning flash. Crane could use a phrase like "the long witches' croon of the shells" with startling effect. As you read notice carefully the many unusual words and phrases.

Stephen Crane never moralized. In this war-tale he draws his picture, brings his story to a dramatic close, without once commenting on the characters or the theme of the story. He is the perfect impartial observer—detached, cool, impersonal. After describing the terrific battle-scene he sums it up: "After the red round eye of the sun had stared long at the little plain and its burden, darkness, a sable mercy, came heavily upon it, and the wan hands of the dead were no longer seen in strange frozen gestures."

As in all of Crane's stories, a thread of irony weaves its way through *The Little Regiment.* Crane pierced quickly to the eternal root of things but his knowledge saddened rather than inspired him. He saw the glory of war—but more than that—its blind futility. *The Little Regiment* was published in 1896 as the title story in a volume of tales of the Civil War. It shows the strong influence of his masterpiece, *The Red Badge of Courage,* written two years before, which stands as one of the great novels of the world.

## THE LITTLE REGIMENT[1]

### I

The fog made the clothes of the men of the column in the roadway seem of a luminous quality. It imparted to the heavy infantry overcoats a new color, a kind of blue which was so pale that a regiment might have been merely a long, low shadow in the mist. However, a muttering, one part grumble, three parts joke, hovered in the air above the thick ranks, and blended in an undertone roar, which was the voice of the column.

The town on the southern shore of the little river loomed spectrally, a faint etching upon the grey cloud-masses which were shifting with oily languor. A long row of guns upon the northern bank had been pitiless in their hatred, but a little battered belfry could be dimly seen still pointing with invincible resolution toward the heavens.

The enclouded air vibrated with noises made by hidden colossal things. The infantry tramplings, the heavy rumbling of the artillery, made the earth speak of gigantic preparation. Guns on distant heights thundered from time to time with sudden, nervous roar, as if unable to endure in silence a knowledge of hostile troops massing, other guns going to position. These sounds, near and remote, defined an immense battle-ground, described the tremendous width

[1] Reprinted from *The Little Regiment* by Stephen Crane, by permission of and special arrangement with Alfred A. Knopf, Inc., authorized publishers.

of the stage of the prospective drama. The voices of the guns, slightly casual, unexcited in their challenges and warnings, could not destroy the unutterable eloquence of the word in the air, a meaning of impending struggle which made the breath halt at the lips.

The column in the roadway was ankle-deep in mud. The men swore piously at the rain which drizzled upon them, compelling them to stand always very erect in fear of the drops that would sweep in under their coat collars. The fog was as cold as wet cloths. The men stuffed their hands deep into their pockets, and huddled their muskets in their arms. The machinery of orders had rooted these soldiers deeply into the mud, precisely as almighty nature roots mullein stalks.

They listened and speculated when a tumult of fighting came from the dim town across the river. When the noise lulled for a time they resumed their descriptions of the mud and graphically exaggerated the number of hours they had been kept waiting. The general commanding their division rode along the ranks, and they cheered admiringly, affectionately, crying out to him gleeful prophecies of the coming battle. Each man scanned him with a peculiarly keen personal interest, and afterward spoke of him with unquestioning devotion and confidence, narrating anecdotes which were mainly untrue.

When the jokers lifted the shrill voices which invariably belonged to them, flinging witticisms at their comrades, a loud laugh would sweep from rank to rank, and soldiers who had not heard would lean forward and demand repetition. When were borne past them some wounded men with grey and blood-smeared faces, and eyes that rolled in that helpless beseeching for assistance from the sky which comes with supreme pain, the soldiers in the mud watched intently, and from time to time asked of the bearers an account of the affair. Frequently they bragged of their corps, their division, their brigade, their regiment. Anon they referred to the mud and the cold drizzle. Upon this threshold of a wild scene of death they, in short, defied the proportion of events with that splendour of heedlessness which belongs only to veterans.

"Like a lot of wooden soldiers," swore Billie Dempster, moving his feet in the thick mass, and casting a vindictive glance indefinitely. "Standing in the mud for a hundred years."

"Oh, shut up!" murmured his brother Dan. The manner of his words implied that this fraternal voice near him was an indescribable bore.

"Why should I shut up?" demanded Billie.

"Because you're a fool," cried Dan, taking no time to debate it; "the biggest fool in the regiment."

There was but one man between them, and he was habituated. These insults from brother to brother had swept across his chest, flown past his face, many times during two long campaigns. Upon this occasion he simply grinned first at one, then at the other.

The way of these brothers was not an unknown topic in regimental gossip. They had enlisted simultaneously, with each sneering loudly at the other for doing it. They left their little town, and went forward with the flag, exchanging protestations of undying suspicion. In the camp life they so openly despised each other that, when entertaining quarrels were lacking, their companions often contrived situations calculated to bring forth display of this fraternal dislike.

Both were large-limbed, strong young men, and often fought with friends in camp unless one was near to interfere with the other. This latter happened rather frequently, because Dan, preposterously willing for any manner of combat, had a very great horror of seeing Billie in a fight; and Billie, almost odiously ready himself, simply refused to see Dan stripped to his shirt and with his fists aloft. This sat queerly upon them, and made them the objects of plots.

When Dan jumped through a ring of eager soldiers and dragged forth his raving brother by the arm, a thing often predicted would almost come to pass. When Billie performed the same office for Dan, the prediction would again miss fulfilment by an inch. But indeed they never fought together, although they were perpetually upon the verge.

They expressed longing for such conflict. As a matter of truth, they had at one time made full arrangement for it, but even with the encouragement and interest of half of the regiment they somehow failed to achieve collision.

If Dan became a victim of police duty, no jeering was so destructive to the feelings as Billie's comment. If Billie got a call to appear at the headquarters, none would so genially prophesy his complete undoing as Dan. Small misfortunes to one were, in truth, invariably greeted with hilarity by the other, who seemed to see in them great reinforcement of his opinion.

As soldiers, they expressed each for each a scorn intense and blasting. After a certain battle, Billie was promoted to corporal. When Dan was told of it, he seemed smitten dumb with astonishment and patriotic indignation. He stared in silence, while the dark blood rushed to Billie's forehead, and he shifted his weight from foot to foot. Dan at last found his tongue, and said: "Well, I'm durned!" If he had heard that an army mule had been appointed to the post of corps commander, his tone could not have had more derision in it. Afterward, he adopted a fervid insubordination, an almost religious reluctance to obey the new corporal's orders, which came near to developing the desired strife.

It is here finally to be recorded also that Dan, most ferociously profane in speech, very rarely swore in the presence of his brother; and that Billie, whose oaths came from his lips with the grace of falling pebbles, was seldom known to express himself in this manner when near his brother Dan.

At last the afternoon contained a suggestion of evening. Metallic cries rang suddenly from end to end of the column. They inspired at once a quick, business-like adjustment. The long thing stirred in the mud. The men had hushed, and were looking across the river. A moment later the shadowy mass of pale blue figures was moving steadily toward the stream. There could be heard from the town a clash of swift fighting and cheering. The noise of the shooting coming through the heavy air had its sharpness taken from it, and sounded in thuds.

There was a halt upon the bank above the pontoons. When the column went winding down the incline, and streamed out upon the bridge, the fog had faded to a great degree, and in the clearer dusk the guns on a distant ridge were enabled to perceive the crossing. The long whirling outcries of the shells came into the air above the men. An occasional solid shot struck the surface of the river, and dashed into view a sudden vertical jet. The distance was subtly illuminated by the lightning from the deep-booming guns. One by one the batteries on the northern shore aroused, the innumerable guns bellowing in angry oration at the distant ridge. The rolling thunder crashed and reverberated as a wild surf sounds on a still night, and to this music the column marched across the pontoons.

The waters of the grim river curled away in a smile from the ends of the great boats, and slid swiftly beneath the planking. The dark, riddled walls of the town upreared before the troops, and from a region hidden by these hammered and tumbled houses came incessantly the yells and firings of a prolonged and close skirmish.

When Dan had called his brother a fool, his voice had been so decisive, so brightly assured, that many men had laughed, considering it to be great humour under the circumstances. The incident happened to rankle deep in Billie. It was not any strange thing that his brother had called him a fool. In fact, he often called him a fool with exactly the same amount of cheerful and prompt conviction, and before large audiences, too. Billie wondered in his own mind why he took such profound offence in this case; but, at any rate, as he slid down the bank and on to the bridge with his regiment, he was searching his knowledge for something that would pierce Dan's blithesome spirit. But he could contrive nothing at this time, and his impotency made the glance which he was once able to give his brother still more malignant.

The guns far and near were roaring a fearful and grand introduction for this column which was marching upon the stage of death. Billie felt it, but only in a numb way. His heart was cased in that curious dissonant metal which covers a man's emotions at such times. The terrible voices from the hills told him that in this wide conflict his life was an insignificant fact, and that his death would be an insignificant fact. They portended the whirlwind to which he would be as necessary as a butterfly's waved wing. The solemnity, the sadness of it came near enough to make him wonder why he was neither solemn nor sad. When his mind vaguely adjusted events according to their importance to him, it appeared that the uppermost thing was the fact that upon the eve of battle, and before many comrades, his brother had called him a fool.

Dan was in a particularly happy mood. "Hurray! Look at 'em shoot," he said, when the long witches' croon of the shells came into the air. It enraged Billie when he felt the little thorn in him, and saw at the same time that his brother had completely forgotten it.

The column went from the bridge into more mud. At this southern end there was a chaos of hoarse directions and commands. Darkness was coming upon the earth, and regiments were being hurried up the slippery bank. As Billie floundered in the black mud, amid the swearing, sliding crowd, he suddenly resolved that, in the absence of other means of hurting Dan, he would avoid looking at him, refrain from speaking to him, pay absolutely no heed to his existence; and this, done skilfully, would, he imagined, soon reduce his brother to a poignant sensitiveness.

At the top of the bank the column again halted and rearranged itself, as a man after a climb rearranges his clothing. Presently the great steel-backed brigade, an infinitely graceful thing in the rhythm and ease of its veteran movement, swung up a little narrow, slanting street.

Evening had come so swiftly that the fighting on the remote borders of the town was indicated by thin flashes of flame. Some building was on fire, and its reflection upon the clouds was an oval of delicate pink.

## II

All demeanour of rural serenity had been wrenched violently from the little town by the guns and by the waves of men which had surged through it. The hand of war laid upon this village had in an instant changed it to a thing of remnants. It resembled the place of a monstrous shaking of the earth itself. The windows, now mere unsightly holes, made the tumbled and blackened dwellings seem skeletons. Doors lay splintered to fragments. Chimneys had flung their bricks everywhere. The artillery fire had not neglected the rows of gentle shade-trees which had lined the streets. Branches and heavy trunks cluttered the mud in driftwood tangles, while a few shattered forms had contrived to remain dejectedly, mournfully upright. They expressed an innocence, a helplessness, which perforce created a pity for their happening into this cauldron of battle. Furthermore, there was under foot a vast collection of odd things reminiscent of the charge, the fight, the retreat. There were boxes and barrels filled with earth, behind which riflemen had lain snugly, and in these little trenches were the dead in blue with the dead in grey, the poses eloquent of the struggles for possession of the town, until the history of the whole conflict was written plainly in the streets.

And yet the spirit of this little city, its quaint individuality, poised in the air above the ruins, defying the guns, the sweeping volleys; holding in contempt those avaricious blazes which had attacked many dwellings. The hard earthen sidewalks proclaimed the games that had been played there during long lazy days, in the careful shadows of the trees. "General Merchandise," in faint letters upon a long board, had to be read with a slanted glance, for the sign dangled by one end; but the porch of the old store was a palpable legend of wide-hatted men, smoking.

This subtle essence, this soul of the life that had been, brushed like invisible wings the thoughts of the men in the swift columns that came up from the river.

In the darkness a loud and endless humming arose from the great blue crowds bivouacked in the streets. From time to time a sharp spatter of firing from far picket lines entered this bass chorus. The smell from the smouldering ruins floated on the cold night breeze.

Dan, seated ruefully upon the doorstep of a shot-pierced house, was proclaiming the campaign badly managed. Orders had been issued forbidding camp-fires.

Suddenly he ceased his oration and, scanning the group of his comrades, said: "Where's Billie? Do you know?"

"Gone on picket."[2]

"Get out! Has he?" said Dan. "No business to go on picket. Why don't some of them other corporals take their turn?"

A bearded private was smoking his pipe of confiscated tobacco, seated comfortably upon a horse-hair trunk which he had dragged from the house. He observed: "Was his turn."

"No such thing," cried Dan. He and the man on the horse-hair trunk held discussion in which Dan stoutly maintained that if his brother had been sent on picket it was an injustice. He ceased his argument when another soldier, upon whose arms could faintly be seen the two stripes of a corporal, entered the circle. "Humph," said Dan, "where you been?"

The corporal made no answer. Presently Dan said: "Billie, where you been?"

His brother did not seem to hear these inquiries. He glanced at the house which towered above them, and remarked casually to the man on the horse-hair trunk: "Funny, ain't it? After the pelting this town got, you'd think there wouldn't be one brick left on another."

[2] ON PICKET—On sentinel duty to guard camp.

"Oh," said Dan, glowering at his brother's back. "Getting mighty smart, ain't you?"

The absence of camp-fires allowed the evening to make apparent its quality of faint silver light in which the blue clothes of the throng became black, and the faces became white expanses, void of expression. There was considerable excitement a short distance from the group around the doorstep. A soldier had chanced upon a hoop-skirt, and arrayed in it he was performing a dance amid the applause of his companions. Billie and a greater part of the men immediately poured over there to witness the exhibition.

"What's the matter with Billie?" demanded Dan of the man upon the horse-hair trunk.

"How do I know?" rejoined the other in mild resentment. He arose and walked away. When he returned he said briefly, in a weather-wise tone, that it would rain during the night.

Dan took a seat upon one end of the horse-hair trunk. He was facing the crowd around the dancer, which in its hilarity swung this way and that way. At times he imagined that he could recognize his brother's face.

He and the man on the other end of the trunk thoughtfully talked of the army's position. To their minds, infantry and artillery were in a most precarious jumble in the streets of the town; but they did not grow nervous over it, for they were used to having the army appear in a precarious jumble to their minds. They had learned to accept such puzzling situations as a consequence of their position in the ranks, and were now usually in possession of a simple but perfectly immovable faith that somebody understood the jumble. Even if they had been convinced that the army was a headless monster, they would merely have nodded with the veteran's singular cynicism. It was none of their business as soldiers. Their duty was to grab sleep and food when occasion permitted, and cheerfully fight wherever their feet were planted until more orders came. This was a task sufficiently absorbing.

They spoke of other corps, and, this talk being confidential, their voices dropped to tones of awe. "The Ninth"—"The First"—"The Fifth"—"The Sixth"—"The Third"—the simple numerals rang with eloquence, each having a meaning which was to float through many years as no intangible arithmetical mist, but as pregnant with individuality as the names of cities.

Of their own corps they spoke with a deep veneration, an idolatry, a supreme confidence which apparently would not blanch to see it match against everything.

It was as if their respect for other corps was due partly to a wonder that organizations not blessed with their own famous numeral could take such an interest in the war. They could prove that their division was the best in the corps, and that their brigade was the best in the division. And their regiment—it was plain that no fortune of life was equal to the chance which caused a man to be born, so to speak, into this command, the keystone of the defending arch.

At times Dan covered with insults the character of a vague, unnamed general to whose petulance and busy-body spirit he ascribed the order which made hot coffee impossible.

Dan said that victory was certain in the coming battle. The other man seemed rather dubious. He remarked upon the fortified line of hills, which had impressed him even from the other side of the river. "Shucks," said Dan. "Why, we—" He pictured a splendid overflowing of these hills by the sea of men in blue. During the period of this conversation Dan's glance searched the merry throng about the dancer. Above the babble of voices in the street a faraway thunder could sometimes be heard, evidently from the very edge of the horizon—the boom-boom of restless guns.

## III

Ultimately the night deepened to the tone of black velvet. The outlines of the fireless camp were like the faint drawings upon ancient tapestry. The glint of a rifle, the shine of a button, might have been of threads of silver and gold sewn upon the fabric of the night. There was little presented to the vision, but to a sense more subtle there was discernible in the atmosphere something like a pulse; a mystic beating which would have told a stranger of the presence of a giant thing—the slumbering mass of regiments and batteries.[3]

With fires forbidden, the floor of a dry old kitchen was thought to be a good exchange for the cold earth of December, even if a shell had exploded in it and knocked it so out of shape that when

[3] ULTIMATELY . . . BATTERIES—Notice the vividness of the description in this paragraph.

a man lay curled in his blanket his last waking thought was likely to be of the wall that bellied out above him, as if strongly anxious to topple upon the score of soldiers.

Billie looked at the bricks ever about to descend in a shower upon his face, listened to the industrious pickets plying their rifles on the border of the town, imagined some measure of the din of the coming battle, thought of Dan and Dan's chagrin, and, rolling over in his blanket, went to sleep with satisfaction.

At an unknown hour he was aroused by the creaking of boards. Lifting himself upon his elbow, he saw a sergeant prowling among the sleeping forms. The sergeant carried a candle in an old brass candlestick. He would have resembled some old farmer on an unusual midnight tour if it were not for the significance of his gleaming buttons and striped sleeves.

Billie blinked stupidly at the light until his mind returned from the journeys of slumber. The sergeant stooped among the unconscious soldiers, holding the candle close, and peering into each face.

"Hello, Haines," said Billie. "Relief?"

"Hello, Billie," said the sergeant. "Special duty."

"Dan got to go?"

"Jameson, Hunter, McCormack, D. Dempster. Yes.—Where is he?"

"Over there by the winder," said Billie, gesturing. "What is it for, Haines?"

"You don't think I know, do you?" demanded the sergeant. He began to pipe sharply but cheerily at men upon the floor. "Come, Mac, get up here. Here's a special for you. Wake up, Jameson. Come along, Dannie, me boy."

Each man at once took this call to duty as a personal affront. They pulled themselves out of their blankets, rubbed their eyes, and swore at whoever was responsible. "Them's orders," cried the sergeant. "Come! Get out of here." An undetailed head with dishevelled hair thrust out from a blanket, and a sleepy voice said: "Shut up, Haines, and go home."

When the detail clanked out of the kitchen, all but one of the remaining men seemed to be again asleep. Billie, leaning on his elbow, was gazing into darkness. When the footsteps died to silence, he curled himself into his blanket.

At the first cool lavender lights of daybreak he aroused again, and scanned his recumbent companions. Seeing a wakeful one he asked: "Is Dan back yet?"

The man said: "Hain't seen 'im."

Billie put both hands behind his head, and scowled into the air. "Can't see the use of these cussed details in the night-time," he muttered in his most unreasonable tones. "Darn nuisances. Why can't they—?" He grumbled at length and graphically.

When Dan entered with the squad, however, Billie was convincingly asleep.

## IV

The regiment trotted in double time along the street, and the colonel seemed to quarrel over the right of way with many artillery officers. Batteries were waiting in the mud, and the men of them, exasperated by the bustle of this ambitious infantry, shook their fists from saddle and caisson,[4] exchanging all manner of taunts and jests. The slanted guns continued to look reflectively at the ground.

On the outskirts of the crumbled town a fringe of blue figures was firing into the fog. The regiment swung out into skirmish lines, and the fringe of blue figures departed, turning their backs and going joyfully around the flank.

The bullets began a low moan off toward a ridge which loomed faintly in the heavy mist. When the swift crescendo had reached its climax, the missiles zipped just overhead, as if piercing an invisible curtain. A battery on the hill was crashing with such tumult that it was as if the guns had quarrelled and had fallen pell-mell and snarling upon each other. The shells howled on their journey toward the town. From short-range distance there came a spatter of musketry, sweeping along an invisible line and making faint sheets of orange light.

Some in the new skirmish lines were beginning to fire at various shadows discerned in the vapour—forms of men suddenly revealed by some humour of the laggard masses of clouds. The crackle of musketry began to dominate the purring of the hostile bullets. Dan, in the front rank, held his rifle poised, and looked into the fog, keenly, coldly, with the air of a sportsman. His nerves were so

[4] CAISSON—Ammunition wagon.

steady that it was as if they had been drawn from his body, leaving him merely a muscular machine; but his numb heart was somehow beating to the pealing march of the fight.

The waving skirmish line went backward and forward, ran this way and that way. Men got lost in the fog, and men were found again. Once they got too close to the formidable ridge, and the thing burst out as if repulsing a general attack. Once another blue regiment was apprehended on the very edge of firing into them. Once a friendly battery began an elaborate and scientific process of extermination. Always as busy as brokers, the men slid here and there over the plain, fighting their foes, escaping from their friends, leaving a history of many movements in the wet yellow turf, cursing the atmosphere, blazing away every time they could identify the enemy.

In one mystic changing of the fog, as if the fingers of spirits were drawing aside these draperies, a small group of the grey skirmishers, silent, statuesque, was suddenly disclosed to Dan and those about him. So vivid and near were they that there was something uncanny in the revelation.

There might have been a second of mutual staring. Then each rifle in each group was at the shoulder. As Dan's glance flashed along the barrel of his weapon, the figure of a man suddenly loomed as if the musket had been a telescope. The short black beard, the slouch hat, the pose of the man as he sighted to shoot, made a quick picture in Dan's mind. The same moment, it would seem, he pulled his own trigger, and the man, smitten, lurched forward, while his exploding rifle made a slanting crimson streak in the air, and the slouch hat fell before the body. The billows of the fog, governed by singular impulses, rolled between.

"You got that feller sure enough," said a comrade to Dan. Dan looked at him absent-mindedly.

## V

When the next morning calmly displayed another fog, the men of the regiment exchanged eloquent comments; but they did not abuse it at length, because the streets of the town now contained enough galloping aides to make three troops of cavalry, and they knew that they had come to the verge of the great fight.

Dan conversed with the man who had once possessed a horse-hair trunk; but they did not mention the line of hills which had furnished them in more careless moments with an agreeable topic. They avoided it now as condemned men do the subject of death, and yet the thought of it stayed in their eyes as they looked at each other and talked gravely of other things.

The expectant regiment heaved a long sigh of relief when the sharp call "Fall in," repeated indefinitely, arose in the streets. It was inevitable that a bloody battle was to be fought, and they wanted to get it off their minds. They were, however, doomed again to spend a long period planted firmly in the mud. They craned their necks, and wondered where some of the other regiments were going.

At last the mists rolled carelessly away. Nature made at this time all provisions to enable foes to see each other, and immediately the roar of guns resounded from every hill. The endless cracking of the skirmishers swelled to rolling crashes of musketry. Shells screamed with panther-like noises at the houses. Dan looked at the man of the horse-hair trunk, and the man said "Well, here she comes!"

The tenor voices of younger officers and the deep and hoarse voices of the older ones rang in the streets. These cries pricked like spurs. The masses of men vibrated from the suddenness with which they were plunged into the situation of troops about to fight. That the orders were long expected did not concern the emotion.

Simultaneous movement was imparted to all these thick bodies of men and horses that lay in the town. Regiment after regiment swung rapidly into the streets that faced the sinister ridge.

This exodus was theatrical. The little sober-hued village had been like the cloak which disguises the king of drama. It was now put aside, and an army, splendid thing of steel and blue, stood forth in the sunlight.

Even the soldiers in the heavy columns drew deep breaths at the sight, more majestic than they had dreamed. The heights of the enemy's position were crowded with men who resembled people come to witness some mighty pageant. But as the column moved steadily to their positions, the guns, matter-of-fact warriors, doubled their number, and shells burst with red thrilling tumult on the crowded plain. One came into the ranks of the regiment, and after the smoke and the wrath of it had faded, leaving motionless figures, every one stormed according to the limits of his vocabulary, for veterans detest being killed when they are not busy.

The regiment sometimes looked sidewise at its brigade companions, composed of men who had never been in battle; but no frozen blood could withstand the heat of the splendour of this army before the eyes on the plain, these lines so long that the flanks were little streaks, this mass of men of one intention. The recruits carried themselves heedlessly. At the rear was an idle battery, and three artillerymen in a foolish row on a caisson nudged each other and grinned at the recruits. "You'll catch it pretty soon," they called out. They were impersonally gleeful, as if they themselves were not also likely to catch it pretty soon. But with this picture of an army in their hearts, the new men perhaps felt the devotion which the drops may feel for the wave; they were of its power and glory; they smiled jauntily at the foolish row of gunners, and told them to go to blazes.

The column trotted across some little bridges, and spread quickly into lines of battle. Before them was a bit of plain, and in back of the plain was the ridge. There was no time left for consideration. The men were staring at the plain, mightily wondering how it would feel to be out there, when a brigade in advance yelled and charged. The hill was all grey smoke and fire-points.

That fierce elation in the terrors of war, catching a man's heart and making it burn with such ardour that he becomes capable of dying, flashed in the faces of the men like coloured lights, and made them resemble leashed animals, eager, ferocious, daunting at nothing. The line was really in its first leap before the wild, hoarse crying of the orders.

The greed for close quarters which is the emotion of a bayonet charge came then into the minds of the men and developed until it was a madness. The field, with its faded grass of a Southern winter, seemed to this fury miles in width.

High, slow-moving masses of smoke, with an odour of burning cotton, engulfed the line until the men might have been swimmers. Before them the ridge, the shore of this grey sea, was outlined, crossed, and re-crossed by sheets of flame. The howl of the battle arose to the noise of innumerable wind demons.

The line, galloping, scrambling, plunging like a herd of wounded horses, went over a field that was sown with corpses, the records of other charges.

Directly in front of the black-faced, whooping Dan, carousing in this onward sweep like a new kind of fiend, a wounded man appeared, raising his shattered body, and staring at this rush of men down upon him. It seemed to occur to him that he was to be trampled; he made a desperate, piteous effort to escape; then finally huddled in a waiting heap. Dan and the soldier near him widened the interval between them without looking down, without appearing to heed the wounded man. This little clump of blue seemed to reel past them as boulders reel past a train.

Bursting through a smoke-wave, the scampering, unformed bunches came upon the wreck of the brigade that had preceded them, a floundering mass stopped afar from the hill by the swirling volleys.

It was as if a necromancer[5] had suddenly shown them a picture of the fate which awaited them; but the line with muscular spasm hurled itself over this wreckage and onward, until men were stumbling amid the relics of other assaults, the point where the fire from the ridge consumed.

The men, panting, perspiring, with crazed faces, tried to push against it; but it was as if they had come to a wall. The wave halted, shuddered in an agony from the quick struggle of its two desires, then toppled, and broke into a fragmentary thing which has no name.

Veterans could now at last be distinguished from recruits. The new regiments were instantly gone, lost, scattered, as if they never had been. But the sweeping failure of the charge, the battle, could not make the veterans forget their business. With a last throe, the band of maniacs drew itself up and blazed a volley at the hill, insignificant to those iron entrenchments, but nevertheless expressing that singular final despair which enables men coolly to defy the walls of a city of death.

After this episode the men renamed their command. They called it the Little Regiment.

---

[5] NECROMANCER—Magician.

## VI

"I seen Dan shoot a feller yesterday. Yes sir, I'm sure it was him that done it. And maybe he thinks about that feller now, and wonders if *he*[6] tumbled down just about the same way. Them things come up in a man's mind."

Bivouac fires[7] upon the sidewalks, in the streets, in the yards, threw high their wavering reflections, which examined, like slim red fingers, the dingy scarred walls and the piles of tumbled brick. The droning of voices again arose from great blue crowds.

The odour of frying bacon, the fragrance from countless little coffee-pails floated among the ruins. The rifles, stacked in the shadows, emitted flashes of steely light. Wherever a flag lay horizontally from one stack to another was the bed of an eagle which had led men into the mystic smoke.

The men about a particular fire were engaged in holding in check their jovial spirits. They moved whispering around the blaze, although they looked at it with a certain fine contentment, like labourers after a day's hard work.

There was one who sat apart. They did not address him save in tones suddenly changed. They did not regard him directly, but always in little sidelong glances.

At last a soldier from a distant fire came into this circle of light. He studied for a time the man who sat apart. Then he hesitatingly stepped closer, and said: "Got any news, Dan?"

"No," said Dan.

The new-comer shifted his feet. He looked at the fire, at the sky, at the other men, at Dan. His face expressed a curious despair; his tongue was plainly in rebellion. Finally, however, he contrived to say: "Well, there's some chance yet, Dan. Lots of the wounded are still lying out there, you know. There's some chance yet."

"Yes," said Dan.

The soldier shifted his feet again, and looked miserably into the air. After another struggle he said: "Well, there's some chance yet, Dan." He moved hastily away.

One of the men of the squad, perhaps encouraged by this example, now approached the still figure. "No news yet, hey?" he said, after coughing behind his hand.

---

[6] *He*—Referring to Dan's brother, Billie, who is among the missing.

[7] BIVOUAC FIRES—Camp-fires.

"No," said Dan.

"Well," said the man, "I've been thinking of how he was fretting about you the night you went on special duty. You recollect? Well, sir, I was surprised. He couldn't say enough about it. I swan, I don't believe he slep' a wink after you left, but just lay awake cussing special duty and worrying. I was surprised. But there he lay cussing. He—"

Dan made a curious sound, as if a stone had wedged in his throat. He said: "Shut up, will you?"

Afterward the men would not allow his moody contemplation of the fire to be interrupted.

"Oh, let him alone, can't you?"

"Come away from there, Casey!"

"Say, can't you leave him be?"

They moved with reverence about the immovable figure, with its countenance of mask-like invulnerability.

## VII

After the red round eye of the sun had stared long at the little plain and its burden, darkness, a sable mercy, came heavily upon it, and the wan hands of the dead were no longer seen in strange frozen gestures.

The heights in front of the plain shone with tiny camp-fires, and from the town in the rear, small shimmerings ascended from the blazes of the bivouac. The plain was a black expanse upon which, from time to time, dots of light, lanterns, floated slowly here and there. These fields were long steeped in grim mystery.

Suddenly, upon one dark spot, there was a resurrection. A strange thing had been groaning there, prostrate. Then it suddenly dragged itself into a sitting posture, and became a man.

The man stared stupidly for a moment at the lights on the hill, then turned and contemplated the faint colouring over the town. For some moments he remained thus, staring with dull eyes, his face unemotional, wooden.

Finally he looked around him at the corpses dimly to be seen. No change flashed into his face upon viewing these men. They seemed to suggest merely that his information concerning himself was not too complete. He ran his fingers over his arms and chest, bearing always the air of an idiot upon a bench at an alms-house door.

Finding no wound in his arms nor in his chest, he raised his hand to his head, and the fingers came away with some dark liquid upon them. Holding these fingers close to his eyes, he scanned them in the same stupid fashion, while his body gently swayed.

The soldier rolled his eyes again toward the town. When he arose, his clothing peeled from the frozen ground like wet paper. Hearing the sound of it, he seemed to see reason for deliberation. He paused and looked at the ground, then at his trousers, then at the ground.

Finally he went slowly off toward the faint reflection, holding his hands palm outward before him, and walking in the manner of a blind man.

## VIII

The immovable Dan again sat unaddressed in the midst of comrades who did not joke aloud. The dampness of the usual morning fog seemed to make the little camp-fires furious.

Suddenly a cry arose in the streets, a shout of amazement and delight. The men making breakfast at the fire looked up quickly. They broke forth in clamorous exclamation: "Well, of all things! Dan! Dan! Look who's coming! Oh, Dan!"

Dan the silent raised his eyes and saw a man, with a bandage of the size of a helmet about his head, receiving a furious demonstration from the company. He was shaking hands, and explaining, and haranguing to a high degree.

Dan started. His face of bronze flushed to his temples. He seemed about to leap from the ground, but then suddenly he sank back, and resumed his impassive gazing.

The men were in a flurry. They looked from one to the other. "Dan! Look! See who's coming!" some cried again. "Dan! Look!"

He scowled at last, and moved his shoulders sullenly. "Well, don't I know it?"

But they could not be convinced that his eyes were in service. "Dan, why can't you look? See who's coming!"

He made a gesture then of irritation and rage. "Curse it! Don't I know it?"

The man with a bandage of the size of a helmet moved forward, always shaking hands and explaining. At times his glance wandered to Dan, who saw with his eyes riveted.

After a series of shiftings, it occurred naturally that the man with the bandage was very near to the man who saw the flames. He paused, and there was a little silence. Finally he said: "Hello, Dan."

"Hello, Billie."

## QUESTIONS

1. Do you think the beginning of the story is effective? If you had written it would you have begun it with action rather than description? Why?
2. What word in the first paragraph reveals to which side, Union or Confederate, the column belongs?
3. Why should Billie take such exception to being called a "fool" in this particular instance? Does the author suggest any explanation?
4. What form of revenge does Billie undertake? Is it just? Is it successful?
5. Upon what occasion and why was the command renamed "The Little Regiment"?
6. Is this a happy ending? Can you suggest a better conclusion?
7. Which seems to be the most important in the story: plot, description, or characterization?
8. What is the theme of *The Little Regiment?* Is the title in keeping with the theme? Explain briefly.
9. Does the author betray, directly or indirectly, his attitude toward war in this story? If so, what is it?
10. What is your own view on the question of war and peace? Has your reading of this story changed it in any way? Explain.

## EXERCISES

Exercises preceded by a star are designed for assignment at the discretion of the teacher, or for any student who volunteers.

1. Give your opinion of the feeling between the two brothers, and illustrate by incidents from the story.
2. Select three of the most realistic passages and show in what way they are realistic.
3. Comment on the irony in the author's remark: "Veterans detest being killed when they are not busy." Find one other example of irony.
4. Make a list of the unusual words, phrases, and images used in *The Little Regiment.*

*5. One writer of blood-and-thunder western stories once declared he had never dared go west of Buffalo for fear of cramping his style. With this in mind, find a reason to explain Crane's greater success in writing war fiction than in "covering" real wars for a newspaper.

*6. Write a short war-narrative, trying to make your descriptions vivid and your incidents realistic.

*7. Compare *The Little Regiment* with one of the following by the same author: *A Grey Sleeve, The Open Boat, The Second Generation.*

Keystone-Underwood

JACK LONDON

One who has sought adventure in far places and found it. His red-blooded tales of sea and wilderness reflect the untamed spirit of the man. London has often been called brutal, but his stories appeal and have the power to thrill.

# THE WHITE SILENCE

## JACK LONDON

## 1876–1916

### THE AUTHOR

Gay, reckless adventurer, storming through the pages of his stories and his life with two-fisted violence, John Griffith (Jack) London holds at once a leading and a unique place among American writers of fiction. The story of his life reads like one of his own virile tales; indeed, his novels and stories are for the most part a refashioning of his own experiences on sea and land.

London was born in San Francisco, January 12, 1876. That his father should be a frontier scout and trapper seems quite fitting. Young Jack fought, rather than grew up, on the San Francisco waterfront, a newsboy and leader of a gang of tough urchins. He left school at fourteen and by his own confession was a ne'er-do-well at seventeen. Yet there was in him a great love for the shock and clamor of life. Existence was a challenge to a red-blooded man. Shipping before the mast as a common sailor, he worked, drank, and fought his way over most of the globe, confident in his strength, learning the barbaric law of survival for the strong, death for the weak. On his return, he became a "knight of the road" and "bummed" his way through the United States and Canada, begging at back doors, tasting too deeply of slums and prisons.

One day something "clicked" in London's mind, and he came to himself with a shock. Aflame with socialistic ideas, he crammed a two-year high school course into three months and entered the University of California, only to leave in his first year, disgusted. But he had found a purpose—he was determined to write. And how he wrote! He was possessed by a creative fever. Ponderous essays, short stories, poems, and blank verse tragedies clicked from his typewriter. Sometimes, he records, he worked fifteen hours a day for days at a stretch, refusing to eat, intent only on the task of putting his turbulent thoughts into words. For a year or two no editor took notice. London was not yet master of himself or of the tools of the writing profession.

Only too often he was without money. At such times he was compelled to abandon his writing and take up any menial job that was available. The famous Klondike gold rush of 1898 saw him hiking over Chilkoot Pass, among the first of the gold-crazed adventurers. Stricken with scurvy, he returned empty-handed but with a mind stocked with memories of the White Silence of the North. He wrote desperately. Finally, at the age of twenty-three, he sold his first story to *The*

*Overland Monthly,* the magazine which had published Bret Harte's first sketches. Four years later (1903) appeared *The Call of the Wild,* followed quickly by *The Sea Wolf*—and Jack London became a vogue and a byword. Until his death he wrote feverishly and, as he admitted, for money. His last publishing contract with the Hearst Company gave him $36,000 a year.

Between periods of intense writing, London led a vagabond life. He set out on what was to have been a seven-year yacht cruise around the world, but the trip was interrupted by a severe tropical illness. The incidents of this journey he has related in *The Cruise of the Snark.* During the Russo-Japanese War he was a newspaper correspondent, and ten years later acted in the same capacity in the war in Mexico. But the pace began to tell. Death came suddenly in 1916 at the age of forty. The trail was ended.

It is the doctrine of "the survival of the fittest" that offers the key to London's life and work. He worked hard, drank hard, played hard, firmly convinced that the best test of a man lies in his ability to dominate, to master man and animal and nature. Steel and brawn and the soul of a fighter—this was his recipe for a man's man and a good story. London was not a profound thinker; he never realized all of life, its necessity for mercy and love as well as the brute force in it. The grim battle of existence was what he saw and painted.

In addition to his novels and stories, Jack London turned his hand to socialistic studies in *The Iron Heel* and *Revolution and Other Essays,* which flame with a militant sincerity against industrial and social evils. *John Barleycorn* is an autobiographical account of his struggle with rum. It will be, however, as the exponent of "the call of the wild," of sea and northland and tropics with their challenge of swift adventure, that he will live.

## THE STORY

*The White Silence* is not a pretty story. Jack London never pretended to write of the sweet and gentle things of life. Like John Masefield, whose *Salt Water Ballads* picture the drab and brutal part of a sailor's existence, his was "the dirt and the dross, the dust and scum of the earth." "By the book reviewers and namby-pambys," writes London, "I am esteemed a sort of primitive beast that delights in the spilled blood of violence and horror." Sometimes through this violence will shine a ray of tenderness. But tenderness *must* not be allowed to dominate. On the frontiers of civilization it is dangerous. It may mean death. In the physical conflict between man and man, between man and nature, the only armor is individual strength, resolution, the will to win.

The most terrifying of all colors is white. Shut out all other hues—the vivid greens of vegetation, the ruddy clouds of sunset, the blue heavens—leave only the cold brilliance of snow beneath brassy skies, and something grips at a man's heart, a terror, a panic that is the more awful because inexplicable. Take away all familiar sounds that speak of men, their habitations and their activities. In this emptiness place three people, one of them a woman. Give them a team of dogs and but little food to carry them over the long trail to safety. Strike one of them down mercilessly, leaving him helpless and hopeless, useless to himself, a fatal burden to his companions. Then, as the white silence enfolds them, see how each faces his own problem and how in the end the will to survive is supreme.

*The White Silence* belongs to London's early work. It opens the volume of short stories entitled, *The Son of the Wolf* (1900), his first published book. The stories had appeared during 1899–1900 in *The Overland Monthly* and *The Atlantic Monthly,* and are filled with recollections of the author's recent experiences in the Klondike. Accustomed to the genteel sentimentality of the 1890's (often called "the mauve decade" because delicacy and refinement were keynotes of the period), readers were shocked by the uncompromising realism of this new writer. Kipling had first jolted them from their stilted drawing-room manner; now this American went a step further, showed them life in the raw, stripped of the pretensions and niceties with which civilization has covered man's real nature. The terrible climax of *The White Silence* "struck the critics of his day like a rawhide whip across the face."

London did not "see life whole," but he saw one sector of it so clearly and portrayed it so vividly that his stories and novels have earned a permanent place in American fiction.

## THE WHITE SILENCE[1]

"Carmen won't last much more than a couple of days." Mason spat out a chunk of ice and surveyed the poor animal ruefully, then put her foot in his mouth and proceeded to bite out the ice which clustered cruelly between the toes.

"I never saw a dog with a highfalutin' name that ever was worth a rap," he said, as he concluded his task and shoved her aside. "They just fade away and die under the responsibility. Did ye ever see one go wrong with a sensible name like Cassiar, Siwash, or Husky? No, sir! Take a look at Shookum here; he's—"

Snap! The lean brute flashed up, the white teeth just missing Mason's throat.

"Ye will, will ye?" A shrewd clout behind the ear with the butt of the dogwhip stretched the animal in the snow, quivering softly, a yellow slaver dripping from its fangs.

[1] Permission for the use of story, *The White Silence,* by Jack London, granted by Charmian K. London, widow of author.

"As I was saying, just look at Shookum, here—he's got the spirit. Bet ye he eats Carmen before the week's out."

"I'll bank another proposition against that," replied Malemute[2] Kid, reversing the frozen bread placed before the fire to thaw. "We'll eat Shookum before the trip is over. What d'ye say, Ruth?"

The Indian woman settled the coffee with a piece of ice, glanced from Malemute Kid to her husband, then at the dogs, but vouchsafed no reply. It was such a palpable truism that none was necessary. Two hundred miles of unbroken trail in prospect, with a scant six days' grub for themselves and none for the dogs, could admit no other alternative. The two men and the woman grouped about the fire and began their meager meal. The dogs lay in their harnesses, for it was a brief midday halt, and fastened their eyes on each mouthful enviously.

"No more lunches after today," said Malemute Kid. "And we've got to keep a close eye on the dogs,—they're getting vicious. They'd just as soon pull a fellow down as not, if they get a chance."

"And I was president of an Epworth[3] once, and taught in the Sunday-school." Having irrelevantly delivered himself of this, Mason fell into a dreamy contemplation of his steaming moccasins, but was aroused by Ruth filling his cup. "Thank God, we've got slathers of tea! I've seen it growing, down in Tennessee. What wouldn't I give for a hot corn-pone just now! Never mind, Ruth; you won't starve much longer, nor wear moccasins either."

The woman threw off her gloom at this, and in her eyes welled up a great love for her white lord—the first white man she had ever seen—the first man she had known to treat a woman as something better than a mere animal or beast of burden.

"Yes, Ruth," continued her husband, having recourse to the macaronic jargon[4] in which it was alone possible for them to understand each other; "wait till we clean up and pull for the Outside. We'll take the White Man's canoe and go to the Salt Water. Yes, bad water, rough water—great mountains dance up and down all the time. And so big, so far, so far away—you travel ten sleep,

---

[2] Malemute—Nickname borrowed from the name of an Eskimo tribe; sometimes applied to an Eskimo dog.

[3] An Epworth—An Epworth League, a Protestant religious organization for young people.

[4] Macaronic jargon—A mixed language, composed of words from two or more tongues, by means of which whites and natives can converse.

twenty sleep, forty sleep" (he graphically enumerated the days on his fingers), "all the time water, bad water. Then you come to great village, plenty people, just the same mosquitoes next summer. Wigwams oh, so high—ten, twenty pines. Hi-yu skookum!"

He paused impotently, cast an appealing glance at Malemute Kid, then laboriously placed the twenty pines, end on end, by sign language. Malemute Kid smiled with cheery cynicism; but Ruth's eyes were wide with wonder, and with pleasure; for she half believed he was joking, and such condescension pleased her poor woman's heart.

"And then you step into a—a box, and pouf! up you go." He tossed his empty cup in the air by way of illustration, and, as he deftly caught it, cried: "And biff! down you come. Oh, great medicine-men! You go Fort Yukon, I go Arctic City—twenty-five sleep—big string, all the time—I catch him string—I say, 'Hello, Ruth! How are ye?'—and you say, 'Is that my good husband?'—and I say, 'Yes'—and you say, 'No can bake good bread, no more soda'—then I say, 'Look in cache,[5] under flour; good-bye.' You look and catch plenty soda. All the time you Fort Yukon, me Arctic City. Hi-yu medicine-man!"

Ruth smiled so ingenuously at the fairy story that both men burst into laughter. A row among the dogs cut short the wonders of the Outside, and by the time the snarling combatants were separated, she had lashed the sleds and all was ready for the trail.

"Mush! Baldy! Hi! Mush on!" Mason worked his whip smartly, and as the dogs whined low in the traces, broke out the sled with the gee-pole.[6] Ruth followed with the second team, leaving Malemute Kid, who had helped her start, to bring up the rear. Strong man, brute that he was, capable of felling an ox at a blow, he could not bear to beat the poor animals, but humoured them as a dog-driver rarely does—nay, almost wept with them in their misery.

"Come, mush on there, you poor, sore-footed brutes!" he murmured, after several ineffectual attempts to start the load. But his patience was at last rewarded, and, though whimpering with pain, they hastened to join their fellows.

---

[5] CACHE—A hiding place for storing things safely.

[6] BROKE OUT . . . GEE-POLE—Freed the sled from the snow by prying with a heavy wooden pike tipped with iron.

No more conversation; the toil of the trail will not permit such extravagance. And of all deadening labours, that of the Northland trail is the worst. Happy is the man who can weather a day's travel at the price of silence, and that on a beaten track.

And of all the heart-breaking labours, that of breaking trail is the worst. At every step the great webbed shoe sinks till the snow is level with the knee. Then up, straight up, the deviation of a fraction of an inch being a certain precursor of disaster, the snowshoe must be lifted till the surface is cleared; then forward, down, and the other foot is raised perpendicularly for the matter of half a yard. He who tries this for the first time, if haply he avoids bringing his shoes in dangerous propinquity and measures not his length on the treacherous footing, will give up exhausted at the end of a hundred yards; he who can keep out of the way of the dogs for a whole day may well crawl into his sleeping-bag with a clear conscience and a pride which passeth all understanding; and he who travels twenty sleeps on the Long Trail is a man whom the gods may envy.

The afternoon wore on, and with the awe, born of the White Silence, the voiceless travelers bent to their work. Nature has many tricks wherewith she convinces man of his finity[7]—the ceaseless flow of the tides, the fury of the storm, the shock of the earthquake, the long roll of heaven's artillery—but the most tremendous, the most stupefying of all, is the passive phase of the White Silence. All movement ceases, the sky clears, the heavens are as brass; the slightest whisper seems sacrilege, and man becomes timid, affrighted at the sound of his own voice. Sole speck of life journeying across the ghostly wastes of a dead world, he trembles at his audacity, realizes that his is a maggot's life, nothing more. Strange thoughts arise unsummoned, and the mystery of all things strives for utterance. And the fear of death, of God, of the universe, comes over him—the hope of the Resurrection and the Life, the yearning for immortality, the vain striving of the imprisoned essence—it is then, if ever, man walks alone with God.

So wore the day away. The river took a great bend, and Mason headed his team for the cut-off across the narrow neck of land. But the dogs balked at the high bank. Again and again, though Ruth and Malemute Kid were shoving on the sled, they slipped back. Then came the concerted effort. The miserable creatures,

[7] FINITY—Mortality, as contrasted with immortality.

weak from hunger, exerted their last strength. Up—up—the sled poised on the top of the bank; but the leader swung the string of dogs behind him to the right, fouling Mason's snowshoes. The result was grievous. Mason was whipped off his feet; one of the dogs fell in the traces; and the sled toppled back, dragging everything to the bottom again.

Slash! the whip fell among the dogs savagely, especially upon the one which had fallen.

"Don't, Mason," entreated Malemute Kid; "the poor devil's on its last legs. Wait, and we'll put my team on."

Mason stayed his hand deliberately till the last word had fallen, then out flashed the long lash, completely curling about the offending creature's body. Carmen—for it was Carmen—cowered in the snow, cried piteously, then rolled over on her side.

It was a tragic moment, a pitiful incident of the trail—a dying dog, two comrades in anger. Ruth glanced solicitously from man to man. But Malemute Kid restrained himself, though there was a world of reproach in his eyes, and bending over the dog, cut the traces. No word was spoken. The teams were double-spanned[8] and the difficulty overcome; the sleds were under way again, the dying dog dragging herself along in the rear. As long as an animal can travel, it is not shot, and this last chance is accorded it—the crawling into camp, if it can, in the hope of a moose being killed.

Already penitent for his angry action, but too stubborn to make amends, Mason toiled on at the head of the cavalcade, little dreaming that danger hovered in the air. The timber clustered thick in the sheltered bottom, and through this they threaded their way. Fifty feet or more from the trail towered a lofty pine. For generations it had stood there, and for generations destiny had had this one end in view—perhaps the same had been decreed of Mason.

He stooped to fasten the loosened thong of his moccasin. The sleds came to a halt, and the dogs lay down in the snow without a whimper. The stillness was weird; not a breath rustled the frost-encrusted forest; the cold and silence of outer space had chilled the heart, and smote the trembling lips of nature. A sigh pulsed through the air—they did not seem to actually hear it, but rather felt it, like the premonition of movement in a motionless void.

---

[8] THE TEAMS WERE DOUBLE-SPANNED—Both dog teams were hitched double to Mason's sled.

Then the great tree, burdened with its weight of years and snow, played its last part in the tragedy of life. He heard the warning crash and attempted to spring up, but, almost erect, caught the blow squarely on the shoulder.

The sudden danger, the quick death—how often had Malemute Kid faced it! The pine-needles were still quivering as he gave his commands and sprang into action. Nor did the Indian girl faint or raise her voice in idle wailing, as might many of her white sisters. At his order, she threw her weight on the end of a quickly extemporized handspike, easing the pressure and listening to her husband's groans, while Malemute Kid attacked the tree with his axe. The steel rang merrily as it bit into the frozen trunk, each stroke being accompanied by a forced, audible respiration, the "Huh!" "Huh!" of the woodsman.

At last the Kid laid the pitiable thing that was once a man in the snow. But worse than his comrade's pain was the dumb anguish in the woman's face, the blended look of hopeful, hopeless query. Little was said; those of the Northland are early taught the futility of words and the inestimable value of deeds. With the temperature at sixty-five below zero, a man cannot lie many minutes in the snow and live. So the sled-lashings were cut, and the sufferer, rolled in furs, laid on a couch of boughs. Before him roared a fire, built of the very wood which wrought the mishap. Behind and partially over him was stretched the rude tent fly—a piece of canvas, which caught the radiating heat and threw it back and down upon him—a trick which men may know who study physics at the fount.

And men who have shared their bed with death know when the call is sounded. Mason was terribly crushed. The most cursory examination revealed it. His right arm, leg, and back were broken; his limbs were paralyzed from the hips; and the likelihood of internal injuries was large. An occasional moan was his only sign of life.

No hope; nothing to be done. The pitiless night crept slowly by—Ruth's portion, the despairing stoicism of her race, and Malemute Kid adding new lines to his face of bronze. In fact, Mason suffered least of all, for he spent his time in Eastern Tennessee, in the Great Smoky Mountains, living over the scenes of his childhood. And most pathetic was the melody of his long-forgotten Southern vernacular, as he raved of swimming-holes and coon-hunts and watermelon raids. It was as Greek to Ruth, but the Kid understood and felt—felt as only one can feel who has been shut out for years from all that civilization means.

Morning brought consciousness to the stricken man, and Malemute Kid bent closer to catch his whispers.

"You remember when we foregathered on the Tanana,[9] four years come next ice-run?[10] I didn't care so much for her then. It was more like she was pretty, and there was a smack of excitement about it, I think. But d'ye know, I've come to think a heap of her. She's been a good wife to me, always at my shoulder in the pinch. And when it comes to trading, you know there isn't her equal. D'ye recollect the time she shot the Moosehorn Rapids to pull you and me off that rock, the bullets whipping the water like hailstones?—and the time of the famine at Nuklukyeto?[11]—or when she raced the ice-run to bring the news? Yes, she's been a good wife to me, better'n that other one. Didn't know I'd been there? Never told you, eh? Well, I tried it once, down in the States. That's why I'm here. Been raised together, too. I came away to give her a chance for divorce. She got it.

"But that's got nothing to do with Ruth. I had thought of cleaning up and pulling for the Outside next year—her and I—but it's too late. Don't send her back to her people, Kid. It's beastly hard for a woman to go back. Think of it!—nearly four years on our bacon and beans and flour and dried fruit, and then to go back to her fish and caribou. It's not good for her to have tried our ways, to come to know they're better'n her people's, and then return to them. Take care of her, Kid. Why don't you—? But no, you always fought shy of them—and you never told me why you came to this country. Be kind to her, and send her back to the States as soon as you can. But fix it so as she can come back—liable to get homesick, you know.

"And the youngster—it's drawn us closer, Kid. I only hope it's a boy. Think of it!—flesh of my flesh, Kid. He mustn't stop in this country. And if it's a girl, why she can't. Sell my furs; they'll fetch at least five thousand, and I've got as much more with the company. And handle my interests with yours. I think that

[9] TANANA—River in Alaska and chief southern tributary of the Yukon.

[10] ICE-RUN—In the spring the ice in the river breaks up and floats down stream.

[11] NUKLUKYETO—Alaskan village on the Yukon River.

bench claim will show up.[12] See that he gets a good schooling; and Kid, above all, don't let him come back. This country was not made for white men.

"I'm a gone man, Kid. Three or four sleeps at the best. You've got to go on. You must go on! Remember, it's my wife, it's my boy—O God! I hope it's a boy! You can't stay by me—and I charge you, a dying man, to pull on."

"Give me three days," pleaded Malemute Kid. "You may change for the better; something may turn up."

"No."

"Just three days."

"You must pull on."

"Two days."

"It's my wife and my boy, Kid. You would not ask it."

"One day."

"No, no! I charge—"

"Only one day. We can shave it through on the grub, and I might knock over a moose."

"No—all right; one day, but not a minute more. And Kid, don't leave me to face it alone. Just a shot, one pull on the trigger. You understand. Think of it! Think of it! Flesh of my flesh, and I'll never live to see him!

"Send Ruth here. I want to say good-by and tell her that she must think of the boy and not wait till I'm dead. She might refuse to go with you if I didn't. Good-by, old man; good-by.

"Kid! I say—a—sink a hole above the pup,[13] next to the slide. I panned out forty cents on my shovel there.

"And Kid!" He stooped lower to catch the last faint words, the dying man's surrender of his pride. "I'm sorry—for—you—know—Carmen."

Leaving the girl crying softly over her dying man, the Kid slipped into his parka[14] and snowshoes, tucked his rifle under his arm, and crept away into the forest. He was no tyro in the stern sorrows of the Northland, but never had he faced so stiff a problem as this. In the abstract, it was a plain, mathematical proposition—

[12] That bench claim will show up—That mineral bed (bench) on which Mason has a claim will yield gold.

[13] Pup—Any small tributary flowing into one of Alaska's large rivers was called a "pup" by Klondike miners.

[14] Parka—An outer garment made of skins.

three possible lives as against one doomed one. But now he hesitated. For five years, shoulder to shoulder, on the rivers and trails, in the camps and mines, facing death by field and flood and famine, had they knitted the bonds of their comradeship. So close was the tie that he had often been conscious of a vague jealousy of Ruth from the first time she had come between. And now it must be severed by his own hand.

Though he prayed for a moose, just one moose, all game seemed to have deserted the land, and nightfall found the exhausted man crawling into camp, light-handed, heavy-hearted. An uproar from the dogs and shrill cries from Ruth hastened him.

Bursting into the camp, he saw the girl in the midst of the snarling pack, laying about her with an axe. The dogs had broken the iron rule of their masters and were rushing the grub. He joined the issue with his rifle reversed, and the hoary game of natural selection was played out with all the ruthlessness of its primeval environment. Rifle and axe went up and down, hit or missed with monotonous regularity; lithe bodies flashed, with wild eyes and dripping fangs; and man and beast fought for supremacy to the bitterest conclusion. Then the beaten brutes crept to the edge of the firelight, licking their wounds, voicing their misery to the stars.

The whole stock of dried salmon had been devoured, and perhaps five pounds of flour remained to tide them over two hundred miles of wilderness. Ruth returned to her husband, while Malemute Kid cut up the warm body of one of the dogs, the skull of which had been crushed by the axe. Every portion was carefully put away, save the hide and offal, which were cast to his fellows of the moment before.

Morning brought fresh trouble. The animals were turning on each other. Carmen, who still clung to her slender thread of life, was downed by the pack. The lash fell among them unheeded. They cringed and cried under the blows, but refused to scatter till the last wretched bit had disappeared—bones, hide, hair, everything.

Malemute Kid went about his work, listening to Mason, who was back in Tennessee, delivering tangled discourses and wild exhortations to his brethren of other days.

Taking advantage of neighbouring pines, he worked rapidly, and Ruth watched him make a cache similar to those sometimes used by hunters to preserve their meat from the wolverines and dogs.

One after the other, he bent the tops of two small pines toward each other and nearly to the ground, making them fast with thongs of moosehide. Then he beat the dogs into submission and harnessed them to two of the sleds, loading the sleds with everything but the furs which enveloped Mason. These he wrapped and lashed tightly about him, fastening either end of the robes to the bent pines. A single stroke of his hunting-knife would release them and send the body high in the air.

Ruth had received her husband's last wishes and made no struggle. Poor girl, she had learned the lesson of obedience well. From a child, she had bowed and seen all women bow, to the lords of creation, and it did not seem in the nature of things for woman to resist. The Kid permitted her one outburst of grief, as she kissed her husband—her own people had no such custom—then led her to the foremost sled and helped her into her snowshoes. Blindly, instinctively, she took the gee-pole and whip, and "mushed" the dogs out on the trail. Then he returned to Mason, who had fallen into a coma; and long after she was out of sight, crouched by the fire, waiting, hoping, praying for his comrade to die.

It is not pleasant to be alone with painful thoughts in the White Silence. The silence of gloom is merciful, shrouding one as with protection and breathing a thousand intangible sympathies; but the bright White Silence, clear and cold, under steely skies, is pitiless.

An hour passed—two hours—but the man would not die. At high noon, the sun, without raising its rim above the southern horizon, threw a suggestion of fire athwart the heavens, then quickly drew it back. Malemute Kid roused and dragged himself to his comrade's side. He cast one glance about him. The White Silence seemed to sneer, and a great fear came upon him. There was a sharp report; Mason swung into his aerial sepulchre; and Malemute Kid savagely lashed the remaining dogs into a wild gallop as he fled across the snow.

## QUESTIONS

1. In what ways do Mason and Malemute Kid differ? What are the qualities which have made them friends for years?
2. Is Mason really cruel? Why did he strike Carmen? What incident or utterance reveals his true nature?
3. What is Mason's attitude toward his wife, Ruth? Of whom is Malemute Kid jealous?

4. Which of the three characters shows the greatest bravery? Support your opinion by evidence gathered from the story.
5. Why does Mason say, "This country was not made for white men"?
6. What is the significance of the last sentence? What happens? Does the conclusion satisfy or repel you? Is it high literary art?
7. Does this story have a purpose; that is, does it try to prove anything? If so, what?
8. Jack London is a realist. Is his a realism of detail, or method, or both?
9. Where in the story do you find the greatest pathos? Be careful to distinguish between mere violence and deep emotion.
10. What similarities do you find between Jack London and Kipling? What differences do you note between *The Man Who Was* and *The White Silence* in matters of style, plot, setting, characters, etc.?
11. What differences can you suggest between the California gold rush of 1849 and the Klondike gold rush nearly half a century later? What American author has written "local color" stories of the mining camps of California?
12. How is "the economy of short story writing" illustrated in *The White Silence?* (See Introduction.)

## EXERCISES

Exercises preceded by a star are designed for assignment at the discretion of the teacher, or for any student who volunteers.

1. Put in your own words the content of the passage in which Mason tells his wife the wonders of the white man's country, explaining what is meant by "white man's canoe," "ten sleep," "wigwams twenty pines high," the "box," and the "big string."
2. In the passage describing the effect of the white silence on travelers (page 736) list the nouns, verbs, and adjectives that contribute greatly to vividness and power.
3. Explain the natural phenomenon mentioned in the second sentence of the last paragraph.

*4. Taking the situation presented in this story—two men and a woman alone in the snowy wastes of Alaska—a writer might construct several entirely different stories. Using this situation, make a brief scenario, listing the chief incidents of a story you would like to write. Note that London refrained from having Malemute Kid fall in love with Ruth. Suggest a reason.

5. Write a description of a snow scene, drawing if possible on your own observation.

*6. Report on one of the following: Chapter 41 ("The Whiteness of the Whale") of Herman Melville's *Moby Dick;* Jack London's *The Call of the Wild* or *The Sea Wolf;* Bret Harte's *The Outcasts of Poker Flat;* Robert Service's *The Spell of the Yukon.*

Keystone View Company, N. Y.

GILBERT KEITH CHESTERTON

One of England's most brilliant authors. Whether he writes short stories, essays, or novels, his works are enlivened by flashes of wit and an animated style. Chesterton's *Father Brown* stories have introduced into modern fiction a new type of amateur detective.

# THE BLUE CROSS

## GILBERT KEITH CHESTERTON

## 1874–

### THE AUTHOR

The year is 1874. In England two boys are born, one in Shropshire, one in London. The former is destined to sing the old sagas of the sea with new power and become poet-laureate—John Masefield. The latter is to tread the "Grub Street" of journalism and emerge a most brilliant master of swift word-play—Gilbert Keith Chesterton.

Chesterton is a big man—physically and as a writer. He has handled the essay, the newspaper column, the poem, the critical review, the drama, and the short story with an amazingly deft touch. It is a truism that to read something of "G.K.C.," as he is called, is to read something clever. The swift arrows of his thought flash out at you from his often startling paragraphs, amusing you with their deftly whimsical humor, arresting you with their keen insight and truth. For example: "The only way of catching a train I have ever discovered is to miss the train before," or, "I sometimes think it is a pity that people travel in foreign countries; it narrows their minds so much," or in a more serious mood, "Every man is dangerous who cares for only one thing."

He has kinship, in his social and political writings, with Masefield in championing the ordinary man, the neglected mass of humanity with its heartaches and often unfair load of work and pain. His newspaper articles and essays stingingly flay despotism and falseness in government and society. Chesterton is unconventional, a rebel, and the careless angle of his battered, black felt hat as he swings down Fleet Street indicates it. Writing voluminously he has sometimes missed the mark, but many good shafts have scored.

"G.K.C." is probably best known as an essayist, particularly in the realm of controversy as illustrated in *Orthodoxy* and *Heretics.* A successful play, *Magic;* several highly imaginative novels, *The Napoleon of Notting Hill, The Flying Inn;* and an amazing series of detective stories centering around a Roman Catholic priest, "Father Brown," illustrate his further genius. He has made excellent studies of Robert Browning, Dickens, and George Bernard Shaw, and has published several thin volumes of poetry, whose merit is greater than their bulk.

Chesterton's father was a real estate agent in West London, an artist and a children's poet in a small but charming way. Gilbert tried art for a time at the Slad Art School with success. Finishing his studies at the famous St. Paul's School where he captured the Milton Prize for English verse, he turned to literature for his career. His first work was reviewing art books for magazines. Literary success was rapid and, stranger yet, permanent. He has been on the staffs of several leading London newspapers but is rather to be regarded as a free lance writer. In 1922 Chesterton was received into the Roman Catholic Church. He has been an able defender of her faith, along with his close friend, the brilliant essayist, Hilaire Belloc.

Perhaps the secret of the power and charm of Chesterton is that he has never lost the "faculty to wonder." He has never outgrown his zest for life, a keen relish in all human experience. His wisdom, however, is not always easy to understand. He dearly loves a paradox—the joining of two ideas that on the surface seem contradictory, as for example:

"The most incredible thing about miracles is that they happen."

"The strong cannot be brave. Only the weak can be brave."

One has to think twice to catch the underlying truth of such apparent contradictions. In a way, Chesterton himself is a paradox, for he has the simple faith that usually goes with placid acceptance of tradition combined with a shrewd wit that takes little for granted. He has punctured false notions and ridiculed pretense with the zest of his chief rival in controversy, George Bernard Shaw.

## THE STORY

Though in a literary sense Father Brown is descended from a long line of amateur detectives, his ancestry is a little obscure. Poe's Dupin (see *The Purloined Letter*) reduced a mystery to an algebraic problem and solved it by the application of pure reason. Sherlock Holmes, the wizard of Baker Street, was pictured by A. Conan Doyle as a high-strung genius who, after playing the violin and smoking innumerable cigarettes, would announce to his confidant, Dr. Watson, that the solution of the crime was merely "elementary." When the versatile Chesterton strayed into the mystery field, he undertook to invent a character who bore the least possible resemblance to these literary ancestors.

Father Brown is a queer little priest whose apparent simplicity invites ridicule. In his round, childish face there is a look of faint surprise. He fumbles continually with a superfluous umbrella. A more innocent, helpless figure is difficult to imagine, yet this appearance disarms suspicion and permits him to conduct his investigations without interference. In reality he combines a shrewd common sense with the mysticism of his faith—not unlike Chesterton. He has forebodings of evil, but from that point on he works on the solid ground of logic. In his rôle of father confessor, he has learned much of the frailties of human nature and applies this knowledge to his pursuit of the criminal.

It was in 1910 that Father Brown made his first bow, quite appropriately in a volume entitled, *The Innocence of Father Brown. The Blue Cross* is the first story in the volume. This book was followed by others in 1914, 1926, and 1927 revealing, respectively, the *wisdom,* the *incredulity,* and the *secret* of the little priest. It was not alone the individuality of the chief character that brought these stories into prominence. Style and thought had a lot to do with it. Phrases leap at you with starlit brilliance. "Between the silver ribbon of morning and the green glittering ribbon of sea—" "The glory of heaven deepened and darkened around the sublime vulgarity of man."

Never before had mystery yarns been clothed in language like this. Never before had detection of crime been combined with religious and philosophical discourses. The ingenious wit that marks Chesterton's essays was not to be sacrificed to the necessity of sticking to a plot. Indeed, the author's commentaries are quite as interesting as the action itself.

Because often in succeeding stories subordinate characters are painted with great skill, it is perhaps unfair to point out that in *The Blue Cross* Valentin, the great detective, and Flambeau, the colossus of crime, show little originality. They are the stock characters of detective stories, of value only as foils to the chief actor. They may be called literary utilities, serving the one purpose of giving Father Brown an opportunity to display his powers. This the little priest does with an ingenuity—and at the same time a simplicity—that is most absorbing.

## THE BLUE CROSS[1]

Between the silver ribbon of morning and the green glittering ribbon of sea, the boat touched Harwich and let loose a swarm of folk like flies, among whom the man we must follow was by no means conspicuous—nor wished to be. There was nothing notable about him, except a slight contrast between the holiday gaiety of his clothes and the official gravity of his face. His clothes included a slight, pale grey jacket, a white waistcoat, and a silver straw hat with a grey-blue ribbon. His lean face was dark by contrast, and ended in a curt black beard that looked Spanish and suggested an Elizabethan ruff. He was smoking a cigarette with the seriousness of an idler. There was nothing about him to indicate the fact that the grey jacket covered a loaded revolver, that the white waistcoat covered a police card, or that the straw hat covered one of the most powerful intellects in Europe. For this was Valentin himself, the head of the Paris police and the most famous investigator of the world; and he was coming from Brussels to London to make the greatest arrest of the century.

[1] *The Blue Cross* from *The Innocence of Father Brown* by G. K. Chesterton. Copyright, 1911, by Dodd, Mead & Company.

Flambeau was in England. The police of three countries had tracked the great criminal at last from Ghent to Brussels, from Brussels to the Hook of Holland; and it was conjectured that he would take some advantage of the unfamiliarity and confusion of the Eucharistic Congress,[2] then taking place in London. Probably he would travel as some minor clerk or secretary connected with it; but, of course, Valentin could not be certain; nobody could be certain about Flambeau.

It is many years now since this colossus of crime suddenly ceased keeping the world in a turmoil; and when he ceased, as they said after the death of Roland,[3] there was a great quiet upon the earth. But in his best days (I mean, of course, his worst) Flambeau was a figure as statuesque and international as the Kaiser. Almost every morning the daily paper announced that he had escaped the consequences of one extraordinary crime by committing another. He was a Gascon[4] of gigantic stature and bodily daring; and the wildest tales were told of his outbursts of athletic humour; how he turned the *juge d'instruction*[5] upside down and stood him on his head, "to clear his mind"; how he ran down the Rue de Rivoli with a policeman under each arm. It is due to him to say that his fantastic physical strength was generally employed in such bloodless though undignified scenes; his real crimes were chiefly those of ingenious and wholesale robbery. But each of his thefts was almost a new sin, and would make a story by itself. It was he who ran the great Tyrolean Dairy Company in London, with no dairies, no cows, no carts, no milk, but with some thousand subscribers. These he served by the simple operation of moving the little milk cans outside people's doors to the doors of his own customers. It was he who had kept up an unaccountable and close correspondence with a young lady whose whole letter-bag was intercepted, by the extraordinary trick of photographing his messages infinitesimally small upon the slides of a microscope. A sweeping simplicity, however, marked many of his experiments. It is said that he once repainted all the numbers in a street in the dead of night merely to divert one traveller

---

[2] Eucharistic Congress—Gathering of clergy and laymen of the Catholic Church to celebrate the Lord's Supper and turn the thoughts of Christians to its mysteries.

[3] Roland—French epic hero, nephew of Charlemagne, whose army was massacred by the infidels. (See *Song of Roland.*)

[4] Gascon—Native of Gascony, France, whose people are given to boasting.

[5] *Juge d'instruction* (zhü'zh dă-strük-syô)—Police magistrate.

into a trap. It is quite certain that he invented a portable pillar-box,[6] which he put up at corners in quiet suburbs on the chance of strangers dropping postal orders into it. Lastly, he was known to be a startling acrobat; despite his huge figure, he could leap like a grasshopper and melt into the tree-tops like a monkey. Hence the great Valentin, when he set out to find Flambeau, was perfectly aware that his adventures would not end when he had found him.

But how was he to find him? On this the great Valentin's ideas were still in process of settlement.

There was one thing which Flambeau, with all his dexterity of disguise, could not cover, and that was his singular height. If Valentin's quick eye had caught a tall apple-woman, a tall grenadier, or even a tolerably tall duchess, he might have arrested them on the spot. But all along his train there was nobody that could be a disguised Flambeau, any more than a cat could be a disguised giraffe. About the people on the boat he had already satisfied himself; and the people picked up at Harwich or on the journey limited themselves with certainty to six. There was a short railway official travelling up to the terminus, three fairly short market gardeners picked up two stations afterwards, one very short widow lady going up from a small Essex town, and a very short Roman Catholic priest going up from a small Essex village. When it came to the last case, Valentin gave it up and almost laughed. The little priest was so much the essence of those Eastern flats; he had a face as round and dull as a Norfolk dumpling; he had eyes as empty as the North Sea; he had several brown paper parcels, which he was quite incapable of collecting. The Eucharistic Congress had doubtless sucked out of their local stagnation many such creatures, blind and helpless, like moles disinterred. Valentin was a sceptic in the severe style of France, and could have no love for priests. But he could have pity for them, and this one might have provoked pity in anybody. He had a large, shabby umbrella, which constantly fell on the floor. He did not seem to know which was the right end of his return ticket. He explained with a moon-calf simplicity to everybody in the carriage that he had to be careful, because he had something made of real silver "with blue stones" in one of his brown-paper parcels. His quaint blending of Essex flatness with

[6] PILLAR-BOX—Letter box on a short pillar.

saintly simplicity continuously amused the Frenchman till the priest arrived (somehow) at Tottenham with all his parcels, and came back for his umbrella. When he did the last, Valentin even had the good nature to warn him not to take care of the silver by telling everybody about it. But to whomever he talked, Valentin kept his eye open for someone else; he looked out steadily for anyone, rich or poor, male or female, who was well up to six feet; for Flambeau was four inches above it.

He alighted at Liverpool Street, however, quite conscientiously secure that he had not missed the criminal so far. He then went to Scotland Yard[7] to regularise his position and arrange for help in case of need; he then lit another cigarette and went for a long stroll in the streets of London. As he was walking in the streets and squares beyond Victoria, he paused suddenly and stood. It was a quaint, quiet square, very typical of London, full of an accidental stillness. The tall, flat houses round looked at once prosperous and uninhabited; the square of shrubbery in the centre looked as deserted as a green Pacific islet. One of the four sides was much higher than the rest, like a daïs; and the line of this side was broken by one of London's admirable accidents—a restaurant that looked as if it had strayed from Soho.[8] It was an unreasonably attractive object, with dwarf plants in pots and long, striped blinds of lemon yellow and white. It stood specially high above the street, and in the usual patchwork way of London, a flight of steps from the street ran up to meet the front door almost as a fire-escape might run up to a first-floor window. Valentin stood and smoked in front of the yellow-white blinds and considered them long.

The most incredible thing about miracles is that they happen. A few clouds in heaven do come together into the staring shape of one human eye. A tree does stand up in the landscape of a doubtful journey in the exact and elaborate shape of a note of interrogation. I have seen both these things myself within the last few days. Nelson does die in the instant of victory;[9] and a man named Williams does quite accidentally murder a man named Williamson; it sounds like a sort of infanticide. In short, there is in life an

[7] SCOTLAND YARD—Headquarters in London of the Metropolitan Police Force, which, upon request, co-operates with the police of other localities.

[8] SOHO—A London district of foreign residents and cheap restaurants.

[9] NELSON . . . VICTORY—Horatio Nelson, England's greatest admiral, was killed in the battle of Trafalgar, 1805, just as his fleet was winning a decisive victory over the French.

element of elfin coincidence which people reckoning on the prosaic may perpetually miss. As it has been well expressed in the paradox of Poe, wisdom should reckon on the unforeseen.

Aristide Valentin was unfathomably French; and the French intelligence is intelligence specially and solely. He was not "a thinking machine"; for that is a brainless phrase of modern fatalism and materialism. A machine only *is* a machine because it cannot think. But he was a thinking man, and a plain man at the same time. All his wonderful successes, that looked like conjuring, had been gained by plodding logic, by clear and commonplace French thought. The French electrify the world not by starting any paradox, they electrify it by carrying out a truism. They carry a truism so far—as in the French Revolution.[10] But exactly because Valentin understood reason, he understood the limits of reason. Only a man who knows nothing of motors talks of motoring without petrol; only a man who knows nothing of reason talks of reasoning without strong, undisputed first principles. Here he had no strong first principles. Flambeau had been missed at Harwich; and if he was in London at all, he might be anything from a tall tramp on Wimbledon Common to a tall toastmaster at the Hôtel Métropole. In such a naked state of nescience,[11] Valentin had a view and a method of his own.

In such cases he reckoned on the unforeseen. In such cases, when he could not follow the train of the reasonable, he coldly and carefully followed the train of the unreasonable. Instead of going to the right places—banks, police stations, rendezvous—he systematically went to the wrong places; knocked at every empty house, turned down every *cul de sac*,[12] went up every lane blocked with rubbish, went round every crescent that led him uselessly out of the way. He defended this crazy course quite logically. He said that if one had a clue this was the worst way; but if one had no clue at all it was the best, because there was just the chance that any oddity that caught the eye of the pursuer might be the same that had caught the eye of the pursued. Somewhere a man must begin, and it had better be just where another man might stop.

[10] THEY CARRY . . . FRENCH REVOLUTION—The doctrine of liberty, fraternity, and equality finally led to the overthrow of the French monarchy—also to the bloodshed of the Reign of Terror.

[11] NESCIENCE—State of not knowing; ignorance.

[12] *Cul de sac*—Blind alley.

Something about that flight of steps up to the shop, something about the quietude and quaintness of the restaurant, roused all the detective's rare romantic fancy and made him resolve to strike at random. He went up the steps, and sitting down at a table by the window, asked for a cup of black coffee.

It was half-way through the morning, and he had not breakfasted; the slight litter of other breakfasts stood about on the table to remind him of his hunger; and adding a poached egg to his order, he proceeded musingly to shake some white sugar into his coffee, thinking all the time about Flambeau. He remembered how Flambeau had escaped, once by a pair of nail scissors, and once by a house on fire; once by having to pay for an unstamped letter, and once by getting people to look through a telescope at a comet that might destroy the world. He thought his detective brain as good as the criminal's, which was true. But he fully realised the disadvantage. "The criminal is the creative artist; the detective only the critic," he said with a sour smile, and lifted his coffee cup to his lips slowly, and put it down very quickly. He had put salt in it.

He looked at the vessel from which the silvery powder had come; it was certainly a sugar-basin; as unmistakably meant for sugar as a champagne-bottle for champagne. He wondered why they should keep salt in it. He looked to see if there were any more orthodox vessels. Yes; there were two salt-cellars quite full. Perhaps there was some specialty in the condiment in the salt-cellars. He tasted it; it was sugar. Then he looked round at the restaurant with a refreshed air of interest, to see if there were any other traces of that singular artistic taste which puts the sugar in the salt-cellars and the salt in the sugar-basin. Except for an odd splash of some dark fluid on one of the white-papered walls, the whole place appeared neat, cheerful and ordinary. He rang the bell for the waiter.

When that official hurried up, fuzzy-haired and somewhat blear-eyed at that early hour, the detective (who was not without an appreciation of the simpler forms of humour) asked him to taste the sugar and see if it was up to the high reputation of the hotel. The result was that the waiter yawned suddenly and woke up.

"Do you play this delicate joke on your customers every morning?" inquired Valentin. "Does changing the salt and sugar never pall on you as a jest?"

The waiter, when this irony grew clearer, stammeringly assured him that the establishment had certainly no such intention; it must be a most curious mistake. He picked up the sugar-basin and looked at it; he picked up the salt-cellar and looked at that, his face growing more and more bewildered. At last he abruptly excused himself, and hurrying away, returned in a few seconds with the proprietor. The proprietor also examined the sugar-basin and then the salt-cellar; the proprietor also looked bewildered.

Suddenly the waiter seemed to grow inarticulate with a rush of words.

"I zink," he stuttered eagerly, "I zink it is those two clergymen."

"What two clergymen?"

"The two clergymen," said the waiter, "that threw soup at the wall."

"Threw soup at the wall?" repeated Valentin, feeling sure this must be some singular Italian metaphor.

"Yes, yes," said the attendant excitedly, and pointing at the dark splash on the white paper; "threw it over there on the wall."

Valentin looked his query at the proprietor, who came to his rescue with fuller reports.

"Yes, sir," he said, "it's quite true, though I don't suppose it has anything to do with the sugar and salt. Two clergymen came in and drank soup here very early, as soon as the shutters were taken down. They were both very quiet, respectable people; one of them paid the bill and went out; the other, who seemed a slower coach altogether, was some minutes longer getting his things together. But he went at last. Only, the instant before he stepped into the street he deliberately picked up his cup, which he had only half emptied, and threw the soup slap on the wall. I was in the back room myself, and so was the waiter; so I could only rush out in time to find the wall splashed and the shop empty. It don't do any particular damage, but it was confounded cheek; and I tried to catch the men in the street. They were too far off though; I only noticed they went round the next corner into Carstairs Street."

The detective was on his feet, hat settled and stick in hand. He had already decided that in the universal darkness of his mind he could only follow the first odd finger that pointed; and this finger was odd enough. Paying his bill and clashing the glass doors behind him, he was soon swinging round into the other street.

It was fortunate that even in such fevered moments his eye was cool and quick. Something in a shop-front went by him like a mere flash; yet he went back to look at it. The shop was a popular greengrocer and fruiterer's, an array of goods set out in the open air and plainly ticketed with their names and prices. In the two most prominent compartments were two heaps, of oranges and of nuts respectively. On the heap of nuts lay a scrap of cardboard, on which was written in bold, blue chalk, "Best tangerine oranges, two a penny." On the oranges was the equally clear and exact description, "Finest Brazil nuts, 4d.[13] a lb." M. Valentin looked at these two placards and fancied he had met this highly subtle form of humour before, and that somewhat recently. He drew the attention of the red-faced fruiterer, who was looking rather sullenly up and down the street, to this inaccuracy in his advertisements. The fruiterer said nothing, but sharply put each card into its proper place. The detective, leaning elegantly on his walking-cane, continued to scrutinise the shop. At last he said, "Pray excuse my apparent irrelevance, my good sir, but I should like to ask you a question in experimental psychology and the association of ideas."

The red-faced shopman regarded him with an eye of menace; but he continued gaily, swinging his cane, "Why," he pursued, "why are two tickets wrongly placed in a greengrocer's shop like a shovel hat[14] that has come to London for a holiday? Or, in case I do not make myself clear, what is the mystical association which connects the idea of nuts marked as oranges with the idea of two clergymen, one tall and the other short?"

The eyes of the tradesman stood out of his head like a snail's; he really seemed for an instant likely to fling himself upon the stranger. At last he stammered angrily: "I don't know what you 'ave to do with it, but if you're one of their friends, you can tell 'em from me that I'll knock their silly 'eads off, parsons or no parsons, if they upset my apples again."

"Indeed?" asked the detective, with great sympathy. "Did they upset your apples?"

"One of 'em did," said the heated shopman; "rolled 'em all over the street. I'd 'ave caught the fool but for havin' to pick 'em up."

"Which way did these parsons go?" asked Valentin.

[13] 4D.—Four pence, 8 cents in U. S. money.
[14] SHOVEL HAT—Reference to the flat headgear worn by priests.

"Up that second road on the left-hand side, and then across the square," said the other promptly.

"Thanks," replied Valentin, and vanished like a fairy. On the other side of the second square he found a policeman, and said: "This is urgent, constable; have you seen two clergymen in shovel hats?"

The policeman began to chuckle heavily. "I 'ave, sir; and if you arst me, one of 'em was drunk. He stood in the middle of the road that bewildered that—"

"Which way did they go?" snapped Valentin.

"They took one of them yellow buses over there," answered the man; "them that go to Hampstead."

Valentin produced his official card and said very rapidly: "Call up two of your men to come with me in pursuit," and crossed the road with such contagious energy that the ponderous policeman was moved to almost agile obedience. In a minute and a half the French detective was joined on the opposite pavement by an inspector and a man in plain clothes.

"Well, sir," began the former, with smiling importance, "and what may—?"

Valentin pointed suddenly with his cane. "I'll tell you on the top of that omnibus," he said, and was darting and dodging across the tangle of the traffic. When all three sank panting on the top seats of the yellow vehicle, the inspector said: "We could go four times as quick in a taxi."

"Quite true," replied their leader placidly, "if we only had an idea of where we were going."

"Well, where *are* you going?" asked the other, staring.

Valentin smoked frowningly for a few seconds; then, removing his cigarette, he said: "If you *know* what a man's doing, get in front of him; but if you want to guess what he's doing, keep behind him. Stray when he strays; stop when he stops; travel as slowly as he. Then you may see what he saw and may act as he acted. All we can do is to keep our eyes skinned for a queer thing."

"What sort of queer thing do you mean?" asked the inspector.

"Any sort of queer thing," answered Valentin, and relapsed into obstinate silence.

The yellow omnibus crawled up the northern roads for what seemed like hours on end; the great detective would not explain further, and perhaps his assistants felt a silent and growing doubt of his errand. Perhaps, also, they felt a silent and growing desire for lunch, for the hours crept long past the normal luncheon hour, and the long roads of the North London suburbs seemed to shoot out into length after length like an infernal telescope. It was one of those journeys on which a man perpetually feels that now at last he must have come to the end of the universe, and then finds he has only come to the beginning of Tufnell Park. London died away in draggled taverns and dreary scrubs, and then was unaccountably born again in blazing high streets and blatant hotels. It was like passing through thirteen separate vulgar cities all just touching each other. But though the winter twilight was already threatening the road ahead of them, the Parisian detective still sat silent and watchful, eyeing the frontage of the streets that slid by on either side. By the time they had left Camden Town behind, the policemen were nearly asleep; at least, they gave something like a jump as Valentin leapt erect, struck a hand on each man's shoulder, and shouted to the driver to stop.

They tumbled down the steps into the road without realising why they had been dislodged; when they looked round for enlightenment they found Valentin triumphantly pointing his finger towards a window on the left side of the road. It was a large window, forming part of the long façade of a gilt and palatial public-house; it was the part reserved for respectable dining, and labelled "Restaurant." This window, like all the rest along the frontage of the hotel, was of frosted and figured glass; but in the middle of it was a big, black smash, like a star in the ice.

"Our cue at last," cried Valentin, waving his stick; "the place with the broken window."

"What window? What cue?" asked his principal assistant. "Why, what proof is there that this has anything to do with them?"

Valentin almost broke his bamboo stick with rage.

"Proof!" he cried. "Good God! the man is looking for proof! Why, of course, the chances are twenty to one that it has *nothing* to do with them. But what else can we do? Don't you see we must either follow one wild possibility or else go home to bed?" He banged his way into the restaurant, followed by his companions, and they were soon seated at a late luncheon at a little table, and looking at the star of smashed glass from the inside. Not that it was very informative to them even then.

"Got your window broken, I see," said Valentin to the waiter as he paid the bill.

"Yes, sir," answered the attendant, bending busily over the change, to which Valentin silently added an enormous tip. The waiter straightened himself with mild but unmistakable animation.

"Ah, yes, sir," he said. "Very odd thing, that, sir."

"Indeed? Tell us about it," said the detective with careless curiosity.

"Well, two gents in black came in," said the waiter; "two of those foreign parsons that are running about. They had a cheap and quiet little lunch, and one of them paid for it and went out. The other was just going out to join him when I looked at my change again and found he'd paid me more than three times too much. 'Here,' I says to the chap who was nearly out of the door, 'you've paid too much.' 'Oh,' he says, very cool, 'have we?' 'Yes,' I says, and picks up the bill to show him. Well, that was a knock-out."

"What do you mean?" asked his interlocutor.

"Well, I'd have sworn on seven Bibles that I'd put 4s.[15] on that bill. But now I saw I'd put 14s., as plain as paint."

"Well?" cried Valentin, moving slowly, but with burning eyes, "and then?"

"The parson at the door he says all serene, 'Sorry to confuse your accounts, but it'll pay for the window.' 'What window?' I says. 'The one I'm going to break,' he says, and smashed that blessed pane with his umbrella."

All three inquirers made an exclamation; and the inspector said under his breath, "Are we after escaped lunatics?" The waiter went on with some relish for the ridiculous story:

"I was so knocked silly for a second, I couldn't do anything. The man marched out of the place and joined his friend just round the corner. Then they went so quick up Bullock Street that I couldn't catch them, though I ran round the bars to do it."

"Bullock Street," said the detective, and shot up that thoroughfare as quickly as the strange couple he pursued.

[15] 4s.—Four shillings. A shilling normally is worth about 25 cents.

Their journey now took them through bare brick ways like tunnels; streets with few lights and even with few windows; streets that seemed built out of the blank backs of everything and everywhere. Dusk was deepening, and it was not easy even for the London policemen to guess in what exact direction they were treading. The inspector, however, was pretty certain that they would eventually strike some part of Hampstead Heath. Abruptly one bulging gas-lit window broke the blue twilight like a bull's-eye lantern; and Valentin stopped an instant before a little garish sweetstuff shop. After an instant's hesitation he went in; he stood amid the gaudy colours of the confectionery with entire gravity and bought thirteen chocolate cigars with a certain care. He was clearly preparing an opening; but he did not need one.

An angular, elderly young woman in the shop had regarded his elegant appearance with a merely automatic inquiry; but when she saw the door behind him blocked with the blue uniform of the inspector, her eyes seemed to wake up.

"Oh," she said, "if you've come about that parcel, I've sent it off already."

"Parcel!" repeated Valentin; and it was his turn to look inquiring.

"I mean the parcel the gentleman left—the clergyman gentleman."

"For goodness' sake," said Valentin, leaning forward with his first real confession of eagerness, "for Heaven's sake tell us what happened exactly."

"Well," said the woman a little doubtfully, "the clergymen came in about half an hour ago and bought some peppermints and talked a bit, and then went off towards the Heath. But a second after, one of them runs back into the shop and says, 'Have I left a parcel?' Well, I looked everywhere and couldn't see one; so he says, 'Never mind; but if it should turn up, please post it to this address,' and he left me the address and a shilling for my trouble. And sure enough, though I thought I'd looked everywhere, I found he'd left a brown paper parcel, so I posted it to the place he said. I can't remember the address now; it was somewhere in Westminster. But as the thing seemed so important, I thought perhaps the police had come about it."

"So they have," said Valentin shortly. "Is Hampstead Heath near here?"

"Straight on for fifteen minutes," said the woman, "and you'll come right out on the open." Valentin sprang out of the shop and began to run. The other detectives followed him at a reluctant trot.

The street they threaded was so narrow and shut in by shadows that when they came out unexpectedly into the void common and vast sky they were startled to find the evening still so light and clear. A perfect dome of peacock-green sank into gold amid the blackening trees and the dark violet distances. The glowing green tint was just deep enough to pick out in points of crystal one or two stars. All that was left of the daylight lay in a golden glitter across the edge of Hampstead and that popular hollow which is called the Vale of Health. The holiday makers who roam this region had not wholly dispersed; a few couples sat shapelessly on benches; and here and there a distant girl still shrieked in one of the swings. The glory of heaven deepened and darkened around the sublime vulgarity of man; and standing on the slope and looking across the valley, Valentin beheld the thing which he sought.

Among the black and breaking groups in that distance was one especially black which did not break—a group of two figures clerically clad. Though they seemed as small as insects, Valentin could see that one of them was much smaller than the other. Though the other had a student's stoop and an inconspicuous manner, he could see that the man was well over six feet high. He shut his teeth and went forward, whirling his stick impatiently. By the time he had substantially diminished the distance and magnified the two black figures as in a vast microscope, he had perceived something else; something which startled him, and yet which he had somehow expected. Whoever was the tall priest, there could be no doubt about the identity of the short one. It was his friend of the Harwich train, the stumpy little *curé*[16] of Essex whom he had warned about his brown paper parcels.

Now, so far as this went, everything fitted in finally and rationally enough. Valentin had learned by his inquiries that morning that a Father Brown from Essex was bringing up a silver cross with sapphires, a relic of considerable value, to show some of the foreign priests at the congress. This undoubtedly was the "silver

[16] *Curé*—Parish priest.

with blue stones"; and Father Brown undoubtedly was the little green-horn in the train. Now there was nothing wonderful about the fact that what Valentin had found out Flambeau had also found out; Flambeau found out everything. Also there was nothing wonderful in the fact that when Flambeau heard of a sapphire cross he should try to steal it; that was the most natural thing in all natural history. And most certainly there was nothing wonderful about the fact that Flambeau should have it all his own way with such a silly sheep as the man with the umbrella and the parcels. He was the sort of man whom anybody could lead on a string to the North Pole; it was not surprising that an actor like Flambeau, dressed as another priest, could lead him to Hampstead Heath. So far the crime seemed clear enough; and while the detective pitied the priest for his helplessness, he almost despised Flambeau for condescending to so gullible a victim. But when Valentin thought of all that had happened in between, of all that had led him to his triumph, he racked his brains for the smallest rhyme or reason in it. What had the stealing of a blue-and-silver cross from a priest from Essex to do with chucking soup at wall paper? What had it to do with calling nuts oranges, or with paying for windows first and breaking them afterwards? He had come to the end of his chase; yet somehow he had missed the middle of it. When he failed (which was seldom), he had usually grasped the clue, but nevertheless missed the criminal. Here he had grasped the criminal, but still he could not grasp the clue.

The two figures that they followed were crawling like black flies across the huge green contour of a hill. They were evidently sunk in conversation, and perhaps did not notice where they were going; but they were certainly going to the wilder and more silent heights of the Heath. As their pursuers gained on them, the latter had to use the undignified attitudes of the deer-stalker, to crouch behind clumps of trees and even to crawl prostrate in deep grass. By these ungainly ingenuities the hunters even came close enough to the quarry to hear the murmur of the discussion, but no word could be distinguished except the word "reason" recurring frequently in a high and almost childish voice. Once over an abrupt dip of land and a dense tangle of thickets, the detectives actually lost the two figures they were following. They did not find the trail again for an agonising ten minutes, and then it led round the brow of a great dome of hill overlooking an amphitheatre of rich and desolate sunset scenery. Under a tree in this commanding yet neglected spot was an old ramshackle wooden seat. On this seat sat the two priests still in serious speech together. The gorgeous green and gold still clung to the darkening horizon; but the dome above was turning slowly from peacock-green to peacock-blue, and the stars detached themselves more and more like solid jewels. Mutely motioning to his followers, Valentin contrived to creep up behind the big branching tree, and, standing there in deathly silence, heard the words of the strange priests for the first time.

After he had listened for a minute and a half, he was gripped by a devilish doubt. Perhaps he had dragged the two English policemen to the wastes of a nocturnal heath on an errand no saner than seeking figs on its thistles. For the two priests were talking exactly like priests, piously, with learning and leisure, about the most aerial enigmas of theology. The little Essex priest spoke the more simply, with his round face turned to the strengthening stars; the other talked with his head bowed, as if he were not even worthy to look at them. But no more innocently clerical conversation could have been heard in any white Italian cloister or black Spanish cathedral.

The first he heard was the tail of one of Father Brown's sentences, which ended: ". . . what they really meant in the Middle Ages by the heavens being incorruptible."

The taller priest nodded his bowed head and said:

"Ah, yes, these modern infidels appeal to their reason; but who can look at those millions of worlds and not feel that there may well be wonderful universes above us where reason is utterly unreasonable?"

"No," said the other priest; "reason is always reasonable, even in the last limbo, in the lost borderland of things. I know that people charge the Church with lowering reason, but it is just the other way. Alone on earth, the Church makes reason really supreme. Alone on earth, the Church affirms that God himself is bound by reason."

The other priest raised his austere face to the spangled sky and said:

"Yet who knows if in that infinite universe—?"

"Only infinite physically," said the little priest, turning sharply in his seat, "not infinite in the sense of escaping from the laws of truth."

Valentin behind his tree was tearing his finger-nails with silent fury. He seemed almost to hear the sniggers of the English detectives whom he had brought so far on a fantastic guess only to listen to the metaphysical[17] gossip of two mild old parsons. In his impatience he lost the equally elaborate answer of the tall cleric, and when he listened again it was again Father Brown who was speaking:

"Reason and justice grip the remotest and the loneliest star. Look at those stars. Don't they look as if they were single diamonds and sapphires? Well, you can imagine any mad botany or geology you please. Think of forests of adamant with leaves of brilliants. Think the moon is a blue moon, a single elephantine sapphire. But don't fancy that all that frantic astronomy would make the smallest difference to the reason and justice of conduct. On plains of opal, under cliffs cut out of pearl, you would still find a notice-board, 'Thou shalt not steal'."

Valentin was just in the act of rising from his rigid and crouching attitude and creeping away as softly as might be, felled by the one great folly of his life. But something in the very silence of the tall priest made him stop until the latter spoke. When at last he did speak, he said simply, his head bowed and his hands on his knees:

"Well, I still think that other worlds may perhaps rise higher than our reason. The mystery of heaven is unfathomable, and I for one can only bow my head."

Then, with brow yet bent and without changing by the faintest shade his attitude or voice, he added:

"Just hand over that sapphire cross of yours, will you? We're all alone here, and I could pull you to pieces like a straw doll."

The utterly unaltered voice and attitude added a strange violence to that shocking change of speech. But the guarder of the relic only seemed to turn his head by the smallest section of the compass. He seemed still to have a somewhat foolish face turned to the stars. Perhaps he had not understood. Or, perhaps, he had understood and sat rigid with terror.

"Yes," said the tall priest, in the same low voice and in the same still posture, "yes, I am Flambeau."

Then, after a pause, he said:

[17] METAPHYSICAL—Philosophical; pertaining to theories of knowledge and existence.

"Come, will you give me that cross?"

"No," said the other, and the monosyllable had an odd sound.

Flambeau suddenly flung off all his pontifical pretensions. The great robber leaned back in his seat and laughed low but long.

"No," he cried, "you won't give it me, you proud prelate. You won't give it me, you little celibate[18] simpleton. Shall I tell you why you won't give it me? Because I've got it already in my own breast-pocket."

The small man from Essex turned what seemed to be a dazed face in the dusk, and said, with the timid eagerness of "The Private Secretary":[19]

"Are—are you sure?"

Flambeau yelled with delight.

"Really, you're as good as a three-act farce," he cried. "Yes, you turnip, I am quite sure. I had the sense to make a duplicate of the right parcel, and now, my friend, you've got the duplicate and I've got the jewels. An old dodge, Father Brown—a very old dodge."

"Yes," said Father Brown, and passed his hand through his hair with the same strange vagueness of manner. "Yes, I've heard of it before."

The colossus of crime leaned over to the little rustic priest with a sort of sudden interest.

"*You* have heard of it?" he asked. "Where have *you* heard of it?"

"Well, I mustn't tell you his name, of course," said the little man simply. "He was a penitent, you know. He had lived prosperously for about twenty years entirely on duplicate brown paper parcels. And so, you see, when I began to suspect you, I thought of this poor chap's way of doing it at once."

"Began to suspect me?" repeated the outlaw with increased intensity. "Did you really have the gumption to suspect me just because I brought you up to this bare part of the heath?"

"No, no," said Brown with an air of apology. "You see, I suspected you when we first met. It's that little bulge up the sleeve where you people have the spiked bracelet."

---

[18] CELIBATE—Unmarried. Roman Catholic priests are sworn to single life.

[19] "THE PRIVATE SECRETARY"—A popular play by Charles Henry Hawtrey, an English actor.

"How in Tartarus,"[20] cried Flambeau, "did you ever hear of the spiked bracelet?"

"Oh, one's little flock, you know!" said Father Brown, arching his eyebrows rather blankly. "When I was a curate in Hartlepool, there were three of them with spiked bracelets. So, as I suspected you from the first, don't you see, I made sure that the cross should go safe, anyhow. I'm afraid I watched you, you know. So at last I saw you change the parcels. Then, don't you see, I changed them back again. And then I left the right one behind."

"Left it behind?" repeated Flambeau, and for the first time there was another note in his voice beside his triumph.

"Well, it was like this," said the little priest, speaking in the same unaffected way. "I went back to that sweet-shop and asked if I'd left a parcel, and gave them a particular address if it turned up. Well, I knew I hadn't; but when I went away again I did. So, instead of running after me with that valuable parcel, they have sent it flying to a friend of mine in Westminster." Then he added rather sadly: "I learnt that, too, from a poor fellow in Hartlepool. He used to do it with handbags he stole at railway stations, but he's in a monastery now. Oh, one gets to know, you know," he added, rubbing his head again with the same sort of desperate apology. "We can't help it being priests. People come and tell us these things."

Flambeau tore a brown-paper parcel out of his inner pocket and rent it in pieces. There was nothing but paper and sticks of lead inside it. He sprang to his feet with a gigantic gesture, and cried:

"I don't believe you. I don't believe a bumpkin like you could manage all that. I believe you've still got the stuff on you, and if you don't give it up—why, we're all alone, and I'll take it by force!"

"No," said Father Brown simply, and stood up also, "you won't take it by force. First, because I really haven't still got it. And, second, because we are not alone."

Flambeau stopped in his stride forward.

"Behind that tree," said Father Brown, pointing, "are two strong policemen and the greatest detective alive. How did they come here, do you ask? Why, I brought them, of course! How did I

[20] TARTARUS—Hades, where wicked spirits are punished.

do it? Why, I'll tell you if you like! Lord bless you, we have to know twenty such things when we work among the criminal classes! Well, I wasn't sure you were a thief, and it would never do to make a scandal against one of our own clergy. So I just tested you to see if anything would make you show yourself. A man generally makes a small scene if he finds salt in his coffee; if he doesn't, he has some reason for keeping quiet. I changed the salt and sugar, and *you* kept quiet. A man generally objects if his bill is three times too big. If he pays it, he has some motive for passing unnoticed. I altered your bill, and *you* paid it."

The world seemed waiting for Flambeau to leap like a tiger. But he was held back as by a spell; he was stunned with the utmost curiosity.

"Well," went on Father Brown, with lumbering lucidity, "as you wouldn't leave any tracks for the police, of course somebody had to. At every place we went to, I took care to do something that would get us talked about for the rest of the day. I didn't do much harm—a splashed wall, spilt apples, a broken window; but I saved the cross, as the cross will always be saved. It is at Westminster by now. I rather wonder you didn't stop it with the Donkey's Whistle."

"With the what?" asked Flambeau.

"I'm glad you've never heard of it," said the priest, making a face. "It's a foul thing. I'm sure you're too good a man for a Whistler. I couldn't have countered it even with the Spots myself; I'm not strong enough in the legs."

"What on earth are you talking about?" asked the other.

"Well, I did think you'd know the Spots," said Father Brown, agreeably surprised. "Oh, you can't have gone so very wrong yet!"

"How in blazes do you know all these horrors?" cried Flambeau.

The shadow of a smile crossed the round, simple face of his clerical opponent.

"Oh, by being a celibate simpleton, I suppose," he said. "Has it never struck you that a man who does next to nothing but hear men's real sins is not likely to be wholly unaware of human evil? But, as a matter of fact, another part of my trade, too, made me sure you weren't a priest."

"What?" asked the thief, almost gaping.

"You attacked reason," said Father Brown. "It's bad theology."

And even as he turned away to collect his property, the three policemen came out from under the twilight trees. Flambeau was an artist and a sportsman. He stepped back and swept Valentin a great bow.

"Do not bow to me, *mon ami*,"[21] said Valentin with silver clearness. "Let us both bow to our master."[22]

And they both stood an instant uncovered while the little Essex priest blinked about for his umbrella.

## QUESTIONS

1. What reason can you suggest to explain why Chesterton chose Brown as the name of his priest-detective?
2. What moved Valentin to enter the restaurant on his first stroll about London? Would you have taken the same chance?
3. What does Valentin mean when he says: "The criminal is the creative artist; the detective only the critic"?
4. Though it is unusual to have a priest play the rôle of detective, what in Father Brown's calling is of great aid to him?
5. How "innocent" is Father Brown? What habits and mannerisms emphasize this apparent innocence?
6. What is the hidden meaning in Father Brown's words: "I saved the cross, as the cross will always be saved"?
7. Of what importance is the setting of the last scene in the story?
8. What sentence presents the climax of the story?
9. A. Conan Doyle has an associate, Dr. Watson, relate the exploits of Sherlock Holmes. Father Brown has no associate. The point of view is that of an all-knowing author. In such a story as "The Blue Cross" is this an advantage or a disadvantage? Why?
10. What part does psychology play in the story?
11. Is there any part of the action that seems incredible to you? What is it?
12. How does Chesterton's style differ from that of other detective story writers with whom you are familiar?

## EXERCISES

Exercises preceded by a star are designed for assignment at the discretion of the teacher, or for any student who volunteers.

1. Write a description and character sketch of Father Brown.
2. Explain the author's statement: "The most incredible thing about miracles is that they happen."
3. Trace the trail Father Brown left for the detectives.

---

[21] *Mon ami*—My friend.

[22] LET US BOTH BOW TO OUR MASTER—In subsequent stories Father Brown unmasks the detective Valentin, who has gone mad, as a murderer, and converts Flambeau from a thief to a private detective.

*4. Chesterton does not hesitate to rely on coincidence. In "The Blue Cross" point out several coincidences on which the tracking of the thief depends. Write an account of an "elfin coincidence" that has happened to you.

5. Comment on the effectiveness of Chesterton's titles. Other story titles in the same volume are: *The Queer Feet, The Wrong Shape, The Hammer of God, The Three Tools of Death.*

*6. Discuss the characters of Valentin and Flambeau (1) as to their reality, and (2) as to their purpose in the story. If you have read *Sherlock Holmes,* compare Valentin with Lestrade of Scotland Yard.

*7. Read one story from *The Father Brown Omnibus* (Dodd, Mead & Company, 1933) or from any one of the Father Brown volumes, and write a book review of it.

# ENGLAND TO AMERICA

## MARGARET PRESCOTT MONTAGUE
## 1878–

### THE AUTHOR

Born in 1878 in White Sulphur Springs, West Virginia, which is still her residence, Margaret Prescott Montague grew up in the traditions of the South. Her father, a well-educated man trained for the law, had taken up farming for the sake of his health. Here, in this agricultural community, Margaret added to a careful home training the impressions received from contacts with the simple inhabitants of the region. She attended the little log schoolhouse and had for her playmates mountain children and darkies. Her sympathies for the under-privileged were heightened by her own slightly defective sight and hearing, and in later years she wrote a number of stories about the deaf and blind.

As her middle name indicates, Miss Montague is related to the famous American historian, William Hickling Prescott. Her mother was a Cary, a name that was also given to her brother. It is easy to understand, therefore, why the hero of *England to America* is called "Lieutenant Skipworth Cary of Virginia." Another connection between the story and her life is to be seen in the choice of Richmond as the hero's home, for at the age of seventeen she herself went to the Virginian capital for study.

Since 1905 Miss Montague has been writing steadily but not rapidly. Four novels and several volumes of short stories and essays comprise her work to date. One of the stories and one of the novels have been adapted for the motion picture screen. She excels in stories of sentiment, for she knows how to keep pathos from sinking into the cheap insincerity of the sentimental school. In delicate treatment of a theme charged with unwept tears she has never surpassed *England to America.*

### THE STORY

War brings out the best and worst in men. In *England to America* Miss Montague shows the best side without glorifying war or denouncing it. It is not a story of physical bravery on the battle-field but of moral courage at home. The theme, nevertheless, goes still deeper than this. It is based on the relations between the two great English-speaking nations, whose differences in temperament make full understanding of each other difficult. Greater than the barriers of custom and manners, however, is the common pride in race, the Anglo-Saxon kinship of Englishmen and Americans.

Britons are noted for their reserve. They have a way of understating things about which they feel deeply that baffles the Yankee, accustomed to give free rein to his feelings. Yet the American idea of the British type is not fair to the original. John Bull is not the caricature we have made of him in novels and musical comedies, any more than an Englishman's notion of Uncle Sam is a true picture of the typical American. Differences in speech and conduct have led to misunderstandings on both sides of the water. To believe that the real Englishman is a high-hatting snob with a monocle whose vocabulary consists of a few phrases such as "My word!" and "Ripping, old top, simply ripping!" is to make the same mistake the English do when they assume that all Americans are boors, that they talk through the nose and ask nothing better than to spend millions of dollars picking up fake antiques all over Europe.

While Miss Montague's story recognizes certain surface differences between the two peoples, it goes beneath these to real national character. After reading it, one cannot help feeling the need of a better understanding between England and America, yet the author disclaims any intentional propaganda. "I felt," she says, "there was a wistful spirit among some of the best elements in England reaching out for American sympathy. They couldn't say what they felt—they were too proud, too reserved. But I wanted to try to interpret them and let them see that we would understand." This she has done with real insight into the English mind and, incidentally, into the hearts of her own Southerners.

Among the stories produced by the World War *England to America* merits the high praise it has received. First published in the *Atlantic Monthly* for September, 1919, only ten months after the signing of the armistice, it was included in the O. Henry Memorial Award Prize Stories for that year. A casual reading will show that style is the least important element in its success. Attempts at finished writing are rare, and even those passages which show some effort in that direction are not particularly distinguished.

There are three things, however, which raise it above the level of ordinary war stories. The first is the invention of a striking situation. It is one of those flashes of genius that come rarely to any author. Its possibilities for arousing emotion are infinite. Even a far less gifted writer than Miss Montague could have used the situation effectively.

Secondly, the method of presenting and unfolding the situation is distinctive. The author chose to reveal the truth gradually, with deft touches anticipating the final disclosure, so that the climax is prepared for yet is stunning when it comes. A different effect, yet none the less powerful, might have been achieved by letting the reader into the secret at the beginning. When the reader shares with one group of characters a secret that is kept from another character, the result is irony. On the stage the same device is called dramatic irony. Whether or not

Miss Montague chose the better method is one of the topics you may discuss after studying the story.

Finally, omission of the more brutal aspects of war and substitution of moral values lifts *England to America* out of the rut. On the whole, the story inspires optimism and emphasizes with singular clarity the bond of race and destiny between the two nations.

## ENGLAND TO AMERICA[1]

### I

"Lord, but the English people are funny!"

This was the perplexed mental ejaculation that young Lieutenant Skipworth Cary, of Virginia, found his thoughts constantly reiterating during his stay in Devonshire.[2] Had he been, he wondered, a confiding fool, to accept so trustingly Chev Sherwood's suggestion that he spend a part of his leave, at least, at Bishopsthorpe, where Chev's people lived? But why should he have anticipated any difficulty here, in this very corner of England which had bred his own ancestors, when he had always hit it off so splendidly with his English comrades at the Front? Here, however, though they were all awfully kind,—at least, he was sure they meant to be kind,—something was always bringing him up short: something that he could not lay hold of, but which made him feel like a blind man groping in a strange place, or worse, like a bull in a china-shop. He was prepared enough to find differences in the American and English points of view. But this thing that baffled him did not seem to have to do with that; it was something deeper, something very definite, he was sure—and yet, what was it? The worst of it was that he had a curious feeling as if they were all—that is, Lady Sherwood and Gerald; not Sir Charles so much—protecting him from himself—keeping him from making breaks, as he phrased it. That hurt and annoyed him, and piqued his vanity. Was he a social blunderer, and weren't a Virginia gentleman's manners to be trusted in England without leading-strings?

He had been at the Front for several months with the Royal Flying Corps,[3] and when his leave came, his Flight Commander,

---

[1] Reprinted from the *Atlantic Monthly* by permission of the author.

[2] Devonshire—A shire, or county, on the southwest coast of England, noted for its beauty of landscape.

[3] Royal Flying Corps—British aviation unit to which a number of Americans were attached.

Captain Cheviot Sherwood, discovering that he meant to spend it in England, where he hardly knew a soul, had said his people down in Devonshire would be jolly glad to have him stop with them; and Skipworth Cary, knowing that, if the circumstances had been reversed, his people down in Virginia would indeed have been jolly glad to entertain Captain Sherwood, had accepted unhesitatingly. The invitation had been seconded by a letter from Lady Sherwood,—Chev's mother,—and after a few days sight-seeing in London, he had come down to Bishopsthorpe, very eager to know his friend's family, feeling as he did about Chev himself. "He's the finest man that ever went up in the air," he had written home; and to his own family's disgust, his letters had been far more full of Chev Sherwood than they had been of Skipworth Cary.

And now here he was, and he almost wished himself away—wished almost that he was back again at the Front, carrying on under Chev. There, at least, you knew what you were up against. The job might be hard enough, but it wasn't baffling and queer, with hidden under-currents that you couldn't chart. It seemed to him that this baffling feeling of constraint had rushed to meet him on the very threshold of the drawing-room, when he made his first appearance.

As he entered, he had a sudden sensation that they had been awaiting him in a strained expectancy, and that, as he appeared, they adjusted unseen masks and began to play-act at something. "But English people don't play-act very well," he commented to himself, reviewing the scene afterward.

Lady Sherwood had come forward and greeted him in a manner which would have been pleasant enough, if he had not, with quick sensitiveness, felt it to be forced. But perhaps that was English stiffness.

Then she had turned to her husband, who was standing staring into the fireplace, although, as it was June, there was no fire there to stare at.

"Charles," she said, "here is Lieutenant Cary"; and her voice had a certain note in it which at home Cary and his sister Nancy were in the habit of designating "mother-making-dad-mind-his-manners."

At her words the old man—and Cary was startled to see how old and broken he was—turned round and held out his hand. "How d'you do?" he said jerkily, "how d'you do?" and then turned abruptly back again to the fireplace.

"Hello! What's up! The old boy doesn't like me!" was Cary's quick, startled comment to himself.

He was so surprised by the look the other bent upon him that he involuntarily glanced across to a long mirror to see if there was anything wrong with his uniform. But no, that appeared to be all right. It was himself, then—or his country; perhaps the old sport didn't fall for Americans.

"And here is Gerald," Lady Sherwood went on in her low remote voice, which somehow made the Virginian feel very far away.

It was with genuine pleasure, though with some surprise, that he turned to greet Gerald Sherwood, Chev's younger brother, who had been, tradition in the corps said, as gallant and daring a flyer as Chev himself, until he got his in the face five months ago.

"I'm mighty glad to meet you," he said eagerly, in his pleasant, muffled Southern voice, grasping the hand the other stretched out, and looking with deep respect at the scarred face and sightless eyes.

Gerald laughed a little, but it was a pleasant laugh, and his hand-clasp was friendly.

"That's real American, isn't it?" he said. "I ought to have remembered and said it first. Sorry."

Skipworth laughed, too. "Well," he conceded, "we generally are glad to meet people in my country, and we don't care who says it first. But," he added, "I didn't think I'd have the luck to find you here."

He remembered that Chev had regretted that he probably wouldn't see Gerald, as the latter was at St. Dunstan's, where they were re-educating the blinded soldiers.

The other hesitated a moment, and then said rather awkwardly, "Oh, I'm just home for a little while; I only got here this morning, in fact."

Skipworth noted the hesitation. Did the old people get panicky at the thought of entertaining a wild man from Virginia, and send an S O S[4] for Gerald, he wondered.

"We are so glad you could come to us," Lady Sherwood said rather hastily just then. And again he could not fail to note that she was prompting her husband.

[4] S O S—Radio or telegraph signal of distress.

The latter reluctantly turned round, and said, "Yes, yes, quite so. Welcome to Bishopsthorpe, my boy," as if his wife had pulled a string, and he responded mechanically, without quite knowing what he said. Then, as his eyes rested a moment on his guest, he looked as if he would like to bolt out of the room. He controlled himself, however, and, jerking round again to the fireplace, went on murmuring, "Yes, yes, yes," vaguely—just like the dormouse at the Mad Tea-Party,[5] who went to sleep, saying, "Twinkle, twinkle, twinkle," Cary could not help thinking to himself.

But after all, it wasn't really funny, it was pathetic. Gosh, how doddering the poor old boy was! Skipworth wondered, with a sudden twist at his heart, if the war was playing the deuce with his home people, too. Was his own father going to pieces like this, and had his mother's gay vivacity fallen into that still remoteness of Lady Sherwood's? But of course not! The Carys hadn't suffered as the poor Sherwoods had, with their youngest son, Curtin, killed early in the war, and now Gerald knocked out so tragically. Lord, he thought, how they must all bank on Chev! And of course they would want to hear at once about him. "I left Chev as fit as anything, and he sent all sorts of messages," he reported, thinking it more discreet to deliver Chev's messages thus vaguely than to repeat his actual carefree remark, which had been, "Oh, tell 'em I'm jolly as a tick."

But evidently there was something wrong with the words as they were, for instantly he was aware of that curious sense of withdrawal on their part. Hastily reviewing them, he decided that they had sounded too familiar from a stranger and a younger man like himself. He supposed he ought not to have spoken of Chev by his first name. Gee, what sticklers they were! Wouldn't his family—dad and mother and Nancy—have fairly lapped up any messages from him, even if they had been delivered a bit awkwardly? However, he added, as a concession to their point of view, "But of course you'll have had later news of Captain Sherwood."

To which, after a pause, Lady Sherwood responded, "Oh, yes," in that remote and colorless voice which might have meant anything or nothing.

At this point dinner was announced.

[5] MAD TEA-PARTY—A scene in Lewis Carroll's *Alice's Adventures in Wonderland.*

Lady Sherwood drew her husband away from the empty fireplace, and Gerald slipped his arm through the Virginian's, saying pleasantly, "I'm learning to carry on fairly well at St. Dunstan's, but I confess I still like to have a pilot."

To look at the tall young fellow beside him, whose scarred face was so reminiscent of Chev's untouched good looks, who had known all the immense freedom of the air, but who was now learning to carry on in the dark, moved Skipworth Cary to generous homage.

"You know my saying I'm glad to meet you isn't just American," he said half shyly, but warmly. "It's plain English, and the straight truth. I've wanted to meet you awfully. The oldsters are always holding up your glorious exploits to us newcomers. Withers never gets tired telling about that fight of yours with the four enemy planes. And besides," he rushed on eagerly, "I'm glad to have a chance to tell Chev's brother—Captain Sherwood's brother, I mean—what I think of him. Only as a matter of fact, I can't," he broke off with a laugh. "I can't put it exactly into words, but I tell you I'd follow that man straight into hell and out the other side—or go there alone if he told me to. He is the finest chap that ever flew."

And then he felt as if a cold douche had been flung in his face, for after a moment's pause, the other returned, "That's awfully good of you," in a voice so distant and formal that the Virginian could have kicked himself. What an ass he was to be so darned enthusiastic with an Englishman! He supposed it was bad form to show any pleasure over praise of a member of your family. Lord, if Chev got the V. C.,[6] he reckoned it would be awful to speak of it. Still, you would have thought Gerald might have stood for a little praise of him. But then, glancing sideways at his companion, he surprised on his face a look so strange and suffering that it came to him almost violently what it must be never to fly again; to be on the threshold of life, with endless days of blackness ahead. Good God! How cruel he had been to flaunt Chev in his face! In remorseful and hasty reparation he stumbled on, "But the old fellows are always having great discussions as to which was the best—you or your brother. Withers always maintains you were."

"Withers lies, then!" the other retorted. "I never touched Chev—never came within a mile of him, and never could have."

[6] V. C.—Victoria Cross, British medal for distinguished bravery.

They reached the dinner-table with that, and young Cary found himself bewildered and uncomfortable. If Gerald hadn't liked praise of Chev, he had liked praise of himself even less, it seemed.

Dinner was not a success. The Virginian found that, if there was to be conversation, the burden of carrying it on was upon him, and gosh! they don't mind silences in this man's island, do they? he commented desperately to himself, thinking how different it was from America. Why, there they acted as if silence was an egg that had just been laid, and everyone had to cackle at once to cover it up. But here the talk constantly fell to the ground, and nobody but himself seemed concerned to pick it up. His attempt to praise Chev had not been successful, and he could understand their not wanting to hear about flying and the war before Gerald.

So at last, in desperation, he wandered off into descriptions of America, finding to his relief, that he had struck the right note at last. They were glad to hear about the States, and Lady Sherwood inquired politely if the Indians still gave them much trouble; and when he assured her that in Virginia, except for the Pocahontas tribe,[7] they were all pretty well subdued, she accepted his statement with complete innocency. And he was so delighted to find at last a subject to which they were evidently cordial, that he was quite carried away, and wound up by inviting them all to visit his family in Richmond, as soon as the war was over.

Gerald accepted at once, with enthusiasm; Lady Sherwood made polite murmurs, smiling at him in quite a warm and almost, indeed, maternal manner. Even Sir Charles, who had been staring at the food on his plate as if he did not quite know what to make of it, came to the surface long enough to mumble, "Yes, yes, very good idea. Countries must carry on together—What?"

But that was the only hit of the whole evening, and when the Virginian retired to his room, as he made an excuse to do early, he was so confused and depressed that he fell into an acute attack of home-sickness.

Heavens, he thought, as he tumbled into bed, just suppose, now, this was little old Richmond, Virginia, U.S.A., instead of being Bishopsthorpe, Avery Cross near Wick, and all the rest of it! And at that, he grinned to himself. England wasn't such an all-fired big country that you'd think they'd have to ticket themselves with

[7] Pocahontas tribe—Cary is "jollying" his hostess. Of course, there is no such tribe.

addresses a yard long, for fear they'd get lost—now, would you? Well, anyway, suppose it was Richmond and his train just pulling into the Byrd Street Station. He stretched out luxuriously, and let his mind picture the whole familiar scene. The wind was blowing right, so there was the mellow homely smell of tobacco in the streets, and plenty of people all along the way to hail him with outstretched hands and shouts of: "Hey, Skip Cary, when did you get back?" "Welcome home, my boy!" "Well, will you *look* what the cat dragged in!" And so he came to his own front door-step, and, walking straight in, surprised the whole family at breakfast; and yes—doggone it! If it wasn't Sunday, and they having waffles! And after that his obliging fancy bore him up Franklin Street, through Monroe Park, and so to Miss Sally Berkeley's door. He was sound asleep before he reached it, but in his dreams, light as a little bird, she came flying down the broad stairway to meet him, and—

But when he waked next morning, he did not find himself in Virginia, but in Devonshire, where, to his unbounded embarrassment, a white housemaid was putting up his curtains and whispering something about his bath. And though he pretended profound slumber, he was well aware that people do not turn brick-red in their sleep. And the problem of what was the matter with the Sherwood family was still before him.

## II

"They're playing a game," he told himself after a few days. "That is, Lady Sherwood and Gerald are—poor old Sir Charles can't make much of a stab at it. The game is to make me think they are awfully glad to have me, when in reality there's something about me, or something I do, that gets them on the raw."

He almost decided to make some excuse and get away; but after all, that was not easy. In English novels, he remembered, they always had a wire calling them to London; but, darn it all! the Sherwoods knew mighty well there wasn't any one in London who cared a hoot about him.

The thing that got his goat most, he told himself, was that they apparently didn't like his friendship with Chev. Anyway, they didn't seem to want him to talk about him; and whenever he tried to express his warm appreciation for all that the older man had done for him, he was instantly aware of a wall of reserve on their part, a holding of themselves aloof from him. That puzzled and hurt him, and put him on his dignity. He concluded that they thought it was cheeky of a youngster like him to think that a man like Chev could be his friend; and if that was the way they felt, he reckoned he'd jolly well better shut up about it.

But whatever it was that they didn't like about him, they most certainly did want him to have a good time. He and his pleasure appeared to be for the time being their chief consideration. And after the first day or so he began indeed to enjoy himself extremely. For one thing, he came to love the atmosphere of the old place and of the surrounding country, which he and Gerald explored together. He liked to think that ancestors of his own had been inheritors of these green lanes, and pleasant mellow stretches. Then, too, after the first few days, he could not help seeing that they really began to like him, which of course was reassuring, and tapped his own warm friendliness, which was always ready enough to be released. And besides, he got by accident what he took to be a hint as to the trouble. He was passing the half-open door of Lady Sherwood's morning-room, when he heard Sir Charles's voice break out, "Good God, Elizabeth, I don't see how you stand it! When I see him so straight and fine-looking, and so untouched, beside our poor lad, and think—and think—"

Skipworth hurried out of earshot, but now he understood that look of aversion in the old man's eyes which had so startled him at first. Of course, the poor old boy might easily hate the sight of him beside Gerald. With Gerald himself he really got along famously. He was a most delightful companion, full of anecdotes and history of the countryside, every foot of which he had apparently explored in the old days with Chev and the younger brother, Curtin. Yet even with Gerald, Cary sometimes felt that aloofness and reserve, and that older protective air that they all showed him. Take, for instance, that afternoon when they were lolling together on the grass in the park. The Virginian, running on in his usual eager manner, had plunged without thinking into an account of a particularly daring bit of flying on Chev's part, when suddenly he realized that Gerald had rolled over on the grass and buried his face in his arms, and interrupted himself awkwardly. "But, of course," he said, "he must have written home about it himself."

"No, or if he did, I didn't hear of it. Go on," Gerald said in a muffled voice.

A great rush of compassion and remorse overwhelmed the Virginian, and he burst out penitently, "What a brute I am! I'm always forgetting and running on about flying, when I know it must hurt like the very devil!"

The other drew a difficult breath. "Yes," he admitted, "what you say does hurt in a way—in a way you can't understand. But all the same I like to hear you. Go on about Chev."

So Skipworth went on and finished his account, winding up, "I don't believe there's another man in the service who could have pulled it off—but I tell you your brother's one in a million."

"Good God, don't I know it!" the other burst out. "We were all three the jolliest pals together," he got out presently in a choked voice, "Chev and the young un and I: and now—"

He did not finish, but Cary guessed his meaning. Now the young un, Curtin, was dead, and Gerald himself knocked out. But, heavens! the Virginian thought, did Gerald think Chev would go back on him now on account of his blindness? Well you could everlastingly bet he wouldn't!

"Chev thinks the world and all of you!" he cried in eager defense of his friend's loyalty. "Lots of times when we're all awfully jolly together, he makes some excuse and goes off by himself; and Withers told me it was because he was so frightfully cut up about you. Withers said he told him once that he'd a lot rather have got it himself—so you can everlastingly bank on him!"

Gerald gave a terrible little gasp. "I—I knew he'd feel like that," he got out. "We've always cared such a lot for each other." And then he pressed his face harder than ever into the grass, and his long body quivered all over. But not for long. In a moment he took fierce hold on himself, muttering, "Well, one must carry on, whatever happens," and apologized disjointedly. "What a fearful fool you must think me! And—and this isn't very pippy for you, old chap." Presently, after that, he sat up, and said, brushing it all aside, "We're facing the old moat, aren't we? There's an interesting bit of tradition about it that I must tell you."

And there you were, Cary thought: no matter how much Gerald might be suffering from his misfortune, he must carry on just the same, and see that his visitor had a pleasant time. It made the

Virginian feel like an outsider and very young, as if he were not old enough for them to show him their real feelings.

Another thing that he noticed was that they did not seem to want him to meet people. They never took him anywhere to call, and if visitors came to the house, they showed an almost panicky desire to get him out of the way. That again hurt his pride. What in heaven's name was the matter with him anyway!

## III

However, on the last afternoon of his stay at Bishopsthorpe, he told himself with a rather rueful grin, that his manners must have improved a little, for they took him to tea at the rectory.

He was particularly glad to go there because, from certain jokes of Withers's, who had known the Sherwoods since boyhood, he gathered that Chev and the rector's daughter were engaged. And just as he would have liked Chev to meet Sally Berkeley, so he wanted to meet Miss Sybil Gaylord.

He had little hope of having a tête-à-tête[8] with her, but as it fell out he did. They were all in the rectory garden together, Gerald and the rector a little behind Miss Gaylord and himself, as they strolled down a long walk with high hedges bordering it. On the other side of the hedge Lady Sherwood and her hostess still sat at the tea-table, and then it was that Cary heard Mrs. Gaylord say distinctly, "I'm afraid the strain has been too much for you—you should have let us have him."

To which Lady Sherwood returned quickly, "Oh, no, that would have been impossible with—"

"Come—come this way—I must show you the view from the arbor," Miss Gaylord broke in breathlessly; and laying a hand on his arm, she turned him abruptly into a side path.

Glancing down at her, the Southerner could not but note the panic and distress in her fair face. It was so obvious that the overheard words referred to him, and he was so bewildered by the whole situation, that he burst out impulsively, "I say, what *is* the matter with me? Why do they find me so hard to put up with? Is it something I do—or don't they like Americans? Honestly, I wish you'd tell me."

[8] TÊTE-À-TÊTE—Private conversation.

She stood still at that, looking at him, her blue eyes full of distress and concern.

"Oh, I am so sorry," she cried. "They would be so sorry to have you think anything like that."

"But what is it?" he persisted. "Don't they like Americans?"

"Oh, no, it isn't that—Oh, quite the contrary!" she returned eagerly.

"Then it's something about me they don't like?"

"Oh, no, no! Least of all, that—*don't* think that!" she begged.

"But what am I to think then?"

"Don't think anything just yet," she pleaded. "Wait a little, and you will understand."

She was so evidently distressed that he could not press her further; and fearing she might think him unappreciative, he said, "Well, whatever it is, it hasn't prevented me from having a ripping good time. They've seen to that, and just done everything for my pleasure."

She looked up quickly, and to his relief he saw that for once he had said the right thing.

"You have enjoyed it, then?" she questioned eagerly.

"Most awfully," he assured her warmly. "I shall always remember what a happy leave they gave me."

She gave a little sigh of satisfaction, "I am so glad," she said. "They wanted you to have a good time—that was what we all wanted."

He looked at her gratefully, thinking how sweet she was in her fair English beauty, and how good to care that he should have enjoyed his leave. How different she was, too, from Sally Berkeley—why she would have made two of his little girl! And how quiet! Sally Berkeley, with her quick glancing vivacity, would have been all around her and off again like a humming-bird before she could have uttered two words. And yet he was sure that they would have been friends, just as he and Chev were. Perhaps they all would be, after the war. And then he began to talk about Chev, being sure that, had the circumstances been reversed, Sally Berkeley would have wanted news of him. Instantly he was aware of a tense listening stillness on her part. That pleased him. Well, she did care for the old fellow all right, he thought; and though she made no response, averting her face, and plucking nervously at the leaves of the hedge as they passed slowly along, he went on pouring out his eager admiration for his friend.

At last they came to a seat in an arbor, from which one looked out upon a green beneficent landscape. It was an intimate secluded little spot—and oh, if Sally Berkeley were only there to sit beside him! And as he thought of this, it came to him whimsically that in all probability she must be longing for Chev, just as he was for Sally.

Dropping down on the bench beside her, he leaned over, and said with a friendly, almost brotherly, grin of understanding, "I reckon you're wishing Captain Sherwood was sitting here, instead of Lieutenant Cary."

The minute the impulsive words were out of his mouth, he knew he had blundered, been awkward, and inexcusably intimate. She gave a little choked gasp, and her blue eyes stared up at him, wide and startled. Good heavens, what a break he had made! No wonder the Sherwoods couldn't trust him in company! There seemed no apology that he could offer in words, but at least, he thought, he would show her that he would not have intruded on her secret without being willing to share his with her. With awkward haste he put his hand into his breast-pocket, and dragged forth the picture of Sally Berkeley he always carried there.

"This is the little girl I'm thinking about," he said, turning very red, yet boyishly determined to make amends, and also proudly confident of Sally Berkeley's charms. "I'd like mighty well for you two to know one another."

She took the picture in silence, and for a long moment stared down at the soft little face, so fearless, so confident and gay, that smiled appealingly back at her. Then she did something astonishing,—something which seemed to him wholly un-English,—and yet he thought it the sweetest thing he had ever seen. Cupping her strong hands about the picture with a quick protectiveness, she suddenly raised it to her lips, and kissed it lightly. "O little girl!" she cried, "I hope you will be very happy!"

The little involuntary act, so tender, so sisterly and spontaneous, touched the Virginian extremely.

"Thanks, awfully," he said unsteadily. "She'll think a lot of that, just as I do—and I know she'd wish you the same."

She made no reply to that, and as she handed the picture back to him, he saw that her hands were trembling, and he had a sudden conviction that, if she had been Sally Berkeley, her eyes would have been full of tears. As she was Sybil Gaylord, however, there were no tears there, only a look that he never forgot. The look of one much older, protective, maternal almost, and as if she were gazing back at Sally Berkeley and himself from a long way ahead on the road of life. He supposed it was the way most English people felt nowadays. He had surprised it so often on all their faces, that he could not help speaking of it.

"You all think we Americans are awfully young and raw, don't you?" he questioned.

"Oh, no, not that," she deprecated. "Young perhaps for these days, yes—but it is more that you—that your country is so—so unsuffered. And we don't want you to suffer!" she added quickly.

Yes, that was it! He understood now, and, heavens, how fine it was! Old England was wounded deep—deep. What she suffered herself she was too proud to show; but out of it she wrought a great maternal care for the newcomer. Yes, it *was* fine—he hoped his country would understand.

Miss Gaylord rose. "There are Gerald and father looking for you," she said, "and I must go now." She held out her hand. "Thank you for letting me see her picture, and for everything you said about Captain Sherwood—for *everything* remember—I want you to remember."

With a light pressure of her fingers she was gone, slipping away through the shrubbery, and he did not see her again.

## IV

So he came to his last morning at Bishopsthorpe; and as he dressed, he wished it could have been different; that he were not still conscious of that baffling wall of reserve between himself and Chev's people, for whom, despite all, he had come to have a real affection.

In the breakfast-room he found them all assembled, and his last meal there seemed to him as constrained and difficult as any that had preceded it. It was over finally, however, and in a few minutes he would be leaving.

"I can never thank you enough for the splendid time I've had here," he said as he rose. "I'll be seeing Chev to-morrow, and I'll tell him all about everything."

Then he stopped dead. With a smothered exclamation, old Sir Charles had stumbled to his feet, knocking over his chair, and hurried blindly out of the room; and Gerald said, *"Mother!"* in a choked appeal.

As if it were a signal between them Lady Sherwood pushed her chair back a little from the table, her long delicate fingers dropped together loosely in her lap; she gave a faint sigh as if a restraining mantle slipped from her shoulders, and, looking up at the youth before her, her fine pale face lighted with a kind of glory, she said, "No, dear lad, no. You can never tell Chev, for he is gone."

*"Gone!"* he cried.

"Yes," she nodded back at him, just above a whisper; and now her face quivered, and the tears began to rush down her cheeks.

"Not *dead!*" he cried. "Not Chev—not that! O my God, Gerald, not *that!*"

"Yes," Gerald said. "They got him two days after you left."

It was so overwhelming, so unexpected and shocking, above all so terrible, that the friend he had so greatly loved and admired was gone out of his life forever, that young Cary stumbled back into his seat, and, crumpling over, buried his face in his hands, making great uncouth gasps as he strove to choke back his grief.

Gerald groped hastily around the table, and flung an arm about his shoulders.

"Steady on, dear fellow, steady," he said, though his own voice broke.

"When did you hear?" Cary got out at last.

"We got the official notice just the day before you came—and Withers has written us particulars since."

"And you *let* me come in spite of it! And stay on, when every word I said about him must have—have fairly *crucified* each one of you! Oh, forgive me! forgive me!" he cried distractedly. He saw it all now; he understood at last. It was not on Gerald's account that they could not talk of flying and of Chev, it was because—because their hearts were broken over Chev himself. "Oh, forgive me!" he gasped again.

"Dear lad, there is nothing to forgive," Lady Sherwood returned. "How could we help loving your generous praise of our poor darling? We loved it, and you for it; we wanted to hear it, but we were afraid. We were afraid we might break down, and that you would find out."

The tears were still running down her cheeks. She did not brush them away now; she seemed glad to have them there at last.

Sinking down on his knees, he caught her hands. "Why did you *let* me do such a horrible thing?" he cried. "Couldn't you have trusted me to understand? Couldn't you *see* I loved him just as you did—No, no!" he broke down humbly. "Of course I couldn't love him as his own people did. But you must have seen how I felt about him—how I admired him, and would have followed him anywhere—and *of course* if I had known, I should have gone away at once."

"Ah, but that was just what we were afraid of," she said quickly. "We were afraid you would go away and have a lonely leave somewhere. And in these days a boy's leave is so precious a thing that nothing must spoil it—*nothing,*" she reiterated; and her tears fell upon his hands like a benediction. "But we didn't do it very well, I'm afraid," she went on presently, with gentle contrition. "You were too quick and understanding; you guessed there was something wrong. We were sorry not to manage better," she apologized.

"Oh, you wonderful, wonderful people!" he gasped. "Doing everything for my happiness, when all the time—all the time—"

His voice went out sharply, as his mind flashed back to scene after scene: to Gerald's long body lying quivering on the grass; to Sybil Gaylord wishing Sally Berkeley happiness out of her own tragedy; and to the high look on Lady Sherwood's face. They seemed to him themselves, and yet more than themselves—shining bits in the mosaic of a great nation. Disjointedly there passed through his mind familiar words—"These are they who have washed their garments—having come out of great tribulation." No wonder they seemed older.

"We—we couldn't have done it in America," he said humbly.

He had a desperate desire to get away to himself; to hide his face in his arms, and give vent to the tears that were stifling him; to weep for his lost friend, and for this great heartbreaking heroism of theirs.

"But why did you do it?" he persisted. "Was it because I was his friend?"

"Oh, it was much more than that," Gerald said quickly. "It was a matter of the two countries. Of course, we jolly well knew you didn't belong to us, and didn't want to, but for the life of us we couldn't help a sort of feeling that you did. And when America was in at last, and you fellows began to come, you seemed like our very own come back after many years, and," he added, a throb in his voice, "we were most awfully glad to see you—we wanted a chance to show you how England felt."

Skipworth Cary rose to his feet. The tears for his friend were still wet upon his lashes. Stooping, he took Lady Sherwood's hands in his and raised them to his lips. "As long as I live, I shall never forget," he said. "And others of us have seen it, too, in other ways—be sure America will never forget, either."

She looked up at his untouched youth out of her beautiful sad eyes, the exalted light still shining through her tears. "Yes," she said, "you see it was—I don't know exactly how to put it—but it was England to America."

## QUESTIONS

1. What is the struggle upon which this story is built? What are the "furtherances and hindrances" (see Introduction to the Short Story) by which the action proceeds to the climax?
2. Did you suspect the true reason behind the Sherwoods' attitude before the author stated it definitely? If so, at what point did you first begin to suspect the truth?
3. Do you think it likely that so cultured an Englishwoman as Lady Sherwood would believe Virginia is still overrun with Indians?
4. Twice Cary gets an intimation of the true state of affairs, both times by overhearing a conversation. What do you think of the double use of this device? Can you suggest another way of handling the problem?
5. What speech of Cary's comes closest to breaking down the morale of the Sherwoods?
6. As the story progresses, Cary shifts from one explanation to another to account for the family's attitude toward him. What are they?
7. Why is it that Cary finds it easier to confide his troubles to Sybil Gaylord than to Gerald?
8. What are the outstanding differences between the English and the Americans as indicated in this story? How are some of these differences illustrated by Sybil Gaylord and Sally Berkeley? What outstanding traits do Englishmen and Americans possess in common?
9. What do you like most about Cary? About Gerald?
10. In what way would the interest differ if, in the opening section, Miss Montague had revealed to the reader the secret of Chev's death? Which method do you think the more effective? Why?
11. Though Chev is dead, his personality pervades the whole story. In what ways do we learn of his qualities?

12. What part does war play in the story? What is the author's attitude toward war?
13. Is the ending of *England to America* happy or tragic? Just what is the main idea Miss Montague is trying to present?

## EXERCISES

**Exercises preceded by a star are designed for assignment at the discretion of the teacher, or for any student who volunteers.**

1. Explain the significance of the title, *England to America.*
2. Miss Montague never quite gives away the secret of Chev's death until that last breakfast. She does, however, furnish a number of clues. Point them out in order from the beginning.
3. Compare Sir Charles with Lady Sherwood as to the manner in which each faces the tragedy and the necessity for concealing it from Cary.
4. Imagining that you are Sybil Gaylord, write a letter to Sally Berkeley, trying to keep it true to character; or write to Sybil as you think Sally would write after she had learned from Cary what happened at Bishopsthorpe.
5. Hold an informal class debate on the proposition: War is a necessary evil.

*6. Report on one of the following suggested readings: James Bryce, *The American Commonwealth,* Part IV, Chap. 80, or Part VI, Chaps. 112–113; Price Collier, *England and the English,* Chap. 4; William Ralph Inge, *England,* Chap. 2; Frank Dilnot, *England after the War,* Chap. 12; Stephen Leacock, *My Discovery of England,* Chaps. 6 and 10.

*7. Turn to page 631 and read Washington Irving's *English Writers on America,* an essay written shortly after the War of 1812. Contrast the conditions which the essay and this story reflect, and state which, in your opinion, is the stronger argument for closer relations between England and America.

# THE GARDEN-PARTY

## KATHERINE MANSFIELD

## 1888–1923

### THE AUTHOR

It is October in Paris in the year 1922. The chill of autumn is in the air, and when the sun hides itself behind the cloudbank, pedestrians pull their wraps closer about them and shiver. Leaves make little wispy noises as they spin downward from the branches.

This is the city to which people come from all over the world to seek pleasure, but Katherine Mansfield is here for a different reason. For months and months she has traveled in search of health. Italy in the winter. England in the summer. Switzerland, where the high mountains put too great a strain on her weakened heart. Now she is under treatment in the French capital.

For longer than she likes to remember the spectre of death has hovered near her. Yet she will not resign herself to the rôle of invalid. Between spells of serious illness she has worked at her stories and written in her Journal. It will not do to let fear take possession. Courage. The miracle may happen and health return. Sometimes, however, the black shadow becomes almost too oppressive to endure. She feels very alone, for her husband is not with her. Work has been the one comfort, but every day it is harder to put pen to paper.

In her Journal she writes for her husband's eyes: "When I say 'I fear'—don't let it disturb you, dearest heart. We all fear when we are in waiting-rooms. Yet we must pass beyond them, and if the other can keep calm, it is all the help we can give each other . . . All this sounds very strenuous and serious. But now that I have wrestled with it, it's no longer so. I feel happy—deep down. *All is well.*"

These were the last words Katherine Mansfield wrote in her Journal. In January, not many weeks later, she was dead. She had passed beyond "the last waiting-room."

Katherine Mansfield's biography has a brevity and a limitedness that reminds one of her stories. Born in New Zealand in 1888, she was sent at the age of thirteen to be educated in England. When she returned to her home land five years later, she found life in that remote part of the British Empire uncongenial. The lure of London proving too strong, she finally won her parents' consent to try living in England on a small allowance.

The next few years were taken up in desperate efforts to establish herself in the arts. She tried music and then shifted to literature, adopting the pen name Katherine Mansfield in place of her own, Kathleen Beauchamp. Her first success grew out of an illness in Bavaria on which the book, *In a German Pension* (1911) is based. Recognition came slowly. Only a few magazines accepted her work, and then she was often poorly paid. In 1911, however, she met a kindred spirit in J. Middleton Murry, editor and critic. They were married, and when eight years later he became editor of *The Athenaeum,* Katherine Mansfield at last had an outlet for her work.

Although her stories, with few exceptions, were written between 1911 and 1922, it was not until 1920 that a collection was published in book form. In that year *Bliss and Other Stories* appeared. Three other volumes, the best known of which is *The Garden-Party,* followed in quick succession. Unfortunately, Katherine Mansfield lived only long enough to have a foretaste of fame. She died before her last two volumes of stories were published. A young woman, only thirty-four, she had not yet reached that maturity which usually produces the best creative work.

J. Middleton Murry thought his wife "the most perfect and accomplished literary artist" of her generation. Even if we discount that estimate considerably, we discover that within her limited sphere she exhibits a unique talent. She has so great a sensitiveness that the little touches of life she invariably treats never seem trivial. Under her deft pen they become more important than the greater events usually chosen by short story writers. Her art has often been compared to that of the Russian, Anton Chekhov, except that one feels a deeper sympathy in her work—yes, and spirituality too; for it is her revelation of the minds of her characters that makes them live in our memory.

## THE STORY

*The Garden-Party* is typical of Katherine Mansfield's method. The thread of action is so slender that it can scarcely be called a plot. The chief character is a young girl whose thoughtless enjoyment of living is disturbed by a note of tragedy—the death of a workman unknown to her except by hearsay. For the first time she realizes the suffering life holds. While some people are making merry, others are sorrowing. It is an idea that strikes her with peculiar force. It leaves her shaken and uncomprehending, the more so because of her own family's inability to understand her feelings. This clash in point of view, to be found in most of Katherine Mansfield's writings, contributes a melancholy that is probably a reflection of the author's own experience.

Although a realist in a true sense, Katherine Mansfield differs from most of her contemporaries. Observation of detail has its place but is subordinate to the revelation of states of mind. Instead of trying to reproduce with photographic accuracy a setting for her characters, she is content to suggest the surroundings with a few carefully chosen details. One feels that her chief characters are not so much a product of physical environment as of personal contacts with other characters. The psychological element is uppermost. Often, as in *The Garden-*

*Party,* there is rebellion against the ideas of a group—in this instance, the family. Laura finds no sympathy. She is left to work out the problem of world sorrow by herself; and the very fact that there is no solution makes her plight the more distressing.

The feminine touch in this author's work is obvious from start to finish. No man could probe the mind of a young girl with the delicacy exhibited by Katherine Mansfield. Her men, on the contrary, often lack robustness. This gives the clue to the writer's limitations. Within certain bounds she is a sure artist, with an insight that is almost intuition. Beyond that she ventures with less confidence.

Written in 1921, little more than a year before her death, *The Garden-Party* represents Katherine Mansfield's mature work. Still it did not satisfy her. Possessing a keen sense of self-criticism, she was striving toward a finer expression of truth when death intervened. This story, which gives its name to the volume published in 1922, *The Garden-Party and Other Stories,* will nevertheless remain as an example of her best work. Notwithstanding the strain of melancholy that runs through it, Katherine Mansfield never descends to the morbid hopelessness that is the stock in trade of many realists. She has, too, a sanity that prevents her from going to the other extreme, the easy optimism of the "Pollyanna" school. Between the two she keeps a delicate balance. Moreover, she refrains from nailing home her moral. The reader will not find the answer to the problem at the back of the book; it is for him to make the interpretation.

## THE GARDEN-PARTY[1]

And after all the weather was ideal. They could not have had a more perfect day for a garden-party if they had ordered it. Windless, warm, the sky without a cloud. Only the blue was veiled with a haze of light gold, as it is sometimes in early summer. The gardener had been up since dawn, mowing the lawns and sweeping them, until the grass and the dark flat rosettes where the daisy plants had been seemed to shine. As for the roses, you could not help feeling they understood that roses are the only flowers that impress people at garden-parties; the only flowers that everybody is certain of knowing. Hundreds, yes, literally hundreds, had come out in a single night; the green bushes bowed down as though they had been visited by archangels.

Breakfast was not yet over before the men came to put up the marquee.[2]

[1] Reprinted from *The Garden-Party* by Katherine Mansfield by permission of and special arrangement with Alfred A. Knopf, Inc., authorized publishers.

[2] MARQUEE—A large tent.

"Where do you want the marquee put, mother?"

"My dear child, it's no use asking me. I'm determined to leave everything to you children this year. Forget I am your mother. Treat me as an honoured guest."

But Meg could not possibly go and supervise the men. She had washed her hair before breakfast, and she sat drinking her coffee in a green turban, with a dark wet curl stamped on each cheek. Jose, the butterfly, always came down in a silk petticoat and a kimono jacket.

"You'll have to go, Laura; you're the artistic one."

Away Laura flew, still holding her piece of bread-and-butter. It's so delicious to have an excuse for eating out of doors, and besides, she loved having to arrange things; she always felt she could do it so much better than anybody else.

Four men in their shirt-sleeves stood grouped together on the garden path. They carried staves covered with rolls of canvas, and they had big tool-bags slung on their backs. They looked impressive. Laura wished now that she had not got the bread-and-butter, but there was nowhere to put it, and she couldn't possibly throw it away. She blushed and tried to look severe and even a little bit short-sighted as she came up to them.

"Good morning," she said, copying her mother's voice. But that sounded so fearfully affected that she was ashamed, and stammered like a little girl, "Oh—er—have you come—is it about the marquee?"

"That's right, miss," said the tallest of the men, a lanky, freckled fellow, and he shifted his tool-bag, knocked back his straw hat and smiled down at her. "That's about it."

His smile was so easy, so friendly that Laura recovered. What nice eyes he had, small, but such a dark blue! And now she looked at the others, they were smiling too. "Cheer up, we won't bite," their smile seemed to say. How very nice workmen were! And what a beautiful morning! She mustn't mention the morning; she must be businesslike. The marquee.

"Well, what about the lily-lawn? Would that do?"

And she pointed to the lily-lawn with the hand that didn't hold the bread-and-butter. They turned, they stared in the direction. A little fat chap thrust out his under-lip, and the tall fellow frowned.

"I don't fancy it," said he. "Not conspicuous enough. You see, with a thing like a marquee," and he turned to Laura in his easy way, "you want to put it somewhere where it'll give you a bang slap in the eye, if you follow me."

Laura's upbringing made her wonder for a moment whether it was quite respectful of a workman to talk to her of bangs slap in the eye. But she did quite follow him.

"A corner of the tennis-court," she suggested. "But the band's going to be in one corner."

"H'm, going to have a band, are you?" said another of the workmen. He was pale. He had a haggard look as his dark eyes scanned the tennis-court. What was he thinking?

"Only a very small band," said Laura gently. Perhaps he wouldn't mind so much if the band was quite small. But the tall fellow interrupted.

"Look here, miss, that's the place. Against those trees. Over there. That'll do fine."

Against the karakas. Then the karaka-trees would be hidden. And they were so lovely, with their broad, gleaming leaves, and their clusters of yellow fruit. They were like trees you imagined growing on a desert island, proud, solitary, lifting their leaves and fruits to the sun in a kind of silent splendour. Must they be hidden by a marquee?

They must. Already the men had shouldered their staves and were making for the place. Only the tall fellow was left. He bent down, pinched a sprig of lavender, put his thumb and forefinger to his nose and snuffed up the smell. When Laura saw that gesture she forgot all about the karakas in her wonder at him caring for things like that—caring for the smell of lavender. How many men that she knew would have done such a thing? Oh, how extraordinarily nice workmen were, she thought. Why couldn't she have workmen for friends rather than the silly boys she danced with and who came to Sunday night supper? She would get on much better with men like these.

It's all the fault, she decided, as the tall fellow drew something on the back of an envelope, something that was to be looped up or left to hang, of these absurd class distinctions. Well, for her part, she didn't feel them. Not a bit, not an atom. . . . And now there came the chock-chock of wooden hammers. Some one whistled, some one sang out, "Are you right there, matey?" "Matey!" The friendliness of it, the—the—— Just to prove how happy she was, just to show the tall fellow how at home she felt, and how she despised stupid conventions, Laura took a big bite of her bread-and-butter as she stared at the little drawing. She felt just like a work-girl.

"Laura, Laura, where are you? Telephone, Laura!" a voice cried from the house.

"Coming!" Away she skimmed, over the lawn, up the path, up the steps, across the veranda, and into the porch. In the hall her father and Laurie were brushing their hats ready to go to the office.

"I say, Laura," said Laurie very fast, "you might just give a squiz at my coat before this afternoon. See if it wants pressing."

"I will," said she. Suddenly she couldn't stop herself. She ran at Laurie and gave him a small, quick squeeze. "Oh, I do love parties, don't you?" gasped Laura.

"Ra-ther," said Laurie's warm, boyish voice, and he squeezed his sister too, and gave her a gentle push. "Dash off to the telephone, old girl."

The telephone. "Yes, yes; oh yes. Kitty? Good morning, dear. Come to lunch? Do, dear. Delighted of course. It will only be a very scratch meal—just the sandwich crusts and broken meringue-shells and what's left over. Yes, isn't it a perfect morning? Your white? Oh, I certainly should. One moment—hold the line. Mother's calling." And Laura sat back. "What, mother? Can't hear."

Mrs. Sheridan's voice floated down the stairs. "Tell her to wear that sweet hat she had on last Sunday."

"Mother says you're to wear that *sweet* hat you had on last Sunday. Good. One o'clock. Bye-bye."

Laura put back the receiver, flung her arms over her head, took a deep breath, stretched and let them fall. "Huh," she sighed, and the moment after the sigh she sat up quickly. She was still, listening. All the doors in the house seemed to be open. The house was alive with soft, quick steps and running voices. The green baize door that led to the kitchen regions swung open and shut with a muffled thud. And now there came a long, chuckling absurd sound. It was the heavy piano being moved on its stiff castors. But the air! If you stopped to notice, was the air always like this? Little faint winds were playing chase, in at the tops of the windows, out at the doors. And there were two tiny spots of sun, one on the inkpot, one on a silver photograph frame, playing too. Darling little spots. Especially the one on the inkpot lid. It was quite warm. A warm little silver star. She could have kissed it.

The front door bell pealed, and there sounded the rustle of Sadie's print skirt on the stairs. A man's voice murmured; Sadie answered, careless "I'm sure I don't know. Wait. I'll ask Mrs. Sheridan."

"What is it, Sadie?" Laura came into the hall.

"It's the florist, Miss Laura."

It was, indeed. There, just inside the door, stood a wide, shallow tray full of pots of pink lilies. No other kind. Nothing but lilies—canna lilies, big pink flowers, wide open, radiant, almost frighteningly alive on bright crimson stems.

"O-oh, Sadie!" said Laura, and the sound was like a little moan. She crouched down as if to warm herself at that blaze of lilies; she felt they were in her fingers, on her lips, growing in her breast.

"It's some mistake," she said faintly. "Nobody ever ordered so many. Sadie, go and find mother."

But at that moment Mrs. Sheridan joined them.

"It's quite right," she said calmly. "Yes, I ordered them. Aren't they lovely?" She pressed Laura's arm. "I was passing the shop yesterday, and I saw them in the window. And I suddenly thought for once in my life I shall have enough canna lilies. The garden-party will be a good excuse."

"But I thought you said you didn't mean to interfere," said Laura. Sadie had gone. The florist's man was still outside at his van. She put her arm round her mother's neck and gently, very gently, she bit her mother's ear.

"My darling child, you wouldn't like a logical mother, would you? Don't do that. Here's the man."

He carried more lilies still, another whole tray.

"Bank them up, just inside the door, on both sides of the porch, please," said Mrs. Sheridan. "Don't you agree, Laura?"

"Oh, I *do,* mother."

In the drawing-room Meg, Jose and good little Hans had at last succeeded in moving the piano.

"Now, if we put this chesterfield against the wall and move everything out of the room except the chairs, don't you think?"

"Quite."

"Hans, move these tables into the smoking-room, and bring a sweeper to take these marks off the carpet and—one moment, Hans——" Jose loved giving orders to the servants, and they loved obeying her. She always made them feel they were taking part in some drama. "Tell mother and Miss Laura to come here at once."

"Very good, Miss Jose."

She turned to Meg. "I want to hear what the piano sounds like, just in case I'm asked to sing this afternoon. Let's try over 'This Life is Weary.'"

*Pom!* Ta-ta-ta *Tee*-ta! The piano burst out so passionately that Jose's face changed. She clasped her hands. She looked mournfully and enigmatically at her mother and Laura as they came in.

> This Life is *Wee*-ary,
> A Tear—a Sigh.
> A Love that *Chan*-ges,
> This Life is *Wee*-ary,
> A Tear—a Sigh.
> A Love that *Chan*-ges,
> And then . . . Good-bye!

But at the word "Good-bye," and although the piano sounded more desperate than ever, her face broke into a brilliant, dreadfully unsympathetic smile.

"Aren't I in good voice, mummy?" she beamed.

> This Life is *Wee*-ary,
> Hope comes to Die.
> A Dream—a *Wa*-kening.

But now Sadie interrupted them. "What is it, Sadie?"

"If you please, m'm, cook says have you got the flags for the sandwiches?"[3]

"The flags for the sandwiches, Sadie?" echoed Mrs. Sheridan dreamily. And the children knew by her face that she hadn't got them. "Let me see." And she said to Sadie firmly, "Tell cook I'll let her have them in ten minutes."

Sadie went.

[3] Flags for the sandwiches—Labels designating the various kinds of sandwiches.

"Now, Laura," said her mother quickly. "Come with me into the smoking-room. I've got the names somewhere on the back of an envelope. You'll have to write them out for me. Meg, go upstairs this minute and take that wet thing off your head. Jose, run and finish dressing this instant. Do you hear me, children, or shall I have to tell your father when he comes home to-night? And—and, Jose, pacify cook if you do go into the kitchen, will you? I'm terrified of her this morning."

The envelope was found at last behind the dining-room clock, though how it had got there Mrs. Sheridan could not imagine.

"One of you children must have stolen it out of my bag, because I remember vividly——cream cheese and lemon-curd. Have you done that?"

"Yes."

"Egg and——" Mrs. Sheridan held the envelope away from her. "It looks like mice. It can't be mice, can it?"

"Olive, pet," said Laura, looking over her shoulder.

"Yes, of course, olive. What a horrible combination it sounds. Egg and olive."

They were finished at last, and Laura took them off to the kitchen. She found Jose there pacifying the cook, who did not look at all terrifying.

"I have never seen such exquisite sandwiches," said Jose's rapturous voice. "How many kinds did you say there were, cook? Fifteen?"

"Fifteen, Miss Jose."

"Well, cook, I congratulate you."

Cook swept up crusts with the long sandwich knife, and smiled broadly.

"Godber's has come," announced Sadie, issuing out of the pantry. She had seen the man pass the window.

That meant the cream puffs had come. Godber's were famous for their cream puffs. Nobody ever thought of making them at home.

"Bring them in and put them on the table, my girl," ordered cook.

Sadie brought them in and went back to the door. Of course Laura and Jose were far too grown-up to really care about such things. All the same, they couldn't help agreeing that the puffs looked very attractive. Very. Cook began arranging them, shaking off the extra icing sugar.

"Don't they carry one back to all one's parties?" said Laura.

"I suppose they do," said practical Jose, who never liked to be carried back. "They look beautifully light and feathery, I must say."

"Have one each, my dears," said cook in her comfortable voice. "Yer ma won't know."

Oh, impossible. Fancy cream puffs so soon after breakfast. The very idea made one shudder. All the same, two minutes later Jose and Laura were licking their fingers with that absorbed inward look that only comes from whipped cream.

"Let's go into the garden, out by the back way," suggested Laura. "I want to see how the men are getting on with the marquee. They're such awfully nice men."

But the back door was blocked by cook, Sadie, Godber's man and Hans.

Something had happened.

"Tuk-tuk-tuk," clucked cook like an agitated hen. Sadie had her hand clapped to her cheek as though she had toothache. Hans's face was screwed up in the effort to understand. Only Godber's man seemed to be enjoying himself; it was his story.

"What's the matter? What's happened?"

"There's been a horrible accident," said cook. "A man killed."

"A man killed! Where? How? When?"

But Godber's man wasn't going to have his story snatched from under his very nose.

"Know those little cottages just below here, miss?" Know them? Of course, she knew them. "Well, there's a young chap living there, name of Scott, a carter. His horse shied at a traction-engine, corner of Hawke Street this morning, and he was thrown out on the back of his head. Killed."

"Dead!" Laura stared at Godber's man.

"Dead when they picked him up," said Godber's man with relish. "They were taking the body home as I come up here." And he said to the cook, "He's left a wife and five little ones."

"Jose, come here." Laura caught hold of her sister's sleeve and dragged her through the kitchen to the other side of the green baize door. There she paused and leaned against it. "Jose!" she said, horrified, "however are we going to stop everything?"

"Stop everything, Laura!" cried Jose in astonishment. "What do you mean?"

"Stop the garden-party, of course." Why did Jose pretend?

But Jose was still more amazed. "Stop the garden-party? My dear Laura, don't be so absurd. Of course we can't do anything of the kind. Nobody expects us to. Don't be so extravagant."

"But we can't possibly have a garden-party with a man dead just outside the front gate."

That really was extravagant, for the little cottages were in a lane to themselves at the very bottom of a steep rise that led up to the house. A broad road ran between. True, they were far too near. They were the greatest possible eyesore, and they had no right to be in that neighbourhood at all. They were little mean dwellings painted a chocolate brown. In the garden patches there was nothing but cabbage stalks, sick hens and tomato cans. The very smoke coming out of their chimneys was poverty-stricken. Little rags and shreds of smoke, so unlike the great silvery plumes that uncurled from the Sheridans' chimneys. Washerwomen lived in the lane and sweeps and a cobbler, and a man whose house-front was studded all over with minute bird-cages. Children swarmed. When the Sheridans were little they were forbidden to set foot there because of the revolting language and of what they might catch. But since they were grown up, Laura and Laurie on their prowls sometimes walked through. It was disgusting and sordid. They came out with a shudder. But still one must go everywhere; one must see everything. So through they went.

"And just think of what the band would sound like to that poor woman," said Laura.

"Oh, Laura!" Jose began to be seriously annoyed. "If you're going to stop a band playing every time some one has an accident, you'll lead a very strenuous life. I'm every bit as sorry about it as you. I feel just as sympathetic." Her eyes hardened. She looked at her sister just as she used to when they were little and fighting together. "You won't bring a drunken workman back to life by being sentimental," she said softly.

"Drunk! Who said he was drunk?" Laura turned furiously on Jose. She said, just as they had used to say on those occasions, "I'm going straight up to tell mother."

"Do, dear," cooed Jose.

"Mother, can I come into your room?" Laura turned the big glass door-knob.

"Of course, child. Why, what's the matter? What's given you such a colour?" And Mrs. Sheridan turned round from her dressing-table. She was trying on a new hat.

"Mother, a man's been killed," began Laura.

"*Not* in the garden?" interrupted her mother.

"No, no!"

"Oh, what a fright you gave me!" Mrs. Sheridan sighed with relief, and took off the big hat and held it on her knees.

"But listen, mother," said Laura. Breathless, half-choking, she told the dreadful story. "Of course, we can't have our party, can we?" she pleaded. "The band and everybody arriving. They'd hear us, mother; they're nearly neighbours!"

To Laura's astonishment her mother behaved just like Jose; it was harder to bear because she seemed amused. She refused to take Laura seriously.

"But, my dear child, use your common sense. It's only by accident we've heard of it. If some one had died there normally—and I can't understand how they keep alive in those poky little holes—we should still be having our party, shouldn't we?"

Laura had to say "yes" to that, but she felt it was all wrong. She sat down on her mother's sofa and pinched the cushion frill.

"Mother, isn't it really terribly heartless of us?" she asked.

"Darling!" Mrs. Sheridan got up and came over to her, carrying the hat. Before Laura could stop her she had popped it on. "My child!" said her mother, "the hat is yours. It's made for you. It's much too young for me. I have never seen you look such a picture. Look at yourself!" And she held up her hand-mirror.

"But, mother," Laura began again. She couldn't look at herself; she turned aside.

This time Mrs. Sheridan lost patience just as Jose had done.

"You are being very absurd, Laura," she said coldly. "People like that don't expect sacrifices from us. And it's not very sympathetic to spoil everybody's enjoyment as you're doing now."

"I don't understand," said Laura, and she walked quickly out of the room into her own bedroom. There, quite by chance, the first thing she saw was this charming girl in the mirror, in her black hat trimmed with gold daisies, and a long black velvet ribbon. Never had she imagined she could look like that. Is mother right? she thought. And now she hoped her mother was right. Am I being extravagant? Perhaps it was extravagant. Just for a moment she had another glimpse of that poor woman and those little children, and the body being carried into the house. But it all seemed blurred, unreal, like a picture in the newspaper. I'll remember it again after the party's over, she decided. And somehow that seemed quite the best plan. . . .

Lunch was over by half-past one. By half-past two they were all ready for the fray. The green-coated band had arrived and was established in a corner of the tennis-court.

"My dear!" trilled Kitty Maitland, "aren't they too like frogs for words? You ought to have arranged them round the pond with the conductor in the middle on a leaf."

Laurie arrived and hailed them on his way to dress. At the sight of him Laura remembered the accident again. She wanted to tell him. If Laurie agreed with the others, then it was bound to be all right. And she followed him into the hall.

"Laurie!"

"Hallo!" He was half-way upstairs, but when he turned round and saw Laura he suddenly puffed out his cheeks and goggled his eyes at her. "My word, Laura! You do look stunning," said Laurie. "What an absolutely topping hat!"

Laura said faintly "Is it?" and smiled up at Laurie, and didn't tell him after all.

Soon after that people began coming in streams. The band struck up; the hired waiters ran from the house to the marquee. Wherever you looked there were couples strolling, bending to the flowers, greeting, moving on over the lawn. They were like bright birds that had alighted in the Sheridans' garden for this one afternoon, on their way to—where? Ah, what happiness it is to be with people who all are happy, to press hands, press cheeks, smile into eyes.

"Darling Laura, how well you look!"

"What a becoming hat, child!"

"Laura, you look quite Spanish. I've never seen you look so striking."

And Laura, glowing, answered softly, "Have you had tea? Won't you have an ice? The passion-fruit ices really are rather special." She ran to her father and begged him. "Daddy darling, can't the band have something to drink?"

And the perfect afternoon slowly ripened, slowly faded, slowly its petals closed.

"Never a more delightful garden-party . . ." "The greatest success . . ." "Quite the most . . ."

Laura helped her mother with the good-byes. They stood side by side in the porch till it was all over.

"All over, all over, thank heaven," said Mrs. Sheridan. "Round up the others, Laura. Let's go and have some fresh coffee. I'm exhausted. Yes, it's been very successful. But oh, these parties, these parties! Why will you children insist on giving parties!" And they all of them sat down in the deserted marquee.

"Have a sandwich, daddy dear. I wrote the flag."

"Thanks." Mr. Sheridan took a bite and the sandwich was gone. He took another. "I suppose you didn't hear of a beastly accident that happened to-day?" he said.

"My dear," said Mrs. Sheridan, holding up her hand, "we did. It nearly ruined the party. Laura insisted we should put it off."

"Oh, mother!" Laura didn't want to be teased about it.

"It was a horrible affair all the same," said Mr. Sheridan. "The chap was married too. Lived just below in the lane, and leaves a wife and half a dozen kiddies, so they say."

An awkward little silence fell. Mrs. Sheridan fidgeted with her cup. Really, it was very tactless of father . . .

Suddenly she looked up. There on the table were all those sandwiches, cakes, puffs, all uneaten, all going to be wasted. She had one of her brilliant ideas.

"I know," she said. "Let's make up a basket. Let's send that poor creature some of this perfectly good food. At any rate, it will be the greatest treat for the children. Don't you agree? And she's sure to have neighbours calling in and so on. What a point to have it all ready prepared. Laura!" She jumped up. "Get me the big basket out of the stairs cupboard."

"But, mother, do you really think it's a good idea?" said Laura.

Again, how curious, she seemed to be different from them all. To take scraps from their party. Would the poor woman really like that?

"Of course! What's the matter with you to-day? An hour or two ago you were insisting on us being sympathetic, and now——"

Oh, well! Laura ran for the basket. It was filled, it was heaped by her mother.

"Take it yourself, darling," said she. "Run down just as you are. No, wait, take the arum lilies too. People of that class are so impressed by arum lilies."

"The stems will ruin her lace frock," said practical Jose.

So they would. Just in time. "Only the basket, then. And, Laura!"—her mother followed her out of the marquee—"don't on any account——"

"What, mother?"

No, better not put such ideas into the child's head! "Nothing! Run along."

It was just growing dusky as Laura shut their garden gates. A big dog ran by like a shadow. The road gleamed white, and down below in the hollow the little cottages were in deep shade. How quiet it seemed after the afternoon. Here she was going down the hill to somewhere where a man lay dead, and she couldn't realize it. Why couldn't she? She stopped a minute. And it seemed to her that kisses, voices, tinkling spoons, laughter, the smell of crushed grass were somehow inside her. She had no room for anything else. How strange! She looked up at the pale sky, and all she thought was, "Yes, it was the most successful party."

Now the broad road was crossed. The lane began, smoky and dark. Women in shawls and men's tweed caps hurried by. Men hung over the palings; the children played in the doorways. A low hum came from the mean little cottages. In some of them there was a flicker of light, and a shadow, crab-like, moved across the window. Laura bent her head and hurried on. She wished now she had put on a coat. How her frock shone! And the big hat with the velvet streamer—if only it was another hat! Were the people looking at her? They must be. It was a mistake to have come; she knew all along it was a mistake. Should she go back even now?

No, too late. This was the house. It must be. A dark knot of people stood outside. Beside the gate an old, old woman with a crutch sat in a chair, watching. She had her feet on a newspaper. The voices stopped as Laura drew near. The group parted. It was as though she was expected, as though they had known she was coming here.

Laura was terribly nervous. Tossing the velvet ribbon over her shoulder, she said to a woman standing by, "Is this Mrs. Scott's house?" and the woman, smiling queerly, said, "It is, my lass."

Oh, to be away from this! She actually said, "Help me, God," as she walked up the tiny path and knocked. To be away from those staring eyes, or to be covered up in anything, one of those women's shawls even. I'll just leave the basket and go, she decided. I shan't even wait for it to be emptied.

Then the door opened. A little woman in black showed in the gloom.

Laura said, "Are you Mrs. Scott?" But to her horror the woman answered, "Walk in please, miss," and she was shut in the passage.

"No," said Laura, "I don't want to come in. I only want to leave this basket. Mother sent——"

The little woman in the gloomy passage seemed not to have heard her. "Step this way, please, miss," she said in an oily voice, and Laura followed her.

She found herself in a wretched little low kitchen, lighted by a smoky lamp. There was a woman sitting before the fire.

"Em," said the little creature who had let her in. "Em! It's a young lady." She turned to Laura. She said meaningly, "I'm 'er sister, miss. You'll excuse 'er, won't you?"

"Oh, but of course!" said Laura. "Please, please don't disturb her. I—I only want to leave——"

But at that moment the woman at the fire turned round. Her face, puffed up, red, with swollen eyes and swollen lips, looked terrible. She seemed as though she couldn't understand why Laura was there. What did it mean? Why was this stranger standing in the kitchen with a basket? What was it all about? And the poor face puckered up again.

"All right, my dear," said the other. "I'll thenk the young lady."

And again she began, "You'll excuse her, miss, I'm sure," and her face, swollen too, tried an oily smile.

Laura only wanted to get out, to get away. She was back in the passage. The door opened. She walked straight through into the bedroom, where the dead man was lying.

"You'd like a look at 'im, wouldn't you?" said Em's sister, and she brushed past Laura over to the bed. "Don't be afraid, my lass,—" and now her voice sounded fond and sly, and fondly she drew down the sheet—" 'e looks a picture. There's nothing to show. Come along, my dear."

Laura came.

There lay a young man, fast asleep—sleeping so soundly, so deeply, that he was far, far away from them both. Oh, so remote, so peaceful. He was dreaming. Never wake him up again. His head was sunk in the pillow, his eyes were closed; they were blind under the closed eyelids. He was given up to his dream. What did garden-parties and baskets and lace frocks matter to him? He was far from all those things. He was wonderful, beautiful. While they were laughing and while the band was playing, this marvel had come to the lane. Happy . . . happy. . . . All is well, said that sleeping face. This is just as it should be. I am content.

But all the same you had to cry, and she couldn't go out of the room without saying something to him. Laura gave a loud childish sob.

"Forgive my hat," she said.

And this time she didn't wait for Em's sister. She found her way out of the door, down the path, past all those dark people. At the corner of the lane she met Laurie.

He stepped out of the shadow. "Is that you, Laura?"

"Yes."

"Mother was getting anxious. Was it all right?"

"Yes, quite. Oh, Laurie!" She took his arm, she pressed up against him.

"I say, you're not crying, are you?" asked her brother.

Laura shook her head. She was.

Laurie put his arm round her shoulder. "Don't cry," he said in his warm, loving voice. "Was it awful?"

"No," sobbed Laura. "It was simply marvelous. But, Laurie——" She stopped, she looked at her brother. "Isn't life," she stammered, "isn't life——" But what life was she couldn't explain. No matter. He quite understood.

"*Isn't* it, darling?" said Laurie.

## QUESTIONS

1. What is the atmosphere of Laura's home? Would you like to be a member of such a family? Why, or why not?
2. How old do you guess Laura to be? What incidents show that her mind is beginning to open to human problems?
3. What is the author's purpose in having the fatal accident occur to an obscure workman instead of to one of the intimate friends of the family?
4. When Laura wants to postpone the party, with whom does your sympathy lie, Laura or Laura's mother and sister? Honestly, what would you do in a similar situation?
5. Of what value is the incident of the new hat? What force does this new hat represent? What is Laura's reaction?
6. Which member of the family comes closest to understanding how Laura feels? Which understands least? What is the father's attitude?
7. How is the gift of food received by the family of the dead man? What effect does the scene in the little house in the lane have on Laura?
8. Judging by what you have learned of Laura, do you think she will grow up to have views different from those of the rest of the family, or will the routine of social life make her forget this experience?
9. What pictures in this story do you remember most vividly? What makes them so clear-cut?
10. How does *The Garden-Party* differ from all the preceding stories in this section? What is unusual about the conclusion?

## EXERCISES

Exercises preceded by a star are designed for assignment at the discretion of the teacher, or for any student who volunteers.

1. Point out passages in the story illustrating how carefully Katherine Mansfield maintains Laura's point of view—always picturing scenes as they would appear to a young girl, not as to an older person.
2. Explain Laura's hesitation in adopting her mother's suggestion to take a basket of food to the family of the dead man.
3. Write a brief character sketch of Laura's mother.
4. The following quotation is printed on the title page of one of Katherine Mansfield's volumes of short stories: "A little bird was asked: Why are your songs so short? He replied: I have many songs to sing, and I should like to sing them all." Explain the application of this to Katherine Mansfield's life and stories.

*5. Compare Katherine Mansfield's style and method with Maupassant's and with Stephen Crane's.

*6 Report on one other story by Katherine Mansfield.

# THE BOOB

## WALTER DE LEON

## 1884–

### THE AUTHOR

When Shakespeare was at the height of his career, the theater as a business was comparatively simple. Some one wrote a play for one of the companies, who put it on with a minimum of effort and expense. Today the show business is a mammoth industry with various departments demanding highly specialized talents. Between the writing of the manuscript and the raising of the curtain for the first performance there is a big gap bridged only through the co-operation of producer, business manager, actors, director, stage manager, designers of stage sets, costume designers, property men, musicians, electricians, scene shifters, and many others. Even after all the money and effort is expended, the play may turn out a "flop," leaving empty pocketbooks and broken hearts along the way. From the vaudeville pair with the comedy patter to the great drama or musical extravaganza there is always this element of chance. How will the public like it?

In this world within a world Walter De Leon is completely at home. He was born in Oakland, California, and, as he observes humorously, "began singing almost immediately." His natural musical talent was developed through years of training. Like many others, he received his first practical experience in a church choir.

At the University of California he showed a growing facility in writing by winning a competition with his first play. Thereafter came years of acting and dancing in musical comedies as a light comedian, one of his engagements being with the first American opera company to tour the Orient. "Big-time" vaudeville was the next step, with Mary Davies, the present Mrs. De Leon, as his partner.

With this experience as a background, De Leon turned to writing—short stories, articles, vaudeville acts, and full-length plays. Eight of his plays reached Broadway. In 1929 a motion picture company became interested in one of his musical successes. Since then he has been in Hollywood writing originals and adaptations for the screen. A number of popular movie hits are to his credit.

Under the circumstances it is only natural that De Leon should turn to the theater world for many of his subjects. He knows these people—the "hoofer" in the light gray suit with straw hat and cane, the musical comedy star thrilled to see her name in incandescent lights at last, the dramatic "heavy" telling the girl in the booking office how good he is. In *The Boob* De Leon takes us behind the scenes and shows us a crisis in the private lives of two public entertainers.

## THE STORY

The house lights slowly dim and then go out. The buzz of voices subsides to an expectant hush. Up front, where the curtain touches the stage, there is a faint glow that gradually increases in brilliance until with slow majesty the curtain rises to disclose the drawing room of Lord and Lady So-and-So. Then, as the audience leans forward to catch the first words, the Play begins.

In the make-believe world behind the footlights there is a glamor that few can resist. For two or three hours we forget ourselves. Even the actors are lost in their several characters, and their lives are submerged in the lives they have borrowed from the dramatist. For a long time we were satisfied with this; then, the public began to take a deep interest in the background of the show business. Behind the stage stories are other stories of the actors themselves—their long struggle up to stardom, their first fright at losing popularity, and in the interval many an episode of real human interest.

In short stories, novels, plays, and motion pictures, show people became good material for authors. The song-and-dance man, the comedian with the broken heart, the little "chorine" trying to earn an honest living—these became stock characters in a vogue that soon grew tiresome. In 1926 the tremendous success of a play called *Broadway* ushered in a whole series of stories dealing with racketeers and night-club entertainers. That field too was presently over-cultivated. Among these various portrayals of stageland, however, there were some that achieved true originality. Later the trend turned toward comic treatment. As so often happens, the serious attitude changed to the satiric. For example, *The Royal Family,* first a play then a motion picture, was a delightful travesty on the life of a distinguished actor family, popularly believed to be the Barrymores.

Walter De Leon's *The Boob* was written before the show business had been exploited as a popular theme. First published in *Hearst's International* and later included in a volume entitled, *The Best Love Stories of 1924,* it was a forerunner of the vogue. In it there is no hook-up with the underworld. There is no wicked producer bargaining for the affections of a lady of the chorus. In place of the usual sordid themes there is a romance of family life.

One of the characters, it should be noted, became a familiar type: the song writer who turns failure into success. The manner in which the Boob makes good is not, however, typical of the average "tin-pan alley" yarn. If at times the child is used to draw a tear in the old melodramatic style, there is still a wholesomeness, a sanity, that lifts the story out of the rut. Frankly romantic in many parts, *The Boob* leaves an impression of reality by its faithfulness to the details of the show world its author knows so well.

## THE BOOB[1]

Good old Billy Renton, who can recall nearly everything that happened during the twenty-five years he played piano in vaudeville and musical comedy orchestras, dropped in the other night with a bundle of phonograph records under his arm.

"Anything especially good?" I asked, pointing to the records.

Billy eased his pudgy self into the deep-cushioned chair beside my desk. "Louise Wickhart's newest," he grunted.

"The same Louise Wickhart who has just made the big hit as the star of Moritz's latest Broadway success?"

Billy nodded. "Did you know she started in vaudeville? With her husband, Bob Carol. Wickhart and Carol was the team and a very nice little act it was, too. We used to call Carol the Boob. Louise came on fast—after the Boob split the act and dropped out."

I scented one of Billy's inside stories of stagefolk, the behind-the-curtain stuff that seldom gets into the newspapers. I shoved a box of cigars toward him.

"It doesn't take long for success to go to some people's heads," I said. "I understand Miss Wickhart won't accept any engagement except in Broadway shows."

"She has her reasons," replied Billy, calmly.

"I'd like to hear them."

"Give me a match to go with this cigar and I'll tell 'em to you." When the cigar was drawing to his satisfaction Billy began as usual without preliminary explanations.

When the Boob stepped into the small reception room adjoining the private office of the great Moritz, that summer day, he was still grinning at his success in kidding the girl at the outside desk into letting him pass. The door to the private office was slightly ajar. The Boob heard the producer's heavy voice arguing persuasively.

"I want you in my new piece because you've got exactly the voice, appearance and personality the part calls for. I can't be franker than that, can I? I've told you I'll give you as much for yourself as the team got in vaudeville. What's keeping you from accepting an engagement that'll mean stardom in a couple of years?"

The Boob shook his head enviously. No manager had ever begged him to sign a contract.

[1] Reprinted by special permission of Walter De Leon, the author.

"I'll be just as frank." A clear, sweet voice broke the silence. The skin on the back of the Boob's long neck prickled as he recognized his wife's voice. "This is the chance I've prayed for. But there's Mr. Carol, my—my partner. I can't very well split the act and—and leave him."

"Why not? He's getting all the benefit out of the partnership. He's no good."

"Pardon me, Mr. Moritz, but I sing better when Mr. Carol plays for me than any other time. Can't you place him, too, in your new show?"

"I wouldn't have that big tramp in my theater. He ain't worth a nickel a week to me. Why, the poor boob—"

"The poor boob you speak of is my husband."

Louise's voice was shaky.

"I'm sorry," apologized Moritz, slowly. "But husband or no husband I can't use him. Now listen, Miss Wickhart—"

The Boob did not linger to hear the producer's new line of argument. He'd heard plenty to keep his mind busy all the way back to Oldtown, the village, two hours by train from New York, where he had grown up, where he and Louise had gone when the advent of their baby had broken off their vaudeville route, and where they had lived now for more than a year.

In Oldtown he walked rapidly up Main Street through the business section and on into the tree-shaded lanes of the older residence section. Turning the corner where St. John's Church stood he hurried past it to the gate in the white picket fence in front of the parsonage. Old Mrs. Seamon, the preacher's wife, answered his ring.

"Can I get my child, please?" The Boob grinned, the lazy, likable grin which, with his drawl and his tall, gangling figure, had inspired his nickname. As close to him as she had been, even his wife didn't know the extent to which the Boob relied on that grin to mask his shyness and almost childlike sensitiveness.

"She's been as good as pie all afternoon," Mrs. Seamon said, giving him the baby.

"Thanks for taking care of her," the Boob replied gratefully. Snuggling the sleeping infant in his long arm, he walked across the street, around the corner to a neat cottage. As he entered the front door the baby woke up, smiled and reached out to pull his long nose.

"Nix on the comedy, Little Lou." The Boob carefully sat his daughter among the pillows of her crib and held out two fingers for her to grab. "I'm up against a tough proposition. I'm going to explain it to you because I need your moral support. You and I have been the closest kind of pals ever since we met each other, and I don't want you to get me wrong on this proposition. Understand?"

Little Lou squirmed.

"All right. Now listen. For a long time your old man has had an inward hunch that he don't amount to much. While he's been silently thinking it, others have been saying it right out loud. For some reason or other your mother likes me too much to tell me that I've disappointed her. But I know I have; in several things—especially money. She thinks I don't realize the responsibility you wished on me; that I ought to be tearing around collecting chunks of money so you can be brought up and educated the very best possible.

"I realize it, all right, kid. Don't worry about that. But I haven't got anything that people want to give me large slabs of money for. That's the trouble; see? Now your mother has. Your beautiful mother, Little Lou, is a very wonderful person, and you and me—we ought to feel very proud just to know her. And you and me—see?—we mustn't do anything to keep her from going ahead and becoming still more wonderful.

"A fellow I know who says exactly what he thinks with the door open has offered her a great opportunity. I'd like nothing better than to go on playing piano for your mother the rest of her life. But that wouldn't be fair. No, ma'am; I've got to split the act. Even for you I'm not going to quarrel with your mother—and bust everything that way. I think I can work it another way. But get this, chicken; I want you to thoroughly understand that whatever I say when your mother comes home today I don't mean. At least, not in the way it sounds. Understand?"

Little Lou laughed. She generally did when her daddy scowled at her and talked gruffly.

"It may be comedy for you, Little Lou, but I'll bet it's a long time before I get a laugh out of it."

The baby was undressed, fed and in bed; the dinner table was set—the Boob knew the dinner was safe in the electric cooker—when his wife arrived home.

"Why didn't you meet me this afternoon?" she asked as they sat down to the table.

"Well, I'll tell you, Lou." The Boob's fingers trembled as he started pulling down his house around him. "I've been thinking things over and I decided this afternoon that I've had enough of show business. I'm no actor. You are; you always carried the act. I was just there to play piano for you and—and fill in while you changed costumes. You kept getting better all the time. I didn't."

"That's not true," said Lou, warmly, her eyes flashing. "The act was going better all the time. We'd had two raises in salary—"

"Yeah, but you were the reason. You've got everything it takes to make a star, honey. You belong on the stage—not at home taking care of a baby."

"Nonsense. I—"

"Wait a second, Lou." A note of impatient irritation, foreign to the Boob, caused Lou to glance sharply at him. "Ever since we've been married you've had your way about everything. I mean —you've run things."

"Bob! How can you say that! We've always talked over every plan—"

"Yeah, but always they've been your plans. I'm not complaining; just explaining why I want you to listen now to a plan I have. The Booking Office wanted us to go back into vaudeville six months ago. You said no."

"I did. The thought of dragging around a seven months baby from town to town, in and out of drafty trains—having to give her different milk and different water every week, trusting her to the care of a different nurse every week, exposing her to all sorts of weather and inconveniences that even we couldn't enjoy—I couldn't do it, Bob. I still feel the same way. That's why I've been trying to place us with a Broadway show, so we could live in one place."

"I know." Again that strangely impatient, fault-finding tone. "But how do you know I'm not perfectly satisfied to stay right here in Oldtown, playing piano in the picture theater and the organ at St. John's on Sundays? I've been supporting us doing that for the last year and—and I like it forty times better than stagework." Keeping his eyes averted from his wife, the Boob gulped a swallow of water to moisten his dry throat.

"But just because I'm quitting show business is no reason for *you* to quit. You're clever and you like it. That's all right. It just means we split the act."

"Split!" Lou's face went white. "Bob, you—"

"Now don't get excited," the Boob drawled. "If you land a job with a show, fine and dandy. If you don't there's nothing to worry about. I can hold my two jobs as long as I want them. That's bread and butter and coal for the winter. What could be sweeter?"

Lou stared at him, recalling a hundred occasions when she had laughingly given up trying to rouse his ambition.

Though it was not ambition the Boob lacked. His fault was a sweetness of disposition which made him content just to be alive; a rare quality which helped him take the bumps of experience serenely and forget them immediately; a Pollyanna ability to put an amber isinglass in front of the spot-light of reality and appreciate its mellowing effect.

Lou had always held a definite purpose before her. Not content to ride to a fair success on the beauty of her face and figure, she had developed by hard study a naturally pretty voice until her singing had become as great an asset professionally as her appearance. Lou was practical. In their act, while she changed costumes, he had sung little songs of his own composition; hardly songs they were; quaintly humorous bits of verse set to droll, ear-tickling tunes. Audiences loved them.

"Why don't you write some regular songs—for me?" Lou often urged. "You can make a lot of money, Bob. We could help the sales by singing them in the act. Try one, won't you, dear?"

Always the Boob promised. But never had he been able to write a song for Lou that satisfied him. And because he was ashamed to confess his failure, Lou believed he was not trying. It was practical Lou who had suggested applying for the movie theater job, a means of earning money instead of drawing further on their small savings. Again it was Lou who suggested to Bob that he offer his services to Doctor Seamon when the regular church organist was called overnight to California. The Reverend Doctor had baptized the Boob, the son of his life-long friend. It was upon the organ in St. John's that the Boob had studied and played a full year before his legs grew long enough to touch the pedals. When the Doctor gratefully accepted his offer to substitute, so beautifully did the Boob play the service, so full-throated did choir and congregation sing, carried along on his swelling chords and stirring rhythms, that preacher and vestrymen knew they could find none better for the small salary the church could afford to pay.

And that was the easy, futureless living the Boob was insisting he was content with. Lou's lips straightened. She squared her shoulders.

"I saw Moritz this afternoon, Bob. He wants me for his new show."

"No!" exclaimed the Boob, softly. "Say, that's wonderful! You signed right up, didn't you?"

"No. He's given me until tomorrow to change my mind—about taking an engagement without you."

"Without me?" The Boob grinned. "I'm through with show business. Ain't it funny how things work out? No sooner do I decide to blow out of the game than you get the big chance you've been wanting. You sign right up, honey. I'm going to stay home and—and take care of the baby." He looked at Lou. She was silently crying. "Gee Whiz, Lou"—he threw his arm across her shoulders—"why the tears? This is an occasion for joy."

"Do"—Lou dabbed her eyes—"do you really *want* me to leave—you?"

The Boob's eyes contracted. "Shucks, honey, it ain't leaving me—exactly. And to think of the money it'll mean for Little Lou!" He glanced at his watch. "Gee, I've got to run right along to the movie house. Good picture they're running today. A lot of laughs in it. See you later, honey." Out in the street, the Boob lit a cigarette with shaking hand, dragged the smoke deep down into his lungs. "If that show isn't a success, I'm going to murder Moritz; that's all," he said, dogging his way toward the smelly picture theater.

A show must be good to stay on Broadway for a solid year. Lou, scoring a personal triumph at every performance, for a year of Saturday nights took a midnight train from New York to Oldtown to spend Sundays and Mondays until three o'clock with Little

Lou and the Boob. But because Sunday was his busy day—what with two church services and his picture house grind—and because Monday mornings Lou was always busy overhauling Little Lou's clothes and talking household matters with Mrs. Margot, the housekeeper-nurse, the Boob really did not see an awful lot of his wife. But even after fourteen months of it, when Lou told him that Moritz had offered her a big increase of salary and feature billing to go on the road with the show, because he realized it meant artistic advancement to Big Lou and a whole lot of money for Little Lou, the Boob said simply, "Fine. You'll go, of course."

The three months road tour stretched into four; then five; then plans for its definite termination were discarded. Missing Big Lou more than he let himself think upon, the Boob devoted himself to Little Lou. Every possible minute he could spare he spent with her, answering her questions. Partly because he was naturally whimsical, partly because looking for the humorous helped raise his own spirits, but mostly because he loved to hear Little Lou laugh, to see the dimples deepen in her fat cheeks and the twinkles come and go in her round eyes, in his explanations of creation as it looks to a child the Boob often slighted the truth to make a good story.

He discovered that Little Lou was quickly sensitive to music. Positively against Mrs. Margot's counsel, he used to sing to her every night after she was put to bed. When she tired of the few nursery songs he knew he wrote special songs for her, simple little tunes with simple little words that sent Little Lou into Dreamland with a smile on her lips.

The organ recitals which later caused so much trouble commenced one night in the Spring—when Big Lou had been away eight months—following a gorgeous party in celebration of Little Lou's third birthday. It was a tired, excited youngster whose interior felt none too comfy, who objected strenuously even to think of bed.

"Tell you what we'll do," said the Boob to Mrs. Margot. "We'll undress her, wrap her up and take her around the corner to the church. That's always a wonderful place to sleep, anyway. Then I'll play something soothing on the organ. Even if it doesn't put her to sleep, I've got a hunch it'll quiet her."

Some minutes later, in the front row of pews, with a few dim lights reflecting softly on the red and purple and green and amber bits of glass in the big memorial window, with the sleepiest music imaginable reaching her as from a long, long way off, Little Lou dropped off to sleep in Mrs. Margot's arms.

The next night at bed-time she insisted the performance be repeated. The Boob laughed and, despite Mrs. Margot's head shaking, bundled her up again. A three cornered compromise was finally reached.

On Tuesdays, Thursdays and Saturdays, subject to good behavior and proper attention to meals, Little Lou knew that at bed-time she would be taken to the pew under the big window where the fuzzy white sheep were eating the grass under the eye of the Shepherd. Then her Daddy would start playing, first a hymn as befitted a church organ. But somehow, in the most surprising way, the hymn would begin sounding farther and farther away, as though it were floating right out of the church; and just when you were straining your ears to see if you could still hear it, it would change to a funny kind of dance, with tiny tinkling bells and the jingle of the silver bangles on the skirts of the fairies who certainly were dancing to that music.

And then you kept very quiet and still because the fairies and the music were coming closer—very close. But always before they flew in through the round hole at the top of the church a dog would bark, or maybe a lion would roar—a loud roar that startled you but didn't make you afraid because you knew it was only a pretend lion that Daddy made roar with his feet. But that would send the fairies scooting away.

Then, each to his own particular kind of a tune, most of the animals in the menagerie would gather. Birds would sing, and monkeys chatter and pretty soon the big elephant would start doing a clumsy dance. Most times, before he finished, though, a bell would ring slowly—seven times—and everybody knows that animals and chickens and children go to bed when the bell rings seven o'clock.

But Daddy never expected her to go to sleep without a song. Sure enough, all of a sudden the music would change and Daddy would start singing, good little songs that only she and Daddy knew. And pretty soon he'd drift into the song about the Man in the Moon looking out of the moon at all the children on the earth and saying, "Now let me see; who's in bed like a good child tonight?

There's little Willie Whiffkins, his foot's sticking out; and naughty Mamie Perkins, gone to sleep in a pout"; but always before he reached her name, something happened. One minute she'd be listening and the next thing she knew it would be morning and the sun would be shining in through the window and her Daddy would be saying, "My Goodness, here it is seven o'clock in the morning and you still in bed. Are you going to sleep all day? Of all the little fat-heads I ever knew—listen, chicken, where did you put your shirt when you went to bed last night?"

"Has Mrs. Carol ever heard you play—like that?" Mrs. Margot asked the Boob as they carried Little Lou home one evening.

"I never played anything like that—before," grinned the Boob. "It's just kid-stuff."

"It's—" But sentimental Mrs. Margot did not say what she thought it was.

Old Doctor Seamon stated his opinion on the matter not only bluntly but militantly when Mr. Grummit, of whom everybody in church always thought when the preacher read that verse in the Bible about the Lord whipping the money-changers out of the temple—anyway, when Mr. Grummit asked the Doctor if he thought it fit that the Boob should play fairy dance music and sacrilegious tunes like that on the church organ, the preacher said:

"There's never a day he plays that my windows aren't open to catch every note. If what Bob plays is sacrilegious, so are my sermons. Because he's expressing the thing I've been pleading with folks for years to express. Love; nothing but love, out of a humble heart."

Then Mrs. Seamon, slipping her hand in that of her husband, smiled gently. "I wish you would come here tomorrow evening and listen with us," she said. "I always get feeling so—so generous toward the world before Little Lou goes to sleep."

Grummit did not go to the parsonage the next evening, but he sent his wife and married daughter, who was visiting them. It was the married daughter, listening to the Boob's songs, who wondered why he didn't publish them. "They're delightful. Can't you persuade him to give me a copy of one or two of them? I'll be glad to pay for them."

The Boob only laughed, embarrassed, when Mrs. Seamon gave him the message.

One day there came a telegram from Lou, playing a return engagement in Boston, the last stand of her season. The wire read: "Cablegram from Moritz states that prima donna of London production won't do. He wants me to take steamer from New York Saturday so I can open in London following week. Have cabled acceptance. Will arrive home tomorrow morning. Love. Lou."

"What do you think!" the Boob said to Little Lou. "Your mother is coming home, tomorrow."

"For real?" asked Little Lou. "To stay wiv you and me?"

"Well, no; not right away, chicken. She's just going to pay us a visit before she goes to London."

"Like de pussy-cat?"[2]

The Boob grinned. "This time the Queen is coming to visit us and our pussy-cat."

Little Lou thought that over. "Daddy, I want to go to Lon'on to visit de Queen wiv Mama."

"And leave me here all alone?"

"No. You come wiv me."

"We'd better wait till your mother invites us, chicken."

When he met Big Lou at the station the next morning she looked more radiantly beautiful than ever as she knelt on the platform and hugged Little Lou to her closely.

"Mama," said her daughter, tearing her eyes from Lou's sparkling ear-drops and the shiny beads around her white throat, "I want to go to Lon'on wiv you."

"Do you, sweetheart?" Lou straightened; looked squarely at the Boob. "I want her, too, Bob."

"That doesn't make it unanimous by a long way," drawled the Boob, remembering Lou hadn't kissed him. "Let's go home and talk it over."

But he knew he was going to lose Little Lou even before her mother stated flatly that she would cancel the London arrangements —break with Moritz—if the alternative meant another six or eight months away from her baby.

"Listen, Bob; why can't you come, too? Pack a trunk and get on the steamer with us—"

---

[2] Pussy-cat—Allusion to the nursery rime beginning:

> "Pussy-cat, pussy-cat, where have you been?"
> "I've been to London to visit the Queen."

She stopped as the Boob shook his head. "I can't leave Doc Seamon and Plunket, at the picture house, in the lurch. I can't do it; that's all. You and Little Lou go. If the play is a hit over there and it looks as though you were going to be there six months or more, I—I'll hop a steamer and—and join you."

The only lie that Bob ever told his daughter was told the morning he took them to the steamer. As he kissed her good-by, for the first time Little Lou realized that her best beloved playmate was being left behind. Tears, large and bitter, a perfect torrent of them, streamed down her plump cheeks. Neither her mother nor Mrs. Margot could quiet her. Convulsively she clung to the Boob.

"Listen, chicken," he picked her up. "You're acting kind of silly for a girl nearly four years old. I'm surprised. I can't go with you today on account of business; understand? As soon as I get through with business, I'll take another big boat and—and"—he gulped—"understand?"

"You mean we go first and you come next?"

"That's it. You first—and me next."

Little Lou, her tears checked, squinted her eyes suspiciously. "How soon—next?"

"Just as soon as I possibly can. Maybe"—the Boob had an inspiration—"maybe I'll get on a boat that goes faster than this boat and maybe I'll get to London before you. Yes, sir; I may get there first. I'll bet you," he dared.

"I bet you," repeated Little Lou, contentedly, long accustomed to win every sporting wager her Daddy proposed.

The Boob stood the empty cottage for a week. Then, at Mrs. Seamon's urging, he moved into a spare room at the parsonage. He and the Doctor were reading in the living room the first Tuesday evening he was there, when Mrs. Seamon entered with her sewing.

"If you don't feel like it, Bob," she said, "don't hesitate to say so; but the Doctor and I do most dreadfully miss the Tuesday, Thursday and Saturday vesper services."

"Vesper services?" inquired the Boob, puzzled.

"The organ recitals you always gave Little Lou. The Doctor claims they're better than his sermons."

"You mean for putting folks to sleep?" asked the Boob, grinning because he felt like crying.

"Why did you ask him to do that?" the Doctor asked his wife as the Boob dragged his unwilling feet across the stretch of lawn between the house and the church.

"He gave up Lou—let her go—a year ago. Now, in his thoughts, he feels that she has taken the baby away from him—permanently. He mustn't give her up in his thoughts. I want him to hold on—tight—to her. Because—"

"Because?" prompted the clergyman as she hesitated.

"Because some day Bob is going to stop groping around in the dark and find the way to show the world his genius. But until that day comes he needs an anchor—ssh!" she cautioned as the first sweet notes of the organ crept through the dusk and in through the open windows.

A few days later came the unexpected cablegram from Lou. "Successful opening. Long run predicted. Critics generous my performance. Send Little Lou songs."

"What does she mean—send Little Lou songs?" the Boob asked Mrs. Seamon.

"The songs you wrote for her," she laughed.

"Oh," said Little Lou's father. "But they're none of them on paper."

"Then you'd better put them on paper as quickly as you can," advised Mrs. Seamon, seizing an opportunity she long had wished.

So the Boob spent many hours writing out all the songs he had done for Little Lou; the words and every note of music he put down neatly and painstakingly. Finally he had them completed, wrapped up for their long voyage, addressed. And, standing in the hallway of the parsonage ready to take them to the post office, suddenly it seemed very clear to the Boob that he was cutting the principal tie that held Little Lou and him together.

He recalled the wording of Lou's cablegram, "*Send* Little Lou songs." If Big Lou had wanted or expected him she would have cabled "*Bring* Little Lou songs."

"Funny I didn't notice that before," he mumbled. "Looks like I was being eased right out of the family." Of a sudden he found himself shaking from head to foot. The hand he raised to his forehead found icy sweat there. "Nerves," said the Boob, through chattering teeth. "Gee, how am I going to play for the pictures this afternoon? I ought to be on my way right now."

As he reached for his hat the bundle of songs rolled unheeded from the stand to the floor.

At a corner drug store he told the clerk—an old friend—to give him some kind of a pick-me-up to carry him through the matinee. With a wink his friend gave him a stout drink of whiskey. And then a second. It was the first drink the Boob had downed since his marriage. The whiskey inside him felt good, steadied him. But he knew its effects would wear off, leave him feeling worse than ever, before his afternoon's work was done. In a poolroom near the theater he bought a flask from another friend. It was in his pocket when he sat down to the piano in the sheltered orchestra pit.

By the time the matinee was over the Boob was hopelessly, miserably drunk. Plunket, the manager, saw him when he staggered out on to Main Street. He placed a steadying hand on the Boob's arm.

"Listen, Bob," he said, not unkindly, "you'd better go home and—"

"Go home? You're crazy." Roughly he shook off Plunket's hand. "I haven't got any home. Understand?" His eyes contracted, narrowed. "I had one—but I couldn't keep it; home and wife and kiddie—but I couldn't hold them. That's the kind of a boob I am."

"That's just the way you're feeling now," said Plunket, placatingly again taking the Boob's arm. With a snarl the Boob shook him off. "Listen," sternly, "you're drunk, Bob—"

"But not nearly drunk enough," the Boob cut in, turned savage. "Not anywhere near drunk enough to forget that nobody gives a damn what happens to me."

The Boob lurched off, down the street toward the railway station, and disappeared, dropped completely out of the sight and ken of every one in Oldtown.

It was not because efforts to locate him were not made that he was not found. Drexell, the music publisher, spent many hours in the parsonage in Oldtown. For Mrs. Seamon, finding the Little Lou songs, had followed her plan to have them copied before the originals were sent across the ocean. These copies she submitted to Drexell. He found in the songs what Mrs. Seamon had found—quaint, irresistible appeal to both old and young—which spelled profits to the publisher. For two months Drexell carried contracts in his pocket, waiting word from the Seamons that the Boob had returned or written to them. Then he made out new contracts containing a larger royalty figure, and inserted advertisements in the trade-papers asking information concerning Bob Carol.

Two months after the Boob had walked into the night, Lou wrote to the Seamons to ask why Bob had not replied to her letter requesting him to join her; and the letter which carried Little Lou's dictated command: "Daddy, you must come—right away quick!" And when another two months passed with no word of the Boob, Lou instructed the Seamons to employ detectives to find him. At the end of six months Mrs. Seamon sensed the mood of desperation in the curt cablegram Lou sent. "Little Lou ill. Returning home. Must find Bob."

The lights in the parsonage burned late the night Little Lou was brought home to toss and fret in the spare room while genial old Doc Runderman shook his head and tried to soothe her mother.

"There's no further danger from the disease," he repeated over and over. "It's a question now of will; whether she wants to fight her way back to health—or not. What is it she keeps mumbling for? What is it she wants?"

"Her father," Big Lou replied, her eyes dark with the shadow of tragedy.

Some sixty miles away, in another small town, at that moment the Boob woke up; woke up on a bench in a deserted park in a steady, drenching downpour of rain; woke up with an urge of purpose fixed uncertainly but tenaciously in his consciousness. There was something, he felt, that he must do; somewhere he must go. It was hard to think straight because of the flashes of heat that shot through his brain and burned the back of his eyes every now and again. All the heat in his body was in his head; legs, arms, chest—they were chilled through. He ought to get a cup of coffee before he started—

Started where? The Boob brushed a hand across his eyes. He had started for many places during the last months; everywhere, nearly, except home. Home? Why, that was it, of course! He must start home. A gust of wind shook a tree branch above him, dislodging its accumulated raindrops to shower down on the Boob. Instinctively he rose, pulled his coat tightly over his chest, and shambled toward the lights of the station.

"How far will this take me toward Oldtown?" he asked the ticket agent, shoving a collection of coins across the wicket-shelf. The agent gave him a pasteboard to a village about two-thirds of the distance to Oldtown, and returned a five-cent piece. Waiting for his train, the Boob spent the coin for a cup of coffee.

At seven o'clock the next morning the Boob alighted from the train and began to walk. It was a day of desolate grayness, of ill-tempered, raw-edged blasts and steady rain, through which the Boob plugged doggedly, obsessed by one thought; he must go home. The sight of him, unshaven, unkempt, his shoes squelching soppily at every step, the greasy brim of his battered felt hat shedding water on his white, set face, deterred many a passing motorist from offering him a lift. So the Boob walked through the day on into the night.

Doc Runderman went to the parsonage about ten o'clock that night.

"She's stopped fussing and fretting, but she refuses to touch any food," the nurse told him.

"That means she's given up," growled the Doc, scowling and pulling his gray beard lest none guess that he, too, had given up.

Up the deserted Main Street tramped the Boob; through the closed-up business section, on into the tree-shaded lanes of the older residence section. Turning the corner where stood St. John's, he stumbled up the steps to the vestry-room. Mechanically he put hand in pocket for a key; unlocked the door. He made his way through the darkness of the vestry-room to the door which gave in to the choir benches, between the altar and the raised pulpit. Opening this door the faint glow of a small light hanging above the altar reached barely to the front row of pews, in the dark, silent church.

Laboriously the Boob pulled himself up on the organ bench. Automatically he turned the switch that filled the big bellows of the organ with air. His numbed feet felt for the pedals. Trembling fingers, icy cold, hesitated over the stops, indecisively. What was he going to play? He didn't feel like playing at all. He was tired, hungry, sick. His head hurt.

Why was he there? Damn the hunch that had driven him through all those miles, through the mud and rain, slogging along like a poor devil of a soldier—mile after mile—without knowing why or wherefore—marching blindly on orders—tramp, tramp—onward, onward—like a soldier—onward tramping—

The Boob's hand swiftly pulled out a stop. His foot pressed on a pedal. His right hand dropped unerringly on the keys.

"Onward, Christian soldiers,
Marching as to war—"

Softly—so had he often played it for Little Lou—as from a great distance, sounded the melody of the old hymn; momentarily more distinct, ever its majestic rhythm, more accentuated, louder, clearer; closer the host approached until with crashing cymbals and triumphant blare of silver bugles its harmonies filled the church. Filled every arched nook and vaulted space and, overflowing into the night, rolled across the glistening lawn and swept into the parsonage.

Doctor Seamon glanced up from his Bible to look with startled eyes into those of his wife. The same prayer rose silently from both hearts. A long minute; two; then the music gradually diminished; the host was marching on.

Through the door of the spare room slipped Big Lou, her face twitching. "Lou wants to hear it again. She—she thinks it's Bob. Will you—could you ask whoever it is—"

Doctor Seamon sprang to his feet. Swiftly he went to the outer door and stepped on to the veranda. His wife was beside him.

"I'll go, Mother. It's raining and—"

"I'll go too. If it should be—"

Hatless, coatless, they hurried across the lawn.

"Thank God!" whimpered Mrs. Seamon as she recognized the Boob. The last reverberations of a long-drawn "Amen" chord were rumbling through the church when the clergyman gently laid his hand on the Boob's shoulder.

"Glad to have you home again, Bob," he said quietly. "Mother and I have been waiting for you. No, don't stop playing," he smiled as the Boob dropped his hands from the keys, "at least not until you've played the hymn once more. Will you, Bob? I'll explain as you play."

Weakly obedient, the Boob's fingers sought the keys. Once again the distant throb of marching feet carried out into the night.

"Bob, old chap, you couldn't have come home at a—a better time. You see, we've a little girl visiting us. She's been a very sick little girl and we've all been trying with all our might to keep her interested in living—so that she will live. But she's so tired it has been very hard to make her want to—until just a moment ago. She heard you playing—she's listening now, Bob; listening to every note—and she wants you to keep playing. It's the first thing she's asked for in days."

"Sure, I'll play for the little girl," the Boob muttered. "That's why I came—through the mud."

When Mrs. Seamon quietly entered the church some minutes later with a tray on which was steaming coffee, cream and sugar, the Boob was playing the dance of the fairies that Mr. Grummit had called sacrilegious. Mrs. Seamon's lips quivered as she saw the expression in the Boob's eyes, the beads of sweat on his forehead, the angry red stains on his cheeks.

"There's hot coffee on the bench beside you, Bob," she spoke slowly, clearly.

With his feet, the Boob made the lion roar, the roar that in a moment would send the fairies scampering in all directions.

"How's the li'l girl?" he asked.

"Actually sitting up in bed—and laughing, Bob. Oh, she is so happy! Pretty soon she'll be ready for a fine long sleep and—"

"You—you tell me," the Boob was annoyed to find he had to hunt for the words he wanted. "You tell me—when she's—'sleep. I—I'll play—till—then."

He played; played with his eyes closed because the light hurt them; played to the steady drumming accompaniment of the rain on the roof; played while the nurse arranged a dainty tray of food, and while Little Lou hungrily polished off every dish and drained the pitcher dry of milk.

And then he began singing; first the song about the silly old Chuckle-headed Huckleberry. Little Lou laughed and then laid her drowsy head on the cool, fresh pillow her mother brought.

Mrs. Seamon hurried across the lawn again. She heard the Boob talking while his fingers sent a rippling melody dancing out into the black shadows; swaying back and forth on the organ bench.

"Listen, here's a new one, Li'l Lou; it's 'bout a—a—I tell you what; I'll sing it 'n' you tell me what it's 'bout. Are you listening, chicken? Here goes."

"If you'll play some sleepy music, Bob," Mrs. Seamon said, "I think she'll go to sleep now."

"I don't want her—go to sleep—'less I know she's—going to wake up; see?"

"Oh, she'll wake up," Mrs. Seamon promised, "because we've promised her that tomorrow you'll play games with her."

"Sure; I always play games with Li'l Lou—every morning." He ran his tongue across his parched lips. "Time for her to—go to sleep. How's that song go—Man in Moon—song? That'll do it—if I can remember how it—sure I know. 'The Man in the Moon looked out of the moon—' "

Doctor Seamon was standing beside the organ bench before the last note of the song floated gently away.

"The little girl is asleep now," he told the Boob. "She's all right—she's going to be all right now."

The Boob's hands slid off the keys. "Then my day's work is done." The next instant he slumped off the bench, a limp, unconscious huddle on the floor.

When he woke up the sun of a brilliant spring morning was flooding the room. Some one was holding his hand. He looked up—into his wife's eyes. Big Lou had to explain that he was not dreaming.

"Little Lou will be in in a few minutes," she finished. Her eyes filled. "Bob, dear, will you please give me the chance to win back the place I once held in your heart?"

The Boob grinned. "Shucks, you don't have to win it back. Just take it, honey."

Billy Renton drew a last puff from his cigar and tossed it in the ash-container.

"You'd be surprised to know what a profitable market there is for kid songs," he said. "And as for those little kid phonograph records—well, the first batch of his songs Bob sang for the phonograph people has already netted him twenty thousand dollars. That's why I'm in town; to get his new records, just out today.

"Maybe you understand now, with the cosy place they bought thirty-five minutes from Times Square so Lou can get home to Bob and Little Lou every night after the show, maybe you can see why she's sort of lost her taste for show business away from Broadway."

## QUESTIONS

1. Of what value is the "frame" in which the story is cast? Does it add any necessary information or is it simply a method of leading up to the story?
2. What trait in the Boob makes children love him? What quality does he lack which would have made financial success easier? Whom do you most admire, the Boob or Big Lou? Why?
3. What is the decision that starts the story moving? What is the decision that leads to the conclusion?
4. What device does the author use to tell the reader what has happened before the story opens? Does this method of Exposition (see Introduction to the Short Story) satisfy you? What other device might he have employed?
5. Why does the author introduce Mr. Grummit into the story? What point of view does Mr. Grummit reflect?
6. When Lou asks the Boob to go to England with her and Little Lou, why does he refuse? Is it only that he cannot leave his work at the church and picture house?
7. Why does the Boob suddenly decide to go home after months of wandering? Is it simply a coincidence that he chooses this moment, or does the author imply some spiritual or telepathic guidance?
8. It is in part irony that makes that last scene at the organ so moving. What does the reader know that the Boob does not know?
9. Did you know before finishing the story whether or not there would be a happy ending? If you did, what clues suggested it?
10. What causes the suffering in this story? Is any single character to blame? Is it the fault of two or more characters? Does it rise from circumstances over which they have no control, or does it come from a good impulse that demands some sacrifice of happiness?

## EXERCISES

Exercises preceded by a star are designed for assignment at the discretion of the teacher, or for any student who volunteers.

1. From the following list choose those topics that in your opinion apply most accurately to the subject or character of the story: love, self-sacrifice, matrimonial troubles, the ladder of success, a little child shall lead them, sentimentality, pathos, realism, romancing, optimism, despair.
2. From your imagination fill in the gap between the Boob's departure from Oldtown and his return. Write an imaginary episode involving a little girl who reminds him of Little Lou.
3. Write a character sketch of one of the following: the Boob, Big Lou, Doctor Seamon, Mr. Grummit.

*4. Contrast *The Boob* with another story or a motion picture dealing with stage life.

*5. Designate the climax of the story, and point out the minor crises that lead up to it.

# THE BIRTHDAY

## THYRA SAMTER WINSLOW

## 1893–

### THE AUTHOR

The second decade of the twentieth century saw the beginning of several new movements in American literature. There was the renaissance of poetry represented by Amy Lowell, Carl Sandburg, Robert Frost, Vachel Lindsay, and others. In fiction, too, new voices were heard, voices that spoke in natural tones of common things. Instead of writing about the unusual, this latter group turned to the typical. Their characters were drawn from the vast middle class of which American society is largely composed: ordinary folks working hard for a living, marrying, settling down, having their small joys and sorrows, and begetting children who repeat the same experiences in their generation. As the characters were typical, so too were the themes. These authors found drama in every-day lives; not the thrill of the unexpected or the sudden change of fortune that so often furnishes a subject for short story writers, but the quiet inconspicuous drama of those whose days are given over to the routine of office and store and kitchen.

Though the stories are written in a detached manner and a matter-of-fact style, there is often an implied sympathy. Through a wealth of detail the reader is made aware that the characters are a product of their surroundings and their position in life. Many of their short-comings are explained by the narrow lives they are forced to live. Again, though there is seldom any outright preaching, one frequently feels criticism of a society responsible for such conditions, as well as a commentary on the persons themselves—their little meannesses and their thoughtless or premeditated cruelty.

We must not think of literary movements as complete in themselves. This type of realism with its slow pace and lack of "big moments" has not crowded out the story of exciting events. Indeed, it forms a comparatively small percentage of the whole. In a strict sense, it is not even new; the French, as illustrated in Maupassant's *The Piece of String,* had long before paid special attention to accuracy of detail. We may say, however, that since 1912 a new spirit has shown itself in the work of a number of American short story writers. It is manifest in the effort to reflect accurately with the least possible distortion a great cross-section of life in the United States. Action, therefore, takes a position subordinate to setting and character, for few lives arrange themselves naturally into full-formed plots. The scope of the action may be extremely limited or very broad. It may comprise a fleeting and comparatively unimportant half-hour in the course of a day, or it may include the larger part of a whole lifetime reported in rapid narration.

In connection with this movement there are two facts worthy of notice. The first is that the Middle West has furnished the majority of the writers; and the second is that many of the writers are women. Though Chicago is inclined to boast that it is the center of this movement, in reality the literary impetus was furnished by the small midwestern town, which suddenly became articulate. Young writers began to speak of things they saw about them—the hum-drum lives of their neighbors and their own youthful experiences. Even before Sinclair Lewis's novel, *Main Street,* inspired a host of imitators, the small town had found itself a literary topic. Though many of the writers have transplanted themselves to Chicago or New York, they still turn from stories of tenement and brown-stone front to depict life as they remember it back home.

Typical of this group is Thyra Samter Winslow. She was born in 1893 at Fort Smith, Arkansas, a thriving industrial town of about 12,000 people situated on the Arkansas River at the extreme western boundary of the state. When only seven years old she wrote a short piece that was printed in the *St. Louis Democrat.* At fourteen she began to write for her town newspaper. After two years of study at the University of Missouri, Miss Samter decided to go to Chicago, already a mecca for young authors. Failing in her first efforts to get a job with the *Chicago Tribune,* she joined the cast of a theatrical company and learned at first hand the inner workings of the show business, an experience that was to be reflected in what is perhaps her most popular book, *Show Business,* once listed as a best-seller. Eventually she earned a post on the *Tribune* and began to write regularly for popular magazines and newspapers. Now she resides at Kew Gardens, Long Island. Among her best known books are *Picture Frames, People Around the Corner,* and *Blueberry Pie.*

## THE STORY

One of the favorite themes of contemporary realism is old age. It is treated, however, without sentimentality. The Old Lady in *The Birthday* is no sweet, white-haired grandmother waiting serenely for death's call while her children and grandchildren shed beautiful tears. She is a vital and at times an assertive personality, fully realizing the lack of sympathy in her family and feeling a sense of superiority over them. Her submissiveness is a rational acceptance of the situation, not an admission of defeat. When it comes to matching wits, she can give them something to think about.

This story is one of the collection comprising *Picture Frames,* a title, by the way, aptly descriptive of the gallery of portraits the author has painted—people whom we can identify and who, if we are honest, may at times show us a fairly accurate reflection of ourselves.

When *Picture Frames* appeared in 1923, Edna Ferber, one of the foremost exponents of contemporary realism, hailed the author as "a new master of the Short Story." She characterized *The Birthday* as a "knowledgeous presentation of the keenness and malice and childishness of old age." In the handling of character, in the graphic clarity of scene, and in the shrewd use of detail to establish the atmosphere of this middle class home and reveal the vacant lives of those who compose it, Thyra Samter Winslow has justified the praise of the critics. Do not read *The Birthday* with the expectation of being thrilled by strange things; read it for the satisfaction of recognizing the familiar: little touches of character, the trivial round of home life, the not always wise attempts at thrift, and above all the craftiness of the Old Lady, who had "a pretty good birthday" after all.

## THE BIRTHDAY[1]

### I

It was the old lady's birthday. She was eighty-two years old and well preserved. To be sure, she was a trifle deaf, but not so deaf as she usually made out. She could hear conversations not intended for her, though she had an annoying way of saying "heh?" when she didn't want to hear a thing. Then, after it had been repeated two or three times she would pass it off as of no consequence, and few things warrant triple repetition.

The old lady was proud of her age. After all, the fact that she had lived so many years was the most remarkable thing about her, as it usually is the most remarkable thing about people who live long. She had outlived her friends, her generation, her welcome.

She was still useful and quite paid her way. She lived with her son, Herman Potter, a thin man of over fifty, who had leather skin and a bald head, and his wife, Minnie, a too-fat woman of the same age, given to useless talk, exclamations and mild hysteria.

There were five children in the family of Herman Potter and one grandchild. They all lived at home except Roger, who was married and in business in Harrington. Fred, the oldest, nearly thirty, had been married but his wife had run away two years before with a soap drummer.[2] Lucius and Phillip, the other sons,

[1] Reprinted from *Picture Frames* by Thyra Samter Winslow by permission of and special arrangement with Alfred A. Knopf, Inc., authorized publishers.

[2] DRUMMER—Traveling salesman.

had never married. Fanny, the one daughter, had had marital misfortunes, also. She had married, at twenty-four, and a couple of years later her husband had "gone out West to try his luck," and she had never heard from him again. Now she had a divorce, granted on grounds of desertion, and was ogling every unattached man in Graniteville. She had one child, a peevish, pale little boy of four, named Elbert.

The old lady had had three children. The older son, Morris, lived in Kansas City, but Morris' wife absolutely refused to consider her husband's mother as a part of her household. In fact, Morris' wife felt that she had married beneath herself by accepting Morris at all, and held herself aloof from Morris' family. The old lady's only daughter, Martha, was dead. Martha had been her favourite child. Martha's husband had married again. Her only child, Helen, was married and lived in Chicago.

The old lady's life was uneventful enough and not unhappy. She was the first one up in the morning because she "didn't need much sleep." She would dress quietly, so as not to wake any one. If, occasionally, she stumbled against a chair, some one would be sure to say, at breakfast, "Didje hear Gramma? She woke me up, knocking around before daylight." The old lady was not very steady and had to hold on to things sometimes when she walked.

There were always unwashed dishes from the night before. The old lady would wash these and then put on the oatmeal for breakfast. There was always oatmeal because it was cheap and filling, and the old lady was there to attend to it. She herself didn't like oatmeal, though she listened each morning to Herman and Minnie who would say, "Gramma, you ought to eat some of this. Fine. Nourishing. Make you grow young."

The old lady would purse her thin lips and then answer, politely enough, "Thank you, but I'm not one that's much for oatmeal."

For breakfast the old lady would drink a cup of coffee without sugar, but with milk in it. She preferred cream but didn't dare say so for the cream pitcher was small and the men helped themselves to it first. After breakfast, if there was any coffee left in the coffee-pot, the old lady would drink another cup, standing up in the kitchen, trying to force a few drops out of the cream pitcher to put into it. If there was fruit for breakfast, the old lady was given the worse piece. She contented herself with one piece of toast, sparsely buttered, for she always felt Minnie's eyes on her when she helped herself to butter. The old lady didn't have a very large appetite.

After breakfast she would help her daughter-in-law with the dishes. Fanny affected delicacy. She was lazy and housework annoyed her. She spent the mornings in her own room reading magazines or running blue ribbon through her lingeries or making rather effeminate little suits for her son.

The old lady was always afraid of her daughter-in-law. Minnie was fat and slow-minded. She was constantly telling the old lady how glad she ought to be because they were all so "well fixed." She liked to spend a long time discussing trifles, how Mrs. Fink's dress hung and didn't Gramma think it was her last year's dress made over—she had a blue dress last year, remember?—and did Gramma think the butcher gave good weight—they had just one meal from that pot-roast, and here there was hardly enough of it left to slice cold.

The Potters lived in a large, square house. Herman had bought it at a forced sale when the children were small. It was painted brown and there were big trees around it. It looked gloomy. It had been one of Graniteville's best streets but the business district had been creeping close until now a garage stood across the street and a store selling cigars and notions just two doors away. There were numerous small rooms in the house and this meant housework. Herman always smiled patronizingly when "the women folks" spoke of the difficulty of keeping the house in order. He was well-to-do in a moderate Graniteville way and was considering changing the Ford for a larger car but he didn't see why three women couldn't keep a house clean without outside help. They gave out the washing, didn't they?

Herman didn't consider that Fanny did none of the housework and that the old lady really was old, that it was almost a task to walk, sometimes, and that on damp days when her shoulders ached it was rather difficult to try to dust, even.

In the afternoon when the house was in order, the old lady would embroider. She did things for all of the family and for the friends of Fanny and Minnie and for church bazaars. She did guest towels, making them even more annoying by the addition of bright blue "blue-birds for happiness" or impossible butterflies; shoe bags with outlines of distorted footwear to explain their use; dresser scarfs with scalloped outlines which didn't launder well.

The old lady did the best she could. She made things people liked and asked for. The only times she ever received praise were when she gave away her finished works of art. She never complained about her eyes, though they did hurt after she bent over her sewing for two or three hours at a time. She preferred to read, though the family took only the cheapest magazines full of sensational stories or articles about motion picture actresses. Sometimes the old lady would go to the Carnegie Library[3] and bring home novels, favourites of thirty years ago, but the family laughed at her when she did that.

In the evening the members of the family would go their various ways without bothering much about her. Fanny would persuade one of the boys to take her to the movies or she would go with a girl friend, loitering on the way home in hopes of being overtaken by masculine admirers. The boys would go to the movies or to a vaudeville show or play pool. They belonged to a couple of lodges, the kind of lodges that are supposed to have international significance—you can give the distress sign to the ticket-seller and get a ticket to Europe in a hurry, though none of the Potters would probably ever want to go to Europe. They liked the idea. A boast of one of the lodges was that none of its members had ever been electrocuted and, though none of the boys looked forward to a life of crime, they accepted the fact eagerly and repeated it as something pretty big for the lodge. The lodge rooms were pleasant places to waste evenings. Minnie and Herman patronized the motion picture theatres, too, but they cared more for cards than for the drama, even in its silent form.[4] Nearly every evening they went to one of the neighbours for a game of bridge or poker or had a few guests in. At ten-thirty there were refreshments of rye bread and cheese and sardines, known as "a little Dutch lunch," and appreciated each night as if it were a novelty.

The old lady didn't go out much evenings. She walked slowly and stumbled a great deal, so no one liked to bother with her. At the movies she couldn't read the captions easily and that meant

---

[3] CARNEGIE LIBRARY—Through the donations of Andrew Carnegie, millionaire steel magnate, many small towns have been able to build public libraries.

[4] DRAMA . . . IN ITS SILENT FORM—This was before the days of the talkies.

some one to read them aloud to her, and the family didn't consider that refined. She could not quite master the intricacies of bridge even enough to fill in when another player was needed, though she tried pitifully hard and her hand shook if she held the cards. The old lady would sew or read. There were socks and stockings to be darned and clothes to be mended, besides the embroidering, so she had enough to do.

About nine she would nod over her sewing, pull herself together, ashamed, and look around to see if any one had observed her, when there was any one at home to observe, which was seldom enough. She would start sewing again, drop off into a doze, start up, finally take her sewing and retire to her bedroom.

The old lady had a fine room. Any of the family would have told her that. It was above the kitchen and got the winter winds rather badly, so that the old lady frequently had sniffy colds, but it was a fine room, nevertheless, with two windows in it. The one bathroom was quite at the other end of the hall, but, after all, one can't have everything.

Two of the boys roomed in the attic, so the old lady could feel that she was having quite the cream of things to be on the second floor. Fanny and her little boy had the front room because Fanny often brought home one of "the girls" to spend the night or her women friends would run up to her room to take off their hats. Her room was done in bird's-eye maple with pink china silk draperies. Herman and Minnie had the next room. They used the furniture they had bought when they first went to housekeeping, a high maple bed and an old-fashioned dresser to match it. On the walls were enlarged crayon portraits of the old lady and of Grandpa Potter, who had died fifteen years before. Didn't having these pictures show what the family thought of the old lady? The pictures had hung in the living-room until Art descended on the household, a few years before, when they had been removed in favour of two Christy heads, a "Reading from Homer," "The Frieze of the Prophets" and "Two's Company."

The old lady didn't have a hard life. She knew that. She was quite grateful for everything that was done for her. She liked housework, even. Of course, Minnie had rather an annoying way of taking all of the pleasure out of it. Minnie did all of the ordering, all of the planning of meals, the preparing of the salad, when there was a salad, all of the interesting, exciting things connected with the kitchen. But, after all, wasn't it Minnie's house? Hadn't she a right? Grandma knew she had liked doing things in her own home. She didn't blame Minnie but it made things a bit monotonous. Not that things weren't nice, though, a room all to herself, even if the furniture was rather haphazard, lots of time to herself, things to embroider. If Grandpa Potter had lived—but, of course, he wasn't alive, any more than any of the other relatives and friends of those other days were alive, the Scotts, the Howards—Martha.

## II

Now it was the old lady's birthday. She thought of it the first thing in the morning when she woke up. She dressed a bit hurriedly as if something were going to happen. She put on a clean morning dress of black and white percale, stiffly starched and, over this, a blue and white checked gingham apron.

She went to the kitchen to straighten things up. There were a lot of dishes for Lu and Phil had brought some boys home after the movies and Fanny had prepared a rarebit for them, using, as is the way of all amateur cooks, quite three times too many dishes.

The old lady had the oatmeal done and the table set, though, when the family came down, one at a time, for breakfast, first Minnie, then her husband, then the boys. Fanny didn't often appear at breakfast.

No one congratulated the old lady on her birthday, though she made a great point of birthdays and they knew it. However, it is easy enough for a family to forget things like that. So, when they were all at the table, making sucking noises over their oatmeal—no one spoke much at meals at the Potters'—Grandma announced, primly,

"To-day's my birthday."

"So it is," said Herman, and, with an appearance of great gallantry put his napkin on the table, arose and went around to the old lady's place. He kissed her with quite a smack.

"Congratulations and good wishes," he said, which the others echoed. Then,

"How old are you, Ma? Over eighty, I know. Quite an age. I'll never live to see eighty."

"I'm eighty-two," said the old lady.

"Don't think for one minute, Ma, that we forgot your birthday," said Minnie. "You know that we ain't. Only this morning, hurrying about breakfast and all, it slipped my mind. I got something for you two weeks ago at the Ladies' Aid Bazaar. You'd rather have it at supper time, wouldn't you?"

The old lady nodded.

"Yes, I would," she said.

It was the custom of the family to have rather a birthday celebration at the evening meal. They were usually together then and gifts were heaped up at the celebrator's plate and there was a cake.

"You're all going to be home to dinner?" asked Minnie. The men nodded.

When the men left the table, Minnie followed them out into the hall and whispered little warnings to them about "not forgetting something for Grandma" and answering whispers of "can't you do it for me, Ma?"

The day passed as the old lady's days generally passed. In the morning she helped Minnie with the birthday cake. It was a chocolate cake, of which the old lady was not especially fond, but the boys all liked chocolate. There was a white icing on it and they stuck marshmallows on that. The old lady hoped not to get a marshmallow—they stick to your teeth so when you wear a plate. There were to be ten candles on the cake, for ten happened to be the number of candles left over from Elbert's Christmas tree, and you can't possibly put eighty-two candles on a cake, anyhow. The candles were of several colours.

Minnie commented on the beauty of the cake when it was finished. She let the old lady see how good the family was to her. It isn't every old lady of eighty-two who has a birthday cake.

About ten o'clock Fanny and Elbert appeared. The old lady brought their breakfast into the dining-room. Fanny and Minnie were going calling and shopping and were going to take Elbert with them. Usually they left him at home with the old lady. He was rather a spoiled child.

Then Fanny and Minnie dressed. The old lady bathed Elbert, who cried because she got soap into his eyes. This annoyed Fanny.

"For Heaven's sake, Gramma, don't get him cross," she scolded. "We're going to meet Mrs. Herron and Grace for lunch, and I want him to act nice. He'll be in an awful temper if he starts crying."

The old lady didn't say anything. She didn't say anything when Elbert pinched her as she was trying to button his suit. She put on his blue reefer and the cap like a sailor's, and buttoned his leggins, though she did wish he'd sit still while she did the buttons.

At half past eleven the others left and the old lady was alone. She peeled the potatoes for supper and put them in water, she straightened up her room, swept the dining-room, dusted a bit, threw away last night's newspapers.

At half past twelve she went into the kitchen for a bite to eat. She could always "feel when lunch-time came." Minnie usually said, when she went out, "There's always plenty in the ice-box for lunch," and the old lady never contradicted her, though she always felt rather sure that Minnie had made a mistake.

Now, she found a dish of pickles—she did not care for pickles—some eggs and some blackberry jam. She was rather fond of eggs but she was afraid that if she did eat one or two of them, Minnie might say something about "never seem able to keep an egg in the house." Eggs were high, just now. So the old lady buttered two slices of not especially fresh bread rather sparingly and spread a little jam on them. She made herself a cup of tea and ate her lunch sitting at the oilcloth-covered table.

She brushed the crumbs off the table, washed the few dishes, went up to her room for a nap. She liked to sleep, when she had a chance, afternoons.

She woke up, an hour later. A long afternoon stretched in front of her. Still, all of her afternoons were long—mornings—evenings, too. She had heard, years before, that time would seem to fly by when you get old. It didn't. Still, there couldn't be many more days now—eighty-two.

She put on her best dress of black silk, with cuffs and collar of lace that Helen had sent years before. Helen—she was some one to think about. Helen—Martha's daughter. Helen was young and lovely and had everything. Twice the old lady had gone to visit Helen. She never felt at home with Helen at any time. Helen's maids were trained automatons; Helen's home was full of strange formalities. Helen's days were full of unusual things. Helen herself, perfectly groomed, cool, impersonal, looked eighteen, though she'd been married six years, did not seem like a human being at all.

It was nice of Helen having her old grandmother visit her, the old lady knew that. She never talked much to Helen, never knew what to say, yet she loved her with a strange yearning that she never felt toward any one else—maybe because the others were so jealous of Helen, of everything she did. The old lady didn't especially like to be at Helen's—she was so afraid of doing the wrong things—yet, though she never figured it out, Helen seemed to belong to her, was more a part of her than any of the others could be. Maybe because she was Martha's child. Martha had always been so much more to her than any of the others.

With fingers that trembled a little, the old lady fastened her dress, the dress that was new the last time she visited Helen. She smoothed her hair with the old brush one of the boys had given her. She looked at the things on her dresser, the cover she had embroidered in violets—they were her favourite flower—the daguerreotype[5] of her and her husband, taken the year they were married, holding hands unashamed. It was coloured, the old lady's cheeks pink and her brooch shining gold. There was a snapshot of Helen on horseback, a stiffly posed picture of little Elbert, a picture of Phil in sailor uniform—he had gone into the navy just before the draft law was put into effect.

The bell rang. The postman!

With quick little steps, the old lady hurried to the door, smiled at the postman as she always did when she took the mail from him and said something about "a cold day," even while she was anxious to close the door so that she could look over the mail. A letter for Herman from an insurance company—a picture post card—a letter in a lavender envelope for Fanny—a post card from Roger—a letter from Kansas City—Morris' wife's writing—yes—she trembled a little—a letter from Helen. She recognized the pale grey envelope, the deeper grey seal. The women Minnie and Fanny went with didn't use grey sealing wax with a crest stamped into it nor grey monogrammed paper—they didn't live in Chicago nor wear lovely pale clothes—didn't do anything the right way.

---

[5] DAGUERREOTYPE—An early kind of photograph produced on a silver surface; named after its inventor, the Frenchman Daguerre.

The old lady put the mail, excepting her post card and two letters, on the hall table, took hers to her room. Morris meant all right—he and his wife—good people in their way—she was glad Morris was doing well—

Helen's letter! She opened it carefully, tearing off the edge in little bits so as not to tear the contents. The old lady got few enough letters. She never knew you could take a letter-opener to them. She took out the letter. There was an inclosure, but the old lady let that lie in her lap while she read Helen's rather smart writing.

She smiled, read it again, put the letter back into the envelope, looked at the bit of paper on her lap—a cheque—twenty-five dollars.

Helen!

## III

The old lady took her work-bag and went down into the living-room. She'd be careful not to get threads around—she knew how Minnie hated that. She was working on a centrepiece, in colours, to be sold at the March sale of the Church Circle. The old lady was glad she could do things like that. Her glasses were of silver and quite bent. The lenses had been fitted for her years before and she had to hold the sewing quite close. She embroidered until it was too dark to see. Then she folded her wrinkled hands in her lap. She didn't believe in "wasting electricity" by turning it on too early.

She sat at the window and thought about things—about Minnie and Herman—how mean Minnie was about little things, about Herman's stupidity and blindness about everything excepting himself. Herman—and the boys, too—never read anything or saw anything they didn't apply to themselves. They were never interested in a single outside thing. All they talked about was what "he said" and how business was going to be. Nothing existed outside of Graniteville. They were so conceited, satisfied. Fanny was just as bad and she whined, too—but she had Elbert. A child is always a little better than nothing. But Helen didn't have any children.

As the old lady grew older the necessity for progeny, so overwhelmingly important in her younger life, had diminished. What difference did it make, anyhow? Elbert, pale and in the sulks, usually—the only one of a fourth generation. Of course the boys might marry and have children. What of it? Of course, if it weren't for Herman, if she hadn't had children, she wouldn't have had a home, might have had to go to the poor-house, maybe. But then, if she hadn't had children, she might have learned a trade and made enough money to get into one of the homes she had read about, where you pay a few thousand dollars and have a nice room and pictures in the evening and company when you like. Still, of course, things couldn't be changed, were all right—there was Helen's letter—

The twilight deepened. The old lady went into the kitchen, turned on a light, put the meat into the oven.

At six Lu came in, then Phil. Then Fanny and Minnie and Elbert. They had gone to call on Mrs. Harden and Elbert had fallen asleep and was cross, now. Fanny was going upstairs to "make herself comfortable," would Gramma undress Elbert?

Fanny put on a pink cotton kimono and went downstairs. The old lady got Elbert to bed, finally. When she got downstairs she saw that Fanny and her mother were busy in the dining-room. She heard the crackle of paper. Discreetly she stayed in the kitchen. They were preparing her birthday presents.

Dinner was ready. Herman had already come home. Herman liked to eat as soon as he got into the house.

The old lady went into the dining-room. The boys were already seated at the table. Herman sat down. Fanny was putting the potatoes on the table. The old lady found a small pile of bundles at her place, the birthday cake on the table.

"This is very nice," she smiled, "I thank you all even before I look."

She sat down, unassisted. She opened the bundles.

There was a bottle of violet toilet water from Fred. She got that every year. It was not her favourite brand—rather a cheaper kind, in fact, but she liked almost any kind of violet. A pale pink satin pin-cushion came next. A card was stuck on it with pins. On this was written in Fanny's rather stupid, slanting hand:

"To great-grandmother from her little great-grandson, Elbert Arthur Longham, on her 82nd birthday."

The present from Minnie was a hand-made camisole of rather coarse lace—the old lady never wore camisoles, a fact of which Minnie should have been faintly aware. Well, she could make

Minnie "take it back" and wear it herself after a month or so. It was Minnie's size, undoubtedly. There was a pound box of chocolates from Lu. Grandma preferred lemon drops or any hard candies that you can suck and make last a long time, but the family liked chocolates. A boudoir cap from Fanny—a present some one had probably given her for Christmas—and a combination drug-store box of soap, dental cream and nail polish from Herman completed the gifts. Phil apologized that he'd been busy every minute and he'd "get something to-morrow."

The old lady put the wrapping paper neatly together and put the things on the sideboard next to the cut-glass punch bowl. She sat down again. Minnie, who served, was filling the plates.

"Thanks, everybody, again," said the old lady. "Your things are very nice and very welcome."

She looked at the group, the selfish, complacent faces. She smiled.

"I—I got a card from Roger and—and two other presents," she said, and took the card and letters from the front of her waist.

She passed the card around the table and opened a letter.

"It's from Morris and Ruby," she explained. "They sent me five dollars."

"Not much for a rich man to send his mother," Herman commented. "He hasn't any expenses from you and all he ever does is to send you five dollars a month for spending money. I hear he's doing better every month and that's all—"

"Now, Herman," soothed Minnie. She wanted to hear the letter. Ruby never wrote to her.

The old lady read the letter, about Ruby's cold and the snow storm and Morris' business success. She folded it and put it on the table.

"This one is from Helen, from Chicago," she said. She added "from Chicago," purposely. She knew how Fanny longed to live in a big city.

"Dear Gammy," she read, and added, "Helen always uses that nickname just like when she was a baby."

She knew the family hated nicknames. They thought Gramma a proper pronunciation.

"To think that you're eighty-two," she continued to read. "Quite out of the flapper class, it seems. This is to welcome the New Year and to send bushels of love and good wishes from the two of us. I wish you were spending your birthday with us, but I know the family do all they can to make you happy."

The old lady glanced at them all. She was glad to see they looked a little uncomfortable.

"We've been awfully busy as usual," the old lady read on. "Since Jimmy's been made president of the company he's getting so conceited that he insists on going to horrid business meetings at night sometimes, so, in self-defence, I have to go to dinners with some of my old beaux."

The old lady looked at Fanny and smiled.

"Helen has a good time," she said, "I like to think of a young girl enjoying herself."

Helen was Fanny's age. Fanny had no "old beaux," nor any other kind to take her to dinner. Fanny was unpopular.

The old lady went on reading:

"But Jim gets an occasional afternoon off and that's compensation. We have heaps of fun driving or just trailing around together. Jim's as devoted as ever—I'll say that for him. I'm afraid we'll never quite settle down, even if we have been married a long time."

"Helen's a great girl," said the old lady. "She and Jim—I never saw a couple like them. She knows how to hold him. I never saw a man so devoted."

The old lady smiled. Fred's wife had eloped with another man. Fanny's husband had "gone out West" and never returned. This would give them something to think about.

"I don't know that I think her husband ought to stand for her going places with other men," said Fanny. "It don't sound right to me. When Helen came down here to visit, when she was seventeen, she was fresh then."

The old lady looked at her.

"Yes. I guess Helen did seem fresh in Graniteville," she agreed. "But Chicago's different. And as most of the folks they go with are millionaires, each owning two or three cars and having boxes at the opera and making a fuss over Helen all the time, I guess her ways are all right up there. I don't blame men wanting to take her places. She's just sweet to every one."

She went on with the letter:

"I don't know what to write that would interest you. We saw Mrs. Blanchard, Mrs. Crowell's mother, at the theatre on Tuesday, and she wanted to be remembered to you. She looked very well. . . . I have a new mink wrap, good-looking. Jim thought it was a Christmas present, but it came the week after so I'm not counting it. It's the only really splurgy thing I've had all winter."

The old lady didn't have to comment. Fanny was wearing her old coat. She'd been begging her brothers and her father for a coat all winter, but they complained about "hard times," as they always did, so she had to make her old seal, bare in spots, do for another year.

"I went to a charity fête last week," the old lady's quavering voice continued, "and wore green chiffon and was symbolic of something or other, but had a good time anyhow. We made nearly eight thousand dollars for the Children's Home."

The old lady knew the church society entertainments in Graniteville. Fanny and Minnie were never important enough, socially, to take part in them, but had to sell tickets as their share.

"I'm enclosing a birthday remembrance. Buy a warm negligée or something else you want. I didn't know what you needed. Let me know if there is anything I can send you. Jim sends a big kiss and a lot of birthday wishes. With love from Helen."

"How much did she send you?" asked Minnie.

The old lady, who was served last, had been handed her plate of food.

"Twenty-five dollars," she answered.

She took the cheque from Helen and the one from Morris, folded them together, made a last gesture.

"Here, you take these, Fanny," she said, "and buy a dress with them. You'll have to have something to wear if you get a chance to go to the Ladies' Aid Ball. With all the things I got and my birthday presents and all, I don't need anything. Anyhow, Helen said to let her know if I did."

It was said so simply that, if the family suspected the old lady, they were silent. Fanny gasped, reached out her hand. She did want a new dress.

"Thanks, Gramma," she said.

IV

The old lady smiled as she ate her dinner. She looked around at the faces. She felt beautifully superior. She knew that, for a moment, their conceit, their satisfaction had been pierced—they had felt something—

The birthday cake was cut and the old lady passed the box of chocolates.

The boys left for a game of pool at the club. Georgina Watson came to get Fanny to go to the movies. Mr. and Mrs. Potter went across the street to play bridge with the Morrises. The old lady promised to go upstairs and look at Elbert who might have caught cold during the afternoon—he had sneezed a couple of times.

The old lady finished the dishes. She read the evening paper. Then she found herself dozing, woke up, dozed again, woke up, put out the living-room light, left one light in the hall, went upstairs. She stopped in Fanny's room to glance at Elbert in his crib. His mouth was slightly open, as always, and he looked pale, but the old lady saw that his condition was not unusual. She went to her room and undressed for bed.

In her high-necked flannel night-gown she stood at her dresser preparatory to putting out the light. She looked at her birthday presents, the cheap violet water, the unwearable camisole and cap, the thoughtless gifts of indifferent people. She looked at her pictures—she and Grandpa when they were first married, Elbert—Helen. Helen—she knew how to write a letter. Why, she couldn't have written a better one if the old lady had told her what to write. The beaux—the car—the mink coat—the charity fête—the attentive husband—

Her birthday was over. She was eighty-two. Long days ahead—housework—sewing—little quarrels—

She thought of Helen's letter again and chuckled. For just a moment Fanny, Minnie, all of them had looked envious, bitter. Nothing she could ever have done or said could have made them as angry as that letter—and none of them dared say what they thought about it. That letter had opened vistas to them that they could never approach. It had lasted only a minute—but even so . . .

"A pretty good birthday," the old lady said to herself as she put out the light, opened the window, and got into bed.

## QUESTIONS

1. What does the story suggest of the town Graniteville—its people and its standard of living?
2. Do you feel that the Potters deserve the fate that keeps their lives so narrow, or that the fault is not wholly theirs? Explain.
3. In what ways does the family impose on Gramma? How does she accept such treatment?
4. What motives inspire the purchase of the birthday gifts for Gramma?
5. How does the Old Lady get revenge for the family's thoughtlessness? Is her method cruel? With whom do you sympathize?
6. Why does the Old Lady like her granddaughter Helen best? Is Helen's sympathy with the Old Lady sincere?
7. What traits of character does Gramma show? How do the others differ from her?
8. Is there a lesson in the story? If you think there is, does the author state it? What is the author's purpose?
9. Do you think this picture is fair to American life? Is it typical or does it refer only to a few homes?
10. What other stories in this section most closely resemble *The Birthday?* What are the marks of resemblance?

## EXERCISES

Exercises preceded by a star are designed for assignment at the discretion of the teacher, or for any student who volunteers.

1. Analyze the four stages of the story indicated by the numbered divisions, and suggest a subtitle for each.
2. Select a paragraph full of detail, and designate those details which show keen observation.
3. In the character of Gramma, reply to Helen's letter, describing the birthday dinner.
4. Write an essay on one of the following topics: *A Day at Home, Grampa, Birthday Presents.*

*5. Explain the differences between *The Birthday* and the majority of the stories in this section, with particular reference to choice of subject, point of view, treatment, plot movement, and conclusion.

# THE SHORT SHORT STORY

As the complexity of business life and the diversions of social life increased, there came a demand for short crisp narratives for both information and entertainment. The rise of the tabloid newspapers with big headlines, many pictures, and only a small amount of actual reading matter is one product of this age of speed. The Short Short Story is another. It is probable that radio broadcasts of brief narratives and dramatic sketches had an influence on the development of the Short Short Story. At any rate, several magazine editors undertook to supply the demand for thumbnail fiction by publishing stories which could be printed on a single page.

In the space of a few years the Short Short Story has become a recognized form of literature. Although the principles of the full-length story apply in general to the briefer narrative, they are more scrupulously observed. Economy and singleness of impression become not merely desirable but inevitable. The single thread of the narrative allows no digressions, no wandering from the main theme. Dialogue is compressed to essentials. Characters must be portrayed deftly and distinctly in a few lines. Even sentences must be pared down to a point where every word and phrase count.

Because of the compactness, there is little room for plot. In most short short stories there is only a situation that is rapidly worked out. Plot, however, is usually implied through exposition. The reader is made aware of events that have taken place before this crucial situation developed. Once this necessary knowledge has been provided, the story advances to its conclusion with breath-taking speed. In the suddenness of the catastrophe or happy ending, as the case may be, lies the peculiar effectiveness of the Short Short Story.

When an author takes this form seriously, selecting a vital subject and applying his best art to its treatment, unexpected possibilities are revealed. Effects difficult to attain in the average short story may be achieved in the swift, one-page narrative. Unfortunately, there is still a tendency to look upon the latter as a passing fad. As a consequence, many writers have been able to sell stories of dubious literary value, "pot-boilers" designed to cash in quickly on the popularity of the type. Yarns based on trivial themes, with a cheap jest for a conclusion like the twist at the end of a vaudeville skit, outnumber the serious efforts.

In spite of this state of affairs, the increasing number of excellent short short stories appearing in magazines compensates for the trash. Writers of recognized talent are finding a challenge in the very limitations which the form imposes, for working in miniature is just as truly an art as working on murals or broad canvases. What the future holds is not easy to predict, but a reading of the following "short shorts" will give an idea of the possibilities.

# APPETITE

## HUGH McNAIR KAHLER

1883–

### THE AUTHOR

Hugh McNair Kahler was born in Philadelphia, in 1883. At the age of twenty-one he was graduated from Princeton, and three years later married Louise Kingsley of Buffalo. He is known as a contributor to the magazines and as the author of several novels. His present home is Princeton, New Jersey, and his summers are spent at Kennebunkport, Maine.

### THE STORY

Two tramps seeking shelter from wind and sleet in a culvert beneath a railroad embankment . . . one cold potato and a lump of stale bread . . . an old newspaper blown in by the wind—these are the simple ingredients of *Appetite,* a short short story that in about 750 words shows how relatively unimportant are the luxuries of life. The tramps, feeling the elemental pangs of hunger and cold, resent the abundance others enjoy until, in a flash, a far worse fate is revealed to them. The change in point of view has a touch of humor that does not, however, destroy the fundamental seriousness of the story.

## APPETITE[1]

It was Joe's turn to rustle for the pokeout,[2] and Link waited for him in the shelter of the low culvert that left a passageway through the railroad embankment for a whimpering little trickle of dirty water.

It was pretty cold in the culvert, but there was shelter from the wind and from the steady slant of sleet, and a newspaper had been blown in far enough to be fairly dry.

The newspaper gave Link the idea of risking a little fire. On a day like this, he thought, the smoke wouldn't be noticed. He found some woody weed stems that felt dry enough to burn and, scouting along the embankment, gathered wet twigs and sticks.

He knew better, though, than to use all his paper for the first attempt. He crumpled half of it and built a careful little pyramid of weed stems above it, and over this arranged the wet wood. He was careful, too, with his match, because he had only three left.



[2] RUSTLE FOR THE POKEOUT—Forage for grub; beg for food.

He cupped his hands close to the sorry little flame that climbed up the paper, so that, if the fire didn't burn, his fingers, at least, would have profited by the brief warmth.

They were blue fingers, broken-nailed; they had stiffened around brakerods[3] so that they wouldn't open all the way, and they were so thick-skinned that they hardly felt the heat of the tiny blaze.

Link nursed and fed his fire cunningly. It stayed alive, and he crouched over it, twisting his head to look for Joe, and every time this happened his lips would pull themselves away from his teeth.

Joe was a long time about it, long enough for the tiny flame to thaw Link's hands so that he forgot to curse the weather and only remembered how hungry he was.

He picked up what was left of the newspaper. Reading was hard work, but sometimes it would keep you from thinking about things—like beefsteaks and big, steaming cups of coffee.

Link smoothed the paper on his knee and began spelling out the words. He did not look up again till Joe clattered up the pebbly creek bed toward the culvert's mouth.

"Here," said Joe, "wrap yourself around this. I got mine back to the house." He pulled a lump of stale bread from one of his coat pockets, and a soapy-looking boiled potato from another.

"Huh," said Link scornfully.

Joe scowled. "What's the big idea? If this pokeout ain't fancy enough for you I can use it all right."

"Go ahead," said Link.

Joe dug his teeth into the bread.

"Listen," said Link. He read aloud, slowly, following the words with a blue, gnarled forefinger.

"Dinner will con-sist of tomato soup, broiled Lake Erie whitefish with cream sauce, sirloin steak with—"

"Can it, will you!" snarled Joe. He glowered down at the soapy-looking potato in his left hand.

"—with mushrooms, French-fried potatoes, mashed boiled turnips and—"

"Can it, will you!" Joe's voice was uglier, now. He dropped the lump of bread on the cinders beside him.

---

[3] FINGERS . . . STIFFENED AROUND BRAKERODS—Hoboes often hop freights and cling perilously to the brakerods beneath the cars. Many have been killed when the cold made them relax their grip.

"—baked macaroni with cheese," Link read on. "Lemon mer-mer[4]—some kind of lemon pie and—"

Joe dropped the potato beside the bread.

"—choc'late ice-cream and mac-mac-aroons—" Link lifted his head. "What's macaroons, Joe?"

"Kind of a cookie. Cocoanut in 'em," said Joe. He kicked a little spurt of cinders into the water.

"Fruit, cheese and coffee will conclude the re-repast, with cigars and cigarettes."

"Gee!" said Joe. "And us out here with a hunk of bread and one lousy potato!" He kicked more cinders into the water. "It ain't right, Link, the way some guys get all the breaks. Sirloin steak! Macaroons! Why should other guys rate a blow-out like that when you and me—"

He paused.

Link's forefinger had plodded farther down the torn page. He had, it seemed to Joe, lost interest in the paper. At least his eyes were now fixed upon the boiled potato. He lifted it, and, thumbing off the cinders that clung to its soapy surface, he ate it.

Joe picked up the scrap of paper and found the place.

"—with cigars and cigarettes," he read. "And promptly at midnight the first of the three doomed men will begin the short march to the death chair."

Thoughtfully he watched Link's hands and teeth at work upon a swiftly dwindling lump of bread.

"Good, huh?" said Joe.

"Yeah," said Link. He swallowed largely. "And say, that potato went good, too."

## QUESTIONS AND EXERCISES

Exercises preceded by a star are designed for assignment at the discretion of the teacher, or for any student who volunteers.

1. To what degree does the setting for *Appetite* contribute to the effectiveness of the story?
2. Write a short essay on the problem which the story presents.

*3. Show how the Short Short Story differs in structure from the longer form.

4. At what point comes the first suggestion of the change in point of view? Why does the author leave the complete revelation until the very end?
5. Which of the two tramps leaves the deeper impression on you? Why does the author limit his characters to Link and Joe? Would the story gain or lose by the introduction of one or more additional characters?

---

[4] MER-MER—Link is trying to pronounce *meringue*.

# FATHOMS DEEP

## OCTAVUS ROY COHEN

1891–

### THE AUTHOR

The name Octavus Roy Cohen is well known to all who read fiction magazines. Besides short stories Cohen has written successful novels and plays. Born in Charleston, South Carolina, in 1891, he was educated at Porter Military Academy and Clemson College in his home state. After two years as a civil engineer, he shifted to journalism, holding editorial jobs in Birmingham, Alabama, Charleston, and Newark, New Jersey. Between 1913 and 1915 he practiced law in South Carolina. Since then he has devoted himself chiefly to writing. Cohen has an easy, colloquial style that appeals to a large audience. Usually a vein of humor runs through his work. A series of Negro stories in dialect has brought him wide popularity. In 1931 he published *Cameos,* a collection of fifty-three short short stories of about 1,000 words each. Though not always profound, they show great dexterity in treatment, especially in the "twist" endings.

### THE STORY

In *Fathoms Deep* Octavus Roy Cohen has written a study of an irresponsible young man who learns wisdom from solitude. It is immediately evident that he has taken the short short story form seriously, treating a significant subject with the earnestness it deserves. It is interesting to note the point at which he picks up the narrative. Instead of starting immediately before the climax, as many short short stories do, *Fathoms Deep* takes off at what is practically the beginning of the adventure. Consequently, the technique is more like that of the full-length story. There is only the situation to present through exposition, for most of the action is included in the story itself. The two twists at the end serve a double purpose, showing character development in the chief actor and a change in material fortunes.

## FATHOMS DEEP[1]

Crazy as a loon, he was, but you couldn't help loving him. Just an overgrown kid with a magnificent body, unruly blond hair, quizzical crow's-feet at the corners of his blue eyes and a manner which made you know that the world could go hang, but he'd make

[1] Copyright 1932 by P. F. Collier & Son Co. Reprinted by permission of the author.

out very well indeed. Good stock, too; but if he was too impulsive, too impetuous and rather too confident of himself—those were virtues, not vices. Don Egerton was different.

His scheme was as wildly impossible and absurd as himself. He paced up and down the office. He made gestures. He said he could hardly wait to be off.

"Across the Pacific—alone—in an eighteen-foot boat!" I gasped. "It's suicide!"

"What of it—if I can't make it? Doesn't the Old Man make a slogan of the fact that he won't let his daughter marry poverty?"

"You said," I hinted darkly, "that you had bet thirty thousand dollars with Tommy Raines: where did you get that much money?"

"Nowhere," he answered. "I was clever. Minute we made the bet he suggested putting up certified checks. 'Never mind, old man,' said I nobly—'it's a gentleman's agreement. We'll shake hands on it.' And we did."

"But the ethics of it, Don: you've tricked Raines into betting thirty thousand dollars against nothing."

"The reward is bigger than ethics," he maintained. "I realize I'm a scoundrel, but I'd be twice one if I passed up this chance for a grubstake. I'm flat broke—flatter than half a pancake. I'm here to borrow from you enough money to outfit the boat—and buy it, too, for that matter. My inheritance has gone the way of many a larger one—bad speculation." Then he became very, very serious: "I've got to make it. Doris' father loves the spectacular. When I reach Japan I'll be something of a hero. He'll regard my thirty thousand as chicken feed, but he'll know I have that much."

"And then?"

"And then I'll make out some way. I always have, haven't I? Besides, Doris will marry me, and once she does that, nothing else matters."

I tried to be severe. I criticized his morals and disparaged his methods. But Don was different, that's all: there's no other way of explaining it. Whatever he did was right simply because he did it, and there was something irresistibly splendid in the prospect of a young man—twenty-five only—embarking on a suicidal effort to achieve a goal which he felt could not be won any other way.

I endeavored to dissuade him. I threatened to betray him to Tommy Raines. I refused to lend him the money to finance his mad enterprise. In the end all my good resolves disappeared: I did not dissuade him, I did not betray him, and I did lend him the money. "You'll never make it," I warned.

"And if I don't, the world will say, 'There went nothing,' and I'll agree."

"Darned fool!" I said.

"Correct! For once."

The daring adventure, the impressive wager, Don's social prominence and the undertone—generally understood—of romance, caught the public imagination. Nautical experts gave advice, small-craft wizards volunteered their services. They learned that they were not dealing with a novice.

Don was a grand sailor and as I watched him supervising work on his boat, shirt unbuttoned at the throat, blue eyes gazing out beyond the horizon, hair blown by the wind, I was reminded of the old Norsemen.

Newspapers and magazines carried hundreds of columns about him; rotogravure sections of Sunday newspapers printed intriguing pictures; he was offered a movie contract in the event he was successful; a great syndicate[2] tried to sign him to write the story of his voyage. Manufacturers mounted the publicity bandwagon and sent materials—more or less useless—in great quantities, gratis. He received sixty-three offers of marriage. A philatelic society[3] intrusted him with a batch of letters to be autographed in Japan and mailed from there—trophies for collectors.

Doris and the Old Man were down to see him off. So, too, was half of San Francisco and scores of newspaper men. Tommy Raines was there—grand sportsman—to wish him luck. The Old Man was proud and fearful. Doris was smiling. She disdained a last-minute appeal. She knew Don better than that. But as his little craft danced bravely into the sunset, its canvas taut in a quartering breeze, Doris' eyes held the light of tragedy; of fierce, helpless, hopeless tragedy which should not come to so young and beautiful a girl.

During the first three or four days Don was reported frequently by wireless. Then came an agonizing wait of more than

[2] SYNDICATE—An association that distributes special news stories and feature articles to magazines and newspapers that subscribe for the service.

[3] PHILATELIC SOCIETY—A society engaged in collecting rare stamps, stamped envelopes, etc.

a week, eight horrible days when columnists speculated about his fate—until a tramp steamer[4] reported that he had halted them and borrowed fresh water to fill his tanks. In good health, reported the master of the tramp; good health and grand spirits.

Then he dropped out. Days dragged interminably, and nothing was heard. We had known it would be that way, but the horror of uncertainty was not mitigated by our intelligence. Tommy Raines—wealthy and indolent and a good fellow—organized a party and chartered accommodations on a west-bound steamer: he felt guilty, and wished Don success. Also, he wanted to be the first to congratulate the lad when—and if—he should succeed.

I sailed with Tommy's party. Doris and her Old Man were on board. Raines was game, Don was game—but Doris was superb. She was standing the strain like the little thoroughbred she was, but I thought then—and I think now—that no man has the right to be a hero if it means torturing the woman who loves him.

And they were all there to greet Don when he sailed proudly into the harbor of Kobe;[5] bronzed and happy—but somehow thinner and older. He didn't talk much about his voyage—even in later years he was reluctant to discuss the typhoon he had weathered, the days when his water supply was low, the week when he was stricken with fever and could scarcely handle the tiller. The men who were in the front line during the World War have little to say about it.

That night Tommy Raines gave a banquet. We were all there—even Doris and her Old Man. Don looked gaunt and worn, but happy. He was sitting next to Doris.

Everybody tried to be light and gay. Tommy had written a check for thirty thousand dollars, and when he presented it to Don we all knew that he was glad he had lost. He wasn't the sort to enjoy gambling with human life.

Don rose and looked at us gravely. Then he tore the check to bits.

"Sorry, Tommy," he said. "I thought I could—but I can't. I didn't have a cent in the world when I made that bet. I couldn't have paid if I'd lost."

---

[4] TRAMP STEAMER—A vessel not making regular trips but getting a cargo wherever it offers.

[5] KOBE—Japanese seaport.

Raines argued with him; insisted that he accept the money anyway. He maintained that Don had done what he set out to do and was entitled to the reward. No use. Don had always been a fine, clean lad and those endless days alone on the Pacific had given him the ability to see clear and straight.

I knew what it meant to him—this refusal to take the money. I knew how he needed it. I knew that Doris would beg him to marry her, just as she had begged him before he embarked on his crazy adventure. And I knew he would refuse.

In fact, I knew everything about everybody—except one person. I failed to take Doris' Old Man into account.

It was the Old Man who saw below the surface. It was the Old Man who called Don and Doris to him and insisted that they marry. It was the Old Man who understood—more clearly than any of us—that Don had done something more important than navigating the Pacific Ocean to win a bet.

## QUESTIONS AND EXERCISES

Exercises preceded by a star are designed for assignment at the discretion of the teacher, or for any student who volunteers.

1. What is it that is "fathoms deep"? Which sentence gives the clue?
2. Contrast Don Egerton with the person from whose point of view the story is told. Give your opinion of Tommy Raines.
3. Next to Don, who is the most important character in *Fathoms Deep?* Why?

*4. What two bits of action compose the climax? Would the story be complete without the second? Explain.

5. What method does the author employ to reveal what happened to Don on his voyage? What principle of short story writing recommends this method instead of direct narration from Don's point of view?
6. Enumerate the several parts of the action and comment on the space the author allows each.

# THE SENATOR RESTS

## M. C. BLACKMAN

1902–

### THE AUTHOR

M. C. Blackman is a Southerner by birth, owning Ida, Louisiana, as his native town. Born in 1902, he may properly be called a product of the new century. After concluding studies at Louisiana State University and the University of Missouri, he entered newspaper work, a profession in which he is still engaged. His duties have taken him from his home state to such widely separated fields as Arkansas, Paris, and Detroit. He now resides in Detroit. Since 1927 Mr. Blackman has written many short stories for the magazines, including the *Forum, Harper's, Collier's, Liberty,* and others. In 1928 his *Hot Copy* won the third O. Henry Prize Award. *The Last Friend,* which he contributed to the *North American Review,* is included in the Roll of Honor in Edward J. O'Brien's *Best Short Stories of 1932.*

### THE STORY

It is peculiarly fitting to close a section of Modern Short Stories with *The Senator Rests.* This short short story, published in *Collier's* for March 5, 1932, indicates how elastic the form established by Poe has become. Though there is practically no external action in it, the reader is aware of progress toward a conclusion. The inner action consists in the revelation of attitudes. A Senator has died. What would be the end of most short stories is in this instance the beginning, for it is the effect of the Senator's death on his associates that makes the story.

In a way, it is like a composite or synthetic portrait; that is, instead of a picture drawn from a single point of view, we are given brief glances from a number of points of view. In the end we have a portrait that represents in its several parts the impression the Senator has made on a half dozen persons of different character and outlook. What makes this process doubly interesting is the fact that while these persons are passing judgment on the Senator they are also revealing themselves. In the brief space in which we see them, they register clear-cut profiles. Though we cannot know them intimately, certain phases of their character are clearly defined.

Even more significant than all this is another idea—an idea which becomes increasingly apparent as each character appears and speaks his few words: the preoccupation of the individual with his own concerns. What does the death of a Senator mean to the extra telegraph operator, to the doctor, to the widow and son, to the Governor, and to the President? It all depends on the person. A few more dollars to buy food for a family. Another patient lost. An obstacle removed from the path of an ambitious politician. Even the grief of those who loved him cannot keep thoughts of the immediate world from intruding. Life goes on. Each one is the center of his own universe, and all that happens is interpreted in the light of its effect upon him. Yet an occasional gleam of understanding and sympathy flashes from one little universe to another.

The author does not say all this, does not even comment. The idea grows out of the testimony of a number of witnesses. For this story is realistic not merely in conception and detail, but in method.

## THE SENATOR RESTS[1]

The nation mourned the Senator's passing—the papers said so. The nation mourned by telegraph, telephone and mail.

The telegraph office in the Senator's home town put on an extra man. The extra operator had a wife and three children, and had worked only eight days in six months. He thought: "Gee, this is a lucky break for me; I ought to get four days out of this."

The doctor was a sick man. He told his wife: "It's not fair. He was getting well, I tell you. Well! How could I foresee that occlusion?[2] They can't blame me for that. And Kenyon went the same way. Two prominent patients lost in two months! And not my fault—not in any way. It's not fair, I say."

The widow kept her eyes full, and through the tears watched the pile of telegrams grow. When no one was looking she shuffled the stack loosely to make them appear even more impressive. She noted the signatures with satisfaction, and placed the one from the President on top.

"That ought to show them," she thought . . . "Adam is dead. Well, well . . . It just doesn't seem possible . . . He'd be surprised if he knew the stir he'd caused just by dying . . . He was too modest, Adam was. Too modest for his own good . . . He could have been President, if he'd had any push about him. If it hadn't been for me—They ought to let me finish his term . . . I could do it as well as he . . . Better, I suspect . . . If it hadn't been for me—"

---

[1] Reprinted by permission of the author.

[2] Occlusion—In medicine, a stoppage, as for example a blood-clot in a vein.

The Governor summoned his most confidential secretary. "Give him the whole works, John. He was all right, that man was. He never crossed my path. Fix up a proclamation; make it flowery, but not sloppy. Order the state-house closed and arrange to have his body lie in state a few hours in the rotunda. Give him a military guard of honor . . . And don't let those buzzards who want his job get to me till after the funeral. What a break for me! I'm gonna grab it myself, if I can get away with it."

The senior member of the undertaking firm said to his partner: "He didn't leave a dime, I hear, and we'll be lucky to get our expenses. But I'd take it for nothing. Think of the publicity! The newspapers'll give us credit, and it'll throw business our way. Plenty of it. I'll bet those cheapskates down the street are tearing their hair. They tried to horn in, but it didn't do 'em no good."

The President of the United States instructed a secretary to send a message of condolence to the widow. "I'll say the things I'm expected to say," he thought, "but nobody will ever know how glad I am that man is out of the way . . . A trouble-maker. Always criticizing. And laughing. That was the worst: the way he poked fun and tried to make me look ridiculous. I wish he'd had my job for a while. That's the worst fate I could wish for him. He might have had it, too, if he had lived. Maybe he's lucky, after all. Lucky to be dead. Oh, well . . ."

The Senator's son had to leave the university during fraternity rush week. He tried not to feel aggrieved at the inconvenience, but the thought kept recurring: "If he could only have waited a week. With me gone, those dumb-bells will mess things up, and the Kappas will grab off our best men . . . I ought to be ashamed of myself. Dad was a good scout, and darned decent to me . . . It's hard, though, to think of its being my father that's dead. I keep thinking of Senator Adam Bentley . . . Headlines . . . Wonder how much insurance he had . . ."

The star reporter sneaked another drink from a bottle secreted in the "morgue,"[3] and began putting smooth phrases together.

It was a hot story, the biggest he'd handled in many dull months, and he gave to it the best he had in him. "That oughta knock 'em

---

[3] Morgue—In journalism, a place where files containing photographs and biographical data concerning distinguished public personages are kept. In case of a sudden death, a complete news story can be drafted in a few minutes.

dead," he thought. "And what a break for us that he died on our time.[4] He always was good copy[5] for us, that old bird was."

The special nurse who had attended the Senator during his stay at the hospital read the papers, reread them, and shook her head wonderingly. She thought: "It don't hardly seem like it could be the same man. He was just a human being, and a nice old duck, I thought. Only it was kind of pathetic the way he'd ask me to sit down and talk to him after all those big guns would leave. And him saying he didn't have a friend to his name. I felt sorry for him. Ha! Me feeling sorry for Senator Adam Bentley, the—" she consulted the paper again—"the great statesman. But I don't care; I did. He was that lonely-like and sad. And he treated me like I was a human being, too. That he did."

She wiped away a tear, and thought she might send flowers. But she decided she wouldn't; there would be so many flowers for a great statesman that her tiny wreath would be lost. Besides, she really couldn't afford it. So she brushed away another tear, and went to see what that cranky old heifer in 42[6] wanted this time.

## QUESTIONS AND EXERCISES

Exercises preceded by a star are designed for assignment at the discretion of the teacher, or for any student who volunteers.

1. What is the double meaning of the title?
2. Give an oral character sketch of each speaker in the story.
3. From the testimony given, describe the sort of person you think the Senator must have been.
4. What is your opinion of the President's comment? Do you condemn the President, or do you sympathize with him? Is it clear just who is to blame for the feeling between the Senator and the President?
5. Which character in the story exhibits the sincerest grief? Why is it extraordinary that of them all this person should be most sympathetic?
6. Write a paragraph explaining in your own words the underlying thought of the story.
7. From a newspaper select two items which in your opinion would make the basis for short short stories. Following class discussion, choose the more promising item and, upon the advice of the teacher, develop it into
   (a) A synopsis for a short short story, *or*
   *(b) A short short story of not more than 500 words. In either case, feel free to change the facts to suit your own purpose.

---

[4] HE DIED ON OUR TIME—He died at an hour when the newspaper could get the report in that day's regular edition.

[5] GOOD COPY—Good source of news.

[6] 42—The number of a hospital room.

## SUGGESTED READING LIST

*The Man Who Was*.................................................Rudyard Kipling

*The Heart of Little Shikara,* Edison Marshall
*Jungle Beasts and Men,* Dhan Gopal Mukerji
*The Man Who Would Be King,* Rudyard Kipling
*The Ship That Found Herself,* Rudyard Kipling

*The Piece of String*.....................................Guy de Maupassant

*The Substitute,* François Coppée
*Rothschild's Fiddle,* Anton Chekhov
*Trifles* (one-act play), Susan Glaspell
*A Coward,* Guy de Maupassant

*The Little Regiment*.............................................Stephen Crane

*Marse Chan,* Thomas Nelson Page
*Horseman in the Sky,* Ambrose Bierce
*The Open Boat,* Stephen Crane

*The White Silence*...................................................Jack London

*Arizona Nights,* Stewart Edward White
*The Frenchwoman's Son,* S. Carleton
*The Son of the Wolf,* Jack London

*The Blue Cross*...................................................G. K. Chesterton

*The Fugitive,* Vincent Starrett
*The Woman at Seven Brothers,* Wilbur Daniel Steele
*Dr. Thorndyke's Cases,* Richard Austin Freeman
*The Hammer of God,* G. K. Chesterton

*England to America*..............................Margaret Prescott Montague

*Contact,* Frances Noyes Hart
*Lady Wipers of Ypres,* Llewellyn Hughes
*Journey's End* (drama), Robert C. Sherriff

*The Garden-Party*.....................................Katherine Mansfield

*Evening,* Zona Gale
*Paul's Case,* Willa Cather
*The Little Girl,* Katherine Mansfield

*The Boob*..................................................Walter De Leon

*Billy,* Mildred Cram
*Banbury Cross,* Frances Noyes Hart
*Merely Players,* Henry Harland

*The Birthday*.......................................Thyra Samter Winslow

*Old Man Minick,* Edna Ferber
*The Wonderful Old Gentleman,* Dorothy Parker
*Home-coming,* Ruth Suckow
*Her Own Room,* Thyra Samter Winslow

Other Short Short Stories:

*The Little House,* Beatrice Blackmer
*At the Barricade,* Murney Mintzer
*The Burned Madonna,* Guy Gilpatric
*The Gift,* David Thibault
*No Errors,* F. R. Buckley
*Expression of Love,* Octavus Roy Cohen
*The Tenth Word,* Dana Burnet
*A Bouquet for Uncle Basil,* Doris Montague
*Awaiting Orders,* Jerome Barry

Short Story Anthologies:

*The Best Short Stories of* (year); an American year book of short stories begun in 1915, Edward J. O'Brien
*Best British Short Stories;* a year book begun in 1922, Edward J. O'Brien
*O. Henry Memorial Award Prize Stories;* a year book begun in 1919
*Best Continental Short Stories;* a year book begun in 1923
*The World's Best Short Stories for 1925*
*The Harper Prize Short Stories* (1924–1925)
*Best Short Stories of the World,* Konrad Bercovici
*Omnibus of Adventure,* John Grove
*Omnibus of Romance,* John R. Colter
Current and back numbers of the *Golden Book Magazine*
*The Fifty Best Short Shorts of* (year); a year book of short short stories begun in 1932, Paul Ernest Anderson and Lionel White
*My Best Story,* An Anthology of Stories Chosen by Their Own Authors